INTRODUCTION TO
MANAGEMENT SCIENCE

Second Edition

INTRODUCTION TO
MANAGEMENT SCIENCE

Second Edition

Sang M. Lee
University of Nebraska—Lincoln

The Dryden Press
Chicago   New York   San Francisco   Philadelphia
Montreal   Toronto   London   Sydney   Tokyo

The Dryden Press
Acquisitions Editor: Mary Fischer
Developmental Editor: Penny Gaffney
Project Editor: Jan Doty/Paula Ransdell
Design Director: Alan Wendt
Production Manager: Barb Bahnsen
Permissions Editor: Doris Milligan
Director of Editing, Design, and Production: Jane Perkins

Chernow Editorial Services, Inc.
Production Supervisor: Douglas Lee Bell
Executive Editor: Barbara A. Chernow
Editorial Coordinator: Alison B. Walker
Illustrations: Textbook Art Associates
Copy Editor: Marsha Scott

Text and Cover Designer: C. J. Petlick, Hunter Graphics
Compositor: The Clarinda Company
Text Type: 10/12 Times Roman

Library of Congress Cataloging-in-Publication Data

Lee, Sang M., 1939–
 Introduction to management science.

 Includes bibliographies and index.
 1. Management science.   I. Title.
T56.L43   1987   658   87–5256
ISBN 0–03–008892–5

Printed in the United States of America
789–039–98765432
Copyright © 1988, 1983 by The Dryden Press, a division of Holt, Rinehart and Winston, Inc.

Address orders:
111 Fifth Avenue
New York, NY 10003

Address editorial correspondence:
One Salt Creek Lane
Hinsdale, IL 60521

The Dryden Press
Holt, Rinehart and Winston
Saunders College Publishing

To Tosca and Amy

THE DRYDEN PRESS SERIES IN MANAGEMENT
Arthur G. Bedeian, Consulting Editor

PREFACE

Management science is concerned with the application of scientific approaches to improve management performance. In management science, special emphasis is placed on the systematic analysis of the nature of the problem, decision environment, objectives of the organization, judgment of the decision maker, and available decision alternatives. Thus, the field of management science encompasses a host of quantitative methodologies as well as behavioral aspects of decision making. The purpose of this text is to provide the student with a comprehensive coverage of how management science concepts and approaches can be applied to improve management decision making.

Management science is no longer a new field of study. Today, such terms as *cost/benefit analysis, simulation, optimization, modeling, computer-based solutions, data base management, artificial intelligence,* and *expert systems* are accepted as standard vocabulary. Management science concepts are no longer the property of trained management scientists. Management science is widely known to practicing managers, government planners, military analysts, space scientists, regional planners, health care administrators, and many other professionals. As the use of management science becomes broader, there is a greater need for a good introductory text. This book is such a text. It explains, in a simple manner with a minimum amount of mathematics, how to formulate management decision problems as models, how to solve them by using management science techniques and computers, and then how to implement the solution results in the actual problem situation.

The emphasis of this book is on the translation of mathematical modeling concepts into a presentation that is palatable to the undergraduate student of business with limited mathematical background. This emphasis is carried out even further in this second edition. All management science topics are introduced by presenting realistic, practical examples in the form of casettes (small cases). Thus, difficult techniques are presented within the framework of working examples, stressing an intuitive understanding of concepts in the decision support perspective rather than mathematical proofs.

In summary, *Introduction to Management Science, Second Edition,* is all of the following:

1. A comprehensive yet easily readable presentation of all important management science techniques.

2. An application orientation to realistic problems through the emphasis of the model formation, computer-based solution, and implementation of the model results.

3. An up-to-date presentation of computer applications, especially using microcomputers.

4. A decision support perspective of management science—supporting the decision maker to be more effective through the use of management science.

5. A managerial perspective of management science—problem formulation, analysis of the decision environment, multiple organizational objectives, and issues involved in implementing model results to improve management effectiveness.

A Note to the Student

Numerous books have been published in the area of management science, operations research, and quantitative methods. Most of these books can be classified into two broad categories: (1) basic surveys that present a cookbook approach of management science techniques and (2) comprehensive theoretical texts that represent the mathematical foundations of various quantitative tools. Few books have presented a comprehensive, introductory, application-oriented, fun-to-read, computer application–oriented, and up-to-date treatment of management science concepts. This book is such a book.

A major objective of this text is to avoid overwhelming you with mathematics. Rather, the purpose is to familiarize you with a wide variety of model building situations so that you come away from the introductory course with an ability to conceptualize the modeling approach in a managerial perspective. I attempt to achieve this purpose through a sound but interesting presentation of the underlying concepts through realistic casettes. I try to make the learning an enjoyable experience for you.

Management science is not simply a collection of quantitative tools. It is a way of thinking and a philosophy of logical problem solving in any decision environment. After studying this book, you should by no means come away with the idea that you now have a set of tools that can be simply plugged into the appropriate situations without carefully considering the assumptions of the model and the realities of the decision environments. Instead, you should develop a broad managerial perspective of management science: its primary purpose is decision support.

All of the techniques presented in this text are selected on the basis of their track record in real-world applications. Although most of the examples and casettes presented are relatively simple as compared to real-world problems, once you master these examples you will be much better prepared to tackle complex problems. Many real-world application examples are provided in the text to give you a general idea about the types of problems in which different techniques can be applied. The most important purpose of this book is to help you sharpen your conceptual skills in dealing with any decision problem. These skills will be invaluable throughout your career, whatever it may eventually be.

A Note to the Instructor

In writing this text, I had three basic objectives: (1) an emphasis on the managerial perspective—the basic role of management science is to improve organizational performance, (2) a comprehensive and interesting discussion of various management science topics through casettes, and (3) an application-oriented text presenting many real-world application examples and computer-based solutions and discussing the factors that are important for successful implementation of management science.

On the basis of two criteria, I selected those topics that are most appropriate for an introductory course in management science: (1) the current track record of the particular technique for solving real-world problems and (2) the capacity of the technique for exposing the student to a variety of different modeling situations. The central theme of the book, which is carried through all of the chapters, stresses the concept of modeling in general. Thus, each chapter presents the identification of the model objective, the decision variables, the model parameters, the underlying assumptions of the model, the decision environment, computer-based solutions, and real-world applications.

In this second edition, the following new chapters are added: Network Models, Forecasting, Markov Analysis, and Decision Support Systems. Also, advanced queuing models and game theory are included as appendices. Each chapter is revised extensively with new materials, casettes, computer-based solutions, real-world applications, glossary, list of references, and problems.

This book is organized so that the most frequently covered topics (most popular topics), such as linear programming and related subjects, are presented first. Although most of the chapters present topics that are independent of other chapters, the topic of linear programming is presented in three chapters, ranging from introductory to more advanced material. Each chapter has the following aids to the student:

1. A brief introduction stating the purpose of the chapter.

2. A list of the learning objectives for the chapter.

3. A brief summary of the topics covered in the chapter.

4. A glossary to enhance the student's understanding of the terminologies.

5. A list of references for further research.

This text has over 60 casettes in the text and over 530 assignment problems at the ends of chapters. In addition, over 200 other problems and cases are presented in the *Study Guide* and the *Instructor's Manual*. Also, the text presents summaries of 34 real-world applications of management science. The *Study Guide* presents a list of suggestions for studying management science, a summary of the important concepts in each chapter, full solutions to all of the odd-numbered assignment problems, additional problems and cases to prepare for tests, and a list of journals that are useful in studying the actual applications of management science.

The *Instructor's Manual* presents solutions to all of the assignment problems, a suggested examination format with problems, discussion of some advanced topics that are not included in the text, and suggested syllabi of the course at different levels. Transparency masters for various figures and tables presented in the text will also be available from the publisher. The text and these accompanying materials present a comprehensive instructional support package for an introductory management science course.

Acknowledgments

In writing this book, I have relied heavily on the suggestions and criticisms of my colleagues and students. I have benefited greatly from discussions with my friends Fred Luthans and Lester Digman at the University of Nebraska. I would like to thank my colleagues Professor Hope Baker (University of North Carolina, Greensboro), Professor James Bartos (Ohio State University), Professor Dale Berggren (Oregon State University), Professor Bruce K. Blaylock (Western Kentucky University), Professor James Cochran (Wright State University), Professor John L. Eatman (University of North Carolina, Greensboro), Professor Spyros Economides (California State University–Hayward), Professor Wayne Ellingson (South Dakota State University), Professor Philip G. Enns (Saint Louis University), Professor Lawrence P. Ettkin (University of Tennessee at Chattanooga), Professor Barry Hiney (Westfield State College), Professor Eugene Kaczka (Clarkson College), Professor C. S. Kim (Miami University), Professor Patrick G. McKeown (University of Georgia), Professor Tom Means (San Jose State University), Professor David Olson (Texas A&M University), Professor James H. Patterson (Indiana University), Professor A. Ravindran (University of Oklahoma), Professor Ahmed Rifari (Northern Illinois University), Professor William E. Pinney (The University of Texas at Arlington), Professor Sam Roy (Moorhead State University), Professor J. P. Shim (Mississippi State University), and Professor Mike Wilson (Eastern Illinois University), who reviewed the entire manuscript several times. Special thanks go to my students, André Everett, S. H. Chung, J. D. Kim, S. O. Lee, K. J. Kim, Q. Guan, E. B. Kim, K. S. Hong, and Bruce Speck at the University of Nebraska. They were indispensable in polishing the book through revisions and in preparing the *Instructor's Manual* and *Study Guide*. I am very grateful to my office staff: Joyce Anderson, Cathy Jensen, and Judee Olson for their expert word-processing skills. A tremendous thanks is expressed to the real professionals at the The Dryden Press: Mary Fischer, Penny Gaffney, Alan Wendt, Jan Doty, and Paula Ransdell, and at Chernow Editorial Services: Douglas Bell, Barbara Chernow, and Alison B. Walker. Finally, I could never have completed this book without the support of my family. I dedicate this book to my daughters Tosca and Amy, who always make book writing a tough task.

Sang M. Lee

ABOUT THE AUTHOR

Sang M. Lee is a University Eminent Scholar, Regents Distinguished Professor, Chairman of the Management Department, and the Executive Director of the Nebraska Center for Productivity and Entrepreneurship. He is an internationally known expert in the fields of decision science and productivity management.

Professor Lee is the author or co-author of 24 books, including *Goal Programming for Decision Analysis, Linear Optimization for Management, Management Science, Micro Management Science, Network Analysis for Management Decisions, Operations Management,* and *Japanese Management.* He has published over 140 research papers in various leading journals of management. He has been a distinguished visiting scholar at numerous universities in the United States, Europe, Japan, Korea, and other nations.

Dr. Lee served as President of the Decision Sciences Institute (DSI) and currently is serving as President of the Pan-Pacific Business Association. He is a Fellow of DSI and received the Distinguished Service Award from DSI in 1980 for his contribution to the decision science profession. He received the Outstanding Research Award and the AMOCO Distinguished Teaching Award at the University of Nebraska. He has organized nine international conferences in the areas of comparative management, productivity, quality control, technology transfer, and international business. He is a frequent consultant to business and nonprofit organizations.

CONTENTS

Chapter 18 MANAGEMENT SCIENCE IMPLEMENTATION AND DECISION SUPPORT SYSTEMS

APPENDICES

INDEX   *793*

SOLUTIONS TO EVEN-NUMBERED ASSIGNMENTS   *798*

1 THE ROLE OF MANAGEMENT SCIENCE

Management is basically a process of achieving a set of objectives in an effective way. To be effective managers, we must be rational in our problem solving and decision making. Management science is a discipline that includes a host of rational approaches to management decision making. In this chapter we will discuss what modern management is and how rational approaches of management science play important roles in today's complex organizations.

Learning Objectives *From the study of this chapter, we will learn the following:*

1. The basic process of management
2. The importance of decision making in management
3. How people ought to make decisions based on rationality
4. How people actually make decisions in reality
5. How management science can assist managers to make better decisions
6. What types of techniques are most widely applied in practice
7. A short historical background of management science
8. How to build a proper perspective about the role of management science
9. The meaning of the following terms:

Management	*Management science*
Decision making	*Operations research*
Rational behavior	*Decision science*
Optimization	*Economic person*
Bounded rationality	*Management information systems*
Satisficing	*Scientific method*
	Systems approach

WHAT'S IT ALL ABOUT?

Life consists of a continuous process of making decisions and solving problems. From the days of childhood to our teenage years and then our adult lives, we try to stay healthy, be happy, and do interesting things. In the process we make numerous types of decisions. The environment in which we live is complex, with various components such as laws, regulations, morality, socioeconomic realities, uncertainty about the future, and diseases. Thus, decision making is never simple.

Although we make decisions every day, we rarely spend time thinking about how we actually do make decisions. Perhaps we are too busy making decisions to think about decision making. Since we want to be successful in almost everything we do, we would like to do the right things at the right times. No one is a perfect decision maker, but each of us would like to be a successful one, at least for important decisions.

As individuals, we are experienced decision makers. Every day we make many routine decisions—how to dress, which road to take to school, where to have lunch, and so on. We also make many important decisions—whether to look for a part-time job at the library or at a local bank, whether to take computer science or engineering as our minor, whether to go to a graduate school or look for a job, and the like. Although the consequences of some of these decisions may be relatively minor, important decisions such as choosing a spouse or a career can change our lives.

Some people believe that good decision makers are born with special abilities. But we believe, and many empirical studies support our position, that decision-making abilities can be acquired through learning and experience. Managerial decision making does not differ too much from personal decision making. However, the magnitude, the nature, and the possible consequences are enormously greater for managerial problems. Thus, our purpose in studying management science is to learn the basics of rational decision making and how they can be applied to solving real-world management problems.

A noted educator once stated that every U.S. child should know at least two foreign languages: English and mathematics. This educator had a rare perceptiveness in his definition of mathematics as a language. Mathematics is the language of rational thought. Thus, we will use mathematics in learning to be rational, consistent, and systematic in generating useful information for decision making. Mathematics allows us to be precise and succinct in expressing our thought. Furthermore, mathematics enables us to manipulate important characteristics of problems in answering "what if" questions. That makes mathematics a perfect tool for rational decision making.

Discussion of mathematics brings up an interesting and practical question: Can we really be perfectly rational in decision making? We know we cannot. Decision making in human organizations is never precise. We must analyze the inexact nature of human problems with imprecise tools and our limited analytical abilities. Managers know this and therefore cannot be total idealists. They must get desired results through practical means. Then, the rational decision-making process based on mathematics must be practical. It can be and has been used in many real-world applications.

MANAGEMENT AND DECISION MAKING

The lifeblood of an organization is **management.** In spite of all else, if management falters, an organization cannot long survive. Although management is vital to our society, we have no universal definition of management; management has different meanings to different people. We know pretty much what a private does in the army, a secretary in an office, an assembly line worker in a General Motors plant, a salesperson in a shoe store, and a nurse in a municipal hospital. However, we have no standard view of a manager's job. Who managers are and what they do depend entirely upon the organization, the geographical location, the department, the expertise of the managers, the number of people working under them, and many other related factors.

Over a half century ago Mary Parker Follet defined management as "getting things done through people." This broad and vague definition is still a very good description of management. Management is a dynamic living system which integrates human, financial, and physical resources in such an effective way that the output becomes greater than the simple sum of its inputs. Thus, management emphasizes the following factors: (1) the determination of definite directions for the organization — a set of objectives; (2) the search for efficient ways to achieve the objectives through evaluating feasible alternatives; and (3) the analysis of the environmental constraints, both external and internal to the organization.

Traditionally, management has been regarded as the art of "getting things done." Thus, it emphasizes the "art" of performing the job. The individual manager's behavioral leadership qualities, with a strong connotation of a military commander's abilities, is an example of the "art" we are talking about. However, many recent studies have emphasized the "science" aspect of management — analytical approaches to problem solving and **decision making.**

In reality, we believe management is a combination of art and science that requires both the behavioral and systematic approaches. In science, we can predict the phenomenon with a definite probability of occurrence when the ingredients of a process are accurately determined. For example, we can foretell with 99.99 percent accuracy the result of a chemical process when certain chemicals are added together in a given environment. However, such accuracy of scientific experimentation or prediction is impossible in a management process, because the ingredients (people and other resources) are unpredictable and the environment is dynamic.

Management is a dynamic system that involves constantly changing environments, technologies, and philosophies. Thus the basic function of modern management has become management of disturbance, problem solving, or decision making. *Decision making is the most fundamental function of management.* As a matter of fact, Herbert A. Simon, an eminent scholar of management and a Nobel laureate in 1978, states that decision making is synonymous with management. Thus, managers are often evaluated on the basis of their performance in decision making.

In order to improve the quality of decision making, organizations and managers constantly seek ways to be more rational and systematic in making decisions. Thus, management science has become an integral part of modern management. Management science is a discipline that includes a host of rational approaches to management decision making. The central theme of management science is the application of scientific and rational methodologies to the process of management.

RATIONALITY IN DECISION MAKING

A well-known scientist decided that he had been a bachelor long enough, or at least that he should seriously consider whether to get married or not, and if so to whom. Being a rational man, he sat down and enumerated the advantages and disadvantages of the marital state and the kind of qualities that he should look for in choosing a wife. As for the advantages — and I quote from his notes, "Children (if it please God), con-

stant companion (and friend in old age), charms of music and female chit-chat." Among the disadvantages — "Terrible loss of time, if many children forced to gain one's bread; fighting about no society." But he continued, "What is the use of working without sympathy from near and dear friends? Who are near and dear friends to the old, except relatives?" And his conclusion was: "My God, it is intolerable to think of spending one's whole life like a neuter bee, working, working, and nothing after all. No, no won't do. Imagine living all one's day solitarily in smokey, dirty London house — only picture to yourself a nice soft wife on a sofa, with good fire and books and music perhaps — compare this vision with the dingy reality of Gt. Marlboro Street." His conclusion: "Marry, marry, marry." Having decided that he ought to get married and having listed the desirable qualities of a future spouse, he then proceeded to look for a suitable candidate. He had several female cousins, so that there was no need to search outside the family circle. He dispassionately compared their attributes with his list of objectives and constraints, made his choice, and proposed to her. Needless to say, he lived happily ever after. The scientist in question — Charles Darwin; the year, 1837.[1]

The above true story points out several important aspects of decision making. The first is that the rational decision-making effort is really nothing new. As a matter of fact, the primary distinguishing characteristic of humanity has been humans' capacity to learn about their environment and to use such knowledge in an organized effort to accomplish desired goals. Some academicians trace the concept of decision making for objectives to the days of the Old Testament or the ancient Greek philosophers. There is no practical value in seeking a detailed genealogy of rational decision making. It should suffice to say that rational decision-making effort has always been a major task of humanity.

The second aspect that we want to point out in the Darwin story is that decision making is constrained by environmental factors. Charles Darwin was a superb scientist. Thus, he was able to be rational in selecting his wife. The six wives of Henry VIII certainly must have wished that he was more rational in solving his marital problems. For some reason, Darwin limited his search for a bride to the family circle. Although he thought he made the best decision, it might not have been the best decision. This special constraint he imposed might have been due to his family training, his personality, or the accepted social norm during that period of time in England. In other words, the way we define the decision environment presents a host of constraints to the decision-making process.

The third aspect of the Darwin story which deserves our attention is that complex real-world problems usually involve multiple, sometimes conflicting, objectives. Indeed, management by multiple objectives is a fact of life in the manager's job. This particular element of complexity presents a host of difficulties in decision making. Management by multiple objectives has been an important area of research in management science during the past 15 years.

Whenever we discuss rationality in decision making, two basic approaches emerge: the scientific method and the concept of the **economic person.** We will now discuss them in detail.

---

[1]S. Eilon, "Goals and Constraints in Decision Making," *Operational Research Quarterly* 23: 1 (1973), 3. Quoted with the permission of the Society of Operational Research.

The Scientific Method

The **scientific method** has evolved over a long period of time as a set of systematic steps for conducting research in the physical sciences — physics, chemistry, biology, astronomy, geology, and so on. It has been said that Sir Francis Bacon was the first person to formally suggest the method, over 400 years ago. Although the scientific method was established for the physical sciences, management scientists have borrowed the concept liberally for management decision making.

Table 1.1 presents the steps of the scientific method and their equivalent phases in management decision making.

Step 1: Define the Decision Problem   This first step is the most crucial and difficult part. It has the preemptive role for the rest of the steps. For example, suppose that you defined your problem as "Should I purchase an IBM PC or a Macintosh?" Your statement excluded not only other personal computers, but also many other types of decisions you face, such as which typewriter to purchase, or whether to spend money on a skiing trip to Colorado, a new camera, and a new sound system.

Suppose you decide to redefine your problem as follows: "I am falling behind in my classes. I must purchase a small computer to complete my term papers and other assignments quickly." Now the nature of the problem has been changed drastically in that it has been opened up to the purchase of all sorts of personal computers — IBM, Apple, Kaypro, Compaq, AT&T, Texas Instruments, NEC, and so on. *Finding a good solution to the right problem is far superior to getting the best solution to the wrong problem.*

Step 2: Search for Data and Information   In order to understand fully the nature of the problem at hand and its relationship to other problems, it is essential to have relevant data and information. Your selection of a personal computer may not be the real problem; perhaps it is your poor management of time: Your too-frequent social activities, declining grade-point average, and extracurricular activities may be interrelated.

It is important to collect relevant data and sort them out in such a way that they will provide information for decision making. For example, you may want to gather information about the different personal computers — price, warranty, software support, compatibility with other computers, versatility, and, perhaps, input from some of your friends who have used these computers concerning their satisfaction with their equipment.

Table 1.1   Steps in the Scientific Method and Their Equivalents in Management Decision Making

The Scientific Method	Management Decision Making
1. Define the problem.	1. Define the decision problem.
2. Collect data.	2. Search for data and information.
3. Develop hypotheses.	3. Generate alternative courses of action.
4. Test hypotheses.	4. Analyze feasible alternatives.
5. Analyze results.	5. Select the best course of action.
6. Draw conclusion.	6. Implement the decision and evaluate results.

Step 3: Generate Alternative Courses of Action   The next step is to generate alternative courses of action that could be taken for the decision problem. Most people limit their search for alternatives to those that are obvious and readily available. It is important to generate additional alternatives so that all feasible courses of action can be evaluated. For example, in searching for the best personal computer, you may want to check local computer dealers, your professors, and mail-order advertisements in appropriate magazines.

Step 4: Analyze Feasible Alternatives   Armed with information about the problem and the available courses of action, you must now turn to analyzing alternatives. The primary standards to be used in the analysis are the objective criteria—the things that you would like to accomplish. For example, you may set several criteria about your personal computer selection, such as price, software availability, and versatility.

You should then evaluate each alternative against the objective criteria. You can easily eliminate several alternatives that are clearly inferior to others. Such alternatives are often referred to as *dominated solutions*. In order to evaluate the nondominated alternatives, you may wish to use your priorities for the objective criteria. For example, suppose that you have the following simple list of priorities written down on the back of an envelope:

1. Price

2. Software support

3. Compatibility with other computers

4. Service availability

5. Warranty

6. Reputation of the manufacturer

Now you should be able to further eliminate some alternatives on the list.

Step 5: Select the Best Course of Action   Once the analysis of alternatives is completed, you can make a decision by selecting the best course of action. The final decision will be based on a number of considerations, some quantitative and some judgmental. For example, the price of a personal computer is a quantitative criterion. However, versatility and the reputation of the manufacturer represent judgmental considerations. Evaluation of decision criteria in terms of their priorities to you is perhaps the most efficient way to select the best course of action.

When we have a set of objective criteria we want to achieve, we often get into a tangle of trade-offs. In other words, sometimes we can achieve an important objective if we give up something else. If you are considering purchasing a personal computer which is loaded with 512K memory and all the software you might need, it may take every penny you have in your savings account for your education.

Step 6: Implement the Decision and Evaluate Results   Decision making means taking a certain action. Implementation of action plans is the final phase of decision making. However, we do not stop there. We must always evaluate the results of the decision and ascertain whether the decision problem is resolved to our satisfaction. Feedback obtained through an evaluation process is a very important element of the scientific method. The implementation phase of management science is fully discussed in Chapter 18.

The Concept of Economic Person

When we study human decision-making behavior in organizations, we find two broad theoretical foundations—**normative** (prescriptive) and **descriptive** (behavioral). The normative theories are concerned with how rational decisions *ought* to be made, whereas the descriptive theories are concerned with how decisions *are* made.

The normative (or classical) theory of rational decision making is conceptually neat. It assumes as decision maker the economic person, who has perfect rationality. In other words, the decision maker is assumed to have complete information on all relevant aspects of the decision environment, to possess a stable system of preferences, and to have the ability to analyze the alternative courses of action. Thus, the decision maker is assumed to be a perfect individual to utilize the scientific method.

The concept of economic person presents a rational individual who always employs the scientific method to obtain the optimum solution for a single objective criterion for the organization. In other words, the economic person always seeks global optimization. Global **optimization** in this context simply means that the decision maker seeks a solution that would result in the best overall organizational measure, such as finding the maximum profit or the least cost. Thus, several economic persons would reach the same solution to a given problem. Clearly, no decision maker in reality behaves like the economic person. Furthermore, decision makers have their own unique ways of approaching a problem, and it is not likely that a number of them would reach the same solution.

Unfortunately, the concept of economic person is not capable of either handling several important features of real-world problems or reflecting the actual decision-making process of management. First, real-world decision problems invariably involve more than a single objective. As a matter of fact, most managerial decision problems involve multiple, competitive, and sometimes incompatible objectives. For example, we have already discussed your personal computer selection problem in relation to your planned ski trip, purchase of a new camera, and a new sound system. Also, it is totally unrealistic to assume that the decision maker has an omniscient rationality, perfect information about the decision problem, and a perfect set of preferences. Decision makers typically have their own unique ways of approaching a problem, personal judgments about the objectives of their organization, very incomplete information about the decision environment, and limited analytical abilities to search for the best solution to the problem.

MANAGEMENT SCIENCE AND THE SYSTEMS APPROACH

Management science is concerned with the application of scientific approaches to generate concrete information that is relevant to the problem solving of the decision maker. Special emphasis is placed on the analysis of the nature of the problem, the decision environment, the objectives of the organization, the judgment of the decision maker, and the economic as well as noneconomic ramifications of the decision environment. As we have already discussed, management science is dedicated to finding the **best**

feasible solution. Feasible implies that the best solution we seek must be workable, or implementable.

Since management science is a systematic and comprehensive approach to decision making, it inevitably involves what is called the **systems approach.** A system is a whole composed of a set of components, their attributes, and certain relationships among components that perform a function. Thus, a manufacturing firm is a person–machine system. A stereo set, however, is a mechanical system; it is made up of components such as transistors, electronic converters, and speakers that transmit sound.

A precise analysis in human organizations, as contrasted to mechanical systems, is not possible because of uncertainties involved in human behavior such as motivation, performance, and cooperation among individuals. This fact further complicates the management decision-making process. Nevertheless, management science attempts to seek the best solution for the organization as a whole. Any managerial problem should be put in proper perspective so that its impact on the whole organization and its environment can be analyzed. In other words, management science should be applied in a systems context.

Upon the solution of the original problem, management science applied in a systems context often uncovers new problems. This is a very important characteristic of management science. Therefore, the most effective way to apply management science is through continuous analysis rather than a one-shot solution approach.

The basic objective of management science is to find a feasible solution which is best for the organization, the global optimization. The process of finding a solution that is best for one or more parts of the organization is usually called **suboptimization.** Management science attempts to find a solution that is close to the global optimum by analyzing interrelationships among the system components that are involved in the problem.

The beginning of management science is unknown, as the birth of science itself is unknown. The roots of management science are as old as mankind's curiosity, civilization, and culture. There is evidence that some forms of scientific approaches to management existed during the era of the industrial revolution. Frederick W. Taylor, the father of **scientific management,** pioneered industrial engineering and systematic approaches to management through his time-and-motion studies in the late nineteenth century.

However, the name **operations research (OR),** a term often used interchangeably with *management science,* began to be used only in the early 1940s. The origin of military operations research activities was in the United Kingdom during the early part of World War II. In order to devise the most effective military tactics and strategies, there was an urgent need for scientific approaches to analyze various logistics problems. The British, and later the U.S., military authorities formed groups of scientists to conduct research on military operations. It has been said that OR studies were instrumental in the victories in the air battle of Britain, the island campaign in the Pacific, the battle of the North Atlantic, and other phases of the war.

Synonyms for the term *management science* are numerous. A frequent substitute is *operations research,* and other terms such as *systems analysis, systems science, operations analysis, quantitative analysis, managerial analysis, decision analysis,* and *decision science* are also used. We have decided to use the term *management science* in this book because we are basically concerned with the systematic analysis of management decision problems. There is no organizational barrier for management science application. In other words, we can use management science for decision problems in government, military service, business and industry, academic institutions, health-care organizations, and many other areas.

HOW MANAGERS ACTUALLY MAKE DECISIONS

Now that we know something about rational decision making and management science, let us focus our attention on how managers actually make decisions in real-world situations. Management science permits the manager to utilize a scientific or analytical approach to problem solving. We believe management science has contributed more toward the acceptance of purpose-oriented management (often referred to as "management by objectives") than is usually appreciated by managers and scholars.

The role of management science is especially important today because of the following factors:

Technology is getting more sophisticated every day (voice recognition systems, artificial intelligence, expert systems, telecommunication systems, lasers, industrial robots, and so on).

There is an increasing shortage of energy and critical materials (fossil fuels, certain vital metals).

Managerial problems involve complex processes (production and inventory control, assembly-line balancing, location allocation, working-capital management, customer-information processing).

Managerial problems are not only complex but are becoming even more important (oil-importing decisions that involve international relations, development of computer-based information systems, design of the MX missile system, negotiations about the trade imbalance with Japan).

The problems managers face are often new, and there is no benefit to be drawn from past experience (the oil embargo of 1973, the Mt. St. Helens eruption, the continuous decline of productivity, and the like).

The emphasis on management planning and long-range objectives requires proactive decision making. Thus, managers attempt to forecast future problems and plan ahead before the problems actually emerge (public transit systems, synthetic fuel development, research on the electrical car, gene-splicing devices).

Although we recognize the importance of management science in analyzing important decision problems, we also realize that management is a human process. There exists an enormous gap between the manager's aspirations for using the scientific method for problem solving and the actuality of trying to sort out a big mess from a disorganized chain of random events. In reality, the manager is not like the economic person who is totally rational and effective in utilizing the scientific method for decision making.

As we discussed earlier, the descriptive theories of decision making are concerned with how decisions *are* actually made. The descriptive theories are based on an abundance of empirical data that propose the now celebrated concept of **bounded rational-**

Figure 1.1   Decision-Making Process

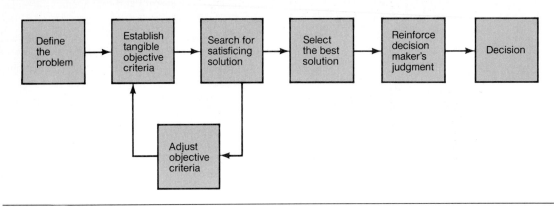

ity. Herbert A. Simon states that under bounded rationality individual decision makers strive to be as efficient as possible in achieving organizational objectives, given their limited information-processing abilities. Clearly, bounded rationality does not mean ir-rationality. The decision maker employs an ''approximate'' or ''intentional'' rationality in the process of attempting to do the best to achieve organizational goals within the given set of constraints.

As we can imagine, management science models developed under the unrealistic conditions of complete rationality have very limited real-world implications. In order to implement decision models, then, either we must sufficiently simplify the model so that the optimum solution can be easily derived or we must design a realistic model and seek satisfactory solutions. The first is the traditional approach, whereas the second approach attempts to retain a richer set of properties of the real decision environment by giving up optimization. Although the two approaches are quite different, they are both ''satisficing'' approaches based on the concept of bounded rationality and have been widely applied by management scientists. The **satisficing** approach attempts to obtain a good solution that is sufficiently satisfactory for a complex decision problem.

The global optimization model based on a single objective criterion (e.g., cost min-imization or profit maximization) is often unrealistic. Perhaps the most practical way to develop a decision model would be to replace the abstract global optimization goal with tangible and measurable subgoals. These subgoals can be formulated on the basis of certain aspiration levels that are related to the organizational goals. Once a decision alternative satisfies a set of aspirations (or at least satisfies important ones), the search activity could be terminated. The satisficing model based on aspiration levels allows for a bounded rational decision by permitting reasonable amounts of analytical effort and incomplete information about the decision environment.

In reality, managers make decisions based not solely on solutions derived from management science models. As a matter of fact, management science models are often used to generate new information or to answer ''what if'' questions. Based on our discussion so far, we can present the decision-making process as shown in Figure 1.1.

THE ROLE OF MANAGEMENT SCIENCE

If managers are not completely rational and systematic in decision making, what then is the role of management science? We can quickly come up with a number of important problems that we have not been able to solve with powerful computer-based management science models — the world population explosion, pollution, the energy shortage, international tension, hunger, decreasing natural resources, and so on. In the role of devil's advocate, let us ask what the world would be like today without systematic analysis of these complex problems. We are sure that the world would be a worse place. We believe management science will play an increasingly more important role in the future, precisely because of the manager's limited ability and rationality.

We are now quite comfortable with the notion that decision making must consider environmental factors, multiple objectives, satisficing, and bounded rationality. We should not view management science as a panacea for managerial decision problems. Decision making is and always will be based on human judgment, intuition, creativity, and perhaps courage, in addition to many systematic approaches. Much of the disillusionment and criticism of management science is the result of unrealistic expectations on the part of those who use it.

Management science plays the following important roles:

Purpose-oriented Decision Making   Management science application requires an organization to be purpose-oriented. Work activities are planned and carried out according to organizational objectives rather than simply rationalizing habits by saying "we have always done it this way." The question "What does this activity contribute toward important organizational objectives?" is frequently asked before resources are committed.

The basic approach of management should be to pursue long-range achievement of the organizational purpose rather than to seek only short-term monetary objectives. One of the primary reasons for the financial and productivity woes of many U.S. corporations is their emphasis on short-term profit objectives, often at the expense of long-term organizational goals.[2] Management science can be a catalyst in coordinating management functions for purpose-oriented decision making in a long-term perspective.

Information- and Analysis-based Decision Making   Decision making based on management science requires an efficient information-processing system. With the ever-increasing complexity of the environment and its vital impact on the organization's survival, information management becomes extremely important. Accurate and timely information must be processed in order to predict the future with an acceptable degree of accuracy. Thus, **management information systems** (MIS) and decision support systems (DSS) have become important for management decision making. We will have a full discussion of DSS in Chapter 18.

Decision Making for Multiple Objectives   Managers should be vitally concerned with the analysis of multiple objectives, not only with their formulation but with their priorities and trade-offs. We are keenly aware of the ever-increasing pressure for the simultaneous satisfaction of such factors as government regulations, economic optimization, industrial relations, and customer demands. Managers must analyze the direct conflict

[2]Bibliographical data for all published material are given in the References at the ends of chapters.

between the organization's economic survival and the other objectives that are related to social responsibilities.

Managers are being held increasingly more accountable for the legitimacy of their objectives, priorities, and resolutions of the conflicts among the objectives of the various interest groups. Thus, we expect to see more widespread application of systematic approaches in dealing with multiple goals and their trade-offs. For example, General Motors Corp. reported that it evaluated several possible sites for its new Saturn plant based on some 60 criteria before it chose Spring Hill, Tennessee, as the best location.

Increased Emphasis on Productivity   The essential purpose of management science is to increase the efficiency of the organization. In order to improve the effectiveness of the management process, three important areas should be evaluated: (1) productivity of human resources; (2) effective management of capital and materials; and (3) efficient decision-making process. Management science can make important contributions to all three areas. We believe that the effective utilization of human resources is the key to the survival and prosperity of the organization.

Increased Attention to Group Behavior   As we focus our attention on the effective utilization of human resources, group decision-making behavior will become increasingly more important. Most management science projects are interdisciplinary in nature. In other words, people from several different departments such as production, finance, marketing, and personnel would work together to solve a common problem.

Many scholars have pointed out that one important reason for the poor showing of U.S. workers in the world productivity race is management's failure to recognize the importance of workers' group behavior. Harvard sociologist Ezra F. Vogel, in his book *Japan as Number One: Lessons for America,* contends that perhaps the most important reason for the phenomenal productivity increase of Japanese workers is their group-conscious behavior patterns. It is extremely important for the Japanese people to belong to groups, and group loyalty and confidence in group objectives are driving forces for Japanese workers. The study of group decision-making behavior, especially the importance of the sense of shared purpose for organizational effectiveness, is receiving greater attention from management in the United States. Thus, participative management based on various group-oriented programs has become popular. Quality circles, quality-of-work-life programs, matrix management, and employee participation programs are good examples.

Efficient Management of Capital, Energy, and Materials   With the increasing scarcity and cost of acquiring capital, energy, and materials, the effective management of these resources is almost as important as the management of human resources. An efficient management of capital, energy, and materials requires systematic approaches based on computer-based information systems and management science. Cost savings from these resources represent a 100 percent contribution to profits, whereas cost savings in other areas (e.g., marketing channels) may represent only a very small net contribution to profits.

More Systematic Contingency Management   In the future, we will probably see more drastic changes in the environment than we have in the past. We will face a shortage of energy, materials, water, clean air, and many other resources. We will also see some important technological breakthroughs—cheaper and more powerful micro-computers, new methods for harnessing energy, new transportation methods, for example. We can also expect many political and economic crises in the international arena. All these changes will have varying degrees of impact on the organizations.

However, an organization cannot be totally reactive to situations, functioning without plans. Nor can it be totally proactive, planning for every possible contingency. But with the aid of management science, management can establish the basic targets and explore the means to get there. With the availability of information systems, management science models, and computational facilities, contingency management can be more systematic and orderly.

Closer Interaction with External Factors   The management process is an open system. It breathes in external factors in the form of environmental constraints, needs, and information. The use of management science requires such information so that the entire system remains current and effective. Thus, management science necessitates that the organization have closer interactions with external forces: government agencies, international situations, socioeconomic factors of the environment, consumer concerns, changing market situations, and the like.

PRACTICAL APPLICATION OF MANAGEMENT SCIENCE

Management science is being applied to a wide range of managerial problems in all types of organizations. Applications of management science have been especially prevalent since the 1960s. However, there have been relatively few published studies about the actual success of management science application. It is therefore somewhat difficult to obtain the true picture of the role of management science in organizations.

A survey conducted by the American Management Association (AMA) in 1957 gave some early indication of the extent of management science application. The survey of 324 organizations that were using management science revealed that 40 percent of the firms reported ''considerable improvement'' in their operations due to management science. Less than 1 percent of the sample indicated the intent to reduce the application of management science.

In a 1966 survey by William Vatter, 360 respondents were questioned about the use of operations research in U.S. companies. This survey asked about any use of operations research and the results obtained from its use. Overall, linear programming, PERT/CPM (Program Evaluation and Review Technique/Critical Path Method), inventory models, simulation, regression analysis, and statistical sampling appeared to be used frequently by the sample companies. Also, the majority of the ratings of tool performance were reported as fair or good.

G. Thomas and J. A. DaCosta surveyed 260 of *Fortune*'s top 500 corporations and 160 of the largest California-based firms in 1978. The results of this survey concerning the corporate use of management science techniques indicate that the most widely used management science techniques were simulation, linear programming, PERT/CPM, and inventory theory. These topics will be thoroughly treated in this text.

A survey was conducted by this author especially for this book. A questionnaire was mailed to 950 nonacademic (practicing) members of the Operations Research Society of America in 1981. Table 1.2 presents the overall results. Based on 142 usable questionnaires returned, this study is similar to previous studies in that statistical analysis, simulation, and linear programming are reported to be the most frequently used

Table 1.2   Results of the Lee Survey

Technique	Use		
	Frequently	Sometimes	Not at All
Statistical analysis	60.6%	37.9%	1.5%
Simulation	45.1	45.1	9.8
Linear programming	29.8	50.4	19.8
Other mathematical programming	23.4	46.1	30.5
PERT/CPM	16.5	45.7	37.8
Inventory models	15.0	42.5	42.5
Multicriteria methods	9.5	34.1	56.4
Search techniques	7.2	35.2	57.6
Queuing models	5.6	45.2	49.2
Game theory	2.4	20.8	76.8

techniques. However, the study also reveals several interesting facts. First, PERT/CPM methods, although still popular, are not so widely applied as previously reported. Second, multicriteria methods are more frequently used now than search techniques, queuing models, or game theory. Third, game theory is not being used much at all in real-world situations. A similar study conducted by S. Lee and J. Shim in 1983 provided the same basic results.

A study conducted by G. Forgionne reinforced Lee and Shim's survey, except that PERT/CPM proved more popular than linear programming. Other mathematical programming techniques tended to be used less, and the conclusion that game theory was used very little in real situations was strongly supported.

BUILDING A PROPER PERSPECTIVE

As you study this book, you will be learning many analytical techniques and will be trying to find exact solutions to various problems. No doubt you will wonder whether it is worth the time and trouble to find *exact* solutions to the problems. For example, you might ask, "Is it necessary to find $x_1 = 1.285714$ or is it sufficient to say that $x_1 = 1.286$?" There is no clear-cut answer, but it all depends on the type of problem. For example, if the variable x_1 represents the number of cups of sugar to put into a cookie mix, either solution would be acceptable. However, if x_1 is the amount of a chemical required to test a chemical reaction, the second solution may not be acceptable.

Managers are often trained to make decisions based on real numbers and to eschew mere qualitative estimates. However, "real" numbers often give wrong or misleading information, and intelligent estimates are often required. For example, let us assess the U.S. health-care system by asking the question, "How many U.S. deaths are attributed to cigarette smoking or old age?" The official statistics give the answer of 0, because neither old age nor cigarette smoking makes the list of the principal causes of death. The key point here is not the precision or the official status of numbers but the understanding of what lies behind them and what they mean. An intelligent estimate based on good understanding is much more useful than precise statistics or exact computations, however authoritative, that are conceptually flawed. This principle should not be neglected in the application of management science.

What we should remember is that a management science model is a simple representation of reality. The purpose of building a model in the first place is to simplify a complex real problem so that we can understand and analyze it. In other words, if a model is almost as complex as the real problem it represents, it has lost its value.

As we shall see in Chapter 2, there is a law of critical few (or Pareto rule) in natural phenomena. We can analyze a management problem by examining critical few variables. The modeling approach is based on this principle. Thus, management science models represent good approximations of the real problems. Solutions we derive by management science are solutions to the approximate models but not solutions to real problems. We must remember this important fact. The role of management science must be put in a proper perspective with this understanding in mind.

When we attempt to build more accurate models and more exact solutions to the models, we must be prepared to expend greater amounts of time, energy, and resources. The critical issue is whether such efforts would be cost-effective. In other words, additional resources required to obtain more accurate solutions should be justified by the benefits derived from the better solutions to the real problems. However, there are other important considerations concerning organizational acceptance of the modeling effort. Generally speaking, complex modeling efforts tend to turn off the interest of those persons who would be implementing the solution. Thus, we must build a proper perspective about modeling in view of the trade-off considerations presented in Table 1.3.

Some people think management science is a panacea for managerial problems. This is far from the truth. Managerial problems usually involve economic, human, physical, engineering, and environmental considerations. Thus, an accurate and completely objective analysis is not possible. Management science must be used as a means to generate new information to improve and sharpen the manager's decision-making abilities, rather than as a black box that spits out solutions to problems.

Successful application of management science requires a considerable amount of artistic creativity and the desire for change. Management problems are like a big mess

Table 1.3   Key Considerations in the Modeling Process

Key Considerations	Modeling Approach	
	Complex Model **Accurate Solutions**	**Simple Model** **Approximate Solutions**
Resources required		
Cost	High	Low
Time	High	Low
Manpower	High	Low
Organizational acceptance		
Involving people	Low	High
Understanding the effort	Low	High
Implementation of the result	Low	High
Solution to the real problem	Good	Approximate

of gelatin that is hard to handle. In order to capture important features of a problem and analyze it for practical application, we must be imaginative, creative, and persistent. Also, we need to find ways to stimulate people who will be using the information generated by models. Management scientists must serve as catalysts in their rejection of the status quo and of any hang-ups about systematic analysis. Such dedication is much needed to implement management science.

SUMMARY

This chapter has provided a broad introduction to management science in terms of its meaning, role, history, and application to decision making. You are not expected to be an expert in management science after reading this chapter, but you should have a good feel for what management science is about. You should also have learned to use several new jargonistic terms such as optimization, economic person, scientific method, bounded rationality, satisficing, and management information systems.

The ideas we have discussed in this chapter are useful in guiding our approaches to management problems and in deriving pertinent information that is essential for decision making. We will be using mathematics throughout this book as a language of rational thought. Mathematical models are effective tools in transforming disorganized and complex real problems into simple and manageable toy problems. Perhaps the most important single item we should remember is that we must keep a proper perspective about the value, role, and limitations of management science.

Glossary

Bounded Rationality   The concept of a person striving to be as efficient as possible in achieving organizational objectives, given limits on the person's ability to process information.

Economic Person   A completely rational individual who attempts to optimize economic payoff.

Global Optimization   The process of finding the best solution for the entire organization or system.

Satisficing   The process of achieving a good solution that is sufficiently satisfactory for a complex decision problem.

Suboptimization   The process of finding a solution that is best for one or more parts of the organization.

System   A consistent whole comprised of a set of components, their attributes, and certain relationships among the components that perform a function.

References

American Management Association. *Operations Research Considered,* Management Report 10. New York: AMA, 1958.

Churchman, C. S., Ackoff, R. L., and Arnoff, E. L. *Introduction to Operations Research.* New York: Wiley, 1957.

Drucker, P. F. *Innovation and Entrepreneurship.* New York: Harper & Row, 1985.

Eilon, S. "Goals and Constraints in Decision Making." *Operational Research Quarterly* 23: 1 (1972), 3–16.

Forgionne, G. A. "Corporate Management–Science Activities: An Update." *Interfaces* 13: 3 (June 1983), 20–23.

Gallagher, C. A., and Watson, J. H. *Quantitative Methods for Business Decisions*. New York: McGraw-Hill, 1980.

Hayes, R. H., and Wheelwright, S. C. *Restoring Our Competitive Edge*. New York: Wiley, 1984.

Lee, S. M. *Management by Multiple Objectives*. Princeton, N.J.: Petrocelli Books, 1982.

Lee, S. M., and Moore, L. J. *Introduction to Decision Science*. New York: Petrocelli-Charter, 1975.

Lee, S. M., Moore, L. J., and Taylor, B. W. *Management Science*. 2d ed. Dubuque, Iowa: W. C. Brown, 1985.

Lee, S. M., and Shim, J. P. "A Note on Microcomputer Applications." *Interface: The Computer Education Quarterly* 6: 3 (1984), 22–27.

Simon, H. A. *Administrative Behavior*. 2d ed. New York: Macmillan, 1957.

Simon, H. A. "Rational Decision Making in Business Organizations." *American Economic Review* 69: 4 (1979), 493–513.

Taylor, F. W. *Principles of Scientific Management*. New York: Harper, 1911.

Thomas, G., and DaCosta, J. A. "A Sample Survey of Corporate Operations Research." *Interfaces* 9: 4 (Aug. 1979), 102–111.

Vatter, W. "The Use of Operations Research in American Companies." *The Accounting Review* 42: 4 (1967), 712–730.

Vogel, E. F. *Japan as Number One: Lessons for America*. Cambridge, Mass.: Harvard University Press, 1979.

Assignments

1.1 What is the difference between management and management science?

1.2 What is the relationship between management science and the broad area of management?

1.3 Try to recall a decision you made today. Discuss how you made the decision. Now follow the steps of the scientific method to see whether you would reach the same decision again.

1.4 Is management an art or science? Discuss your own ideas.

1.5 What are the advantages and disadvantages of the scientific method?

1.6 Contrast the normative and descriptive theories of decision making.

1.7 What is the relationship between management science and the systems approach?

1.8 What are three basic skills of management?

1.9 What are the most widely used synonyms for management science?

1.10 In your opinion, what are three of the most important reasons behind the expanding role of management science?

1.11 Consider a personal problem you have right now. Are there multiple objectives involved? Are they congruent, complementary, or in conflict? Discuss in detail.

1.12 In your opinion, what are the three most important roles of management science?

1.13 "Management science is not a panacea for management problems, but it is the best medicine we have." Discuss your ideas about this statement.

1.14 "Management science must provide the precise answers to the problem." Discuss your opinions about this statement.

2 MODELING IN MANAGEMENT SCIENCE

In management science we approach various managerial problems in the context of models. We attempt to scale down complex real problems to approximate simple relationships so that we can understand and analyze them. Because models play such an important role in management science, this chapter is devoted to modeling and its functions in the process of management science.

Learning Objectives *From the study of this chapter, we will learn the following:*

1. The meaning and classifications of models
2. The advantages and limitations of management science models
3. Classifications of decision-making models
4. The process of management science
5. The meaning of the following terms:

Models	*Iconic model*
Deterministic	*Critical few*
Probabilistic	*Decision making under certainty*
Static	*Decision making under risk*
Dynamic	*Decision making under uncertainty*
Mental model	*Decision making under conflict*
Verbal models	*Independent variables*
Symbolic models	*Dependent variables*
Mathematical models	*Model parameters*
Analog models	*Random parameters*

INTRODUCTION TO MODELING

"Man is a thinking animal"; "I think, therefore, I am." We have heard these old sayings many times. The primary characteristic distinguishing human beings from other animals is that they can think. The ability to think is the source of our ability to solve problems. Imagination and creativity enable human beings to recognize their existence in the environment. Imagination is basically the ability to build mental images of complex objects without actually observing them. In other words, human beings can solve problems by building **models.**

While taking your morning shower, you no doubt think about all the things you need to do during the day: Go to classes in the morning, finish the computer programming project, play a game of racquetball at Wallbanger's, and go to work in the afternoon. As you think about these activities, you are organizing them in a sequence based on the geographic locations of where you need to be, the duration of expected activity times, and the scheduled times of the activities. After a short period of mental modeling, you can decide the sequence of activities for the day.

The **mental model** you constructed above is, of course, quite incomplete and fuzzy. You might ask the question, "Should I make the model more complete by analyzing all the details of the events?" We should say not. You have a simple abstraction of the actual situation, and the simplicity of the model allows you to solve the scheduling problem. If you were to spend 5 hours developing a detailed model, you would not gain anything. The advantage of modeling is that the model we build captures pertinent details of the problem but is simpler than the complex reality. In essence, then, modeling is a process used to develop a simple representation of a problem; the model's solution is then applied to the situation in reality that it represents.

What Is a Model?

There are all types of models around us. Perhaps the models we see and use most often are photographs, road maps, model airplanes, and Raggedy Anns. Mathematical equations, chemical molecule relations, conceptual theories, and our own mental images are also some examples of models. Every model has one basic purpose—to represent some aspects of reality by means of a simple object. So, let us state it one more time: The primary purpose of modeling is to understand a complex problem through a simpler, less expensive, and less cumbersome object.

Model Classification

There are many different ways to classify models. However, the most widely accepted taxonomy for models is *abstract* and *exact*. Abstract models are extremely fuzzy and ill-structured representations of reality. As with your mental model discussed earlier, they have no physical or symbolic configuration. Exact models, on the other hand, have some physical characteristics that resemble the reality under study. Physical models include such things as model airplanes, dolls, and an architect's scaled-down buildings. Between these two extremes there are **symbolic models** such as theories, written statements, and mathematical relationships. Figure 2.1 presents the classifications of models based on their degree of abstraction.

1. *Mental Models.* Mental models are the most abstract representation of reality, such as imagination, as we discussed previously.

2. *Verbal Models.* **Verbal models** use written models to represent mental models with words, such as poetry, plays, novels, theories, and a police officer's report of a traffic accident.

3. *Mathematical Models.* **Mathematical models** are also symbolic models, but they consist of mathematical relationships rather than words. Most management science models we will be studying in this book are mathematical models.

Figure 2.1   Model Classification

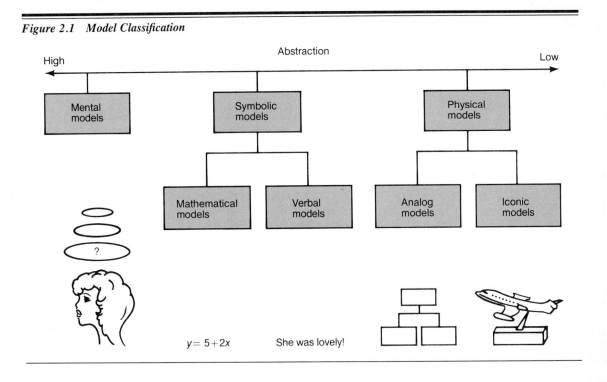

4. *Analog Models.*   **Analog models** are also physical models that may look like the reality they represent. Typically, they focus on certain basic functions or relationships. Maps, blueprints, and organizational charts are good examples of analog models.

5. *Iconic Models.*   **Iconic models** are physical replicas of a reality, usually smaller or bigger in scale than the actual object. Many three-dimensional models such as model airplanes, buildings, and dolls or two-dimensional paintings and photographs are good examples of iconic models.

MANAGEMENT SCIENCE MODELING

Among all the models discussed above, only mathematical models enable us to communicate precisely with the model builder without any misunderstanding. For example, we cannot always comprehend accurately what others have in mind when they verbalize their mental models, but if someone presents his or her annual income as $I = 12x$, where $x =$ monthly income of \$2,000, there is no communication problem as to what the person's yearly income is.

Since mathematical models employ the language of mathematics in describing the system under study, we can also manipulate the models so that we can test the behavior of a system under varying conditions. For example, in the income model $I = 12x$, we can easily determine a new annual income when x is increased from \$2,000 to \$2,500. We can easily expand the model by adding other variables such as interest earned, dividends, and other income.

Management science models are good examples of mathematical models. They are formulated and used to understand or predict certain management systems. One obvious disadvantage of a management science model is that it is something less than the real system it represents. However, this aspect of a model is also an advantage. Since a model is simple, by analyzing it we can understand how the complex system functions. Thus, we can test the behavior of the system under different conditions. The real challenge of modeling is to build as simple a model as possible while including all pertinent attributes of the system.

Determining which model to build for a certain problem is an art in itself. Designing an appropriate model depends on the nature of the problem under study and the desired outcome of the study. For example, a production scheduling model can be formulated only after the production system is thoroughly analyzed and the purpose of the scheduling system is clearly established.

In the natural phenomenon there exists the basic law of **critical few.** According to this law, there are a handful of critical attributes or variables that explain the major portion of the system's functions. For example, several key employees contribute 80 percent of the new ideas, two or three persons are responsible for the project delays, and 10 percent of the items contribute 85 percent of sales. Thus, we must identify these critical few attributes and include their performance in the model. The art of modeling can be mastered only through a good knowledge of management science, experience in model building, and creativity in fitting available tools to complex problems.

The Model Structure

Management science models are usually in the form of mathematical relationships such as equations or inequalities. For example, your disposable income can be expressed as a relationship between your gross income (wages, bonuses, dividends, interest income, and so on) and deductions (taxes, insurance premiums, pension payments, and so on) as follows:

$$DI = G - D$$

where
$$DI = \text{disposable income}$$
$$G = \text{total gross income}$$
$$D = \text{deductions}$$

The above model is perhaps the simplest example of a mathematical model. The complexity as well as the nature of the model will, of course, depend on the nature of the problem under study and the purpose of the analysis. We will discuss many other types of models later in this chapter.

The Model Components

When we attempt to construct a model, the first step is to abstract important components that explain the behavior of the system we are about to analyze. Such components are usually referred to as **variables.** In your disposable income model, G and D are good examples of variables. In a broad sense, we classify variables into two categories: dependent and independent.

The Dependent Variables The **dependent variables** are sometimes referred to as "criterion variables." The value taken on by a dependent variable reflects the level of performance achievement of the system. For example, in the disposable income model,

DI is the dependent variable. When your *DI* = 0, we know what kind of situation you are in—dead broke. If your *DI* = $2,000, either you have been successful in bringing in more income or your deductions have been greatly reduced. The value of the dependent variable is based on the values of the independent variables in the model.

In business organizations we can find a number of widely recognized dependent or criterion variables. Figure 2.2 shows some examples of dependent variables in a production environment: quantity of products processed, quality of products, customer satisfaction, total profit, market share, and return on investment.

The Independent Variables   The **independent variables** are those that are not dependent on other variables in the model. In general, there are two types of independent variables: the **decision** (controllable) variables and the **exogenous** (uncontrollable) variables.

The Decision Variables   The decision variables are often the most important components in management science models. It is the values of these variables for which a solution is sought. For example, let us formulate your total wage earnings model as follows:

$$W = 5.00H$$

where
$$W = \text{total wage earnings}$$
$$5 = \text{wage rate per hour}$$
$$H = \text{number of hours worked}$$

After evaluating the prospects of a loan and your parents' support, you decided that you need at least $700.00 from the part-time job during the next 2 months. Now you are trying to determine how many hours you have to work to earn $700.00. Thus, *H* is your decision variable in this model. You can easily determine the value of *H* as follows:

$$700 = 5H$$
$$H = 700/5$$
$$H = 140$$

Some of the typical decision variables in a production situation are also presented in Figure 2.2.

The Exogenous Variables   The second type of independent variables, the exogenous variables, affect the outcome of the model and the system, but we have very little control over them. For a production problem, exogenous variables may include the cost of materials, availability of materials and human resources, and pollution-control regulations.

Model Parameters   The **parameters** are the remaining components of the model that are essential in developing the relationships among the variables. Parameters are generally classified into two categories: constant and random.

Constant Parameters   The parameters are often assumed to be constant; that is, there exists a **static** state. Such an assumption may be valid for a short time before major environmental or organizational factors change. In the example of your disposable income model, the functional relationship of the total wage *(W)* and the hours worked *(H)* contains a parameter of $5, the hourly wage rate.

Figure 2.2   A Production Scheduling Model

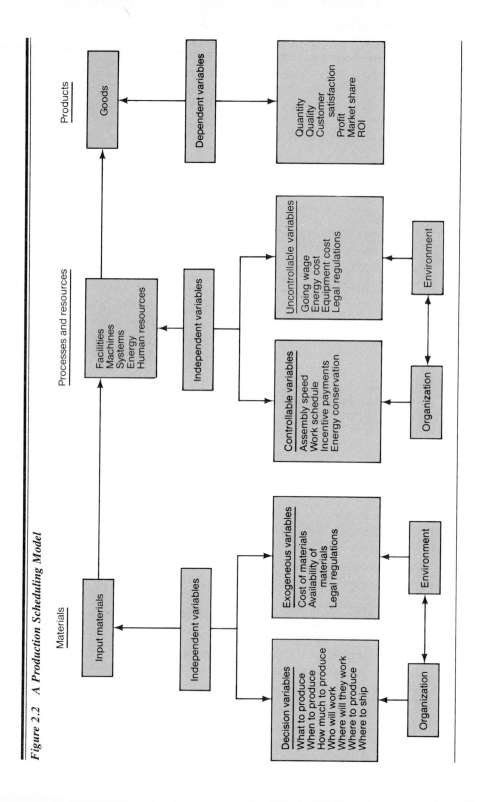

Random Parameters   In a more dynamic or complex situation, the model parameters may not have a constant relationship, but rather the parameters themselves vary according to some probability distribution. For example, in your total wage model let us assume that you accepted the option of getting 100 percent of your wages in tips rather than the $5/hour constant wage rate. In this case your total wage may be expressed as:

$$W = tH$$

where t = amount of tip received per hour

Obviously, t is not a constant parameter but a random parameter.

Relationships within the Model

The essence of management science models is the representation of the relationships among the various components of the model. The relationship *can be illustrated graphically*. For example, your wage model $W = 5H$ can be presented graphically as shown in Figure 2.3.

Most of the management science models presented in this introductory text will be relatively complete so that we can derive a solution. When such a complete model cannot be constructed because of either lack of data or complexity of the system, computer programs may be employed as tools for analysis. The computer-based simulation to analyze waiting lines at a bank is a good example of such an approach.

Figure 2.3   Graphical Representation of the Wage Model

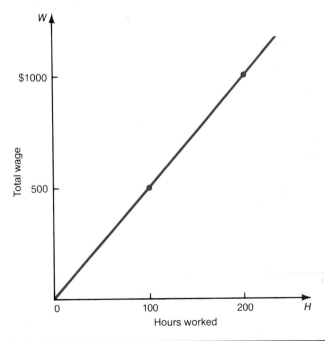

DECISION-MAKING ENVIRONMENT

Management science is primarily concerned with searching for information about feasible courses of action. The type of management science models used may be based both on the nature of the problem at hand and on the decision environment. Basically, there are four different states of decision environment: **certainty, risk, uncertainty,** and **conflict.** In Table 2.1 a summary is presented about the types of decision environments, the expected solutions, and some of the typical management science techniques applied. We shall discuss each decision environment in greater detail.

Decision Making under Certainty

If we have all the information required to make a decision, we have **decision making under certainty.** In other words, under certainty we can predict exactly the outcome of each alternative course of action. For example, in the linear programming problem presented in Chapters 3, 4, and 5, we know exactly how much of different resources are required to produce a product; thus, we can accurately predict its unit profit.

Many of the decision problems we face daily are under certainty. Where to purchase a calculator—K-Mart, Sears, or University Bookstore? Where to have lunch—McDonald's, Burger King, the Crib, or the University Club? You know exactly how much a calculator or a meal costs at each of the locations, and you know the quality you will receive for your money.

Most of the management science techniques we will be studying in this book are for decision making under the condition of certainty. For example, linear programming; goal programming; transportation and assignment models; and analytical approaches of inventory, queuing, and PERT/CPM models are all **deterministic** models for decision making under certainty.

Table 2.1 *Decision Environment, Solutions, and Management Science Techniques*

Decision Environment	Solutions	Typical Techniques
Certainty	Deterministic	Linear programming Integer programming Goal programming Transportation and assignment models Dynamic programming Inventory models under certainty Some queuing and network models
Risk	Probabilistic	Probabilistic decision models Probabilistic inventory models Queuing models Simulation models
Uncertainty	Unknown	Decision analysis under uncertainty
Conflict	Contingent upon opponents' actions	Various custom-built models Game theory

Decision Making under Risk

Decision making under risk refers to the situation in which the probabilities of certain decision outcomes occurring are known. For example, suppose that a computer store is considering stocking a new microcomputer just introduced in the market. The manager's immediate concern is to decide how many units of the microcomputer to stock. The microcomputer costs $1,500 and the suggested retail price is $2,200. Any unsold microcomputer can be sold to the local high school for $1,200.

After a discussion with the manufacturer's representative and analysis of past sales records of new microcomputers, the manager arrived at the following estimate of sales for the next month:

Microcomputers	Probability
2	0.10
3	0.25
4	0.30
5	0.25
6	0.10
	1.00

With the above data, the manager will be able to determine the number of microcomputers to purchase for the next month.

For decision problems under risk, the theory of probability is used extensively. Decision theory, decision trees, **probabilistic** linear programming, stochastic inventory, queuing models, and simulation are some of the examples of decision-making models under risk.

Decision Making under Uncertainty

Decision making under uncertainty refers to the condition in which the probabilities of certain outcomes occurring are not known. Under uncertainty it is impossible even to estimate the probabilities of the various consequences. In the microcomputer purchase case, for example, sales may be totally unpredictable because too many factors affect the sales — reputation of the manufacturer, software availability, price, warranty, service, and the like.

Although it may sound like a helpless case, in reality, decision making under uncertainty is perhaps the most prevalent situation. Obviously, we cannot just give up decision making because uncertainty exists. We must find ways to reduce uncertainty, and there have been several approaches suggested for decision making under uncertainty.

The first approach is to obtain additional information about the problem. This process may yield at least partial probabilities of consequences. Then the problem is not completely a "shot in the dark" but rather a "shot in a fog." Although additional information can make the problem clearer, the question of the cost of additional information becomes important. The benefit derived from additional information must exceed the cost of obtaining such information.

Another approach for handling decision making under uncertainty is to reduce it to a problem under risk by incorporating our own subjective feelings or estimates as probabilities. There are several strategies we can employ for this purpose. We will discuss this topic thoroughly in Chapter 9 when we study decision theory.

Decision Making under Conflict

A condition of conflict exists when the interests of two or more decision makers compete. For example, if decision maker A benefits from a course of action, it is possible only because decision maker B has also taken a certain course of action. Hence, in the decision analysis the decision makers are interested not only in what they do individually but also in what both of them do. There are many such situations when firms are involved in competitive market strategies, new product development, recruitment of experienced executives, or advertising campaigns.

Although **decision making under conflict** may sound simple, in reality it is extremely complex. We may have a decision-making problem under uncertainty that is further compounded by fierce opponents or competitors. Game theory has been suggested as a theoretical approach to decision making under conflict. However, in real-world applications game theory has been disappointingly ineffective, as clearly shown by the surveys we reviewed in Chapter 1. In a conflict situation the problem is usually analyzed by designing custom-built models or by using other management science techniques rather than game theory. Therefore, game theory, which is theoretically neat but which has little practical value, will be discussed only briefly in Appendix 7.

THE PROCESS OF MANAGEMENT SCIENCE MODELING

Management science is the application of scientific approaches to management decision making. There is no one correct way to apply management science. All practitioners of management science have their own ways of doing things. However, there are several major steps that almost everyone agrees are important in management science application:

1. Formulation of the problem
   A. Orientation period
   B. Definition of problem components
      (1) The decision maker
      (2) The decision objectives
      (3) The decision environment
      (4) Alternative courses of action

2. Development of the model

3. Model validation

4. Solution of the model

5. Implementation of the solution

Let us discuss these major phases as outlined above to investigate the role of modeling in management science.

Formulation of the Problem

One aspect of the scientific approach that is absolutely necessary is determining what one is trying to do. As an old saying goes, a problem well put is half solved. As a matter of fact, understanding the problem seems to be the most difficult aspect of management decision making. Quite often when we are faced with a problem, we tend to deal with symptoms rather than a diagnosis. For example, suppose that a machine tool company has been experiencing a rapid decline in sales during the last 2 years. The company has reduced prices, sales force, and inventories and increased promotional efforts. The employees' job satisfaction, morale, and competitive spirit have gradually declined during the same period. These are important symptoms of the problem, but we cannot diagnose (understand and define) the nature of the problem without obtaining additional information, such as the quality of the products, competitors' products, employees' productivity, and so on.

Although management science application begins with the formulation of a problem, this step must be a continuous process until the completion of the project. Once an initial formulation of the problem is completed and subsequent steps proceed, the problem under study is subjected to continuous modification and refinement. Consequently, a continuous updating or modification of the problem is necessary to assure the validity of the model solution.

Each decision-making problem may require a unique approach to formulate it. However, there are several generalized steps in the problem formulation phase.

Orientation Period   The orientation period provides us with an opportunity to assess the overall picture of the problem. During this period we can obtain a broad understanding of the organizational climate, the objectives of the organization, and the purpose of the management science analysis. The orientation period can be used to specify the conditions that are required to carry out the analysis, such as time and resource requirements, administrative arrangements, and the scope of the application.

Definition of Problem Components   Before the problem can be formulated, its components must be clearly defined. The first component to be defined is the decision maker who is not satisfied with the current state of affairs. The second component to be analyzed is the objectives of the decision maker. What are the things that the decision maker is trying to achieve through the analysis? The third component is the decision environment or decision system that embraces the problem in question. Finally, a problem cannot be evaluated unless the decision maker has alternative courses of action. We shall now discuss these components in greater detail.

The Decision Maker   For any decision analysis we must identify the decision maker who has the authority to initiate, modify, and terminate the activities that control the system or organization under study. In some instances the authority of decision making may rest upon more than one individual. In such an event it is essential to acquire a good understanding of how the decision group reaches certain decisions. Is the decision process based on majority vote or unanimous vote? Who has the authority to approve or veto their decision? These questions must be cleared up at this stage.

The Decision Objectives Perhaps the most crucial factor in decision analysis is the identification of decision objectives (or criteria). The decision maker may have a specific set of objectives that she or he wants to achieve through the analysis. In such a case analysis of the objectives is relatively simple. However, sometimes the decision maker cannot specify objectives for the problem. Then it may be necessary to list all the possible outcomes of the project and obtain the decision maker's ideas concerning the desirability of obtaining certain outcomes. Based on this analysis, and the approval of the decision maker, we can establish objectives.

In analyzing the objectives of the decision maker, two distinct types of objectives must be evaluated. First, it is necessary to consider objectives that the decision maker has already obtained and wants to retain, for example, a stable employment level or good community image. These are **maintenance objectives.** The second type of objectives involves the achievement of a higher degree of performance or achievement from either existing or new activities. For example, the decision maker may want to increase the market share, increase profits, decrease personnel turnover, decrease production costs, or install a new computer system. These are **innovative objectives.**

In most managerial problems there are some objectives that are to be improved and others that are to be maintained. In addition to the identification of objectives, it is also essential to obtain the decision maker's priority structure for the objectives. Since it is not always possible to achieve all the objectives to the degree desired by the decision maker, the priority consideration allows a concentration of efforts on the higher-priority objectives. We will discuss this topic thoroughly in Chapter 6.

The Decision Environment Any organized system involves several key components, such as managers (administrators), employees who carry out policies, financial and other resources necessary for policies to be carried out, outsiders who are affected by the organization, and the social and ecological environment in which the organization functions. It is essential, therefore, to analyze the effects and repercussions of the decision from the system's perspective. For example, the decision maker's objectives for the problem may be in conflict with the interests of outsiders and the social environment (e.g., profit maximization while neglecting pollution). Through the analysis of the system components and their objectives, the initial set of the decision maker's objectives may be further modified.

Alternative Courses of Action A problem cannot exist unless the decision maker has a choice of actions. A number of possible courses of action is usually disclosed in the process of going through the steps of formulating the problem. However, the list of alternatives uncovered in this way might not be exhaustive. It may be necessary, therefore, to develop new alternatives through a thorough system analysis. It is extremely difficult to determine how extensive the alternative search should be, since the process may cost a great deal of money, time, and effort.

Development of the Model

Modeling is the crux of the management science approach. It is as important as laboratory experiments in physical science. We are getting into the fine details of the problem in this phase. Developing a model allows a comprehensive analysis by means of a logical expression of the complexities, unique characteristics, and possible uncertainties of the problem. The logical expression requires a mathematical formula to represent the interrelationships among the system's elements.

The model serves as a convenient vehicle that helps to analyze a complex reality in a concise and relatively simple manner. A model clarifies the feasible decision alternatives, the economic and noneconomic consequences of these alternatives, and the optimum alternative for the problem. A systematic analysis is possible only when the relationships among the components and their objective criteria are expressed in a comprehensive but manageable mathematical model.

Model Validation and Data Collection

Once the model is developed, it is important to test the model concerning the validity of its assumptions. The problem at hand may change over time, and thus a continuous updating and validating of the model components, their relationships, and the objective criteria may be necessary. It is imperative that the objective criteria be continuously evaluated, as management goals often change in time with the changes in the decision environment.

Frequently it is necessary to modify a model, even when the model is correctly developed, because required data are not available or are too costly to obtain. Such data are often uncontrollable input or parameters to the model. Sometimes, raw data must be analyzed and rearranged by statistical techniques before they become useful input to the model.

Although the initial model development may be simple, its modification may be extremely difficult. Thus, it may be necessary to go through several cycles of model validation and search for more data. Each model leads to a search for data that may not always yield the required information. However, the search process often reveals how the model should be modified to use the available data.

Solution of the Model

Once a mathematical model is formulated, the next phase is deriving an optimum solution from the model. The **optimum solution** presents the model result that optimizes the given decision criterion (objective). As pointed out earlier, a mathematical model is a simple abstract of reality. If the model represents almost every characteristic of the problem, it may be too complex to allow easy formulation, manipulation, and solution. However, if the model is too simple, it may not represent all the relevant aspects of the problem. Therefore, the model solution phase may point out whether the model is an appropriate one for the problem. This phase may give rise to a continuous review of the problem-formulation/model-development/model-solution/model-validation cycle until a satisfactory solution is found.

Implementation of the Solution

The true value of management science is realized when the model solution is put to actual use. This phase usually requires a translation of the solution into a set of management policies or operating procedures that can be easily implemented by the operating personnel. A problem that plagues most management science practitioners is that the system under investigation keeps changing. Consequently, a control process must be established over the solution so that the model can be updated continuously.

Implementation of an important management science model usually affects the entire organization. Such an organizational change requires modification of management practices, which in turn necessitates behavioral changes on the part of employees affected. It is only natural to expect that employees will resist change, whether it is good for the organization or not. It is imperative, therefore, that many key employees be directly involved in the management science project. Such an employee involvement, coupled with strong top management support for implementation, appears to be the key to the success of management science application. Chapter 18 will discuss the implementation process of management science.

We should always remember that the model does not yield the optimum solution to the real problem under analysis. Instead, the model provides only an optimum or approximately optimum solution to the model we formulated from the problem. Thus, we should never expect that the problem will be solved exactly as the model solution indicates.

KEEPING A PROPER PERSPECTIVE ABOUT MODELS

In this chapter we have discussed the modeling concept and the management science modeling process. Now let us try to put modeling in proper perspective.

Modeling is the crux of management science. Without models it is virtually impossible to analyze complex business systems. Determining which modeling approach to use and building a custom-made model for a particular problem involve much more than just management science knowledge. Artistic creativity and humanistic skills are also required to build and implement a useful model.

Perhaps the most important aspect of modeling is that a model represents something less than the true reality under study. In other words, a model must be simpler and less precise than the reality. Always keep this in mind. Of primary importance is the decision of how simple we want to build a model and how much precision we want to sacrifice. The trade-off considerations we must contemplate lead us to a modeling approach somewhere between the so-called quick-and-dirty and the slow-and-clean modeling approaches.

In the quick-and-dirty modeling approach, a model is built by identifying only the key variables with relatively small amounts of effort, time, and cost. This approach is especially useful when an emergency situation requires a quick overall analysis, when there are insufficient time and personnel for the study, or when the study is not important enough to draw heavily on organizational resources.

The slow-and-clean approach attempts to build a model in the most deliberate and intricate manner. This approach is appropriate when analyzing a long-term policy issue, when there are sufficient organizational resources for a long-term study, or when the study is so important that it deserves the most elaborate and careful analysis. As mentioned above, in most real-world situations the modeling approach taken would be somewhere between the quick-and-dirty and the slow-and-clean extremes. The modeling effort may be based on a host of situational variables such as the importance of the problem, the work burden of the management science personnel, the time and cost required to finish the study, and the availability of the necessary data.

Another important point to remember about modeling is that the optimum solution to a model is the best solution only with respect to the model. In other words, the optimum model solution is not necessarily the best solution to the real problem. At best it could be an approximate optimum solution to the real problem. Therefore, the efforts required to build a very intricate model must be weighed against the costs and benefits associated with such efforts.

Management scientists are often denounced by practicing managers for their "hang-up" or passion for building complex and incomprehensible models. However, managers often want certain information on a moment's notice regardless of where and how it is obtained. Now you can see why developing a proper perspective about modeling is so important. We must view a model as what it is — a convenient vehicle to help us understand a complex business system. But a modeling effort costs money and human resources. Thus, we must develop a model that is an effective and economical way to analyze important decision problems.

SUMMARY

Management science utilizes mathematical relationships to analyze the real-world problem. Mathematical models represent only one group of models that are abstract representations of reality. This chapter has provided a broad introduction to models, management science modeling, model structure, and components. Keeping a proper perspective about the models, that they are simplified representations of the real problem, is an important requirement for an effective application of management science.

This chapter has also discussed the four basic decision-making environments: certainty, risk, uncertainty, and conflict. The approach and methodologies we use for analyzing a problem differ a great deal under different decision environments. Thus, understanding the environment under which the decision problem exists is an essential part of management science application. This chapter also provided a comprehensive discussion of the management science modeling process. The process involves a set of steps that are essential in developing a model which accurately and succinctly represents the real problem and then implementing the solution derived by the model.

Glossary

Analog Model   A physical representation that performs certain functions of reality.

Certainty Condition   A situation in which the outcome of each decision alternative can be predicted exactly.

Conflict Condition   A situation in which the interests of two or more decision makers compete.

Decision Variable   An independent variable under the control of a decision maker.

Dependent Variable   A variable also referred to as a "criterion variable" whose value is based on the value of independent variables.

Exogenous Variable   An independent variable outside the control of a decision maker.

Iconic Model   A physical replica of a real object or situation.

Independent Variable   A variable whose value is not dependent on that of other variables.

Law of Critical Few   Also known as Pareto rule (as suggested by V. Pareto): any natural system has a handful of critical variables that explain the basic behavior of the system.

Mathematical Model   Mathematical relationships that represent reality.

Model   A representation of an object or reality.

Parameter   A value that determines the relationships among the variables.

Random Parameter   A parameter that varies according to some probability distribution.

Risk Condition   A situation in which the probabilities of decision outcomes are known.

Uncertainty Condition   A situation in which the probabilities of decision outcomes are not known.

Variable   A component that explains some of a system's behavior.

Verbal Model   A representation of reality in written words.

References

Beer, S. *Management Sciences: The Basic Use of Operations Research*. Garden City, N.Y.: Doubleday, 1968.

Churchman, C. W., Ackoff, R. L., and Arnoff, E. L. *Introduction to Operations Research*. New York: Wiley, 1957.

Lee, S. M., Moore, L. J., and Taylor, B. W. *Management Science*. 2d ed. Dubuque, Iowa: W. C. Brown, 1985.

Turban, E., and Meredith, J. R. *Fundamentals of Management Science*. 2d ed. Dallas: Business Publications, 1981.

Assignments

2.1 Define the term *model* and give some examples of models you see around you every day.

2.2 Classify models based on the degree of their abstraction, and provide some examples of such models.

2.3 What are the primary advantages of a mathematical model over other models? Why are these advantages important?

2.4 What are the components of a management science model? Define them and discuss their relationships.

2.5 Let us assume that you are about to deposit $1,000 in a passbook savings account that pays an annual interest of 8 percent. Develop a model that will determine the total amount of money you will have in the account at the end of the first year. Also, define all the model components.

2.6 You were just notified by the Student Aid and Scholarships Office that you would receive a regents' scholarship of $1,000 for the coming academic year. Furthermore, your application for a work-study program was also accepted. You will be allowed to work up to 15 hours a week at an hourly wage rate of $3.40. The academic year has a total of 30 weeks of school. You estimate that the total deductions from the scholarship and work-study wages would be as follows: scholarship, 5 percent handling charges; work-study, 12 percent tax and 5 percent health insurance. Develop a model that will determine your total cash situation during the next academic year, and define all the model components.

2.7 The Department of Revenue estimates that the average tax revenue from each citizen is as follows: income tax, $800; sales tax, $150; personal property tax, $250. In addition, the average corporate tax is $7,500 per company. Develop a model that will determine the total tax revenue for the state, and define all the model components.

2.8 Define four primary states of the decision-making environment.

2.9 Provide examples of decision problems you face frequently under the four different states of the decision environment.

2.10 What are the primary differences between the deterministic and probabilistic models?

2.11 What is the role of modeling in the management science process?

2.12 Define the process of management science. Discuss a simple decision problem you face frequently in relation to the process of management science.

2.13 Most objectives can be classified into two types: maintenance and innovative. Classify the objectives you have for the coming year into the two types.

2.14 Many decision problems have multiple and often conflicting objectives. Discuss your objectives for this school year and set priorities by assigning A for the most important objective, B for the second most important objective, and so on.

2.15 What is the most important consideration in keeping a proper perspective about management science models?

3 INTRODUCTION TO LINEAR PROGRAMMING

The allocation of limited resources to competing demands is the most prevalent decision problem in organizations. Resource allocation problems may range from a simple daily work-scheduling problem to a complex capital-budgeting problem that encompasses several years. Mathematical programming is the general term used for a host of management science techniques developed to solve management problems involving resource allocation. Linear programming is the most popular and most widely applied technique of mathematical programming. This chapter will introduce the basic concepts, the model formulations, and the graphical solution method of linear programming.

Learning Objectives *From the study of this chapter, we will learn the following:*

1. The basic approach and history of linear programming
2. The types of management problems that can be analyzed by linear programming
3. The formulation of various types of problems as linear programming models
4. The solution of simple linear programming models by the graphical method
5. The meaning of the following terms:

Mathematical programming	*Divisibility*
Linear programming	*Proportionality*
Objective function	*Equality and inequality*
Constraints	*Graphical method*
Area of feasible solutions	*Additivity*
Slack variables	*Surplus variables*

BASIC CONCEPTS OF LINEAR PROGRAMMING

Organizations constantly face decisions regarding allocation of their resources among various projects. Most resources are limited or scarce—including money, labor, materials, machine capacity, facilities, technology, and the like. The decision maker's objective is to achieve the best possible outcome given the available resources. The desired outcome may be measured by such things as profits, costs, market shares, sales, return on investment, time, distance, or welfare of the public.

The desired outcome, expressed as a mathematical relationship of decision variables, forms the **objective function.** The available amounts of resources, also expressed as mathematical relationships, become **constraints** that restrict the range of possible solutions. **Linear programming** determines the best solution, serving as a powerful decision-making aid to management.

A Brief History

The origins of **mathematical programming** techniques may go far back in mathematical antiquity to the theories of mathematical equations. However, George B. Dantzig is widely recognized as the person who pioneered the technique of linear programming. Dantzig began his pioneering work when he was involved in military logistics problems of the U.S. Air Force during World War II. There were other scholars who complemented Dantzig's work, such as J. von Neumann, L. Kantorovich, T. C. Koopmans, and L. Hurwicz.

Dantzig named the technique "linear programming" after it was first introduced as "programming of interdependent activities in a linear structure." The basic solution technique of linear programming, the simplex method, was developed by Dantzig in 1947. Since then many scholars have joined Dantzig in developing the technique and exploring the applications of linear programming. Some of the best known of these scholars are Marshall Wood, Alex Orden, A. Charnes, W. W. Cooper, A. Henderson, and W. Orchard-Hays.

In 1979, L. G. Khachian, a young Russian mathematician, developed a new linear programming solution algorithm known as the "ellipsoid algorithm." The ellipsoid algorithm was praised a great deal as an efficient algorithm for large-scale linear programming problems. However, it has proved to be less efficient than the simplex technique.

Another new algorithm of linear programming was developed in 1984 by Narendra Karmarkar, a mathematician at AT&T Bell Laboratories. Based on an initial test of a 5,000-decision-variable problem, the Karmarkar algorithm was said to be about 50 times faster than the fastest simplex program available. This algorithm may prove to be a truly effective tool for large-scale linear programming problems.

During its early stage of development, linear programming was applied primarily to military logistics problems such as transportation, assignment, and deployment decisions. However, after the war linear programming became a popular technique in business organizations. One of the earliest industrial applications of linear programming was conducted by A. Charnes and W. W. Cooper for the gasoline-blending problem. Since then it has become one of the most widely applied management science techniques in business organizations, governmental agencies, and nonprofit institutions, as we learned in Chapter 1. Today numerous organizations apply linear programming to such diverse managerial problems as petroleum blending, animal-feed blending, food processing, production scheduling and inventory control, personnel assignment and development, transportation of goods and services, and capital investments.

Basic Requirements

In order to apply linear programming to a particular problem, we must ascertain that the problem under analysis meets several requirements. These requirements restrict the applicability of linear programming. However, understanding the limitations of linear programming imposed by these requirements is very important for keeping a proper perspective about the true value of the technique.

The Objective Criterion   A linear programming problem must have one explicit (quantitatively defined) objective criterion — to optimize. Examples of objective criteria that a decision maker might want to optimize include profit, cost, market share, product exposure, productivity, and defective items. Thus, the objective function must be one of either maximization or minimization of the criterion, but never both. The single-objective optimization is an important requirement of linear programming.

Limited Resources   Linear programming is a useful technique for analyzing decision problems that involve activities requiring the consumption of limited resources. The limited resources could be money, production capacity, personnel, time, or technology. The amounts of limited resources are expressed as constraints for the linear programming problem. The constraints impose restrictions on the activities (decision variables) in optimizing the objective function.

Linear Relationships   Another requirement of linear programming is that all relationships among the variables in the model must be mathematically linear. The term *linear* simply implies that relationships among the decision variables (products, activities, etc.) must be directly proportional. **Proportionality** means that the relationship between outcome and resource usage is constant. In a production problem, for example, if we increase the required materials by 10 percent, we can expect a 10 percent increase in production.

Linear relationships also require that the total measure of the objective criterion and the total sum of resource usage must be additive. For example, suppose that we have a profit maximization problem for a furniture company that produces two products — desks and chairs. **Additivity** requires that the total profit must be the sum of the profits earned from desks and chairs. Also, the amount of resources used for production must exactly equal the sum of the resources required for producing desks and chairs.

Divisibility   Another requirement of linear programming is that the solution values for the decision variables and the amount of resources used need not be integer (whole-number) valued but can be continuous. In other words, fractional values for the decision variables and resources must be permissible in obtaining an optimum solution. In the furniture production case, a production program requiring 100.79 oak boards and 25.27 hours of labor to produce 29.13 desks and 15.25 chairs should be acceptable. In many decision problems it is perfectly acceptable to have fractional values for decision variables and resources. For example, we can use 2.75 cups of sugar and 1.33 pounds of flour to make 3.15 dozens of cookies. However, there are occasions when decision variables have physical significance or meaning only if they are in integer values. For example, we cannot assign 1.29 persons to a job, we cannot construct 67 percent of a power plant, and we cannot take 1.33 credit hours. Other extensions of linear programming will handle these problems, and they will be discussed in Chapter 6.

Deterministic Parameters   In linear programming all the model coefficients (e.g., the profit contribution of each product, the amount of resources required per unit of product, and the amount of available resources) are assumed to be known with certainty. In other words, linear programming implicitly assumes a decision problem in a static state. In real-world situations, however, model parameters are never completely deterministic but vary over time. Techniques have been developed to handle linear programming problems with uncertain parameters.

Nonnegativity   Most linear programming models implicitly require that all decision variables take on nonnegative values. In other words, negative production of certain goods, negative investments, negative amounts of foods served, and the like are not permissible. The nonnegative requirement certainly makes sense in most problems. If we need a decision variable which can be negative (e.g., the rate of change in the unemployment level), we must make a slight adjustment to the decision variable so that the model satisfies the nonnegativity requirement.

Application Areas

As we discussed earlier, linear programming has been a very popular technique that has been widely applied to all types of decision-making problems. As a matter of fact, it is difficult to find a decision problem that has not been analyzed by linear programming. Thus, it would be a major undertaking to list all the functional problem areas that have seen linear programming applications. Instead we will simply look at broad classifications of problem types that have been solved by linear programming.

Resource Allocation Problems   Most business organizations are involved in the production of goods or services. General Motors Corporation, Texas Instruments, IBM, McDonald's, Kentucky Fried Chicken, Mutual of Omaha, The First National Bank, and St. Elizabeth's Hospital are all engaged in the production of goods or services. There may be many different types of limited resources these organizations use in producing a number of different possible outcomes. The typical decision problem would be to determine a combination of input resources that will result in the optimum outcome. Linear programming is perfectly suited for this type of resource allocation problem.

Some of the most widely known resource allocation problems that have been analyzed by linear programming follow:

Manufacturing
   Production mix determination
   Blending (e.g., concrete mixing, cattle feed, sausage blending)
   Assembly line scheduling
   Inventory control

Marketing
   Sales effort allocation
   Sales territory determination
   Advertising budget allocation
   Sales quota allocation

Finance
   Capital budgeting
   Working capital management
   Investment portfolio determination
   Cash flow analysis

Personnel
   Work force allocation and assignment
   Wage and salary administration
   Personnel mix determination

Hospital Administration
   Budget allocation
   Personnel allocation
   Space allocation (e.g., work space determination)

University Administration
   Faculty and staff allocation
   Office space and classroom allocation
   Allocation and reallocation of the operating budget
   Admissions procedure

Planning and Scheduling Problems   Most decision problems involve some degree of planning and/or scheduling. In order to achieve certain objectives in the future, a decision must be made concerning present and future actions that would contribute to the objectives. Stated in a different way, to accomplish the desired results, the optimum combination of inputs in certain time periods must be determined. Linear programming is effective for analyzing such problems as production scheduling, financial planning, work force planning, construction scheduling, traveling salesperson scheduling, course offering scheduling, and student flow scheduling.

Diet Problems   The diet problem is so labeled because one of the earliest applications of linear programming was in determining the most economical diet for human beings. Various food-related problems are concerned with the determination of the most economical (least total cost) mix of ingredients that meets the desired nutrient values. We are familiar with this type of problem from our experience in college dining halls, hospitals, military chow halls, and summer camps.

For example, let us consider a diet problem in a local hospital. In planning a menu for the maternity ward patients, the hospital dietitian is considering 30 different types of food. Because she is concerned about the minimum nutritional requirements for new mothers, she analyzes the amount of nutrient in a unit of each of the foods being considered. The dietitian may formulate a linear programming problem that will specify a menu that meets all the nutritional requirements while minimizing the total cost.

Transportation Problems   In a typical transportation problem we attempt to determine the quantities of a particular good to be transported from a number of origins (e.g., plants) to a number of destinations (e.g., retail outlets) in such a way that we can minimize the total transportation cost. The solution to the problem must satisfy the supply capacity of each origin and the demand requirement of each destination.

For example, let us consider the transportation problem of a concrete-mixing firm. The company has three plants where concrete is mixed and four construction sites where concrete must be supplied. The firm has determined the unit transportation cost (cost involved in transporting a truckload of concrete from each plant to each construction site). Also, the firm has a concrete-mixing capacity at each plant and a contracted agreement for supply to each site. The decision problem is to determine how many truckloads of concrete should be transported from each plant to each construction site so that the total transportation cost is minimized.

Assignment Problems   In assignment problems, we attempt to identify the most efficient way to assign certain objects (e.g., people, machines, or tools) to various destinations to optimize the objective criterion. For example, in a machine-loading problem, linear programming can be applied to determine the optimum assignment of jobs to various machines so that the total production cost can be minimized. Assignment of police patrol cars to various areas of a city to minimize the total time required to reach trouble spots and assignment of snowplows to various spots in an area to minimize the total time required to clear all major roads are also good examples of assignment problems.

MODEL FORMULATION

During the past 15 years linear programming has become more readily available for practical use, primarily because of the continuous development of computer technology. Most of the major computer manufacturers have developed large-scale ''canned'' linear programming packages for their clients, and a large number of linear programming packages are available for applications on mini- or microcomputers. The solution process, therefore, is not the difficult part of linear programming application. The most difficult aspect of linear programming application is model formulation—formulating a linear programming model for a complex real-world problem.

In order to gain some experience and insight in formulating linear programming models, we will examine a variety of examples in this section. One key to successful application of the technique is the ability to recognize when a problem can be solved by linear programming and to formulate the corresponding model.

Casette 3.1   *GALAXY ELECTRONICS, INC.*

Galaxy Electronics, Inc., is a specialist in the emerging field of microcomputers. The firm currently produces two products: a personal computer with the label GE-1000 and a small business-oriented computer with the label GE-2000. The company has set up two modern production assembly lines. The assembly time requirements, the production capacities of assembly lines, and the unit profit for the two products are as follows:

	Production Process (Hours/Unit)		Production Capacity (Hours/Week)
	GE-1000	GE-2000	
Assembly line 1	4	2	80
Assembly line 2	1	3	60
Unit profit	$150	$250	

The marketing department reports that the maximum number of each type of computers that can be sold in a given week is: GE-1000 — 15; GE-2000 — 18.

The management of Galaxy Electronics is attempting to determine the best possible weekly production schedule for GE-1000 and GE-2000 to maximize total profit. To formulate a linear programming model for Galaxy, we must first define the decision variables.

Decision Variables

The variables whose values we are trying to determine in the model are the quantities of the two computers Galaxy should produce on a weekly schedule. Thus, there are two decision variables.

x_1 = the number of GE-1000 computers to be produced per week

x_2 = the number of GE-2000 computers to be produced per week

Model Constraints

Model constraints represent limited resources or other restrictions that are imposed on the decision variables. In this problem, constraints are the limited production hours available in each of the two assembly lines and the sales capabilities. Since each product requires assembly time in each line, the total production time required in assembly line 1 will be the sum of the production time required to produce GE-1000 and the production time for GE-2000. A unit of GE-1000 requires 4 hours in assembly line 1. Thus, the total production time required in assembly line 1 to produce GE-1000 will be $4x_1$. Similarly, we can easily determine the production time required in assembly line 1 for GE-2000 as $2x_2$.

Since the number of available production hours per week in assembly line 1 is 80, the amount of production time we utilize for producing both GE-1000 and GE-2000 units must be limited to 80 hours. In order to express the limited resources, we can use a mathematical symbol $\leq$, which simply means that the left side must be *less than or equal to* the value on the right side. Then we can express the production time constraint for assembly line 1 as

$$4x_1 + 2x_2 \leq 80 \qquad \textit{Assembly line 1}$$

The constraint for assembly line 2 can be formulated in a similar manner. A GE-1000 unit requires 1 hour and a GE-2000 unit takes 3 hours in assembly line 2. The available production capacity for assembly line 2 is 60 hours of operation time on a weekly basis. Thus, the second constraint is

$$x_1 + 3x_2 \leq 60 \qquad \textit{Assembly line 2}$$

The sales capability constraints are as follows:

$$x_1 \leq 15 \qquad \textit{Sales capability for GE-1000}$$

$$x_2 \leq 18 \qquad \textit{Sales capability for GE-2000}$$

As discussed in the section on the requirements of linear programming, a linear programming model also needs nonnegativity constraints. In other words, the quantities of GE-1000 and GE-2000 computers cannot be negative. These nonnegative constraints can be expressed as

$$x_1 \geq 0, \qquad x_2 \geq 0 \qquad \textit{Nonnegativity constraints}$$

The Objective Function

The objective of Galaxy is to maximize total profit. The total profit Galaxy can expect is simply the sum of the profits from GE-1000 and GE-2000. The profit that can be gained by GE-1000 is the unit profit, $150, times the quantity of GE-1000 units produced for sale, or 150x_1$. Similarly, profit from GE-2000 will be 250x_2$. If we express total profit by the symbol Z, the objective function of this problem becomes

$$\text{Maximize } Z = 150x_1 + 250x_2 \qquad \textit{Objective function}$$

Now we can formulate the complete linear programming model for the Galaxy Electronics product mix problem as follows:

$$\text{Maximize } Z = 150x_1 + 250x_2$$
$$\text{subject to} \quad 4x_1 + 2x_2 \leq 80$$
$$x_1 + 3x_2 \leq 60$$
$$x_1 \leq 15$$
$$x_2 \leq 18$$
$$x_1, x_2 \geq 0$$

The solution of this model will determine the optimum values for the decision variables x_1 and x_2. From the optimum solution we can easily calculate the maximum possible profit Z based on the production schedule determined by the model.

Now we can examine the above linear programming model and ascertain whether it satisfies the requirements of linear programming.

1. *The Objective Criterion.* The Galaxy Electronics model has a single objective for maximizing total profits. The objective function is expressed by: Maximize $Z = 150x_1 + 250x_2$.

2. *Limited Resources.* In the Galaxy Electronics problem, the limited resources are expressed by the available production hours in assembly lines 1 and 2 and sales capabilities for GE-1000 and GE-2000.

3. *Linear Relationships.* The objective function and the four constraints are all expressed as linear functions.

4. *Divisibility.* The number of GE-1000 and GE-2000 computers to be determined by the model can take fractional values.

5. *Deterministic.* In the Galaxy Electronics problem, the unit contribution rates of the two computers, the amount of resources required to produce each computer, and the sales limit for each computer are known with certainty.

6. *Nonnegativity.* The quantity of GE-1000 and GE-2000 computers to be produced must be nonnegative.

Casette 3.2   **THE ORIENTATION PROGRAM FOR FIRST-YEAR STUDENTS**

The university is planning the annual orientation program for first-year students during the first week of June. All prospective first-year students and their parents have been invited to the campus for a 3-day period. Since the summer school will not start until the third week of June, the university will make the dormitories available for most participants in the program.

In order to provide an ample amount of free time for the participants to roam around the campus and downtown areas on their own, the dormitories will serve only breakfast. For lunch and dinner, participants will be encouraged to explore a number of interesting restaurants on and around the campus. The dietitians at the dining halls are planning breakfast for the first day of the orientation period. Once the first day's breakfast menu is determined, the second and third days' breakfasts will be decided upon. The dietitians are attempting to provide the participants with a menu that not only is appetizing but also satisfies the nutrient requirements at the lowest possible cost.

The dietitians easily come up with the beverages to serve: orange juice, tomato juice, coffee, tea, and milk. However, based on their experience in recent years, there has been some disagreement among the dietitians concerning the types of food to serve. After a lengthy discussion, they decide to provide a very simple breakfast: scrambled eggs and "smokies" sausage.

The dietitians' responsibility is to provide an adequate amount of the following nutrients in the breakfast: vitamin A, vitamin B, and iron. Another important consideration is that the menu must be provided at the lowest possible cost. The nutritional contents, expressed in milligrams (mg) per scoop of scrambled eggs and per smokie, the minimum nutrient requirements, and the unit cost of the foods being considered are as follows:

Nutrient	Food Nutrient Content (mg)		Nutrient Requirement (mg)
	Scrambled Egg	Smokie	
Vitamin A	3	3	30
Vitamin B	4	2	24
Iron	1	2	12
Unit cost	8¢	10¢	

Decision Variables

The dietitians attempt to determine how much of each type of food to serve in order to meet the nutrient requirements and also minimize the total cost. Since there are only two types of food to be served (not including beverages), there are two decision variables in the problem:

$$x_1 = \text{number of scoops of scrambled eggs served}$$
$$x_2 = \text{number of smokies served}$$

Model Constraints

In this diet problem, the model constraints represent the nutrient requirements that need to be satisfied for vitamin A, vitamin B, and iron. The dietitians have already determined the nutritional content for each unit of food being considered for breakfast. For example, a scoop of scrambled eggs contains 3 milligrams of vitamin A, and one smokie sausage also contains 3 milligrams of vitamin A. Since the minimum requirement for vitamin A is 30 milligrams, the total amount of vitamin A provided by the scrambled eggs and smokies must be *equal to or greater than* 30 milligrams. Thus, we can formulate the constraint for vitamin A as:

$$3x_1 + 3x_2 \geq 30 \qquad \textit{Vitamin A}$$

The constraint for vitamin B can be formulated in a similar manner. A scoop of scrambled eggs contains 4 milligrams, and a smokie, 2 milligrams of vitamin B. The minimum requirement for vitamin B is 24 milligrams. The constraint for vitamin B is:

$$4x_1 + 2x_2 \geq 24 \qquad \textit{Vitamin B}$$

The constraint for iron can be easily constructed in a similar way:

$$x_1 + 2x_2 \geq 12 \qquad \textit{Iron}$$

The Objective Function

The objective of the breakfast menu problem for the student orientation program is to minimize the total cost of breakfast. The total cost of breakfast is simply the sum of the costs of the eggs and smokies to be served. Since we already know that a scoop of scrambled eggs costs 8 cents, we can determine the total cost of serving scrambled eggs by multiplying 8 cents by the number of scoops of scrambled eggs, or $8x_1$. Similarly, the total cost of serving smokies will be $10x_2$. If we express the total cost by the symbol Z, the objective function of this diet problem becomes

$$\text{Minimize } Z = 8x_1 + 10x_2 \qquad \textit{Objective function}$$

Now we can formulate the complete linear programming model for the breakfast menu problem of the orientation program as follows:

$$\text{Minimize } Z = 8x_1 + 10x_2$$
$$\text{subject to} \quad 3x_1 + 3x_2 \geq 30$$
$$4x_1 + 2x_2 \geq 24$$
$$x_1 + 2x_2 \geq 12$$
$$x_1, x_2 \geq 0$$

The solution of this linear programming model will enable the dietitians to determine the optimum values for the decision variables x_1 and x_2. From the optimum solution determined by the model, they can easily calculate the minimum total cost possible based on the menu of scrambled eggs and smokie sausages.

Casette 3.3   UR#1 LIMOUSINE SERVICE COMPANY

UR#1 is a newly chartered transportation corporation in town. UR, as the company is known in financial circles, will be the primary limousine service between the municipal airport and the hotels in the downtown area. The company has done extensive research on the air traffic, passenger flows, hotel occupancy rates, vehicle costs, operation costs, vehicle maintenance costs, facility requirements, and personnel requirements. However, one aspect of the problem that needs an immediate decision is the exact number of different types of vehicles that should be placed on order.

Terry Anderson, the company treasurer and a CPA, has been charged with the decision problem. After examining the company's research material several times, he was able to come up with the following basic data:

1. There are three types of vehicles under consideration by UR: station wagons, vans, and buses. Each vehicle will serve a different purpose. A station wagon will be dispatched to the airport when small airplanes of regional airlines need transportation service or when individual requests are received. Vans will be used as regularly scheduled limousines at 45-minute intervals between the airport and the hotels. Buses will be used at specific times of the day when national airline flights are scheduled and a large number of passengers need the service.

2. If an order is placed immediately, the purchase price for each type of vehicle will be:

Station wagon	$9,500
Van	$12,500
Bus	$45,000

3. The board of directors has authorized $1 million for the purchase of vehicles.

4. The company has already hired 40 new drivers who will complete their 8-week training program before the new vehicles arrive from the manufacturer. The drivers will be fully qualified to operate all three types of vehicles. The company is planning a 16-hour-a-day operation schedule (6 a.m.–10 p.m.). It is expected that the maximum number of drivers on duty at any given time will be 30. Thus, the company does not wish to purchase more than 30 vehicles.

5. The maintenance shop will be fully functional when the company begins its limousine service. The department will have the capacity for performing maintenance service for 80 station wagons. In terms of using the maintenance resources, a van is estimated to be equivalent to 1.5 station wagons, and a bus is equivalent to 3 station wagons.

6. The cost-accounting department has estimates of the expected net annual profit of the vehicles as follows:

Station wagon	$2,500 per vehicle
Van	$3,500 per vehicle
Bus	$10,000 per vehicle

7. Based on the experience of other airport transportation companies in other cities, the board of directors has adopted the following policies:
    a. In view of rising energy costs, the number of station wagons should be at least 30 percent of all the vehicles.

b. Since buses are often required to handle large tourist groups, the company should purchase at least 2 buses.

c. The regularly scheduled limousine service will be provided by vans. Thus, the company should have at least 10 vans in its fleet of vehicles.

The vehicle purchasing problem of UR is to determine the number of station wagons, vans, and buses to purchase, while meeting various constraints, in order to maximize the total profit. Since Terry Anderson could not solve the problem, he consulted with the systems specialist, Susan Kraft, who has just completed her master's degree in management science. After a lengthy discussion with Terry, Susan studied her old class notes and came up with a linear programming model.

Decision Variables

In this problem, the model should determine the number of each type of vehicle to be purchased. Thus, the decision variables are:

$$x_1 = \text{number of station wagons to be purchased}$$
$$x_2 = \text{number of vans to be purchased}$$
$$x_3 = \text{number of buses to be purchased}$$

Model Constraints

There are a number of constraints in this problem. Susan Kraft decided to formulate the constraints as follows:

1. *Budget for the Vehicles to Be Purchased.*   The board of directors allocated $1 million for the purchase of the vehicles. Since station wagons cost $9,500, vans $12,500, and buses $45,000, the budget constraint becomes

$$9,500x_1 + 12,500x_2 + 45,000x_3 \leq 1,000,000$$

2. *The Number of Drivers.*   Although the company will have a total of 40 drivers, the maximum number of drivers on duty at any given time will be 30. Thus, there is no reason to purchase more than 30 vehicles. The constraint is

$$x_1 + x_2 + x_3 \leq 30$$

3. *The Maintenance Department Capacity.*   One of the important considerations that requires attention is the maintenance capacity. Since the vehicles must be used virtually constantly to secure the expected return on investment, maintenance is a very important aspect of the total operation at UR. The capacity of the maintenance shop is equivalent to 80 station wagons. In terms of using the maintenance resource, a van accounts for 1.5 station wagons, and a bus is equivalent to 3 station wagons. Thus, Susan formulates the constraint as

$$x_1 + 1.5x_2 + 3x_3 \leq 80$$

4. *The Board of Directors' Policy Constraints.* Based on other firms' experience and its judgment about the composition of the vehicle fleet, the board has further imposed these additional constraints:

a. *The number of station wagons.* The board decided that the number of station wagons should be at least 30 percent of all the vehicles. Thus, Susan initially formulated this constraint as

$$x_1 \geq .30 \ (x_1 + x_2 + x_3)$$

Susan decided to further simplify the constraint as follows:

$$x_1 \geq .30x_1 + .30x_2 + .30x_3$$
$$x_1 - .30x_1 - .30x_2 - .30x_3 \geq 0$$
$$.70x_1 - .30x_2 - .30x_3 \geq 0$$

b. *The minimum number of buses.* The board also decided to purchase at least 2 buses. This simple constraint is

$$x_3 \geq 2$$

c. *The minimum number of vans.* The board would like to purchase at least 10 vans as the regularly scheduled limousines. This constraint is

$$x_2 \geq 10$$

The Objective Function

The objective of UR in this problem is to maximize the total annual profit from the limousine service operation. The cost-accounting department estimates the net annual profit per vehicle as follows:

Station wagon	$2,500
Van	$3,500
Bus	$10,000

Thus, the objective function can be formulated as

$$\text{Maximize } Z = 2,500x_1 + 3,500x_2 + 10,000x_3$$

Now the complete model can be presented:

$$\text{Maximize } Z = 2,500x_1 + 3,500x_2 + 10,000x_3$$
$$\text{subject to} \quad 9,500x_1 + 12,500x_2 + 45,000x_3 \leq 1,000,000$$
$$x_1 + x_2 + x_3 \leq 30$$
$$x_1 + 1.5x_2 + 3x_3 \leq 80$$
$$.70x_1 - .30x_2 - .30x_3 \geq 0$$
$$x_3 \geq 2$$
$$x_2 \geq 10$$
$$x_1, x_2, x_3 \geq 0$$

Casette 3.4   **LEON'S GROCERIES**

Leon's Groceries is a well-known, privately owned food store. Since it was first opened in 1935 by the late Herschel Leon, Leon's has been best known for its fine meat department. Leon's store hours have increased steadily over the years. Rufus Leon, the new president, fresh out of the university with an MBA degree, has decided to keep the store open 24 hours a day. He has been able to make the necessary arrangements with vendors, the trucking company, and the local banks for the expanded store operation.

One of Leon's nagging problems has been the scheduling for the workers. Rufus has tentatively set up the management teams and workers for three daily shifts as shown in Figure 3.1. Since 5 meat cutters need to work for the 8 a.m. to 4 p.m. daily schedule, the most critical problem is scheduling cashiers and baggers/stockers on a daily basis. Based on the experience of Leon's and that of other stores operating on a 24-hour basis, Rufus has been able to determine the minimum necessary labor for each 4-hour period as follows:

Time Period	Cashiers	Baggers/Stockers
8 a.m.–noon	3	5
Noon–4 p.m.	4	4
4 p.m.–8 p.m.	6	6
8 p.m.–midnight	3	3
Midnight–4 a.m.	1	2
4 a.m.–8 a.m.	2	7

One of the factors complicating the problem is that cashiers and baggers/stockers are not interchangeable. Cashiers need special training for dealing with money and operating the cash register, and baggers/stockers need physical strength to handle the stocking carts and the weight of goods. Leon's has only full-time employees who report to work for an 8-hour shift. Overtime work and part-time work are available only in emergencies or during holiday seasons.

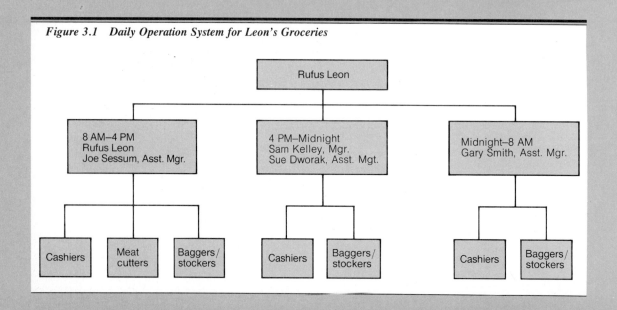

Figure 3.1   Daily Operation System for Leon's Groceries

The employees usually report for work at 8 a.m., noon, 4 p.m., 8 p.m., midnight, and 4 a.m. and work for an 8-hour shift. The wages for employees working at different time periods are as follows:

Time Period	Wage Cashiers	Baggers/Stockers
8 a.m.–noon	$4.00	$3.60
Noon–4 p.m.	4.00	3.60
4 p.m.–8 p.m.	4.20	4.00
8 p.m.–midnight	4.60	4.40
Midnight–4 a.m.	5.00	4.80
4 a.m.–8 a.m.	4.80	4.60

Rufus believes that the total number of cashiers and baggers/stockers should not be more than 60, since the current work force for the 16-hour-a-day operation is 45.

The decision problem is to determine how many cashiers and baggers/stockers should be scheduled to work in order to meet the minimum manpower requirement of the store and also to minimize the total daily wages.

Decision Variables

In this problem, Rufus attempts to determine the number of cashiers and baggers/stockers who will report at the beginning of each of the 4-hour segments during the 24-hour period. We can describe the decision variables schematically as shown in Figure 3.2. The variables can be defined as follows:

x_i = number of cashiers reporting to work during the day at the ith 4-hour intervals starting at 8 a.m. ($i = 1,2,\cdots,6$)

y_i = number of baggers/stockers reporting to work during the day at the ith 4-hour intervals starting at 8 a.m. ($i = 1,2,\cdots,6$)

Model Constraints

In this problem, there are basically two types of constraints: the required minimum number of employees during certain time periods of the day, and the total work force limit of 60 per day. For the first type of constraint, let us consider the number of cashiers needed during the 8 a.m. to noon period. The number of cashiers working during that period (see Figure 3.2) is the total number of cashiers who reported at 4 a.m. and those who reported at 8 a.m. For example, we can easily show the cashiers working from 8 a.m. to noon and the minimum number of cashiers required as follows:

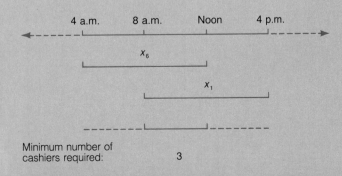

Figure 3.2   Decision Variables of the Leon's Groceries Manpower Scheduling Problem

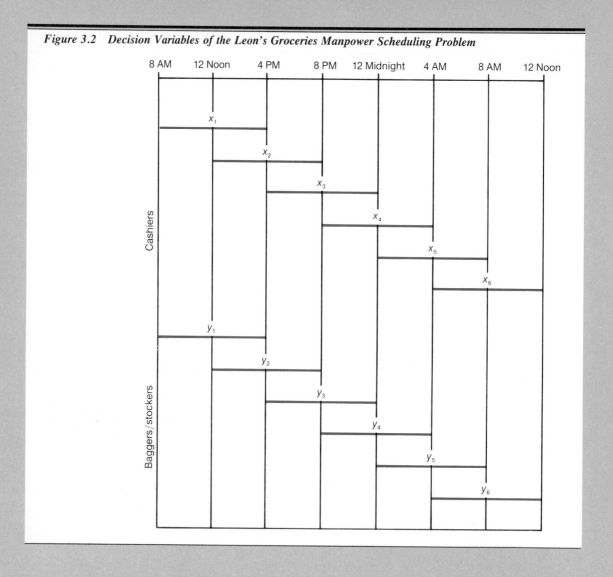

Since the minimum number of cashiers required for the 8 a.m. to noon period is 3, the constraint can be expressed as

$$x_1 + x_6 \geq 3$$

The same reasoning can be applied to all the other constraints for the cashiers. In a similar manner, the required numbers of baggers/stockers can be expressed as constraints. Thus, we can formulate the following constraints:

Cashiers	$x_1 + x_2 \geq 4$	Noon–4 p.m.
	$x_2 + x_3 \geq 6$	4 p.m.–8 p.m.
	$x_3 + x_4 \geq 3$	8 p.m.–midnight
	$x_4 + x_5 \geq 1$	Midnight–4 a.m.
	$x_5 + x_6 \geq 2$	4 a.m.–8 a.m.

Figure 3.3   *Average Wage Rate for the Cashiers at Leon's Groceries*

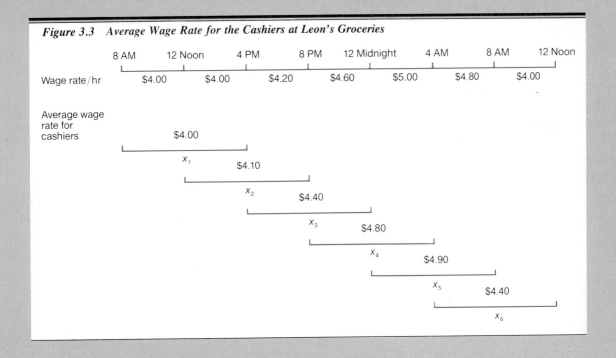

$$
\begin{array}{llll}
\textit{Baggers/} & y_1 + y_6 \geq 5 & \text{8 a.m.–noon} \\
\textit{Stockers} & y_1 + y_2 \geq 4 & \text{Noon–4 p.m.} \\
& y_2 + y_3 \geq 6 & \text{4 p.m.–8 p.m.} \\
& y_3 + y_4 \geq 3 & \text{8 p.m.–midnight} \\
& y_4 + y_5 \geq 2 & \text{Midnight–4 a.m.} \\
& y_5 + y_6 \geq 7 & \text{4 a.m.–8 a.m.}
\end{array}
$$

Another constraint we need to develop is the maximum number of 60 cashiers and baggers/stockers Rufus set as the ceiling for the work force. This constraint can be formulated as

$$x_1 + x_2 + x_3 + x_4 + x_5 + x_6 + y_1 + y_2 + y_3 + y_4 + y_5 + y_6 \leq 60$$

The Objective Function

The objective of the Leon's Groceries scheduling problem is to minimize the total daily payroll cost. Since the total daily payroll is the sum of hours worked times the wage rate for the employees, we must first analyze the wage rates for the employees during the different time periods. For example, Figure 3.3 indicates the hourly rates during the different 4-hour periods and the average wage rate for the cashiers during their respective 8-hour shifts. Thus, the total payroll Z will be:

$$
\begin{aligned}
Z = \; & 32.00x_1 + 32.80x_2 + 35.20x_3 + 38.40x_4 + 39.20x_5 + 35.20x_6 \\
& + 28.80y_1 + 30.40y_2 + 33.60y_3 + 36.80y_4 + 37.60y_5 + 32.80y_6
\end{aligned}
$$

In the above expression, the first parameter, \$32.00 for variable x_1, is simply the average hourly wage rate of \$4.00 for cashiers working the 8 a.m. to 4 p.m. shift multiplied by 8 hours for the shift. For example, if 3 cashiers work during the 8 a.m.

to 4 p.m. shift ($x_1 = 3$), the total wage for the 3 cashiers would be 32.00×3, or $96.00.

We can write the objective function as follows:

$$\text{Minimize } Z = 32.00x_1 + 32.80x_2 + 35.20x_3 + 38.40x_4 + 39.20x_5 + 35.20x_6$$
$$+ 28.80y_1 + 30.40y_2 + 33.60y_3 + 36.80y_4 + 37.60y_5 + 32.80y_6$$

Now the complete model can be formulated as follows:

$$\text{Minimize } Z = 32.00x_1 + 32.80x_2 + 35.20x_3 + 38.40x_4 + 39.20x_5 + 35.20x_6$$
$$+ 28.80y_1 + 30.40y_2 + 33.60y_3 + 36.80y_4 + 37.60y_5 + 32.80y_6$$

$$\begin{aligned}
\text{subject to } \quad & x_1 + x_6 \geq 3 & & y_1 + y_6 \geq 5 \\
& x_1 + x_2 \geq 4 & & y_1 + y_2 \geq 4 \\
& x_2 + x_3 \geq 6 & & y_2 + y_3 \geq 6 \\
& x_3 + x_4 \geq 3 & & y_3 + y_4 \geq 3 \\
& x_4 + x_5 \geq 1 & & y_4 + y_5 \geq 2 \\
& x_5 + x_6 \geq 2 & & y_5 + y_6 \geq 7
\end{aligned}$$

$$x_1 + x_2 + x_3 + x_4 + x_5 + x_6 + y_1 + y_2 + y_3 + y_4 + y_5 + y_6 \leq 60$$

$$x_1, x_2, x_3, x_4, x_5, x_6, y_1, y_2, y_3, y_4, y_5, y_6 \geq 0$$

GRAPHICAL SOLUTION METHOD

Two basic solution methods of linear programming will be presented in this text: the **graphical method** and the simplex method. The main purpose of presenting the graphical method is to provide you with a conceptual knowledge of the linear programming approach. Neither the graphical method nor the simplex method is used for real-world applications of linear programming. Any real problem is solved by using a computer; linear programming solution packages are available for mainframes, minicomputers, and personal computers.

We can effectively depict on a graph those linear programming problems that involve only two dimensions (decision variables). We will therefore study the graphical method through simple problems that have only two decision variables. We can depict three-variable problems graphically, but the procedure becomes quite tedious when they have many constraints. Consequently, even for a moderate-size problem, we apply computer-based simplex programs. The graphical solution method, however, provides us with a conceptual framework for understanding the solution process of linear programming. Thus, we gain much insight into the linear programming approach and the type of information we can generate from the model.

A Simple Maximization Problem

To demonstrate the graphical solution method, we will use a simple maximization problem which we formulated in Casette 3.1. The management of Galaxy Electronics attempts to determine the number of GE-1000 (personal microcomputers) and GE-2000 (business-oriented microcomputers) to be produced in order to maximize total profit. In this problem, there are four constraints representing limited production hours available in assembly line 1 and assembly line 2 and sales capacity constraints. The linear programming model we developed for Galaxy was:

$$\text{Maximize } Z = 150x_1 + 250x_2$$
$$\text{subject to} \quad 4x_1 + 2x_2 \leq 80$$
$$x_1 + 3x_2 \leq 60$$
$$x_1 \leq 15$$
$$x_2 \leq 18$$
$$x_1, x_2 \geq 0$$

where
$$x_1 = \text{number of GE-1000s to be produced}$$
$$x_2 = \text{number of GE-2000s to be produced}$$

The process of the graphical method, whether it is used for a maximization or a minimization problem, consists of the following steps:

1. Graphical representation of constraints

2. Identification of the area of feasible solutions

3. Identification of the optimum solution

We will follow these steps in solving the Galaxy Electronics problem by the graphical method.

Step 1: Graphical Representation of Constraints   The problem has four linear inequalities as constraints. They are:

$4x_1 + 2x_2 \leq 80$	*Constraint 1 (assembly line 1)*
$x_1 + 3x_2 \leq 60$	*Constraint 2 (assembly line 2)*
$x_1 \leq 15$	*Constraint 3 (sales capacity for GE-1000)*
$x_2 \leq 18$	*Constraint 4 (sales capacity for GE-2000)*

Let us analyze these constraints one at a time. For plotting constraints on the graph, we will treat variable x_1 as the horizontal axis and x_2 as the vertical axis.

Initially, the constraints will be plotted on the graph by treating them as linear equalities; then the appropriate inequality conditions will be indicated by the shaded areas. For example, let us consider the first constraint as an equality $4x_1 + 2x_2 = 80$. We can arrange the equality in the customary way, solving for the vertical axis x_2 as

$$4x_1 + 2x_2 = 80$$
$$2x_2 = 80 - 4x_1 \text{ (transposing } 4x_1)$$
$$x_2 = 40 - 2x_1 \text{ (dividing both sides by 2)}$$

The above equality indicates an x_2 intercept of 40 and a slope of -2. We can easily determine the x_1 intercept as 20 by assuming $x_2 = 0$ in the equality: $0 = 40 - 2x_1$; $2x_1 = 40$; $x_1 = 20$. Before we plot the equality on the graph, we must remember the nonnegativity constraint which requires that all decision variables be nonnegative. In other words, variables can take on only positive or 0 values. Thus, the

Figure 3.4   Graphing of $4x_1 + 2x_2 = 80$

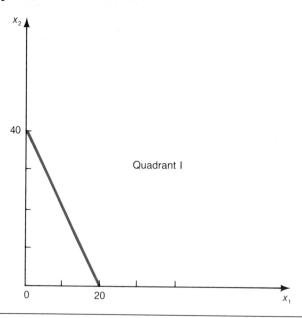

graphical solution requires only the first quadrant of a rectangular coordinate system. Now the equality can be plotted on the graph as shown in Figure 3.4. Next, the inequality condition of the constraint must be satisfied. If we solve for x_2, as we did above, while maintaining the inequality sign, it becomes

$$4x_1 + 2x_2 \leq 80$$
$$2x_2 \leq 80 - 4x_1$$
$$x_2 \leq 40 - 2x_1$$

In the above inequality function, x_2 must be equal to or less than the straight line $x_2 = 40 - 2x_1$. Thus, the inequality condition can be satisfied by the shaded area shown in Figure 3.5. Any point within the shaded area satisfies the constraint, and any point outside does not meet the requirement. For example, let us examine the following three points, also shown in Figure 3.5.

Point A: $(x_1 = 10, x_2 = 10)$
$$4 \times 10 + 2 \times 10 \leq 80$$
$$60 < 80 \qquad\qquad \textit{Satisfies the constraint}$$

Point B: $(x_1 = 10, x_2 = 20)$
$$4 \times 10 + 2 \times 20 \leq 80$$
$$80 = 80 \qquad\qquad \textit{Satisfies the constraint}$$

Point C: $(x_1 = 30, x_2 = 20)$
$$4 \times 30 + 2 \times 20 \leq 80$$
$$160 > 80 \qquad\qquad \textit{Does not satisfy the constraint}$$

Figure 3.5   *Graphing of $4x_1 + 2x_2 \leq 80$ and Test Points*

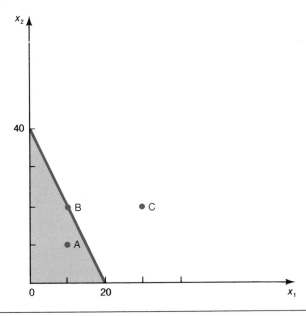

It should be apparent that any production combination of GE-1000 and GE-2000 computers within the shaded area can be processed in assembly line 1 with the available production time. Any production combination outside the shaded area cannot be handled with the given production capacity.

Also, it is important to recognize that the constraint equation line $x_2 = 40 - 2x_1$ represents the maximum possible production for assembly line 1. In other words, if a solution point happened to be exactly on this equation line, as solution point B is in Figure 3.5, we will use up the entire available amount of resources in this constraint. However, if a solution is below the constraint equation line (such as solution point A), there will be an unused amount, or slack, of the resource in the constraint.

In a similar manner, we can plot the second constraint as follows:

$$x_1 + 3x_2 \leq 60$$
$$3x_2 \leq 60 - x_1 \quad \text{(transposing } x_1\text{)}$$
$$x_2 \leq 20 - \frac{1}{3}x_1 \quad \text{(dividing both sides by 3)}$$

The second equality is plotted on the graph, and the inequality condition of $x_2 \leq 20 - (1/3)x_1$ is satisfied by the shaded area, as shown in Figure 3.6. The remaining two sales constraints are simple to plot on the graph. They are plotted in Figure 3.7.

Step 2: Identification of the Area of Feasible Solutions   Production of either microcomputer requires satisfying all the constraints. Thus, the only feasible production area will satisfy all four constraints simultaneously. Such an area can be easily identified

Figure 3.6   Graphing of $x_1 + 3x_2 \leq 60$

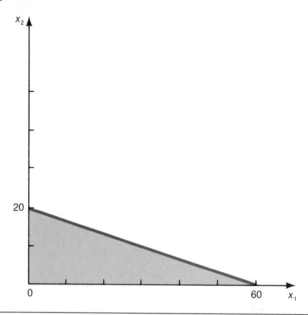

Figure 3.7   Graphing of $x_1 \leq 15$ and $x_2 \leq 18$

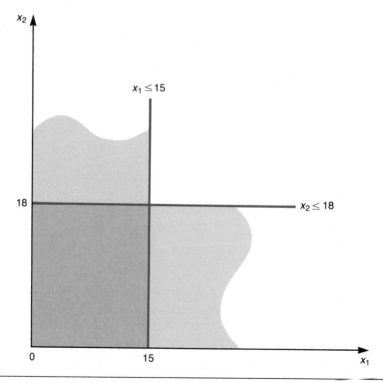

Figure 3.8   Graphing of the Constraints

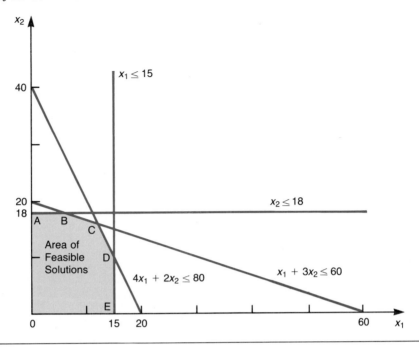

graphically as the region where all four constraints overlap, as in Figure 3.8. This area
is the **area of feasible solutions** or a **feasible region.**

The area of feasible solutions represents a region that satisfies conditions specified
by all the model constraints. Any point within the area is a feasible solution, and any
point external to it is an infeasible solution. For example, in Figure 3.8 the area of
feasible solutions is 0ABCDE.

Step 3: Identification of the Optimum Solution

The Search Approach   The simplest way to identify the optimum solution is to examine all the possible candidate solutions in the feasible region. For example, in the
Galaxy Electronics problem the area of feasible solutions is formed by six corner points,
0, A, B, C, D, and E, as shown in Figure 3.9. Corner point 0, the origin, cannot be
the optimum solution in a maximization problem because the total profit will be 0 when
$x_1 = 0$ and $x_2 = 0$.

Let us now examine a feasible solution, point F ($x_1 = 10$, $x_2 = 10$), inside the
area of feasible solutions as shown in Figure 3.9. The total profit at point F will be
$Z = \$150(10) + \$250(10) = \$4,000$. However, point F is not optimum. We can
increase production of x_2 to 16 2/3 units by moving up to point G. We can also increase
production of x_1 to 15 units if we move over to point D. Or we can increase production
of both x_1 and x_2 by moving up diagonally toward point C.

Figure 3.9   The Area of Feasible Solutions

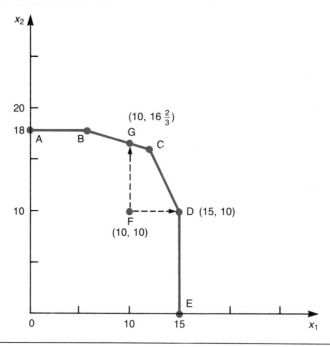

The total profits at points F, G, and D are computed as follows:

Point F: $Z = \$150(10) + \$250(10) = \$4,000.00$

Point G: $Z = \$150(10) + \$250(16\ 2/3) = \$5,666.67$

Point D: $Z = \$150(15) + \$250(10) = \$4,750.00$

From this computation, it should be apparent that points G and D are superior to point F. In other words, solution points on the boundary of the feasible region are always superior to solution points inside the feasible region. Consequently, *the optimum point must be on the boundary*, and it must also be at a *corner point* (also referred to as an *extreme point*) formed by the intersection of two constraints.

The concept of corner points (extreme points) is a very important property of linear programming. The boundary of the area of feasible solutions of a maximization problem is made up of straight lines (or planes) that are maximum possible production lines. Thus, the boundary has no indentions. This is why the feasible region is sometimes referred to as a *convex set*. Because of this property (i.e., convexity) of the feasible region, the optimum solution must be at a corner point. Owing to this property, linear programming is sometimes referred to as an *extremal optimization method*.

Now we are ready to examine the other (excluding the origin) corner points A, B, C, D, and E.

Total profits at points A and E can be easily calculated, since the exact values of x_1 and x_2 are already known. We can calculate total profits at these points as follows:

Point A: $x_1 = 0,\ x_2 = 18$

$Z = 150 \times 0 + 250 \times 18$

$Z = 4,500$

$$\text{Point E:} \quad x_1 = 15, x_2 = 0$$
$$Z = 150 \times 15 + 250 \times 0$$
$$Z = 2{,}250$$

At point A, Galaxy specializes in producing GE-2000 computers. On the other hand, at point E only GE-1000 computers are being produced. Since $2,250 more profit is made at point A, if Galaxy desires to specialize in producing only one computer, it should be GE-2000.

Now we can proceed to calculate the total profit at point B. Before we can do this, we must first calculate the exact values of x_1 and x_2 at this point. Point B is the intersecting point of two straight lines. Thus, we can solve the two equalities simultaneously as follows:

$$x_2 = 20 - \frac{1}{3}x_1$$

$$x_2 = 18$$

Then

$$18 = 20 - \frac{1}{3}x_1$$

$$\frac{1}{3}x_1 = 2$$

$$x_1 = 6$$

Now, the total profit at point B can be derived as $Z = 150 \times 6 + 250 \times 18 = 5{,}400.$

At point C, the two production constraints intersect. Thus, we can solve the two equalities simultaneously.

$$x_2 = 40 - 2x_1 \qquad \textbf{\textit{(1) Assembly line 1}}$$

$$x_2 = 20 - \frac{1}{3}x_1 \qquad \textbf{\textit{(2) Assembly line 2}}$$

$$40 - 2x_1 = 20 - \frac{1}{3}x_1$$

$$-\frac{5}{3}x_1 = -20$$

$$x_1 = 12$$

Substituting this value of x_1 into (1), we have

$$x_2 = 40 - 2 \times 12$$

$$x_2 = 16$$

The total profit at point C is $Z = 150 \times 12 + 250 \times 16 = 5{,}800.$

In a similar manner we found the total profit at point D earlier:

$$x_2 = 40 - 2x_1$$

$$x_1 = 15$$

Thus,

$$x_2 = 40 - 2 \times 15$$

$$x_2 = 10$$

The total profit at point D is: $Z = 150 \times 15 + 250 \times 10 = 4{,}750.$

The maximum profit of $5,800 is found at point C. At point C, Galaxy would produce 12 GE-1000 computers and 16 GE-2000 computers.

The search approach we have discussed is obviously a very simple method for determining the optimum solution when the problem under study has a small number of constraints and thus very few corner points of the feasibility area. However, if a problem has a large number of constraints that form the area of feasible solutions, there would be a large number of corner points to search. Hence, the graphical search procedure is not a practical approach to identifying the optimum solution.

The Iso-profit Function Approach   Perhaps the most practical approach to identifying the optimum solution through the graphical method is concerned with an analysis of the iso-profit function. As the prefix *iso-* implies, the *iso-profit function* is a straight line on which every point has the same total profit. We can derive the iso-profit function (or iso-cost function in a minimization problem) when the objective function is solved for the vertical axis variable (x_2 in our Galaxy Electronics problem). The objective function can be solved for x_2 as follows:

$$Z = 150x_1 + 250x_2 \qquad \textit{Objective function}$$

$$250x_2 = Z - 150x_1$$

$$x_2 = \frac{Z}{250} - \frac{150}{250}x_1$$

$$x_2 = \frac{Z}{250} - \frac{3}{5}x_1 \qquad \textit{Iso-profit function}$$

The iso-profit function derived above has an x_2 intercept of $Z/250$ and a slope of $-3/5$. The x_2 intercept $Z/250$ can be determined only when a total profit value Z is known. For example, if $Z = 1,500$, we can easily determine the x_2 intercept as $Z/250 = 1500/250 = 6$. Thus, the iso-profit function will be $x_2 = 6 - (3/5)x_1$. If the total profit is doubled, then $Z = 3,000$, and the iso-profit function becomes $x_2 = 12 - (3/5)x_1$. Although the x_2 intercept changes as the total profit Z is changed, the slope of the iso-profit function remains constant.

We can plot an infinite number of total profit lines on the graph. As we increase the total-profit value Z, the total-profit function moves gradually upward from the origin. In this maximization problem, then, we should attempt to move upward from the origin with the slope of the iso-profit function as far as we can within the feasibility area. Then, the optimum point is the last point we go through in the feasibility area. For example, let us plot a series of total-profit lines as shown in Figure 3.10. As we move upward from the origin the total profit increases; thus, $Z_1 < Z_2 < Z_3 < Z_4$. The maximum feasible profit is found to be $Z_3 = \$5,800$ at point C. The total profit $Z_4 = \$7,500$ is much greater than the $5,800 we found at point C. However, this profit is infeasible because the profit line is outside of the feasibility area. The iso-profit function approach further reinforces the property of corner points we discussed earlier in the search method section.

The Slope Comparison Approach   Another approach that can be effective in solving simple linear programming problems is the slope comparison approach. In this approach, we compare the slope of the iso-profit function with the slopes of the constraints that form the area of feasible solutions. In the Galaxy Electronics problem, the slopes of the four constraints are $-\infty$, -2, $-1/3$, and 0. As long as the slope of the iso-profit function ($-3/5$) falls between any two slopes, the optimum point is the intersecting

Figure 3.10   Total Profit Functions with Various Intercepts

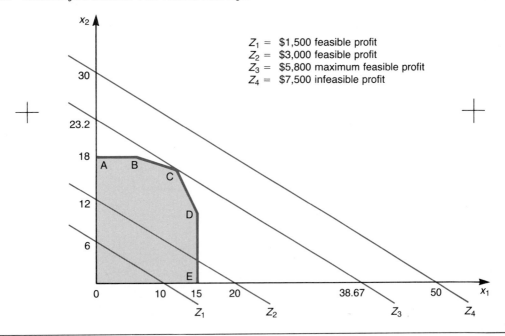

point of the two constraints, as shown in Figure 3.11. The slope $-3/5$ is not as steep as $-\infty$ or -2 but is steeper than $-1/3$ or 0; therefore, the iso-profit function will pass through the intersecting point of the two constraints with slopes of -2 and $-1/3$ at the tip of the area of feasible solutions.

If the iso-profit function had a slope of -3, which falls between -2 and $-\infty$, the optimum point would be at point D. By applying the same reasoning, if the iso-profit function had a slope of $-1/4$, which falls between $-1/3$ and 0, the optimum solution would be at point B.

If the iso-profit function has a slope that is identical to one of the slopes of the *critical constraints* (constraints that form the feasibility area), the optimum solution would be a portion of that constraint. For example, if the slope of the iso-profit function were $-1/3$ in the Galaxy problem (e.g., $Z = 100x_1 + 300x_2$), any point on the line segment BC would be the optimum solution. In such a case, obviously, we have multiple optimum solutions. Usually, however, the decision maker is faced with a choice between points B and C.

Now we can summarize the slope comparison approach for a maximization problem as follows:

Iso-profit Function Slope	Optimum Solution
Flatter than all constraint slopes	Extreme point on vertical axis
Steeper than all constraints	Extreme point on horizontal axis
Between two slopes of constraints	Intersecting point of the two constraint lines
Identical to the slope of a constraint	Multiple optimum solutions on the line segment of the constraint

Figure 3.11   *Graphical Representation of the Slope Comparison Approach*

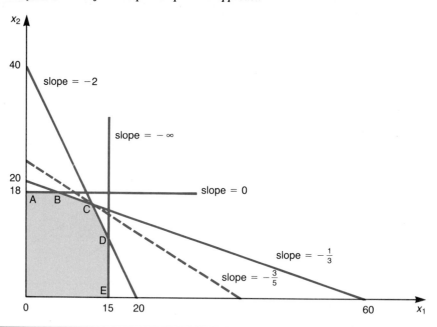

Thus far in our discussion of the slope comparison approach, we have emphasized that we should consider the slopes of only those constraints that form the boundary of the area of feasible solutions. In other words, we must graph all the constraints and identify the feasibility area before attempting to compare slopes. Otherwise, we may consider slopes of the *redundant constraints* (constraints that are not critical and do not form the feasibility area). Consequently, we may possibly identify a solution that is infeasible (a solution outside of the feasibility area) or one that violates the nonnegativity condition (one or more solution values of the decision variables are negative).

It should also be noted here that care must be taken in using the slope comparison approach if the problem involves mixed constraints. For example, suppose we have a linear programming model as follows:

$$\text{Maximize } Z = 12x_1 + 8x_2$$
$$\text{subject to} \quad x_1 + x_2 \le 20$$
$$3x_1 + x_2 \ge 30$$
$$2x_1 + 6x_2 \ge 60$$
$$2x_1 - x_2 \ge 0$$
$$x_1, x_2 \ge 0$$

This maximization problem has mixed constraints—one is a less-than-or-equal-to type and three are the greater-than-or-equal-to type of constraint. Furthermore, one constraint has a right-hand side value of 0. It should be noted here that *a maximization problem does not need to have only less-than-or-equal-to constraints, and a minimization prob-*

Figure 3.12   A Problem with Mixed Constraints

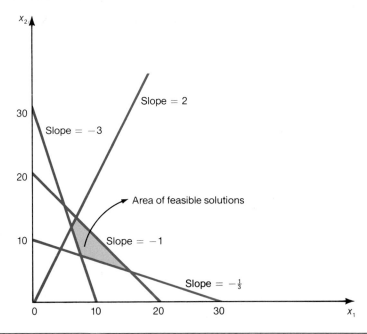

lem does not need to have only greater-than-or-equal-to constraints. A linear programming problem, whether it is a maximization or a minimization problem, can have any combination of the three possible types of constraints: $\leq$, $=$, or $\geq$.

The maximization problem with mixed constraints presented above has the area of feasible solutions as shown in Figure 3.12. In this problem, you may have difficulty in finding the optimum solution by simply comparing slopes. For such problems it is more appropriate to use the iso-profit (or iso-cost) function approach.

Analysis of Slack Variables

In addition to determining the optimum solution, the decision maker is often interested in obtaining additional information about the use of available resources. The optimum solution does not always use up all available resources. If some resources are left, they can be better used in the more critical constraints. Such analysis can be performed through investigating **slack variables.**

In the Galaxy Electronics problem, the optimum solution values were: $x_1 = 12$; $x_2 = 16$. By substituting these values for the decision variables in each of the constraints, we obtain the following:

Constraint	Actual Resource Used	Available Resource	Unused Resource
Assembly line 1	4(12) + 2(16) = 80	80	0
Assembly line 2	1(12) + 3(16) = 60	60	0
Sales for GE-1000	1(12) = 12	15	3
Sales for GE-2000	1(16) = 16	18	2

Now the Galaxy management knows that production of 12 GE-1000 computers and 16 GE-2000 computers will require all available productive resources in assembly lines 1 and 2. However, the sales capacity constraints are not fully utilized; the idle sales capacity for GE-1000 is 3 and for GE-2000 is 2.

The unused or idle capacity in a less-than-or-equal-to constraint is a slack variable. Slack variables simply take up the difference between the available amount of resource (or the right-hand side value) and the actual use of the resource. Thus, we add slack variables on the left side of the constraint and change the $\leq$ to an $=$. Since slack variables do not contribute to profit, their contribution rates in the objective function will be 0.

Now we can reformulate the Galaxy Electronics problem as follows:

$$\text{Maximize } Z = 150x_1 + 250x_2 + 0s_1 + 0s_2 + 0s_3 + 0s_4$$
$$\text{subject to} \quad 4x_1 + 2x_2 + s_1 = 80$$
$$x_1 + 3x_2 + s_2 = 60$$
$$x_1 \qquad\quad + s_3 = 15$$
$$x_2 + s_4 = 18$$
$$x_1, x_2, s_1, s_2, s_3, s_4 \geq 0$$

In any linear programming problem, the final solution must have as many solution variables as the number of constraints. Such variables are called the *basic variables*. The optimum solution of this problem has the following basic variables: $x_1 = 12$; $x_2 = 16$; $s_3 = 3$; and $s_4 = 2$. The nonbasic variables have solution values of 0: $s_1 = 0$; $s_2 = 0$.

Slack-variable analysis can be used for the following important purposes:

1. *Identification of Critical or Binding Constraints.*   The critical constraints are those where all available amounts of resources have been exhausted. Since $s_1 = s_2 = 0$, we have used up all the available resources in assembly lines 1 and 2. In other words, the optimum solution is the intersecting point of the first two constraints as shown in Figure 3.13.

The above reasoning certainly makes sense. As we discussed earlier, a constraint equation line represents the maximum possible production line. Since point C is on the maximum possible production line for each of the first two constraints, there should be no slack in these constraints.

2. *Identification of Noncritical or Nonbinding Constraints.*   Noncritical constraints are those where some idle resources remain. In our problem, $s_3 = 3$ and $s_4 = 2$. Thus, the third and fourth constraints are noncritical. In other words, the optimum solution is not on these constraint lines but below them, as shown in Figure 3.13.

3. *Resource Reallocation Decision.*   Now that we have identified the critical and noncritical constraints, we can determine whether we can make a resource reallocation decision. For example, if the management of Galaxy Electronics wants to increase re-

Figure 3.13   Slack Variables

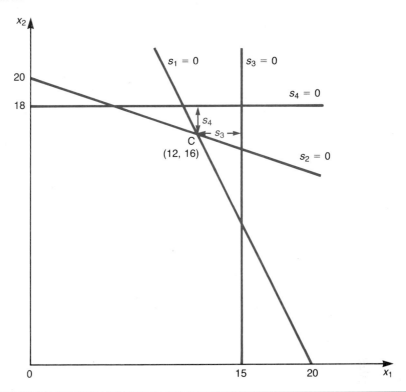

sources, the increase should not be equally divided among the resources nor allocated on the basis of same proportion. We already have slack resources in the third and fourth constraints. Consequently, any increase should be in the first two constraints.

Any decrease in resources should be in the third and fourth constraints rather than across-the-board (as government agencies often practice). Hence, if we can effectively reallocate some resources (e.g., labor) from the last two constraints to the first two constraints, the optimum solution may move up and the total profit would be increased.

A Simple Minimization Problem

Thus far we have discussed the graphical method of linear programming for a maximization problem. The basic approaches used for a maximization problem can also be applied to a minimization problem. Let us consider the model that we formulated in Casette 3.2 for the orientation program. The problem is concerned with the determination of the number of scoops of scrambled eggs and the number of smokie sausages to serve for breakfast in order to minimize the cost per serving. The constraints involved in the problem are to meet vitamin A, vitamin B, and iron requirements.

The diet problem we formulated was

$$\text{Minimize } Z = 8x_1 + 10x_2$$

$$\text{subject to} \quad 3x_1 + 3x_2 \geq 30 \qquad \textit{Vitamin A}$$

$$4x_1 + 2x_2 \geq 24 \qquad \textit{Vitamin B}$$

$$x_1 + 2x_2 \geq 12 \qquad \textit{Iron}$$

$$x_1, x_2 \geq 0$$

where x_1 = number of scoops of scrambled eggs served

x_2 = number of smokies served

The objective function is expressed in terms of cents rather than dollars. The right-hand side values of the constraints specify the *minimum* requirements for the three nutrients. Thus, the inequalities are shown as greater-than-or-equal-to constraints.

Based on the knowledge we have gained so far, we can easily plot the three constraints and identify the area of feasible solutions on a graph, as shown in Figure 3.14, by going through the following procedure:

$$3x_1 + 3x_2 \geq 30 \qquad \textit{(1) Vitamin A}$$

$$3x_2 \geq 30 - 3x_1$$

$$x_2 \geq 10 - x_1$$

$$4x_1 + 2x_2 \geq 24 \qquad \textit{(2) Vitamin B}$$

$$2x_2 \geq 24 - 4x_1$$

$$x_2 \geq 12 - 2x_1$$

$$x_1 + 2x_2 \geq 12 \qquad \textit{(3) Iron}$$

$$2x_2 \geq 12 - x_1$$

$$x_2 \geq 6 - \frac{1}{2}x_1$$

The area of feasible solutions is represented by the shaded area on and above the lines outlined by ABCD. The problem can be solved by using any of the three approaches we have discussed. The optimum solution is the point where the total cost is minimum. If we did not have the model constraints, the optimum solution would be at the origin, point 0. Hence, the optimum solution within the area of feasible solutions must be one of those corner points that are close to the origin and that form the feasibility area.

If we use the *search approach,* we can simply examine the total cost at each of the four corner points A, B, C, and D. If the *iso-cost function approach* is used ("cost" because this is a cost minimization problem), the optimum point will be the first point we touch within the feasibility area as we move out from the origin with the slope of the iso-cost function $-4/5$. For example, the iso-cost function can be developed as follows:

$$Z = 8x_1 + 10x_2$$

$$10x_2 = Z - 8x_1$$

$$x_2 = \frac{Z}{10} - \frac{4}{5}x_1$$

Figure 3.14   The Graphical Presentation of the Diet Problem

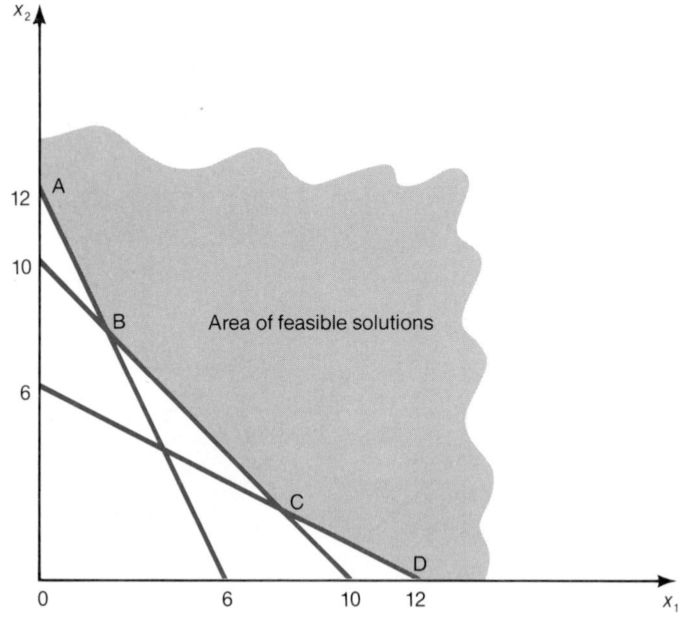

If the *slope comparison approach* is used, the slopes of the three constraints $(-2, -1,$ and $-1/2)$ should be compared with the slope of the iso-cost function, $-4/5$.

Let us use the iso-cost function approach to identify the optimum point. We can move out from the origin with a number of total-cost functions, as shown in Figure 3.15. The total cost of the three iso-cost functions have the relationship $Z_1 < Z_2 < Z_3$. We can easily identify point C as the optimum solution. Exact values of x_1 and x_2 at point C can be easily calculated when the two constraint equalities are solved simultaneously. The two constraints are the vitamin A and iron requirements.

We can solve for x_1 and x_2 as

$$x_2 = 10 - x_1 \tag{1}$$

$$x_2 = 6 - \frac{1}{2} x_1 \tag{3}$$

Thus,

$$10 - x_1 = 6 - \frac{1}{2} x_1$$

$$-\frac{1}{2} x_1 = -4$$

$$x_1 = 8$$

Substituting this value of x_1 into (1), we have

$$x_2 = 10 - 8$$

$$x_2 = 2$$

Figure 3.15   Graphical Solution of the Diet Problem by the Iso-cost Function Approach

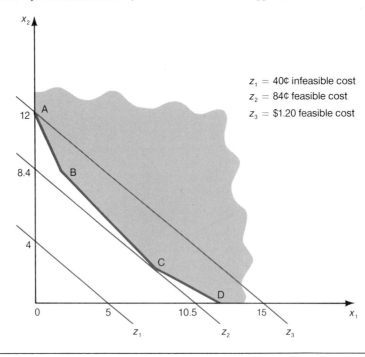

Now the total cost at point C can be derived as

$$Z = 8 \times 8 + 10 \times 2 = 84$$

Analysis of Surplus Variables

The analysis of slack variables discussed earlier is similar to that of **surplus variables.** The optimum solution to the orientation program problem was: $x_1 = 8$, $x_2 = 2$, $Z = 84$. By substituting solution values of the decision variables in each of the constraints, we obtain the following:

Constraint	Actual Nutrient Provided	Minimum Requirements	Surplus
Vitamin A	3(8) + 3(2) = 30	30	0
Vitamin B	4(8) + 2(2) = 36	24	12
Iron	1(8) + 2(2) = 12	12	0

In a less-than-or-equal-to constraint, a slack variable is added to the left side, and the constraint is made an equality. In a greater-than-or-equal-to constraint, the right-hand side value represents the minimum requirement. Thus, the left side can have a value which is greater than the right-hand side value. To make the constraint an equality, therefore, we need to subtract a variable in the left side. This variable is referred to as the *surplus variable*.

After including surplus variables, the orientation program model becomes:

$$\text{Minimize } Z = 8x_1 + 10x_2 + 0s_1 + 0s_2 + 0s_3$$

$$\text{subject to} \quad 3x_1 + 3x_2 - s_1 = 30$$

$$4x_1 + 2x_2 - s_2 = 24$$

$$x_1 + 2x_2 - s_3 = 12$$

$$x_1, x_2, s_1, s_2, s_3 \geq 0$$

The basic variables of the optimum solution are: $x_1 = 8$; $x_2 = 2$; and $s_2 = 12$. Consequently, the nonbasic variables are $s_1 = s_3 = 0$. By providing 8 scrambled eggs and 2 smokies, we are barely meeting the minimum requirements for vitamin A and iron (surplus variables in these constraints have 0 values). However, this solution provides 12 milligrams of surplus in excess of the minimum requirement for vitamin B.

A Problem with an Equality Constraint

In our discussion thus far we have dealt with linear programming problems having only **inequality** constraints. However, in certain problems we may actually have **equality** constraints. Let us consider the following simple maximization problem:

$$\text{Maximize } Z = \$18x_1 + \$12x_2$$

$$\text{subject to} \quad 2x_1 + x_2 \leq 40$$

$$x_2 \geq 10$$

$$x_1 + x_2 = 20$$

$$x_1, x_2 \geq 0$$

This problem, which is illustrated graphically in Figure 3.16, has all three types of constraints: $\leq$, $\geq$, and $=$. We already know how to define the feasibility area for an inequality constraint. For an equality constraint, the feasibility area is simply the straight line itself. Thus, the feasibility area for this problem is the line segment AB.

The iso-profit function of this problem is

$$Z = 18x_1 + 12x_2$$

$$x_2 = \frac{Z}{12} - \frac{3}{2}x_1$$

Since the slope of the iso-profit function is $-3/2$ and the slope of the line segment AB is -1, the optimum solution is point B. Now we can easily determine the optimum solution as $x_1 = 10$, $x_2 = 10$, $Z = \$300$.

Some Complications

Several situations present some difficulty in analyzing linear programming problems. This section discusses several of these complications.

1. *Negative Right-Hand Side Value.*   Many real-world problems involve constraints with negative right-hand side values. The solution value for the basic variable must be nonnegative throughout the solution process. Consider the following constraint:

$$2x_1 - x_2 + 3x_3 \leq -10$$

Figure 3.16   A Problem with an Equality Constraint

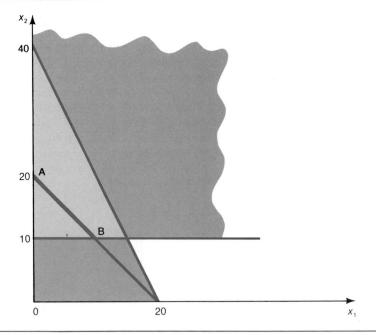

If the initial solution is at the origin, $x_1 = 0$, $x_2 = 0$, and $x_3 = 0$. Thus, the constraint equality with the appropriate slack variable becomes

$$2x_1 - x_2 + 3x_3 + s_1 = -10$$
$$2(0) - 0 + 3(0) + s_1 = -10$$
$$s_1 = -10$$

Since $s_1 \geq 0$, the above condition is not acceptable. This problem can be easily resolved by multiplying both sides by -1 and handling the constraint as follows:

$$2x_1 - x_2 + 3x_3 \leq -10$$
$$(-1)(2x_1 - x_2 + 3x_3) \leq (-1) - 10$$
$$-2x_1 + x_2 - 3x_3 \geq 10$$
$$-2x_1 + x_2 - 3x_3 - s_1 = 10$$

2. *An Infeasible Problem.* A linear programming problem is infeasible when it has conflicting or mutually exclusive constraints. Such a problem has no feasible region because there is no area where all constraints overlap. For example, let us consider the following problem:

$$\text{Minimize } Z = 10x_1 + 8x_2$$
$$\text{subject to } \quad 2x_1 + 2x_2 \leq 6$$
$$x_1 + 2x_2 \geq 10$$
$$x_1, x_2 \geq 0$$

Figure 3.17   An Infeasible Problem

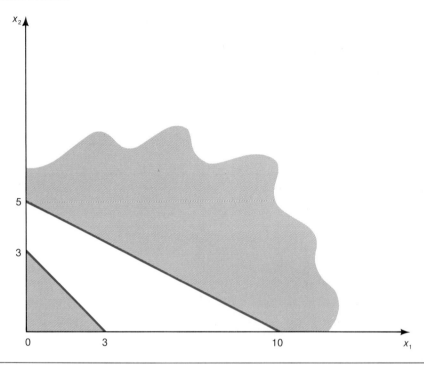

The problem is illustrated graphically in Figure 3.17. Since the two constraints do not overlap, there is no feasible region. Thus, this problem is infeasible and cannot be solved by linear programming.

3. *An Unbounded Problem.*   In a maximization problem of linear programming, if total profit can increase indefinitely without violating any constraints, the problem is termed as *unbounded*. An unbounded problem occurs only when the model is improperly formulated while leaving out important other constraints. Every management problem exists in the condition of scarce resources. Thus, it is not possible to keep on increasing total profit without a bound. For example, let us consider the following problem:

$$\text{Maximixe } Z = 5x_1 + 7x_2$$
$$\text{subject to} \quad 2x_1 + 2x_2 \geq 16$$
$$x_2 \leq 5$$
$$x_1, x_2 \geq 0$$

The problem is illustrated graphically in Figure 3.18. As the iso-profit function moves out gradually, total profit increases without a bound. Thus, this is an unbounded problem.

Figure 3.18   An Unbounded Problem

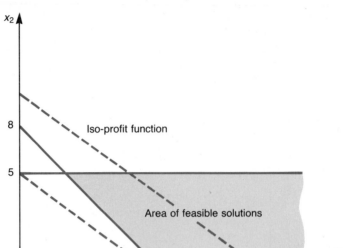

REAL-WORLD APPLICATIONS OF LINEAR PROGRAMMING

Since linear programmimg is a systematic method of selecting the best alternative among a large number of solution combinations, it is reasonable to expect extensive real-world applications of this technique. Indeed, there have been a large number of papers published about the application of linear programming to various management decision problems. However, it is extremely difficult to determine the number of real-world applications of linear programming in actual decision-making settings. It is even harder to ascertain what percentage of these applications were actually implemented and resulted in positive consequences.

Since many business firms consider any innovative application of management science as a comparative advantage, they do not often reveal their management science applications. The profession of management science, however, has emphasized the publication of real-world applications. For example, The Institute of Management Science (TIMS) has an annual award for the best paper describing a real-world application of management science. In this section we will introduce three real-world applications of linear programming.

Rationalizing Milk Processing with Linear Programming

Milk processing involves complicated trade-offs among customer demands, production equipment time, and storage capacity. Supply is generally not a problem, and once consumer demand is met, the government will buy the excess. Thus, maximizing production is the primary objective. The main material is raw milk, and the many inter-related products include cheese, whey, butter, cream, and powdered milk. Most decisions tend to be based on experience and intuition, rather than coordinated planning.

The dairy cooperative for which the model was formulated is in Tulare, California.[1] The total development cost — including purchase of a microcomputer — was under $15,000. Daily input at the cooperative is 5 million pounds of raw milk, making it the largest single milk-processing plant in the United States.

In the model, the objective function is to maximize total milk processed. The 36 constraints include product relationships, product conversions, capacity limitations, and demand–supply restrictions. The milk flow analysis program has increased daily processing by about 150,000 pounds, for an estimated annual increase in profits of about $48,000. In addition, plant supervisors have been relieved of 4 hours of hand calculations per day.

U.S. Forest Service Resource Allocation Planning

The U.S. Forest Service is responsible for the management of nearly 200 million acres of land, which produce about one-fifth of our annual timber harvest, shelter millions of animals, and provide recreational opportunities for millions of people.[2] To administer the 154 national forests, 121 headquarters have been established, each supported by ranger district offices. The National Forest Management Act of 1976 (NFMA) requires the development of comprehensive plans to guide the management of each forest. Earlier plans addressed only specific problems, such as harvesting strategies to maximize timber production, but NFMA was interpreted as requiring plans that would maximize benefits in an environmentally sound manner.

A consultant, with considerable Forest Service support, developed the FORPLAN (FORest PLANning) system, using a commercial linear programming solution package. The Forest Service offices can access the computers via remote terminals, and the FORPLAN models are being customized for each forest's specific needs. The models simultaneously allocate land to various objectives and schedule the results, costs, and market prices.

In the early 1980s, roughly 150 analysts worked on linear programming models involving up to 6,000 constraints and 120,000 variables. Hundreds of resource specialists developed technical input and interpreted the results. Although implementation is being contested by both political and ecological groups, valuable knowledge has been gained, and numerous procedures have been improved. As middle managers more readily accept advanced technology, the applications and acceptance of FORPLAN models should increase.

Water Pollution Management in the Netherlands

Although some aspects of the water management needs of the Netherlands are unique, many of the Dutch government's concerns are universal: providing enough clean water for the population, agriculture, and industry, for example. Pollution enters Dutch waters from three sources: the North Sea (via river tides and groundwater seepage), from the Rhine River (courtesy of upstream residents), and from the Dutch people themselves. Water pollution in the Netherlands consists primarily of salt, heat, fertilizers, algae and decaying biological matter, and industrial chemicals.

---

[1] Robert Sullivan and Stephen Secrest, "A Simple Optimization DSS for Production Planning at Dairyman's Cooperative Creamery Association," *Interfaces* 15:5 (1985), 46–53.

[2] Richard C. Field, "National Forest Planning Is Promoting U.S. Forest Service Acceptance of Operations Research," *Interfaces* 14:5 (1984), 67–76.

Water management has a long history in the Netherlands; the most common problem has been controlling excess water. However, a severe drought in 1976, coupled with water quality problems, highlighted the need for major policy revisions and increased control. In 1976, over $2.5 billion of agricultural losses were blamed on the drought—a staggering 4 percent of the gross domestic product. The Rand Corporation, the Dutch water agency, and a leading Dutch research organization formed PAWN (Policy Analysis for the Water Management of the Netherlands).[3]

The PAWN project gathered a huge database and developed an integrated system of 50 models, four of which involved linear programming. One model employing linear programming optimization evaluates heat discharge at electric power generators to reallocate national power production. The model contains four kinds of constraints: power production capacity of each generator, satisfaction of power demand in various regions, transmission capabilities of the power grid, and thermal standards at each point in the network. The cost of fuel was included for each site.

By late 1984, many of the changes and programs suggested by PAWN had been incorporated into Dutch national water management policy. Implementation is expected to save millions of dollars annually, channel investments into the most cost-effective projects, and allow for adherence to more stringent environmental controls.

SUMMARY

Linear programming is a powerful mathematical technique for determining the optimum solutions to decision problems that involve linear objective functions and linear constraints. Linear programming has been widely applied by industry, government, and nonprofit organizations. Two reasons for this popularity appear to be its relatively simple concept and its applicability to many real-world problems. Another very important reason is the availability of the simplex technique as a solution algorithm. Today, there are numerous simplex-based computer programs available. These programs enable the decision maker to solve complex linear programming problems with relative ease. The most critical problem in applying linear programming is the model formulation. It requires a good understanding of the basic concept, requirements, and application areas of linear programming.

In this chapter, we have seen how linear programming assists the decision maker in selecting the most effective course of action from various alternatives. We have studied the important aspects of linear programming through various casette examples and the graphical solution method. We have also learned how a decision maker can gain clearer insight into the nature of a problem by performing sensitivity analysis.

Glossary

Additivity   The concept that solution values within a formula must be expressed in the same kind of units, so that the sum of the values is logical and reasonable. For example, dollars and dollars are additive, but dollars and chairs are not.

[3]Bruce F. Goeller and the PAWN Team, "Planning the Netherlands' Water Resources," *Interfaces* 15:1 (1985), 3–33.

Area of Feasibility   The solution area which satisfies all the constraints simultaneously is known as the area of feasible solutions, or area of feasibility, particularly when employing the graphical method.

Constraint   Limits imposed on resources, time, requirements, and other aspects of a decision are expressed as formulae which restrict or constrain the possible solutions.

Divisibility   Linear programming frequently results in fractional solution values, and the variables must be able to accept this restriction. For example, 15.32 pounds of sand is feasible, but, because people are not divisible, we cannot accept a solution of 2.37 engineers.

Equality   A mathematical expression in which the left side exactly equals the right side is an equality. On a graph, an equality is represented by a line, for example: $4x_1 + 2x_2 = 37$.

Graphical Method   A solution technique suitable for linear programming models with two variables, the graphical method plots the constraints on a graph to visualize their relationships and to determine feasible and optimum solutions.

Inequality   A mathematical expression in which the left side does not always equal the right side is an inequality. On a graph, an inequality is represented by an area, for example: $x_1 + 3x_2 \leq 15$.

Infeasible Problem   An infeasible problem has no solution that satisfies all the constraints. This situation occurs when some of the constraints are in conflict.

Nonnegativity   Nonnegativity requires that all variables of the model are 0 or positive, that is, not negative.

Objective Function   The goal or objective of the decision maker is expressed as an equation representing the effect of potential choices on the achievement of that goal.

Optimum Solution   An optimum solution is a feasible solution that maximizes the value of the objective function for a maximization problem or minimizes the value of the objective function for a minimization problem.

Slack Variable   Added to less-than-or-equal-to constraints, a slack variable represents unused resources; its inclusion permits conversion of the inequality to an equality.

Surplus Variable   A slack variable in reverse, a surplus variable represents how much the left side exceeds the right side in a greater-than-or-equal-to constraint; its inclusion permits conversion of the inequality to an equality.

Unbounded Problem   An unbounded problem's objective function value can increase indefinitely without bounds. This situation occurs when important constraints are left out by mistake.

References

Charnes, A., and Cooper, W. W. *Management Models and Industrial Applications of Linear Programming*. New York: Wiley, 1961.

Dantzig, G. B. *Linear Programming and Extensions*. Princeton, N.J.: Princeton University, 1963.

Karmarkar, N. "A New Polynomial-Time Algorithm for Linear Programming." Technical Report, AT&T Laboratories, 1984.

Khachian, L. G. "A Polynomial Algorithm in Linear Programming." *Doklady* 244:6 (1979), 1093–1096.

Lee, S. M., Moore, L. J., and Taylor, B. *Management Science*. 2d ed. Dubuque, Iowa: W. C. Brown, 1985.

Loomba, N. P., and Turban, E. *Applied Programming for Management*. New York: Holt, Rinehart & Winston, 1974.

Assignments

3.1 What are the most important reasons that linear programming is one of the most widely applied techniques of management science?

3.2 List six major requirements of linear programming.

3.3 Define the following terms by using examples: *proportionality, additivity, divisibility, nonnegativity*.

3.4 Discuss a problem you are familiar with that can be solved by linear programming.

3.5 Discuss the three different types of constraints that are used in linear programming.

3.6 What is the main difference between a linear equality and a linear inequality?

3.7 What is the iso-profit function? Why is it useful for the graphical method?

3.8 What is a redundant constraint?

3.9 When do we face a case of multiple optimum solutions?

3.10 When is the slope comparison approach not appropriate?

3.11 What is the difference between an infeasible problem and an unbounded problem?

3.12 Graph the following equalities:
    a. $7x_1 + 7x_2 = 28$ **d.** $x_1 + 2x_2 = 18$
    b. $12x_1 + 8x_2 = 72$ **e.** $x_2 = 9$
    c. $x_1 = 6$

3.13 Graph the following inequalities:
    a. $2x_1 + 2x_2 \leq 16$ **d.** $6x_1 + 4x_2 \leq 48$
    b. $2x_1 \leq 24$ **e.** $1/2x_1 + x_2 \leq 6$
    c. $x_2 \geq 6$

3.14 Graph the following constraints and indicate the area of feasible solutions:

$$\text{subject to} \quad 3x_1 + 3x_2 \leq 300$$
$$6x_1 + 3x_2 \leq 480$$
$$3x_1 + 3x_2 \leq 480$$
$$x_1, x_2 \geq 0$$

3.15 Graph the following constraints and indicate the area of feasible solutions:

$$\text{subject to} \quad 7x_1 + 14x_2 \leq 56$$
$$42x_1 + 28x_2 \leq 168$$
$$x_1, x_2 \geq 0$$

3.16 Solve the following linear programming problem by the graphical method:

$$\text{Maximize } Z = \$18x_1 + \$14x_2$$
$$\text{subject to} \quad 4x_1 + 2x_2 \leq 80$$
$$2x_1 + 6x_2 \leq 60$$
$$x_1, x_2 \geq 0$$

3.17 Solve the following linear programming problem by the graphical method:

$$\text{Maximize } Z = \$9x_1 + \$15x_2$$
$$\text{subject to} \quad 3x_2 \leq 18$$
$$9x_1 + 6x_2 \leq 54$$
$$x_1, x_2 \geq 0$$

3.18 Solve the following linear programming problem by the graphical method:

$$\text{Minimize } Z = 6x_1 + 5x_2$$
$$\text{subject to} \quad 5x_1 + 2x_2 \geq 20$$
$$5x_1 + 12x_2 \geq 60$$
$$x_1, x_2 \geq 0$$

3.19 Given the following linear programming model:

$$\text{Maximize } Z = \$40x_1 + \$44x_2$$
$$\text{subject to} \quad 16x_1 + 12x_2 \leq 96$$
$$12x_1 + 16x_2 \leq 96$$
$$14x_1 + 14x_2 = 88$$
$$x_1, x_2 \geq 0$$

a. Solve it by using the graphical method.
b. Change the first constraint from less-than-or-equal-to to greater-than-or-equal-to. Does this change the optimum solution? If it does, identify the new optimum.
c. Would the optimum solution change if the third constraint were less-than-or-equal-to? Hint: Use the slope comparison approach.

3.20 The Gloria Haig Company is a producer of two lines of designer jeans, Chic and Fancy. Ms. Haig supervises two production operation departments—design and cut, and sewing. The company has a definite commitment to Bloomdust Department Store for 800 jeans. There is no inventory for the new season's designer jeans. Thus, the company must produce at least 800 new jeans for the coming season. Production of one lot of 100 jeans requires the following operations:

	Chic	Fancy
Design and cut	20 hr	40 hr
Sewing	40 hr	40 hr

The company has secured the necessary labor to operate the two departments for the following number of hours during the next month: design and cut department, 400 hours; sewing department, 600 hours. Gloria is confident, as usual, that she can sell all the jeans to be produced next month. The expected unit profits are: Chic, $13; Fancy, $20.

a. Formulate a linear programming model to determine the mix of Chic and Fancy designer jeans that will maximize profits.

b. Solve the above problem using the graphical method.

3.21 The Artful Dodger Sports Shop is sponsoring a weekly boomerang-throwing contest as part of its spring promotions. Anyone may enter, but the boomerangs used must be purchased at the Artful Dodger. Because a smooth finish on the boomerang is essential to ensure accurate flights, most competitors are expected to buy a new boomerang every few weeks. The Artful Dodger thus expects to sell all that it can produce.

Two models can be made: the regular model (with a profit of $2 each) and the "Super Bender" (which yields a $5 profit). However, production facilities are limited. A regular boomerang requires 1 hour of carving and 2 hours of finishing; a "Super Bender" takes 3 hours to carve and 2 hours to finish. The skilled crafters employed by Artful Dodger have indicated they will spend no more than 75 hours carving and 100 hours finishing boomerangs per week.

a. Formulate a linear programming model to determine the number of each type of boomerang that should be produced each week to maximize profits.

b. Solve the above problem using the graphical method.

3.22 Cheery Fruitcake Supply dries various types of fruit for a prestigious fruitcake manufacturer. Cheery has increased production annually for the last 25 years, with bright prospects for the future. However, an official from the Environmental Protection Agency appeared, demanding a reduction in the river pollution caused by Cheery's operations.

The manager was preparing to rename the company Gloomy when you suggested that linear programming might help make the best out of the situation. Analysis showed that two types of pollution are involved: thermal and biochemical. Water used to cool the drying engines and blowers is released into the stream, and unprocessed fruit waste constitutes the biochemical pollution.

Only two kinds of fruit have been found to be at fault. Analysis shows that apricots contribute 5 units of thermal pollution and 2 units of biochemical pollution per pound of dried fruit produced. A pound of oranges, however, produces 2 units of thermal pollution and 7 units of biochemical pollution. Regulations indicate that 900 units of thermal and 700 units of biochemical pollution per week would not adversely affect the environment, and would satisfy the inspector.

a. Formulate a linear programming model to determine the mix of apricots and oranges which will allow for maximum total production (in pounds).

b. Solve this model using the graphical method.

c. Due to market fluctuations, the price Cheery can obtain for a pound of dried apricots has risen to 140 percent of the price obtainable for oranges. Would this change the production mix?

d. Cheery has received an order for 75 pounds of oranges and 150 pounds of apricots. The order must be ready in 1 week; no inventory is on hand. Can Cheery deliver?

3.23 The dietitian at a camp is planning breakfast for the first day of camp. The dietitian has the responsibility of providing a menu that satisfies the minimum nutrient requirements at the lowest cost. Two types of foods are being considered for the breakfast: toast and sausage.

A piece of toast contains 2 milligrams of vitamin A, 3 milligrams of vitamin B, and 2 milligrams of iron. A sausage contains 4 milligrams of vitamin A, 1.5 milligrams of vitamin B, and 2 milligrams of iron. The minimum breakfast requirements of these nutrient elements are estimated to be:

Nutrient	Requirement (mg)
Vitamin A	20
Vitamin B	15
Iron	16

The American Medical Association has published an article which reported that having more than four sausages for breakfast is not recommended for young people. The dietitian considers this one of the most important constraints. The unit costs of the food are: toast, 4 cents; sausage, 8 cents.

a. Formulate a linear programming model for the problem.

b. Solve this problem graphically.

3.24 The Browning Clothing Store is making plans for its annual shirt and pants sale. The owner, Mr. Jarvis, is planning to use two forms of advertising — radio and newspaper — to promote the sale. Based on past experience, Mr. Jarvis feels confident that each newspaper ad will reach 40 shirt customers and 80 pants customers. He estimates that each radio ad will reach 30 shirt customers and 20 pants customers.

The cost of each newspaper ad is $100, and the cost of each radio spot is $150. An advertising agency will prepare the advertising, and it will require 5 worker-hours of preparation for each newspaper ad and 15 worker-hours of preparation for each radio spot.

Mr. Jarvis's sales manager says that a minimum of 75 worker-hours should be spent on the preparation of advertising to fully utilize the services of the advertising agency. Mr. Jarvis feels that, to have a successful sale, the advertising must reach at least 360 shirt customers and at least 400 pants customers.

a. Formulate a linear programming model to determine how much advertising should be done using each of the two forms of media to minimize costs and still attain the objectives Mr. Jarvis has set.

b. Solve the above problem using the graphical method.

3.25 Lee Fortune Cookies Inc. produces two types of fortune cookies: love and happiness. The major decision problem to be solved is the product mix determination in order to maximize profits. The production of a dozen fortune cookies requires the following resources and capacity (the available resources and capacity are presented in the last column):

Requirement per Dozen	Love	Happiness	Available
Cookie mix	1.0 lb	0.6 lb	120 lb
Icing mix	0.4 lb	0 lb	32 lb
Labor	0.15 hr	0.10 hr	15 hr
Oven capacity	1 doz	1 doz	120 doz

The expected profit for love cookies is 40 cents per dozen, and for happiness cookies it is 30 cents per dozen.

a. Formulate a linear programming model for the problem.

b. Solve the above problem graphically.

c. Provided that the profit per dozen for love cookies remains at 40 cents, what kind of profit range should happiness cookies have in order for 80 dozen love cookies and 30 dozen happiness cookies to be the optimum solution?

3.26 Scoutmaster Tom D. Harry wishes to lead his troop of 15 scouts on a 2-week wilderness hike. Upon consulting his quartermaster, he learns that the typical camp menu would weigh about 45 pounds per scout. Each scout would also be carrying camping equipment and personal gear, so the total weight would be unduly restrictive. A new menu is clearly required.

The local camping center offers two brands of dehydrated foods. Each brand offers a variety of complete meals, with ProLight foods weighing 3 ounces per meal and EatRight meals weighing 5 ounces each. Each scout will eat three meals per day and must obtain an average of at least 3,500 calories per day (averaged over the 2-week period). ProLight meals average 1,100 calories, and EatRight pouches yield 1,500.

To further complicate matters, the treasury is low, so no more than $75 per scout can be spent. One ProLight meal costs $2.25, and the price of an EatRight package is $1.50.

a. Formulate a linear programming model to determine what mix of the two brands of dehydrated foods will minimize the weight the scouts must carry.

b. Solve this model using the graphical method. Interpret the solution in terms of weight, cost, and quantity of each type of meal that each scout will carry.

c. Scoutmaster Harry has been offered a promotional discount by the camping center: The scouts can have any 42 meals they desire for $60 each. Is there a new optimum solution? If so, identify it and interpret the solution.

3.27 The Cover Girl Company is expanding its operations and attempting to expand its sales territory. The sales manager has a staff of experienced salespersons who are each paid $200 per week. He is planning to hire some new sales trainees for $100 per week.

Based on past experience, an experienced salesperson can generate $10,000 worth of sales per week. A sales trainee can generate an average of $6,000 worth of sales per week. The company has budgeted $800 for a training program for the new trainees. The estimated cost of training is $100 per trainee. The sales manager's payroll budget is $1,600 per week. Furthermore, the company has decided that the sales force should be limited to 10 or fewer salespeople. The decision problem of the sales manager is to determine the optimum number of experienced salespersons and new trainees in order to maximize total sales.

a. Formulate a linear programming model for the problem.

b. Identify the optimum solution and the total sales by using the graphical method.

c. If the weekly sales of the experienced salespersons remain relatively constant at $10,000 per week but the weekly sales of the trainees fluctuate widely, how much should the average sales per trainee per week be before the company should limit its sales staff to two experienced salespersons and eight trainees?

d. In the original problem, if the training cost per trainee is $200 rather than $100, how would the optimum solution be changed?

e. In the original problem, if the company increases the number of salespeople from 10 to 12, how would the solution be changed?

3.28 Carolina Industrial Chemicals Inc. (CIC) has purchased a new processor which promises great savings in raw materials wasted (lost in processing). However, as the union was quick to point out, the new system also uses far less labor, and CIC is bound to employ its 50 workers a full 5 days per week. CIC does not believe in operating overtime, as the higher costs would ruin the competitiveness of its product.

The new processor loses only one-fifth the amount lost in the old system, due primarily to better valves and seals, as well as a more controlled thermal scrubber. The new system produces 1 batch per worker-day, whereas the old system produces one batch per 3 worker-days. A batch from the new processor weighs 1 ton, but a batch from the old weighs 2 tons. CIC has a contract to provide 200 tons per week; if more is produced, it can be sold without any problems.

CIC wishes to know what the best combination of batches would be, minimizing raw materials lost in processing, subject to the above restrictions.

a. Formulate a linear programming model for this problem.

b. Solve this model using the graphical method.

c. The labor contract will expire in 11 months. At that time, CIC will be free to employ as many or as few workers as it chooses and may operate partial days if needed. Should CIC change its processor use mix, or will the current mix still provide the most savings in materials lost? If there is a new optimum mix, identify it.

3.29 Old Dominion Chemicals Inc. produces two products: formula Y and formula Z. Production of both products requires the same two processes. A unit of formula Y requires 3 hours in the first process and 4 hours in the second process. A unit of formula Z requires 5 hours in the first process and 2 hours in the second process. The maximum available production time in each of the two processes is: first process, 60 hours; second process, 70 hours.

The production of formula Z results in a by-product, formula ZX. Some of formula ZX can be marketed at a profit. However, production of formula ZX in excess of 10 units is not desirable because of the limited market. The production process for formula Z yields 4 units of formula ZX for each unit of formula Z. The unit profits of formula Y and formula Z are $5 and $10 respectively. The by-product, formula ZX, yields a $3 unit profit. If formula ZX cannot be sold, it should be destroyed, at a unit cost of $2. The marketing department reports that the demand for formula Y and formula Z is unlimited, but that only 10 units of formula ZX can be sold at the present time.

Formulate a linear programming model that will determine the maximum number of units of formula Y, formula Z, and formula ZX to be produced in order to maximize total profits.

3.30 The Appalachian Mining Company operates two gold mines. The mines are located in different parts of the country, and they have different production capacities. After crushing, the ore is graded into three classes: premium, good, and regular. There is some demand for each grade of ore.

The company has a contract to provide a smelting plant with 18 tons of premium, 12 tons of good, and 36 tons of regular grade ore per week. The first mine costs $3,000 per day to operate, whereas the second mine costs only $2,400 per day. The average production per day for the first mine is 9 tons of premium, 3 tons of good, and 6 tons of regular grade ore. The second mine produces 3 tons of premium, 3 tons of good, and 18 tons of regular grade ore daily. The management's problem is to determine how many days a week the company should operate each mine in order to fulfill its contract obligations most economically.

a. Formulate a linear programming model for the problem.
b. Illustrate the model graphically by identifying the following: axis of graph, constraints, area of feasible solutions, point of optimum solution, and values of the decision variables at the optimum point.
c. Given the optimum solution, determine the operation cost per week, and for each mine determine the number of tons of each grade of ore produced each week.
d. Would there be any change in the optimum solution if the daily operation cost of the first mine is reduced to $2,250 while the daily operation cost of the second mine remains at $2,400?
e. In the original problem, what would be the effect if the firm has to ship only 9 tons of good grade instead of 12 tons?

3.31 Your grandfather has just left you $1 million. You plan to invest this money in four investment plans: stocks, bonds, savings, and real estate. Investments in stocks and bonds are available at the beginning of each of the next 6 years. Each dollar invested in stocks at the beginning of each year returns an average of $1.20 (a profit of $.20) in time for immediate reinvestment 2 years later. Each dollar invested in bonds at the beginning of each year returns $1.40 3 years later for reinvestment.

In addition, money-making investments in savings (in a credit union) and in real estate will be available at the beginning of each year. Each dollar invested in the credit union at the beginning of each year returns \$1.10 1 year later. Each dollar invested in real estate at the beginning of a year hence returns \$1.30 2 years later.

You would also like to diversify your investments in order to minimize the risk. The total amount invested in stocks should not exceed 30 percent of the total investment in the other alternatives. Furthermore, you wish to invest at least 25 percent of the total investment in the credit union savings plan. In addition, you are planning to get married at the end of the third year, and you would like to make sure that the amount of cash you will have at that time (to show off to your bride but not to spend) would be at least \$150,000.

If you are attempting to maximize the amount of money (cash) you will have at the end of the sixth year, how would you formulate a linear programming model?

3.32 A major federal agency charged with collecting reports from the public has just felt the budget axe. As head of the telephone-answering service, you have been instructed to minimize the number of operators you use, while still providing a specified service level to the agency.

Your operators work two phone centers. One center is known as the complaint line, and the other is an information line. A typical call on the complaint line takes 12 minutes to resolve, whereas an information call takes only 8 minutes. The purpose of the service is to reduce the number of errors made by the people completing the reports. Per 100 calls on the complaint line, an average reduction of 34 late forms and 18 errors is achieved. For every 100 calls answered on the information line, 10 late forms and 45 errors are avoided. Your daily goal is to reduce late forms by 1,000 and errors by 2,000.

If each operator can be on the phone for 6 hours per day, how few operators do you need? (Hint: Operators come in whole-person units only, so round your answer for each center to the next highest integer.)

4 SIMPLEX METHOD OF LINEAR PROGRAMMING

In this chapter, we get into the nitty-gritty part of linear programming—the simplex method. The simplex method is the general solution technique of linear programming. It is a systematic procedure that seeks the optimum solution to a problem through progressive operations. We will study the simplex solution procedure and its application to a wide range of linear programming problems.

Learning Objectives   *From the study of this chapter, we will learn the following:*

1. The simplex method as the general solution technique of linear programming
2. The simplex solution procedure
3. Interpretation of the simplex tableau
4. Solution of any type of linear programming problem by the simplex method
5. Ways to resolve several types of complications faced in linear programming
6. The meaning of the following terms:

Simplex method	*Leaving variable*
Pivot element	*Degeneracy*
Pivot column	*Testing the optimality*
Pivot row	*Artificial variable*
Entering variable	*Big M method*

THE SIMPLEX METHOD

The graphical method of linear programming that we studied in Chapter 3 is a straightforward technique for solving simple linear programming problems. However, most real-world management problems are too complex to be solved by the graphical method. As a matter of fact, many resource allocation problems faced by management may involve several thousand variables and several hundred constraints. Systematic procedures have been developed to solve complex linear programming problems. The best-known technique is the **simplex method.**

The simplex method of linear programming was developed by George B. Dantzig in 1947 and has since been further refined by many other contributors. This method is simply a mathematical procedure that employs an iterative process so that the optimum solution is achieved through progressive operations. In other words, in a maximization

Figure 4.1   The Simplex Solution Process

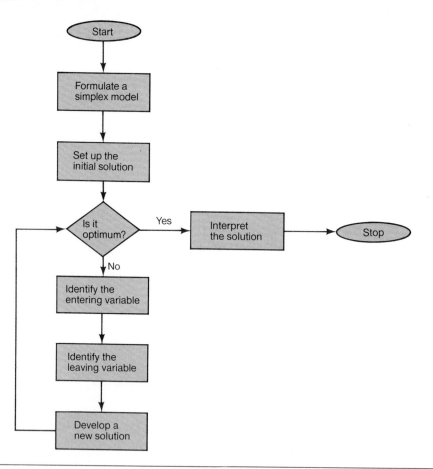

problem, the last solution yields a total profit that is equal to or greater than the profit yielded by the previous solution. Although it may sound like a formidable task, the basic procedure is quite simple. In fact, if you follow the simplex procedure outlined in this chapter, a lack of knowledge of algebra will not be a problem.

The simplex method is nothing more than the repeated solution process of a set of linear equations. The simplex method is similar to the graphical method in that they both test optimality at extreme points within the area of feasible solutions. The simplex method starts the search for the optimum solution from the origin and moves to another corner point whose objective value is equal to or better than that of the current solution. This process continues until there is no better solution to be found in the feasibility area.

The overall process of the simplex method is shown in Figure 4.1. Once the problem is properly arranged, an initial solution is set up in the simplex tableau and is tested for optimality. If the solution is not optimum (the initial solution is, of course, usually not optimum), a new solution is derived in the second simplex tableau by identifying the incoming and outgoing variables as well as by completing the simplex operations. The new solution is also tested for optimality. If it is the optimum solution, its interpretation will terminate the process. If it is not optimum, the procedure is repeated until an optimum solution is found.

The simplex tableau at each step represents a new solution. Thus, the first (initial) solution is determined in the first tableau and the optimum solution in the final tableau. The movement from one solution point (or tableau) to another is referred to as an *iteration*. The value of the objective function in any tableau must always be *equal to or greater than* that of the previous solution in a maximization problem and *equal to or less than* that of the previous solution in a minimization problem.

THE SIMPLEX SOLUTION PROCEDURE

In this section we will go through the details of the solution procedure. In learning about the simplex method, the important thing is to *understand* the underlying concepts rather than *memorize* the solution mechanics. Computers are used to solve real problems in a fraction of the time a manual solution would require, but the basic simplex process is the same. Understanding the simplex concept will allow you to better interpret the solution and to realize how it was obtained. First we will walk slowly through the method until you get the general idea, and then we will breeze through other examples. As a vehicle to explain the simplex procedure, let us discuss the following simple problem.

Casette 4.1   *CANDEX CAMERA WORKS LTD.*

Candex Camera Works Ltd. specializes in precision photographic equipment. The company currently produces two well-known 35-millimeter cameras: Candex A1 and Candex ZX. The modern production process involves two assembly lines. The production time requirements in the two assembly lines for each camera and the production capacities in the assembly lines are as follows:

Production Resource	Time Requirements		Production Capacity
	Candex A1	Candex ZX	
Assembly line 1	3 hr	3 hr	90 hr
Assembly line 2	2 hr	4 hr	80 hr

The unit profit is $40 for the Candex A1 and $50 for the Candex ZX.

The decision problem facing the Candex management is to determine the product mix for Candex A1 and Candex ZX that will maximize the total profit with the given weekly production capacities in the two assembly lines.

With the model formulation experience we have had, we can easily develop the following linear programming model for Candex:

$$\text{Maximize } Z = \$40x_1 + \$50x_2$$
$$\text{subject to} \quad 3x_1 + 3x_2 \leq 90$$
$$2x_1 + 4x_2 \leq 80$$
$$x_1, x_2 \geq 0$$

where
$$x_1 = \text{number of Candex A1 to be produced}$$
$$x_2 = \text{number of Candex ZX to be produced}$$

Step 1: Develop the Simplex Model

The first step of the simplex method procedure is to develop the simplex model. The regular linear programming model usually includes a number of linear inequalities, such as $\leq$ or $\geq$. It is necessary to transform such inequalities to equalities so that we can develop equality constraints, as we discussed in Chapter 3.

For example, let us review the two assembly line constraints for Candex.

$$3x_1 + 3x_2 \leq 90 \qquad \qquad \textit{Assembly line 1}$$
$$2x_1 + 4x_2 \leq 80 \qquad \qquad \textit{Assembly line 1}$$

It is quite possible that the optimum product mix solution may not use up all the production time in the two assembly lines. For example, if an optimum solution happened to be at $x_1 = 30$, $x_2 = 0$, then the resource usage would be as follows:

$$3(30) + 3(0) = 90 \qquad \qquad \textit{Assembly line 1}$$
$$2(30) + 4(0) < 80 \qquad \qquad \textit{Assembly line 2}$$

In assembly line 1 we need all 90 hours of the available production time. But, in assembly line 2 we require only 60 hours, and thus 20 of the 80 available production hours will not be used.

In a less-than-or-equal-to constraint, the left-hand-side value of the inequality could be *less than* the right-hand-side value. Thus, in order to convert the constraint into an equality, we must add a slack variable to the left-hand side so that it can be brought up to the value on the right-hand side. We need as many slack variables as there are less-than-or-equal-to constraints.

In the two assembly line constraints of the Candex problem, we need the following two slack variables:

$$s_1 = \text{slack variable for assembly line 1}$$
$$s_2 = \text{slack variable for assembly line 2}$$

Now we can transform the two inequality constraints to equalities as follows:

$$3x_1 + 3x_2 + s_1 = 90 \qquad \qquad \textit{Assembly line 1}$$
$$2x_1 + 4x_2 + s_2 = 80 \qquad \qquad \textit{Assembly line 2}$$

The use of slack variables allows the equalities to be general enough to hold under any situation.

Now we can formulate the simplex model as follows:

$$\text{Maximize } Z = 40x_1 + 50x_2 + 0s_1 + 0s_2$$
$$\text{subject to} \quad 3x_1 + 3x_2 + s_1 + 0s_2 = 90$$
$$2x_1 + 4x_2 + 0s_1 + s_2 = 80$$
$$x_1, x_2, s_1, s_2 \geq 0$$

Step 2: Determine the Initial Solution

The Initial Solution   We are now ready to start the solution process by determining the first extreme solution point of the linear programming problem. In the simplex method, we initiate the solution procedure from the origin (where we do not produce any product). Since the values of the two decision variables are 0 at the origin ($x_1 = 0$, $x_2 = 0$), the two constraint equalities will be

$$3x_1 + 3x_2 + s_1 + 0s_2 = 90$$
$$3(0) + 3(0) + s_1 + 0s_2 = 90$$
$$s_1 = 90$$

and

$$2x_1 + 4x_2 + 0s_1 + s_2 = 80$$
$$2(0) + 4(0) + 0s_1 + s_2 = 80$$
$$s_2 = 80$$

In the initial solution, the slack variables take on the values shown on the right-hand side. In other words, the only variables with nonzero values are s_1 ($s_1 = 90$) and s_2 ($s_2 = 80$). These nonzero-value variables are often referred to as *basic* or *basis* variables. We will explain this in greater detail later when we use the simplex tableau.

The objective function, then, becomes

$$\text{Total profit } Z = 40x_1 + 50x_2 + 0s_1 + 0s_2$$
$$= 40(0) + 50(0) + 0(90) + 0(80)$$
$$= 0$$

Obviously, the total profit is 0 when the production plant is completely idle at Candex.

The Simplex Tableau   As we discussed earlier, the simplex method is based on an iterative process. It is essential, therefore, to employ a simplified tableau for analysis and iteration. Although many different formats of the simplex tableau have been suggested, the functions of the tableau are basically the same. The simplex tableau we will use is shown in Table 4.1. In Table 4.1 we can observe the following important points:

1. *The Variable Columns.*   There are as many variable columns as there are variables (decision variables, slack variables, and so on). The variable columns are vertical and list first decision variables and then slack variables, in the subscript sequence (x_1, x_2, s_1, s_2).

2. *The Basic Variable Rows.*   There are as many horizontal basic variable rows as there are constraints. Each row will hold one basic variable and its substitution rates.

Table 4.1   The Simplex Tableau

c_b $\diagdown$ c_j	Basis	Solution	x_1	x_2	$\ldots$	s_1	s_2	$\ldots$
z_j $c_j - z_j$								

c_j = the unit contribution rate associated with each of the variables in the objective function.
c_b = the unit contribution rate of each of the basis variables (variables in the solution basis).
Basis = the variables of the current solution. These variables usually have nonzero values.
Solution = the current solution values of the basic variables.

3. *The c_j Row.* The c_j represents the unit contribution rate associated with each variable. We obtain c_j values from the objective function and list them above the variable labels in each of the variable columns.

4. *The c_b Column.* The c_b represents the unit contribution rate of each of the basic (basis) variables. The basic variables are those in the solution set. In the initial solution (at the origin), s_1 and s_2 are the two basic variables.

5. *The Basis Column.* The basis column is reserved for listing the basic variables. In our example, s_1 and s_2 are the two basic variables in the initial solution. In the simplex tableau, regardless of its iteration order, there are as many basic variables as the number of model constraints. In our example, we have two constraints. Thus, we have two basic variables in the simplex tableau at each iteration. The nonbasic variables are those that are not in the solution basis. In our example, x_1 and x_2 are not in the solution basis. Thus, x_1 and x_2 are the nonbasic variables. By definition, values of the nonbasic variables are 0 (where $x_1 = 0$, $x_2 = 0$ at the initial solution). There are as many nonbasic variables in the simplex tableau as the number of variables minus the number of basic variables. In our example problem, we have four variables and two basic variables (two constraints). Thus, the number of nonbasic variables will be $4 - 2 = 2$.

6. *The Solution Column.* The solution column is reserved for the solution values of the basic variables. In the initial solution of our example problem, the solution values of the two basic variables are $s_1 = 90$ and $s_2 = 80$. Thus, we list 90 in the s_1 row and 80 in the s_2 row.

The First Simplex Tableau   The first simplex tableau contains the initial solution (solution at the origin) of the linear programming problem. As we found out earlier, in the initial solution $x_1 = 0$, $x_2 = 0$, $s_1 = 90$, and $s_2 = 80$. Since the nonzero-value variables are s_1 and s_2, they are the *basic* variables. Their solution values are 90 for s_1

Table 4.2   *Basic Variables, C_j, and C_b, and Technological Coefficients in the Initial Tableau*

C_b	c_j Basis	Solution	40 x_1	50 x_2	0 s_1	0 s_2
0	s_1	90	3	3	1	0
0	s_2	80	2	4	0	1
	z_j					
	$c_j - z_j$					

and 80 for s_2. We can now enter the variables and their solutions in the tableau, as shown in Table 4.2.

The objective function in the simplex model is: Maximize $Z = 40x_1 + 50x_2 + 0s_1 + 0s_2$. Thus, we can list c_j values for all the variables in the simplex tableau accordingly. We can also determine the c_b values, which represent the contribution rates of the basic variables. The two basic variables we determined are s_1 and s_2. Their contribution rates in the objective function are both 0. The contribution rates are shown in the tableau in Table 4.2.

The next step is to list the coefficients of the model variables in the main body of the tableau. The two constraints of the simplex model are

$$3x_1 + 3x_2 + s_1 + 0s_2 = 90$$
$$2x_1 + 4x_2 + 0s_1 + s_2 = 80$$

We list the coefficient of each variable in the appropriate columns and rows. For example, in the first constraint equality the coefficient of x_1 is 3. Thus, it should be listed in the x_1 column of the first row (the s_1 row). All the variable coefficients are also entered in Table 4.2.

The coefficients listed in each of the variable columns represent the *marginal rates of substitution* between the variables headed by the columns and rows. For example, in the x_1 column we have coefficients of 3 and 2 in the s_1 and s_2 rows respectively. In order to produce one unit of x_1 (one Candex A1 camera), we must use 3 units of s_1 (3 hours of idle production time in assembly line 1) and 2 units of s_2 (2 hours of idle production time in assembly line 2). The marginal rates of substitution between x_2 and s_1 and s_2 are 3 and 4 respectively. The marginal rate of substitution between s_1 and s_1 and between s_2 and s_2 will be, of course, 1. Since s_1 and s_2 are not related to each other, their substitution rates are 0.

The next step is to calculate z_j and $c_j - z_j$ values. The z_j and $c_j - z_j$ can be defined as follows:

z_j *(Solution Column):* The total profit (or total cost in a minimization problem) of the given solution

z_j *(Variable Column):* The amount of profit lost for each unit of variable that is brought into the solution at the current iteration

$c_j - z_j$: The *net* increase in profit (or cost in a minimization problem) associated with one unit of each product (variable) that is brought into the solution at the current iteration

Now we can proceed to calculate values in the z_j row. First, we will calculate the z_j value in the solution column. The z_j value is the sum of c_b times the appropriate solution-column values. For example, we can calculate the z_j (solution) as follows:

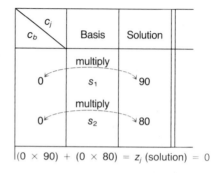

$(0 \times 90) + (0 \times 80) = z_j \text{ (solution)} = 0$

We can calculate the z_j values in various variable columns by following the same procedure except that we multiply c_b with the coefficients in each column rather than the solution-column values. For example, the z_j value in the x_1 column can be calculated as follows:

c_b	c_j Basis	Solution	x_1
0	s_1	90	3
0	s_2	80	2

$(0 \times 3) + (0 \times 2) = z_j(x_1) = 0$

We can calculate z_j in the x_2 column in a similar manner:

c_b	c_j Basis	Solution	x_1	x_2
0	s_1	90		3
0	s_2	80		4

$(0 \times 3) + (0 \times 4) = z_j(x_2) = 0$

The same computational procedure is used for $z_j(s_1)$ and $z_j(s_2)$. Now we can list the z_j values in the tableau, as shown in Table 4.3.

Table 4.3   The Complete Initial Simplex Tableau

c_b	c_j / Basis	Solution	40 x_1	50 x_2	0 s_1	0 s_2
0	s_1	90	3	3	1	0
0	s_2	80	2	4	0	1
	z_j	0	0	0	0	0
	$c_j - z_j$		40	50	0	0

We should note here once again that the coefficients listed in each of the variable columns represent the marginal rates of substitution. In order to bring one unit of x_1 into the solution, we need 3 units of s_1 and 2 units of s_2. Thus, the total profit we must give up for producing one unit of x_1 will be: $c_b(s_1) \cdot 3 + c_b(s_2) \cdot 2 = 0 \cdot 3 + 0 \cdot 2 = 0$. In this case, $z_j(x_1) = 0$ because slack variables have zero unit contribution rates. The total profit we must give up in order to bring one unit of a variable into the solution can be regarded as the implicit cost involved in the production process.

$c_j - z_j$ represents the net increase in profit (or cost in a minimization problem) associated with one unit of each product. In the tableau we have the c_j value at the top and the z_j value at the bottom of each column. For example, in the x_1 column a Candex A1 camera brings in $40 profit ($c_1$). At the initial solution, where the firm has idle production time, no profit is lost in producing the Candex A1 camera ($z_1 = 0$). Therefore, the net per-unit profit contribution for Candex A1 is $40. In other words, $c_1 - z_1$ ($c_j - z_j$ in the first variable column) is $40 - 0 = $40, as shown below.

c_b	c_j / Basis	Solution	40 x_1
0	s_1	90	
0	s_2	80	minus
	z_j	0	0
	$c_j - z_j$		40

$c_1 - z_1 = 40 - 0 = 40$

The same procedure can be applied to all other variable columns. Now we list the $c_j - z_j$ values in the tableau, and the complete initial simplex tableau is presented in Table 4.3.

Step 3: Test the Optimality

Now that we have completed the initial simplex tableau, we are ready to **test the optimality.** The optimality test is concerned with ascertaining whether the current solution is the optimum solution. This can be accomplished by analyzing the simplex criterion, the $c_j - z_j$ row.

As we discussed earlier, a $c_j - z_j$ value indicates the net per-unit contribution for each variable. If any one of the $c_j - z_j$ values is positive, it implies that we can further improve the total profit. Thus, the current solution is not optimum. On the other hand, if all $c_j - z_j$ values are either 0 or negative, the current solution cannot be improved. Thus, we have reached the optimum solution.

The initial solution shown in Table 4.3 is obviously not an optimum solution. We have two positive $c_j - z_j$; the x_1 column shows 40, and the x_2 column, 50.

Step 4: Identify the Entering Variable

Deciding which product we should introduce into the solution first is the process of identifying the **entering variable.** Since our objective is profit maximization, the first product we should introduce is the one that would increase total profit at the fastest rate.

The net increase of profit per unit of each product is represented by $c_j - z_j$. Then, the product to be introduced first will be the one with the largest positive value of $c_j - z_j$. Examining Table 4.3, we find that the largest positive $c_j - z_j$ value is \$50 in the x_2 column. This indicates that x_2 (Candex ZX cameras) should be produced first in order to increase total profit at the fastest rate.

The column with the largest $c_j - z_j$ (x_2 in this problem) is usually called the **pivot column.** The variable in the pivot column is the variable entering into the solution basis

Figure 4.2   The Entering and Leaving Variables for the Second Solution

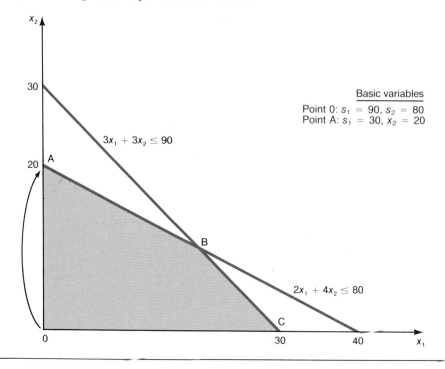

in the next simplex tableau. Since x_2 is the entering variable, we will be moving vertically on the x_2 axis from the origin to point A in Figure 4.2. In other words, in the second solution, Candex will specialize in producing only Candex ZX cameras.

There are two points we should note concerning the selection procedure of an entering variable. First, we must remember that the basic variables are those that are already in the basis with certain solution values assigned to them. For example, in the initial solution, s_1 and s_2 are the basic variables with solution values of 90 and 80, respectively. Since basic variables are already in the solution, one of them cannot be chosen as an entering variable. Therefore, the entering variable *must* be one of the nonbasic variables that have 0 solution values.

The second point, as we can see in Table 4.3, is that all the basic variable columns (s_1 and s_2 columns) have a $c_j - z_j$ value of 0. This is another reason that one of the nonbasic variables will always be selected as the entering variable.

Step 5: Determine the Leaving Variable

The Candex problem has two constraints, and thus there are only two basic variables. Since x_2 is the variable coming into the solution basis, one of the two basic variables must become 0 in value and leave the solution basis.

Since we are trying to maximize profit at the fastest rate, we would like to produce as many Candex ZX cameras (x_2) as the constraints allow. Now, let us examine the maximum number of x_2's that can be processed in assembly line 1. This maximum number can be determined if we use all of the available resource in assembly line 1 to produce only Candex ZX. Thus, we can analyze as follows:

$$3x_1 + 3x_2 + s_1 + 0s_2 = 90 \qquad \textit{Assembly line 1}$$
$$3(0) + 3x_2 + 0 + 0s_2 = 90$$
$$3x_2 = 90$$
$$x_2 = 30$$

In assembly line 1, if we produce only x_2, the maximum number we can process is 30. We can also check the maximum quantity of Candex ZX we can process in assembly line 2 as follows:

$$2x_1 + 4x_2 + 0s_1 + s_2 = 80 \qquad \textit{Assembly line 2}$$
$$2(0) + 4x_2 + 0s_1 + 0 = 80$$
$$4x_2 = 80$$
$$x_2 = 20$$

In assembly line 2, we can process up to 20 units of x_2. Since we must use both assembly lines to produce a camera, and assembly line 1 can process up to 30 units while assembly line 2 can produce only up to 20 units, the *maximum* number of units of x_2 we can produce is limited to 20.

In Table 4.4, we can see clearly that a unit of x_2 requires 3 hours of s_1 and 4 hours of s_2, as we already know from the marginal rates of substitution. The available idle production hours in the two assembly lines are 90 and 80 respectively, as shown in the solution column. Then, by dividing the solution values of s_1 and s_2 by the marginal

Table 4.4   The Pivot Column and the Pivot Row

c_b	Basis	Solution	40 x_1	50 x_2	0 s_1	0 s_2
0	s_1	90	3	3	1	0
0	s_2	80	2	④	0	1
	z_j	0	0	0	0	0
	$c_j - z_j$		40	50	0	0

substitution rates, we can also determine the maximum number of x_2 (Candex ZX) that each assembly line can produce. The computation is shown below.

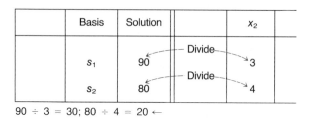

$$90 \div 3 = 30; \, 80 \div 4 = 20 \leftarrow$$

In order to determine the maximum quantity of a variable that can be introduced to the solution, the only thing we have to do is identify the *minimum nonnegative value* when the solution values are divided by the coefficients (substitution rates) in the pivot column. *Thus, the rows with either 0 or negative coefficients in the pivot column must be excluded from consideration.* This is a very important point to remember.

The row that indicates the minimum nonnegative value is the s_2 row. This is the **pivot row,** and s_2 is the **leaving variable.** In other words, in the second tableau, x_2 (Candex ZX) comes into the solution basis, and it replaces s_2 (idle production time in assembly line 2). We can easily see this logic if we substitute $x_2 = 20$ into the two constraint equalities while holding x_1 to 0 as follows:

$$3x_1 + 3x_2 + s_1 + 0s_2 = 90 \qquad \textit{Assembly line 1}$$
$$3(0) + 3(20) + s_1 + 0s_2 = 90$$
$$60 + s_1 = 90$$
$$s_1 = 30$$

$$2x_1 + 4x_2 + 0s_1 + s_2 = 80 \qquad \textit{Assembly line 2}$$
$$2(0) + 4(20) + 0s_1 + s_2 = 80$$
$$80 + s_2 = 80$$
$$s_2 = 0 \leftarrow \text{pivot row}$$

In the first constraint (assembly line 1), we will still have 30 hours of idle production time when we produce the maximum possible quantity of 20 units of x_2. In the second constraint (assembly line 2), however, we will be using all 80 of the available

Table 4.5   The Partially Completed Second Simplex Tableau

c_b \\ c_j	Basis	Solution	40 x_1	50 x_2	0 s_1	0 s_2
0	s_1					
50	x_2	20	1/2	1	0	1/4

production hours, and thus $s_2 = 0$. When a variable has a 0 value, it is relegated to a nonbasic variable. Now we know why x_2 comes into the solution basis and replaces s_2.

In Figure 4.2 we can reinforce our analysis. At the initial solution (the origin), we know that $x_1 = 0$ and $x_2 = 0$, and thus $s_1 = 90$ and $s_2 = 80$. When the entering variable x_2 comes into the solution basis and replaces s_2, the new solution is at point A. At point A, we are on the maximum possible production line for the second constraint. Thus, we will be using all of the available resources in assembly line 2, and consequently $s_2 = 0$. However, point A is below the maximum possible production line for the first constraint. Hence, $s_1 > 0$. In fact, the exact value of $s_1 = 30$. In Figure 4.2 we can easily see the change in the basic variables as we move from the origin to solution point A.

Step 6: Develop a New Solution

To develop the second solution, let us refer to Table 4.4, which indicates the pivot column and the pivot row by blue numbers. The variable in the pivot column (x_2) is the entering variable, and the variable in the pivot row (s_2) is the leaving variable. The coefficient at the intersection of the pivot column and the pivot row is called the **pivot element.**

Then, in the second simplex tableau the first thing we should do is substitute x_2 for s_2. The unit contribution rate (c_j) of x_2 is \$50. This figure is entered as c_b for x_2 in Table 4.5.

The pivoting procedure is demonstrated below in Tableau 1 and 2, with x_2 pivoting into the second row as we move from the initial tableau to the second tableau.

Basis	Solution	x_1	x_2	s_1	s_2
s_2	80	2	(4)	0	1

Basis	Solution	x_1	x_2	s_1	s_2
x_2	20	1/2	1	0	1/4

$$80 \div 4 = 20 \quad 2 \div 4 = 1/2 \quad 4 \div 4 = 1 \quad 0 \div 4 = 0 \quad 1 \div 4 = 1/4$$

Dividing all row values by the pivot element of 4, as shown above, yields new row values. The new values in the x_2 row are also listed in Table 4.5. Now we can write the computational procedure as:

$$\text{New value (pivot row)} = \text{old value} \div \text{pivot element}$$

The next step in completing the second simplex tableau is to calculate new values in the other constraint rows. First, let us calculate the new solution value for s_1. In the initial solution there were 90 hours of idle production time in assembly line 1 (s_1). However, when we produce 20 Candex ZX cameras ($x_2 = 20$), the idle production capacity in assembly line 1 must be decreased. Since it requires 3 units of s_1 and 4 units of s_2 to produce a Candex ZX, production of 20 Candex ZX cameras will require 60 units of s_1 and 80 units of s_2. After producing 20 Candex ZX cameras, there will be $90 - 60 = 30$ hours available in line 1 ($s_1 = 30$), and $80 - 80 = 0$ hours available in line 2 ($s_2 = 0$, and thus s_2 is no longer in the solution basis).

Now, let us replay in slow motion the operation we have just performed. From the 90 units of s_1, which is the old solution value in the initial tableau, we substracted the product of the *row element* (3) and the new solution value in the pivot row (20). We can summarize the calculations as follows:

$$\text{New value (other rows)} = \text{old value} - (\text{row element} \times \text{new value in pivot row})$$

In order to maintain consistency, we must use the same procedure for calculating the new coefficients. After a period of practice, you will become so proficient in calculating the new row values that you may not even need a scrap of paper to write out the calculations. However, until that time comes you can use the following easy procedure:

Column	Old Row Value	−	(Row Element	×	New Value in Pivot Row)	=	New Row Value
Solution	90	−	(3	×	20)	=	30
x_1	3	−	(3	×	1/2)	=	3/2
x_2	3	−	(3	×	1)	=	0
s_1	1	−	(3	×	0)	=	1
s_2	0	−	(3	×	1/4)	=	−3/4

In this procedure, the row element is the element at the intersection of the pivot column and the row under consideration (the s_1 row in this case). Thus, each row has its own element as the pivot row has the pivot element. Now we can list the new row values for the s_1 row, as shown in Table 4.6.

Now that we have found all of the new values in the simplex tableau, we can proceed to complete the second simplex tableau, as shown in Table 4.6. The z_j value in the solution column ($\$1,000$) indicates the total profit of the second solution, where we produce 20 Candex ZX cameras and have 30 hours of idle production time in assembly line 1.

Table 4.6   The Complete Second Simplex Tableau

c_b / c_j	Basis	Solution	40 x_1	50 x_2	0 s_1	0 s_2
0	s_1	30	3/2	0	1	−3/4
50	x_2	20	1/2	1	0	1/4
	z_j	1,000	25	50	0	12.50
	$c_j - z_j$		15	0	0	−12.50

To make sure that you still remember the procedure for calculating z_j values, the following computations are presented:

c_b / c_j	Basis	Solution	40 x_1	50 x_2	0 s_1	0 s_2
0	s_1	30	3/2	0	1	−3/4
50	x_2	20	1/2	1	0	1/4

$$\frac{0 \cdot 30}{50 \cdot 20}$$
$$z_j \text{ (solution)} = \$1,000$$

$$\frac{0 \cdot 3/2}{50 \cdot 1/2}$$
$$z_j(x_1) = \$25$$

$$\frac{0 \cdot 0}{50 \cdot 1}$$
$$z_j(x_2) = \$50$$

$$\frac{0 \cdot 1}{50 \cdot 0}$$
$$z_j(s_1) = \$0$$

$$\frac{0 \cdot -3/4}{50 \cdot \ \ 1/4}$$
$$z_j(s_2) = \$12.50$$

The z_j and $c_j - z_j$ values are also shown in Table 4.6, which is the complete second simplex tableau. There are two points we should examine in Table 4.6. First, s_1 and x_2 are the basic variables, and x_1 and s_2 are the nonbasic variables in the second solution. In each of the basic-variable columns (x_2 and s_1), there is only one nonzero coefficient, a coefficient of 1 at the intersection of its row and column. For example, at the intersection of the s_1 row and the s_1 column there is a unit (1) coefficient. Also, at the intersection of the x_2 row and the x_2 column there is a coefficient of 1. That is precisely why c_j and z_j values are identical, and thus $c_j - z_j = 0$, in the basic-variable columns. Second, in the nonbasic-variable column (x_1 and s_2), there usually are a number of nonzero coefficients, and thus $c_j - z_j$ values usually are also nonzero.

Before we move on to the next step, let us examine more carefully the second simplex tableau presented in Table 4.6. In the original problem, production of a Candex A1 camera (x_1) required 3 hours in assembly line 1 and 2 hours in assembly line 2, as shown in Table 4.4. Then, why do we now have coefficients of 3/2 in the s_1 row and 1/2 in the x_2 row in Table 4.6? These coefficients represent the new marginal rates of substitution between x_1 and the basic variables s_1 and x_2.

In the second simplex tableau we are producing 20 units of x_2 (Candex ZX cameras) by using 60 hours of s_1 and 80 hours of s_2. Thus, there is no production capacity left over in assembly line 2 to produce any x_1, although we still have 30 hours left over in assembly line 1. That is why s_2 has been removed from the solution basis while s_1 remains. Now it is obvious that the only way we can produce any x_1 is by sacrificing some units of x_2.

We have idle capacity of 30 hours in assembly line 1 ($s_1 = 30$). Therefore, the critical constraint is assembly line 2, where we have no slack time. A unit of x_1 requires 2 hours and a unit of x_2 requires 4 hours in assembly line 2. Therefore, to secure 2 hours that are required to produce one unit of x_1, we must sacrifice 1/2 unit of x_2. This rate of substitution is shown by the coefficient 1/2 in the x_1 column and x_2 row.

How about the coefficient 3/2 in the s_1 row? When we sacrifice 1/2 unit of x_2, we also get back 3/2 hours of production time in assembly line 1, as shown below.

Production Resource	Time Requirement for One Unit of x_2	Time Recovered When 1/2 Unit of x_2 Is Sacrificed
Assembly line 1	3 hr	3/2 hr
Assembly line 2	4 hr	2 hr

A unit of x_1 requires 3 hours in assembly line 1. If we use the 3/2 hours that we get back from sacrificing 1/2 unit of x_2, then the actual use of s_1 required to produce one unit of x_1 will be 3/2 hours ($3/2 + 3/2 = 3$ hours). Now the whole thing makes sense. The total amount of profit lost when we sacrifice 1/2 unit of x_2 is $1/2 \cdot \$50 = \$25$. Since the unit contribution of x_1 is \$40, the net contribution of one unit of x_1 at this solution point is \$15 ($40 - 25 = 15$). This is precisely the $c_j - z_j$ value of the x_1 column.

We can also examine the marginal rates of substitution for the x_2 column. In the x_2 column, we have coefficients of 0 in the s_1 row and 1 in the x_2 row. These coefficients indicate that production of one unit of x_2 requires, at this stage of the simplex solution, 0 unit of s_1 and 1 unit of x_2. In other words, the only way we can produce one additional unit of Candex ZX camera is by sacrificing a Candex ZX we have produced. This same relationship exists for every basic variable.

How about the coefficients in the s_2 column? s_2 is a nonbasic variable. Thus, $s_2 = 0$. s_2 became 0 when we produced 20 units of x_2. In order to make $s_2 = 1$, we must sacrifice some units of x_2. A whole unit of x_2 requires 4 hours in assembly line 2. Thus, if we want to make $s_2 = 1$, we must sacrifice 1/4 unit of x_2. This coefficient, 1/4, is shown at the intersection of the s_2 column and the x_2 row.

When we sacrifice 1/4 unit of x_2 to create one hour of idle production time in assembly line 2 ($s_2 = 1$), we also get back 3/4 hour in assembly line 1 because a whole unit of x_2 requires 3 hours in assembly line 1. The coefficient, $-3/4$, at the intersection of the s_2 column and the s_1 row indicates this relationship. The negative substitution rate shows that the solution value of s_1 will be increased by 3/4 if we make $s_2 = 1$. In other words, if we decide to make $s_2 = 1$, then the solution values of the basic variables will be $s_1 = 30\ 3/4$, $x_2 = 19\ 3/4$.

The net effect of making $s_2 = 1$ will be the lost profit incurred from the sacrifice of 1/4 unit of x_2. Since a whole unit of x_2 contributes \$50, the 1/4 unit of x_2 we sacrifice results in a loss of \$12.50 profit. This lost profit (\$12.50) is shown as the $c_j - z_j$ value in the s_2 column.

Step 7: Test the Optimality and Repeat the Procedure

Now that we have completed one iteration, we must test the optimality of the solution, and if the solution is not optimal, repeat the solution procedure. As we discussed earlier, the optimality test checks for any positive $c_j - z_j$ value, which indicates a potential increase in the solution. In Table 4.7, there is a positive $c_j - z_j$ value of \$15 in the x_1 column. Thus, the second solution is not optimum.

Now we prepare the second iteration by identifying the entering variable (the pivot column) and the leaving variable (the pivot row). The pivot column has already been identified. Since the x_1 column is the only column with a positive $c_j - z_j$, it is the pivot column. The entering variable is x_1. To determine the leaving variable, we divide the solution values of the basic variables by their corresponding coefficients in the pivot column as follows:

Row	Solution Value		Coefficient		
s_1	30	÷	3/2	=	20 ←
x_2	20	÷	1/2	=	40

The minimum nonnegative (i.e., minimum positive or 0) value we find is 20, in the s_1 row. Thus, the pivot row is the s_1 row, and s_1 is the leaving variable. The pivot element is 3/2, as identified in Table 4.7.

Table 4.7   The Pivot Column and Pivot Row in the Second Tableau

c_b	c_j Basis	Solution	40 x_1	50 x_2	0 s_1	0 s_2
0	s_1	30	③/2	0	1	−3/4
50	x_2	20	1/2	1	0	1/4
	z_j	1,000	25	50	0	12.50
	$c_j - z_j$		15	0	0	−12.50

To determine new values, we can easily perform the following pivot operation. For the s_1 row (pivot row):

Column	Old Value	$\div$	Pivot Element	$=$	New Row Value
Solution	30	$\div$	3/2	$=$	20
x_1	3/2	$\div$	3/2	$=$	1
x_2	0	$\div$	3/2	$=$	0
s_1	1	$\div$	3/2	$=$	2/3
s_2	$-3/4$	$\div$	3/2	$=$	$-1/2$

For the x_2 row:

Column	Old Row Value	$-$	(Row Element	$\times$	New Value in Pivot Row)	$=$	New Row Value
Solution	20	$-$	(1/2	$\times$	20)	$=$	10
x_1	1/2	$-$	(1/2	$\times$	1)	$=$	0
x_2	1	$-$	(1/2	$\times$	0)	$=$	1
s_1	0	$-$	(1/2	$\times$	2/3)	$=$	$-1/3$
s_2	1/4	$-$	(1/2	$\times$	$-1/2$)	$=$	1/2

The new row values are listed in the third simplex tableau shown in Table 4.8. The z_j and $c_j - z_j$ values are determined in a manner similar to the previous two simplex tableaux.

Now that a new solution has been identified, the simplex procedure is repeated: Test the optimality, identify the entering variable, determine the leaving variable, complete a new solution tableau. When we test the optimality in Table 4.8, it is immediately obvious that there is no positive $c_j - z_j$ value. In the x_1 and x_2 columns, the $c_j - z_j$ values are 0 as they are the basic-variable columns. In the nonbasic-variable columns,

Table 4.8　The Third Simplex Tableau

c_b	c_j / Basis	Solution	40 x_1	50 x_2	0 s_1	0 s_2
40	x_1	20	1	0	2/3	$-1/2$
50	x_2	10	0	1	$-1/3$	1/2
	z_j	1,300	40	50	10	5
	$c_j - z_j$		0	0	-10	-5

Figure 4.3   The Optimum Solution

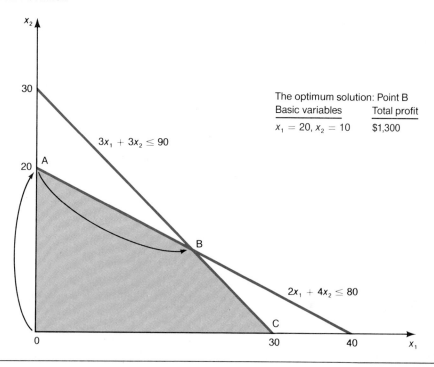

s_1 and s_2, the $c_j - z_j$ values are negative. Thus, there is no nonbasic variable that can improve the total profit. In other words, we have found the optimum solution.

The optimum solution, also shown graphically in Figure 4.3, is:

$$x_1 = 20$$
$$x_2 = 10$$
$$Z = \$1,300$$

Since the optimum point B is at the intersecting point of the two constraint lines, there will be no idle resources. Thus, at point B, $s_1 = 0$ and $s_2 = 0$.

Step 8: Interpret the Optimum Solution

The linear program solution procedure does not end at simply getting the optimum solution. We may want to ask a series of "what if" questions about the stability of the optimum solution in the fickle decision environment. A detailed discussion of the optimum-solution interpretation will be presented in Chapter 5 when we study duality and sensitivity analysis. Here we will limit our discussion to some simple, obvious, but important matters. From the final simplex tableau we can easily identify the following:

Basic Variables	Nonbasic Variables	Total Profit
$x_1 = 20$	$s_1 = 0$	$Z = \$1,300$
$x_2 = 10$	$s_2 = 0$	

"How about the two negative $c_j - z_j$ values we see in the s_1 and s_2 columns?" you will ask. That is a very constructive question. The $c_j - z_j$ values are -10 in the s_1 and -5 in the s_2 column, respectively. Thus, if we attempt to enter 1 unit of s_1 into the solution basis (i.e., making 1 production hour idle in assembly line 1), the total profit will decrease by \$10. Similarly, if we introduce s_2 into the solution basis, the total profit will decrease by \$5 per unit of s_2.

Now, you may wonder how we get such information. Let us examine the partial tableau of the final solution as shown below:

c_j c_b	Basis	Solution	x_1	x_2	0 s_1	0 s_2
40	x_1	20			2/3	$-1/2$
50	x_2	10			$-1/3$	1/2
	z_j	1,300			10	5
	$c_j - z_j$				-10	-5

When we say that we want to introduce s_1 into the solution, that simply means that we want to pick s_1 as the pivot column. Although we would not pick s_1 as the pivot column because it has a negative $c_j - z_j$, let us assume that we would do this for a test. The rates of substitution between s_1 and the basic variables x_1 and x_2 are 2/3 and $-1/3$. Thus, when we introduce 1 unit of s_1 into the solution, we have to reduce the solution value of x_1 by 2/3 unit (from 20 to 19 1/3) and also increase the solution value of x_2 by 1/3 unit (from 10 to 10 1/3). A positive substitution rate will decrease the solution value, and a negative substitution rate will increase the solution value for the corresponding basic variables.

Then, in the optimum solution, if we let $s_1 = 1$ (i.e., take away 1 production hour in assembly line 1 and make only 89 hours available instead of the previous 90 hours), the change in the solution values will be:

$$x_1 = 20 \quad \rightarrow x_1 = 19\ 1/3$$
$$x_2 = 10 \quad \rightarrow x_2 = 10\ 1/3$$
$$Z = 1{,}300 \quad Z = 1{,}290$$

The change in the total profit can be more easily calculated by:

Product	Unit Profit	Change in Profit
x_1: decrease of 2/3 unit	\$40	$-80/3$
x_2: increase of 1/3 unit	\$50	$+50/3$
	Net change in profit $=$	$-\$10$

We can easily see the change in solution values in the graph shown in Figure 4.4. Since we are reducing the right-hand-side value of the constraint from 90 to 89 hours, the intercepts of the first constraint will be changed accordingly. Thus, the new feasible

Figure 4.4   A New Optimum Solution with a Changed Right-hand-side Value of Constraint 1

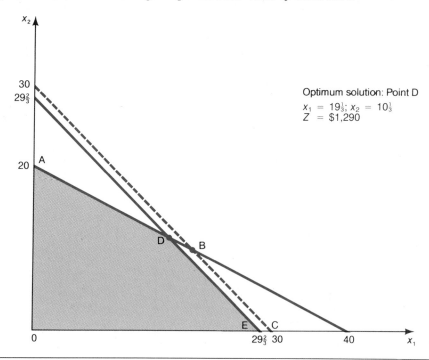

Optimum solution: Point D
$x_1 = 19\frac{1}{3}$; $x_2 = 10\frac{1}{3}$
$Z = \$1,290$

region is 0ADE and the optimum solution will be point D. When we move from point B to point D, the value of x_1 will be decreased by 2/3 and the value of x_2 will be increased by 1/3. We can see these changes clearly in the figure.

We can make a similar interpretation for s_2. If we let $s_2 = 1$, the solution value of x_1 will increase by 1/2 (from 20 to 20 1/2) and the solution value of x_2 will decrease by 1/2 (from 10 to 9 1/2). The net change in total profit will be $-\$5$. The $c_j - z_j$ values of the nonbasic-variable columns are often referred to as *shadow prices*. The reason is that the same $c_j - z_j$ value applies whether we increase or decrease the resource in a given constraint.

For example, if we reduce the available production time in assembly line 1 by 1 hour (from 90 to 89), the total profit will be *decreased* by \$10. However, if we increase the available resource by 1 unit (from 90 hours to 91 hours), the total profit will be *increased* by the identical \$10. Thus, the shadow price is like a mirror image.

Now, suppose Candex is thinking about expanding its production capacity by 2 percent by hiring additional labor. How should this increase be allocated to the two assembly lines? From the analysis of shadow prices in the s_1 and s_2 columns, we can logically conclude that additional workers must be allocated to assembly line 1. If Candex is considering a reduction in production capacity, we also know that the reduction must be initiated in assembly line 2.

As we discussed earlier, many organizations (especially notorious are the government and nonprofit agencies) often increase or decrease the resources of various departments on an equal proportion basis. For example, if a state government wants to reduce its overall budget by 5 percent, each department is ordered to reduce its budget by 5 percent. Obviously it is assumed that all departments have exactly the same shadow price. This is, of course, a fallacy. Thus, a careful interpretation of the final simplex tableau is a very important part of the linear programming solution process.

Summary of the Simplex Solution Procedure

Now that we have completed our discussion of the simplex solution procedure through the Candex example, let us summarize all the steps we have taken.

Step 1: Develop the Simplex Model   We convert all the linear programming constraints into equalities by introducing appropriate slack variables. The objective function is also modified to include all slack variables.

Step 2: Determine the Initial Solution   The initial solution is at the origin. Thus, all of the decision variables have 0 values, and the slack variables become the basic variables. The initial simplex tableau is developed at this step, and all elements are computed.

Step 3: Test the Optimality   The current solution is tested as to whether it is optimum. This is accomplished by looking for positive $c_j - z_j$ values. If no positive $c_j - z_j$ is found, the solution is optimum. Go to Step 8. If there exists at least one positive $c_j - z_j$, the solution is not optimum. Continue with the procedure.

Step 4: Identify the Entering Variable   We identify the nonbasic-variable column with the largest positive $c_j - z_j$ value. This is the pivot column. The nonbasic variable in this column is the entering variable.

Step 5: Determine the Leaving Variable   The solution values of the basic variables are divided by the corresponding coefficients in the pivot column. The row that yields the minimum nonnegative value is the pivot row. The variable in the pivot row is the leaving variable.

Step 6: Develop a New Solution   The entering variable replaces the leaving variable in the solution basis. New values are computed in the following manner:

New value (pivot row) = old value ÷ pivot element

New value (other rows) = old value − (row element × new value in pivot row)

The z_j and $c_j - z_j$ values are also computed.

Step 7: Test the Optimality and Repeat the Procedure   For the new solution that we have derived, we again test the optimality. Thus, this step is simply a return to Step 3.

Step 8: Interpret the Optimal Solution   We examine the final simplex tableau and find the optimum solution in terms of the basic variables and their values as well as the total profit derived by the solution. We analyze shadow prices and may also want to perform the appropriate sensitivity analysis.

SIMPLEX SOLUTION OF A PROBLEM WITH MIXED CONSTRAINTS

Thus far, we have solved only one type of linear programming problem—a maximization problem with less-than-or-equal-to constraints. However, in many real-world problems there are other types such as exactly-equal-to or greater-than-or-equal-to constraints. In this section we will tackle one such problem.

Example 4.1   A MAXIMIZATION PROBLEM WITH MIXED CONSTRAINTS

Let us examine the following simple problem that has all three types of constraints:

$$\text{Maximize } Z = 5x_1 + 7x_2$$
$$\text{subject to}\quad x_1 + 2x_2 = 50$$
$$x_1 \geq 20$$
$$x_2 \leq 20$$
$$x_1, x_2 \geq 0$$

In this problem, the first constraint may be a production constraint. It implies that the second product (x_2) requires twice as much productive resource as the first product (x_1). It also indicates that the firm has 50 units of productive resource, and it must use precisely what it has, no less and no more. Many production process constraints are often *exactly-equal-to* types, especially those of chemical processes.

The second and third constraints could be sales constraints. If we want to produce and market the first product, we must produce a minimum of 20 units. For the second product, however, the market is quite limited. Thus, the maximum quantity we can produce and sell is limited to 20 units.

The first step of the simplex procedure is to set up a simplex model for the problem. In order to convert all constraints to simplex equalities, let us examine the first constraint.

We normally start by converting an inequality constraint to an equality function, but the first constraint is already an equality. How should we convert it to an equality? We could leave it as it is, but we remember, of course, that the initial solution of the simplex method is at the origin, where $x_1 = 0$ and $x_2 = 0$. If we substitute these values into the constraint, we obtain

$$x_1 + 2x_2 = 50$$
$$0 + 2(0) = 50$$
$$0 = 50$$

This result is obviously an unacceptable outcome. First of all, $0 \neq 50$! Thus, the equality does not hold. Clearly, we need to add a variable on the left side of the equality so that we can assign some value to this variable when $x_1 + 2x_2$ is less than 50. We may be tempted to add a slack variable. However, we remember that slack variables are used only to satisfy the less-than ($<$) inequality sign. For example, in Casette 4.1 we had a constraint $3x_1 + 3x_2 \leq 90$. In order to convert the inequality into an equality and eliminate the "$<$" sign, we added a slack variable to derive $3x_1 + 3x_2 + s_1 = 90$.

In the constraint under consideration, $x_1 + 2x_2 = 50$, we do not have an inequality sign to eliminate by adding a slack variable. For cases like this, we need to create a new variable, often referred to as an **artificial variable.** With the addition of an artificial variable, the equation becomes

$$x_1 + 2x_2 = 50 \rightarrow x_1 + 2x_2 + A_1 = 50$$

The function of A_1 can be seen in Figure 4.5. Since the constraint equality indicates that solutions must be on the straight line AB exactly, this line segment itself represents the area of feasible solutions. However, the initial solution is at the origin. In other words, the initial solution is outside the area of feasible solutions. To facilitate preliminary solutions outside the feasibility area, we must use the artificial variable. For example, at the origin the constraint will be as follows:

$$x_1 + 2x_2 + A_1 = 50$$
$$0 + 2(0) + A_1 = 50$$
$$A_1 = 50$$

At the origin, $x_1 = 0$, $x_2 = 0$, and $A_1 = 50$. Thus, the constraint equality holds.

The second constraint of the problem, $x_1 \geq 20$, presents a new difficulty. This is the first time we are facing a greater-than-or-equal-to constraint in conjunction with the simplex method. Since x_1 can be greater than or equal to 20, x_1 can be as much as 100, 1,000, or more. As we discussed in Chapter 3, we must subtract a surplus variable from the left-hand-side of the constraint to make it an equality. The word *surplus* is appro-

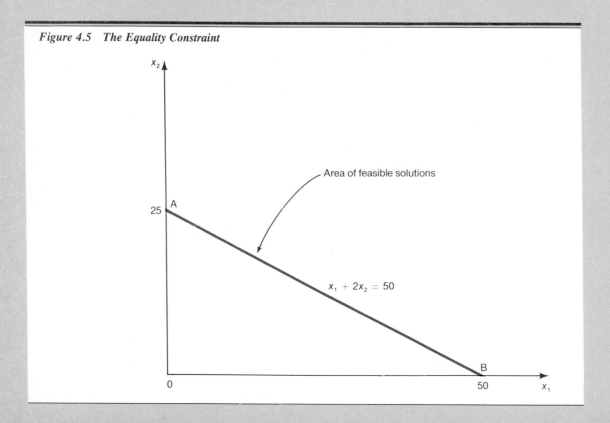

Figure 4.5   The Equality Constraint

priate in that the variable takes a positive value only when $x_1 > 20$. For example, if $x_1 = 100$, then the equality becomes

$$x_1 - s_1 = 20$$
$$100 - s_1 = 20$$
$$s_1 = 80$$

The use of s_1 has solved the problem nicely. However, there is one more problem that we did not discuss in Chapter 3. At the initial solution (at the origin), $x_1 = 0$. Therefore, the equality will be

$$x_1 - s_1 = 20$$
$$0 - s_1 = 20$$
$$s_1 = -20$$

Since the nonnegativity constraint applies to all variables, including slack, surplus, and artificial variables, the above situation is unacceptable. Figure 4.6 depicts our predicament. At the origin, the solution is clearly outside the feasibility area for the second constraint. To facilitate preliminary solutions until we get into the area of feasible solutions, we must introduce an artificial variable (A_2). Thus, the equality becomes $x_1 - s_1 + A_2 = 20$. At the origin, the equality will be

$$x_1 - s_1 + A_2 = 20$$
$$0 - 0 + A_2 = 20$$
$$A_2 = 20$$

In this relationship, $s_1 = 0$ at the origin because s_1 can take a positive value only when $x_1 > 20$. This reasoning should be obvious—remember that a surplus variable is subtracted to remove the greater-than sign from the relationship $x_1 \geq 20$. Now we can test several points where x_1 takes on different values and see whether our new simplex equality holds up.

If $x_1 = 10$,

$$x_1 - s_1 + A_2 = 20$$
$$10 - 0 + A_2 = 20$$
$$A_2 = 10$$

If $x_1 = 20$,

$$x_1 - s_1 + A_2 = 20$$
$$20 - 0 + 0 = 20$$
$$20 = 20$$

If $x_1 = 100$,

$$x_1 - s_1 + A_2 = 20$$
$$100 - s_1 + 0 = 20$$
$$s_1 = 80$$

In these tests, when $x_1 = 20$, the value of A_2 becomes 0, because the solution is now feasible for the $x_1 \geq 20$ constraint. But, since x_1 is not yet greater than 20, s_1 is also 0. When $x_1 = 100$, this solution is feasible and thus $A_2 = 0$. However, since $x_2 > 20$, s_1 takes a positive value. Figure 4.6 explains our reasoning quite clearly.

Figure 4.6   Graphical Presentation

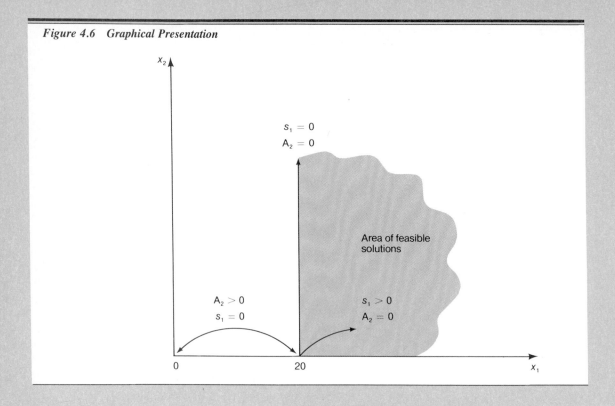

It is very easy to convert the third constraint of the problem, $x_2 \leq 20$, into a simplex equality. Simply by adding a slack variable, we can generate the equality $x_2 + s_2 = 20$.

Let us restate the conditions needed for the use of a slack, surplus, or an artificial variable:

Type of Variable	Purpose
Slack or surplus	To remove an inequality sign ($<$ or $>$) and create an equality relationship
Artificial	To facilitate preliminary solutions outside the feasibility area for the given constraint

We can further summarize the conversion process for linear programming constraints into simplex equalities as follows:

Type of Constraint	Adjustment Required
Less than or equal to ($\leq$)	Add a slack variable.
Exactly equal to ($=$)	Add an artificial variable.
Greater than or equal to ($\geq$)	Subtract a surplus variable and add an artificial variable.

We are now about ready to formulate the complete simplex model. In the objective function, we must also include all the variables in the constraint equalities. There is no problem in assigning a 0 c_j value to the slack or surplus variable. But how about the artificial variable? If we assign a 0 value to c_j, the artificial variable may be in the solution basis of the optimum solution. What we do not want or need is to have an artificial variable in the final solution.

One way we can be assured of an optimum solution without an artificial variable is by assigning a very large negative c_j value to the artificial variable. In this way the artificial variable becomes so costly that we will try to take it out of the solution basis as soon as possible. This approach is known as the **big M method,** because the c_j value assigned to the artificial variable is a large negative-value M (negative million or billion dollars, let us say).

Now we are finally ready to formulate a simplex model for the problem as follows:

$$\text{Maximize } Z = 5x_1 + 7x_2 + 0s_1 + 0s_2 - MA_1 - MA_2$$
$$\text{subject to }\quad x_1 + 2x_2 + A_1 = 50$$
$$x_1 - s_1 + A_2 = 20$$
$$x_2 + s_2 = 20$$
$$x_1, x_2, s_1, s_2, A_1, A_2 \geq 0$$

In the initial solution, we are once again at the origin ($x_1 = 0$, $x_2 = 0$). The three simplex equalities will be

$$x_1 + 2x_2 + A_1 = 50 \qquad\qquad \textit{Constraint 1}$$
$$0 + 2(0) + A_1 = 50$$
$$A_1 = 50$$
$$x_1 - s_1 + A_2 = 20 \qquad\qquad \textit{Constraint 2}$$
$$0 - 0 + A_2 = 20$$
$$A_2 = 20$$
$$x_2 + s_2 = 20 \qquad\qquad \textit{Constraint 3}$$
$$0 + s_2 = 20$$
$$s_2 = 20$$

The basic variables are A_1, A_2, and s_2. Note that whenever there is an artificial variable in a simplex equality it becomes a basic variable and consequently appears in the solution basis in the initial solution. The solution values for A_1, A_2, and s_2 are 50, 20, and 20, respectively. They are listed in the appropriate column in Table 4.9.

In the initial tableau, z_j values are computed in the usual manner. For example, in the solution column, z_j is calculated as follows:

c_b	Basis	Solution	
$-M$	A_1	50	$-M \cdot 50$
$-M$	A_2	20	$-M \cdot 20$
0	s_2	20	$+ 0 \cdot 20$
			$z_j = -70M$

Table 4.9   *The Initial Solution for the Mixed Constraint Problem*

c_b / c_j	Basis	Solution	5 x_1	7 x_2	0 s_1	0 s_2	$-M$ A_1	$-M$ A_2
$-M$	A_1	50	1	2	0	0	1	0
$-M$	A_2	20	1	0	-1	0	0	1
0	s_2	20	0	①	0	1	0	0
	z_j	$-70M$	$-2M$	$-2M$	M	0	$-M$	$-M$
	$c_j - z_j$		$5 + 2M$	$7 + 2M$	$-M$	0	0	0

The z_j values in the variable columns are calculated in a similar fashion.

The $c_j - z_j$ values are also computed in the usual manner. For example, in the x_1 column, c_j is 5 and z_j is $-2M$. Therefore, $c_1 - z_1 = 5 - (-2M) = 5 + 2M$. Then, $c_j - z_j$ for the x_2 column will be $c_2 - z_2 = 7 - (-2M) = 7 + 2M$.

In Table 4.9 we can easily identify the pivot column and the pivot row. The pivot column is the x_2 column, since it has the largest $c_j - z_j$ value. Thus, the entering variable is x_2. To determine the pivot row, we divide the solution values by each of the corresponding coefficients. As we discussed earlier, we can use only *positive* coefficients. The minimum nonnegative value of 20 is found in the s_2 row. Hence, this is the pivot row, and s_2 is the leaving variable.

In Table 4.10 we find the second solution to the problem. In completing the second simplex tableau, you might use the following helpful tips. In the pivot row:

1. s_2 is replaced by x_2.

2. c_b is now 7 instead of 0.

3. Since all row values are divided by the pivot element 1, the new values will be the same as the old ones.

In other rows:

1. Find new row values with this operation: old value $-$ (row element $\times$ new value in pivot row).

2. The old row values will remain the same in those rows where there is 0 value in the pivot column.

In Table 4.10 we can easily identify the x_1 column as the pivot column and the A_1 row as the pivot row. In Table 4.11, which presents the third solution, we notice that

Table 4.10 The Second Solution for the Mixed Constraint Problem

c_b	c_j Basis	Solution	5 x_1	7 x_2	0 s_1	0 s_2	$-M$ A_1	$-M$ A_2
$-M$	A_1	10	①	0	0	-2	1	0
$-M$	A_2	20	1	0	-1	0	0	1
7	x_2	20	0	1	0	1	0	0
	z_j	$140 - 30M$	$-2M$	7	M	$2M + 7$	$-M$	$-M$
	$c_j - z_j$		$5 + 2M$	0	$-M$	$-2M - 7$	0	0

Table 4.11 The Third Solution for the Mixed Constraint Problem

c_b	c_j Basis	Solution	5 x_1	7 x_2	0 s_1	0 s_2	$-M$ A_2
5	x_1	10	1	0	0	-2	0
$-M$	A_2	10	0	0	-1	②	1
7	x_2	20	0	1	0	1	0
	z_j	$190 - 10M$	5	7	M	$-3 - 2M$	$-M$
	$c_j - z_j$		0	0	$-M$	$3 + 2M$	0

the A_1 column has been completely eliminated from the tableau. When an artificial variable is replaced by a decision, slack, or surplus variable in the solution basis, that artificial variable is no longer needed and can be discarded from the tableau. This is completely logical because the artificial variable is used only to facilitate preliminary solutions outside the feasible area for a given constraint. When an artificial variable is being kicked out of the solution, we know immediately that the new solution is now in the feasible solution area for the constraint.

For example, in the first constraint, A_1 is replaced by x_1 in Table 4.11. The quantity of x_1 being produced is 10, and x_2 has 20 units in the third solution. The first constraint of the problem, $x_1 + 2x_2 = 50$, suggests that the left-hand side should exactly equal 50. Since we began the solution at the origin, we needed A_1 until we moved up to the equation line $x_1 + 2x_2 = 50$. Now, however, we no longer need A_1 as we are on this line (the feasibility area). In subsequent iterations, we will not and cannot go back into an infeasible area for the constraint. Thus, we can eliminate A_1 from the tableau.

Table 4.12 presents the fourth solution. Since A_2 is replaced by s_2, we eliminated the A_2 column in the tableau. The optimum solution, derived in Table 4.13, is: $x_1 = 50$, $x_2 = 0$, $s_1 = 30$, $s_2 = 20$, and $Z = \$250$. The simplex solution process of the problem can be seen clearly in Figure 4.7.

Table 4.12   The Fourth Solution for the Mixed Constraint Problem

c_b	c_j / Basis	Solution	5 x_1	7 x_2	0 s_1	0 s_2
5	x_1	20	1	0	−1	0
0	s_2	5	0	0	−1/2	1
7	x_2	15	0	1	(1/2)	0
	z_j	205	5	7	−1.5	0
	$c_j - z_j$		0	0	1.5	0

Table 4.13   The Optimum Solution for the Mixed Constraint Problem

c_b	c_j / Basis	Solution	5 x_1	7 x_2	0 s_1	0 s_2
5	x_1	50	1	2	0	0
0	s_2	20	0	1	0	1
0	s_1	30	0	2	1	0
	z_j	250	5	10	0	0
	$c_j - z_j$		0	−3	0	0

Figure 4.7   The Mixed Constraint Problem

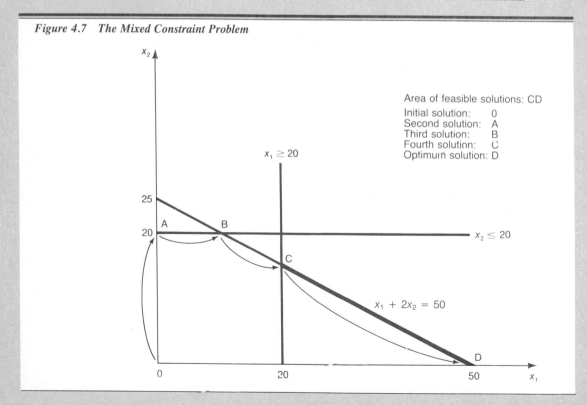

SIMPLEX SOLUTION OF A MINIMIZATION PROBLEM

Thus far, we have solved two maximization problems by the simplex method. The same solution procedure can be applied to minimization problems. Let us review the minimization problem we formulated and solved graphically in Chapter 3.

Example 4.2   *THE ORIENTATION PROGRAM FOR FIRST-YEAR STUDENTS*

This problem is concerned with the determination of scoops of scrambled eggs and number of smokie sausages to serve for breakfast to meet vitamin A, vitamin B, and iron requirements while minimizing the cost per serving. The problem was formulated as

$$\text{Minimize } Z = 8x_1 + 10x_2$$

$$
\begin{aligned}
\text{subject to} \quad 3x_1 + 3x_2 &\geq 30 & \textit{Vitamin A} \\
4x_1 + 2x_2 &\geq 24 & \textit{Vitamin B} \\
x_1 + 2x_2 &\geq 12 & \textit{Iron} \\
x_1, x_2 &\geq 0
\end{aligned}
$$

where
$x_1 =$ number of scoops of scrambled eggs served

$x_2 =$ number of smokies served

The first step of the simplex solution procedure is, of course, to formulate a simplex model by introducing appropriate slack, surplus, and/or artificial variables. Since the problem has three greater-than-or-equal-to constraints, we need to subtract a surplus variable and add an artificial variable in each of the constraints as follows:

$$
\begin{aligned}
3x_1 + 3x_2 - s_1 + A_1 &= 30 \\
4x_1 + 2x_2 - s_2 + A_2 &= 24 \\
x_1 + 2x_2 - s_3 + A_3 &= 12
\end{aligned}
$$

In a maximization problem, we assign a large negative c_j value, $-M$, to the artificial variable in the model. In a minimization problem, however, we must assign to the artificial variable a large positive M as a c_j value. Since we are trying to minimize total cost, the positive M value assigned to the artificial variable would make it very costly, and thus the procedure assures us a final solution without the artificial variable. Now, the simplex model is formulated as:

$$\text{Minimize } Z = 8x_1 + 10x_2 + 0s_1 + 0s_2 + 0s_3 + MA_1 + MA_2 + MA_3$$

$$
\begin{aligned}
\text{subject to} \quad 3x_1 + 3x_2 - s_1 + A_1 &= 30 \\
4x_1 + 2x_2 - s_2 + A_2 &= 24 \\
x_1 + 2x_2 - s_3 + A_3 &= 12 \\
x_1, x_2, s_1, s_2, s_3, A_1, A_2, A_3 &\geq 0
\end{aligned}
$$

The first solution is at the origin, where we do not provide any eggs or sausage for breakfast. We can determine the basic variables in the first simplex tableau as shown in Table 4.14.

Table 4.14   The Initial Solution of the Orientation Program Problem

c_b	c_j Basis	Solution	8 x_1	10 x_2	0 s_1	0 s_2	0 s_3	M A_1	M A_2	M A_3
M	A_1	30	3	3	−1	0	0	1	0	0
M	A_2	24	④	2	0	−1	0	0	1	0
M	A_3	12	1	2	0	0	−1	0	0	1
	z_j	66M	8M	7M	−M	−M	−M	M	M	M
	$z_j - c_j$		8M − 8	7M − 10	−M	−M	−M	0	0	0

With the simplex knowledge we have gained, it is now a simple task to complete the initial tableau presented in Table 4.14. You will notice one obvious change in the simplex tableau. We reversed the simplex criterion from $c_j - z_j$ to $z_j - c_j$. By reversing the computation procedure, we can still identify the pivot column by selecting a non-basic-variable column with the *largest positive* $z_j - c_j$. The $z_j - c_j$ value in each of the nonbasic-variable columns represents the net per-unit decrease of cost for each corresponding variable. The pivot column is the x_1 column, and the pivot row is the A_2 row, as identified in Table 4.14.

The second simplex tableau is obtained in Table 4.15. Since A_2 was replaced by x_1 in the solution basis, we can eliminate the A_2 column. The second solution is an infeasible solution, because we still have artificial variables in the basis. Also, it is not an optimum solution because we still have positive $z_j - c_j$ values in some of the nonbasic-variable columns. The entering variable is x_2, and the leaving variable is A_3.

The third solution is presented in Table 4.16. This solution is still infeasible, because A_1 remains in the solution basis. The fourth solution, shown in Table 4.17, indicates that it is a feasible solution because all artificial variables have been eliminated from the solution basis. However, this solution is not an optimum solution because there exists a positive $z_j - c_j$ value in the s_2 column. One more iteration gives us the final solution, as shown in Table 4.18. The nonbasic-variable columns (s_1 and s_3) indicate

Table 4.15   The Second Solution of the Orientation Program Problem

c_b	c_j Basis	Solution	8 x_1	10 x_2	0 s_1	0 s_2	0 s_3	M A_1	M A_3
M	A_1	12	0	3/2	−1	3/4	0	1	0
8	x_1	6	1	1/2	0	− 1/4	0	0	0
M	A_3	6	0	③/2	0	1/4	−1	0	1
	z_j	18M + 48	8	3M + 4	−M	M − 2	−M	M	M
	$z_j - c_j$		0	3M − 6	−M	M − 2	−M	0	0

Table 4.16   The Third Solution of the Orientation Program Problem

c_b \ c_j	Basis	Solution	8 x_1	10 x_2	0 s_1	0 s_2	0 s_3	M A_1
M	A_1	6	0	0	−1	1/2	①	1
8	x_1	4	1	0	0	−1/3	1/3	0
10	x_2	4	0	1	0	1/6	−2/3	0
	z_j	6M + 72	8	10	−M	1/2 M − 1	M − 4	M
	$z_j - c_j$		0	0	−M	1/2 M − 1	M − 4	0

Table 4.17   The Fourth Solution of the Orientation Program Problem

c_b \ c_j	Basis	Solution	8 x_1	10 x_2	0 s_1	0 s_2	0 s_3
0	s_3	6	0	0	−1	⑴/2	1
8	x_1	2	1	0	1/3	−1/2	0
10	x_2	8	0	1	−2/3	1/2	0
	z_j	96	8	10	−4	1	0
	$z_j - c_j$		0	0	−4	1	0

Table 4.18   The Final Solution of the Orientation Program Problem

c_b \ c_j	Basis	Solution	8 x_1	10 x_2	0 s_1	0 s_2	0 s_3
0	s_2	12	0	0	−2	1	2
8	x_1	8	1	0	−2/3	0	1
10	x_2	2	0	1	1/3	0	−1
	z_j	84	8	10	−2	0	−2
	$z_j - c_j$		0	0	−2	0	−2

negative $z_j - c_j$ values. Thus, we have reached the optimum solution. The simplex solution process is graphically presented in Figure 4.8.

The optimum solution to the diet problem is $x_1 = 8$, $x_2 = 2$, $s_2 = 12$, and $Z = 84¢$. This solution corresponds with the solution we derived in Chapter 3 by the graphical method. The dietitians should provide 8 scoops of scrambled eggs and 2 smokies for breakfast with the per-serving cost of 84¢. Since s_1 and s_3 are nonbasic variables,

Figure 4.8   The Orientation Program Problem Solution Process

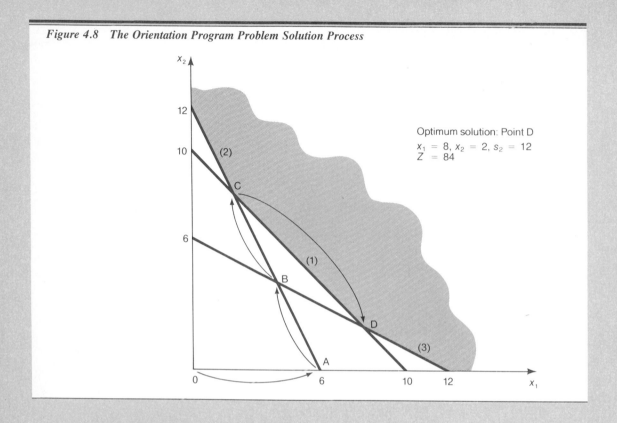

Optimum solution: Point D
$x_1 = 8$, $x_2 = 2$, $s_2 = 12$
$Z = 84$

we know that the breakfast does not provide any surplus vitamin A and iron requirements. In other words, the breakfast will provide precisely the minimum requirements of 30 milligrams of vitamin A and 12 milligrams of iron. However, since $s_2 = 12$ in the solution base, the breakfast provides 12 milligrams beyond the minimum requirement of 24 milligrams of vitamin B. Thus, the total vitamin B content of the breakfast would be 36 milligrams.

Another interesting piece of information we can derive from the final simplex tableau is that the shadow prices of s_1 and s_3 are identical: -2. Thus, if we can decrease the minimum requirement of vitamin A from 30 milligrams to 29 milligrams, the cost of the breakfast can be reduced by 2¢ (from 84¢ to 82¢). Similarly, if the minimum requirement of iron is reduced by 1 milligram (from 12 milligrams to 11 milligrams), the cost of the breakfast will decrease by 2¢. If, however, the minimum requirement for vitamin A or iron is increased by 1 milligram, the per-serving cost of the breakfast will increase by 2¢.

SOME PROBLEM SITUATIONS

Several situations might give us some trouble when solving linear programming problems by the simplex method. Once we learn how to take care of these situations, we will be completely ready to tackle any linear programming problem.

Tie in Selecting the Entering Variable

Selection of the entering variable or the pivot column is based on the $c_j - z_j$ value of the nonbasic-variable columns. If two or more nonbasic-variable columns have the identical largest $c_j - z_j$ (or $z_j - c_j$ in a minimization problem) value, we have a tie in selecting the entering variable. In such a situation, the selection of the entering variable can be made arbitrarily. Selection of one of the tied variable columns will carry us eventually to the optimum solution. To minimize the number of iterations required to reach the optimum solution, the following simple steps would be helpful:

Step 1   If there is a tie between two decision variable columns, an arbitrary selection can be made.

Step 2   If there is a tie between a decision variable and a slack (or surplus) variable, the decision variable should be selected as the entering variable.

Step 3   If there is a tie between two slack (or surplus) variables, again, the choice can be made arbitrarily.

Tie in Selecting the Leaving Variable (Degeneracy)

To determine the leaving variable, or the pivot row, the solution values of the basic variables are divided by the coefficients in the pivot column. Then, the row with the minimum nonnegative value is selected. The occurrence of two or more basic-variable rows with identical minimum nonnegative values presents the problem of **degeneracy.**

The degeneracy case can be best explained by an example. Suppose we have the following linear programming problem:

$$\text{Maximize } Z = 80x_1 + 70x_2$$
$$\text{subject to} \quad 2x_1 + x_2 \le 120$$
$$x_1 \quad\;\; \le 70$$
$$x_1 + x_2 \le 60$$
$$x_1, x_2 \ge 0$$

We can easily determine the initial solution as shown in Table 4.19. The pivot column is the x_1 column because it has the largest positive $c_j - z_j$. When we divide the solution values by the coefficients in the pivot column, we find a tie between the s_1 and s_3 rows

Table 4.19   The Initial Solution of the Degeneracy Case

c_b	Basis	Solution	80 x_1	70 x_2	0 s_1	0 s_2	0 s_3
0	s_1	120	2	1	1	0	0
0	s_2	70	1	0	0	1	0
0	s_3	60	1	1	0	0	1
	z_j	0	0	0	0	0	0
	$c_j - z_j$		80	70	0	0	0

Table 4.20   The Second Solution of the Degeneracy Case

c_b	c_j Basis	Solution	80 x_1	70 x_2	0 s_1	0 s_2	0 s_3
80	x_1	60	1	1/2	1/2	0	0
0	s_2	10	0	−1/2	−1/2	1	0
0	s_3	0	0	(1/2)	−1/2	0	1
	z_j	4,800	80	40	40	0	0
	$c_j - z_j$		0	30	−40	0	0

as candidates for the pivot row. If we select the s_1 row as the pivot row, the second solution we obtain as shown in Table 4.20.

In the second solution, the basic variable s_3 has a solution value of 0. As we discussed earlier, only nonbasic variables are to have 0 solution values. In the case of degeneracy, however, a basic variable with 0 value remains in the solution basis. This fact does not present any serious problem. The case of degeneracy in the two-variable case can occur any time a combination of three constraints and/or axes meet at an extreme point. For example, in Figure 4.9 we can see clearly that the first and third constraint lines and the x_1 axis intersect at an extreme point A ($x_1 = 60$, $x_2 = 0$).

Figure 4.9   A Case of Degeneracy

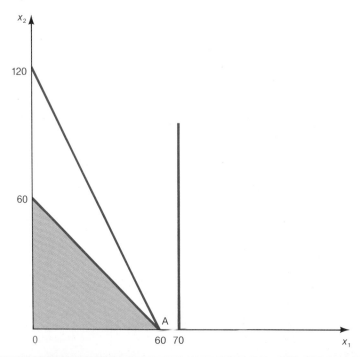

Theoretically, a degeneracy problem can generate an indefinite number of iterations without improving the solution. Fortunately, in most real-world problems only rarely do we face any difficulty with degeneracy.

Multiple Optimum Solutions

A case of multiple optimum solutions occurs when the slope of the iso-profit function (or the iso-cost function in a minimization problem) is identical to the slope of a constraint that forms the area of feasible solutions, as we already discussed in Chapter 3. Let us examine the following problem with multiple optimum solutions:

$$\text{Maximize } Z = 60x_1 + 60x_2$$
$$\text{subject to} \quad 3x_1 + 3x_2 \leq 90$$
$$2x_1 + 4x_2 \leq 80$$
$$x_1, x_2 \geq 0$$

This problem is illustrated graphically in Figure 4.10. The slope of the iso-profit function is -1. Thus, the optimum solution is the line segment BC. Consequently, we have a case with multiple optimum solutions.

When we solve a linear programming problem by the simplex method, we cannot examine the slopes as such. However, there is another way we can detect a case of multiple optimum solutions. Let us consider the final simplex solution to the above problem, as shown in Table 4.21. Since there is no positive $c_j - z_j$ value, the optimum

Figure 4.10   A Problem with Multiple Optimum Solutions

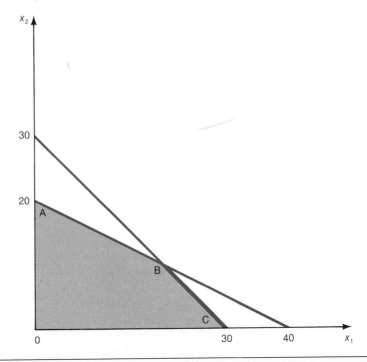

Table 4.21   A Problem with Multiple Optimum Solutions

c_b	c_j Basis	Solution	60 x_1	60 x_2	0 s_1	0 s_2
60	x_1	20	1	0	2/3	−1/2
60	x_2	10	0	1	−1/3	1/2
	z_j	1,800	60	60	20	0
	$c_j - z_j$		0	0	−20	0

Table 4.22   An Alternate Optimum Solution

c_b	c_j Basis	Solution	60 x_1	60 x_2	0 s_1	0 s_2
60	x_1	30	1	1	1/3	0
0	s_2	20	0	2	−2/3	1
	z_j	1,800	60	60	20	0
	$c_j - z_j$		0	0	−20	0

solution has been found, and thus the simplex procedure is terminated. The usual final simplex solution yields 0 values for $c_j - z_j$ in all basic-variable columns and negative $c_j - z_j$ values in all nonbasic-variable columns. However, the s_2 column, which is a nonbasic-variable column, indicates a $c_j - z_j$ value of 0.

We recall that a $c_j - z_j$ value represents the per-unit profit increase for a nonbasic variable. Since $c_j - z_j$ is 0 for a nonbasic variable s_2, entering s_2 in the solution will yield a different solution with the same total profit. For example, the new solution is shown in Table 4.22. The decision maker now has the option of deciding which optimum solution to implement on the basis of noneconomic factors.

An Infeasible Problem

As we discussed in Chapter 3, a problem is infeasible when it has conflicting or mutually exclusive constraints. Such a problem is simple to identify if it involves only two decision variables because we can plot the constraints graphically.

When we use the simplex method, an infeasible problem is not that easily detected, especially for large-scale problems. When a problem is completely solved by the simplex method, the final simplex tableau indicates 0 or negative $c_j - z_j$ values. But if one or more artificial variables are in the solution basis with positive solution values, it is an infeasible problem. However, if the problem is degenerate (involving a tie in selecting the leaving variable) and the artificial variable in the solution basis has a 0 value, it is not an infeasible problem.

Table 4.23   Simplex Solution of an Infeasible Problem

c_b / c_j	Basis	Solution	10 x_1	8 x_2	0 s_1	0 s_2	M A_1
8	x_2	3	1	1	1/2	0	0
M	A_1	4	-1	0	-1	-1	-1
	z_j	$24 + 4M$	$8 - M$	8	$4 - M$	$-M$	M
	$z_j - c_j$		$-2 - M$	0	$4 - M$	$-M$	0

For example, let us consider the following problem:

$$\text{Minimize } Z = 10x_1 + 8x_2$$
$$\text{subject to} \quad 2x_1 + 2x_2 \le 6$$
$$x_1 + 2x_2 \ge 10$$
$$x_1, x_2 \ge 0$$

The final simplex solution tableau for the problem is shown in Table 4.23. Since the $c_j - z_j$ values of all the nonbasic-variable columns are negative, it is the final simplex tableau. However, an artificial variable A_1 is still in the basis with a solution value of 4. Thus, this is an infeasible problem.

An Unbounded Problem

If a maximization problem is unbounded, total profit can increase indefinitely without a bound as presented in Chapter 3. When we use the simplex method, the solution procedure continues until the unbounded condition becomes obvious. Suppose we select a pivot column (the column with the largest positive $c_j - z_j$ value). The next step is to determine the pivot row (the row with the minimum nonnegative value when the solution values are divided by the positive coefficients in the pivot column). If the pivot column has only 0 or negative coefficients, there is no pivot row. Thus, the problem can be detected as unbounded. For example, let us consider the following unbounded problem:

$$\text{Maximize } Z = 20x_1 + 30x_2$$
$$\text{subject to} \quad -4x_1 + 4x_2 \le 32$$
$$x_2 \le 12$$
$$x_1, x_2 \ge 0$$

The final simplex tableau for this problem is presented in Table 4.24. The tableau indicates that we have not yet reached the optimum solution because the s_1 column indicates a positive $c_j - z_j$ value of 5. Thus, the s_1 column is the pivot column. However, there is no positive coefficient in the s_1 column. Therefore, we cannot select a pivot row. Hence, this problem is an unbounded problem.

Table 4.24   Simplex Solution of an Unbounded Problem

c_b	c_j Basis	Solution	20 x_1	30 x_2	0 s_1	0 s_2
30	x_2	12	0	1	0	1
20	x_1	4	1	0	$-1/4$	1
	z_j	440	20	30	-5	50
	$c_j - z_j$		0	0	5	-50

SUMMARY

In this chapter, we have learned about the simplex method of linear programming. We have studied the simplex solution procedure through a maximization problem, a problem with mixed constraints, and a case of minimization. We have also discussed several types of situations that often present us with problems, and we have seen how we can resolve these difficulties when solving linear programming problems by the simplex method.

The simplex solution procedure presented in this chapter is the key to understanding the topics to be discussed in subsequent chapters. Thus, if you have some difficulty in understanding the simplex method at this point, you should go back and study the chapter again.

Glossary

Artificial Variable   Introduced into equal-to or greater-than-or-equal-to constraints when converting them into simplex equalities, the artificial variable enables temporarily "feasible" solutions.

Big M Method   Artificial variables in the solution basis indicate infeasible solutions. Assigning a contribution coefficient of M (for million or billion) to the artificial variables ensures that the simplex procedure will drive them out, provided a solution is feasible.

Degeneracy   When there is a tie in selecting the pivot row (leaving variable), the situation is degenerate, and a basic variable has a solution value of 0 in the subsequent simplex tableau. Degeneracy can theoretically continue forever, but real-world problems rarely encounter this difficulty.

Entering Variable   In the pivoting operation of the simplex method, the entering variable is the nonbasic variable selected to become part of the solution basis based on the superiority of its potential contribution to the objective function.

Leaving Variable   In the pivoting operation of the simplex method, the leaving variable is the basic variable selected to be removed from the solution basis because it is the most restrictive on the incoming variable.

Pivot Column   The column containing the entering variable is the pivot column.

Pivot Element   The intersection of the pivot column and pivot row is the pivot element. It is used in calculating new values for the pivot row.

Pivot Row   The row containing the leaving variable is the pivot row.

Simplex Method   Typically, linear programming problems are solved via the simplex method, which consists of a series of mathematical operations which are repeated until an optimum solution is obtained or the problem is shown to be infeasible. Each iteration (repetition of the operations) produces a solution equally close or closer to the optimum than the previous iteration's solution.

Testing the Optimality   Whenever a simplex solution is reached, it must be tested to ascertain whether it is the optimum solution. Positive $c_j - z_j$ values indicate that better solutions exist.

References

Charnes, A., and Cooper, W. W. *Management Models and Industrial Applications of Linear Programming.* New York: Wiley, 1961.

Kwak, N. K. *Mathematical Programming with Business Applications.* New York: McGraw-Hill, 1973.

Lee, S. M., and Moore, L. J. *Introduction to Decision Science.* New York: Petrocelli-Charter, 1975.

Lee, S. M., Moore, L. J., and Taylor, B. W. *Management Science.* 2d ed. Dubuque, Iowa: W. C. Brown, 1985.

Assignments

4.1 Why do you think we have to study the simplex method, knowing that linear programming problems are usually solved by the computer?

4.2 What is the major difference between the graphical method and the simplex method of linear programming?

4.3 Convert the following constraints into simplex equalities:

$$2x_1 + 3x_2 \leq 36 \qquad\qquad x_1 + x_2 + 3x_3 = 45$$
$$4x_1 + x_2 - x_3 \geq 10 \qquad -x_1 + x_2 + 2x_3 \geq -5$$
$$3x_1 - 2x_2 + x_3 \geq -2$$

4.4 How is the pivot column determined in a maximization problem?

4.5 How is the pivot row determined?

4.6 In selecting the pivot column in a maximization problem, if there is a tie between two nonbasic variables both having the largest positive $c_j - z_j$ value, how would you break this tie?

4.7 When does a degeneracy occur and how would you handle the situation?

4.8 What is an infeasible problem? How is such a situation identified during the simplex solution process?

4.9 What is an unbounded problem? How can a problem be identified as unbounded?

4.10 Solve the following linear programming problem by the simplex method:

$$\text{Maximize } Z = \$40x_1 + \$30x_2$$
$$\text{subject to} \quad 2x_1 + 2x_2 \leq 240$$
$$2x_1 \leq 120$$
$$2x_2 \leq 80$$
$$x_1, x_2 \geq 0$$

4.11 Solve the following linear programming problem by the simplex method:

$$\text{Maximize } Z = \$48x_1 + \$64x_2$$
$$\text{subject to} \quad 16x_1 + 12x_2 \leq 96$$
$$8x_1 + 16x_2 \leq 80$$
$$4x_1 \leq 16$$
$$x_1, x_2 \geq 0$$

4.12 Solve the following linear programming problem by the simplex method:

$$\text{Minimize } Z = \$2x_1 + \$3x_2$$
$$\text{subject to} \quad 2x_1 + 5x_2 \geq 30$$
$$4x_1 + 2x_2 \geq 28$$
$$x_1, x_2 \geq 0$$

4.13 Solve the following linear programming problem by the simplex method:

$$\text{Maximize } Z = \$70x_1 + \$80x_2$$
$$\text{subject to} \quad -2x_1 + x_2 \geq -20$$
$$x_1 + x_2 \leq 14$$
$$x_1 + 2x_2 \leq 20$$
$$x_1, x_2 \geq 0$$

4.14 American Meatless Sausage Inc. prepares its famous meatless sausage from two ingredients: soy concentrate and cornmeal. Each kilogram of soy concentrate contains 90 milligrams of protein, 6 milligrams of iron, and 120 calories. Each kilogram of cornmeal contains 45 milligrams of protein, 18 milligrams of iron, and 120 calories. To satisfy the nutritional requirements of the USDA, each kilogram of sausage must contain at least 90 milligrams of protein and 18 milligrams of iron. Also, in order to appeal to the weight-watcher segment of the market, a kilogram of sausage should not exceed 360 calories. The soy concentrate costs 72¢/kilogram and the cornmeal costs 18¢/kilogram.

    a. Formulate a linear programming model for this problem.

    b. Find the optimum solution (by the graphical method) that minimizes the total cost while satisfying all the constraints.

c. What are the basic variables and their values in the optimum solution? What are the nonbasic variables and their values?

d. If the USDA changed the minimum requirement of iron from 18 to 24 milligrams for each kilogram of sausage, what would be the change in the optimum solution?

e. In the original problem, if the cost of cornmeal is increased to 54¢/kilogram, how would the optimum solution change?

4.15 The Uptown Haberdashery is having its Annual After Holiday Dog Day Sale of unsold winter garments. Due to a very mild winter, Mr. Brown, the store manager, has the following inventory for sale: 5,000 men's overcoats, 7,500 women's wool sweaters, and 2,250 children's wool sweaters.

Mr. Brown is designing an advertising campaign for the sale. The types of advertising he plans to use and the estimated number of customers that each type is expected to reach are: newspaper, 1,000 customers per ad; radio, 750 customers per ad; and mail, 1,500 customers per ad. The cost of each type of advertising is: newspaper, $120 per ad; radio, $90 per spot; and mail, $200 per ad.

The Hutter Advertising Agency has conducted an advertising survey and found the percentage of the market for men, women, and children reached by each type of advertising to be as follows:

Market	Type of Advertising		
	Newspaper	Radio	Mail
Men	45%	20%	50%
Women	40	55	40
Children	15	25	10

Mr. Brown has decided that to sell his inventory he must reach at least 6,000 men, 8,500 women, and 3,500 children.

a. Formulate a linear programming model to determine how much of each type of advertising Mr. Brown should use to minimize the total advertising cost and still sell his inventory.

b. Use the simplex method and go through one iteration (two simplex tableaux, including the initial tableau).

c. Solve this problem by using a computer, if one is available.

4.16 Kay Manning, manager of sales, has two salespeople working for her. The ability of each salesperson to secure new accounts had historically been as follows. Salesperson 1: 4 new accounts per 10 visits to prospects, and salesperson 2: 3 new accounts per 10 visits to prospects. As of May 1, salesperson 1 has 20 established customers that he must call on each month if he is to retain their monthly orders. Salesperson 2 has 15 established accounts that he is attempting to maintain.

The average time each salesperson spends with each type of customer per visit is as follows:

	Type of Customer	
Salesperson	New Account	Established Account
1	10	5
2	8	6

Each new order yields the company an average profit of $150, whereas orders from established accounts are usually smaller and yield an average profit of $50 an order. Salesperson 1 has a larger area to cover than salesperson 2, and as a result he has only 120 hours (hr) (net of traveling time) to spend with his customers each month. Salesperson 2 has 135 hr available to spend with his customers, since his traveling time is less.

a. Formulate a linear programming model to determine how many new and how many old customers each salesperson should call on in May to maximize profits.

b. Solve this problem by the simplex method.

4.17 Ms. Osborne, marketing manager of the Midwest Typewriter Company, is trying to decide how to allocate her salespeople to the company's three primary markets. Market 1 is an urban area, and the salespeople can sell, on the average, 40 typewriters per week. The salespeople in the other two markets can sell, on the average, 36 and 25 typewriters per week, respectively.

For the coming week, three salespeople will be on vacation, leaving only 12 people available for duty. Also, because of a limited number of company cars, a maximum of 5 salespeople can be allocated to market 1. The selling expenses per week for each salesperson in each area are: $80/week for market 1, $70/week for market 2, and $50/week for market 3. The budget for the next week is $750. The profit margin per typewriter is $15.

a. Formulate a linear programming model to determine how many salespeople should be assigned to each area next week to maximize profits.

b. Use the simplex method and go through one iteration.

4.18 The new cars for the upcoming year are about to be introduced, and Mr. Weimer, sales manager of Roadside Motors, has a very large stock of last year's cars. Almost all the current stock is large luxury cars that are not selling because of their poor gas mileage. To move these cars, Mr. Weimer is planning a large advertising campaign and sale. He plans to use the following types of advertising: (1) radio spots, which cost $40 per spot and reach an estimated 200 potential customers per ad; (2) newspaper ads, which cost $50 per ad and reach an estimated 300 potential customers per ad; and (3) mail ads, which cost $45 per ad and reach an estimated 325 potential customers per ad.

Mr. Weimer has estimated that he must reach at least 5,000 potential customers to reduce his inventory. At present, the company has a contract for a minimum of 10 radio spots, 5 newspaper ads, and 5 mail ads.

a. Formulate a linear programming model to determine how many ads of each type Mr. Weimer should purchase to minimize total costs.

b. Solve this problem using the simplex method.

4.19 The Downing Plastics Company has just received a government contract to produce three plastic valves: exhaust, intake, and bypass. These valves will be used in the Explorer spacecraft. The valves must be highly heat and pressure resistant. The company has developed a three-stage production process that will provide the valves with the necessary properties.

The process involves work in three different chambers. Chamber 1 provides the necessary pressure resistance and can process valves for 1,200 minutes each week. Chamber 2 provides heat resistance and can process valves for 900 minutes a week. Chamber 3 tests the valve and can operate for 1,300 minutes a week. The three valve types and their time requirements in each chamber are:

Valve	Time Requirement (min)		
	Chamber 1	Chamber 2	Chamber 3
Exhaust	5	7	4
Intake	3	2	10
Bypass	2	4	5

The government will purchase all the valves that can be produced, and the company will receive the following profit on each valve: exhaust, $1.50; intake, $1.35; and bypass, $1.00.

a. Formulate a linear programming model to determine how many valves of each type the company should produce each week to maximize profits.

b. Go through one iteration by the simplex method.

4.20 The Willis Office Furniture Company is a small business operating in Rhode Island. It has two warehouses in the state from which it fills customers' orders. Due to a recent business slump, the company is attempting to institute a cost reduction campaign. A customer has just ordered 10 desks and 8 tables, and Mr. North, the distribution manager, wishes to minimize shipping costs. The shipping costs of tables and desks from each warehouse are:

Furniture	Shipping Cost	
	Warehouse 1	Warehouse 2
Desk	$15	$12
Table	7	9

The company delivers all orders using their own trucks. Trucks coming from warehouse 2 can haul no more than 7 tables and desks, but trucks coming from warehouse

1 can transport up to 14 tables and desks. Mr. North has also instituted another policy that he hopes will reduce shipping costs: He has decided that the inventories at the two warehouses should be approximately equal. Therefore, he says that the difference in the number of tables and desks shipped from either warehouse cannot exceed 2.

    a. Formulate a linear programming model to determine how many tables and desks should be shipped from each warehouse to minimize total shipping costs.

    b. Solve this problem by the simplex method.

4.21 The Venus Candy Company makes three different candy bars: Saturn, Moon, and Venus. The ingredients for each candy bar are as follows:

	Ingredients		
Candy Bar	**Chocolate**	**Nuts**	**Caramel**
Saturn	12 g	4 g	15 g
Moon	6 g	10 g	8 g
Venus	10 g	2 g	15 g

The company's suppliers have limited the company to the following ingredients per week: chocolate, 25,000 grams; nuts, 15,000 grams; and caramel, 30,000 grams. The marketing department estimates that the maximum demand for the Saturn will be 900 per week and for the Moon, 700 per week. The Venus is a relatively new product, and demand for this bar appears to be very large at the present time. Per-unit profit contributions for each candy bar are as follows: Saturn, 2¢; Moon 2.5¢; and Venus, 1.5¢. The company would like to know how many candy bars of each type to produce next week to maximize total profits. Solve this problem by the simplex method.

4.22 Consider the following linear programming problem:

$$\text{Minimize } Z = \$15x_1 + \$25x_2$$
$$\text{subject to } \quad 3x_1 + 4x_2 \geq 12$$
$$2x_1 + x_2 \geq 6$$
$$3x_1 + 2x_2 \geq 9$$
$$x_1, x_2 \geq 0$$

    a. Solve this problem by the simplex method.

    b. Is the optimum solution valid? Why or why not?

4.23 The General Bulb Company produces three kinds of light bulb: a 60-watt soft-light bulb, a 60-watt regular bulb, and a 100-watt bulb. The bulbs each take 1 hour per case in production line 1. In production line 2, a case of the soft-light takes 2 hours, and a case of each of the others takes 1 hour. Production line 1 has 25 hours per week available, and production line 2 has 40 hours per week available.

    The company has determined that the two types of 60-watt bulb are considered substitute products by most people and that their combined demand will not be more than 25 cases per week. The demand for the 100-watt bulbs will never be greater than 60 cases per week. If the soft-light bulbs earn a profit of $7 per case and the other two types of bulbs earn a profit of $5 per case, how many cases per week should the company produce of each type to maximize total profits?

4.24 The American Inland Oil Company is faced with a problem. It has only enough oil to keep its refineries operating for 1 more year. The company has determined that it has three possible alternatives for increasing its oil supply, but it can spend no more than $6 million, and this investment must provide at least 2.5 million barrels of oil a year for at least the next 75 years.

Alternative 1 is to invest in more oil wells in this country. The company has determined that the total cost of a new well is $200,000 with an expected yield of 500,000 barrels per year for 10 years. Alternative 2 is to invest in oil wells in South America. A well there costs $800,000 initially and will yield 1 million barrels a year for 25 years. Alternative 3 is to invest in research for the recovery of shale oil. It is estimated that this research will cost $2 million but will yield 1.5 million barrels a year for 50 years. Unlike the other alternatives, only one research project is possible.

a. Formulate a linear programming model to determine the optimum choice of alternative that will maximize the company's oil supply.

b. Solve this problem by the simplex method.

4.25 The Ozark Brewing Company produces custom-blended whiskey to order. The components of the blend are rye whiskey and bourbon. The company has received an order for a minimum of 600 gallons of custom-blended whiskey. The customer has specified that the order must contain at least 40 percent rye and not more than 375 gallons of bourbon. The customer has also specified that the blend should be mixed in the ratio of two parts rye to one part bourbon.

The company can produce at the rate of 750 gallons a week, regardless of the blend, and it wishes to fill the order in 1 week of production. The company has agreed to furnish the blend for a price of $15 a gallon. Its cost per gallon of rye and bourbon used are $6 and $3, respectively. To meet the customer's requirements and maximize total profits, the management wishes to determine the blend the company should produce during 1 week's production. Formulate the problem as a linear programming problem and solve it by the simplex method. Now answer the following:

a. How much total blend should be produced?

b. How much of each component should be used?

c. What is the maximum profit yielded?

d. Which restrictions are constraining the solution?

e. If the Ozark Brewing Company could sell only 600 gallons, how much of each component would they produce, and what would be the total profit?

4.26 The Roller Products Company produces roller skates and skateboards. It has three production lines. Production line 1 makes skateboard platforms. Production line 2 makes skate assemblies. Production line 3 mounts wheels on both products. The marketing department has determined virtually unlimited demand for both products. Profit per pair of roller skates is $10 and per skateboard, $6. Production line 1 can produce 6 skateboard platforms per day, and production line 2 can produce 5 pairs of shoes per day. Production line 3 can mount 20 wheel sets per day. Each skateboard requires 2 wheel sets, and each pair of roller skates requires 4 wheel sets.

a. How many skateboards and roller skates should be scheduled per day to maximize total profits?

b. Solve this problem by the simplex method.

4.27 A gardener has 1,000 square yards of land available to devote to cash crops. Profits for the planned crops are as follows: lima beans, $20 per 10 square yards; spinach, $10 per 10 square yards; zucchini, $15 per 10 square yards.

The gardener has $200 available to invest. Total preparation costs for 10 square yards are $4 for lima beans, $2 for spinach, and $1 for zucchini. The gardener has 200 hours available for gardening. Each 10 square yards requires the following amounts of time: lima beans, 2 hours; spinach, 1 hour; and zucchini, 3 hours.

a. Formulate a linear programming model to determine the optimum areas in square yards for each of the three crops.

b. Using the simplex method, go through three iterations.

4.28 The Ladies Haven Inc. produces two types of ladies bathing suits—bikini and backless. These two products are manufactured in three sewing centers (SC). On the average, a bikini requires 6 minutes in SC I, 6 minutes in SC II, and 4 minutes in SC III. A backless bathing suit requires 4 minutes in SC I, 7.5 minutes in SC II, and 10 minutes in SC III. The maximum time available for production per day is: SC I, 2 hours; SC II, 2.25 hours; and SC III, 2.5 hours. The expected profits are $12 from a bikini and $14 from a backless.

a. Using the graphical technique, find the optimum product mix that will maximize total profits.

b. What are the basic and nonbasic variables in the optimum solution?

c. If the firm has to cut labor, where should it cut and by how many minutes without sacrificing the total profit?

4.29 Jack Phillips is the social chairperson of the Sigma Delta Sigma Fraternity. He is planning a special drink for the upcoming open house. He has decided to serve Phillips screwdrivers. Although some friends swear that a Phillips screwdriver contains one part vodka and two parts Phillips Milk of Magnesia, the 5-ounce drink contains vodka and frozen orange juice.

For the open house, Jack has obtained the following ingredients: premium vodka, 400 ounces; cheap vodka, 500 ounces; premium orange juice, 800 ounces; and cheap orange juice, 400 ounces. Jack plans four different-quality Phillips screwdrivers. The recipes for the drinks and the prices that will be charged are as follows:

Drinks	Vodka	Orange Juice	Price
Phillips screwdriver—The Thing	4 oz premium	1 oz premium	$2.50
Phillips screwdriver—Deluxe	3 oz premium	2 oz cheap	2.20
Phillips screwdriver—Regular	3 oz cheap	2 oz premium	2.00
Phillips screwdriver—All the Way	2 oz cheap	3 oz cheap	1.70

From past experience, Jack knows that the maximum number of drinks he can sell are 125 drinks that contain cheap vodka and 150 drinks that contain cheap orange juice. He also feels that he can sell at least 40 of The Thing.

Formulate a linear programming model to determine the optimum quantity of each type of drink to prepare to maximize total revenue.

4.30 Solve the following linear programming problem by the simplex method:

$$\text{Minimize } Z = 7x_1 + 4x_2 + 8x_3$$

$$\text{subject to} \quad 16x_1 + 12x_2 + 10x_3 \geq 120$$

$$8x_1 + 10x_2 + 14x_3 \geq 112$$

$$x_2 \qquad\qquad \leq 10$$

$$x_3 \geq 4$$

$$x_1, x_2, x_3 \geq 0$$

5 DUALITY, SENSITIVITY ANALYSIS, AND COMPUTER SOLUTIONS OF LINEAR PROGRAMMING

The purpose of linear programming is not just to derive an optimum solution. Since we live in an environment of uncertainty, we seek additional information from the solution process to answer "what if" contingency questions. For example, a linear programming model may be formulated to analyze the impacts of inflation, materials shortage, increase or decrease of the budget, technological improvements, change in market situations, and integer requirements for certain variables. Since most linear programming problems are solved using computers, discussion of how we can apply mainframes or microcomputers to analyze linear programming problems is essential. In this chapter, we will study three major topics: duality, sensitivity analysis, and computer solutions of linear programming.

Learning Objectives   *From the study of this chapter, we will learn the following:*

1. The concept and purpose of duality
2. The relationship between primal and dual models of linear programming
3. How to formulate a dual model for any linear programming problem
4. How to perform sensitivity analysis
5. How to solve linear programming problems by using computers
6. The meaning of the following terms:

Duality   *Dual solution*
Graphical sensitivity analysis   *Primal solution*
Simplex-based sensitivity analysis

DUALITY IN LINEAR PROGRAMMING

Duality simply means that every linear programming problem can be formulated and analyzed in two ways. The first form is the ordinary linear programming model, often referred to as the *primal*. The second model is the other side of the primal, often called the *dual*. Every primal linear programming model can be formulated as a dual model. For example, a profit maximization problem can be formulated as a problem of cost minimization. Or, a cost minimization can be viewed as a problem of maximizing the efficiency of using available resources.

Thus far, our discussion of linear programming has been limited to seeking the optimum solution to the primal. Each primal maximization problem has a corresponding minimization problem. Similarly, each primal minimization problem has a corresponding dual maximization problem. Therefore, the dual of a dual problem is the primal of the given problem.

You may ask, "Why should we worry about another way to solve the same problem?" Most management science texts offer two primary reasons. First, the **dual solution** provides valuable information concerning economic ramifications of the problem. Second, for certain problems the dual approach requires less computational effort than the primal because fewer iterations are required to reach the optimum solution.

If we are proficient in interpreting the primal solution, however, we can obtain all the information the dual model provides, thus the first argument is not really valid. Second, in general the number of iterations required, and thus the computation time, is proportional to the number of constraints. Consequently, although a dual model to a certain problem may require less computation time, spending 2 hours to formulate a dual model to save 10 seconds of computation certainly does not accomplish anything significant. Thus, our discussion of duality will be relatively brief, and our emphasis will be on formulating the dual model and explaining the relationship between the primal and the dual.

The Primal-Dual Relationship

The **primal solution** provides us with the optimum values for the basic variables and the objective function. We can interpret the final simplex tableau to identify the shadow prices discussed in Chapter 4. To begin our discussion, let us go back to the familiar Candex Camera Works problem.

Example 5.1   CANDEX CAMERA WORKS LTD.

$$\text{Maximize } Z = 40x_1 + 50x_2$$
$$\text{subject to}\quad 3x_1 + 3x_2 \leq 90$$
$$2x_1 + 4x_2 \leq 80$$
$$x_1, x_2 \geq 0$$

where
$$x_1 = \text{number of Candex A1 cameras produced}$$
$$x_2 = \text{number of Candex ZX cameras produced}$$

To formulate a dual model for this problem, the following chart of the primal-dual relationship can be used:

Model Feature	Primal	Dual
1. Objective function	Maximization Minimization	Minimization Maximization
2. Number of variables	Number of decision variables (x_j)	Number of model constraints
3. Number of constraints	Number of model constraints	Number of decision variables (u_i)
4. Objective function coefficients	Unit contribution rates in the objective function	Right-hand-side value
5. Resources	Right-hand-side value	Unit contribution rates in the objective function
6. Coefficient matrix	Technological coefficients	Transposed technological coefficients
7. Direction of constraints	$\leq, \geq$	$\geq, \leq$

Table 5.1   The Primal and Dual Candex Problem

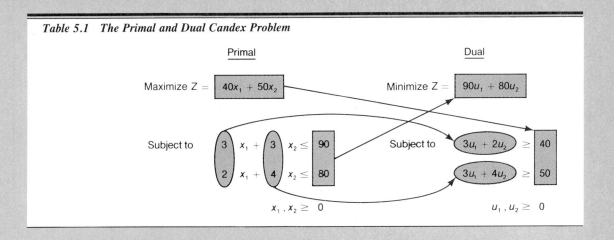

Now we can formulate the dual model for the Candex problem, as shown in Table 5.1. Let us follow the primal-dual relationship summarized above to make some sense out of the dual model formulation process.

1. Since the primal problem is for maximization, the dual problem becomes a minimization problem.

2. The primal problem has two decision variables; thus, the dual model will have two model constraints.

3. The primal model has two constraints; thus, the dual model will have two decision variables, u_1 and u_2. We can define these variables as follows:

u_1 = the marginal value of 1 hour of production time in assembly line 1

u_2 = the marginal value of 1 hour of production time in assembly line 2

4. The objective function coefficients in the primal model are \$40 and \$50 for x_1 and x_2, respectively. Thus, these two coefficients become the right-hand-side values (resources) of the dual constraints.

5. The amounts of resources available in the primal model are 90 hours in assembly line 1 and 80 hours in assembly line 2. These figures become the unit contribution rates in the objective function for u_1 and u_2.

6. The technological coefficients in the primal model are transposed for the dual model. In other words, the column-wise coefficients in the primal become the row-wise coefficients in the dual.

Interpretation of the Dual Model

In the dual model, decision variables u_1 and u_2 represent the marginal value of a resource unit (1 production hour) in the two assembly lines. Since a Candex A1 (x_1) requires 3 hours in assembly line 1 and 2 hours in assembly line 2, the total cost of resources committed to produce one Candex A1 will be $3u_1 + 2u_2$. The unit profit for

Figure 5.1   Optimum Solutions for the Primal and Dual Problems

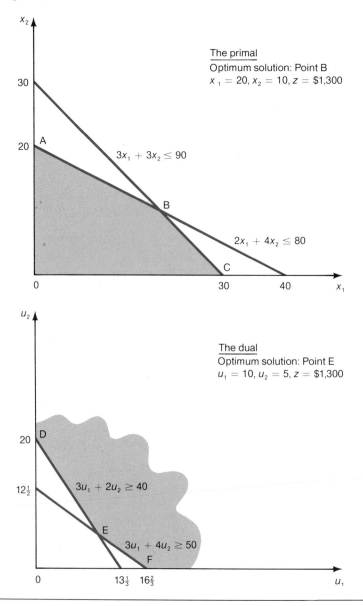

The primal
Optimum solution: Point B
$x_1 = 20, x_2 = 10, z = \$1{,}300$

$3x_1 + 3x_2 \le 90$

$2x_1 + 4x_2 \le 80$

The dual
Optimum solution: Point E
$u_1 = 10, u_2 = 5, z = \$1{,}300$

$3u_1 + 2u_2 \ge 40$

$3u_1 + 4u_2 \ge 50$

x_1 is \$40, as shown in the primal objective function. The condition necessary to commit $3u_1 + 2u_2$ worth of resources to produce a Candex A1 is that it produce at least \$40 profit. If the resources committed in producing a Candex A1 do not return at least \$40 profit, then the management of Candex should use the resources for other purposes. Thus, the first constraint of the dual model is expressed as

$$3u_1 + 2u_2 \ge 40$$

Table 5.2 The Optimum Solution of the Primal Problem

c_b	c_j / Basis	Solution	40 x_1	50 x_2	0 s_1	0 s_2
40	x_1	20	1	0	2/3	$-1/2$
50	x_2	10	0	1	$-1/3$	1/2
	z_j	1,300	40	50	10	5
	$c_j - z_j$		0	0	-10	-5

Dual solution $Z = 1,300$ $s_1 = 0$ $s_2 = 0$ $u_1 = 10$ $u_2 = 5$

Table 5.3 The Optimum Solution of the Dual Problem

c_b	c_j / Basis	Solution	90 u_1	80 u_2	0 s_1	0 s_2
90	u_1	10	1	0	$-2/3$	1/3
80	u_2	5	0	1	1/2	$-1/2$
	z_j	1,300	90	80	-20	-10
	$z_j - c_j$		0	0	-20	-10

Primal solution $Z = 1,300$ $s_1 = 0$ $s_2 = 0$ $x_1 = 20$ $x_2 = 10$

The second constraint of the dual model can be formulated in a similar manner. Production of a Candex ZX camera (x_2) requires 3 hours in assembly line 1 and 4 hours in assembly line 2. Therefore, the total worth of resources committed to the production of one Candex ZX will be $3u_1 + 4u_2$. The unit contribution rate of Candex ZX is $50. Hence, the second constraint becomes

$$3u_1 + 4u_2 \geq 50$$

In the primal model, the available production resources are 90 hours in assembly line 1 and 80 hours in assembly line 2. The objective function is to minimize the total cost involved in producing Candex A1 and Candex ZX cameras by utilizing these available resources. Thus, the objective function is

$$\text{Minimize } Z = 90u_1 + 80u_2$$

The optimum solutions for the primal and dual problems are presented graphically in Figure 5.1. The simplex solutions are also presented for the primal and dual problems in Tables 5.2 and 5.3, respectively. The shadow prices are shown as the $c_j - z_j$ values of the nonbasic-variable columns in the primal optimum solution. These shadow prices (without minus signs) correspond to the basic-variable solution values in the dual optimum solution. We can contrast the two optimum solutions and analyze their relationship as follows:

Primal Solution	Dual Solution
Basic variables $x_1 = 20$ $x_2 = 10$	Nonbasic variable $z_j - c_j$ (shadow price) s_1 column: -20 s_2 column: -10
Nonbasic variable $c_j - z_j$ (shadow price) s_1 column: -10 s_2 column: -5	Basic variables $u_1 = 10$ $u_2 = 5$
Slack column coefficients	Slack column coefficients ($-$transposed)

$$
\begin{array}{cc}
s_1 & s_2 \\
2/3 & -1/2 \\
-1/3 & 1/2
\end{array}
\qquad
\begin{array}{cc}
s_1 & s_2 \\
-2/3 & 1/3 \\
1/2 & -1/2
\end{array}
$$

The Dual of a Problem with Mixed Constraints

As we discussed in Chapter 4, frequently the primal problem may have mixed constraints. Although some constraints will be less-than-or-equal-to or greater-than-or-equal-to types, others will be equality constraints. In such a case the formulation of a dual model becomes somewhat complicated. As we discussed previously, the direction of the dual constraints must be exactly opposite to the direction of the primal constraints. This procedure is not easy to follow when the primal model has mixed constraints. Perhaps the easiest way to resolve this problem is to adjust the primal constraint so that the directions of all the constraints are the same. Let us consider the following primal problem.

Example 5.2

$$\text{Maximize } Z = 10x_1 + 8x_2 + 6x_3$$
$$\text{subject to} \quad 2x_1 + x_2 + 3x_3 \leq 90$$
$$x_2 + x_3 \geq 20$$
$$x_1 + x_2 + x_3 = 10$$
$$x_1, x_2, x_3 \geq 0$$

In order to formulate the dual model for the above problem, let us try to make all the primal constraints $\leq$ types. The first constraint is already a $\leq$ type. The second constraint is a $\geq$ type. The direction of this constraint can be changed as follows:

$$x_2 + x_3 \geq 20$$
$$-x_2 - x_3 \leq -20 \text{ (multiplying both sides by } -1)$$

The third constraint is an equality ($=$) constraint. Thus, the third dual variable is unrestricted in sign. In order to avoid this complexity, we can easily replace an equality constraint with two inequality constraints. For example, $x_1 + x_2 + x_3 = 10$ can be expressed by the following two inequalities:

$$x_1 + x_2 + x_3 \leq 10$$
$$x_1 + x_2 + x_3 \geq 10$$

If the model satisfies the two inequality constraints, the original equality constraint will be completely satisfied. Now we change the direction of the second constraint as follows:

$$x_1 + x_2 + x_3 \geq 10$$
$$-x_1 - x_2 - x_3 \leq -10$$

Now we can formulate the dual model for the problem as follows:

$$\text{Minimize } Z = 90u_1 - 20u_2 + 10u_3 - 10u_4$$
$$\text{subject to} \quad 2u_1 + u_3 - u_4 \geq 10$$
$$u_1 - u_2 + u_3 - u_4 \geq 8$$
$$3u_1 - u_2 + u_3 - u_4 \geq 6$$
$$u_1, u_2, u_3, u_4 \geq 0$$

In addition to facilitating the economic interpretation of the problem, the dual is often formulated for computational purposes. Let us consider a problem with 10 decision variables and 30 constraints. The number of constraints usually (not always) determines the maximum number of iterations required to solve the problem. The primal solution, therefore, can take the maximum of about 30 iterations. However, if we formulate a dual model for the problem, it will involve 30 decision variables and 10 constraints. Thus, the computation time required to solve it can be reduced significantly.

Another reason we study duality is that the mathematical property of the primal-dual relationship can be useful in developing advanced models of management science. For example, the *ellipsoid algorithm* of linear programming, proposed by the Russian mathematician L. G. Khachian, utilizes the primal-dual relationship in developing the algorithm. However, the mathematical property of the primal-dual relationship is obviously beyond the scope and purpose of this book.

SENSITIVITY ANALYSIS

The optimum solution we obtain for a given linear programming model represents a solution under a set of restrictive assumptions, such as the certainty of the decision environment. In real-world situations, the decision environment is dynamic rather than static. Thus, the decision maker is vitally interested in the "what if" questions concerning the effects of change in model parameters on the optimum solution.

Sensitivity analysis is a postoptimality analysis which attempts to evaluate the sensitivity of the optimum solution to discrete changes in the model parameters. If the optimum solution is very sensitive to changes in certain parameters, special efforts should be directed to accurately forecasting the future values of those parameters. However, if the optimum solution is not very sensitive to changes in a parameter, estimating the value of that parameter more accurately would waste time and effort.

In this section, we will first consider a simple sensitivity analysis based on the graphical method of linear programming. Then we will discuss sensitivity analysis based on the simplex method of linear programming.

Simple Graphical Sensitivity Analysis

Simple **graphical sensitivity analysis** examines the effects of changes in: (1) unit contribution rates of the objective function, (2) the right-hand-side values (e.g., amount of resources), and (3) technological coefficients (e.g., use of resources).

Example 5.3

By way of introducing sensitivity analysis, let us examine the following problem:

$$\text{Maximize } Z = 100x_1 + 80x_2$$
$$\text{subject to} \quad x_1 + x_2 \leq 100$$
$$2x_1 + x_2 \leq 160$$
$$x_1 + 2x_2 \leq 160$$
$$x_1, x_2 \geq 0$$

Figure 5.2 depicts this problem on a graph. The three constraints have slopes of -2, -1, and $-1/2$, respectively. The iso-profit function has a slope of $-5/4$. Thus, the optimum solution is at the intersecting point of constraints (1) and (2) in Figure 5.2. At point C, the solution is $x_1 = 60$, $x_2 = 40$, and $Z = 9,200$.

Figure 5.2   *Graphical Solution of the Sensitivity Analysis Problem*

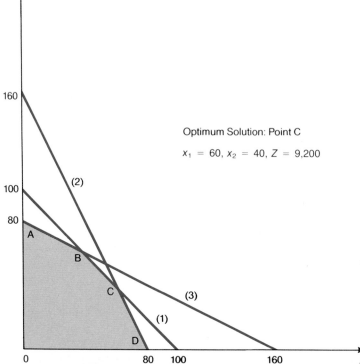

Does the optimum solution remain the same when there are changes in unit profits, technological coefficients, or resource levels? We are trying to answer these questions by sensitivity analysis.

Change in Contribution Rates   In many real-world problems, contribution rates (unit profits or unit costs of the decision variables in the objective function) change frequently. For example, on Wall Street the prices of most stocks change daily, in grocery stores the cost of food seems to go up every month, and hospital care costs vary considerably depending on the location and reputation of the hospital.

In our example, suppose the unit profit of x_1 changes from \$100 to \$120 while the unit profit of x_2 remains at \$80. Notice that the only change is in the unit contribution rate of x_1 in the objective function. In other words, the area of feasible solutions remains exactly the same, but the slope of the iso-profit function is changed from $-5/4$ to $-3/2$. If we denote the unit contribution rates of x_1 and x_2 as c_1 and c_2, respectively, the slope of the iso-profit function is simply $-(c_1/c_2)$. Thus, if we employ the slope comparison method, it is evident that point C ($x_1 = 60$, $x_2 = 40$) remains as the optimum solution. Of course, the total profit is increased from \$9,200 to \$10,400.

From our knowledge of the slope comparison approach, which we discussed in Chapter 3, clearly point C would remain the optimum solution as long as the iso-profit function has a slope between -1 and -2. If the iso-profit function has a slope of -2, any point on the line segment CD will be an optimum solution (a case of multiple optimum solutions). However, if the slope of the iso-profit function is -1, any point on the line segment BC can be an optimum solution (note that this is also a case of multiple optimum solutions). Consequently, we can summarize the combination of optimum solutions and the slopes of the iso-profit function as follows:

Slope of the Iso-profit Function	Optimum Solution
$-\dfrac{c_1}{c_2} > -\dfrac{1}{2}$	Point A
$-\dfrac{c_1}{c_2} = -\dfrac{1}{2}$	Line segment AB
$-1 < -\dfrac{c_1}{c_2} < -\dfrac{1}{2}$	Point B
$-\dfrac{c_1}{c_2} = -1$	Line segment BC
$-2 < -\dfrac{c_1}{c_2} < -1$	Point C
$-\dfrac{c_1}{c_2} = -2$	Line segment CD
$-\dfrac{c_1}{c_2} < -2$	Point D

Now we can ask a simple question. If the unit profit of x_2 remains constant at \$80 but the unit profit of x_1 fluctuates, what kind of profit range should there be for x_1 in order for us to select point B as the optimum solution? We can easily analyze the problem as follows:

$$c_1 = ?, \quad c_2 = 80$$

The requirement for point B being the optimum solution,

$$-1 \le -\frac{c_1}{c_2} \le -\frac{1}{2}$$

$$-1 \le -\frac{c_1}{80} \le -\frac{1}{2}$$

The upper limit of the range can be found by

$$-1 \le -\frac{c_1}{80}; \quad c_1 \le 80$$

The lower limit of the range can be found by

$$-\frac{c_1}{80} \le -\frac{1}{2}; \quad c_1 \ge 40$$

If the unit profit of x_2 remains constant at \$80, the required range of the unit profit of x_1 is $40 \le c_1 \le 80$ in order for point B ($x_1 = 40$, $x_2 = 60$) to be the optimum solution.

Change in the Right-hand-side Value   The right-hand-side value of a constraint usually represents the available resource. A change in the right-hand-side value of a constraint will produce changes in the intercepts of the constraint function and consequently may affect the area of feasible solutions. For example, in our original problem let us suppose the third constraint is changed from $x_1 + 2x_2 \le 160$ to $x_1 + 2x_2 \le 120$. The change in the intercepts and consequently in the area of feasible solutions is shown in Figure 5.3. Note that a change in the right-hand side does not affect the slope of the constraint. The new area of feasible solutions, as shown in Figure 5.3, is 0FGD. By applying the slope comparison method, it is clear that the optimum solution is point G ($x_1 = 66 \ 2/3$, $x_2 = 26 \ 2/3$), where $Z = \$8,800$. Once again, a change in the right-hand-side value does not always result in a change in the optimum solution.

In Figure 5.2 we identified the optimum solution as point C, where constraints 1 and 2 intersect. Thus, the critical (binding) constraints are 1 and 2. The noncritical (unbinding) constraint for the optimum solution is constraint 3. Thus, if we can increase our resources in any of the three constraints, an increase in the right-hand-side value should be made in either constraint 1 or constraint 2 but not in constraint 3.

To decide whether we should increase the right-hand-side value in constraint 1 or constraint 2, we can simply check which choice yields a greater increase in profit. For example, if we increase the right-hand-side value of constraint 1 by one unit of resource, a new optimum solution becomes:

$$x_1 + x_2 \le 101 \qquad \qquad \textit{Constraint 1}$$
$$2x_1 + x_2 \le 160 \qquad \qquad \textit{Constraint 2}$$

The optimum point is the intersecting point of constraints 1 and 2: $x_1 = 59$, $x_2 = 42$, where $Z = \$9,260$.

Figure 5.3   Effect of a Change in Resource in the Optimum Solution

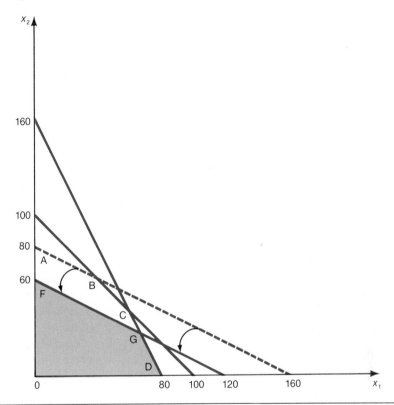

However, if we increase the right-hand-side value of constraint 2 by one unit of resource, a new optimum solution will be:

$$x_1 + x_2 \leq 100 \qquad \textit{Constraint 1}$$
$$2x_1 + x_2 \leq 161 \qquad \textit{Constraint 2}$$

The optimum point is still the intersecting point of constraints 1 and 2: $x_1 = 61$, $x_2 = 39$, where $Z = \$9,220$.

From the above analysis, it is obvious that we should increase our resource in constraint 1, rather than in constraint 2, to maximize the total profit. Now we can see clearly that an across-the-board increase (an increase of the resources in all three constraints by the same proportions), which we see so often in many organizations, is not always the best way to allocate resources.

We can also analyze the problem in the same manner when resources must be reduced from constraints. Any reduction in resources (the right-hand-side value) must come first in the noncritical constraints. In this problem, the right-hand-side should be reduced in constraint 3. Once again, we can see that an across-the-board decrease in resources really is inefficient.

From the above discussion, the net change in the total profit when we increase or decrease one unit of resource in each of the two binding constraints is as follows:

Constraint 1: $60 ($9260 − $9200 = $60)

Constraint 2: $20 ($9220 − $9200 = $20)

These two figures represent the marginal value of additional units of exhausted resources, or shadow prices.

Change in Technological Coefficients   Technological coefficients are those parameters that are associated with the decision variables in model constraints. For example, in our problem the second constraint is $2x_1 + x_2 \leq 160$. Thus, the technological coefficients for x_1 and x_2 in this constraint are 2 and 1, respectively. Changes in technological coefficients occur frequently as the result of technological innovations (e.g., new types of machines require shorter production time in assembly line 1), the learning curve or a higher employee morale (e.g., employees become more efficient on the job), or new product specifications or government regulations. Such changes may have profound effects on the problem solution.

Changes in technological coefficients have no effect on the objective function of the problem. Thus, the iso-profit (or iso-cost) function will not be altered. Changes in technological coefficients affect the constraints and thereby usually bring changes in the area of feasible solutions. For example, suppose the second constraint is changed from $2x_1 + x_2 \leq 160$ to $2x_1 + 2/3\, x_2 \leq 160$. The coefficient of x_2 is changed from 1 to 2/3 in the constraint. This change will effect changes in the slope of the constraint and the x_2 intercept, as shown in Figure 5.4. The new area of feasible solutions is now 0ABED. Thus, the new optimum solution will be point E ($x_1 = 70$, $x_2 = 30$), where $Z = \$9,400$.

A change in a technological coefficient does not always result in a change in the optimum solution. For example, if point B were the previous optimum solution, the change in the technological coefficient of x_2 in the second constraint discussed above (i.e., $2x_1 + x_2 \leq 160$ is changed to $2x_1 + 2/3\, x_2 \leq 160$) would have no effect on the optimum solution. In this case, point B remains the optimum solution.

Simplex-Based Sensitivity Analysis

With the availability of many efficient interactive computer programs for linear programming, sensitivity analysis is often performed by solving the problem again with changes in the model parameters. This process can be simplified by establishing a data file in which changes can be easily made. However, if we need to perform sensitivity analysis of many small changes in the parameters, the interactive approach may be both costly and time consuming. Thus, the **simplex-based sensitivity analysis** can be a very useful tool.

We will limit our discussion of sensitivity analysis to the following: (1) change in the unit contribution rates (c_j); (2) change in available resources (b_i); (3) change in the technological coefficients (a_{ij}); (4) addition of a new constraint; and (5) addition of a new variable.

Figure 5.4   Effect of a Change in the Technological Coefficient on the Optimum Solution

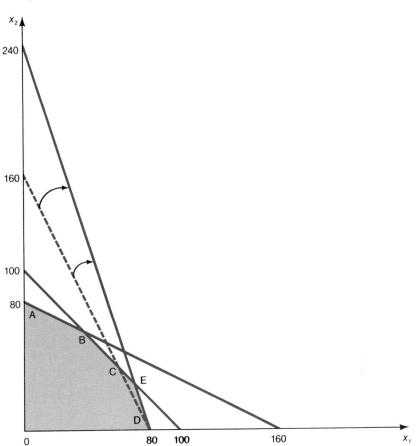

Example 5.4

$$\text{Maximize } Z = 6x_1 + 7x_2 + 9x_3$$
$$\text{subject to} \quad 2x_1 + 3x_2 + 2x_3 \leq 240$$
$$3x_1 + 2x_2 + 4x_3 \leq 200$$
$$x_1 + x_2 + x_3 \leq 80$$
$$x_1, x_2, x_3 \geq 0$$

The three constraints in the above model can be easily converted into equalities by adding appropriate slack variables as follows:

$$2x_1 + 3x_2 + 2x_3 + s_1 = 240$$
$$3x_1 + 2x_2 + 4x_3 + s_2 = 200$$
$$x_1 + x_2 + x_3 + s_3 = 80$$

Table 5.4　The Final Simplex Tableau for Example 5.4

c_b	Basis	Solution	6 x_1	7 x_2	9 x_3	0 s_1	0 s_2	0 s_3
0	s_1	20	$-1/2$	0	0	1	1/2	-4
9	x_3	20	1/2	0	1	0	1/2	-1
7	x_2	60	1/2	1	0	0	$-1/2$	2
	z_j	600	8	7	9	0	1	5
	$c_j - z_j$		-2	0	0	0	-1	-5

The optimum simplex solution tableau is presented in Table 5.4. The optimum solution is $x_2 = 60$, $x_3 = 20$, $s_1 = 20$, and $Z = 600$. Our discussion of sensitivity analysis will use the solution tableau presented in Table 5.4.

Change in the Unit Contribution Rates　One thing we should remember about a change in a unit contribution rate (c_j) is that it does not affect the area of feasible solutions. Thus, the only thing we have to check is the optimality — that is, whether all nonbasic variables have nonpositive $c_j - z_j$ values. We will discuss the change of a unit contribution rate first for a nonbasic variable and then for a basic variable.

Change in the Contribution Rate of a Nonbasic Variable　The determination as to whether a decision variable appears in the optimum solution, and if so in what quantity, is based on two things: (1) the contribution rate of the decision variable in relation to the contribution rates of the other variables and (2) the use of resources to produce a unit of the product in relation to the resource uses of the other products.

Among the decision variables in our example, x_1 is the only one not in the solution basis. In other words, x_1 is a nonbasic variable. The fact that x_1 is a nonbasic variable indicates that its unit contribution rate, $c_1 = \$6$, is not sufficient, in relation to its relative resource requirements, to warrant its production. Consequently, if c_1 decreases for some reason, x_1 would remain a nonbasic variable. However, if c_1 increases by a substantial amount, x_1 may become attractive enough to warrant its introduction into the solution base.

The only thing we have to check, then, is whether the *positive* change in the contribution rate of x_1 will be sufficient to make the $c_j - z_j$ value positive in the column. Since the current $c_j - z_j$ value in the x_1 column is -2, the positive change in the contribution rate of x_1 should be at least 2 before x_1 can become a basic variable.

If we express the change in the contribution rate of x_1 as Δc_1, the following statements can be made:

$\Delta c_1 > -(c_1 - z_1)$	A new solution results in x_1 as a basic variable.
$\Delta c_1 = -(c_1 - z_1)$	The previous optimum solution is still optimum but an alternate optimum solution exists.
$\Delta c_1 < -(c_1 - z_1)$	The previous optimum solution is still optimum.

Change in the Contribution Rate of a Basic Variable   When the contribution rate of a basic variable is changed, there are three possible consequences: (1) the change in the contribution rate is not sufficient to change the optimum solution; (2) the change in the contribution rate is sufficient to warrant a new optimum solution; or (3) the change in the contribution rate does not affect the total profit (or cost), but there is an alternate optimum solution (a case of multiple optimum solutions).

Since the variable under consideration is a basic variable, a change in its contribution rate will affect the z_j (and thus the $c_j - z_j$) values in the nonbasic-variable columns. In a basic-variable row, there are only nonzero coefficients in its own column and in the nonbasic-variable columns. For example, in Table 5.4 we can easily see that in the x_2 row there are nonzero coefficients of 1 in the x_2 column itself and in the nonbasic-variable columns x_1, s_2 and s_3. Consequently, when the unit contribution rate of a basic variable changes, the results are as shown below:

Change in c_j	The Nonbasic-Variable Column	
	With Positive Coefficient	With Negative Coefficient
Increase $(+\Delta)$	Becomes less attractive	Becomes more attractive
Decrease $(-\Delta)$	Becomes more attractive	Becomes less attractive

If a nonbasic variable becomes less attractive, it remains a nonbasic variable. In other words, the previous optimum solution remains optimum. Therefore, we are primarily concerned with the circled conditions in the above summary: If the contribution rate *increases*, we want to examine the nonbasic-variable columns where there are *negative* coefficients in the basic-variable row; if the contribution rate *decreases*, we want to analyze the nonbasic-variable columns where there are *positive* coefficients in the basic-variable row.

Now we are ready to examine a change in the unit contribution rate of a basic variable in our example. Let us suppose that the contribution rate of x_2 (c_2) is increased by a certain amount Δ. We can substitute $7 + \Delta$ for the previous contribution rate c_2 ($\$7.00$), as shown in Table 5.5. Notice that this change will affect the z_j (and consequently the $c_j - z_j$) values of the three nonbasic-variable columns x_1, s_2, and s_3. Since c_2 is being increased, the x_1 and s_3 columns become less attractive because of their

Table 5.5   Change in the Contribution Rate of x_2

c_b \ c_j	Basis	Solution	6 x_1	$7+\Delta$ x_2	9 x_3	0 s_1	0 s_2	0 s_3
0	s_1	20	$-1/2$	0	0	1	1/2	-4
9	x_3	20	1/2	0	1	0	1/2	-1
$7+\Delta$	x_2	60	1/2	1	0	0	$-1/2$	2
	z_j	600	$8+\Delta/2$	$7+\Delta$	9	0	$1-\Delta/2$	$5+2\Delta$
	$c_j - z_j$		$-2-\Delta/2$	0	0	0	$-1+\Delta/2$	$-5-2\Delta$

positive coefficients of 1/2 and 2 in the x_2 row. Thus, we can concentrate our attention on the s_2 column.

As soon as the $c_j - z_j$ value of the s_2 column becomes 0 or positive as c_2 increases, we can have a new optimum solution. Then, we can analyze as follows the value of Δ that will make the $c_j - z_j$ value in the s_2 column positive:

s_2 column:
$$c_j - z_j \geq 0$$
$$-1 + \Delta/2 \geq 0$$
$$\Delta/2 \geq 1$$
$$\Delta \geq 2$$

Clearly, if c_2 increases by \$2, the $c_j - z_j$ value in the s_2 column becomes 0—a case of multiple optimum solutions. If the increase of c_2 is over \$2, s_2 becomes a basic variable, and we have a new solution. Thus, the upper limit of change in c_2 becomes

$$\text{Upper limit} = \text{current contribution rate} + \text{required change} = \$7 + \$2$$
$$\text{Upper limit } (c_2) = \$9$$

If c_2 decreases, we can substitute $7 + \Delta$ for 7 and evaluate the nonbasic-variable columns that have positive coefficients in the x_2 row. There are two positive coefficients in the x_2 row: 1/2 in the x_1 column and 2 in the s_3 column (other than 1 in its own column, x_2). We can perform our analysis as follows:

x_1 column:
$$c_j - z_j \geq 0$$
$$-2 - \Delta/2 \geq 0$$
$$\Delta/2 \leq -2$$
$$\Delta \leq -4$$

s_3 column:
$$c_j - z_j \geq 0$$
$$-5 - 2\Delta \geq 0$$
$$-2\Delta \geq 5$$
$$\Delta \leq -2.5$$

Since the required change is the maximum of $\Delta \leq -4$ or $\Delta \leq -2.5$, if c_2 is decreased by \$2.50, the $c_j - z_j$ value of the x_1 column will become 0, and a new optimum solution could result. Thus, the lower limit of change in c_2 is

$$\text{Lower limit} = \text{current contribution rate} + \text{required change} = \$7 - \$2.50$$
$$\text{Lower limit } (c_2) = \$4.50$$

The range of c_2 is \$4.50 (lower limit) to \$9.00 (upper limit). If the contribution rate of x_2 is within this range, the current optimum solution remains optimum. If c_2 increases above \$9, a new optimum solution will result, since the $c_j - z_j$ value of the s_2 column becomes positive. However, if the contribution rate of x_2 is exactly equal to either \$4.50 or \$9, there will be an alternate optimum solution.

A similar analysis can be made for the contribution rate of x_3. If there exists no negative coefficient in a basic decision variable row, there will be no upper limit. However, if the row has no positive coefficient, there is no lower limit.

To simplify the process, use the following simple procedure for deriving the upper or lower limits of contribution rates:

$$\text{Lower limit:} \quad c_{kl} = \max \left(c_k + \frac{c_j - z_j}{a_{kj}} \right) \text{ for } a_{kj} > 0$$

$$\text{Upper limit:} \quad c_{ku} = \min \left(c_k + \frac{c_j - z_j}{a_{kj}} \right) \text{ for } a_{kj} < 0$$

where

c_k = contribution rate of the kth basic variable in the solution basis

$c_j - z_j$ = the $c_j - z_j$ value of the jth variable that is nonbasic

a_{kj} = the coefficient in the kth basic-variable row and jth variable column that is nonbasic

In our example, we can again find the range of the contribution rate of x_2 as follows:

$$c_{2l} = \max \left(c_2 + \frac{c_{x1} - z_{x1}}{a_{3,x1}}; \ c_2 + \frac{c_{s3} - z_{s3}}{a_{3,s3}} \right) \quad \text{(There are two positive}$$

coefficients in the x_2 row: one in the x_1 column and the other in the s_3 column.)

$$= \max \left(7.00 + \frac{-2}{1/2}; \ 7.00 + \frac{-5}{2} \right)$$

$$= \max (7.00 - 4.00; \ 7.00 - 2.50)$$

$$= \max (3.00; \ 4.50)$$

$$= 4.50$$

$$c_{2u} = \min \left(c_2 + \frac{c_{s2} - z_{s2}}{a_{3,s2}} \right) \quad \text{(There is only one negative coefficient in the } x_2$$

row—in the s_2 column.)

$$= \left(7.00 + \frac{-1}{-1/2} \right)$$

$$= 7.00 + 2.00$$

$$= 9.00$$

We can summarize our sensitivity analysis of changes in the unit contribution rates of decision variables as follows:

Decision Variable	Contribution Rate Ranging		
	Lower Limit	Current Rate	Upper Limit
x_1	No limit	$6.00	$ 8.00
x_2	$4.50	7.00	9.00
x_3	7.00	9.00	14.00

Changes in the Available Resources In this section we will discuss the effect of a change in the right-hand-side value *(b_i)* of a constraint on the optimum solution. A change in b_i does not affect $c_j - z_j$. You will remember from our discussion of graphical sensitivity analysis that a change in b_i affects only the intercepts of the constraint. Thus, the only thing we have to check is whether the new solution values of the basic variables are still nonnegative after a change in b_i. If they are nonnegative, the previous optimum solution mix is still optimum. If there is a negative solution value for a basic variable, the previous optimum solution is infeasible. Thus, we are not interested in checking the optimality but rather the *feasibility*.

We can develop a simple approach for determining a b_i range within which the previous optimum solution mix of basic variables would remain in the solution basis. For example, let us assume that the second constraint of the model has been changed from $3x_1 + 2x_2 + 4x_3 + s_2 = 200$ to $3x_1 + 2x_2 + 4x_3 + s_2 = 200 + \Delta$. In other words, b_2 has been increased by Δ units. If we substitute $b_2 = 200 + \Delta$ for the original b_2 and solve the problem, the simplex solution results in the final simplex tableau shown in Table 5.6.

Notice that in Table 5.6, none of the coefficients in the model change, except for the solution values for the s_1, x_2, and x_3 rows. The coefficients of Δ in the solution column correspond to the coefficients in the s_2 column, as shown below:

Basis	Δ Coefficient in Solution Column	Coefficient in s_2 Column
s_1	$1/2(\Delta)$	$1/2$
x_3	$1/2(\Delta)$	$1/2$
x_2	$-1/2(\Delta)$	$-1/2$

The above result is no accident. The slack variable s_2 appears only in the second constraint, where b_2 has been changed. Therefore, the coefficients in the s_2 column indicate what multiples of b_2 have been added to the solution values of the other rows.

Table 5.6   *The Final Simplex Tableau ($b_2 = 200 + \Delta$)*

	c_j	Basis	Solution	6 x_1	7 x_2	9 x_3	0 s_1	0 s_2	0 s_3
c_b									
0		s_1	$20 + \Delta/2$	$-1/2$	0	0	1	$1/2$	-4
9		x_3	$20 + \Delta/2$	$1/2$	0	1	0	$1/2$	-1
7		x_2	$60 - \Delta/2$	$1/2$	1	0	0	$-1/2$	2
		z_j	$600 + \Delta$	8	7	9	0	1	5
		$c_j - z_j$		-2	0	0	0	-1	-5

Now let us refer to Table 5.6. As long as a change in b_2 expressed by Δ does not result in a negative solution value in the basis, the previous solution mix remains the optimum mix. Thus, we can easily determine the range of Δ as follows:

$$s_1 \text{ row:} \quad 20 + \Delta/2 \geq \quad 0$$
$$\Delta/2 \geq -20$$
$$\Delta \geq -40$$

$$x_3 \text{ row:} \quad 20 + \Delta/2 \geq \quad 0$$
$$\Delta/2 \geq -20$$
$$\Delta \geq -40$$

$$x_2 \text{ row:} \quad 60 - \Delta/2 \geq \quad 0$$
$$-\Delta/2 \geq -60$$
$$\Delta \leq \quad 120$$

We can arrange the value of Δ as follows:

$$-40 \leq \Delta \leq 120$$

Since the current value of $b_2 = 200$, the range of b_2 is

$$200 - 40 \leq b_2 \leq 200 + 120$$
$$160 \leq b_2 \leq 320$$

Within the above range of b_2, the solution mix of basic variables remains in the optimum solution. However, the solution values of the basic variables do not remain the same. For example, suppose that b_2 is changed from 200 to 220. Then the optimum solution will be as follows:

Previous Optimum Solution		New Optimum Solution	
Basis	**Solution**	**Basis**	**Solution**
s_1	20	s_1	$20 + 1/2(20) = 30$
x_3	20	x_3	$20 + 1/2(20) = 30$
x_2	60	x_2	$60 - 1/2(20) = 50$
	$Z = \$600$		$Z = \$620$

From our discussion thus far it is easy to ascertain that when a b_i increases, the solution value of the basic-variable row that has a negative coefficient in the corresponding slack-variable column decreases. For example, when b_2 was increased from 200 to 220, as illustrated above, the solution values for the x_2 row decreased because of their negative coefficients in the s_2 column. Thus, we should be primarily concerned with the circled conditions in the following summary box:

	Basic-variable Solution Values	
Change in b_i	**Positive Slack Coefficients**	**Negative Slack Coefficients**
Increase $(+\Delta)$	Increase	(Decrease)
Decrease $(-\Delta)$	(Decrease)	Increase

To simplify the process of determining the right-hand-side value ranging, you are provided with the following simple procedure. Do not try to memorize the formulas, but simply learn to use them. The actual sensitivity analysis is usually performed by computer.

$$\text{Lower limit:} \quad b_{il} = \max \left(b_i - \frac{B_k}{a_{ki}^*} \right) \text{ for } a_{ki}^* > 0$$

$$\text{Upper limit:} \quad b_{iu} = \min \left(b_i - \frac{B_k}{a_{ki}^*} \right) \text{ for } a_{ki}^* < 0$$

where
b_i = the original right-hand-side value of the ith constraint
B_k = the solution value of the kth basic variable
a_{ki}^* = the coefficient in the kth row and ith slack variable column where b_i has been changed

Now let us go back to our example. The optimum solution was presented in Table 5.4. The interpretation of the shadow price (the $c_j - z_j$ value of the nonbasic slack variable) is that the objective function will be changed by the amount shown by the shadow price within the right-hand-side range for that particular constraint. For example, the interpretation of the shadow price in the s_2 column is that one additional unit in b_2 would be worth \$1. Thus, if we relax this constraint by one unit, our total profit would be increased by \$1. However, if we tighten the constraint by reducing b_2 by one unit, our profit would be decreased by \$1. This shadow price is valid within the lower and upper limits of b_2. The range can be calculated as

$$b_{2l} = \max \left(b_2 - \frac{B_{s1}}{a_{s1,\ s2}};\ b_2 - \frac{B_{x3}}{a_{x3,\ s2}} \right) \quad \text{(There are two positive}$$

coefficients in the s_2 column.)

$$= \max \left(200 - \frac{20}{1/2};\ 200 - \frac{20}{1/2} \right)$$

$$= \max (160;\ 160) = 160$$

$$b_{2u} = \min \left(b_2 - \frac{B_{x2}}{a_{x2,\ s2}} \right) \text{(There is only one negative coefficient}$$

in the s_2 column—in the x_2 row).

$$= \left(200 - \frac{60}{-1/2} \right)$$

$$= (200 + 120)$$

$$= 320$$

The range of b_2 is 160 (lower limit) to 320 (upper limit). If b_2 is within this range, the current optimum solution mix remains the same. Within this range, therefore, the shadow price of \$1 for the x_2 column remains valid. By using the same procedure, we can determine the right-hand-side value ranging for all constraints as follows:

Constraint Number	Right-hand-side Ranging		
	Lower Limit	Current Value	Upper Limit
1	220	240	No limit
2	160	200	320
3	50	80	85

Changes in the Technological Coefficients   The decision maker is interested in the impact of changes in technological coefficients on the optimum solution. The effect of a change in an a_{ij} depends on whether the coefficient is for a basic decision variable or a nonbasic decision variable.

Change in an a_{ij} of a Nonbasic Decision Variable   When the a_{ij} coefficient of a nonbasic decision variable is changed, it does not affect the feasibility of the previous optimum solution. In other words, if we repeat the simplex solution with the changed a_{ij} coefficient of a nonbasic decision variable, the only possible changes would be in the coefficients of that nonbasic-variable column. Thus, the same solution must be obtained, and it must be feasible. Since the variable is nonbasic ($x_j = 0$ in the final solution), the only thing we have to check is whether the new coefficients in this variable column have made the $c_j - z_j$ value positive.

For example, suppose that coefficient a_{21} is changed from 3 to $3 + \Delta$. Then, the constraint becomes $(3 + \Delta)x_1 + 2x_2 + 4x_3 + s_2 = 200$. Table 5.7 presents the final simplex tableau with $a_{21} = 3 + \Delta$ substituted in the model. Notice that coefficients are changes in the x_1 column.

For example, we can contrast the old and new coefficients as follows:

Row	Old Coefficient in x_1 Column	Coefficient in s_2 Column	New Coefficient in x_1 Column
s_1	$-1/2$	$1/2$	$-1/2 + (1/2)\Delta$
x_3	$1/2$	$1/2$	$1/2 + (1/2)\Delta$
x_2	$1/2$	$-1/2$	$1/2 - (1/2)\Delta$

Table 5.7   The Final Simplex Tableau ($a_{21} = 3 + \Delta$)

c_b	c_j Basis	Solution	6 x_1	7 x_2	9 x_3	0 s_1	0 s_2	0 s_3
0	s_1	20	$-1/2 + (1/2)\Delta$	0	0	1	1/2	-4
9	x_3	20	$1/2 + (1/2)\Delta$	0	1	0	1/2	-1
7	x_2	60	$1/2 - (1/2)\Delta$	1	0	0	$-1/2$	2
	z_j	600	$8 + \Delta$	7	9	0	1	5
	$c_j - z_j$		$-2 - \Delta$	0	0	0	-1	-5

It should be apparent that the Δ coefficients in the x_1 column correspond exactly to the coefficients in the s_2 column. As long as the $c_j - z_j$ value of the x_1 column remains nonpositive, the previous optimum solution remains optimum. The range of a_{21}, over which the previous optimum solution remains optimum, can be determined by analyzing the optimality condition as follows:

$$c_j - z_j \leq 0$$
$$-2 - \Delta \leq 0$$
$$\Delta \geq -2$$

Since $a_{21} = 3 + \Delta$,

$$\Delta = a_{21} - 3$$

Thus

$$a_{21} - 3 \geq -2$$
$$a_{21} \geq 1$$

If a_{21} is less than 1, the $c_j - z_j$ value becomes positive in the x_1 column, and thus x_1 is the entering variable. One more iteration would yield a new optimum solution. As long as $a_{21} \geq 1$, the previous solution is still optimum.

Change in an a_{ij} ***of a Basic Decision Variable***   Analyzing the impact of a change in an a_{ij} is more complex when the variable involved is a basic variable. Since $x_j > 0$ in the final solution because it is a basic variable, a change in an a_{ij} will have some effect on the solution values of other basic variables. Therefore, a new solution must be checked for its feasibility as well as its optimality.

First, we must calculate the new coefficients of x_j in the simplex tableau by the same procedure we have already described when a change in an a_{ij} occurs for a nonbasic variable. Since x_j is a basic variable, all coefficients in the x_j column should be 0 except for a coefficient of 1 in its own basic-variable row. This condition must be restored algebraically to test the feasibility and optimality of the revised solution.

To illustrate the procedure, let us go back to our problem. Suppose the second constraint is changed from the original $3x_1 + 2x_2 + 4x_3 + s_2 = 200$ to $3x_1 + 2x_2 + 3x_3 + s_2 = 200$ (coefficient a_{23} is changed from 4 to 3). We can easily determine the required change as follows:

Row	Old Coefficient in x_3 Column	Coefficient in s_2 Column	New Coefficient in x_3 Column	
s_1	0	1/2	$0 + (1/2)(-1)$	$= -1/2$
x_3	1	1/2	$1 + (1/2)(-1)$	$= 1/2$
x_2	0	$-1/2$	$0 + (-1/2)(-1)$	$= 1/2$

Since the change in a_{23} is -1, $\Delta = -1$. Thus, the coefficients in the s_2 column are multiplied by -1. That is how, in Table 5.8, we determine $-1/2$ and $1/2$ in the s_1 and x_2 rows, respectively. To restore the condition of the basic-variable column coefficients, in Table 5.8 we must pick the x_3 column as the pivot column and the x_3 row as the pivot row.

A new optimum solution is derived in Table 5.9. This solution also restored the condition of the basic-variable column coefficients in the x_3 column. If a new solution

Table 5.8   The Simplex Tableau ($a_{23} = 3$)

c_b	Basis	Solution	6 x_1	7 x_2	9 x_3	0 s_1	0 s_2	0 s_3
0	s_1	20	$-1/2$	0	$-1/2$	1	1/2	-4
9	x_3	20	1/2	0	(1/2)	0	1/2	-1
7	x_2	60	1/2	1	1/2	0	$-1/2$	2
	z_j	600	8	7	8	0	1	5
	$c_j - z_j$		-2	0	1	0	-1	-5

Table 5.9   New Optimum Solution ($a_{23} = 3$)

c_b	Basis	Solution	6 x_1	7 x_2	9 x_3	0 s_1	0 s_2	0 s_3
0	s_1	40	0	0	0	1	1	-5
9	x_3	40	1	0	1	0	1	-2
7	x_2	40	0	1	0	0	-1	3
	z_j	640	9	7	9	0	2	3
	$c_j - z_j$		-3	0	0	0	-2	-3

derived has a negative solution value, it is an infeasible solution. Whenever we encounter a negative solution value, we pick this as the pivot row first. Then, we pick the pivot column by dividing only negative $c_j - z_j$ values by their corresponding negative coefficients in the row. The column with the minimum positive value is the pivot column.

A similar analysis can be made for the remaining basic decision variable x_2. Since we have to check both the feasibility and the optimality of the solution when the a_{ij} of a basic variable changes, we cannot simply determine the coefficient ranging. However, we can determine the coefficient ranging for the solution feasibility. Such a solution may not be optimum, however, and it may require additional iterations to determine the optimum solution.

Addition of a New Constraint   After the optimum solution has been obtained for a linear programming problem, it may become necessary to add a new constraint. Such a situation may result from new government regulation, a new company policy, a new organizational structure, a change in the economic situation, or an error in overlooking a resource constraint in the model formulation process. If the decision maker decides to add a new constraint after the final solution has been reached, the solution mix may be changed.

The addition of a new constraint does not affect the objective function. If the new constraint is binding, it will further reduce the area of feasible solutions, and thus the total profit, z_j, will decrease. However, if the new constraint is not binding (i.e., if it is redundant), the previous optimum solution is still feasible and optimum. Always remember that a new constraint can only further reduce the solution space, but it can never expand the feasibility area.

The only thing we have to check, when we add a new constraint, is whether the previous optimum solution is still feasible: Examine whether the solution values of the basic variables satisfy the new constraint. If the new constraint is not satisfied, the previous optimum solution is now an infeasible solution. Let us consider the following two cases.

A New Constraint, $x_2 \leq 70$ Suppose that we decide to add a new constraint, $x_2 \leq 70$, to the model. This constraint simply says that we should restrict production of x_2 to 70 units. The previous optimum solution indicates that currently we are scheduled to produce 60 units of x_2. We can easily check the previous optimum solution and see that it satisfies the new constraint. Thus, the previous solution is still optimum.

A New Constraint, $x_2 \leq 50$ Let us suppose that we decide to add a new constraint, $x_2 \leq 50$. The current optimum solution shows $x_2 = 60$. Consequently, the new constraint is not satisfied, and the current solution is infeasible.

First, we develop a new simplex equality, $x_2 + s_4 = 50$. Then, we introduce s_4 into the solution basis and list the appropriate coefficients in the simplex tableau, as shown in Table 5.10. In the x_2 column, since x_2 is a basic variable, the only nonzero coefficient must be the 1 in the x_2 row. To restore this condition, we select the x_2 column as the pivot column and the x_2 row as the pivot row.

The new solution, after the iteration, is shown in Table 5.11. This solution is clearly infeasible because the solution value of s_4 is negative (-10). Now, we select the s_4 row as the pivot row and the s_3 column as the pivot column. The new optimum solution is obtained in Table 5.12.

Table 5.10 *Addition of a New Constraint* ($x_2 \leq 50$)

c_b	Basis	Solution	6 x_1	7 x_2	9 x_3	0 s_1	0 s_2	0 s_3	0 s_4
0	s_1	20	$-1/2$	0	0	1	1/2	-4	0
9	x_3	20	1/2	0	1	0	1/2	-1	0
7	x_2	60	1/2	①	0	0	$-1/2$	2	0
0	s_4	50	0	1	0	0	0	0	1
	z_j	600	8	7	9	0	1	5	0
	$c_j - z_j$		-2	0	0	0	-1	-5	0

Table 5.11   An Infeasible New Solution

c_b	c_j Basis	Solution	6 x_1	7 x_2	9 x_3	0 s_1	0 s_2	0 s_3	0 s_4
0	s_1	20	$-1/2$	0	0	1	1/2	-4	0
9	x_3	20	1/2	0	1	0	1/2	-1	0
7	x_2	60	1/2	1	0	0	$-1/2$	2	0
0	s_4	-10	$-1/2$	0	0	0	1/2	$\left(-2\right)$	1
	z_j	600	8	7	9	0	1	5	0
	$c_j - z_j$		-2	0	0	0	-1	-5	0

Table 5.12   The New Optimum Solution

c_b	c_j Basis	Solution	6 x_1	7 x_2	9 x_3	0 s_1	0 s_2	0 s_3	0 s_4
0	s_1	40	1/2	0	0	1	$-1/2$	0	-2
9	x_3	25	3/4	0	1	0	1/4	0	$-1/2$
7	x_2	50	0	1	0	0	0	0	1
0	s_3	5	1/4	0	0	0	$-1/4$	1	$-1/2$
	z_j	575	27/4	7	9	0	9/4	0	5/2
	$c_j - z_j$		$-3/4$	0	0	0	$-9/4$	0	$-5/2$

Addition of a New Variable   After we solve a linear programming problem, we may discover, for example, that we omitted an important decision variable in the model or that the firm decided to introduce a new product that uses the same basic production resources. Including an additional variable in the model requires an appropriate c_j coefficient in the objective function and appropriate a_{ij} coefficients in the constraints.

The important question is whether the new variable is attractive enough to be brought into the solution basis. This question can be answered simply by analyzing the new product's resource requirements and its contribution rate. For example, let us suppose that a new variable, x_4 is to be added. Let us assume that the new variable x_4 requires 3 units of resource in constraint 1, 2 units of resource in constraint 3, and has a unit profit of $6.

From Table 5.4, the shadow price for resource 1 (in the s_1 column) is $0; resource 3's shadow price (s_3 column) is $5. Thus, the cost of producing one unit of x_4 is found by multiplying each resource requirement by its respective shadow price and adding:

$$Z(x_4) = (3 \times 0) + (2 \times 5) = \$10$$

With a c_j of \$6 for x_4, the net contribution becomes

$$c_j - z_j = 6 - 10 = -4$$

Thus, x_4 will not be brought into the solution basis, and the previous solution is still optimum.

If the $c_j - z_j$ value for the new variable is positive, we can solve the problem again with the new model. Most computer programs have the interactive option to change the model input. Thus, a new solution can be derived quite easily with the addition of a new decision variable.

COMPUTER SOLUTIONS IN LINEAR PROGRAMMING

The graphical method presented in Chapter 3 and the simplex method discussed in Chapter 4 are effective in solving linear programming problems manually, but in this day and age we certainly do not solve them by hand. As a matter of fact, a computer-based solution is a prerequisite for any meaningful application of linear programming.

The popularity and wide application of linear programming are primarily due to the standardized solution procedure of electronic computers. Today, literally hundreds of user-friendly linear programming programs are available for mainframes, minicomputers, and microcomputers. We have witnessed an explosion of microcomputer-based applications of linear programming. The user-friendly, menu-driven interactive programs on the microcomputer have become so widely available that even the simplest linear programming problem is solved by computer.

The standardized computer solution programs are often referred to as *linear programming codes* or *canned linear programming software packages*. Almost every major computer manufacturer has developed a linear programming software for its computer system. Mainframe computer software is available from IBM, UNIVAC, RCA, Control Data, and other companies. Also, many microcomputer programs have recently become very popular, such as *LINDO, Micro Manager,* and *STORM.* In this section we will present the use of *Micro Manager.*

Micro Manager is a comprehensive software package developed by S. M. Lee and J. P. Shim for IBM PCs and compatible microcomputers. It contains 23 programs for various management science techniques, including linear programming. This program is a completely user-friendly package based on a menu-driven and query-driven system.

Micro Manager leads you step by step through the program by providing an "information" option which demonstrates the solution procedure of an example problem. Also, you have the option to input through either an interactive query-driven mode or a batch data file mode.

We will solve the Candex Camera problem of Casette 4.1 using *Micro Manager.* Figure 5.5 presents the input and output of the model. The program provides three output options: (1) the optimum solution only; (2) the final simplex tableau and solution; and (3) all simplex tableaux and the final solution. The figure presents the second option. Clearly this is the same solution derived in Casette 4.1.

Figure 5.5   Micro Manager *Data Input and Solution Printout*

```
PROGRAM: Linear Programming I

***** INPUT DATA ENTERED *****
Max  Z =  40 x 1 + 50 x 2

Subject to:

C 1   3 x 1 + 3 x 2 <=  90
C 2   2 x 1 + 4 x 2 <=  80

*****   PROGRAM OUTPUT   *****
Simplex tableau: Iteration 2
```

\Cj			40.00	50.00	0.00	0.00
Cb	Basis	Bi	x 1	x 2	s 1	s 2
40.00	x 1	20.00	1.00	0.00	0.67	-0.50
50.00	x 2	10.00	0.00	1.00	-0.33	0.50
	Zj	1300.00	40.00	50.00	10.00	5.00
	Cj-Zj		0.00	0.00	-10.00	-5.00

```
Final optimal solution
```

Variable	Value
x 1	20.00
x 2	10.00
Z	1300.00

```
Sensitivity Analysis
```

Right-hand side Ranging

Constraint Number	Lower Limit	Current Value	Upper Limit
1	60.00	90.00	120.00
2	60.00	80.00	120.00

Contribution Rate Ranging

Variable	Lower Limit	Current Rate	Upper Limit
x 1*	25.00	40.00	50.00
x 2*	40.00	50.00	80.00

```
* indicates basic variable
```

SUMMARY

Every linear programming problem, whether a maximization or a minimization problem, has a dual model corresponding to its primal. The optimum solution to the dual model provides useful information for the decision maker. The values of the objective functions (z_j in the solution column) in the primal and dual models are always the same when the optimum solutions are reached. The dual decision variables in the optimum solution are the shadow prices.

The graphical and simplex solution methods are techniques used to derive the optimum solution to a linear programming problem with constant model parameters. However, in real-world situations, model parameters change frequently. Sensitivity analysis is perhaps as important a part of linear programming as the derivation of the optimum primal solution. The decision maker is extremely concerned with the sensitivity of the optimum solution to changes in the model parameters. This chapter discussed sensitivity analysis based on the graphical and simplex approaches.

Today, even the smallest real-world linear programming problem is solved by computer, using software such as *LINDO* and *Micro Manager*.

Glossary

Duality   Every linear programming problem has a standard, or primal, formulation and an alternative formulation called the *dual model*. The dual is the opposite of the primal and, as such, can furnish marginal values and trade-off information helpful in analyzing the primal model.

Dual Solution   The solution obtained from a dual model will correspond to that from the matching primal model. Marginal contribution rates (or shadow prices) in the dual represent solution values in the primal, and vice versa.

Graphical Sensitivity Analysis   Problem solving that analyzes changes in model parameters through graphing. The process of determining the reaction of the solution to various model changes is *sensitivity analysis*.

Primal Solution   The typical initial formulation of a linear programming problem is the primal model; solutions prepared from this primal model are primal solutions.

Simplex-based Sensitivity Analysis   Using the simplex approach, changes in model parameters may be analyzed using information provided on the final simplex tableau. The process of determining the reaction of the solution to various model changes is *sensitivity analysis*.

References

Ackoff, R. L., and Sasiani, M. F. *Fundamentals of Operations Research*. New York: Wiley, 1968.

Baumol, W. J. *Economic Theory and Operational Analysis*. 2d ed. Englewood Cliffs, N.J.: Prentice-Hall, 1965.

Charnes, A., and Cooper, W. W. *Management Models and Industrial Applications of Linear Programming*. New York: Wiley, 1961.

Dantzig, G. B. *Linear Programming and Extensions*. Princeton, N.J.: Princeton University, 1963.

Hillier, F. S., and Lieberman, G. J. *Introduction to Operations Research*. 4th ed. San Francisco: Holden-Day, 1986.

Kim, C. *Introduction to Linear Programming*. New York: Holt, Rinehart & Winston, 1971.

Kwak, N. K. *Mathematical Programming with Business Applications*. New York: McGraw-Hill, 1973.

Lee, S. M. *Linear Optimization for Management*. New York: Petrocelli-Charter, 1976.

Lee, S. M., Moore, L. J., and Taylor, B. W. *Management Science*. 2d ed. Dubuque, Iowa: W. C. Brown, 1985.

Lee, S. M., and Shim, J. P. *Micro Management Science*. Dubuque, Iowa: W. C. Brown, 1986.

Lee, S. M., and Shim, J. P. *Micro Manager*. Dubuque, Iowa: W. C. Brown, 1986.

Loomba, N. P., and Turban, E. *Applied Programming for Management*. New York: Holt, Rinehart & Winston, 1974.

Schrage, L. *Linear, Integer, and Quadratic Programming with LINDO*. Palo Alto, Calif.: The Scientific Press, 1984.

Simonnard, M. *Linear Programming*. Englewood Cliffs, N.J.: Prentice-Hall, 1966.

Wagner, H. M. *Principles of Operations Research*. 2d ed. Englewood Cliffs, N.J.: Prentice-Hall, 1975.

Assignments

5.1 What are the important benefits of formulating and solving a dual model?

5.2 Can one determine the dual solution based on the simplex solution of a primal problem?

5.3 If a primal model has 10 constraints and 15 decision variables, how many constraints and decision variables would its corresponding dual model have?

5.4 Is the dual model faster to solve than the primal model?

5.5 What are some possible benefits of studying the primal-dual relationships?

5.6 Why is sensitivity analysis useful in analyzing linear programming problems?

5.7 What are some of the possible reasons for changes in the technological coefficients in real-world situations?

5.8 What are some of the possible reasons for changes in the right-hand-side (available resources) values?

5.9 A manufacturing firm is considering the adoption of the Japanese just-in-time production system. In this system, materials and components are purchased just in time to be used in the assembly plant. What type of changes will be necessary in their linear programming model for aggregate production planning?

5.10 Can we use sensitivity analysis when the model parameters change continuously?

5.11 How do graph-based and simplex-based sensitivity analysis differ?

5.12 Discuss a case where we may need to add a new constraint to the problem.

5.13 Discuss a case where we may want to add a new decision variable to the problem.

5.14 Formulate the dual of the following linear programming problem:

$$\text{Maximize } Z = 240x_1 + 225x_2$$
$$\text{subject to} \quad 3x_1 + 9x_2 \le 12$$
$$6x_1 + 15x_2 \le 24$$
$$x_1, x_2 \ge 0$$

5.15 Formulate the dual of the following linear programming problem:

$$\text{Maximize } Z = 80x_1 + 120x_2$$
$$\text{subject to} \quad 4x_1 + 8x_2 \le 240$$
$$8x_1 - 4x_2 \ge 36$$
$$x_1, x_2 \ge 0$$

5.16 Formulate the dual of the following linear programming problem:

$$\text{Maximize } Z = 40x_1 + 36x_2$$
$$\text{subject to} \quad 16x_1 + 8x_2 = 80$$
$$2x_2 \le 8$$
$$x_1, x_2 \ge 0$$

5.17 Formulate the dual of the following linear programming problem:

$$\text{Minimize } Z = -20x_1 + 40x_2$$
$$\text{subject to} \quad -2x_1 + 2x_2 \le 2$$
$$6x_1 + 4x_2 \le 24$$
$$x_1, x_2 \ge 0$$

5.18 Paul, the butcher at the local meat market, has a meat loaf mixing problem that requires linear programming. He is attempting to determine the optimum mix of two types of meat loaf: regular and hot.

A tray of regular meat loaf requires 1 hour of mixing, and a tray of hot meat loaf takes 2 hours. A tray of regular meat loaf takes 3 feet of shelf space, and a tray of hot meat loaf requires only 2 feet. From past experience, Paul has determined that the profit per tray is $8 for regular and $12 for hot meat loaf. He estimates that the maximum mixing time available per day is 9 hours, and the shelf space available is 16 feet. The maximum daily sale of meat loaf is estimated to be 6 trays.

a. Formulate the primal linear programming model and solve it by the graphical method.

b. Formulate the dual model for this problem.

c. Solve the primal problem by the simplex method.

d. If we assume that the profit per tray of hot meat loaf is steady at $12 but that the profit per tray of regular meat loaf fluctuates considerably, what profit range should there be for a tray of regular meat loaf in order for Paul to mix and sell 4 trays of regular and 2 trays of hot meat loaf?

e. In the original problem, formulated and solved above in (c), if Paul hires an assistant and the mixing time is increased to 12 hours, what will be the change in the optimum solution?

f. Again in the original problem, if Paul purchases a new mixer that can mix a tray of hot meat loaf in 1 hour (everything else remaining the same), what will be the effect on the optimum solution?

5.19 The Student Center is preparing a special breakfast for the visiting high school seniors. The center's dietitians have decided to serve only two types of food: eggs and toast (plus all the water one wishes to drink). The minimum vitamin requirements for the breakfast and the vitamin content in a unit of each food follow.

Vitamin	Vitamin Content per Unit (mg)		Minimum Requirement (mg)
	Egg	Toast	
A	4	5	20
B	12	3	30
C	3	2	12

a. If the unit cost is 3¢ for an egg and 2¢ for toast, find the optimum solution by the graphical method.
b. Formulate the dual model for this problem.
c. If the minimum requirement for vitamin C is increased from 12 to 18 milligrams, what will be the change in the final solution?
d. In the original problem solved above in (a), if the unit cost for toast is increased to 4¢, what will be the impact of this change on the optimum solution?

5.20 The Craft Shop is sponsoring its annual yo-yo contest. All yo-yos must be purchased from the shop. The shop sells two models of yo-yos—Super Climber and Hugging Yo. Each model requires three production processes: molding, painting, and finishing. The shop has secured the maximum of 100 hours for molding, 40 hours for painting, and 20 hours for finishing.

Production of a batch of 100 Super Climbers requires 2 hours of molding, 30 minutes of painting, and 30 minutes of finishing. Production of a batch of 100 Hugging Yos requires 2 hours of molding, 1 hour of painting, and 15 minutes of finishing. The sales manager reports that the maximum expected sales for Super Climber is 3,500 (35 batches of 100 each), since to use this yo-yo requires a special skill. The manager also reports that they can sell all the Hugging Yos that the shop produces. The management of the firm has decided to use this number of expected sales as a model constraint.

The expected profit from the sale of one batch (100) of Super Climbers is $30 and for a batch (100) of Hugging Yos, $20.

a. Solve this problem by using the graphical method, and determine the exact number of batches of each type of yo-yo to be produced.
b. What are the basic variables and their values at the optimum point?
c. Because of the unexpected popularity of the Hugging Yo, its unit profit per batch has increased from $20 to $35. What will be the impact of this change on the optimum solution?
d. Solve the original problem in (a) above by the simplex method, and identify the shadow prices. Within what ranges are these shadow prices valid?

5.21 The local credit union has \$500,000 to invest in various investment alternatives. The credit union does not wish to invest in mutual funds or common stocks, as it views these as risky alternatives in view of the current economic instability. Instead, it prefers to diversify its investments by allocating the funds among the following alternatives: personal loans to the members of the credit union, government bonds, deposits in a savings and loan association, and preferred stock.

The credit union is simply trying to determine the optimum allocation of funds to be invested in the four alternatives so that the maximum return can be realized. The actual investment in a specific choice (e.g., preferred stock of General Motors Corp.) within the given investment area will be determined at a later date.

The current yield rates for each of the four alternatives are: personal loans, 7.0 percent; government bonds, 8.0 percent; savings and loan association, 6.5 percent; and preferred stocks, 7.5 percent. The credit union wishes to invest the entire \$500,000 so that there will be no idle funds.

Because of the risk elements and the lengths of investment periods required, the management of the credit union has set the following guidelines:

a. Investment in preferred stock should not exceed the amount invested in government bonds or the amount invested in the savings and loan association.

b. The amount of loans to the members should not exceed the total investment in the other three alternatives.

c. At least 30 percent of the total investment funds should be allocated for personal loans to the members.

    (1) Formulate the primal model for this problem.

    (2) Solve the model with a computer program, if one is available.

    (3) Suppose the management has decided to introduce the additional constraint that the total investment in government bonds should be at least \$50,000. What would be the effect of this new constraint on the optimum solution?

5.22 Consider the following final simplex tableau for a linear programming problem:

c_b	c_j Basis	Solution	40 x_1	24 x_2	52 x_3	23 x_4	0 s_1	0 s_2	0 s_3	0 s_4	0 s_5	0 s_6
24	x_2	50	0	1	1/2	0	-1/5	2/5	0	0	0	-1
0	s_4	10	0	0	-1	0	-3/5	1/5	0	1	0	-3
0	s_3	530	0	0	2 1/2	0	-5	0	1	0	0	-13
40	x_1	10	1	0	1	0	3/5	-1/5	0	0	0	3
0	s_5	16	0	0	1	0	0	0	0	0	1	0
23	x_4	10	0	0	0	1	0	0	0	0	0	-1
	z_j	1830	40	24	52	23	19.20	1.60	0	0	0	73
	$c_j - z_j$		0	0	0	0	-19.20	-1.60	0	0	0	-73

a. Identify the optimum solution.

b. What is the marginal value of an additional unit of resource in the first constraint? What is the range of b_1 within which the marginal value is valid ($b_1 = 120$)?

c. Is there an alternate optimum solution? If so, identify the new solution.

d. Suppose that the firm can obtain 10 additional units of resource for the fourth constraint at \$10 each ($b_4 = 20$). Should it obtain these additional units? Why or why not?

e. Suppose that the firm can obtain additional resources for the second constraint at \$1 per unit ($b_2 = 160$). Should it purchase the additional resources? If so, how many units?

f. Suppose the firm signed a trade agreement with its competitor, and the agreement resulted in a new constraint, $x_1 \leq 8$. Derive the new solution with this additional constraint.

5.23 Solve the following problem using a computer program or the simplex method:

$$\text{Maximize } Z = 12x_1 + 15x_2 + 9x_3$$
$$\text{subject to} \quad 8x_1 + 16x_2 + 12x_3 \leq 250$$
$$4x_1 + 8x_2 + 10x_3 \geq 80$$
$$7x_1 + 9x_2 + 8x_3 = 105$$
$$x_1, x_2, x_3 \geq 0$$

5.24 Solve the following problem by using a computer program or the simplex method:

$$\text{Maximize } Z = 51x_1 + 68x_2$$
$$\text{subject to} \quad 17x_1 + 17x_2 \leq 8{,}500$$
$$17x_1 + 17x_2 \geq 6{,}800$$
$$102x_1 - 68x_2 \geq 0$$
$$17x_1 - 34x_2 = 0$$
$$x_1, x_2 \geq 0$$

5.25 Solve the following problem by using a computer program or the simplex method:

$$\text{Maximize } Z = 4x_1 + 20x_2 + 17x_3$$
$$\text{subject to} \quad 9x_1 + 10x_2 + 7x_3 \geq 90$$
$$19x_1 + 18x_2 + 11x_3 \geq 120$$
$$32x_1 + 36x_2 + 27x_3 \leq 1{,}100$$
$$17x_1 + 21x_2 + 18x_3 \leq 700$$
$$x_1, x_2, x_3 \geq 0$$

5.26 Solve the following problem by using a computer program or the simplex method:

$$\text{Maximize } Z = 3x_1 + 4x_2 + 2x_3$$
$$\text{subject to} \quad x_1 + x_2 + x_3 \leq 650$$
$$x_1 + x_2 + x_3 \geq 500$$
$$x_1 - 2x_2 + 4x_3 = 0$$
$$6x_1 + 3x_2 + 5x_3 \leq 1{,}900$$
$$x_1, x_2, x_3 \geq 0$$

5.27 The dietitian at the local hospital is preparing the breakfast menu for the maternity ward patients. She is planning a special nonfattening diet and has chosen cottage cheese and scrambled eggs for breakfast. She is primarily concerned with the vitamin E and iron requirements for the breakfast.

According to the American Medical Association (AMA), new mothers must get at least 12 milligrams of vitamin E and 24 milligrams of iron from breakfast. The AMA handbook reports that a scoop of cottage cheese contains 3 milligrams of vitamin E and 3 milligrams of iron. An average scoop of scrambled eggs contains 2 milligrams of vitamin E and 8 milligrams of iron. The AMA handbook also recommends that new mothers eat at least two scoops of cottage cheese for breakfast. The dietitian considers this to be one of the model constraints.

The hospital accounting department estimates that a scoop of cottage cheese costs 5¢ and a scoop of scrambled eggs also costs 5¢. The dietitian is attempting to determine the optimum breakfast menu that satisfies all the requirements and minimizes the total cost.

    a. Formulate the primal model for the problem.

    b. Formulate the dual model.

    c. Determine the contribution coefficient ranges for cottage cheese and eggs.

    d. Determine the right-hand-side value ranges for all the constraints.

5.28 Given the following linear programming problem:

$$\text{Maximize } Z = 3x_1 + 10x_2 + 6x_3$$
$$\text{subject to} \quad 7x_1 + 2x_2 + x_3 \leq 8$$
$$-x_1 + 2x_2 + 6x_3 \leq 12$$
$$x_1 + 2x_2 + x_3 \geq 4$$
$$x_1, x_2, x_3 \geq 0$$

    a. Find the ranges for all b_i values for which the solution remains feasible.

    b. Find the ranges for all c_j values for which the solution remains optimum.

    c. How will the solution be affected if a_{11} is changed from 7 to 4?

    d. If the right-hand-side value of the third constraint is changed from 4 to 6, what happens to the previous optimum solution?

5.29 The following linear programming problem was solved by *Micro Manager*.

$$\text{Maximize } Z = 2x_1 + 6x_2 + 2x_3$$
$$\text{subject to} \quad 10x_1 + 12x_2 + 7x_3 \leq 20{,}000$$
$$7x_1 + 10x_2 + 8x_3 \leq 7{,}000$$
$$x_1 + x_2 + x_3 = 1{,}000$$
$$x_1, x_2, x_3 \geq 0$$

```
Simplex tableau: Iteration 2

       \Cj              2.00    6.00    2.00    0.00    0.00  -9999.00
    Cb   Basis   Bi      x 1     x 2     x 3     s 1     s 2     A 1
    ------------------------------------------------------------------
    0.00  s 1 10000.00   0.00    0.00   -3.67    1.00   -0.67   -5.33
    6.00  x 2     0.00   0.00    1.00    0.33    0.00    0.33   -2.33
    2.00  x 1  1000.00   1.00    0.00    0.67    0.00   -0.33    3.33
    ------------------------------------------------------------------
          Zj    2000.00   2.00    6.00    3.33    0.00    1.33   -7.33
          Cj-Zj            0.00    0.00   -1.33    0.00   -1.33 -9991.67
```

a. Is the solution at iteration 2 optimum? Why or why not?

b. Find the ranges for all c_j values for which the solution remains optimum.

c. Find the feasible ranges for all b_i values within which the shadow prices remain the same.

d. If an additional constraint $4x_1 + 3x_2 \geq 4{,}000$ is added to the problem, what will happen to the previous solution?

5.30 The following linear programming problem was solved by a computer program:

$$\text{Maximize } Z = 60x_1 + 90x_2 + 90x_3 + 55x_4$$

$$\text{subject to} \quad 3x_1 + 2x_2 \leq 40$$

$$4x_3 + x_4 \leq 25$$

$$10x_1 + 12.5x_3 \leq 100$$

$$x_2 + 2x_4 \leq 22$$

$$x_1, x_2, x_3, x_4 \geq 0$$

Simplex tableau: Iteration 3

Cb	Basis	Bi	$\backslash$Cj 60.00 x 1	90.00 x 2	90.00 x 3	55.00 x 4	0.00 s 1	0.00 s 2	0.00 s 3	0.00 s 4
90.00	x 2	20.00	1.50	1.00	0.00	0.00	0.50	0.00	0.00	0.00
90.00	x 3	6.00	0.19	0.00	1.00	0.00	0.06	0.25	0.00	-0.13
0.00	s 3	25.00	7.66	0.00	0.00	0.00	-0.78	-3.13	1.00	1.56
55.00	x 4	1.00	-0.75	0.00	0.00	1.00	-0.25	0.00	0.00	0.50
	Zj	2395.00	110.63	90.00	90.00	55.00	36.88	22.50	0.00	16.25
	Cj-Zj		-50.63	0.00	0.00	0.00	-36.88	-22.50	0.00	-16.25

a. Is the solution optimum at iteration 3?

b. What kind of increase in c_1 do we need in order to have x_1 as a basic variable?

c. What will happen if c_2 is changed to 75?

d. Find the feasible ranges for all b_i values.

e. If a new constraint $2x_2 + x_3 + 10x_4 \geq 55$ is added to the problem, is the previous solution still optimum?

f. Suppose a new variable x_5 is added to the problem with a contribution rate of 60. This variable requires 2 units of resource in constraint 2 and 2 units of resource in constraint 4. Should we produce this new product? Show your reasoning.

5.31 Princess Racquet Company produces four types of tennis racquets: graphite, fiberglass, steel, and power. The profit on each racquet type is: graphite, $7; fiberglass, $6; steel, $7; and power, $2. The company's current production capacity is 32 racquets per day. Mr. Simon, the production manager, believes that the demand per day for each line of product is graphite, 20; fiberglass, 15; and steel, 17. The demand for power racquets cannot be determined because that line has just been placed on the market. With the given information, Mr. Simon wants to determine what production mix will maximize total profit.

a. Formulate a linear programming model for this problem.

b. Solve the problem by using a computer program or the simplex method.

c. Mr. Simon wonders how much the total profit would change as demand for each racquet changed. Explain the profit change according to potential changes in demand.

d. Because of the lack of demand, Mr. Simon decided to drop the line of power racquets. What will happen to the solution?

6

INTEGER PROGRAMMING, GOAL PROGRAMMING, AND OTHER TOPICS OF LINEAR PROGRAMMING

Chapters 3, 4, and 5 discussed linear programming as a decision-making technique for problems that require continuous solution values for the decision variables and a single objective criterion. However, many real-world problems must have either integer solution values or multiple objectives, and decision making with integer solution values or multiple, and sometimes conflicting, objectives has been a new challenge of management science during the past two decades. Chapter 6 focuses on all-integer and zero–one integer programming and on the concept and solution methods of goal programming, and briefly reviews several other advanced topics of linear programming.

Learning Objectives *From the study of this chapter, we will learn the following:*

1. The basic concept and approaches of integer programming
2. The concept and approach of goal programming
3. The types of management problems that can be analyzed by integer or goal programming
4. The formulation of various decision problems as integer- or goal-programming models
5. The solution of simple integer- and goal-programming problems by the graphical method
6. The solution of complex integer- and goal-programming problems by the simplex method
7. Computer-based solution of integer- and goal-programming problems
8. The meaning of the following terms:

Integer programming	*Zero-one programming*
Goal programming	*Cost of indivisibility*
Multiple objectives	*Deviational variables*
Incompatible objectives	*Overachievement*
Priority structures	*Underachievement*
Preemptive priorities	*System constraints*
Cardinal weights	*Goal constraints*
Multiple-objective linear programming	*Parametric programming*
Game theory	*Stochastic programming*
Branch-and-bound approach	*Chance-constrained programming*

INTEGER PROGRAMMING

Linear programming assumes that all variables can take any nonnegative continuous values in the solution. The divisibility requirement presents no special difficulty for most decision problems. For example, it is perfectly acceptable to spend $129.79 to pour 1.25 cubic feet of concrete, or to use 1.679 ounces of a chemical in an experiment. In certain problems, however, decision variables cannot take continuous values. For example, we cannot take 1.337 courses at the university, it is impossible to construct 0.29 nuclear power plant, and we cannot assign 2.79 people to complete a task. For these types of problems, linear programming is not directly applicable.

One approach we can take to derive an integer solution is simply to round off the linear programming solution. However, it is not a simple task to round off the fractional solution values of the basic variables while satisfying all the constraints of the model. As a matter of fact, a rounded solution may actually be infeasible with the given set of constraints, or a rounded solution may be inferior to the optimum integer solution.

Integer programming is a special extension of linear programming that was developed to derive the optimum integer solution to linear programming problems. The integer-programming model must have the following characteristics: (1) a linear objective function; (2) a set of linear constraints; (3) a nonnegativity constraint for model variables; and (4) integer-value constraints for certain variables. When the model requires all integer values for the basic variables, it is referred to as an *all-integer problem*. If the model requires only certain variables to be integers, it is a *mixed-integer problem*. A special case of integer-programming problem requires that each decision variable equal 0 or 1. Such a problem is often referred to as a *zero–one integer-programming problem*.

There are many different types of integer-programming techniques available. The best known and perhaps most widely applied techniques are the **branch-and-bound** and **zero–one** methods. Thus, our discussion will be centered around these two methods. We will begin our discussion of integer programming with the rounding approach and the graphical method of all-integer programming.

The Rounding Approach

The easiest and often the most practical approach to solving integer-programming problems is the rounding approach. This approach is simple and certainly economical in terms of the effort and cost required to derive an integer solution. In this approach, we first use the ordinary linear programming method to derive the optimum continuous (or fractional) solution. Then, the solution values of the basic variables are rounded off to their nearest integer values.

The major disadvantage of this approach is that the rounded solution may not correspond to the true integer optimum solution. Because the rounded solution may be significantly inferior to the optimum integer solution, the cost and effort required to find the best integer solution may be fully warranted. Or, the rounded solution may be an infeasible solution with the given set of constraints.

Let us examine the following two problems:

$$\text{Problem A:} \quad \text{Maximize } Z = 9x_1 + 10x_2$$
$$\text{subject to} \quad 3x_1 + 4x_2 \le 30$$
$$2x_1 + x_2 \le 12$$
$$x_1, x_2 \ge 0$$

Table 6.1   *Comparison of Continuous, Rounded, and Integer Solutions*

Problem	Continuous Solution	Rounded Integer Solution	Optimum Integer Solution
A	$x_1 = 3\ 3/5$ $x_2 = 4\ 4/5$ $Z = \$81.40$	$x_1 = 4$ $x_2 = 5$ $Z = \$86$ (infeasible)	$x_1 = 2$ $x_2 = 6$ $Z = \$78$
B	$x_1 = 1\ 9/11$ $x_2 = 3\ 3/11$ $Z = \$90.18$	$x_1 = 2$ $x_2 = 3$ $Z = \$86$ (feasible)	$x_1 = 0$ $x_2 = 4$ $Z = \$88$

$$\text{Problem B:}\quad \text{Maximize } Z = 10x_1 + 22x_2$$
$$\text{subject to}\quad 2x_1 + 5x_2 \le 20$$
$$6x_1 + 4x_2 \le 24$$
$$x_1, x_2 \ge 0$$

Table 6.1 presents a comparison of the standard simplex solution with no integer requirements, rounded solutions, and optimum integer solutions for these two problems. For Problem A, the rounded solution yields a total profit of $86, which is $4.60 more than the profit in the continuous solution. Obviously, this is an infeasible solution. Always remember that *an integer solution is never better than a continuous solution, and in most cases the integer solution is inferior to the continuous solution.* The reason is, of course, that the additional integer requirement was imposed upon the model. Additional constraints can only shrink the solution space, never expand it. The difference between the continuous and integer solutions is often referred to as the **cost of indivisibility.**

For Problem B, the rounded solution is feasible, but it is inferior to the optimum integer solution. The rounded solution indicates a total profit that is only $2 less than the total profit derived by the optimum integer solution. However, if the unit contribution rates happen to be expressed in millions of dollars, it certainly is cost effective to invest the necessary effort and time to derive the optimum integer solution rather than use the rounded solution.

The Graphical Approach

If an integer-programming problem involves only two decision variables, we can easily solve it by the graphical method. This approach is no different from the graphical method of linear programming we discussed in Chapter 3, except that we must satisfy the integer requirements. The best way to apply the graphical approach of integer programming is to use graph paper and plot all the integer points within the area of feasible solutions. Then, identify the optimum integer solution through either the iso-profit (or iso-cost) function or the search approaches.

Casette 6.1   CREATIVE DESIGNER JEANS, INC.

Julia Klein, a college junior majoring in Textiles and Design at the university, has decided to create designer jeans and sell them at several boutiques in town. Julia has developed two distinct and simple designs called "Coed" and "Julia." The designs are changed slightly every week so that each boutique will have different jeans to market. Currently, Creative Designer Jeans has orders for the next 6 months' production.

Julia has set up two production processes: Process 1, cutting and patching, and process 2, final sewing. With the help of a friend, Julia has set up the following operations:

Process	Time Requirement per Pair		Production Capacity
	Coed	Julia	
Cutting and patching	2 hrs	3 hrs	12 hrs
Sewing	5 hrs	3 hrs	15 hrs
Unit profit	$20	$16	

Since the designs are changed every week, the weekly production requires an integer solution. Julia is attempting to determine the optimum number of Coed and Julia

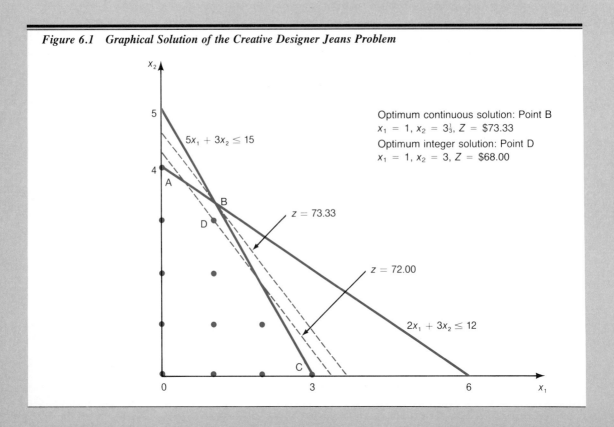

Figure 6.1   *Graphical Solution of the Creative Designer Jeans Problem*

Optimum continuous solution: Point B
$x_1 = 1, x_2 = 3\frac{1}{3}, Z = \$73.33$
Optimum integer solution: Point D
$x_1 = 1, x_2 = 3, Z = \$68.00$

$5x_1 + 3x_2 \le 15$

$z = 73.33$

$z = 72.00$

$2x_1 + 3x_2 \le 12$

jeans to produce every week to maximize total profit. A noninteger solution is not acceptable for this problem.

We can formulate the problem as an integer-programming model as follows:

$$\text{Maximize } Z = 20x_1 + 16x_2$$
$$\text{subject to} \quad 2x_1 + 3x_2 \leq 12$$
$$5x_1 + 3x_2 \leq 15$$
$$x_1, x_2 = \quad 0 \text{ or nonnegative integer}$$

where x_1 = number of Coed jeans produced per week

x_2 = number of Julia jeans produced per week

This model is the same as any linear programming model except for the last constraint, which specifies the integer requirement for the decision variables. The graphical solution to this problem is presented in Figure 6.1.

The area of feasible solutions is 0ABC. The optimum continuous solution is identified as point B, where $x_1 = 1$, $x_2 = 3\ 1/3$, and $Z = \$73.33$. To determine the integer optimum solution, we must depart from the continuous optimum point (point B) and retreat toward the origin with the slope of the iso-profit function ($-5/4$). The optimum integer solution is the first integer point intersecting the iso-profit function. This point is point D, where $x_1 = 1$, $x_2 = 3$, and $Z = \$68.00$

The Branch-and-Bound Method

The general solution method most widely used for integer programming is the branch-and-bound method. Since a problem has a certain finite number of integer solutions, we can use an enumeration procedure to pick the best solution. The branch-and-bound method is basically a systematic search routine of enumeration that greatly reduces the solution combinations to be examined.

The basic steps of the branch-and-bound method of integer programming for a maximization problem can be outlined as follows:

Step 1 Solve the problem by the standard simplex method without the integer requirements.

Step 2 Examine the optimum solution. If the basic variables with integer requirements are all integer valued, the optimum integer solution is found. Stop. If any of the basic variables does not satisfy the integer requirements, continue the process.

Step 3 The set of feasible noninteger solution values is branched into two subproblems. This *branching* is accomplished by introducing two mutually exclusive constraints that are necessary to satisfy the integer requirement of a chosen variable.

Step 4 The *bounding* procedure is as follows: For each subproblem, the objective function value of the optimum noninteger solution is determined as the *upper bound*. The best integer solution derived in any subproblem becomes the *lower bound*. Those subsets having upper bounds that are less than (inferior to) the current lower bound are excluded from further analysis. If there is a feasible integer solution, one that is as good as or better than the upper bound for any subset, it is the optimum integer solution. If no such solution exists, a subproblem with the best upper bound is selected to continue branching. Repeat the process by returning to step 3.

To illustrate the branch-and-bound method, let us consider the Creative Designer Jeans problem:

$$\text{Maximize } Z = 20x_1 + 16x_2$$
$$\text{subject to} \quad 2x_1 + 3x_2 \leq 12$$
$$5x_1 + 3x_2 \leq 15$$
$$x_1, x_2 = 0 \text{ or nonnegative integer}$$

Step 1   The optimum solution to the problem without the integer requirements was derived in Figure 6.1. The optimum solution is $x_1 = 1$, $x_2 = 3 \ 1/3$, $Z = \$73.33$.

Step 2   The optimum solution that is derived is not an integer solution. Thus the branch-and-bound process must continue.

Step 3   To branch the problem into two subproblems, the variable with the noninteger solution value that has the greatest fractional part is selected. In our solution, only x_2 has a fractional value. Thus, x_2 is selected to develop two mutually exclusive constraints for the two subproblems.

To eliminate the fractional part of x_2, two new constraints are developed. The two integer values closest to 3 1/3 are 3 and 4. Thus, we develop two subproblems by introducing one additional constraint to the original problem, $x_2 \leq 3$ or $x_2 \geq 4$ in each of the subproblems. These two mutually exclusive constraints eliminate all possible fractional values for x_2 between 3 and 4. The two subproblems are as follows:

$$\text{Subproblem A:} \quad \text{Maximize } Z = 20x_1 + 16x_2$$
$$\text{subject to} \quad 2x_1 + 3x_2 \leq 12$$
$$5x_1 + 3x_2 \leq 15$$
$$x_2 \leq 3$$
$$x_1, x_2 \geq 0$$

$$\text{Subproblem B:} \quad \text{Maximize } Z = 20x_1 + 16x_2$$
$$\text{subject to} \quad 2x_1 + 3x_2 \leq 12$$
$$5x_1 + 3x_2 \leq 15$$
$$x_2 \geq 4$$
$$x_1, x_2 \geq 0$$

Step 4   The two subproblems are solved by the graphical method of linear programming, as shown in Figure 6.2. Subproblem A yields a noninteger solution with a total profit of \$72.00. This is the upper bound. Subproblem B, on the other hand, has an integer solution. Thus, this integer solution ($x_1 = 0$, $x_2 = 4$, $Z = \$64.00$) is the lower bound. The noninteger solution of subproblem A has a total profit (\$72.00) that is greater than the lower bound (\$64.00). Therefore, a further branching of Subproblem A may yield an integer solution that is better than the lower bound.

Bounding is achieved by setting the lower bound (\$64.00) of the integer solution derived in subproblem B. Any subproblem that yields solutions with less than \$64.00 total profit will be eliminated from further consideration. We now branch subproblem A into two parts: A1 and A2; A1 has an additional constraint, $x_1 \leq 1$, and A2 has an additional constraint, $x_1 \geq 2$.

Figure 6.2   Graphical Solutions of Subproblems A and B

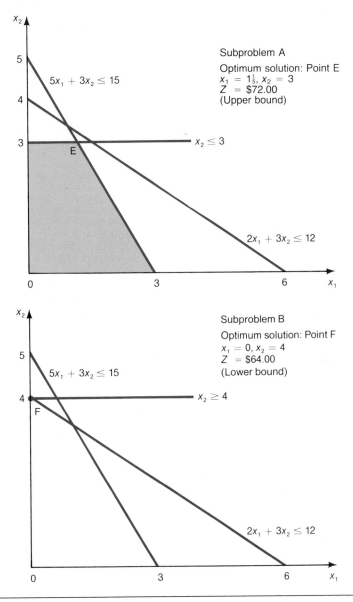

Subproblem A
Optimum solution: Point E
$x_1 = 1\frac{1}{5}, x_2 = 3$
$Z = \$72.00$
(Upper bound)

$5x_1 + 3x_2 \leq 15$

$x_2 \leq 3$

$2x_1 + 3x_2 \leq 12$

Subproblem B
Optimum solution: Point F
$x_1 = 0, x_2 = 4$
$Z = \$64.00$
(Lower bound)

$5x_1 + 3x_2 \leq 15$

$x_2 \geq 4$

$2x_1 + 3x_2 \leq 12$

$$
\begin{aligned}
\text{A1:} \quad &\text{Maximize } Z = 20x_1 + 16x_2 \\
&\text{subject to} \quad 2x_1 + 3x_2 \leq 12 \\
&\qquad\qquad\quad\; 5x_1 + 3x_2 \leq 15 \\
&\qquad\qquad\qquad\qquad\; x_2 \leq 3 \\
&\qquad\qquad\qquad\qquad\; x_1 \leq 1 \\
&\qquad\qquad\qquad\; x_1, x_2 \geq 0
\end{aligned}
$$

Figure 6.3   Graphical Solutions of Subproblems A1 and A2

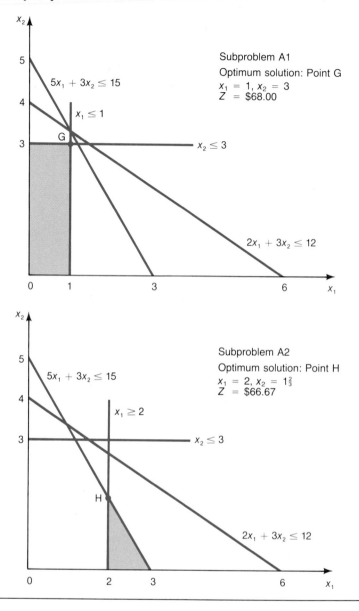

$$\text{A2:}\quad \text{Maximize } Z = 20x_1 + 16x_2$$
$$\text{subject to}\quad 2x_1 + 3x_2 \le 12$$
$$5x_1 + 3x_2 \le 15$$
$$x_2 \le 3$$
$$x_1 \ge 2$$
$$x_1,\, x_2 \ge 0$$

Figure 6.4   Complete Branch and Bound Solution

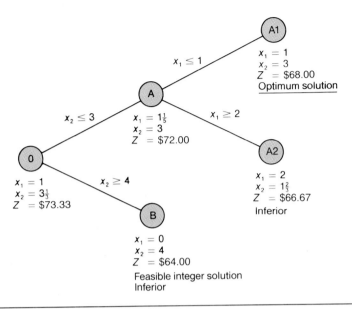

The graphical solutions for A1 and A2 are shown in Figure 6.3. A1 yields an integer solution ($x_1 = 1$, $x_2 = 3$, $Z = \$68.00$), and since this solution is better than the current lower bound, it becomes the new lower bound. A2 yields a noninteger solution ($x_1 = 2$, $x_2 = 1\ 2/3$, $Z = \$66.67$). This solution, however, is inferior to the current lower bound ($68.00 derived in A1). Thus, no further branching will be necessary from A2. There is no upper-bound solution that is better than the lower bound. The optimum integer solution has been obtained. The optimum integer solution is the current lower bound $x_1 = 1$, $x_2 = 3$, $Z = \$68.00$.

In the branch-and-bound procedure, further analysis is terminated when (1) a subproblem results in a solution that is inferior to the current lower-bound solution, and (2) further branching yields infeasible solutions.

When the search process is completed, the best integer solution is selected as the optimum solution. The branch-and-bound procedure for the Creative Designer Jeans problem is presented in Figure 6.4.

Computer Solution of Integer-Programming Problems

Many popular integer-programming computer programs are available today, including *LINDO* and *Micro Manager*. In this section, we will present the computer solution of the Creative Designer Jeans problem discussed as Casette 6.1 through *Micro Manager*.

Figure 6.5 presents the model input and the solution. The solution is $x_1 = 1$, $x_2 = 3$, and $Z = 68.00$; this solution is identical to the graphical solution we derived in Figure 6.3.

Figure 6.5   Computer Input and Solution for Casette 6.1

```
PROGRAM: All Integer Programming

***** INPUT DATA ENTERED *****

Max  Z =  20 x 1 + 16 x 2

Subject to:

C 1   2 x 1 + 3 x 2 <=  12
C 2   5 x 1 + 3 x 2 <=  15

*****   PROGRAM OUTPUT   *****

Level 0  node  0 :  Optimal solution =      73.33334

                           x 1 = 1
                           x 2 = 3.333334

Level 1  node  1 :  Optimal solution =      72.00000

                           x 1 = 1.2
                           x 2 = 3

Level 2  node  2 :  Optimal solution =      68.00000

                           x 1 = 1
                           x 2 = 3

Level 2  node  3 :  Optimal solution =      66.66667

                           x 1 = 2
                           x 2 = 1.666667

Level 1  node  4 :  Optimal solution =      64.00000

                           x 1 = 0
                           x 2 = 4

Final optimal solution =      68.00000

        x 1 = 1
        x 2 = 3
```

Zero–One Programming

Many real-world problems require not only integer solutions but also solution values of either 0 or 1 for the decision variables. Personnel assignment, capital budgeting, portfolio selection, project-scheduling, fixed-cost, location–allocation, knapsack, and traveling salespeople problems are good examples of zero–one problems. In a zero–one problem, if a decision variable is selected, its solution value is 1; if it is not selected, its value is 0.

Example 6.1   A CAPITAL-BUDGETING PROBLEM

A commercial bank is considering five possible investment alternatives. Table 6.2 presents pertinent information about the five projects under consideration. Alternatives 3 and 4 are mutually exclusive real estate development projects using the same plot of land. Thus, only one of the two alternatives can be selected. If we denote x_j for each investment alternative, the two mutually exclusive alternatives can be expressed as

$$x_3 + x_4 \leq 1$$

The objective of this capital-budgeting problem is to maximize the total present value of investment alternatives selected. Thus, the model is:

$$\text{Maximize } Z = 400x_1 + 750x_2 + 380x_3 + 170x_4 + 900x_5$$

$$\begin{aligned}
\text{subject to} \quad 1{,}000x_1 + 1{,}600x_2 + 700x_3 + 250x_4 + 2{,}400x_5 &\leq 4{,}000 \\
6x_1 + 10x_2 + 4x_3 + 2x_4 + 15x_5 &\leq 28 \\
200x_1 + 320x_2 + 150x_3 + 40x_4 + 750x_5 &\geq 450 \\
160x_1 + 280x_2 + 140x_3 + 60x_4 + 500x_5 &\geq 400 \\
x_3 + x_4 &\leq 1 \\
x_j &= 0 \text{ or } 1
\end{aligned}$$

Table 6.2   Investment Opportunities and Capital Budgeting

	Initial Investment ($ thousands)	Personnel Requirement	Expected Annual Cash Flow ($ thousands)	Expected Annual Profit ($ thousands)	Net Present Value ($ thousands)
Investment:					
1	1,000	6	200	160	400
2	1,600	10	320	280	750
3	700	4	150	140	380
4	250	2	40	60	170
5	2,400	15	750	500	900
Requirements or constraints	Maximum $4,000	Maximum 28	Minimum $450	Minimum $400	Maximize

The general solution method of zero–one integer-programming problems is the implicit enumeration method developed by Egon Balas. The technique starts the solution process from the origin where all variables are assigned 0 values. Thus, the initial solution is infeasible. The procedure then forces the solution toward feasibility while optimizing the objective function. Discussion of the implicit enumeration technique is beyond the scope of this text. If you are interested in learning more about this method, consult the works by Lee, Moore, and Taylor cited in the References.

Computer Solution of Zero–One Integer Problems

A number of zero–one programs are available for mainframe or microcomputer systems. We will solve Example 6.1, previously discussed, using *Micro Manager*.

Figure 6.6 presents the solution by *Micro Manager*. The program output presents only feasible solutions, and assigned values are the following: 1 is assigned a value of 1; -1 is assigned a value of 0; and 0 has no value assigned and thus is the same as 0. The optimum solution is $x_1 = 0$, $x_2 = 1$, $x_3 = 0$, $x_4 = 0$, $x_5 = 1$, and $Z = \$1,650$. Thus, only projects 2 and 5 are selected for investment.

GOAL PROGRAMMING

As we learned in Chapters 1 and 2, decision making is the primary task of management. In the past, management practice has been based primarily on experience and intuition. There is no denying that experience is often the foundation of knowledge. We always try to learn from others' experiences in order to avoid making the same mistakes ourselves. For example, we have learned a great deal from our grandpas' storytelling, from nonfiction books, from "how to" handbooks, and from management case studies.

Confucius, some 2,400 years ago, told us the value of experience when he said, "I hear and I forget, I see and I remember, I do and I understand." However, the value of experience is decreasing because of the rapidly changing decision environment. We cannot use the decision-making approach we used last year to solve a similar problem we will face 5 years from now.

In Chapter 1, we discussed the concept of economic person. In the traditional normative approach to decision making, the student of management science has been taught that the systematic way to solve a decision problem is to follow faithfully a set of rules such as:

1. Determine the decision variables.

2. Formulate an objective function, which is either to maximize or to minimize a single objective criterion.

3. Develop a set of constraints representing resource limitations and environmental restrictions.

4. Seek the global optimum solution for the single objective.

Figure 6.6   Computer Solution of Zero–One Programming Problem

```
PROGRAM: Zero One Programming

##### INPUT DATA ENTERED #####

Max  Z =  400 x 1 + 750 x 2 + 380 x 3 + 170 x 4 + 900 x 5

Subject to:

C 1   1000 x 1 + 1600 x 2 + 700 x 3 + 250 x 4 + 2400 x 5 <=  4000
C 2   6 x 1 + 10 x 2 + 4 x 3 + 2 x 4 + 15 x 5 <=  28
C 3   200 x 1 + 320 x 2 + 150 x 3 + 40 x 4 + 750 x 5 >=  450
C 4   160 x 1 + 280 x 2 + 140 x 3 + 60 x 4 + 500 x 5 >=  400
C 5   1 x 3 + 1 x 4 <=  1

#####   PROGRAM OUTPUT   #####

Iteration :  2
Assigned Variables:  1  1  0  0  0
The value of this combination is  1150

Iteration :  8
Assigned Variables:  1 -1 -1  1  1
The value of this combination is  1470

Iteration :  9
Assigned Variables:  1 -1 -1 -1  1
The value of this combination is  1300

Iteration :  11
Assigned Variables: -1  1  1  0  0
The value of this combination is  1130

Iteration :  14
Assigned Variables: -1  1 -1 -1  1
The value of this combination is  1650

Iteration :  18
Assigned Variables: -1 -1  1 -1  1
The value of this combination is  1280

Iteration :  20
Assigned Variables: -1 -1 -1  1  1
The value of this combination is  1070

Iteration :  21
Assigned Variables: -1 -1 -1 -1  1
The value of this combination is  900

The optimal solution is 1650

The solution values of decision variables are as follows:

   0   1   0   0   1
```

This general approach has become so ingrained that we tend to follow the procedure without even pausing to consider the real-world problem, the cognitive limitations of the decision maker, the complexity of the environment, or the assumptions of the model formulation process. Today, we have a large mass of data that supports the descriptive approach to decision making. Thus, we try to develop new ways to solve management problems.

The descriptive approach to decision making is based on the bounded rationality that we discussed in Chapter 1: The idea of intentionally rational decision behavior is the foundation of bounded rationality. Under bounded rationality, the satisficing approach replaces the optimizing approach. In the satisficing approach, an abstract single objective for the organization is replaced by tangible and measurable goals. These measurable goals may be formulated on the basis of certain aspiration levels that are related to organizational goals.

Today, *management by multiple objectives* (also referred to as *multicriteria decision making* or *multiobjective decision making*) is one of the most important areas of management science. There have been various techniques introduced for multiple-objective decision making, such as multiattribute utility theory, multicriteria linear programming, heuristic search methods, goal programming, and learning models. Of these, **goal programming** is one of the most powerful and popular techniques for multiple-objective decision making.

Initially, goal programming was developed as an extension of the optimization technique of linear programming, but goal programming is much more than a mere extension of linear programming. It has the additional capabilities to analyze the decision maker's multiple aspiration levels, to relax some of the model constraints, and to incorporate the decision maker's preference system for multiple conflicting goals. Thus, goal programming can transform a decision model into a satisficing model. This special feature of goal programming allows the decision maker to incorporate environmental, organizational, and judgmental considerations into the model through the determination of aspiration levels and their priorities.

The concept of goal programming was originally introduced by A. Charnes and W. W. Cooper (see References) and was further developed as a distinct management science technique for multiple-objective decision problems through the efforts of many other scholars, especially the contributions of Y. Ijiri and S. M. Lee. Goal programming can be applied to various decision problems having a single goal and multiple subgoals as well as to problems with multiple conflicting goals and subgoals.

If there are multiple conflicting goals in a model, it may not be possible to achieve every goal to the desired extent. In such a case, the goal-programming model attempts to obtain satisfactory levels of goal attainment that would be the best feasible solution in view of the importance of these goals to the organization. Thus, there is a need for a weighting system for the goals such that the less important goals are considered only after the very important goals have been achieved at levels beyond which no further improvements are desired. These weights can be established on the basis of absolute ordinal priorities or on **cardinal** (numerical) **weights** such as utility.

The ordinal weighting scheme is based on the **preemptive priority weights** for the goals. Thus, the most important objective is sought before the other goals are considered. Once the most important goal has been attained as desired or to the maximum extent possible within the constraints of the problem, the second most important objective will be sought. This sequential approach continues until the most satisfactory solution is identified.

The numerical weighting scheme, however, is based on a system that converts all the goals into a universal criterion such as number of points, utilities, or effectiveness values. For example, the military services have established many job or performance evaluation systems based on points. This scheme allows a conversion of **multiple objectives** to a single criterion by considering the *perceived degree of magnitude or importance* of the various goals. However, this approach has many inherent difficulties and has not been widely accepted by practicing managers.

Goal programming and linear programming are similar in many aspects. They have the same basic limitations, assumptions, and requirements. As in linear programming, goal programming can apply the graphical method or the simplex method but in a modified form. Although goal programming is a powerful and flexible technique for multiple-objective decision problems, it is by no means a panacea for problems of this type. It is still a relatively new technique, and many areas are open to further development. Nevertheless, it is an increasingly popular technique among the practitioners of management science.

Application Areas

In general, a goal-programming model performs three types of analysis: (1) it determines the required resources to achieve a set of desired objectives; (2) it determines the degree of attainment for the established goals with given resources; and (3) it provides the best satisficing solution under the varying amounts of resources and the **priority structures** for the goals. If the goal-programming approach is to be taken for a decision problem, it must be carefully examined by the decision maker to fully utilize its advantage.

Goal programming has been applied to a wide range of decision problems in business firms, government agencies, and nonprofit organizations. The most popular application areas of goal programming have been resource allocation, planning and scheduling, and policy analysis problems. Applications of goal programming include the following examples:

Academic planning	Location–allocation decisions
Advertising-media planning	Marketing strategy planning
Blood bank logistics	Police force deployment
Economic policy analysis	Production planning and inventory control
Environmental protection	
Financial analysis	Transportation logistics
Health-care-delivery planning	Work force planning
Insurance planning	Zero-base budgeting

It is impossible to provide even a brief summary of all these goal-programming examples here. However, later in this chapter we will examine two real-world applications of goal programming. It should suffice to state that goal programming is one of the most popular techniques for multiple-objective decision making among scholars and practitioners of management science.

Model Formulation

To gain some experience in formulating multiple-objective decision problems as goal-programming models, we will examine several decision situations in casettes. It is important to recognize quickly which of the problems under consideration can be solved by goal programming, and then be able to formulate a corresponding model for those that can be solved.

A Single-Objective Problem   We will start our discussion of goal-programming model formulation with the simplest possible case, one in which we have a single objective. You may quickly recognize that such a problem can be formulated as a linear programming model. Goal programming can solve any single-objective or multiple-objective problem as long as it satisfies the basic requirements. Therefore, goal programming is capable of solving any linear programming problem as well as many different types of problems that involve multiple objectives.

Casette 6.2   ***CENTURY ELECTRONICS INC.***

Century Electronics Inc. is a small manufacturer of video players. The company produces only two types of video players: cassette and disc. Century has a production plant where all its players are processed, and production of either a cassette player or a disc player requires an average of 1 hour in the plant. The plant has a normal production capacity of 40 hours per week.

The marketing department of Century reports that a maximum of 24 cassette and 30 disc players can be sold each week. The expected profit from the sale of a cassette player is $60 and is $40 from the sale of a disc player. Currently, the company has only one goal—maximizing the total profit from its weekly operation under normal production and market conditions.

Linear Programming Model

This problem can be easily formulated as a linear programming problem as follows:

$$\text{Maximize } Z = 60x_1 + 40x_2$$

$$
\begin{aligned}
\text{subject to} \quad x_1 + x_2 &\le 40 &&\textit{Production constraint} \\
x_1 &\le 24 &&\textit{Sales constraint} \\
x_2 &\le 30 &&\textit{Sales constraint} \\
x_1, x_2 &\ge 0
\end{aligned}
$$

where x_1 = number of cassette players produced per week

x_2 = number of disc players produced per week

This problem can be solved by the graphical method, as shown in Figure 6.7. The solution indicates that the company should produce 24 cassette players and 16 disc players, and the total weekly profit will be $2,080. It is obvious that Century has some

Figure 6.7   The Century Electronics Problem

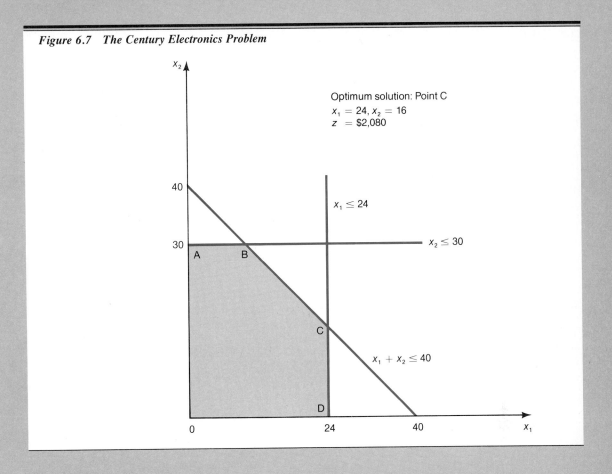

Optimum solution: Point C
$x_1 = 24$, $x_2 = 16$
$z = \$2{,}080$

$x_1 \le 24$

$x_2 \le 30$

$x_1 + x_2 \le 40$

slack market for disc players, as it produces only 16 units when the market can accommodate 30 units.

Goal-Programming Model

The above single-objective problem can also be formulated and solved by goal programming. Let us discuss each component of the model.

System Constraints.   A goal-programming model has two types of constraints: system and goal. System constraints represent absolute restrictions imposed by the decision environment on the model. For example, there are only 7 days in a week (time constraint), the production or sales capacity in the short run is limited to certain existing conditions (capacity constraint), and the production should be limited to demand and storage capacity (physical constraint). System constraints must be satisfied before any of the goal constraints can be considered.

In this problem, there are three system constraints:

$$x_1 + x_2 \le 40 \qquad \textit{Production constraint}$$
$$x_1 \le 24 \qquad \textit{Sales constraint for cassette players}$$
$$x_2 \le 30 \qquad \textit{Sales constraint for disc players}$$

Goal Constraints. Goal constraints represent aspiration levels for certain goals or objectives. Desired level of profit, desired level of pollution control, desired market share, and desired diversification of investments among various alternatives are several illustrations of goal constraints.

In the Century Electronics problem, there is only one goal constraint because there is a single goal. The only goal is to maximize the total weekly profit. The company has no specific desired level of profit, but it seeks to maximize the total profit. Therefore, the right-hand-side value is not set. To maximize the total profit, we can set the right-hand-side value unrealistically high (say $100,000) and then try to achieve this level. Now we can formulate the goal constraint for profit maximization as follows:

$$60x_1 + 40x_2 + d_1^- - d_1^+ = \$100,000$$

where
$$d_1^- = \text{underachievement of the \$100,000 profit goal}$$
$$d_1^+ = \text{overachievement of the \$100,000 profit goal}$$

We need to explain the d_1^- and d_1^+ variables in greater detail. These variables, referred to as **deviational variables,** can be thought of as slack and surplus variables. For example, if the total profit attained is less than $100,000, then the negative deviational variable d_1^- will have a certain value while the positive deviational variable d_1^+ will be 0. However, if the total profit achieved happens to exceed $100,000, then d_1^+ will have a certain value while d_1^- will be 0.

Since we are attempting to maximize the total profit, we must minimize d_1^- as much as possible. If we could minimize it all the way to 0, then our total profit would be at least $100,000. However, if we were interested in limiting our profit level to $100,000, then we must minimize d_1^+. If we could minimize it all the way to $d_1^+ = 0$, then our total profit would be $100,000 or less. If both of the deviational variables, d_1^- and d_1^+, are minimized to 0, then the total profit level will be exactly $100,000.

From the above discussion, it should be obvious that at least one deviational variable is always 0. Also, since d_1^- and d_1^+ are complementary to each other if $d_1^- > 0$, then $d_1^+ = 0$, and if $d_1^+ > 0$, then $d_1^- = 0$. Thus, it is always true that $d_1^- \times d_1^+ = 0$.

Now, we can summarize as follows the three options open for the goal constraints and their corresponding consequences:

Minimize	Goal	If Goal Achieved
d_1^-	$60x_1 + 40x_2 \geq 100,000$	$d_1^- = 0, d_1^+ \geq 0$
d_1^+	$60x_1 + 40x_2 \leq 100,000$	$d_1^- \geq 0, d_1^+ = 0$
$d_1^- + d_1^+$	$60x_1 + 40x_2 = 100,000$	$d_1^- = 0, d_1^+ = 0$

Objective Function. The Century Electronics problem has a single goal of profit maximization. This goal can be achieved if d_1^- is minimized. Thus, the objective function becomes

$$\text{Minimize } Z = d_1^-$$

Now, the complete model can be developed as follows:

$$\text{Minimize } Z = d_1^-$$
$$\text{subject to} \quad x_1 + x_2 \leq 40$$
$$x_1 \leq 24$$
$$x_2 \leq 30$$
$$60x_1 + 40x_2 + d_1^- - d_1^+ = 100{,}000$$
$$x_1, x_2, d_1^-, d_1^+ \geq 0$$

In this model, we have used an arbitrarily large profit figure of \$100,000, which is totally unattainable. Thus, we can easily eliminate d_1^+ in the goal constraint, because d_1^+ will always be 0.

The same goal-programming model formulation approach can be applied to any problem which has a single objective, whether it be a maximization or a minimization problem. For example, if the problem were a cost minimization instead of a profit maximization problem, we could formulate it in the following manner, with slight changes to the sales constraints:

$$\text{Minimize } Z = d_1^+$$
$$\text{subject to} \quad x_1 + x_2 \geq 40$$
$$x_1 \geq 24$$
$$x_2 \geq 30$$
$$60x_1 + 40x_2 + d_1^- - d_1^+ = 0$$
$$x_1, x_2, d_1^-, d_1^+ \geq 0$$

In the goal constraint described above, the right-hand-side value of 0 is an unrealistic total cost. As we attempt to minimize d_1^+, the positive deviation from 0 cost, the process becomes a cost minimization approach.

Solution of the Goal-Programming Model. The goal-programming model we formulated for Century Electronics to maximize profit can be easily solved by the graphical method. As the goal constraint has such a large right-hand-side value, this constraint line will be far above the other system constraints. However, the slope of the goal constraint is $-3/2$, exactly the same as the slope of the iso-profit function of the linear programming model.

The first step of the solution process is to identify the area of feasible solutions defined by the system constraints. Figure 6.8 shows the feasibility area 0ABCD. The next step is to minimize d_1^- from the goal constraint line. We plotted the goal constraint line unrealistically close to the feasibility area for the purpose of illustration. To minimize the value of d_1^-, we must move in toward the origin with the slope of the goal constraint ($-3/2$). Actually, this is the same procedure as the iso-profit function approach except that it moves from the opposite direction (toward the origin rather than away from the origin).

The optimum solution can be found by identifying the first point within the feasibility area as we move in toward the origin with the slope of the goal constraint. The optimum solution point is identified as point C in Figure 6.8. The optimum solution is $x_1 = 24$, $x_2 = 16$, $d_1^- = \$97{,}920$, and total profit $= \$2{,}080$.

Figure 6.8   Graphical Solution of the Century Electronics Problem

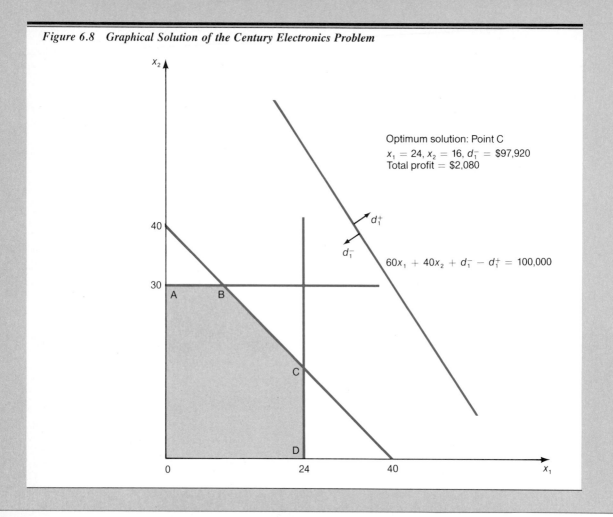

Optimum solution: Point C
$x_1 = 24$, $x_2 = 16$, $d_1^- = \$97,920$
Total profit $= \$2,080$

$60x_1 + 40x_2 + d_1^- - d_1^+ = 100,000$

A Multiple-Objective, Multiple-Subgoal Problem   The next case of goal programming we will study is a multiple-objective, multiple-subgoal problem. Such a problem
may have both system and goal constraints or it may have only a set of goal constraints.
When there are multiple and often conflicting objectives, a preference-weighting system
must be introduced. If there are definite reasons and sufficient information to allow
conversion of all the objectives into a common criterion such as utility or profit, the
multiple-objective problem can be reduced to a single-objective problem.

   Many real-world problems, however, involve both **incompatible objectives** and
incommensurable ones. For example, a problem may have an employment goal (measured in number of full-time employees), a profit goal (measured in dollars), and a
pollution control goal (measured in terms of tons of chemical wastes). Thus, it is often
impossible to convert these goals into a common criterion such as utility or profit. A
powerful alternative approach is to weight the multiple objectives based on *ordinal
weights* or **preemptive priorities.**

The preemptive priority system can be simply explained as a process in which the objectives are pursued in an ordinal sequence based on their importance. Let us suppose that a problem has five goals. The most important objective is pursued first until it is attained as fully as desired or until it reaches a point beyond which further improvement is impossible because of the system constraints. Then, the second goal is sought within the solution space defined by the system constraints and the first priority goal. This process continues until all five goals have been considered.

Certain goal-programming problems may have several subgoals at a certain priority level. For example, let us suppose the second goal of a problem is to maintain the firm's current market share for its products. If the firm currently has five products, the second-priority goal will involve five subgoals — market share goals for the five products.

If we are totally indifferent about market share goals for the five products, we can assign the same numerical weight to each of the five subgoals. However, if there is a good reason to assign different numerical weights (e.g., there are different unit profits for the five products), differential weights can be assigned. Thus, it is necessary for multiple subgoals at a given priority level to be commensurable.

Casette 6.3   BIG SOUND RECORDS INC.

Big Sound Records Inc. is a popular record store located next to the university campus. It is by far the largest record shop in town, in terms of both total sales and record selections. The owner of the shop, Robert Ryman, was an MBA student who conducted a feasibility study for a record shop next to the campus as a term project in the small-business management course. After receiving his degree, Bob Ryman was convinced that he could actually implement his feasibility study. He opened Big Sound Records 2 years ago with a $10,000 loan from the U.S. Small Business Administration. He has been a very successful small-business owner ever since.

The record shop employs 10 full-time and 8 part-time salespeople. Every salesperson is trained on the job to handle both sales and cash registers. The normal numbers of working hours per month are 160 for a full-time salesperson and an average of 80 hours per month for a part-time salesperson.

According to the past sales records, average sales have been 10 records per hour for the full-time salespeople and 6 records per hour for the part-time salespeople. The average hourly wage rates are $6 for full-time employees and $4 for part-time employees. The average gross profit from the sale of a record is $1.50.

In view of past sales records, aggressive promotional efforts, and an increased enrollment at the university, Bob feels that the sales goal for the next month should be 22,000 records. Since the store is open 6 days a week, overtime work is often required of the salespeople (not necessarily overtime, but extra hours for the part-time salespeople).

Bob is convinced that good employer-employee relations have been an essential factor in his business success. Therefore, he feels that a stable employment level with an occasional overtime requirement is a better practice than an unstable employment level with no overtime. However, he also believes that overtime of more than 200 hours per month among the full-time employees should be avoided because fatigue is related to declining sales effectiveness.

Bob has established the following goals for the next month's operation in the order of their priority:

1. The first goal is to achieve sales of 22,000 records in the next month.

2. The second goal is to limit the overtime of full-time salespersons to 200 hours.

3. The third goal is to provide job security for the salespeople. Bob feels that full utilization of full-time employees is twice as important as full utilization of part-time salespeople.

4. The fourth goal is to achieve a gross profit of $31,000 for the next month.

5. The last goal is to minimize the overtime work of the full-time and part-time employees. Bob wants to assign differential weights to the minimization of overtime given to full-time and part-time salespeople according to their marginal profit ratios per hour.

The Big Sound Records problem involves no system constraints, only goal constraints.

Sales Goal

Achievement of the sales goal, which is set at 22,000 records, is a function of the total working hours of the full-time and part-time salespeople and their productivity (sales per hour) rates:

$$10x_1 + 6x_2 + d_1^- - d_1^+ = 22,000$$

where

$$x_1 = \text{total full-time salespeople hours per month}$$
$$x_2 = \text{total part-time salespeople hours per month}$$
$$d_1^- = \text{underachievement of the sales goal}$$
$$d_1^+ = \text{overachievement of the sales goal}$$
$$10 = \text{sales of records per hour for full-time salespeople}$$
$$6 = \text{sales of records per hour for part-time salespeople}$$
$$22,000 = \text{sales goal for month}$$

The sales goal will be achieved if we minimize d_1^-, the underachievement of the sales goal of 22,000 records.

Overtime Work for Full-time Salespeople

In the goal-programming approach, to achieve a certain goal we must have a deviational variable to minimize. If we do not have such a deviational variable, we must create one by formulating a new goal constraint. In the Big Sound Records problem, Bob's second goal is to limit the overtime of the full-time employees to 200 hours during the next month.

We do not have a deviational variable to limit the overtime work of the full-time employees. Thus, we must first determine the regular working hours for the full-time employees. We have defined x_1 as the total full-time salespeople's hours per month. With 10 full-time employees, the total regular working hours per month will be $10 \times 160 = 1,600$ hours:

$$x_1 + d_2^- - d_2^+ = 1,600$$

where

d_2^- = underutilization of regular full-time salespeople hours per month

d_2^+ = overtime given to full-time salespeople hours per month

To limit the overtime work of the full-time salespeople to 200 hours, we should introduce the following constraint:

$$d_2^+ + d_3^- - d_3^+ = 200$$

where

d_3^- = underutilization of the allowed overtime of 200 hours for full-time salespeople

d_3^+ = overtime in excess of 200 hours for full-time salespeople

We have introduced both the negative and positive deviations from the allowed overtime of 200 hours because the actual overtime work for the full-time salespeople may, in fact, be less than, equal to, or even greater than 200 hours. Now we have a deviational variable (d_3^+) to minimize in order to achieve the second goal. It should be noted that this constraint can also be expressed in a different way. For example, we can add the allowed overtime of 200 hours to the right-hand-side value of the regular working-hour constraint of the full-time salespeople and obtain the following:

$$x_1 + d_3^- - d_3^+ = 1,800$$

In this problem, either of the above constraints can be used to formulate a goal-programming model. The second goal can be achieved by minimizing d_3^+ (overtime in excess of 200 hours for full-time employees).

Job Security Goal

Bob would like to provide job security for his full-time and part-time salespeople. This goal can be achieved if the salespeople are provided with at least their regular working hours and if no one is laid off. We have already formulated the regular working hours for the full-time salespeople $(x_1 + d_2^- - d_2^+ = 1,600)$. The total regular working hours for the 8 part-time salespeople will be $8 \times 80 = 640$ hours/month. Thus, we can formulate the following constraint:

$$x_2 + d_4^- - d_4^+ = 640$$

where

d_4^- = underutilization of the total regular part-time salespeople hours per month

d_4^+ = extra working hours given to part-time salespeople per month

The third goal can be achieved by minimizing d_2^- and d_4^- (underutilization of the regular working hours for full-time and part-time salespeople, respectively).

Profit Goal

Bob's fourth goal is to achieve a gross profit of $31,000 for the next month. Big Sound Records has an average gross profit margin per record of $1.50. Thus, the total gross profit will be a function of the total expected sales of records and the average profit per record. The expected sales of records per hour for the full-time and part-time salespeople are 10 and 6 respectively. Thus, the goal constraint becomes:

$$15x_1 + 9x_2 + d_5^- - d_5^+ = 31,000$$

where

$$d_5^- = \text{underachievement of the profit goal}$$
$$d_5^+ = \text{overachievement of the profit goal}$$
$$15 = \text{gross profit per hour generated by full-time salespeople}$$
$$(10 \text{ records} \times \$1.50 = \$15)$$
$$9 = \text{gross profit per hour generated by part-time salespeople}$$
$$(6 \text{ records} \times \$1.50 = \$9)$$

The profit goal can be achieved by minimizing d_5^- (the underachievement of the profit goal of $31,000).

Overtime Minimization Goal

The last goal of the owner of Big Sound Records is to minimize the overtime work of the full-time and part-time employees. We have already formulated the regular working-hour constraints for the full-time and part-time salespeople. Thus, there is no need to reformulate these constraints in order to identify the deviational variables being minimized to achieve this goal. The two constraints that contain the overtime work as deviational variables are as follows:

$$x_1 + d_2^- - d_2^+ = 1,600$$
$$x_2 + d_4^- - d_4^+ = 640$$

The overtime minimization goal can be achieved by minimizing d_2^+ and d_4^+ (overtime work assigned to full-time and part-time employees, respectively).

The Objective Function

Now we are ready to formulate the objective function for the problem. Let us formulate the function by adding the priority goals in the sequence of their ordinal ranking.

Sales Goal.   In order to achieve the sales goal, we must minimize the underachievement of the sales goal to 0 in the following goal constraint:

$$10x_1 + 6x_2 + d_1^- - d_1^+ = 22,000$$

Thus, the highest priority factor P_1 should be assigned to the minimization of d_1^-. The objective function becomes

$$\text{Minimize } Z = P_1 d_1^-$$

Overtime Work for Full-time Salespeople.   Bob wants to limit the overtime work of the full-time salespeople to 200 hours. This goal can be achieved if we minimize the deviational variable that represents overtime in excess of 200 hours in either of the following constraints:

$$d_2^+ + d_3^- - d_3^+ = 200$$

or

$$x_1 + d_3^- - d_3^+ = 1,800$$

The second priority factor, P_2, should be assigned to the minimization of d_3^+. The objective function now becomes

$$\text{Minimize } Z = P_1 d_1^- + P_2 d_3^+$$

Job Security.   Bob's third goal is to provide job security to the full-time and part-time employees. Since we must consider two separate goal constraints, we have multiple subgoals at the third priority level. If Bob were completely indifferent to a preferential handling of the job security of full-time and part-time employees, we could assign the same weight to these subgoals. However, he has already indicated that he would like to assign twice the weight to providing job security for full-time employees as for part-time employees. The two goal constraints involved in the third priority level are:

$$x_1 + d_2^- - d_2^+ = 1,600$$
$$x_2 + d_4^- - d_4^+ = 640$$

To achieve the job security goal, we must minimize d_2^- and d_4^- but with differential weights assigned as follows:

$$\text{Minimize } Z = P_1 d_1^- + P_2 d_3^+ + 2P_3 d_2^- + P_3 d_4^-$$

Profit Goal.   The fourth goal is to achieve a gross profit of $31,000. This goal can be achieved by minimizing d_5^- in the following goal constraint:

$$15x_1 + 9x_2 + d_5^- - d_5^+ = 31,000$$

The fourth priority goal is assigned to the minimization of d_5^- as follows:

$$\text{Minimize } Z = P_1 d_1^- + P_2 d_3^+ + 2P_3 d_2^- + P_3 d_4^- + P_4 d_5^-$$

Overtime Minimization Goal.   The last goal is concerned with minimization of overtime work for full-time and part-time salespeople. Once again, we have a case of multiple subgoals at a given priority level. We could achieve this goal if we could minimize d_2^+ and d_4^+ to 0 in the following goal constraints:

$$x_1 + d_2^- - d_2^+ = 1,600$$
$$x_2 + d_4^- - d_4^+ = 640$$

We are interested in determining the differential weights to be assigned to d_2^+ and d_4^+. Full-time salespeople receive an average hourly wage of $6. Thus, an overtime hourly wage rate will be $9, time-and-a-half pay. With this payroll cost, Big Sound Records can expect sales of 10 records, which would result in $15 gross profit. Thus, the expected profit–payroll ratio is

$$\frac{\$15}{\$9} = \frac{5}{3}$$

Part-time salespeople do not receive overtime pay but rather the regular hourly wage rate of $4 for any work beyond their normal monthly working schedule of 80 hours. With an extra overtime hour, a part-time salesperson is expected to sell 6 records, resulting in $9 gross profit. Thus, the expected profit/payroll ratio is

$$\frac{\$9}{\$4} = \frac{9}{4}$$

It should be clear now that if we have to provide overtime in order to achieve the higher-priority goals, we should provide overtime to the part-time employees rather than to the full-time employees. The profit–payroll ratios for full-time and part-time salespeople are as follows:

	Salespeople	
Ratio	Full-time	Part-time
Actual	$\frac{5}{3}$	$\frac{9}{4}$
Integer (multiply by 4 × 3)	20	27

Since the profit–payroll ratio is lower for the full-time employee group, the relative cost of overtime is higher for the full-time salespeople. Thus, we can reverse the differential weight assignment so that minimization of overtime for the full-time salespeople will be given a greater weight than that for the part-time salespeople. The objective function becomes

$$\text{Minimize } Z = P_1 d_1^- + P_2 d_3^+ + 2P_3 d_2^- + P_3 d_4^-$$
$$+ P_4 d_5^- + 27P_5 d_2^+ + 20P_5 d_4^+$$

Now the complete goal-programming model for the Big Sound Records problem can be formulated as follows:

$$\text{Minimize } Z = P_1 d_1^- + P_2 d_3^+ + 2P_3 d_2^- + P_3 d_4^- + P_4 d_5^- + 27P_5 d_2^+ + 20P_5 d_4^+$$

$$\begin{aligned}
\text{subject to} \quad 10x_1 + 6x_2 + d_1^- - d_1^+ &= 22{,}000 \\
x_1 \qquad\quad + d_2^- - d_2^+ &= 1{,}600 \\
d_2^+ + d_3^- - d_3^+ &= 200 \\
x_2 + d_4^- - d_4^+ &= 640 \\
15x_1 + 9x_2 + d_5^- - d_5^+ &= 31{,}000 \\
x_1, x_2, d_i^-, d_i^+ &\geq 0 \quad (i = 1, 2, \ldots, 5)
\end{aligned}$$

A Problem with System Constraints and Multiple Objectives In this section, we will examine a more complex case involving a number of system constraints and multiple objectives. With the model formulation experience we have accumulated thus far, it should be relatively simple to formulate a goal-programming model for an additional problem.

Casette 6.4   ***BLEEKER COLLEGE FOUNDATION***

Bleeker College is a private fine arts college with a long tradition. With decreasing student enrollment and rising educational cost, Bleeker has been very aggressively engaged in alumni fund-raising activities. Recently, Dr. Joseph Anthony's estate informed the college that the late physician had left his entire Western art collection to Bleeker.

The Bleeker College Foundation has been successful in negotiating with the Guggenheim Museum for the sale of the entire collection of 42 fine paintings by early Western artists. The basic agreement is that Bleeker will receive a total of $2 million during the next 4 years. The payment schedule will be as follows: year 1, $1.2 million; year 2, $500,000; year 3, $200,000; year 4, $100,000.

The conditions of this gift are complex. The most restrictive condition is that funds from the sale of the paintings must be safely invested. The bequest specifically indicated that the funds could be invested only in real estate, government bonds, money market funds, and local bank stocks. The current annual yield rates of the investment alternatives are as follows: real estate, 15 percent; government bonds, 12 percent; money market funds, 16 percent; and bank stocks, 10 percent. The Anthony family also specified the following required expenditures from the gift during the first 5 years:

1. Establish a distinguished professorship with the name of Joseph Anthony Professor of Free Enterprise in the school of business with a salary of at least $40,000 per academic year. Also, provide an operating budget of $10,000 for the clerical and office expenses of the professorship. Both the professorship and the operating budget must be increased by 10 percent per year during the next 5 years.

2. Establish at least two $2,000 scholarships in each of the following departments: basic science, premed, fine arts, Romance languages, and business management. Starting in the third year, at least three scholarships should be provided in each department.

3. Create a dean's discretionary account in the school of business during the third year at an annual allocation of $100,000.

The board of directors of the Bleeker College Foundation decided to set the following goals for the Anthony gift in the order of their importance:

1. Invest at least 50 percent of all funds available in the most liquid investment vehicles — government bonds and money market funds.

2. Invest at least $200,000 in The First National Bank stocks, which have shown the most stable growth of the available alternatives during the past several years.

3. Establish the chaired professorship, Joseph Anthony Professor of Free Enterprise, and the operating budget for this professorship; secure enough funds for all of the required scholarships; and create the school of business discretionary fund.

4. Maximize the cash value of this gift by the end of the fifth year.

The Bleeker College Foundation would like to determine how the cash proceeds of the Anthony gift should be invested during the next 5 years to achieve the established objectives.

System Constraints

In this problem, the cash inflow and outflow during the 5-year period can be visualized as shown in Figure 6.9. Cash outflow in a given year must be limited to available cash. It is assumed that the Foundation will normally invest all of the funds available after

Figure 6.9   Cash Flows for the Bleeker College Foundation Problem

Cash Inflows	Year					
	1	2	3	4	5	6
Cash	$1,200,000	$500,000	$200,000	$100,000		
Real estate		$1.15RE_1$	$1.15RE_2$	$1.15RE_3$	$1.15RE_4$	$1.15RE_5$
Government bonds		$1.12B_1$	$1.12B_2$	$1.12B_3$	$1.12B_4$	$1.12B_5$
Money market fund		$1.16M_1$	$1.16M_2$	$1.16M_3$	$1.16M_4$	$1.16M_5$
Bank stock		$1.1BS_1$	$1.1BS_2$	$1.1BS_3$	$1.1BS_4$	$1.1BS_5$

Cash Outflows	Year				
	1	2	3	4	5
Real estate	RE_1	RE_2	RE_3	RE_4	RE_5
Government bonds	B_1	B_2	B_3	B_4	B_5
Money market fund	M_1	M_2	M_3	M_4	M_5
Bank stock	BS_1	BS_2	BS_3	BS_4	BS_5
Professorship & operating budget	$50,000	$55,000	$60,500	$66,550	$73,205
Scholarships	$20,000	$20,000	$30,000	$30,000	$30,000
Dean's fund, School of Business			$100,000	$100,000	$100,000

cash expenses for the professorship, scholarships, and dean's fund have been deducted from the available money. Thus, we can formulate the following system constraints:

Year 1: $RE_1 + B_1 + M_1 + BS_1 \leq 1,200,000$

Year 2: $RE_2 + B_2 + M_2 + BS_2 \leq 500,000 + 1.15RE_1 + 1.12B_1 + 1.16M_1 + 1.1BS_1$

Year 3: $RE_3 + B_3 + M_3 + BS_3 \leq 200,000 + 1.15RE_2 + 1.12B_2 + 1.16M_2 + 1.1BS_2$

Year 4: $RE_4 + B_4 + M_4 + BS_4 \leq 100,000 + 1.15RE_3 + 1.12B_3 + 1.16M_3 + 1.1BS_3$

Year 5: $RE_5 + B_5 + M_5 + BS_5 \leq 1.15RE_4 + 1.12B_4 + 1.16M_4 + 1.1BS_4$

Goal Constraints

In addition to the system constraints listed above, the Bleeker College Foundation has the following goal constraints:

1. At least 50 percent of all funds invested should be in government bonds and money market funds. Thus, the constraint is

$$\sum_{i=1}^{5} B_i + \sum_{i=1}^{5} M_i \geq .5 \left(\sum_{i=1}^{5} RE_i + \sum_{i=1}^{5} B_i + \sum_{i=1}^{5} M_i + \sum_{i=1}^{5} BS_i \right)$$

By introducing deviational variables and rearranging the variables, we obtain the following constraint, in which we minimize d_1^-:

$$-.5 \sum_{i=1}^{5} RE_i + .5 \sum_{i=1}^{5} B_i + .5 \sum_{i=1}^{5} M_i - .5 \sum_{i=1}^{5} BS_i + d_1^- - d_1^+ = 0$$

2. At least \$200,000 should be invested in The First National Bank stocks. This investment is assumed to satisfy the gift condition that some money should be invested in local bank stocks. Thus, we have the following constraint:

$$\sum_{i=1}^{5} BS_i + d_2^- - d_2^+ = 200,000$$

In this constraint, we should minimize d_2^-.

3. Sufficient funds should be secured for the chaired professorship and other cash expenditures. This constraint can be satisfied if cash inflow exceeds cash outflow by at least \$70,000 in the first year. The constraint for the first year is

$$1,200,000 - RE_1 - B_1 - M_1 - BS_1 \geq 70,000$$

Thus, we can develop the following goal constraint and minimize d_3^+:

$$RE_1 + B_1 + M_1 + BS_1 + d_3^- - d_3^+ = 1,130,000$$

Goal constraints for the remaining 4 years can be formulated in a similar manner. Note that the amount of cash expenditures differs for each year (refer to Figure 6.9):

$$RE_2 + B_2 + M_2 + BS_2 - 1.15RE_1 - 1.12B_1 - 1.16M_1 - 1.1BS_1$$
$$+ d_4^- - d_4^+ = 425,000$$

$$RE_3 + B_3 + M_3 + BS_3 - 1.15RE_2 - 1.12B_2 - 1.16M_2 - 1.1BS_2$$
$$+ d_5^- - d_5^+ = 9,500$$

$$1.15RE_3 + 1.12B_3 + 1.16M_3 + 1.1BS_3 - RE_4 - B_4 - M_4 - BS_4$$
$$+ d_6^- - d_6^+ = 96,550$$

$$1.15RE_4 + 1.12B_4 + 1.16M_4 + 1.1BS_4 - RE_5 - B_5 - M_5 - BS_5$$
$$+ d_7^- - d_7^+ = 203,205$$

In the above constraints, d_4^+, d_5^+, d_6^-, and d_7^- should be minimized. We transformed the sixth and seventh goal constraints because their right-hand-side values were negative. We simply multiply both sides by -1 and then minimize the negative deviational variable rather than the positive deviational variable.

4. The cash value of the Anthony gift should be maximized by the end of the fifth year. In Figure 6.9 it is obvious that the cash inflow by the end of the fifth year will be determined by the sum of $1.15RE_5 + 1.12B_5 + 1.16M_5 + 1.1BS_5$. We can set an arbitrarily large right-hand-side value of \$100,000,000 and then attempt to minimize the underachievement, or d_8^-:

$$1.15RE_5 + 1.12B_5 + 1.16M_5 + 1.1BS_5 + d_8^- - d_8^+ = 100,000,000$$

Now we formulate the complete goal-programming model for the Bleeker College Foundation problem as follows:

Minimize $Z = P_1 d_1^- + P_2 d_2^- + P_3(d_3^+ + d_4^+ + d_5^+ + d_6^- + d_7^-) + P_4 d_8^-$

subject to

$$RE_1 + B_1 + M_1 + BS_1 \leq 1,200,000$$
$$-1.15RE_1 + RE_2 - 1.12B_1 + B_2 - 1.16M_1 + M_2 - 1.1BS_1 + BS_2 \leq 500,000$$
$$-1.15RE_2 + RE_3 - 1.12B_2 + B_3 - 1.16M_2 + M_3 - 1.1BS_2 + BS_3 \leq 200,000$$
$$-1.15RE_3 + RE_4 - 1.12B_3 + B_4 - 1.16M_3 - M_4 - 1.1BS_3 + BS_4 \leq 100,000$$
$$-1.15RE_4 + RE_5 - 1.12B_4 + B_5 - 1.16M_4 - M_5 - 1.1BS_4 + BS_5 \leq 0$$
$$-.5\sum_{i=1}^{5} RE_i + .5\sum_{i=1}^{5} B_i + .5\sum_{i=1}^{5} M_i - .5\sum_{i=1}^{5} BS_i + d_1^- - d_1^+ = 0$$
$$\sum_{i=1}^{5} BS_i + d_2^- - d_2^+ = 200,000$$

$$RE_1 + B_1 + M_1 + BS_1 + d_3^- - d_3^+ = 1{,}130{,}000$$

$$RE_2 + B_2 + M_2 + BS_2 - 1.15RE_1 - 1.12B_1 - 1.16M_1 - 1.1BS_1 + d_4^- - d_4^+ = 425{,}000$$

$$RE_3 + B_3 + M_3 + BS_3 - 1.15RE_2 - 1.12B_2 - 1.16M_2 - 1.1BS_2 + d_5^- - d_5^+ = 9{,}500$$

$$1.15RE_3 + 1.12B_3 + 1.16M_3 + 1.1BS_3 - RE_4 - B_4 - M_4 - BS_4 + d_6^- - d_6^+ = 96{,}550$$

$$1.15RE_4 + 1.12B_4 + 1.16M_4 + 1.1BS_4 - RE_5 - B_5 - M_5 - BS_5 + d_7^- - d_7^+ = 203{,}205$$

$$1.15RE_5 + 1.12B_5 + 1.16M_5 + 1.1BS_5 + d_8^- - d_8^+ = 100{,}000{,}000$$

$$RE_i, B_i, M_i, BS_i, d_i^-, d_i^+ \geq 0$$

The Graphical Method of Goal Programming

Let us remember that the objective of goal programming is not the maximization or minimization of a single-objective criterion. Instead, the objective is to achieve a set of multiple goals as close to the desired levels as possible. The basic approach we will take is to minimize the deviations between the goals and what we can achieve within the given set of system constraints. The deviation from the goal with the highest priority factor will be minimized to the fullest possible extent, the deviation from the second goal will be minimized after considering the first goal, and so on. Thus, in goal programming, *the optimum solution is optimum only in the sense that it is the most attractive satisficing solution for multiple objectives.*

The goal-programming model is, therefore, always a minimization problem. To explain the graphical solution of goal programming, let us consider the following problem.

Casette 6.5   **AN ELECTRONICS MANUFACTURING FIRM**

A small electronics manufacturing firm produces AM-FM and AM radios. Production of a radio, regardless of its type, requires an average of 1 hour in the production plant. Currently, the company has a normal production capacity of 40 hours per week. The expected weekly sales for each type of radio are: AM-FM, 20; AM, 30. The unit profit for each type of radio is: AM-FM, $40; AM, $30.

The plant manager has the following goals for next week's plant operation, listed in the order of their importance:

1. Minimize underutilization of normal production capacity

2. Achieve the sales goal for AM-FM radios by producing at least 20 radios

3. Avoid overtime operation of the plant in excess of 10 hours

4. Achieve a weekly profit goal of $1,800

5. Achieve the sales goal for AM radios by producing at least 30 radios

Figure 6.10 Achievement of the First Goal

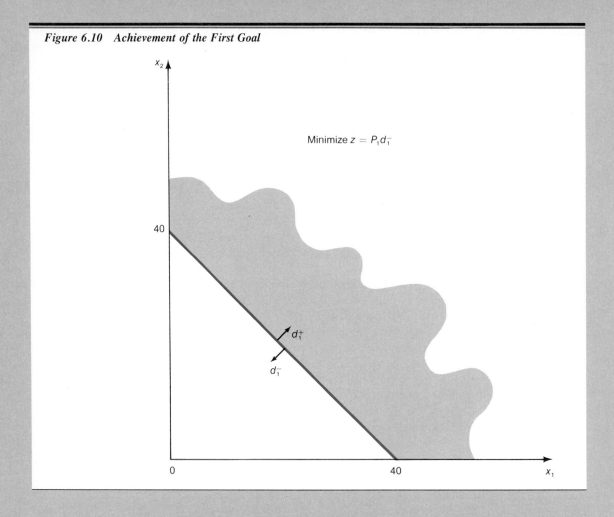

With the model formulation experience we have acquired in this chapter, we can easily formulate the following goal-programming model for the problem:

$$\text{Minimize } Z = P_1 d_1^- + P_2 d_2^- + P_3 d_3^+ + P_4 d_4^- + P_5 d_5^-$$

$$\text{subject to} \quad x_1 + x_2 + d_1^- - d_1^+ = 40$$

$$x_1 + d_2^- - d_2^+ = 20$$

$$x_1 + x_2 + d_3^- - d_3^+ = 50$$

$$40x_1 + 30x_2 + d_4^- - d_4^+ = 1,800$$

$$x_2 + d_5^- - d_5^+ = 30$$

$$x_1, x_2, d_i^-, d_i^+ \geq 0$$

Figure 6.11   Achievement of the First and Second Goals

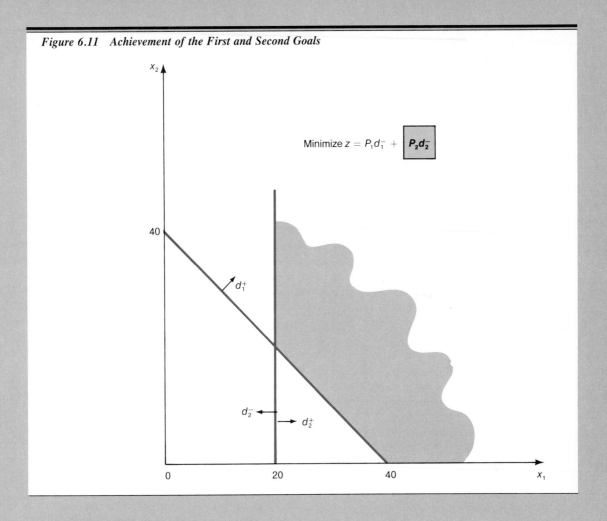

where

$$x_1 = \text{number of AM-FM radios to be produced}$$

$$x_2 = \text{number of AM radios to be produced}$$

To solve this problem, we will plot one constraint at a time, following the order of the objective function. For example, the most important goal is to minimize the under-utilization of capacity (the negative deviation) in the first constraint. Thus, we can plot the normal production capacity constraint and minimize d_1^-, as shown in Figure 6.10. When we minimize d_1^-, the feasible area becomes the shaded area. Any point in the shaded area will satisfy the first goal because the total production hours will be 40 or more.

The second goal is to minimize the underachievement of the sales goal for AM-FM radios. This can be accomplished by minimizing d_2^- in the second constraint. However, this goal must be sought within the feasible area already defined by satisfying the first goal. Thus, the feasible area becomes further reduced, as shown in Figure 6.11.

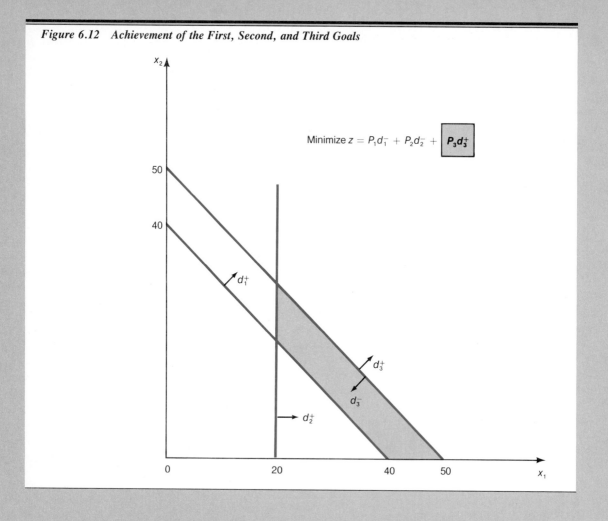

Figure 6.12   Achievement of the First, Second, and Third Goals

The third goal is to limit overtime operation of the plant to 10 hours. This goal would be achieved if we could minimize d_3^+ to 0 within the feasible area. As can be seen in Figure 6.12, the third goal is achieved, and the feasible area is now a narrow strip. Within this shaded area, any solution would satisfy the first three most important goals.

The fourth goal, to achieve the weekly profit goal of $1,800, can be satisfied by minimizing d_4^- in the fourth constraint. The process further reduces the feasible area. The narrow space of feasible area that remains is shown in Figure 6.13.

The last goal of the problem is to achieve the sales goal for AM radios. We must minimize d_5^- as much as possible. In the feasible area already defined by ABC in Figure 6.14, it is impossible to minimize d_5^- all the way to 0. Thus, we must search for the point, within the feasible area, that is closest to the $x_2 = 30$ line. It is obvious that point A is the optimum solution.

At point A, we can easily derive the values of x_1 and x_2 by solving the two intersecting equalities simultaneously. We obtain $x_1 = 30$ and $x_2 = 20$. By substituting

Figure 6.13 *Achievement of the First, Second, Third, and Fourth Goals*

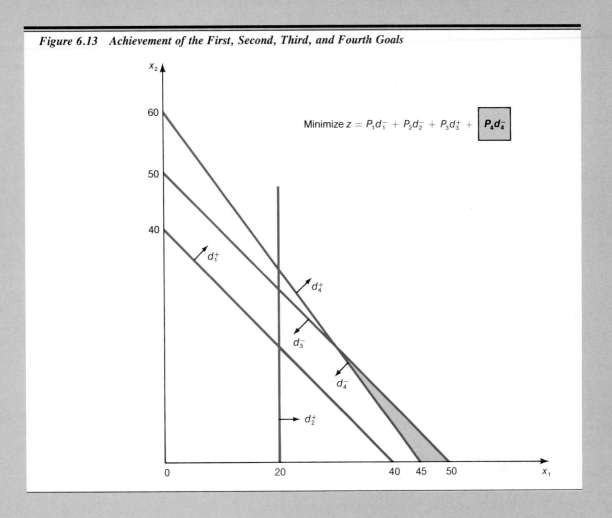

these values in all of the goal constraints, we find the following basic variables:

$x_1 = 30$, $x_2 = 20$, $d_1^+ = 10$, $d_2^+ = 10$, $d_5^- = 10$, and all other variables $= 0$

Based on the solution values, we can interpret the degree of goal attainment as follows:

P_1:   Attained (plant is in operation for 50 hours)

P_2:   Attained (30 AM-FM radios sold)

P_3:   Attained (overtime operation of the plant is limited to 10 hours)

P_4:   Attained (profit of $1,800 is attained)

P_5:   Not attained (produced only 20 AM radios—underachievement of 10 AM radios)

Figure 6.14   *The Optimum Solution for the Electronics Firm Problem*

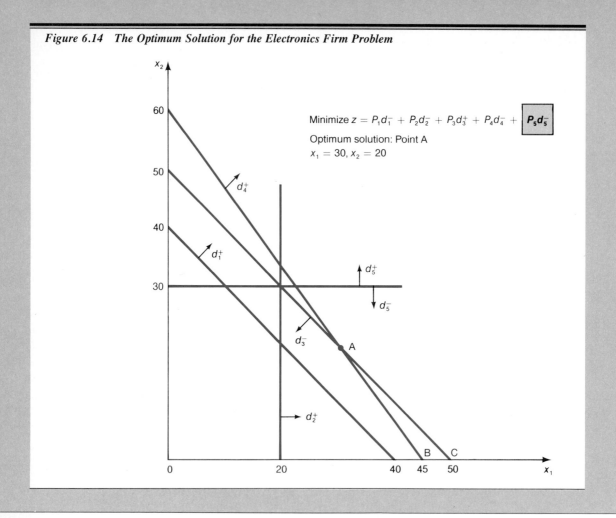

The Modified Simplex Method of Goal Programming

There have been several solution methods introduced for goal programming. Some methods are more efficient in terms of computation time on the computer. However, almost every solution technique is based on the basic solution approach known as the *modified simplex method*. This method, developed by S. M. Lee, takes advantage of the unique features of the goal-programming model in applying the simplex technique.

Some of the best-known solution techniques of goal programming, such as the goal-partitioning algorithm and the revised simplex method of goal programming, are based on the modified simplex method framework augmented by efficient-matrix manipulation methods. We will summarize the steps involved in the modified simplex method of goal programming in a later section of this chapter. However, the basic steps we will be following are presented in the simple flow diagram shown in Figure 6.15.

Figure 6.15   Goal Programming Solution Process by the Modified Simplex Method

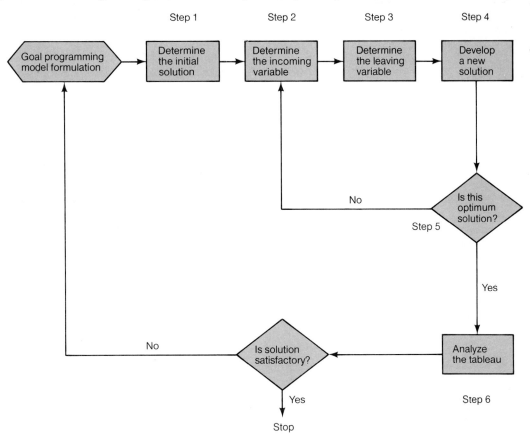

Consider the following problem:

$$\text{Minimize } Z = P_1 d_1^- + P_2 d_4^+ + 5P_3 d_2^- + 3P_3 d_3^- + P_4 d_1^+$$

$$\text{subject to} \quad x_1 + x_2 + d_1^- - d_1^+ = 80 \text{ (hours)}$$

$$x_1 \qquad + d_2^- - d_2^+ = 70 \text{ (production of item 1)}$$

$$x_2 + d_3^- - d_3^+ = 45 \text{ (production of item 2)}$$

$$x_1 + x_2 + d_4^- - d_4^+ = 90 \text{ (hours of overtime)}$$

$$x_1, x_2, d_i^-, d_i^+ \geq 0$$

Before we jump into the modified simplex method of goal programming, we must remember several key features of the goal-programming model:

1. In a goal-programming model, our objective is not to optimize one criterion but to achieve multiple objectives. The basic approach we take is to minimize the deviational variables through the use of priority factors and differential weights.

2. Since the objective function is expressed by priorities and associated differential weights, c_j or c_b values are represented by these weights rather than by unit contribution rates.

3. The preemptive priority weights are not one-dimensional values but multidimensional values. Therefore, z_j or $z_j - c_j$ requires a matrix because it cannot be represented by a single row.

4. Since the simplex criterion $z_j - c_j$ is a matrix, the selection of the pivot column must be determined by the priority factors. In other words, we must select the pivot column that would improve the highest unachieved priority goal by the greatest amount.

5. The modified simplex method of goal programming attempts to satisfy the system constraints, if there are any, by assigning the superpriority P_0 to the appropriate deviational variables. Then, it proceeds to achieve the most important goal to the fullest possible extent, then the second goal, and so on in sequence.

6. A goal-programming model is a minimization problem. Thus, we must calculate $z_j - c_j$ rather than $c_j - z_j$.

Developing the Initial Simplex Tableau This step is similar to that of the simplex method of linear programming. We assume that the initial solution is at the origin, where we do not produce anything. Thus, $x_1 = 0$ and $x_2 = 0$. Substituting these values of the decision variables in the constraints, we can determine the basic variables.

In the first constraint, because $x_1 = 0$ and $x_2 = 0$, then d_1^+ (e.g., overtime operation to produce the two products) must be 0. Thus, d_1^- will take the right-hand-side value as shown:

$$x_1 + x_2 + d_1^- - d_1^+ = 80$$
$$0 + 0 + d_1^- - 0 = 80$$
$$d_1^- = 80$$

The basic variable for the first constraint is d_1^-, and the solution value is 80.

In a similar manner, we can determine that d_2^-, d_3^-, and d_4^- are also basic variables. As a matter of fact, it is a rule that the negative deviational variables (d_i^-) in each of the constraints become the basic variables in the initial tableau.

The initial simplex tableau is presented in Table 6.3. The c_j and c_b values are obtained from the objective function of the model. For example, P_1 was assigned to d_1^- in the objective function. Thus, P_1 is listed as c_j in the d_1^- column and in the d_1^- row. The z_j matrix is omitted to simplify the simplex tableau. The simplex criterion $z_j - c_j$ is calculated in one operation, first z_j and then subtracting c_j.

In the basis column, we list the priorities in ascending order, from the lowest at the top to the highest at the bottom. In this way we can determine the pivot column from the bottom of the tableau.

In the solution column, we simply calculate the z_j value. The z_j value in the solution column is calculated by the same procedure we used in linear programming:

Table 6.3   The Initial Simplex Tableau

c_b	c_j Basis	Solution	0 x_1	0 x_2	P_1 d_1^-	$5P_3$ d_2^-	$3P_3$ d_3^-	0 d_4^-	P_4 d_1^+	0 d_2^+	0 d_3^+	P_2 d_4^+
P_1	d_1^-	80	1	1	1	0	0	0	-1	0	0	0
$5P_3$	d_2^-	70	①	0	0	1	0	0	0	-1	0	0
$3P_3$	d_3^-	45	0	1	0	0	1	0	0	0	-1	0
0	d_4^-	90	1	1	0	0	0	1	0	0	0	-1
	P_4	0	0	0	0	0	0	0	-1	0	0	0
$z_j - c_j$	P_3	485	5	3	0	0	0	0	0	-5	-3	0
	P_2	0	0	0	0	0	0	0	0	0	0	-1
	P_1	80	1	1	0	0	0	0	-1	0	0	0

$$z_j \text{ (solution)} = \Sigma \, (c_b \times \text{solution values})$$
$$= (P_1 \times 80) + (5P_3 \times 70) + (3P_3 \times 45) + (0 \times 90)$$
$$= 80P_1 + 485P_3$$

The z_j value in the solution column represents the unattained portion of each goal. For example, in the initial tableau, z_j values in the solution column are $P_1 = 80$, $P_2 = 0$, $P_3 = 485$, and $P_4 = 0$. In other words, the first and third goals are not completely attained, but the second and fourth goals are completely attained. How can this be possible when our solution is at the origin, where we are not even operating? When we examine the objective function, it is clear that the second and fourth goals are to minimize the **overachievement** of operating-hours limits as much as possible. Since we are not even operating, there is no overachievement.

The **underachievement** of the first goal is 80 because our goal is to operate for at least 80 hours, and we are idle. The unattained portion of the third goal is 485. This value is a bit difficult to explain. The third goal is concerned with achieving the production goals. We assigned differential weights of 5 and 3 to the achievement of the production goals for two items. These two subgoals are commensurable (i.e., they are measured in number of units). Since we have not achieved the production goal of 70 of the first item and 45 of the second item, the total unattained portion of this goal will be $(70 \times 5) + (45 \times 3) = 485$.

For the variable columns, we must calculate the $z_j - c_j$ value in one operation. First, we must compute the z_j value in each of the variable columns. We must remember that the $z_j - c_j$ value is 0 in the basic-variable columns. Therefore, we can eliminate the d_1^-, d_2^-, d_3^-, and d_4^- columns from the $z_j - c_j$ calculation. Calculation of z_j in a variable column can be accomplished by the following procedure:

$$z_j \text{ (variable column)} = \Sigma \, (c_b \times \text{coefficients})$$

Thus, the z_j value in the x_1 column is

$$z_j \, (x_1) = (P_1 \times 1) + (5P_3 \times 1) + (3P_3 \times 0) + (0 \times 1)$$
$$= P_1 + 5P_3$$

The c_j value in the x_1 column is 0, as shown at the top of the column. Thus, $z_j - c_j$ for the x_1 column is $(P_1 + 5P_3) - 0 = P_1 + 5P_3$.

Since P_1 and P_3 are not commensurable, we must list them separately in the P_1 and P_3 rows of the simplex criterion. Thus, we list *1* at the P_1 level and *5* at the P_3 level. In a similar manner, we can derive the $z_j - c_j$ value in the x_2 column:

$$z_j (x_2) = (P_1 \times 1) + (5P_3 \times 0) + (3P_3 \times 1) + (0 \times 1)$$
$$= P_1 + 3P_3$$

The c_j value is also 0 in the x_2 column. Therefore, $z_j - c_j = P_1 + 3P_3$. We also list *1* at the P_1 level and *3* at the P_3 level.

The $z_j - c_j$ values in the basic-variable columns d_1^-, d_2^-, d_3^-, and d_4^- will all be 0. For the d_1^+ column, the z_j value is $-P_1$. Since the c_j value of the column is P_4, the $z_j - c_j$ value will be $-P_1 - P_4$. Therefore, -1 is listed in the P_1 row and also in the P_4 row. It should be a simple task to calculate $z_j - c_j$ in the d_2^+ and d_3^+ columns. They are $-5P_3$ and $-3P_3$ respectively. In the last column, d_4^+, the z_j value is 0. But its c_j value is P_2. Thus, the $z_j - c_j$ value will be $-P_2$. Accordingly, we list -1 in the P_2 row.

As we discussed earlier, we combined into one the calculational procedures for determining z_j and $z_j - c_j$ in the simplex tableau. The single procedure obviously requires more mental calculations, but it certainly makes the tableau simpler to handle. If a problem containing 5 preemptive priorities and 20 variables is being analyzed, we can avoid a 5×20 matrix by calculating $z_j - c_j$ in one operation.

Now, let us move on to the selection of the pivot column and the pivot row. The criterion we use in determining the pivot column is the rate of contribution of each nonbasic variable in achieving the highest unattained objective in terms of the priorities. In Table 6.3, the highest unattained priority goal is P_1, where we have 80 hours of unattained goal. Thus, we are searching for a nonbasic-variable column that has the largest positive $z_j - c_j$ value at the P_1 level.

In Table 6.3, there are two identical positive values in the x_1 and x_2 columns. To break this tie, we check the next-lower priority level. Since there is a greater value (5) in the x_1 column at the P_3 level as compared to the x_2 column (3), we select x_1 as the pivot column.

The pivot row selection procedure is exactly the same as that employed in linear programming. The pivot row is the row that has the minimum nonnegative value when we divide the solution values by the positive coefficients in the pivot column. For example, we have three positive coefficients in the x_1 column in the d_1^-, d_2^-, and d_4^- rows. Thus, we can divide the solution values by the positive coefficients as follows:

Row	Solution	÷	Coefficient	=	Quotient
d_1^-	80	÷	1	=	80
d_2^-	70	÷	1	=	70 ← pivot row
d_4^-	90	÷	1	=	90

The pivot row is selected as the d_2^- row. In Table 6.3, the blue numbers identify x_1 as the pivot column and d_2^- as the pivot row.

The First Iteration   Now we are ready to develop the second simplex tableau. We can apply the regular simplex procedure to complete the first iteration.

In the initial tableau shown in Table 6.3, we identified x_1 as the incoming variable and d_2^- as the outgoing variable. The pivot element is also identified by the circle. To find the new values in the pivot row and in the other rows, we use the following procedures:

Pivot Row: New value = old value ÷ pivot element

Other Rows: New value = old value − (row value × new value in pivot row)

Table 6.4 presents the simplex tableau after the first iteration. The solution indicates that we operate for 70 hours to produce 70 units of item 1, and thus $x_1 = 70$. Therefore, the underutilization of the normal operating hours is 10 hours ($d_1^- = 10$). We have now completely achieved the production goal for item 1, and, therefore, d_2^- has been removed from the solution basis.

Since we have not yet produced any item 2, underachievement of the production goal for item 2 is 45 ($d_3^- = 45$). Currently, we are in operation for 70 hours. Since the acceptable overtime operation is 10 hours (see the fourth constraint), we are underutilizing 20 hours from the total allowed operation hours of 90 ($d_4^- = 20$).

The z_j values in the solution column in Table 6.4 indicate that the unattained portion of the first goal has been decreased considerably, from 80 to 10. This is a good sign because the goal-programming model is a minimization problem, and the value of z_j should decrease at each step toward the optimum solution. As our immediate concern is the achievement of the most important goal, we can simply examine whether z_j has decreased at the P_1 level at each iteration. When z_j is at the P_1 level and is completely minimized to 0, we can then focus our attention on the z_j value at the P_2 level, and so on. In Table 6.4, z_j at the P_3 level has also decreased by 350, as the production of 70 units of item 1 enables the achievement of the production goal for that item.

Table 6.4   The Second Simplex Tableau

c_b	c_j Basis	Solution	0 x_1	0 x_2	P_1 d_1^-	$5P_3$ d_2^-	$3P_3$ d_3^-	0 d_4^-	P_4 d_1^+	0 d_2^+	0 d_3^+	P_2 d_4^+
P_1	d_1^-	10	0	①	1	−1	0	0	−1	1	0	0
0	x_1	70	1	0	0	1	0	0	0	−1	0	0
$3P_3$	d_3^-	45	0	1	0	0	1	0	0	0	−1	0
0	d_4^-	20	0	1	0	−1	0	1	0	1	0	−1
	P_4	0	0	0	0	0	0	0	−1	0	0	0
$z_j - c_j$	P_3	135	0	3	0	−5	0	0	0	0	−3	0
	P_2	0	0	0	0	0	0	0	0	0	0	−1
	P_1	10	0	1	0	−1	0	0	−1	1	0	0

Table 6.5   The Third Simplex Tableau

c_j			0	0	P_1	$5P_3$	$3P_3$	0	P_4	0	0	P_2
c_b	Basis	Solution	x_1	x_2	d_1^-	d_2^-	d_3^-	d_4^-	d_1^+	d_2^+	d_3^+	d_4^+
0	x_2	10	0	1	1	-1	0	0	-1	1	0	0
0	x_1	70	1	0	0	1	0	0	0	-1	0	0
$3P_3$	d_3^-	35	0	0	-1	1	1	0	1	-1	-1	0
0	d_4^-	10	0	0	-1	0	0	1	①	0	0	-1
	P_4	0	0	0	0	0	0	0	-1	0	0	0
$z_j - c_j$	P_3	105	0	0	-3	-2	0	0	3	-3	-3	0
	P_2	0	0	0	0	0	0	0	0	0	0	-1
	P_1	0	0	0	-1	0	0	0	0	0	0	0

The Second Iteration   In the second simplex tableau shown in Table 6.4, we can identify x_2 as the pivot column. The best way to achieve the most important goal is by producing 10 units of item 2, thereby operating for a total of 80 hours. Thus, the pivot row is the d_1^- row.

Table 6.5 presents the third simplex tableau. The solution indicates that production of 70 units of item 1 and 10 of item 2 is sufficient to achieve the first, second, and fourth goals. However, the third goal is not completely attained, since the production goal of item 2 is still 35 short ($d_3^- = 35$, shown in the solution basis).

A very interesting point we discover in Table 6.5 is that when a goal is attained there should be only 0 or negative $z_j - c_j$ values at the given priority level. For example, we can ascertain that the P_1 goal is attained when z_j at the P_1 level is 0. Therefore, all $z_j - c_j$ values at the P_1 level are either 0 or negative. The same result is found at the P_2 and P_4 levels. However, since the P_3 goal is not attained (i.e., the z_j value is 105), there should be at least one positive $z_j - c_j$ value at the P_3 level. We can find a positive $z_j - c_j$ value of 3 in the d_1^+ column.

The Optimum Solution   The selection of the pivot column should be determined at the P_3 level. The d_1^+ column is the pivot column, and d_4^- is the pivot row. The fourth simplex tableau is presented in Table 6.6. This solution is the optimum solution. Notice that the z_j value at the P_3 level was decreased from 105 to 75. To decrease the underachievement of the third goal, we sacrificed the attainment of the fourth goal by 10 units, as shown by the z_j value at the P_4 level.

The optimum solution is $x_1 = 70$, $x_2 = 20$, $d_3^- = 25$, and $d_1^+ = 10$. In other words, the company should produce 70 of item 1 and 20 of item 2 with 10 hours of overtime operation, missing item 2's production goal by 25. With this solution, the company's goal attainment will be as follows:

P_1:   Attained

P_2:   Attained

P_3:   Not attained (underachievement of sales goal for item 2 by 25)

P_4:   Not attained (10 hours of overtime operation)

Table 6.6   The Optimum Solution Tableau

c_b	Basis	Solution	0 x_1	0 x_2	P_1 d_1^-	$5P_3$ d_2^-	$3P_3$ d_3^-	0 d_4^-	P_4 d_1^+	0 d_2^+	0 d_3^+	P_2 d_4^+
0	x_2	20	0	1	0	-1	0	1	0	1	0	-1
0	x_1	70	1	0	0	1	0	0	0	-1	0	0
$3P_3$	d_3^-	25	0	0	0	1	1	-1	0	-1	-1	1
P_4	d_1^+	10	0	0	-1	0	0	1	1	0	0	-1
	P_4	10	0	0	-1	0	0	1	0	0	0	-1
$z_j - c_j$	P_3	75	0	0	0	-2	0	-3	0	-3	-3	3
	P_2	0	0	0	0	0	0	0	0	0	0	-1
	P_1	0	0	0	-1	0	0	0	0	0	0	0

In Table 6.6, since the third goal is not attained, there is a positive $z_j - c_j$ value at the P_3 level. This value is 3 in the d_4^+ column. Obviously, we can attain the third goal if we introduce d_4^+ into the solution. We find, however, a negative $z_j - c_j$ value (-1) at a higher priority level (i.e., at the P_2 level). This implies that if we introduce d_4^+ into the solution, we would improve the achievement of the third goal (P_3) at the expense of achieving the second goal (P_2). Of course, we are not willing to accept this trade-off. Thus, we cannot introduce d_4^+ into the solution.

The same logic applies to the d_4^- column. We find a positive $z_j - c_j$ value of 1 at the P_4 level in the d_4^- column. However, there is a negative $z_j - c_j$ value of -3 at a higher priority level (i.e., P_3). Therefore, d_4^- cannot be selected as the pivot column. The optimum solution must satisfy one of the following two conditions:

1. The z_j values in the solution column are 0 at all priority levels. This is a case in which all priority goals are attained. This case can occur only when there is no conflict among the goals.

2. There is no pivot column to be selected because all the positive $z_j - c_j$ values at the various priority levels have accompanying negative $z_j - c_j$ values below them (i.e., at higher priority levels). This is a case in which some of the goals are in conflict. Thus, all goals cannot be achieved as desired.

The complete modified simplex solution procedure is shown in Figure 6.16.

Goal Conflicts   We can derive some valuable information from the final simplex tableau. From an analysis of the $z_j - c_j$ values, we can point out where conflict exists among the goals. For example, in Table 6.6 we can easily identify the conflict between the second and third goals in the d_4^+ column. Also, there is a conflict between the third and fourth goals in the d_4^- column. Now we can determine precisely how we must rearrange the priority structure if the underachieved goals at the lower levels are to be attained. This process of analyzing goal conflicts provides an opportunity for us to evaluate the soundness of our priority structure for the goals.

Figure 6.16   The Modified Simplex Solution Procedure for the Jeans Galore Problem

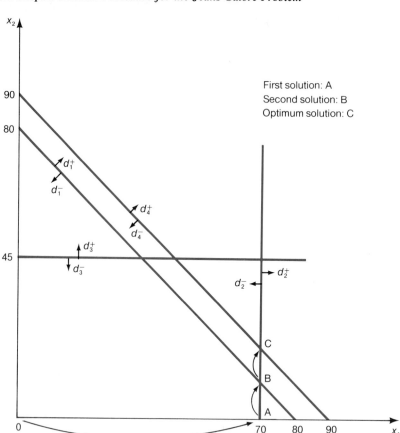

We can also analyze the coefficients in the main body of the final simplex tableau in order to identify the exact trade-offs between the goals that are in conflict. For example, in Table 6.6 we can see that if we introduce 25 units of d_4^+ into the solution, the third goal will be completely attained by reducing the unattained portion of this goal by 75. However, this procedure will "undo" the second goal by 25 units, and the degree of attainment of the fourth goal will also deteriorate by 25 units. The marginal substitution rate in this case is 3:1, as can be seen by the coefficients shown below:

c_b	c_j Basis	Solution	. . .	P_2 d_4^+	Effects of 25 units of d_4^+
	$\vdots$	$\vdots$			
$z_j - c_j$	P_4	10	$\vdots$	-1	25
	P_3	75		3	-75
	P_2	0		-1	25
	P_1	0		0	0

The same type of analysis can be made in the d_4^- column. The trade-off rate between the third and fourth goals is 3:1. An analysis of the final simplex tableau provides a great deal of information about and insight into the decision environment and the decision maker's goal priority structure.

Some Goal-Programming Complications

As in linear programming, there are several unique situations in goal programming. Some of these situations are common to all linear optimization techniques. However, certain unique features of goal programming provide us with ways to resolve some of these complications.

Negative Right-hand-side Value   It is possible that the right-hand-side value of a certain goal constraint may be negative. In such a case, we must first multiply both sides by -1 and then introduce the appropriate deviational variables. For example, let us consider the following goal constraint:

$$-2x_2 + x_3 - x_4 \geq -10$$

The goal is to make the left-hand side of the inequality greater than or equal to -10. Now we multiply both sides by -1 and obtain

$$2x_2 - x_3 + x_4 \leq 10$$

Then, we introduce the deviational variables and attempt to minimize the positive deviation in the goal constraint:

$$2x_2 - x_3 + x_4 + d_1^- - d_1^+ = 10$$

A Tie in Selecting the Pivot Column   This situation has already been clarified. If there is a tie in selecting the pivot column, the $z_j - c_j$ values at the lower priority levels of the two tied columns should be compared. If the tie cannot be broken, select the column that has a lower priority factor as its c_j value. If the tie is still not broken, select between the contending variable columns arbitrarily.

A Tie in Selecting the Pivot Row   This situation has also been explained previously. To determine the pivot row, the solution values are divided by the positive coefficients in the pivot column. The row that has the minimum nonnegative value is the pivot row. If two or more rows have the identical minimum nonnegative quotient, the tie is broken by selecting the variable row with the highest priority factor.

Multiple Optimum Solutions   For certain problems, it is possible that two or more extreme points yield solutions that achieve exactly the same goal levels. Such a situation never occurs if: (1) there is a single goal at each of the priority levels; (2) differential weights are assigned among the subgoals when there is more than one goal at a given priority level; and (3) conflicts exist among some of the goals.

An Unbounded Problem   For some problems, it is theoretically possible that lack of system constraints or realistic goal levels may allow one or more variables to increase without bound. However, in most real-world situations such a situation never occurs because of restrictive system constraints or goal conflicts.

An Infeasible Problem   When there is a conflict among the system constraints, the problem is infeasible. We can assign the superpriority P_0 to the deviational variables in the system constraints. Then, in the final simplex tableau, the z_j value in the solution

Figure 6.17   Results of Interactive Mode of Goal Programming Using **Micro Manager**

PROGRAM: Goal Programming

INPUT DATA ENTERED

Min $Z = P 1 \, dn \, 1 + P 2 \, dp \, 4 + 5 P 3 \, dn \, 2 + 3 P 3 \, dn \, 3 + P 4 \, dp \, 1$

Subject to:

```
C 1    1 x 1 + 1 x 2 + dn 1 - dp 1  =  80
C 2    1 x 1 + dn 2 - dp 2  =  70
C 3    1 x 2 + dn 3 - dp 3  =  45
C 4    1 x 1 + 1 x 2 + dn 4 - dp 4  =  90
```

PROGRAM OUTPUT

Initial tableau

C#	Cb	Basis	Bi
C 1	1P 1	-d 1	80.00
C 2	5P 3	-d 2	70.00
C 3	3P 3	-d 3	45.00
C 4	0	-d 4	90.00

\Cj C#	1P 1 -d 1	5P 3 -d 2	3P 3 -d 3	0 -d 4	1P 4 +d 1	0 +d 2	0 +d 3	1P 2 +d 4	0 x 1	0 x 2
C 1	1.00	0.00	0.00	0.00	-1.00	0.00	0.00	0.00	1.00	1.00
C 2	0.00	1.00	0.00	0.00	0.00	-1.00	0.00	0.00	1.00	0.00
C 3	0.00	0.00	1.00	0.00	0.00	0.00	-1.00	0.00	0.00	1.00
C 4	0.00	0.00	0.00	1.00	0.00	0.00	0.00	-1.00	1.00	1.00
P 4	0.00	0.00	0.00	0.00	-1.00	0.00	0.00	0.00	0.00	0.00
P 3	0.00	0.00	0.00	0.00	0.00	-5.00	-3.00	0.00	5.00	3.00
P 2	0.00	0.00	0.00	0.00	0.00	0.00	0.00	-1.00	0.00	0.00
P 1	0.00	0.00	0.00	0.00	-1.00	0.00	0.00	0.00	1.00	1.00

column should be 0 if the problem is to be feasible. If the z_j value at the P_0 level is positive, the problem is infeasible. In such a case, the system constraints must be carefully analyzed to determine whether the conflict among system constraints can be resolved.

Computer Solution of Goal-Programming Problems

Because of the nature of goal programming, even a small problem can be quite cumbersome to solve using the modified simplex method. Consequently, even small goal-programming problems are solved with computers.

The most widely used mainframe program for goal programming is *GPGO*, developed by Sang M. Lee. This program is especially useful to solve relatively large goal-

Figure 6.17 *(continued)*

Final tableau (iteration 4)

C#	Cb	Basis	Bi
C 1	0	x 2	20.00
C 2	0	x 1	70.00
C 3	3P 3	-d 3	25.00
C 4	1P 4	+d 1	10.00

\Cj C#	1P 1 -d 1	5P 3 -d 2	3P 3 -d 3	0 -d 4	1P 4 +d 1	0 +d 2	0 +d 3	1P 2 +d 4	0 x 1	0 x 2
C 1	0.00	-1.00	0.00	1.00	0.00	1.00	0.00	-1.00	0.00	1.00
C 2	0.00	1.00	0.00	0.00	0.00	-1.00	0.00	0.00	1.00	0.00
C 3	0.00	1.00	1.00	-1.00	0.00	-1.00	-1.00	1.00	0.00	0.00
C 4	-1.00	0.00	0.00	1.00	1.00	0.00	0.00	-1.00	0.00	0.00
P 4	-1.00	0.00	0.00	1.00	0.00	0.00	0.00	-1.00	0.00	0.00
P 3	0.00	-2.00	0.00	-3.00	0.00	-3.00	-3.00	3.00	0.00	0.00
P 2	0.00	0.00	0.00	0.00	0.00	0.00	0.00	-1.00	0.00	0.00
P 1	-1.00	0.00	0.00	0.00	0.00	0.00	0.00	0.00	0.00	0.00

Analysis of deviations

Constraint	RHS Value	d+	d-
C 1	80.00	10.00	0.00
C 2	70.00	0.00	0.00
C 3	45.00	0.00	25.00
C 4	90.00	0.00	0.00

Analysis of decision variables

Variable	Solution value
x 2	20.00
x 1	70.00

Analysis of the objective function

Priority	Nonachievement
P 1	0.00
P 2	0.00
P 3	75.00
P 4	10.00

programming problems. The most user-friendly microcomputer program for goal programming is contained in *Micro Manager*.

Figure 6.17 presents the results of the interactive mode of goal programming using *Micro Manager*. The computer printout presents the input data, simplex tableaux, and the analysis of the model results. To save space, we present only the initial and the final simplex tableaux.

The final result indicates that $x_1 = 70$, $x_2 = 20$, $d_1^+ = 10$, and $d_3^- = 25$. The first two goals are completely achieved, the third goal has a nonachievement of 75, and the fourth goal has a nonachievement of 10. This is the exact result we obtained with the modified simplex method.

OTHER TOPICS IN ADVANCED LINEAR PROGRAMMING

In this section we will briefly review several topics of advanced linear programming for those who would like to conduct independent studies. Some of these topics relate to the development and extension of the theory of linear programming; others relate to the new applications of linear programming.

Linear Programming under Uncertainty

As we have discussed earlier, the general linear programming approach is deterministic. This assumption makes linear programming an extremely simple technique to use. However, this assumption is also a source of limitation in the practical application of linear programming. The true value of model parameters is usually not known until after the decision based on a linear programming solution is actually implemented, primarily because frequently all or some of the parameters are random variables — variables that are influenced by random events in the decision environment.

Several different approaches have been suggested for the solution of the linear programming problem under uncertainty. However, we can express their common characteristic as the "extreme difficulty of solution." There is no general solution method of linear programming under uncertainty, such as the simplex method for the deterministic linear programming problem.

There are basically two approaches to linear programming under uncertainty. The first approach, which is generally referred to as **stochastic programming,** attempts to solve the problem through making two or more decisions by selecting model parameters at different points in time. This approach sounds very logical. Its practical application, however, is enormously complex, especially when the model is large.

The second approach, called **chance-constrained programming,** is a deterministic model equivalent to the problem-under-uncertainty model and is developed by analyzing the probability distribution of the parameter values. If you are interested in studying this topic further, you should consult the works of Charnes and Cooper; Lee, Moore, and Taylor; and Madansky (see References at the end of this chapter).

Linear Programming and Game Theory

The relationship between linear programming and **game theory** was first explored by von Neumann and Dantzig in 1947. The formal relationships between the two fields were further analyzed by A. W. Tucker and his associates. These studies received tremendous attention from management scientists because of their great potential for practical application and because of their theoretical breakthrough in game theory. Although the linear programming formulation of a game problem is very interesting mathematically, it has yet to expand the existing knowledge of game theory in any significant way. Those interested in studying this area should consult the many advanced books on mathematical programming, such as the works of Dantzig, and Lee, Moore, and Taylor (see References).

Multiple-Objective Linear Programming

In linear programming, we can handle only one basic objective—maximize or minimize an objective criterion subject to a set of constraints. In most real-world problems, it is only rarely that we find a decision problem that has a single objective. Most decision problems we face in life have multiple, sometimes conflicting, objectives. For example, you are going to a university or a college to gain valuable knowledge in many different areas. Academic programs for a degree, extracurricular activities for your personal interests, dating or meeting many different people in order to socialize and grow, having a part-time job at a local bank to gain some work experience, and living with others to develop friendships—these could be some examples of your objectives. It is extremely difficult or almost impossible to analyze a problem involving multiple objectives by linear programming.

We have seen some recent advances in the area of multiple-objective linear programming. The basic procedure is to optimize one objective at a time. For example, let us suppose that we have three objectives, arranged according to priority, as follows:

1. Minimize payroll cost

2. Achieve a profit level of $150,000

3. Provide a 10 percent bonus to employees

The linear programming model can initially be solved to achieve the first objective subject to a set of constraints. When the first objective is achieved as desired or to the extent possible with the given set of constraints, it can be used as an additional constraint. Then, the second objective is pursued. This procedure is repeated until all of the objectives are pursued, and then the final result is analyzed in terms of the attainment of the objectives. Those interested in this topic should consult the work of Steuer (see References).

Parametric Programming

In many decision problems, model parameters change simultaneously and continuously, rather than discretely, as in sensitivity analysis. Parametric programming is also a post-optimum analysis, like sensitivity analysis, but it is concerned with the analysis of continuous changes in the model parameters. A detailed discussion of parametric programming is certainly beyond the scope of this book. However, readers interested in parametric programming are encouraged to read the works of Lee, Moore, and Taylor (see References).

REAL-WORLD APPLICATIONS OF INTEGER AND GOAL PROGRAMMING

There have been a number of interesting real-world applications of integer and goal programming reported in management literature. Some of these applications have been for decision problems in business firms, and others have been for decision problems in government agencies and nonprofit organizations. Most of these applications are primarily concerned with resource allocations, planning or scheduling, and policy analysis.

Maximizing Scores Through Integer Programming

Intercollegiate women's gymnastics meets tend to be very competitive, with winning margins frequently below 1 percent and sometimes below 0.25 percent. The National Collegiate Athletics Association (NCAA) stipulates four events, with each team allowed up to six gymnasts in each event. The top five from each team are counted in the team score. At least four gymnasts must compete in all four events.

Utah State University developed an integer-programming model of the lineup selection.[1] Five sets of constraints are needed, as well as integer restrictions. Needed inputs included expected ratings of each gymnast in each event, predicted by past performance averages and modified by the coach's judgment of the competitor's emotional and physical state. Changes in the input would produce new solutions from new situations—such as injury to a gymnast. An added benefit was the reduction in perceived personal preferences in making a selection.

Validation of the model was accomplished by comparing actual results based on the coach's decision with model predictions for the same lineup and with the model's optimum solution. The actual score matched the predicted score, but the model showed that a few changes could have produced a higher total score.

Scheduling by Integer Programming for Office Construction

The owners of a 90-acre plot of land next to Irvine Stadium in Dallas planned an office complex of four high-rise and three low-rise (or garden) buildings. Named *Texas Plaza*, the project would provide 4.5 million square feet of office space, a large hotel, and some retail space. Based on comparable current construction bids, total cost would easily exceed $400 million.

For both financial and construction requirements, a schedule showing construction starting times for each building was needed. Demand for office space was estimated for 7 years, so that buildings would not remain idle or be available too late to satisfy potential tenants. The goal of the owners was to maximize net present value of profit, through optimal building starting dates.[2]

An integer-programming model (with 98 variables and 77 constraints) provided the required schedule, including partial space-leasing amounts for each year and the sale value of each building. Integer programming was called for because buildings come in whole units only and can't be partially opened for leasing. The original schedule for Texas Plaza predicted a $30.8 million present net profit, whereas the integer programming solution provided $37.1 million. Costs to set up the program were $6,000 to $8,000, with subsequent solution runs costing $1,000 to $2,000 each.

Navy Recruitment Managed by Goal Programming

Among the most valuable tools of military recruiters is the offer of delayed entry into the service, with recruits reporting up to 1 year after signing up. Recruits obtained in this fashion "spread the word" in a grapevine effect, producing much higher recruiting rates in areas with many delayed-entry recruits.

[1]Peter Ellis and Raymond Corn, "Using Bivalent Integer Programming to Select Teams for Intercollegiate Women's Gymnastics Competition," *Interfaces* 14:3 (1984), 41–46.

[2]Richard Peiser and Scot Andrus, "Phasing of Income-Producing Real Estate," *Interfaces* 13:5 (1983), 1–9.

To balance its recruiting efforts in various sections of the country, the U.S. Navy has implemented a goal-programming model which allocates delayed-entry spaces to its recruiting districts.[3] The model is solved monthly, using fresh data on current results and goal changes when appropriate. Constraints include meeting but not exceeding: monthly national enlistment goals, number of national year-end delayed-entry program pool members, and delayed-entry versus regular recruit proportions. The overall goal is to eliminate imbalances in the delayed-entry recruits per recruiter among the different areas in every time period.

In its first year of operation, the program reduced the mean average absolute deviation from 18.72 to 7.55 percent for the six areas, relative to the national average. A Navy recruiting office representative states that the project has "helped this organization improve the equity and cost effectiveness of its recruiting management system."

Maximizing Services for Crippled Children

The State of Georgia administers its assistance programs for physically handicapped children under 21 through the Crippled Children's Service (CCS).[4] Supported primarily by state funds, the CCS conducts more than 800 clinic sessions yearly, maintaining 14 permanent locations statewide. Many services must be purchased in the private sector, including surgery, hospitalization, prosthetic devices, and medication. CCS itself has over 100 employees, of which about 85 are scattered throughout the state.

Goal programming was selected as a method of satisficing six to seven conflicting goals set within CCS. The goals included such considerations as increase in service, increase in programs, increase in wages and professional compensation, and cost minimization and budget limitations. For this study, three priority structures were arranged to analyze optimum results under alternative situations. The model showed that to reach all the service and compensation goals, CCS would require funding that was approximately double its current budget. With a 5 percent budget increase restriction, none of the goals were fully achieved. Revising the priorities for a more realistic analysis, the modeller met several goals, revised others, and partially met some goals. One of the major benefits perceived from construction of the model was a more realistic view of the trade-off between cost and social programs.

SUMMARY

Integer programming is a special type of linear programming in which all or some of the model variables are required to have integer values in the optimum solution. The branch-and-bound method is a useful tool for general integer programming problems, especially when the variables are constrained by upper and lower bounds. Zero–one programming is a special case of integer programming where solution values of the decision variables must be either 0 or 1.

[3]Richard C. Morey, "Managing the Armed Services' Delayed Entry Pools to Improve Productivity in Recruiting," *Interfaces* 15:5 (1985), 81–90.

[4]Carl Joiner and Albert Drake, "Governmental Planning and Budgeting with Multiple Objective Models," *OMEGA* 11:1 (1983), 57–66.

In recent years an increasing amount of attention has been given to goal programming as a decision-making tool for problems that involve multiple and conflicting objectives. Goal programming is a powerful technique that allows the decision makers to incorporate into the model their judgment about the unique decision environment, the bureaucratic decision process, and the organizational goals and their priorities. The goal-programming solution process yields valuable information about goal conflicts, soundness of the priority structure for goals, and trade-offs among the conflicting objectives.

During the past several years there have been a number of important advances made in the area of goal programming, including sensitivity analysis, integer goal programming, interactive goal programming, decomposition goal programming, separable goal programming, chance-constrained goal programming, and several advanced solution methods. If you are interested in doing some research in these topics, consult the References.

In this chapter, we also reviewed several advanced topics of linear programming — linear programming under uncertainty, linear programming and game theory, multiple objective linear programming, and parametric programming. Although these topics are interesting and also useful for special cases, they are beyond the level of this introductory text. Those interested in these topics should consult the References at the end of this chapter.

Glossary

Aspiration Levels   Levels of goals that are used as right-hand-side values in goal constraints.

Branch-and-Bound   An integer solution procedure that applies a sequential branching scheme to partition the set of feasible solutions into subproblems until the optimum integer solution is found.

Cardinal Weights   Numerical weights assigned to the subgoals at a given priority level.

Chance-constrained Programming   An approach to linear programming under uncertainty that uses the probability distribution of uncertain parameters to formulate an equivalent deterministic model.

Cost of Indivisibility   The difference in the objective function values of a continuous solution and an integer solution for the same problem.

Deviational Variable   A variable that represents either a negative or positive deviation from the stated goal level.

Goal Constraints   Constraints that are formulated to achieve desired goals that have been assigned certain priorities.

Goal Programming   A multiple-objective programming technique that seeks the best satisficing solution based on priorities assigned to the objectives.

Incompatible Objectives   Objectives that are in direct conflict or competition for available resources.

Integer Programming   A mathematical programming technique that seeks an optimum solution with the values of decision variables that satisfy integer requirements.

Overachievement   The level by which a goal is achieved beyond the desired level.

Parametric Programming   A postoptimum analysis, like sensitivity analysis, involving the analysis of continuous changes in the model parameters.

Preemptive Priorities   A set of hierarchical or lexicographic priorities assigned to various goals or objectives.

Priority Structure   The set of priorities assigned to the goals involved in a multiple-objective decision problem.

Stochastic Programming   Linear programming under the condition of uncertainty.

System Constraints   Absolute boundaries within which a satisficing solution is sought.

Underachievement   The extent to which a goal is not achieved.

Zero–One Programming   An integer-programming technique that seeks an optimum solution with the values of decision variables that are either 0 or 1.

References

Balas, E. "An Additive Algorithm for Solving Linear Programs with Zero–One Variables." *Operations Research* 13 (1965), 517–546.

Charnes, A., and Cooper, W. W. *Management Models and Industrial Applications of Linear Programming.* New York: Wiley, 1961.

Ignizio, J. P. *Goal Programming and Extensions.* Lexington, Mass.: Lexington, Books, 1976.

Ijiri, Y. *Management Goals and Accounting for Control.* Chicago: Rand-McNally, 1965.

Land, A. H., and Doig, A. G. "An Automatic Method of Solving Discrete Programming Problems." *Econometrica* 28 (1960), 497–520.

Lee, S. M. *Goal Programming for Decision Analysis.* Philadelphia: Auerbach, 1972.

Lee, S. M. *Goal Programming Methods for Multiple Integer Programs.* Atlanta: American Institute of Industrial Engineers, 1979.

Lee, S. M. *Management by Multiple Objectives.* Princeton, N.J.: Petrocelli Books, 1981.

Lee, S. M., Moore, L. J., and Taylor, B. W. *Management Science.* 2d ed. Dubuque, Iowa: W. C. Brown, 1985.

Lee, S. M., Shim, J. P., and Lee, C. S. "The Signal Flow Graph Method of Goal Programming." *Computers and Operations Research* 11:3 (1984), 253–265.

Madansky, A. "Method of Solution of Linear Programs under Uncertainty." *Operations Research* 10:4 (1962), 463–471.

Mitten, L. G. "Branch-and-Bound Methods: General Formulation and Properties." *Operations Research* 18 (1970), 24–34.

Spronk, J. *Interactive Multiple Goal Programming.* Boston: Martinus Nijhoff, 1981.

Steuer, R. E. "An Interactive Multiple Objective Linear Programming Procedure." *TIMS Studies in Management Science* 6 (1979), 225–239.

Zeleny, M. *Multiple Criteria Decision Making.* New York: McGraw-Hill, 1982.

Assignments

6.1 What is the cost of indivisibility? Explain through an example.

6.2 What are some real-world problems for which we need integer solution values?

6.3 Discuss a problem that would require a mixed-integer or zero–one integer-programming model.

6.4 The rounding approach is a simple and practical approach to solving some integer-programming problems. What possible dangers are involved in using the rounding approach?

6.5 What is the set of steps that has been advocated for decision making in the traditional normative approach of decision making?

6.6 What is the foundation of the descriptive approach of decision making? How is this approach different from the normative approach?

6.7 Contrast satisficing and optimizing.

6.8 What are the major differences between linear programming and goal programming?

6.9 Outline a problem you face frequently that involves multiple conflicting objectives.

6.10 What are the major differences between system and goal constraints?

6.11 Explain the difference between cardinal weights and preemptive priority weights.

6.12 What are the major differences between the ordinary simplex method of linear programming and the modified simplex method of goal programming?

6.13 What is a trade-off? Is there a trade-off between two goals only when they are in conflict?

6.14 Solve the following integer-programming problem by using the branch-and-bound method.

$$\text{Maximize } Z = 3x_1 + 4x_2$$
$$\text{subject to} \quad x_1 + x_2 \leq 500$$
$$x_1 + x_2 \geq 400$$
$$x_1 - 2x_2 \geq 0$$
$$6x_1 - 4x_2 \geq 0$$
$$x_1, x_2 = 0 \text{ or nonnegative integer}$$

6.15 Solve the following integer-programming problem by using the branch-and-bound method.

$$\text{Maximize } Z = 4x_1 + 20x_2$$
$$\text{subject to} \quad x_1 + 10x_2 \leq 20$$
$$x_1 \qquad\quad \leq 2$$
$$x_1, x_2 = 0 \text{ or nonnegative integer}$$

6.16 Solve the following integer-programming problem by the branch-and-bound method.

$$\text{Minimize } Z = 0.5x_1 + 0.5x_2$$
$$\text{subject to} \quad 3x_1 + 2x_2 \geq 12$$
$$3x_1 + 8x_2 \geq 24$$
$$x_1 \qquad\quad \geq 2$$
$$x_1, x_2 = 0 \text{ or nonnegative integer}$$

6.17 Solve the following integer-programming problem by using the branch-and-bound method.

$$\text{Minimize } Z = 3x_1 + 4x_2 + 6x_3$$
$$\text{subject to} \quad 6x_1 + 12x_2 + 6x_3 \geq 24$$
$$7x_1 + 3x_2 + 5x_3 \geq 60$$
$$3x_1 + 3x_2 + 2x_3 \geq 25$$
$$x_1, x_2, x_3 = 0 \text{ or nonnegative integer}$$

6.18 Solve the following zero–one integer-programming problem by using a computer program.

$$\text{Maximize } Z = 5x_1 + 6x_2 + 7x_3$$
$$\text{subject to} \quad 2x_1 + 3x_2 - x_3 \leq 30$$
$$x_1 + x_2 + x_3 \leq 10$$
$$x_1 \geq 2$$
$$x_1 + 2x_2 \leq 15$$
$$x_1, x_2, x_3 = 0 \text{ or } 1$$

6.19 Solve the following goal-programming problem by the graphical method:

$$\text{Minimize } Z = P_1 d_2^- + P_2 d_1^- + P_3 d_1^+ + P_4 d_3^-$$
$$\text{subject to} \quad x_1 + x_2 + d_1^- - d_1^+ = 80$$
$$x_1 + d_2^- - d_2^+ = 100$$
$$x_2 + d_3^- = 45$$
$$x_j, d_i^-, d_i^+ \geq 0$$

6.20 Solve the following goal-programming problem by the graphical method:

$$\text{Minimize } Z = P_1 d_1^- + P_2 d_4^+ + 3P_3 d_2^- + P_3 d_3^- + P_4 d_2^+ + 3P_4 d_3^+$$
$$\text{subject to} \quad 5x_1 + 2x_2 + d_1^- - d_1^+ = 550$$
$$x_1 + d_2^- - d_2^+ = 80$$
$$x_2 + d_3^- - d_3^+ = 32$$
$$x_1 + d_4^- - d_4^+ = 90$$
$$x_j, d_i^-, d_i^+ \geq 0$$

6.21 Solve the Big Sound Records Inc. problem, Casette 6.3 in this chapter, by the graphical method.

6.22 The manufacturing plant of an electronics firm produces two types of television sets: color and black-and-white. Past experience indicates that production of either set requires an average of 3 hours in the plant. The plant has a normal production capacity of 120 hours a week. The marketing department reports that the estimated number of color and black-and-white sets that can be sold each week are 25 and 30, respectively.

The gross profit from the sale of a color set is $80, whereas it is $40 from the sale of a black-and-white set. The president of the company has set the following goals, arranged in the order of their importance to the organization:

   a. Avoid any underutilization of normal production capacity (no layoffs of production workers).

   b. Sell as many television sets as estimated by the marketing department. Since the gross profit from the sale of a color television set is twice the amount from a black-and-white set, the president has twice as much desire to achieve the sales goal for color sets as for black-and-white sets.

   c. Minimize the overtime operation of the plant as much as possible.

Solve this problem by the graphical method of goal programming.

6.23 Oriental Rugs Inc. produces the world's finest factory-made oriental rugs. The company's production facility consists of two production lines. Line 1 is staffed with skilled workers who can produce an average of 2 rugs per hour. Line 2 is capable of producing an average of 1.5 rugs per hour, as it is staffed with relatively new employees. The regular production capacity for the next week is 40 hours for each line. The profit from an average rug is $200. It is estimated that the operating costs of the two lines are virtually the same. The president of the firm has listed, in ordinal ranking of importance, the following multiple goals to achieve in the coming week:

   a. Meet the production goal of 170 rugs for the week.

   b. Limit the overtime operation of line 1 to 5 hours.

   c. Avoid the underutilization of the regular working hours of line 1 as specified by the union contract.

   d. Limit the overtime operation for each of the production lines. (Apply differential weights according to the relative cost of overtime.)

Formulate a goal-programming model for the problem and solve it by the graphical method.

6.24 The director of County Social Services faces the problem of job allocation between her two teams of social workers. The processing rate of the first team is 5 cases per week, and the processing rate of the second team is 6 cases per week. Each team usually works 46 weeks per year. The director has the following goals for the next year, arranged in order of importance:

   a. Avoid any underachievement of the case-processing level, which is set at 55 for the next year.

   b. Avoid any "yearly" overtime for team 2 beyond 1 week.

   c. The total overtime should be minimized. (Assign differential weights according to the relative cost of overtime work. Assume that the service cost for the two teams is identical.)

   d. Any underutilization of regular working weeks should be avoided. (Again assign weights according to the relative productivity of the two teams.)

First formulate a goal-programming model to determine the working weeks of the two teams for the next year, and then solve this problem by the graphical method.

6.25 Sunny Electronics Inc. produces the most sophisticated color television sets on the market. The company has two production lines. The production rate of line 1 is 4 sets per hour, whereas it is 3 sets per hour in line 2. The regular production capacity is 40 hours a week for each line. The expected profit from an average color television set is $100. The top management of the firm has set the following goals for the week (in ordinal ranking):

a. Meet the production goal of 360 sets for the week.

b. Limit the overtime of line 1 to 10 hours.

c. Avoid the underutilization of the regular working hours for both lines. (Assign differential weights according to the production rate of each line.)

d. Limit the overtime operation for each line. (Assign differential weights according to the relative cost of an overtime hour. Assume that the cost of operation is identical for the two production lines.)

Formulate a goal-programming model for this problem. If top management desires to put the profit goal of $38,000 for the week as the first-priority goal over the stated four goals, how would the model be changed? If top management has only the one goal of profit maximization, subject to the regular production capacity of both lines, how would the goal-programming model be formulated?

6.26 Valley Products Inc. plans to schedule its annual advertising campaign. The total advertising budget is set at $1 million. The firm can purchase local radio spots at $50 per spot, local television spots at $300 per spot, or local newspaper advertising at $100 per insertion. The payoff from each advertising medium is a function of its audience size and audience characteristics. The generally accepted objective criterion for advertising is audience points. Audience points for the three advertising vehicles are:

Radio: 50 points per spot

Television: 250 points per spot

Newspaper: 200 points per insertion

The president of the firm has established the following goals for the advertising campaign, listed in the order of their importance:

a. The total budget should not exceed $1 million.

b. The contract with the local radio and television station requires that the firm spend at least $300,000 for television and radio ads.

c. The company does not wish to spend more than $200,000 for newspaper ads.

d. Audience points from the advertising campaign should be maximized.

Formulate a goal-programming model for this problem.

6.27 Otani Electronics produces two types of radios: AM and FM. According to past experience, production of either type of radio requires an average of 30 minutes in the plant. The plant has a normal production capacity of 80 hours a week. The marketing department reports that the *maximum* number of AM and FM radios that can be sold each week are 80 and 100 respectively. The unit profits are: AM, $30; FM, $20. The president of the company has set the following multiple goals, listed in the order of their importance:

a. Avoid any underutilization of the normal production capacity.

b. Achieve the sales goals of 80 AM and 100 FM radios. (Assign differential weights according to the unit profits.)

c. Minimize the overtime operation of the plant as much as possible.

If the president of the firm had only the single goal of profit maximization within the normal production capacity and sales constraints, how would you set up a goal-programming model? Formulate a goal-programming model for this problem and solve it by the simplex method.

6.28 Omaha Computer Hardwares Inc. produces three types of computers: Epic, Galaxie, and Utopia. The production of all computers is conducted in a complex and modern assembly line. The production of an Epic requires 5 hours in the assembly line, a Galaxie requires 8 hours, and a Utopia requires 12 hours. The normal number of operating hours of the assembly line is 200 per month. The marketing department and the accounting department have estimated that profits per unit for the three types of computers are $100,000 for the Epic, $120,000 for the Galaxie, and $150,000 for the Utopia. The marketing department further reports that demand is such that the firm can expect to sell all the computers it produces in the next month. The president of the firm has established the following goals, listed according to their importance:

    a. Avoid underutilization of the production capacity of the assembly line.
    b. Meet the demand of the northeastern sales district for 5 Epics, 5 Galaxies, and 8 Utopias (no differential weights).
    c. Limit the overtime operation of the assembly line to 20 hours.
    d. Meet the sales goal for each type of computer: Epic, 15; Galaxie, 12; and Utopia, 12 (no differential weights).
    e. Minimize the total overtime operation of the assembly line.

Formulate a goal-programming model for this problem. Work through two iterations (three tableaux) by the simplex method of goal programming.

6.29 Your grandmother has just won $40,000 in the "Lifebuoy Sweepstakes." Because of her advanced age, you plan to "have fun" helping her to invest in these five alternatives: stock options, real estate, bonds, savings accounts, and diamonds. Real estate and bonds yield an estimated 17 percent and 12 percent per year, respectively, and the savings account yields 6 percent. Since options and diamonds are risky, you cannot assume they will have any yield. You have established the following goals, in order of their importance:

    a. Minimize the risk by diversifying the investment. No more than 40 percent of the total investment should be in any one alternative.
    b. Since diamonds are rumored to be profitable, try to invest at least $10,000 in this alternative.
    c. The amount invested in speculative ventures (options and diamonds) should not exceed the amount invested in safer plans.
    d. Guarantee that Granny will earn at least $5,000 annually from your investments.

Formulate a goal-programming model that will determine the amount of money to be invested in each of the various alternatives.

6.30 Old Dominion Electronics Inc. produces two types of tape players: cassette players and 8-track players. The production of both products is done in two assembly centers. Each cassette player requires 4 hours in assembly center 1 and 2 hours in assembly center 2. Each 8-track player requires 2 hours in assembly center 1 and 6 hours in assembly center 2. Additionally, each product requires some in-process inventory. Each cassette player requires $100 worth of in-process inventory; an 8-track player requires $60 worth of in-process inventory. The normal monthly operation capacity for assembly center 1 is 240 hours and for assembly center 2 is 300 hours. The average monthly in-process inventory is $8,000. According to the marketing department, the estimated sales for the cassette player and 8-track player are 55 and 65, respectively, for the coming month.

a. If the president of the firm is simply trying to maximize profit, how would you set up a linear programming model within the limits of the normal monthly production capacity, average inventory level, and forecast sales? (Assume unit profits of $100 for cassette players and $60 for 8-track players.)

b. Solve this problem by the graphical method of linear programming.

c. The president of the firm has established the following multiple goals according to their importance:

(1) Achieve the sales goal of 55 cassette players for the month.

(2) Not more than $8,500 may be tied up in in-process inventory.

(3) Avoid any underutilization of the regular operation hours of both assembly centers (no differential weights).

(4) Limit the overtime operation of assembly center 1 to 40 hours.

(5) Achieve the sales goal of sixty-five 8-track players.

(6) Limit the overtime operation of each assembly center (no differential weights).

Set up a goal-programming model and work through three tableaux by the simplex method.

6.31 Lancelot Chemical, Inc. (LCI) has just developed a mouthwash—Misty Wink. The advertising department of LCI is in the process of designing a major promotional campaign for Misty Wink. The company has decided to use television, radio, and magazine ads. The advertising department has compiled the following cost information:

	Cost per Ad
Television	$4,000
Radio	1,200
Magazine	1,500

The amount of effective exposures per unit of advertising in each medium is dependent upon the region reached by the LCI advertising. LCI has decided to direct its advertising to two regions—Midwest and Southwest. The expected effective exposures per unit of ad in each region is presented below:

	Midwest	Southwest
Television	100,000	700,000
Radio	120,000	400,000
Magazine	80,000	500,000

The company's two major customer target groups for the advertising campaign are singles and young married people. The expected effective exposures per unit of ad to the two target groups are:

	Singles	Young Marrieds
Television	100,000	350,000
Radio	90,000	50,000
Magazine	95,000	300,000

LCI has established the following goals, arranged by priority, for the advertising campaign:

a. Achieve at least 3 million effective exposures in the Midwest and 9.5 million exposures in the Southwest region.

b. The maximum desired number of ads are: television, 12; radio, 40; magazine, 25.

c. Achieve at least 2.5 million effective exposures among the young marrieds.

d. Achieve a maximum of 3 million effective exposures among singles.

e. Limit the advertising campaign budget to $70,000.

Formulate a goal-programming model for this problem.

6.32 The Midtown City Council is reviewing housing proposals for a new development area. There is some dispute among various interest groups as to what goals should be sought. The Zoning Committee has recommended three types of housing: one-family houses, deluxe condominiums, and apartments. The Zoning Committee has compiled the following data for each type of housing:

	Housing Type		
	One-family	Deluxe Condo	Apartment
Land usage per unit (acres)	0.25	0.30	0.125
Families housed per unit	1	4	6
Tax base generated per unit ($)	50,000	100,000	25,000
Taxes required for city services ($)	4,000	8,000	6,000

Twenty acres are available for zoning. The League for Better Housing has conducted a campaign to gain housing for at least 500 families. The Taxpayers' Union has strongly lobbied for an added tax base of $4 million. The Gray Panthers have disrupted the City Council meetings and demanded that taxes for city services be no more than $250,000.

The City Council hired a public-opinion survey company to assess the priorities of the citizens. The poll results are as follows:

	Priority		
Goal	1	2	3
Housing for 500 families	55%	35%	10%
Tax base of $4 million	40	30	30
Taxes for services, $250,000	15	20	65

Based on this survey, the City Council has established the following priorities:

P_1:   Provide housing for at least 500 families.

P_2:   Establish at least $4 million worth of new tax base.

P_3:   Limit taxes for city services to $250,000.

Formulate this problem as a goal-programming model. Solve this problem by computer program if available.

6.33 Donald White was recently named by Governor Wilson as the campaign director for his upcoming reelection campaign. Governor Wilson thinks that if he can get his message to 2 million people in the state, he has a good chance to win a large chunk of votes at the Republican Convention.

Donald White has obtained the following information about advertising media availability and their costs:

Medium	Voter Exposure per $1,000 Spent	Cost per Insertion	Maximum Units Available
Television (prime-time)	20,000	$500	60
Television (nonprime-time)	8,000	400	60
Radio	7,000	300	100
Newspaper	5,000	200	120
Billboards	750	100	150

Governor Wilson has a campaign fund of $160,000 available, which, according to the state election law, cannot be exceeded. Furthermore, no more than $60,000 can be spent on television ads (a legal limit of 60 units).

Governor Wilson's priorities are as follows:

P_1:   Obtain exposure to 2 million voters.

P_2:   Avoid spending over $160,000.

P_3:   Spend at least $15,000 on newspaper ads.

P_4:   Maximize voter exposure.

Donald White is attempting to formulate the advertising strategies for Governor Wilson. As a special consultant, you have been asked to help. Formulate this problem as a goal-programming model.

6.34 A goal-programming problem has been solved by using the *GPGO* computer program. The computer printout on pages 234 and 235 presents the data input and solution output.

    a. Formulate the goal-programming model for the problem.

    b. What are the basic variables and their values of the optimum solution?

    c. Discuss the degree of goal attainment.

    d. Are there any goal conflicts? If so, between which goals? What are their trade-offs?

GPGO Computer Program: Data Input and Solution Output

```
FILE: J00      GPOUTPUT A1        VM/SP CONVERSATIONAL MONITOR SYSTEM        PAGE 00001

0PAGE-01
THE RIGHT HAND SIDE-INPUT
      1    2000.000000
      2    5280.000000
      3    5400.000000
      4     500.000000

0PAGE-02
THE SUBSTITUTION RATES-INPUT
ROW 1   1.000   0.000   0.000  -1.000   0.000   0.000   0.000   2.500   3.000
ROW 2   0.000   1.000   0.000   0.000  -1.000   0.000   0.000   5.000   8.000
ROW 3   0.000   0.000   1.000   0.000   0.000  -1.000   0.000   0.000   1.000
ROW 4   0.000   1.000   0.000   0.000   0.000   0.000  -1.000   1.000   0.000

0PAGE-03
THE OBJECTIVE FUNCTION-INPUT
PRIORITY 4   0.000   1.000   0.000   0.000   0.000   0.000   0.000
PRIORITY 3   0.000   0.000   1.000   0.000   0.000   0.000   0.000
PRIORITY 2   0.000   0.000   0.000   1.000   0.000   0.000   0.000
PRIORITY 1   0.000   0.000   0.000   0.000   0.000   0.000   0.000

0PAGE-04 SUMMARY OF INPUT INFORMATION
NUMBER OF ROWS.......:   4
NUMBER OF VARIABLES..:  10
NUMBER OF PRIORITIES.:   4
ADDED PRIORITIES.....:   0
THE INITIAL ZJ-CJ MATRIX
PRIORITY 4   0.000   0.000   0.000   0.000   0.000  -1.000   1.000   0.000   0.000
PRIORITY 3   0.000   0.000   0.000  -1.000   0.000   0.000   0.000   0.000   1.000
PRIORITY 2   0.000   0.000   0.000   0.000  -1.000   0.000   0.000   0.000   0.000
PRIORITY 1   0.000  -1.000   0.000   0.000   0.000   0.000   0.000   2.500   3.000

1 ITERATIONS........:      4

0PAGE-05
THE SIMPLEX SOLUTION
THE BASIC VARS.       THE RIGHT HAND SIDE
   30C+XD13           416.000000
   10C+XD40           240.000000
  104C+XD40           400.000000
                       34.000000

THE SUBSTITUTION RATES
ROW    0.000   0.200   0.000   0.000   0.000  -0.200   1.600   1.000   0.000
ROW   -1.000   0.500   1.000   0.000   0.000  -0.500   1.000   0.000   0.000
```

```
FILE: J00        GPOUTPUT A1            VM/SP CONVERSATIONAL MONITOR SYSTEM                PAGE 00002

ROW   3
      0.000    0.000    1.000    0.000    0.000    0.000   -1.000    0.000    1.000
ROW   4
      0.000   -0.200    1.600    1.000    0.200   -1.600   -1.600   -1.000    0.000    0.000
THE ZJ-CJ MATRIX
PRIORITY   4
      0.000   -0.200    1.600    0.000    0.200   -1.600   -1.600   -1.000    0.000    0.000
PRIORITY   3
      0.000    0.000   -1.000    0.000    0.000   -1.600   -1.600   -1.000    0.000    0.000
PRIORITY   2
      0.000    0.000    0.000    0.000    0.000   -1.000    0.000    0.000    0.000    0.000
PRIORITY   1
     -1.000    0.000    0.000    0.000    0.000    0.000    0.000    0.000    0.000    0.000

AN EVALUATION OF THE OBJECTIVE FUNCTION
     84.000
     80.000
      0.000
      0.000

OPAGE-06
ANALYSIS OF DEVIATIONS
ROW    RHS-VALUE          D+             D-
 1     200.00000      240.00000       0.00000
 2    5280.00000        0.00000       0.00000
 3     430.00000        0.00000       0.00000
 4     500.00000        0.00000      84.00000

OPAGE-07
ANALYSIS OF DECISION VARIABLES
VARIABLE    AMOUNT
 1        416.00000
 2        400.00000

OPAGE-08
ANALYSIS OF THE OBJECTIVE FUNCTION
PRIORITY    NON-ACHIEVEMENT
 4          84.000000
 3           0.000000
 2           0.000000
 1           0.000000
```

6.35 The Big Sound Records problem, presented as Casette 6.3, was solved by *Micro Manager*. The model and the final solution tableau are presented below and on page 237.

    a. Determine the basic variables and their values in the final simplex tableau.

    b. Discuss the goal attainment.

    c. Discuss goal conflicts and their trade-offs.

```
PROGRAM: Goal Programming

***** INPUT DATA ENTERED *****

Min Z = P 1 dn 1  + P 2 dp 3  +  2 P 3 dn 2  + P 3 dn 4  + P 4 dn 5  + 27 P 5
dp 2  +  20 P 5 dp 4

Subject to:

C 1    10 x 1 + 6 x 2 + dn 1 - dp 1  =  22000
C 2    1 x 1 + dn 2 - dp 2  =  1600
C 3    1 x 1 + dn 3 - dp 3  =  1800
C 4    1 x 2 + dn 4 - dp 4  =  640
C 5    15 x 1 + 9 x 2 + dn 5 - dp 5  =  31000


Final tableau (iteration 6 )
```

C#	Cb	Basis	Bi
C 1	0	+d 5	2000.00
C 2	0	x 1	1800.00
C 3	27P 5	+d 2	200.00
C 4	0	x 2	666.67
C 5	20P 5	+d 4	26.67

\Cj C#	1P 1 -d 1	2P 3 -d 2	0 -d 3	1P 3 -d 4	1P 4 -d 5	0 +d 1
C 1	1.50	0.00	0.00	0.00	-1.00	-1.50
C 2	0.00	0.00	1.00	0.00	0.00	0.00
C 3	0.00	-1.00	1.00	0.00	0.00	0.00
C 4	0.17	0.00	-1.67	0.00	0.00	-0.17
C 5	0.17	0.00	-1.67	-1.00	0.00	-0.17
P 5	3.33	-27.00	-6.33	-20.00	0.00	-3.33
P 4	0.00	0.00	0.00	0.00	-1.00	0.00
P 3	0.00	-2.00	0.00	-1.00	0.00	0.00
P 2	0.00	0.00	0.00	0.00	0.00	0.00
P 1	-1.00	0.00	0.00	0.00	0.00	0.00

\Cj	27P 5	1P 2	20P 5	0	0	0
C#	+d 2	+d 3	+d 4	+d 5	x 1	x 2
C 1	0.00	0.00	0.00	1.00	0.00	0.00
C 2	0.00	-1.00	0.00	0.00	1.00	0.00
C 3	1.00	-1.00	0.00	0.00	0.00	0.00
C 4	0.00	1.67	0.00	0.00	0.00	1.00
C 5	0.00	1.67	1.00	0.00	0.00	0.00
P 5	0.00	6.33	0.00	0.00	0.00	0.00
P 4	0.00	0.00	0.00	0.00	0.00	0.00
P 3	0.00	0.00	0.00	0.00	0.00	0.00
P 2	0.00	-1.00	0.00	0.00	0.00	0.00
P 1	0.00	0.00	0.00	0.00	0.00	0.00

Analysis of deviations

Constraint	RHS Value	d+	d-
C 1	22000.00	0.00	0.00
C 2	1600.00	200.00	0.00
C 3	1800.00	0.00	0.00
C 4	640.00	26.67	0.00
C 5	31000.00	2000.00	0.00

Analysis of decision variables

Variable	Solution value
x 1	1800.00
x 2	666.67

Analysis of the objective function

Priority	Nonachievement
P 1	0.00
P 2	0.00
P 3	0.00
P 4	0.00
P 5	5933.33

7 THE TRANSPORTATION PROBLEM

A prevalent managerial decision problem for many organizations is the transportation of goods and services from sources to destinations while minimizing the total transportation cost. In this chapter, we will study various techniques that are useful in analyzing the transportation problem. The graphical and simplex methods presented in Chapters 3 and 4 are for general linear programming problems. Some special types of linear programming problems can be analyzed more efficiently by using special techniques. The transportation method is such a special technique. In this chapter, we will study the transportation solution method as a tool to determine the optimum transportation of goods from a number of sources to a number of destinations at a minimum total cost.

Learning Objectives From the study of this chapter, we will learn the following:

1. The basic nature of the transportation problem
2. The formulation of a linear programming model for the transportation problem
3. The development of an initial solution to the transportation problem
4. The solution of the transportation problem
5. The analysis of an unbalanced transportation problem
6. Computer solution of transportation problems
7. The application of the transportation method to real-world problems
8. The meaning of the following terms:

Balanced transportation problem
Unbalanced transportation problem
Northwest corner method
Minimum-cell-cost method
Vogel's approximation method
Opportunity cost
Stepping-stone path
Modified distribution method

Cost-improvement index
Degeneracy
Multiple optimum solutions
Prohibited transportation route
Transshipment problem
Transportation problem with multiple objectives

THE NATURE OF THE TRANSPORTATION PROBLEM

The transportation problem is concerned with the transportation of a product (or service) from a number of sources that have specific quantities of supply to a number of destinations with certain quantities of demand. For example, a petroleum company has six refineries (sources) and twenty fuel depots (destinations) at various locations. For a given period of time, each refinery has a specific capacity of supply of gasoline and each depot has a specific demand for gasoline. If we know the unit transportation cost from each refinery to each depot, we may be able to determine the quantity of gasoline to be transported from specific refineries to specific depots in order to minimize the total transportation cost.

The transportation method has a wide spectrum of real-world applications. One such application would be the military logistics problem of transporting troops and supplies from various camps and supply depots to several hot spots (such as the Persian Gulf, the Middle East, and the Far East) while minimizing the total transportation time. You can easily identify with the problem of locating dormitories on campus to accommodate student residence requirements while minimizing the average distance that students must walk around the campus.

Mathematical analysis of the transportation problem was not undertaken until 1941, when F. L. Hitchcock published his study, "The Distribution of a Product from Several Sources to Numerous Localities." Since then, the transportation problem has been further studied by such scholars as T. C. Koopmans, George B. Dantzig, A. Charnes, W. W. Cooper, and many others (see References). As a matter of fact, many variations of the transportation method have been developed. Examples include the assignment method, location-allocation problems, and distribution problems. In this chapter, we will study the more widely used techniques for transportation problems.

To illustrate the transportation method, we will examine a simple problem in Casette 7.1.

Casette 7.1   GULF COAST OIL COMPANY INC.

Gulf Coast Oil Company Inc. is a petroleum refinery company headquartered in Dallas, Texas. The company does not operate its own oil wells. Instead, it purchases crude oil from a number of small offshore drilling companies on a long-term contract basis. The company has three refineries, located in Houston, Corpus Christi, and Fort Worth, and it has three distribution depots, located in San Antonio, Texarkana, and El Paso. The company's most important product is gasoline for automobiles.

The transportation problem faced by Gulf Coast Oil is to supply the required quantity of gasoline to each of the distribution depots from the three refineries, each with specific production capacity, to minimize total transportation costs. The transportation problem can be visualized on the map in Figure 7.1. We must remember here that only refineries can produce and supply gasoline to depots. A depot cannot supply gasoline to another depot.

The problem is further illustrated by the network in Figure 7.2. The network also presents the supply capacity at each of the refineries, the demand requirements at each of the distribution depots, and the unit transportation costs. The decision variables can be defined as follows:

x_{ij} = quantity of gasoline to be transported from refinery i to distribution depot j

	where	$i = 1$	Houston	$j = 1$	San Antonio
		$i = 2$	Corpus Christi	$j = 2$	Texarkana
		$i = 3$	Fort Worth	$j = 3$	El Paso

Figure 7.1   Gulf Coast Oil Transportation Problem

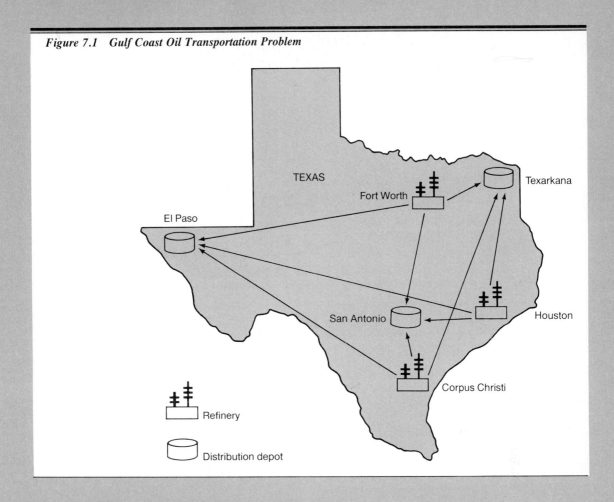

As can be seen in Figure 7.2, this is a balanced transportation problem in which total supply exactly equals total demand. We can formulate a linear programming model that will minimize the total transportation costs subject to the supply-and-demand constraints as follows:

$$\text{Minimize } Z = 20x_{11} + 9x_{12} + 5x_{13} + 6x_{21} + 10x_{22} + 18x_{23} + 2x_{31}$$
$$+ 15x_{32} + 12x_{33}$$

$$\text{subject to } \left. \begin{array}{l} x_{11} + x_{12} + x_{13} = 150 \\ x_{21} + x_{22} + x_{23} = 100 \\ x_{31} + x_{32} + x_{33} = 250 \end{array} \right\} \text{ Supply}$$

$$\left. \begin{array}{l} x_{11} + x_{21} + x_{31} = 200 \\ x_{12} + x_{22} + x_{32} = 120 \\ x_{13} + x_{23} + x_{33} = 180 \end{array} \right\} \text{ Demand}$$

$$x_{ij} \geq 0$$

The formulated linear programming model for the Gulf Coast Oil transportation problem can be solved quite easily by using one of the many available linear program-

Figure 7.2   *Gulf Coast Oil Transportation Network*

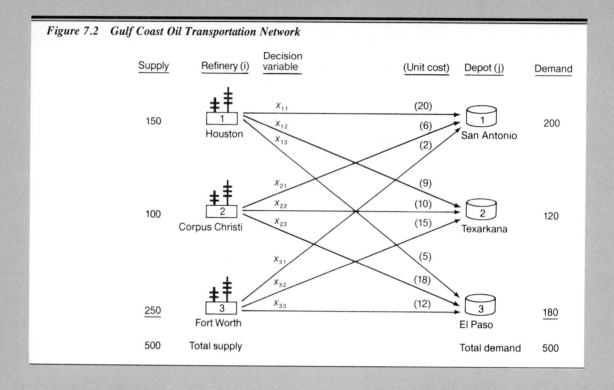

ming codes. The problem can be succinctly summarized in tableau form, as shown in Table 7.1. The tableau indicates the sources, destinations, supply capacity (in 1,000 gallons) at each of the sources, demand requirements (in 1,000 gallons) at each of the distribution depots, and unit transportation costs from each source to each destination.

Table 7.1   *Tableau Form of the Gulf Coast Oil Problem*

Sources \ Destinations	1 San Antonio	2 Texarkana	3 El Paso	Supply (1,000 gallons)
1 Houston	$20	$9	$5	150
2 Corpus Christi	6	10	18	100
3 Fort Worth	2	15	12	250
Demand (1,000 gallons)	200	120	180	500

THE BALANCED TRANSPORTATION PROBLEM

In a balanced transportation problem, the total supply at sources and the total demand at destinations are exactly equal. Although not many real-world transportation problems are balanced cases, once we learn to solve a balanced case, any unbalanced case can be easily solved by making simple modifications.

To illustrate the balanced transportation problem, let us once again consider the Gulf Coast Oil transportation problem. This balanced transportation problem can be summarized in tableau form, as shown in Table 7.2. The numbers in the "From" column indicate the refineries that are the sources of the gasoline, and the numbers in the "To" row refer to the distribution depots that are the final destinations of the gasoline.

Each cell at the intersection of a source and a destination is where we are attempting to allocate some quantity to be transported. For example, if cell (1,1) has the number *40* recorded in it, then 40,000 gallons of gasoline will be transported from source 1 (Houston) to destination 1 (San Antonio). Each cell also has a boxed-in number in the upper left corner. This number indicates the unit transportation cost from a source to a destination. For example, cell (1,1) has a cost figure of 20. This figure tells us that the transportation cost of 1,000 gallons from source 1 (Houston) to destination 1 (San Antonio) is $20.

The solution procedure for the general transportation problem is as follows:

Step 1: Define the Problem and Set Up the Transportation Tableau   The first step of the transportation method is to analyze the problem and set up the transportation tableau with all the following information: supply capacity at each source, demand requirement at each destination, and unit transportation cost from each source to each destination.

Table 7.2   Transportation Tableau for the Gulf Coast Oil Problem

To / From	1	2	3	Supply
1	20 x_{11}	9 x_{12}	5 x_{13}	150
2	6 x_{21}	10 x_{22}	18 x_{23}	100
3	2 x_{31}	15 x_{32}	12 x_{33}	250
Demand	200	120	180	500

Quantity of shipment from source 2 to destination 1

Total supply and total demand

Step 2: Develop an Initial Solution   Just as in linear programming, we need an initial solution to start the solution process. In linear programming, the initial solution is always at the origin. However, in a transportation problem we need an initial solution other than the origin because we are using a tableau format that requires satisfaction of the supply and demand constraints. Several approaches can be used to generate an initial solution.

Step 3: Determine the Optimum Solution   Once an initial solution is derived, we are ready to use the transportation method to generate improved solutions until we determine the optimum solution. This step may require a number of iterations as we move toward the optimum solution.

Step 4: Evaluate the Optimum Solution   The final step of the transportation method is to analyze the optimum solution in terms of the transportation schedule, the total transportation cost, and alternative optimum solutions. Since we have already discussed the transportation problem of Gulf Coast Oil and set up the transportation tableau, we will focus our attention on Step 2.

Developing an Initial Solution

As we discussed earlier, in a transportation problem the initial solution cannot be at the origin because of the tableau form of analysis we use. In developing an initial solution, a number of different methods can be used. We will discuss the three most widely used methods: the northwest corner method, the minimum-cell-cost method, and Vogel's approximation method.

Northwest Corner Method   The northwest corner method is the simplest way to develop an initial solution. Although other methods may provide better initial solutions, none is as simple and straightforward as the northwest corner method. The northwest corner method, although a very systematic method, is not based on logic or even on common sense. Thus, an initial solution derived by the northwest corner method usually yields the largest total transportation cost among the three methods we will be studying here.

The steps of the northwest corner method can be summarized as follows:

1. Starting from the northwest corner (upper left corner) of the transportation tableau, allocate as much quantity as possible to cell (1,1) from source 1 to destination 1 within the supply constraint of source 1 and the demand constraint of destination 1.

2. The first allocation will satisfy either the supply capacity of source 1 or the demand requirement of destination 1. If the demand requirement for destination 1 is satisfied but the supply capacity for source 1 is not exhausted, move on to cell (1,2) for the second allocation. If the demand requirement for destination 1 is not satisfied but the supply capacity for source 1 is exhausted, move on to cell (2,1) for the second allocation. If the demand requirement for destination 1 is satisfied and the supply capacity for source 1 is also exhausted, move on to cell (2,2) for the second allocation.

3. Continue the allocation process in the same manner toward the southeast corner (lower right corner) of the transportation tableau until the supply capacities of all sources are exhausted and the demand requirements of all destinations are satisfied.

One distinctive feature of the northwest corner solution is that the occupied cells usually form a stair-step effect from the upper left corner, as shown in Table 7.3 by the shaded cells. Now we are ready to calculate the total transportation cost of the initial solution we obtained in Table 7.3 as follows:

Cell	Σ (Quantity Transported	×	Unit Cost)	=	Total Cost
(1,1)	150	×	$20	=	$3,000
(2,1)	50	×	6	=	300
(2,2)	50	×	10	=	500
(3,2)	70	×	15	=	1,050
(3,3)	180	×	12	=	2,160
			Total transportation cost	=	$7,010

The total transportation cost of this initial solution is $7,010. Of course, we remember that this is just an initial solution, a solution from which we initiate our search for the optimum solution. The northwest corner method is the simplest way to obtain an initial solution. However, this method usually yields the least attractive initial solution, because it does not consider the unit transportation costs in making allocations. Consequently, when we initiate the solution process with the northwest corner method, the number of iterations required to reach the optimum solution will be greater than the number required by other methods.

Minimum-Cell-Cost Method   A simple way to develop an initial solution is to use good common sense. For example, since the objective of the problem is to minimize total cost, we must try to allocate as much as possible to those cells in the tableau that

Table 7.3   *The Initial Solution by the Northwest Corner Method*

From \ To	1	2	3	Supply
1	20 150	9	5	150
2	6 50	10 50	18	100
3	2	15 70	12 180	250
Demand	200	120	180	500

have minimum unit transportation costs. This approach is referred to as the *minimum-cell-cost method*.

The steps of the minimum-cell-cost method can be summarized as follows:

1. Select the cell with the minimum cell cost in the tableau and allocate as much to this cell as possible within the supply and demand constraints.

2. Select the cell with the next minimum cell cost and allocate as much to this cell as possible within the demand and supply constraints.

3. Continue this procedure until all the supply and demand requirements are satisfied. In a case of tied minimum cell costs between two or more cells, the tie can be broken by selecting the cell that can accommodate the greater quantity.

Let us consider the Gulf Coast Oil problem once again. In the entire transportation tableau, we can easily identify the minimum cell cost as \$2 in cell (3,1). We can make the initial allocation of 200 in cell (3,1) because the supply capacity of source 3 is 250 and the demand requirement of destination 1 is 200. We always select the lesser of the supply and demand quantities as the amount of allocation. When we make this initial allocation, the demand requirement of destination 1 is completely satisfied and the supply capacity of source 3 is reduced to 50, as shown in Table 7.4. The shaded column in Table 7.4 indicates that we can eliminate this column from further consideration because the demand requirement is satisfied for destination 1.

The cell with the next minimum cell cost in the unshaded cells is \$5 in cell (1,3). The maximum quantity we can allocate to cell (1,3) is 150, since source 1 has a supply

Table 7.4   *Initial Allocation by the Minimum-Cell-Cost Method*

From \ To	1	2	3	Supply
1	20	9	5	150
2	6	10	18	100
3	2 200	15	12	~~250~~ 50
Demand	200	120	180	500

capacity of 150 even though destination 3 has a demand requirement of 180. The second allocation is made in Table 7.5.

The next cell we allocate to is cell (2,2), which has the minimum cell cost among the remaining four cells. The maximum quantity we can allocate is 100, as shown in Table 7.6. By allocating 100 to cell (2,2), we will exhaust the supply capacity of source 2. Because we have exhausted the supply capacities of sources 1 and 2, it is clear in Table 7.6 that the only source that still has some supply capacity is source 3. It has 50

Table 7.5   *First and Second Allocations by the Minimum-Cell-Cost Method*

From \ To	1	2	3	Supply
1	20	9	5 150	150
2	6	10	18	100
3	2 200	15	12	50 ~~250~~
Demand	200	120	30 ~~180~~	500

Table 7.6   *First, Second, and Third Allocations by the Minimum-Cell-Cost Method*

From \ To	1	2	3	Supply
1	20	9	5 150	150
2	6	10 100	18	100
3	2 200	15	12	50 ~~250~~
Demand	200	20 ~~120~~	30 ~~180~~	500

Table 7.7   The Initial Solution by the Minimum-Cell-Cost Method

From \ To	1	2	3	Supply
1	20	9	5 — 150	150
2	6	10 — 100	18	100
3	2 — 200	15 — 20	12 — 30	250
Demand	200	120	180	500

available. However, destinations 2 and 3 still have demand requirements of 20 and 30, respectively. Thus, we have no further choice but to allocate 20 to cell (3,2) and 30 to cell (3,3). Table 7.7 presents the complete initial solution by the minimum-cell-cost method. The total transportation cost of the initial solution shown in Table 7.7 is $2,810.

As we compare the total transportation costs derived by the northwest corner method ($7,010) and the minimum-cell-cost ($2,810) method, it is clear that the commonsense approach of the minimum-cell-cost method has resulted in a savings of $4,200. Thus, we can conclude that the optimum solution could be reached a great deal faster by using the minimum-cell-cost method rather than the northwest corner method.

Vogel's Approximation Method   Another technique to develop an initial solution is Vogel's approximation method (VAM). This method makes allocations based on a rational approach — minimization of the **penalty** (or **opportunity**) **cost.** The penalty cost can be defined as the amount we lose because of our failure to select the best alternative. For example, suppose you are considering two job offers. One offer is from a large electronics firm with an annual salary of $28,000. The second offer is from a family-owned wholesale restaurant equipment company with an annual salary of $16,000. Because of your desire to work in a small organization, you decide to accept the second offer. The penalty cost of this career decision is $12,000 in terms of the first year's salary.

The steps of VAM, which is also referred to as the *penalty,* or *regret, method,* can be summarized as follows:

1. Calculate the penalty cost for each row and each column. The penalty cost is simply the difference between the minimum cell cost and next minimum cell cost in a given row or column. Thus, the penalty cost represents the per-unit opportunity cost associated with the failure to allocate to the cell with the minimum cell cost in a given row or column.

2. Select the row or column that has the largest penalty cost. Allocate as much quantity as possible to the cell with the minimum cell cost in the selected row or column. This procedure assures that we avoid paying the largest penalty cost. If there is a tie in selecting the largest penalty cost, select the row or column whose minimum cost cell can accommodate the greatest quantity.

3. Adjust the demand and supply requirements after the allocation. Eliminate any rows and columns that have satisfied the demand or supply requirements and thus eliminate them from further consideration.

4. If there are additional allocation choices, recalculate the penalty costs and continue the allocation process. If all demand and supply requirements are fully satisfied, the initial solution has been determined.

Now, let us apply VAM to set up the initial solution for the Gulf Coast Oil problem. In Table 7.8, we have calculated the penalty costs for the rows and columns. In the first row (source 1), the minimum cell cost is \$5 in cell (1,3). The next minimum cell cost is \$9 in cell (1,2). Therefore, the penalty cost for the first row will be

Table 7.8   *Penalty Costs and the Initial Allocation by VAM*

From \ To	1	2	3	Supply	Row penalty cost
1	20	9	5	150	4
2	6	10	18	100	4
3	2 ⎵ 200	15	12	50 ~~250~~	10*
Demand	200	120	180	500	
Column penalty cost	4	1	7		

$9 - $5 = 4. This penalty cost of $4 is the extra amount we have to pay per unit if we fail to allocate to cell (1,3) and subsequently allocate to cell (1,2). The same procedure is used for calculating the penalty costs for all the rows and columns.

The largest penalty cost in Table 7.8 is $10 in row 3. This penalty cost indicates that if we fail to allocate to the cell with the minimum cost, (3,1), we have to allocate to the next best cell, (3,3), and pay a $10 penalty per unit. To avoid paying this penalty, we must allocate as much as possible to cell (3,1). The maximum quantity we can allocate to cell (3,1) is 200, since the demand requirement of destination 1 is only 200 whereas the supply capacity of source 3 is 250. After making the initial allocation, we can eliminate column 1 from further consideration as we have met its demand requirement, as shown in Table 7.8. Next, we adjust the supply capacity of source 3 from 250 to 50 (250 − 200 = 50), as also shown in Table 7.8.

Now that we have eliminated column 1 from further consideration, the row penalty costs must be recalculated. In Table 7.9, it is obvious that row 2 has the largest penalty cost. To avoid paying this penalty, we must allocate as much as possible to cell (2,2). The maximum quantity we can allocate to this cell is 100. This allocation will completely exhaust the supply capacity of source 2. Thus, we can eliminate row 2 from further consideration. The demand requirement of column 2 is adjusted to 20. All the adjustments are shown in Table 7.9.

In Table 7.10, we recalculate the column penalty costs because we have eliminated row 2. The maximum penalty cost now appears in column 3. Therefore, we must allocate as much as possible to cell (1,3). The maximum quantity we can allocate to cell (1,3) is 150. Table 7.10 presents the adjustments after this third allocation. Now, there are only two empty cells. We need to allocate 20 to cell (3,2) and 30 to cell (3,3). We

---

Table 7.9   The Second Allocation by VAM

From \ To	1	2	3	Supply	Row penalty cost
1	20 / 9	5		150	4
2	6 / 10 / 100	18		100	8*
3	2 / 200	15	12	50 ~~250~~	3
Demand	200	20 ~~120~~	180	500	

Column penalty cost: 1   7

Table 7.10   The Third Allocation by VAM

To From	1	2	3	Supply	Row penalty cost
1	20	9	5 150	150	4
2	6	10 100	18	100	
3	2 200	15	12	50 ~~250~~	3
Demand	200	20 ~~120~~	30 ~~180~~	500	

| Column
penalty
cost | | 6 | 7* | | |

do not have a further allocation choice. Thus, we can make these allocations and identify the initial solution derived by VAM, as shown in Table 7.11. The total transportation cost of this initial solution derived by VAM is $2,810. This total transportation cost happens to be the same as the cost of the initial solution derived by the minimum-cell-cost method; the solutions are identical.

Table 7.11   The Initial Solution by VAM

To From	1	2	3	Supply
1	20	9	5 150	150
2	6	10 100	18	100
3	2 200	15 20	12 30	250
Demand	200	120	180	500

VAM uses the concept of opportunity cost in developing the initial solution. This method is more logical than the minimum-cell-cost method because it takes into account the relative cost of current and subsequent allocations. In general, VAM yields a better initial solution than other methods. As a matter of fact, for simple transportation problems, VAM frequently yields the optimum solution or a solution that is a good approximate optimum solution. This is why this method is named Vogel's *approximation* method. As we will see later, the initial solution derived by VAM is in fact the optimum solution to our example.

Determining the Optimum Solution—the Modified Distribution Method

Once we develop an initial solution for the transportation problem, the next step is to improve the solution and eventually determine the optimum solution. To check whether we can improve the solution by further reducing the total transportation cost, we must analyze the possibility of reallocation to some of the empty cells. We will study the most widely used technique: the *modified distribution method* (MODI). This method is essentially a variation of the simplex method with different procedures for computing the improvement index of an empty cell.

To evaluate all the empty cells in the tableau, we must meet one requirement. The number of occupied cells must be exactly equal to the sum of the number of rows (sources) and the number of columns (destinations) minus 1:

Number of occupied cells = (number of rows + number of columns) − 1

The occupied cells are none other than the basic variables in the simplex approach. Accordingly, the empty cells are the nonbasic variables. In the simplex tableau, the number of basic variables is exactly equal to the number of constraints. In a transportation problem, the total number of constraints is equal to the number of rows plus the number of columns.

Now you may wonder why the number of occupied cells (i.e., the basic variables) is 1 less than the sum of the rows and columns. In a balanced transportation problem, total supply is equal to total demand. Now let us consider a three-row and three-column transportation problem. When two supply constraints and two demand constraints have been satisfied and an allocation is made to satisfy the third supply constraint, that allocation will simultaneously satisfy the third demand constraint. In other words, one of the six constraints becomes a redundant constraint. This is why we need only five occupied cells for a 3 × 3 problem.

The MODI method, originated by George B. Dantzig, is based on the dual formulation of the primal transportation problem. To demonstrate this method, let us start with an initial solution obtained by the northwest corner method for the Gulf Coast Oil problem (Table 7.12). For the MODI operation, we must make a slight modification in the tableau. We add the r_i column for row values and the k_j row for column values, as shown in Table 7.12.

For the *occupied cells* [cells where some quantities have been allocated, e.g., cells (1,1), (2,1), (2,2), (3,2), and (3,3)], the following relationships exist:

$$c_{ij} = r_i + k_j$$

Table 7.12   Initial Transportation Tableau by the MODI Method Showing Stepping-Stone Path for Cell (1,3)

r_i	From \ To	1	2	3	Supply
	k_j	$k_1 = 20$	$k_2 = 24$	$k_3 = 21$	
$r_1 = 0$	1	20 / 150	9	5	150
$r_2 = -14$	2	6 / 50	10 / 50	18	100
$r_3 = -9$	3	2	15 / 70	12 / 180	250
	Demand	200	120	180	500

Total transportation cost = $7,010

where

$$c_{ij} = \text{unit transportation cost at the occupied cell } ij$$
$$r_i = i\text{th row value}$$
$$k_j = j\text{th column value}$$

For example, the unit transportation cost for the five occupied cells can be described as follows:

$$c_{11} = r_1 + k_1 = 20 \qquad \text{cell (1,1)}$$
$$c_{21} = r_2 + k_1 = 6 \qquad \text{cell (2,1)}$$
$$c_{22} = r_2 + k_2 = 10 \qquad \text{cell (2,2)}$$
$$c_{32} = r_3 + k_2 = 15 \qquad \text{cell (3,2)}$$
$$c_{33} = r_3 + k_3 = 12 \qquad \text{cell (3,3)}$$

In these equations, we have six unknown variables (row and column values) and five equations. To solve for the six unknown variables, one of the variables must be selected and assigned an arbitrary value. The usual procedure is to select r_1 and assign a 0 value to it. With $r_1 = 0$, it is a simple task to identify the values of the remaining variables as follows:

Occupied Cell	$c_{ij} = r_i + k_j$	Row or Column Value
$r_1 + k_1 = 20$	$0 + k_1 = 20,$	$k_1 = 20$
$r_2 + k_1 = 6$	$r_2 + 20 = 6,$	$r_2 = -14$
$r_2 + k_2 = 10$	$-14 + k_2 = 10,$	$k_2 = 24$
$r_3 + k_2 = 15$	$r_3 + 24 = 15,$	$r_3 = -9$
$r_3 + k_3 = 12$	$-9 + k_3 = 12,$	$k_3 = 21$

All the row and column values are determined. As we can see in the above calculations, the row and column values are not always positive. We list these values in the transportation tableau, as shown in Table 7.12. We are now ready to evaluate all the empty cells.

For the *empty cells,* the **cost-improvement index (CII),** which represents the net change in cost and a $c_j - z_j$ value in the simplex tableau, can be determined as follows:

$$\text{CII} = c_{ij} - r_i - k_j$$

If a cell has a negative CII, it indicates that an improved solution is possible. When all the CII values are 0 or positive, an optimum solution is obtained. We can calculate the CII for each of the empty cells as follows:

Empty Cell	$c_{ij} - r_i - k_j$	CII
(1,2)	$9 - 0 - 24$	-15
(1,3)	$5 - 0 - 21$	-16
(2,3)	$18 - (-14) - 21$	$+11$
(3,1)	$2 - (-9) - 20$	-9

The empty cell with the largest negative CII is cell (1,3) with $-\$16$. Every unit we transfer to cell (1,3) will reduce the total transportation cost by \$16. Since only sources can transport goods to destinations, transfers can be made only row-wise but never column-wise. Furthermore, a transfer must use only occupied cells. The set of occupied cells used to make a transfer is referred to as a **stepping-stone path.**

The stepping-stone path for cell (1,3) as shown in Table 7.12 is as follows:

$$(1,3) = \; + \, (1,3) - (1,1) + (2,1) - (2,2) + (3,2) - (3,3)$$

The stepping-stone path can be easily determined by checking the supply and demand requirements as we transfer 1 unit. For example, when we transfer 1 unit from cell (1,1) to cell (1,3), we must increase 1 unit in destination column 1. Since we can only step on occupied cells, the only cell where we can increase 1 unit is cell (2,1). This required transfer of 1 unit must be made row-wise. Thus, a transfer of 1 unit can be made from cell (2,2) to cell (2,1). Likewise, the final tranfer of 1 unit should be made from cell (3,3) to cell (3,2).

How much can we transfer to cell (1,3) along the stepping-stone path? The maximum is exactly the *minimum quantity* we find in the negative stones of the stepping-stone path. The negative stones are cells (1,1), (2,2), and (3,3) as shown in Table 7.12. The minimum quantity in these cells is 50 in cell (2,2).

After we implement this transfer, we derive the second solution. The second solution is evaluated by recalculating the row and column values and the CII as shown below:

Occupied Cell	$c_{ij} = r_i + k_j$	Row or Column Value
(1,1)	$20 = 0 + k_1$	$k_1 = 20$
(1,3)	$5 = 0 + k_3$	$k_3 = 5$
(2,1)	$6 = r_2 + 20$	$r_2 = -14$
(3,2)	$15 = 7 + k_2$	$k_2 = 8$
(3,3)	$12 = r_3 + 5$	$r_3 = 7$

Empty Cell	$c_{ij} - r_i - k_j$	CII
(1,2)	$9 - 0 - 8$	$+1$
(2,2)	$10 - (-14) - 8$	$+16$
(2,3)	$18 - (-14) - 5$	$+27$
(3,1)	$2 - 7 - 20$	-25

Table 7.13 presents the second solution with the row and column values. The cell with the best CII is cell (3,1) with $-$\$25. By tracing its stepping-stone path, as shown

Table 7.13   *The Second Solution by the MODI Method*

Total transportation cost = \$6,210

in Table 7.13, we can easily determine that the maximum quantity we can transfer is 100 [in cell (1,1)].

We repeat the process and derive the third solution, as shown in Table 7.14. The new row and column values and the CIIs are determined as follows:

Occupied Cell	$c_{ij} = r_i + k_j$	Row or Column Value
(1,3)	$5 = 0 + k_3$	$k_3 = 5$
(3,3)	$12 = r_3 + 5$	$r_3 = 7$
(3,2)	$15 = 7 + k_2$	$k_2 = 8$
(3,1)	$2 = 7 + k_1$	$k_1 = -5$
(2,1)	$6 = r_2 + (-5)$	$r_2 = 11$

Empty Cell	$c_{ij} - r_i - k_j$	CII
(1,1)	$20 - 0 - (-5)$	$+25$
(1,2)	$9 - 0 - 8$	$+1$
(2,2)	$10 - 11 - 8$	-9
(2,3)	$18 - 11 - 5$	$+2$

Table 7.14 presents the third solution with row and column values. The cell with the best CII is cell (2,2) with $-\$9$. We trace the stepping-stone path for cell (2,2), as shown in Table 7.14. The maximum quantity we can transfer to cell (2,2) is 100 [in cell (2,1)]. When we transfer 100 units to cell (2,2), we obtain the fourth solution, as shown in Table 7.15.

Now we repeat the evaluation process by the MODI method and determine the row and column values and the CIIs for the empty cells as follows:

Occupied Cell	$c_{ij} = r_i + k_j$	Row or Column Value
(1,3)	$5 = 0 + k_3$	$k_3 = 5$
(3,3)	$12 = r_3 + 5$	$r_3 = 7$
(3,2)	$15 = 7 + k_2$	$k_2 = 8$
(3,1)	$2 = 7 + k_1$	$k_1 = -5$
(2,2)	$10 = r_2 + 8$	$r_2 = 2$

Empty Cell	$c_{ij} - r_i - k_j$	CII
(1,1)	$20 - 0 - (-5)$	$+25$
(1,2)	$9 - 0 - 8$	$+1$
(2,1)	$6 - 2 - (-5)$	$+9$
(2,3)	$18 - 2 - 5$	$+11$

The CII values calculated for the empty cells indicate that they are all positive. Therefore, we have reached the optimum solution. The optimum solution of the Gulf Coast Oil problem has the transportation network shown in Figure 7.3.

Table 7.14   The Third Solution by the MODI Method

k_j		$k_1 = -5$	$k_2 = 8$	$k_3 = 5$	
r_i	To / From	1	2	3	Supply
$r_1 = 0$	1	20	9	5 — 150	150
$r_2 = 11$	2	6 — 100	10	18	100
$r_3 = 7$	3	2 — 100	15 — 120	12 — 30	250
	Demand	200	120	180	500

Total transportation cost = $3,710

Table 7.15   The Optimum Solution Obtained by the MODI Method

k_j		$k_1 = -5$	$k_2 = 8$	$k_3 = 5$	
r_i	To / From	1	2	3	Supply
$r_1 = 0$	1	20	9	5 — 150	150
$r_2 = 2$	2	6	10 — 100	18	100
$r_3 = 7$	3	2 — 200	15 — 20	12 — 30	250
	Demand	200	120	180	500

Total transportation cost = $2,810

Figure 7.3   Optimum Transportation Network for Gulf Coast Oil

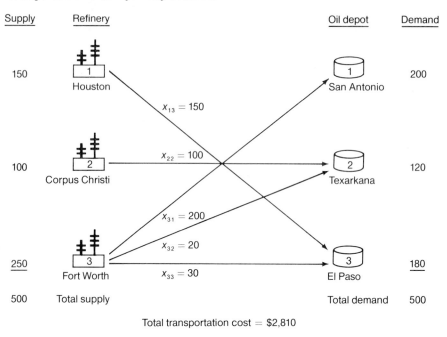

Total transportation cost = $2,810

We can summarize the MODI method as follows:

1. Starting with a solution, compute the row (r_i) and column (k_j) values by using the relationship $c_{ij} = r_i + k_j$ for all the occupied cells. Assign $r_1 = 0$ and determine all the r_i and k_j values.

2. Compute the CIIs for all the empty cells by using the formula CII $= c_{ij} - r_i - k_j$.

3. Trace the stepping-stone path for the empty cell that has the largest negative CII. If there is no negative CII, the optimum solution is found.

4. Transfer to the selected empty cell the minimum quantity in the negative stones of the stepping-stone path.

5. Develop a new solution and repeat the procedure by going back to step 1.

THE UNBALANCED TRANSPORTATION PROBLEM

Our discussion thus far has focused on the balanced transportation problem, in which total supply equals total demand. In real-world situations, however, a balanced case is the exception rather than the rule. As a matter of fact, most transportation problems are unbalanced cases in which either supply exceeds demand or demand exceeds supply. To analyze an unbalanced transportation problem, we must make a minor modification in the transportation tableau so that the case becomes a balanced case. First we will discuss the case in which demand exceeds supply and then the case in which supply exceeds demand.

Demand Exceeds Supply

Let us consider the original transportation problem of Gulf Coast Oil Company. Suppose the demand for gasoline at the third destination (El Paso) has increased to 240 from the original demand of 180. The total demand from the three destinations is now 560, while the total supply remains at 500. This problem can be formulated as a linear programming model as follows:

$$\text{Minimize } Z = 20x_{11} + 9x_{12} + 5x_{13} + 6x_{21} + 10x_{22} + 18x_{23} + 2x_{31} + 15x_{32} + 12x_{33}$$

$$\text{subject to } \left.\begin{array}{r} x_{11} + x_{12} + x_{13} = 150 \\ x_{21} + x_{22} + x_{23} = 100 \\ x_{31} + x_{32} + x_{33} = 250 \end{array}\right\} \text{Supply}$$

$$\left.\begin{array}{r} x_{11} + x_{21} + x_{31} \leq 200 \\ x_{12} + x_{22} + x_{32} \leq 120 \\ x_{13} + x_{23} + x_{33} \leq 240 \end{array}\right\} \text{Demand}$$

$$x_{ij} \geq 0$$

Since the demand is greater than (>) the supply, we will use every unit supplied by the sources. However, all the quantity demanded by a destination may not be satisfied. In any unbalanced problem, whichever is the lesser quantity between the demand and supply requirements will always have an equal-to (=) constraint, whereas the greater of the two will always have a less-than-or-equal-to ($\leq$) constraint.

To make the unbalanced case a balanced problem, we can create an imaginary refinery (source) that can accommodate the excess demand. We introduce a *dummy* source to supply the increased demand of 60 at destination 3. Now we can balance supply and demand. Since the dummy source is only an imaginary refinery, the unit transportation costs of all of the cells in the dummy row are 0.

The initial solution for the problem can be determined by the northwest corner, minimum-cell-cost, or Vogel's approximation method. In using the northwest corner method or VAM, we treat the dummy row (or dummy column in a case of supply > demand) as if it were one of the regular rows. However, if we use the minimum-cell-cost method, we cannot make the first unique assignment among the three zero-cost cells in the dummy row. For example, the supply quantity of 60 in the dummy row can be assigned to cell (4,1), (4,2), or (4,3) at the minimum cost of 0. Therefore, for the minimum-cell-cost method it is better that we leave the dummy row (or dummy column) for consideration at the end.

Let us consider the modified transportation tableau shown in Table 7.16. Notice that the unbalanced case has been modified to become a balanced case. We exclude the dummy row and start with the minimum-cell-cost method. The cell with the minimum transportation cost is cell (3,1). We make the maximum possible assignment of 200 in this cell and continue as we did earlier in the minimum-cell-cost method procedure. After all assignments are made in the regular rows, as shown in Table 7.16, we consider the unique assignment in the dummy row. Obviously, the last assignment has to be made in cell (4,3).

Table 7.16   *Initial Solution by the Minimum-Cell-Cost Method for the Unbalanced Problem*

From \ To	1	2	3	Supply
1	20	9	5 150	150
2	6	10 100	18	100
3	2 200	15 20	12 30	250
4 Dummy	0	0	0 60	60
Demand	200	120	240	560

Now we can proceed to solve the problem by using the MODI method. If the optimum solution calls for the dummy row to transport some quantity to one or more destinations, this implies that the destination(s) will receive less than the quantity required. For example, if the optimum solution shows the dummy row supplying 60 units to destination 3, in reality destination 3 would receive only 180 units rather than the 240 it demanded.

Supply Exceeds Demand

Now we can analyze the opposite case in which supply exceeds demand. Suppose, again in the Gulf Coast Oil problem, that the demand requirement at destination 1 has decreased to 160 from the original 200. The total demand from the three destinations now amounts to only 460, whereas the total supply remains at 500. Clearly, this is a case in which supply exceeds demand. We can formulate a linear programming model for the unbalanced case as follows:

$$\text{Minimize } Z = 20x_{11} + 9x_{12} + 5x_{13} + 6x_{21} + 10x_{22} + 18x_{23} + 2x_{31} + 15x_{32} + 12x_{33}$$

$$\text{subject to} \quad
\left.\begin{array}{l}
x_{11} + x_{12} + x_{13} \le 150 \\
x_{21} + x_{22} + x_{23} \le 100 \\
x_{31} + x_{32} + x_{33} \le 250
\end{array}\right\} \text{Supply}$$

$$\left.\begin{array}{l}
x_{11} + x_{21} + x_{31} = 160 \\
x_{12} + x_{22} + x_{32} = 120 \\
x_{13} + x_{23} + x_{33} = 180
\end{array}\right\} \text{Demand}$$

$$x_{ij} \ge 0$$

Table 7.17   Initial Solution by the Northwest Corner Method for the Second Unbalanced Problem

From \ To	1	2	3	4 Dummy	Supply
1	20 / 150	9	5	0	150
2	6 / 10	10 / 90	18	0	100
3	2	15 / 30	12 / 180	0 / 40	250
Demand	160	120	180	40	500

To balance the supply and demand requirements for the problem, we must create a dummy destination to absorb the excess supply of 40 units. The dummy column is added in the tableau and unit transportation costs of 0 are assigned to the cells in the dummy destination column, as shown in Table 7.17. The initial solution by the northwest corner method is also presented in Table 7.17. As usual, we can proceed to improve the solution by using the MODI method.

If destination 4 (dummy column) receives some quantity from a source (or sources) in the final solution, this implies that the source (or sources) is not supplying up to its productive capacity. For example, if the dummy destination receives 40 units from source 3, as shown in Table 7.17, source 3 in reality is supplying only 210 units, or 40 below its supply capacity of 250. Thus, source 3 (refinery at Fort Worth) may either produce gasoline up to its productive capacity and store the unsold quantity of 40 units or produce 40 units less than its productive capacity and simply meet the demand.

SOME UNIQUE SITUATIONS

In many transportation problems, we face situations that may cause some difficulty. In this section, we will discuss some of these situations.

Degeneracy

To improve a solution, we must evaluate all the empty cells and determine their CII values. For the MODI method, the number of occupied cells should be exactly $m + n - 1$ (m = number of rows, n = number of columns). If a transportation tableau has less than $m + n - 1$ occupied cells, the solution is referred to as *degenerate*. In a degenerate problem, we cannot evaluate all the empty cells because degeneracy would prohibit us from developing a sufficient number of $c_{ij} = r_i + k_j$ relationships to determine the row and column values to use the MODI method.

Degeneracy can occur at any time during the transportation solution process, either in the initial solution or during the iterations. The cause of degeneracy is a unique allocation that satisfies the demand and supply requirements simultaneously. Let us discuss degenerate cases in the initial solution and also during the iterations.

Degeneracy in the Initial Solution   Suppose the Gulf Coast Oil problem has been slightly modified as shown in Table 7.18. The initial solution is derived by the northwest corner method. Since the demand at destination 3 and supply at source 3 are an identical 160 units, the unique allocation in cell (3,3) satisfies the demand and supply requirements simultaneously. We have only four occupied cells, which results in a degenerate solution. We know from our previous discussion that the northwest corner method usually yields an initial solution with a chain of occupied cells that form a step effect. This chain is broken in Table 7.18.

To remedy the problem of degeneracy, we must restore the condition of $m + n - 1$ number of occupied cells for the solution. By assigning a very small quantity, ϵ (epsilon), to an empty cell, we will connect the broken chain of occupied cells. In our solution, shown in Table 7.18, there are two candidates, cell (2,3) and cell (3,2). By assigning ϵ to either cell (2,3) or cell (3,2), we can proceed with the solution process in the usual manner.

There are two characteristics of ϵ that we must know about. First, ϵ is such a small value that if we add some quantity to ϵ the sum will be exactly equal to the quantity just added. For example, let us consider the stepping-stone path for an empty cell as shown in Table 7.19(a). The ϵ cell is a positive stone. Thus, when we add the transfer

Table 7.18   Degeneracy in the Initial Solution

From \ To	1	2	3	Supply
1	20 / 150	9	5	150
2	6 / 50	10 / 140	18	190
3	2	15	12 / 160	160
Demand	200	140	160	500

Table 7.19   A Positive ε Cell in the Stepping-Stone Path

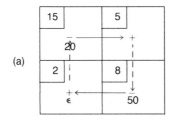   (a)   (b)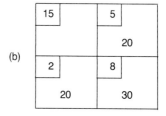

Table 7.20   A Negative ε Cell in the Stepping-Stone Path

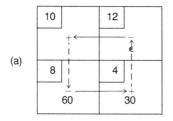   (a)   (b)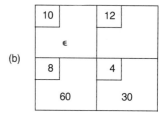

---

quantity of 20 to ε, the new quantity in the ε cell becomes 20, as shown in Table 7.19(b). This transfer actually eliminated ε, as the problem is no longer degenerate.

The second characteristic of ε is that if ε is in a negative stone of the stepping-stone path, the quantity we can transfer to the empty cell will be ε. For example, let us consider the stepping-stone path shown in Table 7.20(a). Since the minimum quantity in the negative stones of the path is ε, this is the quantity that must be transferred, as shown in Table 7.20(b). When ε is subtracted from the quantities of the occupied cells in the path, the old quantities remain the same because ε is such a minimal value. Thus, this transfer serves *no purpose*. Therefore, whenever ε is in a negative stone, we should ignore this path evaluation and move on to the next path that shows the greatest CII.

Degeneracy in Subsequent Iterations   Let us suppose that the Gulf Coast Oil problem has been modified as shown in Table 7.21. The initial solution is derived by the northwest corner method. This solution is not degenerate. From a brief analysis of the CII values, indicated by the circled numbers in each empty cell, it is obvious that cell (1,3) is where we must make a transfer. The stepping-stone path is also indicated in Table 7.21.

The maximum quantity we can transfer to cell (1,3) is 120. However, when this transfer is made, both cell (1,1) and cell (2,2) become empty, since these two negative stones have the identical minimum quantity of 120 in the negative cells of the stepping-stone path. The iteration yields a degenerate solution, as shown in Table 7.22. We can assign ε to one of the two negative cells that have become empty, namely cell (1,1) and cell (2,2). Now we can proceed with the solution process in the usual manner.

Table 7.21   The Initial Solution by the Northwest Corner Method

From \ To	1	2	3	Supply
1	20 / 120	9 / (−15)	5 / (−16)	120
2	6 / 30	10 / 120	18 / (+11)	150
3	2 / (−9)	15 / 20	12 / 210	230
Demand	150	140	210	500

Table 7.22   The Second Solution Tableau

From \ To	1	2	3	Supply
1	20	9	5 / 120	120
2	6 / 150	10 / ϵ	18	150
3	2	15 / 140	12 / 90	230
Demand	150	140	210	500

If a solution is degenerate, we cannot determine all the row (r_i) and column (k_j) values when we apply the MODI method. From an analysis of the relationship $c_{ij} = r_i + k_j$, we can easily determine to which empty cell we must assign ϵ in order to calculate the r_i and k_j values. Once ϵ is assigned to an appropriate empty cell, we can proceed in the usual manner.

Prohibited or Impossible Transportation Routes

In certain transportation problems, shipment from a certain source to a certain destination is either prohibited by local traffic ordinances or physically impossible because of a union strike, road construction, seasonal hazards of the road (snow, flooding, etc.), weight limits on bridges, and the like. A transportation problem with prohibited or impossible routes can be handled by assigning a large unit transportation cost M (similar to the large M method we used in linear programming) to each of the prohibited cells. The same result can be obtained if we block out those cells altogether. In such a case, the blocked-out cells are skipped over in the evaluation of the empty cells.

Multiple-Optimum Solutions

In a transportation tableau, the optimum solution is obtained when all the CII values for the empty cells are 0 or positive. If there are one or more empty cells with CII values of 0, the problem has alternate optimum solutions. Since the empty cells represent the nonbasic variables and their CII values are $c_j - z_j$ in the simplex concept, we can easily identify with the multiple-optimum-solution case. We can make a transfer to an empty cell with a CII value of 0 and obtain an entirely different solution but with exactly the same total transportation cost.

For example, let us suppose that the optimum solution to a modified version of the Gulf Coast Oil problem is obtained as shown in Table 7.23. The circled CII values for the empty cells are also presented in the table. Cell (1,2) has a CII value of 0. Thus, there is an alternate optimum solution.

From a brief analysis of the stepping-stone path for cell (1,2), shown in Table 7.23, we can easily determine that the maximum quantity we can transfer to cell (1,2) is 20.

Table 7.23   An Optimum Solution Tableau

From \ To	1	2	3	Supply
1	20 (+24)	9 (0)	6 150	150
2	6 (+9)	10 100	18 (+16)	100
3	2 200	15 20	12 30	250
Demand	200	120	180	500

Table 7.24   An Alternate Optimum Solution

From \ To	1	2	3	Supply
1	20	9 20	6 130	150
2	6	10 100	18	100
3	2 200	15	12 50	250
Demand	200	120	180	500

After this transfer, a new optimum solution is derived, as shown in Table 7.24. The total transportation cost remains the same, but an alternate optimum solution is identified. If management has a preference for a given solution, in consideration of such noneconomic factors as road conditions, traffic accident figures for certain routes, and union contracts, an analysis of multiple optimum solutions may be valuable.

The Transshipment Problem

In a typical transportation problem, only sources can transport goods to destinations. However, in many real-world problems, destinations can be intermediate points of transportation. For example, gasoline can be transported from a refinery in Houston to an oil depot in San Antonio, and then the San Antonio depot can transport it to another depot in El Paso. The *transshipment method* has an enormous potential for practical application. A special procedure is available to solve the transshipment problem by the regular transportation method, with some minor adjustments.

Transshipment problems use the basic transportation tableau, expanding it to accommodate the new routes. The resulting tableau is four times the size of the simple transportation tableau; thus, a linear programming formulation would involve four times as many decision variables, as Figure 7.4 illustrates. Note that the original transportation tableau appears as the upper right quadrant of the transshipment tableau.

Each cell in the transshipment tableau must be assigned its own c_{ij} (contribution coefficient). These are not mirror images of the simple transportation tableau, and they require fresh input. For example, shipping from 1 to A may cost $20, but the reverse route from A to 1 may cost only $5. Such differences may result from load capacities, shipment frequencies, standardized routes, upstream/downstream considerations, or a variety of other factors. Each c_{ij} must be determined individually. In cases where a given route is impossible, the large M method will work; alternatively, the impossible cell can simply be blocked out. The cost of shipping from any location to itself is always 0.

Figure 7.4   Comparison of Transportation and Transshipment Tableaus

Destinations

From \ To	A	B	C	Supply
1	x_{1A}	x_{1B}	x_{1C}	
2	x_{2A}	x_{2B}	x_{2C}	
3	x_{3A}	x_{3B}	x_{3C}	
Demand				

Sources (left label for rows 1, 2, 3)

Destinations

	(Sources)			(Destinations)			
From \ To	1	2	3	A	B	C	Supply
1	x_{11}	x_{12}	x_{13}	x_{1A}	x_{1B}	x_{1C}	
2	x_{21}	x_{22}	x_{23}	x_{2A}	x_{2B}	x_{2C}	
3	x_{31}	x_{32}	x_{33}	x_{3A}	x_{3B}	x_{3C}	
A	x_{A1}	x_{A2}	x_{A3}	x_{AA}	x_{AB}	x_{AC}	
B	x_{B1}	x_{B2}	x_{B3}	x_{BA}	x_{BB}	x_{BC}	
C	x_{C1}	x_{C2}	x_{C3}	x_{CA}	x_{CB}	x_{CC}	
Demand							

Sources [(Sources) for rows 1–3, (Destinations) for rows A–C]

GULF COAST OIL—TRANSSHIPMENT

To demonstrate the transshipment solution procedure, we will expand the Gulf Coast Oil problem to allow for transportation between refineries, between depots, and from depots to refineries. These new routes form the three additional quadrants needed to constitute a transshipment tableau. The new shipping situation is reflected in Figure 7.5, including the shipping costs along each route in each direction.

Figure 7.5   Gulf Coast Oil Transshipment Problem

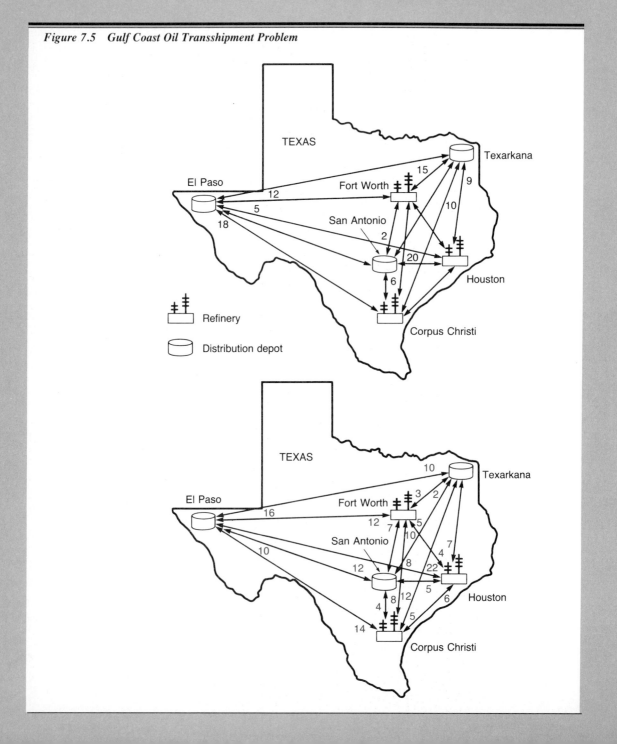

Transshipment allows a source or a destination to serve as an intermediate point for some of or all the items being transported. Every source and every destination can thus supply the total supply as well as its own supply; every source and every destination can also demand the total demand plus its own demand. In the Gulf Coast Oil problem, total supply (and total demand) equals 500,000 gallons, represented by 500 in the model. Houston could supply 150,000 gallons in the simple transportation problem; now, it can supply 650,000. Likewise, El Paso's demand was 180,000; it is now 680,000. Notice the addition of 500 to every supply row and to every demand column, illustrated in Table 7.25. This table represents the complete transshipment tableau, with an initial solution derived using VAM.

Table 7.26 presents the optimal solution, obtained using standard transportation techniques. The quantities on the zero–cost diagonal are meaningless—ignore them. The remaining values, highlighted by a circle, represent the actual shipments that would

Table 7.25   *Transshipment Tableau with Initial Solution Using VAM*

From \ To	1 Houston	2 Corpus Christi	3 Fort Worth	A San Antonio	B Texarkana	C El Paso	Supply
1 Houston	0 500	5	5	20	9	5 150	650
2 Corpus Christi	6	0 500	10	6	10 100	18	600
3 Fort Worth	4	8	0 500	2 250	15	12	750
A San Antonio	5	4	7	0 450	2 20	10 30	500
B Texarkana	7	12	3	8	0 500	16	500
C El Paso	22	14	12	12	10	0 500	500
Demand	500	500	500	700	620	680	3,500

Table 7.26   Optimal Solution of Gulf Coast Oil Transshipment Problem

From \ To	1 Houston	2 Corpus Christi	3 Fort Worth	A San Antonio	B Texarkana	C El Paso	Supply
1 Houston	0	5	5	20	9	5	
	470					(180)	650
2 Corpus Christi	6	0	10	6	10	18	
	(30)	500		(70)			600
3 Fort Worth	4	8	0	2	15	12	
			500	(250)			750
A San Antonio	5	4	7	0	2	10	
				380	(120)		500
B Texarkana	7	12	3	8	0	16	
					500		500
C El Paso	22	14	12	12	10	0	
						500	500
Demand	500	500	500	700	620	680	3,500

occur. Calculating the total cost gives a new Z of $2,240. Gulf could save $570 over the optimal simple transportation solution by routing 30,000 gallons from Corpus Christi through Houston to El Paso and 120,000 gallons from Fort Worth through San Antonio to Texarkana.

THE TRANSPORTATION PROBLEM WITH MULTIPLE OBJECTIVES

Many practical transportation problems often involve multiple conflicting objectives rather than the single objective of transportation cost minimization. In such cases, since the transportation method can handle only one objective criterion (i.e., the transportation cost), we must abandon this approach and instead apply the goal-programming methodology. Many transportation-related problems with multiple objectives have been analyzed by goal programming in recent years. Some of these applications are location-allocation, labor scheduling and allocation, school busing logistics, and product transportation or transshipment problems. If you are interested in this topic, you should consult the References at the end of this chapter.

COMPUTER SOLUTIONS FOR TRANSPORTATION PROBLEMS

Although linear programming computer programs will solve transportation and transshipment problems, programs especially formulated for these techniques produce solution outputs that are easier to interpret and that frequently use less computing time.

Knowledge of the tableau format helps to interpret the computer output, particularly in transshipment problems. The input and output for the Gulf Coast Oil transportation problem (Casette 4.1) is shown in Figure 7.6, using the *Micro Manager* program.

The transshipment problem formulated in Casette 4.2 would be entered on the computer as a transportation problem with six sources and six destinations. Summary input and output tableaux are shown in Figure 7.7, again using the *Micro Manager* package. As in our manually created tableaux, the original transportation problem is the upper right quadrant of the transshipment tableaux. Compare these two figures with Tables 7.15 and 7.26, the manually derived optimal solution tableaux for these problems.

REAL-WORLD APPLICATION

There have been numerous real-world applications of the transportation method. Many transportation and transportation-related problems, such as location-allocation problems, are often formulated in the general transportation model framework and solved by linear programming. In this section, we will examine one example of a real-world application.

Samkjoringen av Kraftverkene i Norge is the national electrical cooperative which organizes and coordinates the electrical power companies that have approximately 95 percent of the generating capacity in Norway.[1] Samkjoringen's primary responsibility is to manage the central electrical network. The central network represents the transmission grid system that is utilized for rational coordination and utilization of the member power stations for each time period. The central network includes approximately 2,540 kilometers of 275-kV lines, 3,640 kilometers of 132-kV lines, and various transformers that connect the different system voltages.

The central network has 75 subscribing companies that use the grid system. The central network is owned by a number of member companies of Samkjoringen. The ownership companies of the central network receive an annual compensation based on

---

[1]O. Aarvik and Paul Randolph, ''The Application of Linear Programming to the Determination of Transmission Fees in an Electrical Power Network,'' *Interfaces* 6:1 (1975), 47–49.

Figure 7.6   Computer Input and Output, Casette 7.1

```
PROGRAM: Transportation

Enter 1 for maximization or 2 for minimization: 2
Enter number of supply (source) points (greater than 1): 3
Enter number of demand (destination) points (greater than 1):  3

Enter available capacity for supply (source) point 1 :  150
Enter available capacity for supply (source) point 2 :  100
Enter available capacity for supply (source) point 3 :  250

Enter available capacity for demand (destination) point 1 :  200
Enter available capacity for demand (destination) point 2 :  120
Enter available capacity for demand (destination) point 3 :  180

Enter unit transportation cost for all routes.

From supply 1 to demand 1 :  20
From supply 1 to demand 2 :  9
From supply 1 to demand 3 :  5


From supply 2 to demand 1 :  6
From supply 2 to demand 2 :  10
From supply 2 to demand 3 :  18

From supply 3 to demand 1 :  2
From supply 3 to demand 2 :  15
From supply 3 to demand 3 :  12



## End of interactive input ##              One moment please...


PROGRAM: Transportation

##### INPUT DATA ENTERED #####

Minimization problem :

        !    1       2       3  !   Supply
    -------------------------------------------
    1   !   20.00    9.00    5.00!    150.00
    2   !    6.00   10.00   18.00!    100.00
    3   !    2.00   15.00   12.00!    250.00
    -------------------------------------------
    Demand!  200.00  120.00  180.00!    500.00

#####   PROGRAM OUTPUT   #####

        !    1       2       3  !   Supply
    -------------------------------------------
    1   !    0.00    0.00  150.00!    150.00
    2   !    0.00  100.00    0.00!    100.00
    3   !  200.00   20.00   30.00!    250.00
    -------------------------------------------
    Demand!  200.00  120.00  180.00!    500.00

Optimal solution  :      2810.00
```

Figure 7.7   Computer Input and Output, Casette 7.2

```
PROGRAM: Transportation

***** INPUT DATA ENTERED *****

Minimization problem :

         !    1        2        3        4        5        6  !   Supply
       ----------------------------------------------------------------
   1   !   0.00     5.00     5.00    20.00     9.00     5.00!   650.00
   2   !   6.00     0.00    10.00     6.00    10.00    18.00!   600.00
   3   !   4.00     8.00     0.00     2.00    15.00    12.00!   750.00
   4   !   5.00     4.00     7.00     0.00     2.00    10.00!   500.00
   5   !   7.00    12.00     3.00     8.00     0.00    16.00!   500.00
   6   !  22.00    14.00    12.00    12.00    10.00     0.00!   500.00
       ----------------------------------------------------------------
Demand!  500.00   500.00   500.00   700.00   620.00   680.00!  3500.00


*****   PROGRAM OUTPUT   *****

         !    1        2        3        4        5        6  !   Supply
       ----------------------------------------------------------------
   1   ! 470.00     0.00     0.00     0.00     0.00   180.00!   650.00
   2   !  30.00   500.00     0.00    70.00     0.00     0.00!   600.00
   3   !   0.00     0.00   500.00   250.00     0.00     0.00!   750.00
   4   !   0.00     0.00     0.00   380.00   120.00     0.00!   500.00
   5   !   0.00     0.00     0.00     0.00   500.00     0.00!   500.00
   6   !   0.00     0.00     0.00     0.00     0.00   500.00!   500.00
       ----------------------------------------------------------------
Demand!  500.00   500.00   500.00   700.00   620.00   680.00!  3500.00

Optimal solution :      2240.00
```

their fixed percentage of the capital invested in the grid system. The total compensation paid to the ownership companies equals the total sum paid by the subscribers to the central network.

The subscribers' annual fees are made up of three primary components: transmission fees, exchange fees, and connection fees. The transmission fees represent approximately 90 percent of the total subscription fees. This study was focused on the determination of the transmission fee for each subscriber. To formulate the transportation model upon which the study was based, the following terms were defined:

Sources: points that feed electricity into the system

Sinks: points that use electricity

x_{ij}:   amount of electricity (megawatts) transmitted from source i ($i = 1, \ldots, m$) to sink j ($j = 1, \ldots, n$)

a_i: amount of electricity (megawatts) supplied by source i to the network

b_j: amount of electricity (megawatts) used by sink j

c_{ij}:   distance in kilometers from source i to sink j

The transportation model formulated was:

$$\text{Minimize } Z = \sum_{i=1}^{m} \sum_{j=1}^{n} c_{ij} x_{ij}$$

$$\text{subject to } \sum_{j=1}^{n} x_{ij} = a_i, \qquad (i = 1, \ldots, m)$$

$$\sum_{i=1}^{m} x_{ij} = b_j, \qquad (j = 1, \ldots, n)$$

$$x_{ij} \geq 0$$

This transportation problem was solved by the Norwegian Computer Center by means of a fast transportation computer code. The largest transportation problem solved had 75 sources and 92 sinks—161 constraints and 6,900 decision variables. The authors claim that the problem was solved in 16 seconds. Once the transportation model was solved, the exact transmission fee could be determined for each subscriber.

In the past, Samkjoringen had used hand methods to solve simplified transportation models, a task often requiring several weeks. In addition to the enormous computation time consumed by using hand calculation, frequently the allocation that was used might not have been the optimum one. Thus, the use of a transportation model greatly improved the efficiency in determining the equitable transmission fees for the subscribers of the central electrical network in Norway.

SUMMARY

The transportation problem is a special type of linear programming problem, and its analysis has constituted one of the major areas of fruitful application of linear programming. The initial work done by F. L. Hitchcock and T. C. Koopmans in the 1940s paved the way for future research. Many scholars have since refined and extended the basic transportation model to include not only the determination of optimum transportation patterns but also the analysis of production scheduling problems, transshipment problems, and assignment problems (to be presented in Chapter 8).

In the general transportation problem, the objective is to minimize total transportation costs. The basic assumption underlying this method is that management is concerned primarily with cost minimization. Thus, linear programming computer programs have been widely applied to the transportation problem. However, this assumption is not always valid. In the transportation problem, there may be multiple objectives, such as the fulfillment of transportation schedule contracts, fulfillment of union contracts, provision for a stable employment level in various plants and transportation fleets, balancing of work among a number of plants, minimization of transportation hazards, and, of course, minimization of cost. The application of goal programming has broadened considerably our ability to solve complex transportation problems.

Glossary

Balanced Transportation Problem   A problem whose total supply exactly equals total demand.

Cost-Improvement Index   In the MODI method, the potential net contribution to the solution by any cell, computed by evaluating its stepping-stone path.

Degenerate Transportation Solution   When the number of occupied cells is less than the number of rows plus columns minus 1, a lack of occupied cells prevents proper use of the MODI technique. An epsilon is typically assigned to allow another iteration.

Minimum-Cell-Cost Method   Technique to provide an initial solution to a transportation problem by meeting supply and demand requirements, starting with the least-cost cell and proceeding to fill the minimum-cost cell remaining.

Modified Distribution Method   MODI is a modified simplex technique for use with transportation tableaux. Evaluation of an empty cell's stepping-stone path leads to its cell improvement index, upon which further iterations are based.

Multiple-Objective Transportation Problem   More than one objective in a transportation situation requires that another technique (such as goal programming) be used.

Multiple Optimum Solutions   More than one solution with equal objective function values will produce a cost-improvement index of 0 in at least one unoccupied cell of the transportation tableau.

Northwest Corner Method   A heuristic which provides an initial solution to a transportation problem by meeting supply and demand requirements in a stepped fashion, starting in the upper left (or northwest) corner of the tableau.

Prohibited Transportation Route   When a given route is infeasible or prohibited, the large *M* method may be implemented by assigning a huge or undesirable value as cost or profit to the prohibited cell.

Stepping-Stone Path   Route along which balanced transfer of units may take place to improve the objective value.

Transshipment Problem   Transportation problem in which some sources or destinations can serve as intermediary points en route to the final destination.

Unbalanced Transportation Problem   A problem where total supply does not equal total demand. Solution requres a dummy source for additional supply or a dummy destination to provide additional demand.

Vogel's Approximation Method (VAM)   VAM provides an initial solution to a transportation problem by considering opportunity costs; frequently provides an optimum or near-optimum solution.

References

Ackoff, R. L., and Sasieni, M. W. *Fundamentals of Operations Research*. New York: Wiley, 1968.

Charnes, A., and Cooper, W. W. *Management Models and Industrial Applications of Linear Programming*. New York: Wiley, 1961.

Churchman, C. W., Ackoff, R. L., and Arnoff, E. L. *Introduction to Operations Research*. New York: Wiley, 1958.

Dantzig, G. B. *Linear Programming and Extensions*. Princeton, N.J.: Princeton University, 1963.

Hillier, F. S., and Lieberman, G. J. *Introduction to Operations Research*. 4th ed. San Francisco: Holden-Day, 1986.

Hitchcock, F. L. "The Distribution of a Product from Several Sources to Numerous Localities." *Journal of Mathematics and Physics* 20 (1941), 224–230.

Koopmans, T. C., ed. *Activity Analysis of Production and Allocation, Cowles Commission Monograph No. 13*. New York: Wiley, 1951.

Kwak, N. K. *Mathematical Programming with Business Applications*. New York: McGraw-Hill, 1973.

Lee, S. M., and Moore, L. J. "Multiple-Criteria School Busing Models." *Management Science* 23:7 (1977), 703–715.

Lee, S. M.; Moore, L. J.; and Taylor, B. W. *Management Science*. 2d ed. Dubuque, Iowa: W. C. Brown, 1985.

Orden, A. "The Transshipment Problem." *Management Science* 2 (1956), 276–285.

Reinfeld, V., and Vogel, R. *Mathematical Programming*. Englewood Cliffs, N.J.: Prentice-Hall, 1958.

Assignments

7.1 Why is the transportation method a special technique of linear programming?

7.2 Describe a problem familiar to you that can be solved by the transportation method.

7.3 What is the primary difference between a balanced and an unbalanced transportation problem?

7.4 In terms of logic or scientific reasoning, distinguish among the following three methods for developing an initial transportation solution: northwest corner method, minimum-cell-cost method, and VAM.

7.5 Describe the opportunity cost concept by giving an example familiar to you.

7.6 What is the theoretical foundation of the MODI method?

7.7 Is there more than one stepping-stone path for each empty cell? Why or why not?

7.8 How do you determine the maximum quantity that can be transferred or reallocated to an empty cell?

7.9 What is the cost-improvement index (CII)?

7.10 What is the difficulty involved in dealing with a degenerate transportation solution? Discuss it for occasions when we solve the problem by the MODI method.

7.11 Is there only one unique empty cell in which we must assign ϵ when a condition of degeneracy exists?

7.12 Discuss the implications of multiple optimum solutions to a transportation problem.

7.13 What is the primary difference between a transportation problem and a transshipment problem?

7.14 What are two approaches that can be used to handle prohibited transportation routes?

7.15 State the equivalent simplex terms or conditions for the following transportation terms: *CII, stepping-stone path, degeneracy, maximum quantity to be transferred to an empty cell.*

7.16 Consider the following transportation problem:

To / From	A	B	C	D	Supply
1	$5	$12	$7	$10	50
2	4	6	7	6	50
3	2	8	5	3	60
Demand	40	20	30	70	

   a. Determine initial solutions using the northwest corner method, the minimum-cell-cost method, and VAM. Compute the total cost for each method.
   b. Solve this problem by the MODI method.

7.17 Consider the transportation problem with the following parameters:

To / From	1	2	3	4	Supply
A	$5	$5	$7	$6	40
B	4	2	3	5	70
C	7	8	4	4	40
Demand	30	20	30	40	

Derive initial solutions by the northwest corner method, minimum-cell-cost method, and VAM. Indicate total transportation costs.

7.18 Consider the following transportation problem:

To / Demand	A	B	C	Supply
1	$80	$90	$100	42
2	90	110	110	30
3	100	120	90	28
Demand	35	40	25	

a. Determine an initial solution using the northwest corner method.
b. Determine an initial solution using the minimum-cell-cost method.
c. Formulate this problem as a general linear programming model.

7.19 Consider the following transportation problem:

To From	A	B	C	D	Supply
1	$50	$75	$30	$45	120
2	65	80	40	60	170
3	40	70	50	55	110
Demand	100	100	100	100	

a. Determine an initial solution by VAM.
b. Using an initial solution by VAM, find the optimum solution using the MODI method.

7.20 Given the following transportation problem:

To From	A	B	C	D	Supply
1	$120	$100	$90	$150	360
2	100	80	20	100	250
3	90	50	130	80	300
Demand	260	400	250	300	

a. Find an initial solution by the northwest corner method.
b. Solve the problem by the MODI method.

7.21 Consider the following transportation problem:

To From	A	B	C	Supply
1	$40	$10	$20	800
2	15	20	10	500
3	20	25	30	600
Demand	1050	500	650	

a. Formulate a linear programming model for this problem.

b. Set up initial solutions by the northwest corner method, minimum-cell-cost method, and VAM.

c. Solve this problem by the MODI method.

7.22 Consider the following transportation problem:

To From	A	B	C	D	E	Supply
1	$21	$12	$28	$17	$9	50
2	15	13	20	50	12	60
3	18	17	22	10	8	40
4	M	2	10	5	1	70
5	33	29	35	27	23	50
Demand	40	30	50	60	50	

a. Determine an initial solution using VAM.

b. Solve this problem by the MODI method.

7.23 Oranges are transported and then stored in warehouses in Tampa, Miami, and Fresno. These warehouses supply oranges to markets in New York, Philadelphia, Chicago, and Boston. The following tableau gives the shipping costs per ton and the supply and demand requirements:

To From	New York	Philadelphia	Chicago	Boston	Supply
Tampa	$9	$14	$12	$17	200
Miami	11	10	6	10	200
Fresno	12	8	15	7	200
Demand	130	170	100	150	

Because of a distributor's agreement, shipments are prohibited from Miami to Chicago.

a. Set up the transportation tableau for this problem and determine an initial solution using the minimum-cell-cost method.

b. Solve this problem by the MODI method.

c. Are there multiple optimum solutions to this problem? If there is an alternate optimum solution, identify it.

7.24 The Yankee Hill Stone Company has a contract to supply gravel for all road repairs in a certain county. The company maintains three stockpiles, each containing the following amounts of gravel: 100 tons, stockpile 1; 60 tons, stockpile 2; and 80 tons, stockpile 3. Because of recent flooding, numerous roads need repair. The company has received instructions to deliver the following amounts to the designated locations: Fremont, 40 tons; Johnstown, 90; and Marion, 110. The company has had this contract for many years, and it is known that the transportation cost per ton from each stockpile to each location is as follows:

	Fremont	Johnstown	Marion
Stockpile 1	$4	$6	$2
Stockpile 2	8	7	10
Stockpile 3	6	1	4

a. Formulate a linear programming model for this problem.
b. Develop initial solutions by the minimum-cell-cost method and VAM.
c. Starting with the initial solution derived by the northwest corner method, identify the cell with the best cost-improvement index and the quantity that can be transferred to that cell.
d. Find the optimum solution by the MODI method.
e. Is there an alternate optimum solution? If so, identify it.

7.25 Owen's Tree Farm is the primary supplier of Christmas trees for a tricity region in Colorado. Christmas trees are grown at three different farm locations and shipped to the three cities as orders are placed. Shipping costs per tree from each farm to each city have been estimated as follows:

	Boulder	Colorado Springs	Denver
Farm 1	25¢	9¢	18¢
Farm 2	13	15	12
Farm 3	20	17	22

This year's supply of trees is very good, and each farm has the following number of trees available: 1,500, farm 1; 800, farm 2; and 1,000, farm 3. Mr. Owen has received orders from tree distributors in the tricity area, and they have requested the following number of trees: Boulder, 700; Colorado Springs, 1,200; and Denver, 1,600.

    a. Formulate an initial solution by the minimum-cell-cost method.
    b. Find the optimum solution by the MODI method.

7.26 REBAL is an organization of students and staff at various local high schools who are interested in rebalancing the environment. REBAL groups in three high schools have conducted an extensive paper-recycling drive during the holidays. They have collected the following amounts of waste paper: East High, 175 tons; Northwest High, 150 tons; and Central High, 125 tons.

Currently, there are three paper-recycling companies in the area. They are, however, relatively small firms and can process a very limited quantity per month. The three firms report that they can buy only up to the following quantities of waste paper: Colonial Recycling, 200 tons; Systems Environment, 100 tons; and Valley Ecology, 100 tons. The companies have their own trucks for transportation. Their shipping costs per ton of waste paper from the three high school locations are as follows:

	Colonial	Systems	Valley
East High	$20	$19	$17
Northwest High	23	21	20
Central High	18	24	22

a. Formulate a linear programming model for the transportation problem.
b. Set up an initial solution by VAM.
c. Is the initial solution derived in part (b) degenerate? If so, what are some of the cells in which ϵ should be assigned?
d. Find the optimum solution by the MODI method.

7.27 The Grover Brewing Company brews an extremely popular brand of beer. However, to preserve quality, it produces beer in only three plants where spring water is available. The company ships to three wholesalers. The current inventory of beer at the three plants is: Colorado plant, 18,000 cases; Minnesota plant, 12,500 cases; and Washington plant, 9,500 cases. The three wholesalers have just placed orders for the following quantities of beer: 15,000 cases for wholesaler 1; 8,500 cases for wholesaler 2; and 16,500 cases for wholesaler 3. Since they are the only customers, the company has the following accurate shipping costs per 100 cases from each plant to each wholesaler:

	Wholesaler 1	Wholesaler 2	Wholesaler 3
Colorado plant	$8	$6	$4
Minnesota plant	4	7	3
Washington plant	5	8	6

The Colorado plant reports that, as a result of a recent snowstorm in the area, it is impossible to ship beer to wholesaler 3.
a. Set up an initial solution by the minimum-cell-cost method.
b. Find the optimum solution by the MODI method.

7.28 The Charmelle Dress Company has been producing summer dresses for the past several months in anticipation of orders from its customers. Charmelle stores its dresses in three warehouses, which at the present time have the following inventories: 2,600 dresses, warehouse 1; 3,500 dresses, warehouse 2; and 1,850 dresses, warehouse 3. Orders have begun to come in, and three large customers have placed the following orders to be shipped to the following cities: Chicago, 2,400 dresses; New York, 1,750 dresses; and Tampa, 3,350 dresses. The distribution manager has computed the following shipping costs per 100 dresses from each warehouse to each city:

	Chicago	New York	Tampa
Warehouse 1	$15	$10	$13
Warehouse 2	15	14	12
Warehouse 3	11	12	15

a. Starting with an initial solution derived by the minimum-cell-cost method, solve the problem by the MODI method.
b. Are there alternate optimum solutions? If so, identify them.

7.29 Through local radio stations, the management of Economy Discount Stores plans to advertise summer sales to be held in its four locations. The cost of advertising per minute varies because of differences in the sizes of the audiences reached. Management has information on the available advertising time for each of four radio stations, required advertising time by the stores, and costs, as shown in the following tableau:

Radio Stations \ Discount Stores	1	2	3	4	Available Time
WAAA	$50	$70	$65	$50	30
WBBB	45	60	75	60	40
WCCC	60	50	55	70	50
WDDD	65	50	60	75	50
Required Time	30	30	40	50	

Using the MODI method, determine the amount of advertising time to be used on each radio station in order to minimize total cost.

7.30 North Carolina Tobacco Company purchases tobacco and stores certain quantities in warehouses located in the following four cities:

Warehouse Location	Capacity (Tons)
A. Charlotte	90
B. Raleigh	50
C. Lexington	80
D. Danville	60

These warehouses supply tobacco to cigarette companies in three cities that have the following demands:

Cigarette Company	Demand (Tons)
1. Richmond	120
2. Winston-Salem	100
3. Durham	110

The following railroad shipping costs per ton have been determined:

To From	1	2	3
A	$7	$10	$5
B	12	9	4
C	7	3	11
D	9	5	7

Because of railroad construction, shipments are temporarily prohibited from Charlotte to Richmond.

    a. Set up the transportation tableau for this problem, determine the initial solution by VAM, and compute the total cost.

    b. Solve this problem by the MODI method.

    c. Are there multiple optimum solutions? If there are alternate optimum solutions, identify them.

7.31 Transglobal International Movers (TIM) operates between six towns in southern Tennessee. A major horse breeder has selected TIM to deliver colts from its three breeding farms to its training pasturages in three other towns. The horses will not mind indirect trips, as they enjoy the beautiful scenery and companionship en route. Because the breeder's stock is basically uniform, the breeder isn't specifying which horses must be delivered to which pasturage, only general supply and capacity. Altogether, 65 horses must be moved, with 25 coming from Fairview, 18 from Hillside, and 22 from Manesville. Green Acres has prepared stalls for 20 horses, while Happy Hollow has 22 empty stalls, and Idylwild will accept 23 new horses.

Transglobal's shipping tariffs are rather involved and at times confusing, so the owner of the horses has requested an analysis. Your assignment is to minimize the total transport cost, based on the following fees charged per horse.

From	To	Cost ($)
Fairview	Hillside	30
	Manesville	10
	Green Acres	20
	Happy Hollow	120
	Idylwild	150
Hillside	Fairview	40
	Manesville	20
	Green Acres	80
	Happy Hollow	100
	Idylwild	70
Manesville	Fairview	50
	Hillside	10
	Green Acres	70
	Happy Hollow	80
	Idylwild	90
Green Acres	Fairview	10
	Hillside	20
	Manesville	30
	Happy Hollow	40
	Idywild	50
Happy Hollow	Fairview	20
	Hillside	10
	Manesville	30
	Green Acres	80
	Idlywild	20
Idylwild	Fairview	90
	Hillside	60
	Manesville	30
	Green Acres	70
	Happy Hollow	100

7.32 Eastern Gobi Enterprises produces fine glass and china at its three large factories. Special sand required as an ingredient in all EGE's products can be collected at three sites. Because of hazardous road conditions, some routes can handle only small trucks, which increases transport costs dramatically. However, sand from one site can be transferred to the trucks departing from another site and can pass through one of the factories en route to another. However, shipping sand from a factory to a collection site is not allowed.

The three factories, Glass, China, and Crystal, have indicated a monthly demand for 170, 240, and 90 tons of sand, respectively. The three sand-mining sites, pits A, B, and C, can furnish only limited amounts of sand per month, due to collection difficulties. Pit A can provide 130 tons; pit B expects to mine 210 tons; and pit C can supply 160 tons. Transportation costs are as follows:

From Pit	To Factory	$/ton	To Other Pit	$/ton
A	Glass	9	B	3
	China	22	C	8
	Crystal	12		
B	Glass	4	A	12
	China	6	C	7
	Crystal	11		
C	Glass	8	A	9
	China	4	B	4
	Crystal	5		

From Factory	To Factory	$/ton
Glass	China	7
	Crystal	2
China	Glass	3
	Crystal	4
Crystal	Glass	3
	China	6

a. Prepare the transshipment tableau.
b. Determine an initial solution by VAM.
c. Find the optimum solution using the MODI method.

7.33 Given the original transportation tableau in problem 7.20, prepare a transshipment tableau based on the following additional transportation costs:

To From	1	2	3
1	—	30	40
2	50	—	20
3	60	20	—

To From	A	B	C	D	1	2	3
A	—	60	30	80	100	40	20
B	30	—	50	40	20	90	50
C	40	20	—	80	50	30	60
D	110	60	40	—	80	20	90

a. Determine an initial solution by VAM. Is this solution superior to the optimum obtained in the original problem? Are further iterations called for, or is the current solution acceptable?

b. Formulate this problem as a linear programming model.

7.34 Given the following computer printout of input and optimum solution, formulate the initial tableau and the linear programming model.

```
PROGRAM: Transportation

***** INPUT DATA ENTERED *****

Minimization problem :

          |    1        2        3   |   Supply
    ------------------------------------------------
    1     |   80.00   120.00    90.00|    50.00
    2     |  100.00    70.00    50.00|    80.00
    3     |   60.00   100.00    70.00|    70.00
    ------------------------------------------------
    Demand|   60.00    90.00    50.00|   200.00

*****    PROGRAM OUTPUT    *****

          |    1        2        3   |   Supply
    ------------------------------------------------
    1     |   50.00     0.00     0.00|    50.00
    2     |    0.00    80.00     0.00|    80.00
    3     |   10.00    10.00    50.00|    70.00
    ------------------------------------------------
    Demand|   60.00    90.00    50.00|   200.00

Optimal solution :     14700.00
```

7.35 Given the following computer printout of input and optimum solution, formulate the initial tableau and the linear programming model.

```
PROGRAM: Transportation

***** INPUT DATA ENTERED *****

Minimization problem :

          !    1       2       3  !   Supply
       -------------------------------------------
        1  !  16.00   10.00    7.00!   110.00
        2  !  12.00   11.00    9.00!    60.00
        3  !  13.00    9.00    8.00!    30.00
        4  !   0.00    0.00    0.00!    30.00
       -------------------------------------------
     Demand!  50.00   80.00  100.00!   230.00


*****   PROGRAM OUTPUT   *****

          !    1       2       3  !   Supply
       -------------------------------------------
        1  !   0.00   10.00  100.00!   110.00
        2  !  20.00   40.00    0.00!    60.00
        3  !   0.00   30.00    0.00!    30.00
        4  !  30.00    0.00    0.00!    30.00
       -------------------------------------------
     Demand!  50.00   80.00  100.00!   230.00

Optimal solution  :      1750.00
```

7.36 Given the following computer printout of input and optimum solution, formulate the initial tableau and the linear programming model.

```
PROGRAM: Transportation

***** INPUT DATA ENTERED *****

Maximization problem :

         |    1       2       3  |   Supply
      --------------------------------------------
      1  |   8.00    3.00    9.00|    17.00
      2  |   6.00    7.00   10.00|    23.00
      3  |   4.00   11.00    8.00|    19.00
      4  |   0.00    0.00    0.00|    31.00
      --------------------------------------------
   Demand|  30.00   30.00   30.00|    90.00


*****   PROGRAM OUTPUT   *****

         |    1       2       3  |   Supply
      --------------------------------------------
      1  |  10.00    0.00    7.00|    17.00
      2  |   0.00    0.00   23.00|    23.00
      3  |   0.00   19.00    0.00|    19.00
      4  |  20.00   11.00    0.00|    31.00
      --------------------------------------------
   Demand|  30.00   30.00   30.00|    90.00

   Optimal solution  :      582.00
```

7.37 Given the following computer printout of input and optimum solution, formulate the initial tableau and the linear programming model.

```
PROGRAM: Transportation

##### INPUT DATA ENTERED #####

Minimization problem :

        |    1       2       3       4       5       6  |   Supply
   -------------------------------------------------------------------
   1    |   0.00   13.00    7.00   12.00   11.00    6.00|   210.00
   2    |   3.00    0.00    5.00    8.00    5.00   15.00|   190.00
   3    |   6.00    9.00    0.00    9.00   11.00   13.00|   200.00
   4    |   2.00    1.00    7.00    0.00    6.00    3.00|   150.00
   5    |   5.00    6.00    4.00    1.00    0.00    5.00|   150.00
   6    |  16.00    8.00   12.00    5.00    2.00    0.00|   150.00
   -------------------------------------------------------------------
 Demand|  150.00  150.00  150.00  220.00  185.00  195.00|  1050.00


#####    PROGRAM OUTPUT   #####

        |    1       2       3       4       5       6  |   Supply
   -------------------------------------------------------------------
   1    | 150.00    0.00    0.00    0.00    0.00   60.00|   210.00
   2    |   0.00  150.00    0.00    0.00   40.00    0.00|   190.00
   3    |   0.00    0.00  150.00   50.00    0.00    0.00|   200.00
   4    |   0.00    0.00    0.00  150.00    0.00    0.00|   150.00
   5    |   0.00    0.00    0.00   20.00  130.00    0.00|   150.00
   6    |   0.00    0.00    0.00    0.00   15.00  135.00|   150.00
   -------------------------------------------------------------------
 Demand|  150.00  150.00  150.00  220.00  185.00  195.00|  1050.00

Optimal solution  :      1060.00
```

7.38 Given the following computer printout of input and optimum solution, formulate the initial tableau and the linear programming model.

```
PROGRAM: Transportation

***** INPUT DATA ENTERED *****

Maximization problem :

        !    1       2       3       4   !   Supply
     --------------------------------------------------
     1  !  16.00   23.00   14.00   19.00!    96.00
     2  !  17.00   16.00   13.00   14.00!   123.00
     3  !  18.00   20.00   17.00   15.00!    79.00
     4  !  25.00   18.00   15.00   17.00!    85.00
     5  !   0.00    0.00    0.00    0.00!   167.00
     --------------------------------------------------
     Demand! 125.00  200.00   75.00  150.00!   550.00

*****   PROGRAM OUTPUT   *****

        !    1       2       3       4   !   Supply
     --------------------------------------------------
     1  !   0.00   96.00    0.00    0.00!    96.00
     2  !  40.00   25.00    0.00   58.00!   123.00
     3  !   0.00   79.00    0.00    0.00!    79.00
     4  !  85.00    0.00    0.00    0.00!    85.00
     5  !   0.00    0.00   75.00   92.00!   167.00
     --------------------------------------------------
     Demand! 125.00  200.00   75.00  150.00!   550.00

Optimal solution  :      7805.00
```

7.39 Given the following computer printout of input and optimum solution, formulate the initial tableau and the linear programming model.

```
PROGRAM: Transportation

***** INPUT DATA ENTERED *****

Maximization problem :

          :    1       2       3       4       5       6  :   Supply
    -----------------------------------------------------------------------
     1    :   12.00   14.00    8.00   16.00   13.00    9.00:   500.00
     2    :   10.00   12.00    6.00   18.00   11.00   11.00:   500.00
     3    :    0.00    0.00    0.00    0.00    0.00    0.00:   850.00
    -----------------------------------------------------------------------
  Demand:    300.00  250.00  400.00  350.00  300.00  250.00:  1850.00

*****    PROGRAM OUTPUT    *****

          :    1       2       3       4       5       6  :   Supply
    -----------------------------------------------------------------------
     1    :    0.00   250.00    0.00    0.00   250.00    0.00:   500.00
     2    :    0.00     0.00    0.00   350.00    0.00   150.00:   500.00
     3    :  300.00     0.00   400.00    0.00    50.00   100.00:   850.00
    -----------------------------------------------------------------------
  Demand:    300.00  250.00  400.00  350.00  300.00  250.00:  1850.00

Optimal solution  :     14700.00
```

8 THE ASSIGNMENT PROBLEM

In the assignment problem, we attempt to find the best way to match each of the given number of objects (people, tasks, etc.) to each of the given number of stations (machines, work areas, etc.). There are many real-world situations in which, for example, we try to assign employees to tasks, crews to projects, and ambulances to first-aid stations. The basic goal of the assignment problem is either to minimize the total cost of completing all the required tasks or to maximize the total payoff (or benefit) from the assignments.

Because of its simple structure, the assignment problem can be solved more efficiently by its unique solution method than by linear programming. In this chapter, we will study the concept, solution approaches, and special features of the assignment problem.

Learning Objectives *From the study of this chapter, we will learn the following:*

1. The basic nature of the assignment problem
2. How to formulate a linear programming model for the assignment problem
3. How to apply the transportation approach to the assignment problem
4. How to solve an assignment problem by the Hungarian method
5. How to solve an assignment problem by the branch-and-bound approach
6. How to solve an assignment problem by using computers
7. The meaning of the following terms:

Hungarian method
Opportunity cost table
Revised opportunity cost table

Impossible assignment
Multiple optimum assignments

THE NATURE OF THE ASSIGNMENT PROBLEM

The assignment problem is simply a variation of the transportation problem in which the numbers of sources and destinations are exactly equal and in which the supply capacity of each source and the demand requirement of each destination equal exactly 1. Pioneers in the development of solution methods for the assignment problem are P. S. Dwyer, M. M. Flood, and H. W. Kuhn (see References). Several variations have been developed for the solution method, the best known of which is the **Hungarian**

method, so named because the underlying theorem was first proved by the Hungarian mathematician, D. König. More recently, the *branch-and-bound* and *zero–one integer-programming* methods have been applied to solve assignment-related problems.

In real-world situations, many managerial problems involve the assignment of people, machines, or objectives. Several examples of assignment problems are:

Employees to machines

Snowplows to areas in a city

Service crews to different districts

Police teams to various precincts

Instructors to undergraduate
  and graduate courses

Scientists to various research projects

Ambulances to first-aid stations

Cashiers to checkout counters

Salespeople to sales districts

Combat divisions to war zones

In the general assignment problem, there are only a finite number of objects (people, crews, etc.) to be assigned to a finite number of stations (machines, projects, etc.). Also, the objects must be assigned to stations on a one-to-one basis. The typical objective criterion of the assignment problem is either to minimize the total cost of the assignment or to maximize the total payoff from the assignment.

Casette 8.1   MARTHA WEINSTEIN COSMETICS INC.

Martha Weinstein Cosmetics Inc. was founded in 1958 by the late Martha Weinstein, a pioneer in cosmetology and beauty care for women. The company has since developed a national chain of personal sales forces, known as "Martha's Crusade." The company has regional sales offices where salespeople are recruited, trained, and assigned to specific territories. The company management believes that the most important factor behind the success of a salesperson, and consequently the success of the company, is effective assignment of each trained salesperson to a territory based on performance evaluation during on-the-job training.

Recently, the Midland district sales office recruited and trained four new salespeople. The new salespeople were assigned to the four sales territories on a monthly rotation system. Each salesperson spent 1 month in each sales territory for the 4-month on-the-job training program. Because of differences in the salespeople's familiarity with each territory as well as differences in their ability to deal with various types of customers, the time required to call on potential clients in each territory varies for each salesperson.

For each salesperson in each of the sales territories during the on-the-job training, the average time required (in minutes) to contact a potential new client is as follows:

Salesperson	Sales Territory			
	A	B	C	D
1	8 min	10 min	12 min	16 min
2	11	11	15	8
3	9	6	5	14
4	15	14	9	7

The task faced by the district sales manager is the assignment of the four salespeople to each of the four sales territories. As an incentive to develop the area, only one person is to be assigned to a specific territory. The basic decision problem, therefore, is to determine how each salesperson should be assigned in order to minimize the total time required to contact potential clients.

THE COMPLETE ENUMERATION METHOD

The assignment problem of Martha Weinstein Cosmetics can be presented in tableau form, as shown in Table 8.1. We note that there are identical numbers of rows and columns. Also, the quantity of supply in each row and the demand requirement in each column are exactly 1. These are unique characteristics of the assignment problem.

In the assignment problem described in Table 8.1, since there are 4 salespeople and 4 territories, the total number of possible assignments would be 4! = 4 × 3 × 2 × 1 = 24. Thus, one way we can identify the optimum assignment is to perform a *complete enumeration* of all possible solutions. Table 8.2 presents the complete enumeration of alternative assignments. Comparing the 24 possible assignments, alternatives 1 and 4 yield the minimum total customer-contact time of 31 minutes. In this problem, we have multiple optimum solutions.

Table 8.1   Tableau Form of the Martha Weinstein Assignment Problem

Territory / Salesperson	A	B	C	D	Supply
1	8	10	12	16	1
2	11	11	15	8	1
3	9	6	5	14	1
4	15	14	9	7	1
Demand	1	1	1	1	4

Table 8.2   Complete Enumeration of Assignment Alternatives

Alternative	Assignment	Total Time
1	1A, 2B, 3C, 4D	8 + 11 + 5 + 7 = 31 ← minimum
2	1A, 2B, 4C, 3D	8 + 11 + 9 + 14 = 42
3	1A, 3B, 2C, 4D	8 + 6 + 15 + 7 = 36
4	1A, 3B, 4C, 2D	8 + 6 + 9 + 8 = 31 ← minimum
5	1A, 4B, 2C, 3D	8 + 14 + 15 + 14 = 51
6	1A, 4B, 3C, 2D	8 + 14 + 5 + 8 = 35
7	2A, 1B, 3C, 4D	11 + 10 + 5 + 7 = 33
8	2A, 1B, 4C, 3D	11 + 10 + 9 + 14 = 44
9	2A, 3B, 1C, 4D	11 + 6 + 12 + 7 = 36
10	2A, 3B, 4C, 1D	11 + 6 + 9 + 16 = 42
11	2A, 4B, 1C, 3D	11 + 14 + 12 + 14 = 51
12	2A, 4B, 3C, 1D	11 + 14 + 5 + 16 = 46
13	3A, 1B, 2C, 4D	9 + 10 + 15 + 7 = 41
14	3A, 1B, 4C, 2D	9 + 10 + 9 + 8 = 36
15	3A, 2B, 1C, 4D	9 + 11 + 12 + 7 = 39
16	3A, 2B, 4C, 1D	9 + 11 + 9 + 16 = 45
17	3A, 4B, 1C, 2D	9 + 14 + 12 + 8 = 43
18	3A, 4B, 2C, 1D	9 + 14 + 15 + 16 = 54
19	4A, 1B, 2C, 3D	15 + 10 + 15 + 14 = 54
20	4A, 1B, 3C, 2D	15 + 10 + 5 + 8 = 38
21	4A, 2B, 1C, 3D	15 + 11 + 12 + 14 = 52
22	4A, 2B, 3C, 1D	15 + 11 + 5 + 16 = 47
23	4A, 3B, 1C, 2D	15 + 6 + 12 + 8 = 41
24	4A, 3B, 2C, 1D	15 + 6 + 15 + 16 = 52

If we have a large number of objects and stations, it is impractical to use the complete enumeration method. For example, if we have 6 salespeople and 6 sales territories, the number of alternatives that must be evaluated will be $6! = 6 \times 5 \times 4 \times 3 \times 2 \times 1 = 720$. Obviously, this is not a useful technique for real-world assignment problems.

A LINEAR PROGRAMMING MODEL FOR THE ASSIGNMENT PROBLEM

We can formulate an assignment problem as a linear (integer) programming problem. If we denote x_{ij} as the decision variable representing the assignment of the ith salesperson to the jth sales territory, it should be clear that x_{ij} must be either 1 or 0. If the ith salesperson is assigned to the jth territory, x_{ij} becomes 1. If the ith salesperson is not assigned to the jth territory, x_{ij} will be 0. If we denote c_{ij} as the time required for the ith salesperson to contact a potential new client in the jth territory, the assignment problem can be formulated as a linear programming problem as follows:

$$\text{Minimize } Z = 8x_{11} + 10x_{12} + 12x_{13} + 16x_{14} + 11x_{21} + 11x_{22}$$
$$+ \; 15x_{23} + 8x_{24} + 9x_{31} + 6x_{32} + 5x_{33} + 14x_{34}$$
$$+ \; 15x_{41} + 14x_{42} + 9x_{43} + 7x_{44}$$

$$\text{subject to} \quad \left.\begin{array}{l} x_{11} + x_{12} + x_{13} + x_{14} = 1 \\ x_{21} + x_{22} + x_{23} + x_{24} = 1 \\ x_{31} + x_{32} + x_{33} + x_{34} = 1 \\ x_{41} + x_{42} + x_{43} + x_{44} = 1 \end{array}\right\} \text{Supply requirement}$$

$$\left.\begin{array}{l} x_{11} + x_{21} + x_{31} + x_{41} = 1 \\ x_{12} + x_{22} + x_{32} + x_{42} = i \\ x_{13} + x_{23} + x_{33} + x_{43} = 1 \\ x_{14} + x_{24} + x_{34} + x_{44} = 1 \end{array}\right\} \text{Demand requirement}$$

$$x_{ij} = 0 \text{ or } 1$$

From this assignment model, we can identify several interesting characteristics of the assignment problem. First, the assignment problem tableau is a square matrix because the problem has n sources and n destinations. Second, since a person (source) can be assigned to only one territory (destination), we have the following relationship:

$$\sum_{i=1}^{n} x_{ij} = \sum_{j=1}^{n} x_{ij} = 1$$

Consequently, the number of positive solution variables for an $n \times n$ problem must be exactly n. In the strict sense of the transportation model, then, the assignment problem is always a degenerate case because we need $2n - 1$ number of occupied cells in the $n \times n$ problem to avoid degeneracy. Third, the total number of possible assignment combinations for an $n \times n$ assignment problem is $n!$.

THE HUNGARIAN METHOD OF ASSIGNMENT

The Hungarian method is based on the concept of opportunity cost, or penalty cost, which we discussed in Vogel's approximation method of transportation in Chapter 7. The opportunity cost is the cost associated with failing to take the best course of action. Thus, the Hungarian method attempts to minimize the opportunity cost of not using (assigning to) the cheapest cells. The Hungarian method consists of the following steps:

Step 1: Develop the Opportunity Cost Table   First derive the opportunity cost table for the rows. This table is constructed by first subtracting the minimum value m in each row from all other values in the same row. Then, follow the same procedure for the columns to develop the complete opportunity cost table. However, opportunity costs for columns should by developed from the already established opportunity cost table for the rows.

Step 2: Analyze the Feasibility of an Optimum Assignment   To test the feasibility of an optimum assignment, draw a minimum number of horizontal and/or vertical lines to cross out all the 0 values in the opportunity cost table. If the number of straight lines required is equal to the number of rows or columns, an optimum assignment can be made. Otherwise, proceed to Step 3.

Step 3: Develop a Revised Opportunity Cost Table   In the opportunity cost table derived in Step 2, identify the minimum value that is not crossed out and subtract this value from all the values not crossed out. This same minimum value is added to all the values at the intersections of two straight lines.

Step 4: Repeat Steps 2 and 3 until an Optimum Solution Is Found

The Opportunity Cost Table

The first step of the Hungarian method of assignment is to develop the opportunity cost table. The initial opportunity table is obtained through row-wise reductions. In the Martha Weinstein problem, if a salesperson is assigned to a sales territory with the minimum customer contact time, obviously we chose the best alternative. For example, in Table 8.3, if salesperson 1 is assigned to territory A, an average of 8 minutes would be required to contact a potential new client. If we assign the same salesperson to territory B, the required time would be 10 minutes. The best possible assignment for salesperson 1, disregarding other employees for the time being, is clearly territory A.

The failure to assign salesperson 1 to territory A and assigning him or her to territory B will cost the firm 2 minutes (10 − 8 = 2) and thus result in a less-than-optimum sales performance. Since we are attempting to minimize the total time required to contact potential clients, our strategy should be to minimize the opportunity cost. First, let us find the initial opportunity cost table by analyzing each row. The procedure we follow in determining the row opportunity costs is to subtract the minimum value in

Table 8.3   The Martha Weinstein Problem

Sales- person \ Territory	A	B	C	D
1	8	10	12	16
2	11	11	15	8
3	9	6	5	14
4	15	14	9	7

Table 8.4   The Initial Row-wise Opportunity Cost Table

Sales-person \ Territory	A	B	C	D
1	0	2	4	8
2	3	3	7	0
3	4	1	0	9
4	8	7	2	0

each row from each of the other values in that row. For example, we can compute the opportunity cost for the first row as follows:

Cell	Cell Value	−	Minimum Row Value	=	Opportunity Cost
(1,A)	8	−	8	=	0
(1,B)	10	−	8	=	2
(1,C)	12	−	8	=	4
(1,D)	16	−	8	=	8

Table 8.4 presents the opportunity cost for each of the rows.

From our discussion thus far, it should be clear that the opportunity cost also exists for columns. Any of the four salespersons can be assigned to territory A. Salesperson 1 has the minimum customer contact time of 8 minutes in territory A. If salesperson 2 is assigned to territory A, we must absorb the opportunity cost of 3 minutes ($11 - 8 = 3$) because we failed to assign salesperson 1 to that territory. The column opportunity cost must be computed from the row opportunity cost table we derived in Table 8.4. For example, the final opportunity costs for column A can be calculated as follows:

Cell	Cell Value	−	Minimum Column Value	=	Opportunity Cost
(1,A)	0	−	0	=	0
(2,A)	3	−	0	=	3
(3,A)	4	−	0	=	4
(4,A)	8	−	0	=	8

The complete opportunity cost table after the column reduction is shown in Table 8.5.

Table 8.5 The Complete Opportunity Cost Table

Salesperson \ Territory	A	B	C	D
1	0	1	4	8
2	3	2	7	0
3	4	0	0	9
4	8	6	2	0

Analysis of Optimum Assignment Feasibility

Once we develop a complete opportunity cost table, the next step is to determine whether an optimum assignment can be made. An optimum assignment is possible if the final opportunity cost table has four *independent 0s* that allow four unique assignments. The "independent" 0 indicates that assigning a salesperson to a cell with opportunity cost of 0 will not exclude assignments to other cells having costs of 0.

When we make an assignment to a cell with 0 opportunity cost, we are assured of the best possible assignment for a given row and a given column. That is why we are

Table 8.6 The First Test of Optimum Assignment Feasibility

Salesperson \ Territory	A	B	C	D
1	~~0~~	~~1~~	~~4~~	~~8~~
2	3	(2)	7	~~0~~
3	~~4~~	~~0~~	~~0~~	~~9~~
4	8	6	(2)	~~0~~

Table 8.7 The Second Test of Optimum Assignment Feasibility

Sales-person \ Territory	A	B	C	D
1	0	(1)	4	8
2	3	2	7	0
3	4	0	0	9
4	8	6	2	0

looking for as many independent 0s as the number of rows or columns. A convenient way to test optimality is to draw a *minimum* number of straight lines, horizontally or vertically but never diagonally, to cross out all the 0 values in the opportunity cost table.

Note that the word *minimum* is significant in this procedure. By minimizing the number of straight lines required to cover all the 0 values, we will be identifying the number of independent 0s in the opportunity cost table. Therefore, *the minimum number of straight lines must equal the number of rows or columns for an optimum assignment.* If the number of straight lines is less than the number of rows or columns, we do not have a sufficient number of independent 0s to make an optimum assignment.

Tables 8.6 and 8.7 present two ways to cover all the 0s in the table. It is evident that we need only three lines to cross out all the 0s. Thus, an optimum assignment is not possible at this point.

The Revised Opportunity Cost Table

Since we need only three lines to cover all the 0s in the opportunity cost table, we have only three independent 0 cells in which assignments can be made. In other words, one salesperson must be assigned to a cell in which we have a positive opportunity cost. To identify the cheapest cell to which the fourth salesperson can be assigned, we must revise the opportunity cost table. The procedure we use can be summarized as follows:

1. In the table identify the minimum opportunity cost that is not crossed out by a straight line.

2. Subtract this value from all the other opportunity costs that are not crossed out by straight lines.

3. Add the same minimum value to those opportunity costs that are at the intersections of two straight lines.

4. Fill the remaining cells with the unchanged opportunity costs from the previous table.

This procedure is repeated, if necessary, until we can make an optimum assignment. This procedure is used to generate additional independent 0s while retaining the previously identified independent 0 values. Each new independent 0 is determined on the basis of the opportunity costs among the cells not crossed out. In other words, we are creating an opportunity cost table within an opportunity cost table. The cell with the minimum opportunity cost that is not crossed out becomes the cell with the 0 opportunity cost.

Let us use the first test table shown in Table 8.6 to develop the revised opportunity cost table. Among the six opportunity costs not crossed out in the table, the minimum cost is 2 in cells (2,B) and (4,C). We subtract this value 2 from all the costs not crossed out, and we also add this value to the two intersection values in cells (1,D) and (3,D). Note that the costs that are crossed out by only one line are unchanged in the revised opportunity cost table. The revised opportunity cost table is presented in Table 8.8.

Table 8.9 presents two ways to cross out all the 0s in the revised opportunity cost table. We need four straight lines to cover all the 0s. Consequently, it is possible to make an optimum assignment for the problem. In the revised opportunity cost table shown in Table 8.8, there are two 0s in each row and each column except the first row

Table 8.8   The Revised Opportunity Cost Table

Sales-person \ Territory	A	B	C	D
1	0	1	4	10
2	1	0	5	0
3	4	0	0	11
4	6	4	0	0

Table 8.9   Two Tests of Optimum Assignment Feasibility

(a)

Sales-person \ Territory	A	B	C	D
1	0	1	4	10
2	1	0	5	0
3	4	0	0	11
4	6	4	0	0

(b)

Sales-person \ Territory	A	B	C	D
1	0	1	4	10
2	1	0	5	0
3	4	0	0	11
4	6	4	0	0

and first column. The first assignment must be made in a row or column where there is *only one* 0 because it represents a unique assignment. Since there is only one 0 in the first row, we will assign salesperson 1 to territory A.

After this assignment, three rows (2, 3, and 4) and three columns (B, C, and D) remain, as shown in Table 8.10. Since each remaining row and column has two 0s, we cannot make a unique assignment. However, there are two optional assignments we can make. First, we can assign salesperson 2 to territory B. Then, the remaining assignments in the one-to-one pairing will be salesperson 3 to territory C and salesperson 4 to territory D. Second, we can assign salesperson 2 to territory D. Then, we have no other choice but to assign salesperson 3 to territory B and salesperson 4 to territory C. Thus, we have two optimum solutions. These solutions correspond to those we identified ear-

Table 8.10   The Opportunity Cost Table after the Assignment of 1A

Sales-person \ Territory	A	B	C	D
1	0	1	4	10
2	1	0	5	0
3	4	0	0	11
4	6	4	0	0

lier by the complete enumeration method. The two possible optimum assignments and their total time are as follows:

Assignment 1		
Salesperson	**Territory**	**Time**
1	A	8 min
2	B	11
3	C	5
4	D	7
	Total time =	31 min

Assignment 2		
Salesperson	**Territory**	**Time**
1	A	8 min
2	D	8
3	B	6
4	C	9
	Total time =	31 min

A MAXIMIZATION ASSIGNMENT PROBLEM

The Hungarian method of assignment can also be applied to a problem in which the basic objective is to maximize a criterion. In a maximization problem, the objective criterion is usually profit, system effectiveness, sales, market share, utility, and the like. When a person is assigned to different tasks, the person's work effectiveness may vary according to experience, expertise, and interest. The work effectiveness of an employee in different tasks (or locations, work groups, projects, etc.) can be expressed by an assignment table. This table can be transformed into an opportunity cost table.

The opportunity cost is the difference between the actual effectiveness realized and the best possible effectiveness measure if the best assignment were to be made. Thus, the objective of the problem is to determine an optimum assignment schedule that will minimize the total opportunity cost.

Casette 8.2   **THE NEIGHBORHOOD TEAM-POLICING ASSIGNMENT**

Harristown is a medium-size city with a population of approximately 120,000. The Harristown Police Department (HPD) recently decided to institute a neighborhood-based team-policing system. The team-policing system is based on the general concept of decentralized management. Under this system, the city is divided into four team areas: northeast, southeast, northwest, and southwest. Each team will be assigned to a given area, and it is totally responsible for all police work on a 24-hours-a-day, 365-days-a-year basis.

The primary incentive behind the neighborhood-based team-policing system is that each team can exercise its own initiative in solving police problems in a given neighborhood. Furthermore, citizen participation in assisting the police department through a grass-roots neighborhood-policing network is expected to be a major benefit of this system. Currently, four field teams have been organized and deployed throughout the city. The HPD headquarters team provides general support to the teams, such as record-keeping, central dispatcher system, public service assistance, computer-based information systems, planning and analysis, as well as the detective team and SWAT team.

Each team has the same organizational setup as shown in Figure 8.1 (page 306). Although all the team personnel assignments have been completed, the police chief has not been able to assign four captains to lead each team. The problem stems from the fact that each of the four captains would like to be the leader of the southwest area, where there tends to be more "action" because of its location. This area has the municipal airport, state penitentiary, and state mental correction institute, in addition to a number of newly opened restaurants and bars.

To be equitable and systematic in assigning the four captains to the four areas, the chief decided to rotate their jobs so that each captain will work for a period of 1 month in each of the four areas. After the 4-month period of job rotation, their work performance in each area will be evaluated on the basis of a complicated scoring system. The scoring system is determined by each team's effectiveness under a given team leader in the following areas: (1) meeting service calls, (2) investigating major crimes, (3) performing preventive patrol duties in the team area, (4) doing community relations work, and (5) cooperating with the headquarters' support team. At the conclusion of the rotation period, the evaluation committee submitted the summary sheet presented in Table 8.11. The police chief now wants to make an optimum assignment of the four captains in order to maximize their total effectiveness score.

Figure 8.1   Organizational Setup of the Team

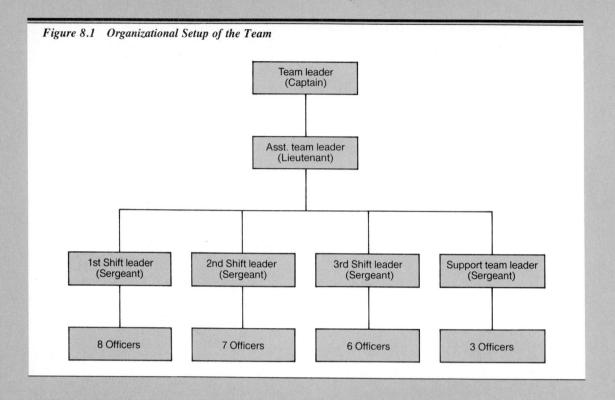

Table 8.11   Effectiveness Score Summary for the Four Captains in the Four Team Areas

Captains \ Team Areas	1	2	3	4
1	20	28	24	26
2	18	15	16	20
3	30	28	25	23
4	17	22	21	22

From a brief examination of Table 8.11, it is clear that captain 1 performed best in team area 2. Thus, the opportunity cost of assigning captain 1 to team area 1 would be 8 points (28 − 20 = 8). Now we can derive a row opportunity cost table by calculating the differences between the *highest* row score and each of the row scores, as shown in Table 8.12.

Table 8.12   *The Initial Row-wise Opportunity Cost Table*

Captains \ Team Areas	1	2	3	4
1	8	0	4	2
2	2	5	4	0
3	0	2	5	7
4	5	0	1	0

The complete opportunity cost table can be obtained from Table 8.12 by subtracting the *smallest* value in each column from each element in that same column. For example, in the third column, the smallest value is 1 in cell (4,3). Thus, subtracting this value of 1 from each element in column 3, we obtain column opportunity costs of 3, 3, 4, and 0. The complete opportunity cost table is presented in Table 8.13.

We now use straight lines to cover all the zero elements in Table 8.12. It is obvious that we need four lines, as shown in Table 8.13. Thus, an optimum assignment can be made. Since there is only one 0 in row 1, we can assign captain 1 to team area 2. Then, captain 2 is assigned to team area 4. Now we have no further choice but to assign

Table 8.13   *The Complete Opportunity Cost Table*

Captains \ Team Areas	1	2	3	4
1	8	0	3	2
2	2	5	3	0
3	0	2	4	7
4	5	0	0	0

captain 3 to team area 1 and captain 4 to team area 3. The optimum assignment schedule and the total effectiveness score are as follows:

Captain	Team Area	Effectiveness Score
1	2	28
2	4	20
3	1	30
4	3	21
	Total score =	99

SOME UNIQUE ASSIGNMENT PROBLEMS

As in the transportation problem, we may face a number of unique situations in real-world assignments. We will discuss several such situations here.

Unequal Rows and Columns

One very important requirement of the Hungarian method of assignment is that the number of rows (supply sources) must be exactly equal to the number of columns (demand destinations). In many practical problems, however, such an assignment problem is a very rare case indeed. For example, the number of employees to be assigned may be greater than the number of tasks to which they can be assigned. Or, there may be more jobs that need to be performed than the number of employees to do the work. In such cases we introduce either a dummy employee (row) or a dummy job (column) and balance the row-column requirements. The unit assignment costs for the dummy row or column will all be zero. This procedure is exactly the same as the one we used for the unbalanced transportation problem in Chapter 7.

Casette 8.3   **MISSISSIPPI BARGE TRANSPORTATION INC.**

Mississippi Barge Transportation Inc. (MBT) is a company located in St. Louis that specializes in loading and unloading cargo being transported by barges on the Mississippi River. The company has four docks on the riverfront with various loading and unloading equipment, crews with different areas of expertise, and different storage capacities. Thus, the efficiency of unloading certain cargo from barges varies among the docks.

MBT has just been notified that three barges are expected to arrive for unloading the next morning. Barge 1 contains coal destined for a public utility company. Barge 2 has a grain cargo to be shipped to a local gasohol plant. Barge 3 contains heavy equipment from Texas. The company wants to determine an optimum assignment of the three barges to three of the four available docks in order to minimize the total time required to unload the cargos from all the barges. In analyzing the past performance records of the four docks in unloading these types of cargos, the dock manager estimated the number of hours required to unload each type of cargo by each of the four docks. His calculations are presented in Table 8.14.

To apply the Hungarian method, a dummy row (barge) is added with 0 unloading hours. This problem is summarized in Table 8.15. Now we are ready to determine the initial row-wise opportunity cost table. The opportunity cost can be calculated by subtracting the minimum number of hours in a given row from each row element. The row-wise opportunity cost table is presented in Table 8.16.

Since the dummy row has all 0 elements, the column opportunity cost will be exactly the same as the one shown in Table 8.16. Therefore, the complete opportunity

Table 8.14   The Cargo Unloading Problem

Dock / Barge	A	B	C	D	Supply
1	5	8	3	6	1
2	4	5	7	4	1
3	6	2	4	5	1
Demand	1	1	1	1	4 / 3

Table 8.15   The Cargo Unloading Problem with a Dummy Row

Dock / Barge	A	B	C	D
1	5	8	3	6
2	4	5	7	4
3	6	2	4	5
4 Dummy	0	0	0	0

Table 8.16   The Row-wise Opportunity Cost Table

Barge \ Dock	A	B	C	D
1	2	5	0	3
2	0	1	3	0
3	4	0	2	3
4 Dummy	0	0	0	0

Table 8.17   The Complete Opportunity Cost Table

Barge \ Dock	A	B	C	D
1	2	5	0	3
2	0	1	3	0
3	4	0	2	3
4 Dummy	0	0	0	0

cost table has been derived. Four straight lines are used to cross out all the 0 elements in Table 8.17; thus, an optimum assignment can be made. The two optimum assignments are shown below.

Barge	Dock	Unloading Time
1	C	3 hr
2	A or D	4
3	B	2
	Total time =	9 hr

Impossible (or Prohibited) Assignments

There are many instances in which certain employees cannot be assigned to certain jobs, certain ships cannot be unloaded at certain docks, and the like. The reasons for such impossible assignments may be the physical requirements of the task, special equipment or facility required at a certain work station, or the personal preference of an individual. As in the transportation problem with prohibited routes, we can assign large costs *(M)* to the impossible assignments and solve the problem by the usual assignment method. Or we can block out those impossible assignments in the table and proceed in the usual manner.

Multiple Optimum Solutions

As we have observed previously, for a given problem there may be two or more ways to cross out all the 0 elements in the final opportunity cost table. This implies that there are more than the required number of independent 0 elements. In such a case, there will be multiple optimum solutions with the same total cost (profit) of assignment. Decision makers can exercise their judgment or preference and select one particular optimum solution for the problem.

Multiple Objectives

It is possible that an assignment problem may involve a set of multiple conflicting objectives. For example, the team leader assignment problem for the Harristown Police Department may involve such multiple objectives as matching each captain's police work experience with each of the team area's major policing problems, or accommodating each of the captain's or team members' preference for a particular assignment. There are many real-world location-allocation problems that are variations of the assignment problem with multiple objectives. Some examples of such problems may be a fire station location, a new school-site decision, a warehouse location decision, and a labor allocation.

The zero–one goal-programming approach has been applied to many assignment-related problems involving multiple objectives. If an employee is assigned to a certain task, the solution value for the variable is 1; otherwise, it would be 0. Those of you who are interested in this topic should consult Lee and Franz (see References).

THE BRANCH-AND-BOUND APPROACH

The assignment problem can also be solved by the branch-and-bound approach of integer programming discussed in Chapter 6. The assignment problem has a finite number of solution possibilities. Thus, we can utilize the branch-and-bound procedure to partition the set of all feasible assignments into smaller, mutually exclusive subsets for analysis. The basic solution procedure of the branch-and-bound method for a minimization assignment problem can be summarized as follows:

Step 1 The set of all feasible solutions is branched into several subsets, starting with the first station (column). Thus, each subset is determined by assigning each object (row) to the first station.

Step 2   For each subset, the *lower bound* is determined. The lower bound is computed by summing the cost of the initial assignment in Step 1 and the minimum costs in each of the remaining unassigned columns. If there are *feasible* assignments, the minimum value among their lower bounds is determined as the *upper bound*.

Step 3   Those subsets having lower bounds that exceed the current upper bound must be excluded from further analysis. A subset with the best lower bound among the remaining subsets is selected and branched further.

Step 4   A feasible solution where the objective function value is not greater than the lower bound for any subset is to be found. This is the optimum solution. If such a solution does not exist, return to Step 3.

To illustrate the branch-and-bound approach to the assignment problem, let us consider the Martha Weinstein Cosmetics problem discussed earlier. The problem is presented in Table 8.18. The objective of the problem is to assign each of the four salespersons to each of the four sales territories so that the total time required to contact potential new clients is minimized. The problem can be represented with a 4×4 matrix. Therefore, the total number of feasible solutions would be $4! = 24$.

In applying the branch-and-bound procedure, we should determine a tight lower bound for all 24 feasible solutions. The best way to determine such a tight lower bound is by summing the minimum costs in each of the columns, regardless of the feasibility of each assignment. In Table 8.18, the minimum column costs are circled. Thus, the lower bound is $8 + 6 + 5 + 7 = 26$.

We can assign any one of the four salespeople to territory A. Hence, all feasible solutions are initially branched into four subsets. If we assign salesperson 1 to territory

---

Table 8.18   The Martha Weinstein Cosmetics Assignment Problem

Territory / Salesperson	A	B	C	D
1	(8)	10	12	16
2	11	11	15	8
3	9	(6)	(5)	14
4	15	14	9	(7)

Table 8.19   The Lower Bound of Branch 1A

Salesperson \ Territory	A	B	C	D
1	⑧			
2		11	15	8
3		⑥	⑤	14
4		14	9	⑦

Lower bound $= 8 + 6 + 5 + 7 = 26$

A, the total number of feasible solutions becomes $3! = 6$. The lower bound for this subset can be determined by summing the circled values in Table 8.19. The lower bound for branch 1A (assigning salesperson 1 to territory A) is 26. This lower bound is not the total time of a feasible solution because salesperson 3 is assigned twice, to territory B and territory C.

In a similar manner, the lower bounds for the subsets 2A, 3A, and 4A can be determined. For example, if salesperson 2 is assigned to territory A, the lower bound would be $11 + 6 + 5 + 7 = 29$, as shown in Table 8.20. The lower bounds of branches 3A and 4A can be determined similarly.

The lower bounds of the four subsets of solutions are presented below.

Subset	Lower Bound
1A	$8 + 6 + 5 + 7 = 26$ ← lower bound
2A	$11 + 6 + 5 + 7 = 29$
3A	$9 + 10 + 9 + 7 = 35$
4A	$15 + 6 + 5 + 8 = 34$

The minimum value among the lower bounds of the four subsets is 26, the lower bound of subset 1A. This value, therefore, is the lower bound in the first-stage branching operation. The upper bound is represented by the minimum value among the lower bounds of the feasible solutions, if there are any at this stage. None of the solutions we have derived in the four subsets is feasible. Thus, there is no upper bound as yet.

Table 8.20   The Lower Bound of Branch 2A

Salesperson \ Territory	A	B	C	D
1		10	12	16
2	⑪			
3		⑥	⑤	14
4		14	9	⑦

Lower bound = 11 + 6 + 5 + 7 = 29

The first-stage branching operation is presented in Figure 8.2. Subset 1A is selected for the second-stage branching operation because it has the current lower bound. Thus, we identify subset 1A by the circled node ①, as shown in Figure 8.2. Salesperson 1 has been assigned to territory A. The next assignment we have to make is to appoint one of the three remaining salespeople to territory B. Let us suppose that we are going to assign salesperson 2 to territory B. Then, the lower bound for this subset would be the sum of the assignment times of cells (1,A), (2,B), and the minimum elements in

Figure 8.2   The First-Stage Branching Operation

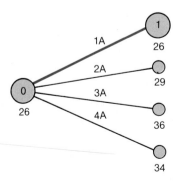

Table 8.21   The Lower Bound of Branch 1A-2B

Salesperson \ Territory	A	B	C	D
1	(8)			
2		(11)		
3			(5)	14
4			9	(7)

Lower bound $= 8 + 11 + 5 + 7 = 31$

the remaining two columns, C and D, after deleting Rows 1 and 2. Therefore, the lower bound for subset 1A-2B is $8 + 11 + 5 + 7 = 31$, as shown in Table 8.21. In a similar manner, we can calculate the lower bounds for the remaining two subsets.

The lower bounds of the three branches from node 1 (1A) are presented below.

Subsets	Lower Bound
1A-2B	$8 + 11 + 5 + 7 = 31 \leftarrow$ upper bound
1A-3B	$8 + 6 + 9 + 7 = 30$
1A-4B	$8 + 14 + 5 + 8 = 35$

The minimum value among the lower bounds of the feasible assignments is identified as the upper bound. Subset 1A-2B is a feasible solution. Therefore, its lower bound, 31, computed above, is the upper bound. Subset 1A-4B should be eliminated from further consideration because it is not a feasible solution and its lower bound (35) is greater than the current upper bound (31). The second-stage branching operation is presented in Figure 8.3.

From Figure 8.3, it is obvious that subsets 3A, 4A, and 1A-4B can all be eliminated from further consideration because their lower bounds are greater than the current upper bound. Now, the lower bound is identified as 29, which is the lower bound of subset 2A. The next branching operation must take place at this node. Since we must

Figure 8.3   The Second-Stage Branching Operation

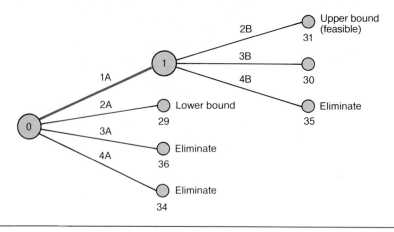

come back to node 0 to examine subset 2A, this procedure is often referred to as *back-tracking*.

In the 2A branch, we can calculate the lower bounds of the three subsets 2A-1B, 2A-3B, and 2A-4B. For example, the lower bound of subset 2A-1B can be calculated as shown in Table 8.22.

Table 8.22   The Lower Bound of Branch 2A-1B

Sales-person \ Territory	A	B	C	D
1		(10)		
2	(11)			
3			(5)	14
4			9	(7)

Lower bound = 11 + 10 + 5 + 7 = 33

Figure 8.4   The Third-Stage Branching Operation

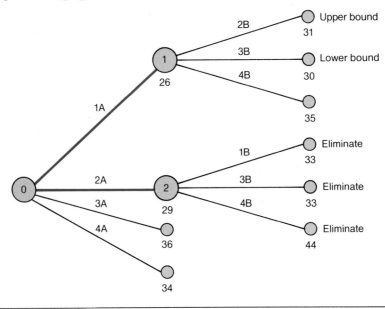

The lower bounds of the three subsets are as follows:

Subset	Lower Bound
2A-1B	11 + 10 + 5 + 7 = 33
2A-3B	11 + 6 + 9 + 7 = 33
2A-4B	11 + 14 + 5 + 14 = 44

None of the above three lower bounds is acceptable because they are all greater than the current upper bound. Thus, we must backtrack to subset 1A-3B, which has the new lower bound as shown in Figure 8.4.

In the 1A-3B branch, we can easily calculate the lower bounds of the two subsets as follows:

Subset	Lower Bound
1A-3B-2C	8 + 6 + 15 + 7 = 36
1A-3B-4C	8 + 6 + 9 + 8 = 31

The above two solutions are both feasible. The lower bound of subset 1A-3B-4C yields the total time, which is identical to the current upper bound. Thus, there are two optimum assignment schedules for this problem, which can be identified as follows:

	Assignment 1			Assignment 2	
Sales-person	Territory	Time	Sales-person	Territory	Time
1	A	8 min	1	A	8 min
2	B	11	2	D	8
3	C	5	3	B	6
4	D	7	4	C	9
	Total time = 31 min			Total time = 31 min	

The above two solutions correspond to the optimum solutions we derived by the Hungarian method of assignment. The complete branch-and-bound analysis for the problem is shown in Figure 8.5. If the total time of the final two subsets (1A-3B-2C-4D and 1A-3B-4C-2D) both exceeded the upper bound (31), these solutions would have been eliminated from further consideration. In that case, a node with the new lower bound, if it were less than the current upper bound, would be selected for further branching. If no node met this requirement, then the subset that yields the upper bound would be the optimum solution.

The branch-and-bound procedure we have discussed thus far can also be applied to a maximization assignment problem. The approach is exactly the same as the one we applied to a minimization problem. The only differences are the calculation process for the lower and upper bounds and the branching procedure.

Figure 8.5 The Complete Branch-and-Bound Solution Procedure

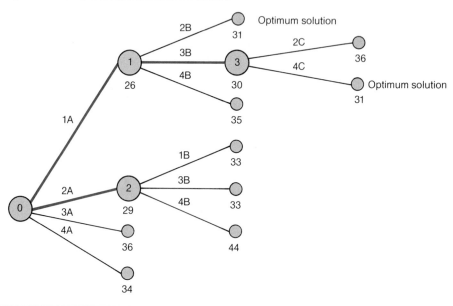

In a maximization, the lower bound is computed by summing the payoff of the actual assignment and the maximum payoffs in each of the remaining unassigned columns. If there are feasible assignments, the maximum value among their lower bounds is determined as the upper bound. Then, only those subsets having lower bounds that exceed the current upper bound are selected for further analysis. A subset with the highest lower bound among the remaining subsets is selected and branched further. In continuing the branch-and-bound process, the optimum solution is found when the objective function value of a subset is not less than the lower bound for any subset.

Computer Solution of Assignment Problems

The Hungarian method and the branch-and-bound approach are effective in solving simple assignment problems. Nevertheless, we rarely solve assignment problems by hand. The assignment problem can be solved by using the computer either through the integer-programming program or the Hungarian method program.

We will use *Micro Manager* to solve the Martha Weinstein Cosmetics problem presented as Casette 8.1. Figure 8.6 presents the Hungarian method solution. Figure 8.7

Figure 8.6   Computer-derived Hungarian Method Solution of Casette 8.1

```
PROGRAM: Assignment

***** INPUT DATA ENTERED *****

Minimization problem:

      |    1       2       3       4   |
      -------------------------------------
   1  |   8.00   10.00   12.00   16.00 |
   2  |  11.00   11.00   15.00    8.00 |
   3  |   9.00    6.00    5.00   14.00 |
   4  |  15.00   14.00    9.00    7.00 |
      -------------------------------------


*****   PROGRAM OUTPUT   *****

      | 1  2  3  4 |
      ----------------
   1  | 1  0  0  0 |
   2  | 0  0  0  1 |
   3  | 0  1  0  0 |
   4  | 0  0  1  0 |
      ----------------

Optimal solution :  31
```

Figure 8.7   Computer-derived Integer Programming Solution of Casette 8.1

```
PROGRAM: All Integer Programming

***** INPUT DATA ENTERED *****

Min Z =  8 x 1 + 10 x 2 + 12 x 3 + 16 x 4 + 11 x 5 + 11 x 6 + 15 x 7 + 8 x 8 +
         9 x 9 + 6 x 10 + 5 x 11 + 14 x 12 + 15 x 13 + 14 x 14 + 9 x 15 + 7 x 16

Subject to:

C 1    1 x 1 + 1 x 2 + 1 x 3 + 1 x 4 =  1
C 2    1 x 5 + 1 x 6 + 1 x 7 + 1 x 8 =  1
C 3    1 x 9 + 1 x 10 + 1 x 11 + 1 x 12 =  1
C 4    1 x 13 + 1 x 14 + 1 x 15 + 1 x 16 =  1
C 5    1 x 1 + 1 x 5 + 1 x 9 + 1 x 13 =  1
C 6    1 x 2 + 1 x 6 + 1 x 10 + 1 x 14 =  1
C 7    1 x 3 + 1 x 7 + 1 x 11 + 1 x 15 =  1
C 8    1 x 4 + 1 x 8 + 1 x 12 + 1 x 16 =  1


*****   PROGRAM OUTPUT   *****

Level 0  node  0 :  Optimal solution =      31.00000

                              x 1 = 1
                              x 2 = 0
                              x 3 = 0
                              x 4 = 0
                              x 5 = 0
                              x 6 = 0
                              x 7 = 0
                              x 8 = 1
                              x 9 = 0
                              x10 = 1
                              x11 = 0
                              x12 = 0
                              x13 = 0
                              x14 = 0
                              x15 = 1
                              x16 = 0
```

presents the solution of the same problem by the all-integer programming method. The optimum solution is identical for both methods and corresponds with the optimum solution we derived in Casette 8.1

REAL-WORLD APPLICATIONS

SCAT and SPAT Assign Students to Interviews or Projects

Two personnel assignment situations at the University of Minnesota involved typical problems encountered by practicing managers: large number of assignees, ranked preferences, and blocked or required choices.[1] In the first situation, students desired assignment to interview slots with corporate recruiters; in the second, MBA students were assigned to field projects as a requirement of their curriculum. Manual procedures in place before development of a computerized solution took up to 4 days, with students "camping out" in the hallways. Frustration, wasted time, and suboptimal assignments were the result.

The student–company assignment problem was formulated as SCAT, and produced an optimal assignment scheme 3.5 hours after the last student preference input. Central processing unit (CPU) time was just over 11 seconds, making 3,015 assignments. In all, 744 students had requested 8,046 interviews, but only 3,142 slots were scheduled because nearly 90 percent of the interviews assigned were within the students' top ten choices.

The student–project assignment problem (SPAT) received similar treatment but required more experienced operators and longer processing time. A total of 155 students were assigned to 40 projects, with nearly 90 percent receiving one of their top five choices. In both SCAT and SPAT applications, students and administrators responded very positively, with few complaints. The solutions were perceived as careful, fair, and incorporating individual preferences. The method was judged cost-effective and expeditious.

Assigning Aerial Spraying Teams to Protect Spruce Forests

The Maine Forest Service sprays approximately 850,000 acres of spruce fir forests annually to control budworm damage. Several types of aircraft flying from six or more airfields spray 250 to 300 infested areas. Weather is an important factor, as is the growth stage of the budworm, limiting the spraying season and influencing the choice of insecticide for each area.

In a linear programming assignment model developed for the Maine Forest Service, the decision variables represented the times assigned to each aircraft team, at each airfield, to spray each block.[2] Limitations included feasibility of specific combinations of blocks for a given trip, operating range of the aircraft type, and aircraft-insecticide compatibility. The objective function involved minimizing total spraying cost, using cost factors determined by flying time per route and aircraft-specific costs.

Implementation of the model on a minicomputer enhanced efficiency of the spray operations and reduced the number of airfields and aircraft teams. The model proved versatile in handling potential additions and deletions of airfields and aircraft. The model, as used in 1984, contained 748 variables and 292 constraints and was solved using a revised simplex algorithm.

---

[1] Arthur Hill, J. David Naumann, and Norman Chervany, "SCAT and SPAT: Large-Scale Computer-Based Optimization Systems for the Personnel Assignment Problem," *Decision Sciences* 14:2 (1983), 207–220.

[2] David Rumpf, Emanuel Melachrinoudis, and Thomas Rumpf, "Improving Efficiency in a Forest Pest Control Spray Program," *Interfaces* 15:5 (1985), 1–11.

Personal Preferences Considered in Assigning Remedial Education Instructors

The Blue Hills Home Corporation, St. Louis Division, faced the assignment of 22 teachers to 22 private schools. Each teacher would provide remedial educational services 4 hours daily at each of two schools. Teachers, supervisors, and school administrators all expressed preferences about particular assignments, and some preferences conflicted with job attitude assessments and productivity observations.

A goal-programming assignment approach was taken, with three priority levels, 44 goal constraints, and 462 decision variables.[3] The first priority level incorporated actual assignments to prevent a double shift at the same school by a given teacher. The second priority included judgmental criteria, with weighted preferences of supervisors, teachers, and administrators. Seniority and experience were considered in weighting conflicting requests. The third priority attempted to minimize traveling costs in terms of distance between school shifts for each teacher.

Various priority arrangements were tested, but no alternative provided a completely satisfactory solution. In the best solution, assignments were made in accordance with supervisor and teacher preferences, at the expense of school administrator preferences. When actually implemented, the program saved considerable manual effort, reduced transportation costs by roughly 15 percent, and lowered resistance to the resulting announced assignments.

SUMMARY

The assignment problem is a variation of the linear programming problem. As a matter of fact, the assignment problem is a special type of transportation problem in which there are equal numbers of sources and destinations and in which the supply of each source and the demand of each destination must equal exactly 1. The objective of the assignment problem is to determine the optimum allocation of resources to various tasks. In this chapter, we have discussed the two widely applied techniques of assignment: the Hungarian method and the branch-and-bound procedure.

Glossary

Hungarian Method   An assignment solution technique based on the concept of opportunity cost. The method's underlying theorem was first proved by D. König, a Hungarian mathematician.

Opportunity Cost Table   The assignment problem tableau with opportunity costs computed, first row-wise and then column-wise.

References

Dwyer, P. S. "Solution to the Personnel Classification Problem with the Method of Optimal Regions." *Psychometrika* 19 (1954), 11–26.

Flood, M. M. "On the Hitchcock Distribution Problem." *Pacific Journal of Mathematics* 2 (1953), 369–386.

Kuhn, H. W. "The Hungarian Method for the Assignment Problem." *Naval Research Logistics Quarterly* 2 (1955), 83–97.

Kwak, N. K. *Mathematical Programming with Business Applications*. New York: McGraw-Hill, 1973.

[3]Sang Lee and Marc Schniederjans, "A Multicriteria Assignment Problem: A Goal Programming Approach," *Interfaces* 13:4 (1983), 75–81.

Lee, S. M. *Linear Optimization for Management*. New York: Petrocelli-Charter, 1976.

Lee, S. M. *Goal Programming Methods for Multiple Objective Integer Programs*. Atlanta: American Institute of Industrial Engineers, 1979.

Lee, S. M., and Franz, L. S. "Optimizing the Location-Allocation Problem with Multiple Objectives." *International Journal of Physical Distribution and Materials Management* 9:6 (1979), 245–255.

Lee, S. M., Moore, L. J., and Taylor, B. W. *Management Science*. 2d ed. Dubuque, Iowa: W. C. Brown, 1985.

Assignments

8.1 Why is the assignment problem a special variation of the transportation problem?

8.2 If we can formulate an assignment problem as a linear programming model, why do we need the assignment method?

8.3 Describe a problem with which you are familiar that can be solved by the assignment method.

8.4 Why is an assignment problem a zero–one programming problem?

8.5 Why do we refer to the general assignment method as the *Hungarian method?*

8.6 What is the logic behind the use of straight vertical and horizontal lines in the Hungarian method?

8.7 State the primary difference(s) between the Hungarian and the branch-and-bound methods.

8.8 In the branch-and-bound approach, how do we determine the lower and upper limits of a minimization assignment problem?

8.9 What is backtracking in the branch-and-bound procedure?

8.10 How can we handle an impossible or prohibited assignment when the Hungarian method is used?

8.11 Three secretaries are available to type three reports. Given below is the typing time (in hours) required for each secretary to type each report. Determine the optimum assignment by the Hungarian method.

Secretary	Report A	B	C
Joyce	12	12	20
Jane	10	12	24
Cindy	15	15	24

8.12 Conformity Systems Inc. has three employees: a typist, a clerk, and a stenographer. Each person will be assigned one of the following tasks: bookkeeping, filing, and report preparation. The manager wishes to assign workers to jobs so that the total cost is minimized. The costs for each possible job assignment are as follows:

Employee	Job Bookkeeping	Filing	Report Preparation
Typist	$40	$50	$70
Clerk	50	40	60
Stenographer	60	50	50

Find the optimum assignment solution by the Hungarian method.

8.13 Given the following table for an assignment problem and using the Hungarian method, find the assignment requiring the least total time.

Job	Machine A	B	C	D
1	10 min	14 min	15 min	13 min
2	12	13	15	12
3	8	12	12	11
4	13	16	18	16

8.14 An insurance firm has five salespeople that the firm wants to assign to five sales regions. Because of previously acquired contacts, each salesperson's efficiency in covering each region varies in terms of expected sales. The estimated sales per month (in thousands of dollars) by each salesperson for each of the regions are as follows:

Salesperson	Region A	B	C	D	E
1	$15	$12	$14	$16	$18
2	14	10	15	10	14
3	16	13	10	19	16
4	18	17	12	17	14
5	12	16	10	14	13

Find the optimum assignment by the Hungarian method.

8.15 Given the following cost table for an assignment problem and using the branch-and-bound procedure, find the minimum-total-cost assignment of workers to machines.

		Machine		
Worker	A	B	C	D
1	$20	$30	$32	$36
2	28	26	32	20
3	22	18	16	36
4	26	26	22	18

8.16 The Checker Cab Company has a taxi waiting at each of four posts. Four customers have called and requested service. The distances, in miles, from the waiting taxis to the four customers are given below:

Cab Post		Customer		
	1	2	3	4
A	16	8	6	14
B	10	12	8	10
C	12	18	14	12
D	8	14	12	16

Using the branch-and-bound method and the Hungarian method, find the optimum assignment of taxis to customers that will minimize the total driving distance.

8.17 In a job shop operation, five jobs may be performed on any of four machines. The hours required for each job on each machine are presented in the following table:

Job		Machine		
	1	2	3	4
A	13	14	16	10
B	12	13	15	12
C	11	12	12	9
D	16	16	18	14
E	10	12	13	12

The plant line supervisor would like to assign the jobs so that the total time is minimized. Find the optimum solution by the Hungarian method.

8.18 Bay Laboratories Inc. has five machines that need to be staffed by five operators. The time in minutes required to complete the given tasks by each operator with a given machine is shown in the following table:

Operator	Machine				
	A	B	C	D	E
1	8	10	10	15	2
2	14	21	17	10	2
3	14	18	22	25	3
4	16	19	20	24	2
5	8	11	11	10	2

a. Identify the optimum solution by the branch-and-bound method.

b. Find the optimum assignment solution by the Hungarian method.

8.19 The personnel director of a company facing severe financial difficulty must relocate four operations researchers from recently closed locations. Unfortunately, there are only three positions available. Salaries are the same throughout the company. Moving expenses will be used as the means of determining who goes where and who gets the opportunity to begin a new career. The estimated moving expenses are:

Operations Researcher	New Location		
	Gary	Salt Lake	San Francisco
Arlene	$5,000	$8,000	$4,000
Benson	7,000	3,000	5,000
Charlene	2,000	1,000	6,000
David	4,000	3,000	1,000

Find the optimum assignment solution by the Hungarian method.

8.20 Given the following payoff table for an assignment problem, use the Hungarian method to find the maximum payoff assignment of employees to machines.

Employee	Machine				
	A	B	C	D	E
1	$12	$9	$8	$7	$12
2	17	15	11	12	6
3	14	10	14	16	8
4	5	4	6	5	5

8.21 A job shop has four machinists to be assigned to four machines. The hourly cost required to operate each machine by each machinist is:

	Machine			
Machinist	A	B	C	D
1	$12	$11	$8	$14
2	10	9	10	8
3	14	8	7	11
4	6	8	10	9

However, due to a lack of experience, machinist 3 cannot operate machine B.

a. Formulate this problem as a general linear programming model.

b. Find the optimum assignment of machinist to machine by the Hungarian method.

c. Formulate an initial solution of the assignment problem by Vogel's approximation method.

d. Go through one iteration by the MODI method based on the initial solution derived with Vogel's approximation method.

8.22 A sergeant must assign four soldiers to duties. Because these four soldiers have been especially recalcitrant, the sergeant decides to assign each soldier to the worst job possible. Each soldier rates the five duties by preference, with 5 being the most favorable rating. Since only one soldier can be assigned to each job, everyone's worst choice cannot be selected. But the assignment method can be used to obtain the worst set of assignments possible. Based on the ratings given below, find the worst assignment (from the viewpoint of the soldiers) by the Hungarian method.

	Duty				
Soldier	KP	Guard Duty	CQ	Driver	Club Guard
Fennegan	1	2	3	4	5
Hennigan	1	2	4	3	5
Lannigan	1	3	2	4	5
O'Toole	2	1	3	4	5

8.23 Brockwinkle's Transport of Poughkeepsie has five transport crews. Today they have four jobs scheduled. The estimated numbers of hours for each of the crews to accomplish the jobs are as follows:

	Crew No.				
Job No.	12	28	37	42	58
1292	9	6	5	4	2
2862	7	6	3	2	Won't
3774	6	7	4	5	3
4921	2	6	4	9	6

Crew 58 refuses to perform job 2862, citing clause 621.32A of its union contract.

   a. Find the assignment requiring the least total time by the Hungarian method.

   b. Are there multiple optimum solutions? If so, identify them.

   c. Solve this problem by the branch-and-bound method.

8.24 The Memphis Police Department has five hard-drug squads available for assignment to five drug cases. The chief of detectives wishes to assign the squads so that the total dollar value of the drugs confiscated from the cases is maximized. The estimated dollar value, in thousands of dollars, of the hard-drugs that can be confiscated by each squad in each case is as follows:

Squad	\multicolumn{5}{c}{Case}
	1	2	3	4	5
A	14	7	3	7	27
B	20	7	12	6	30
C	10	3	4	5	21
D	8	12	7	12	21
E	13	25	24	26	8

Each squad has a different composition of personnel, expertise, equipment, and so on. Solve this maximization assignment using the Hungarian method.

8.25 Matthews Insurance Company has been given four additional districts in recognition of its outstanding performance. Mr. Matthews has five agents with varying degrees of training and experience whom he can assign to handle this new business. He would like to assign only one agent to each district. Mr. Matthews has estimated the costs involved in contacting ten potential customers by each agent as follows:

Agent	\multicolumn{4}{c}{District}
	1	2	3	4
A	$38	$32	$60	$36
B	34	44	48	50
C	40	38	52	60
D	38	58	42	46
E	35	39	45	48

Which agent should be assigned to which district in order to minimize total costs?

8.26 Trans-American Air Cargo Co. has five types of airplanes that it must assign to five different routes. Because of variations among the routes (distances, cargo characteristics, weather, airport facilities, etc.), the airplanes are not all equally adaptable to each route. The cost (in thousands of dollars) for each airplane over each route is as follows:

Airplane	Omaha–Chicago	Los Angeles–Denver	Detroit–Kansas City	New York–Reno	St. Louis–Phoenix
DC3	$10	$15	$17	$40	$45
DC7	8	12	20	38	43
B707	7	14	18	34	37
B727	6	13	12	30	32
B747	9	12	21	42	41

How should the airplanes be assigned in order to minimize the total costs?

8.27 A manufacturing firm has five employees and six machines. The firm is attempting to assign the employees to the machines in a manner that will minimize the total cost. A cost table showing the cost incurred by each employee on each machine is presented below:

Employee	Machine					
	A	**B**	**C**	**D**	**E**	**F**
1	$12	$7	$10	$14	$8	$10
2	10	14	13	20	9	11
3	5	3	6	9	7	10
4	9	11	7	16	9	10
5	10	6	14	8	10	12

However, due to union rules regarding departmental transfers, employee 3 cannot be assigned to machine E and employee 4 cannot be assigned to machine B.

a. Solve this problem by indicating the optimum assignment and computing the total minimum cost.

b. Formulate this problem as a general linear programming model.

8.28 Ms. Jane Sano is trying to decide where to locate three new machines that she has ordered for her shop. Some locations are more desirable than others for particular machines because of their proximity to work centers that would have heavy work flows to and from these machines. Sano has come up with the following table of estimated handling costs:

Machine	Location		
	A	**B**	**C**
1	$33	$15	$39
2	24	30	33
3	27	36	21

a. Which machines should be placed at which locations to minimize the handling costs? Solve this problem by the Hungarian method.

b. Solve this problem by the branch-and-bound method.

8.29 The Public Works Department of Saratoga Springs has seven snowplows. The director wants to assign these plows to seven districts in the city to clean up the new snow in the shortest possible time. The amount of time (in minutes) required to clean up all major streets in each district by different snowplows is given in the following table. Solve the assignment problem.

	Districts						
Plow	A	B	C	D	E	F	G
1	44	52	27	41	60	22	35
2	58	47	65	33	42	39	51
3	43	36	50	41	53	32	25
4	49	55	34	46	40	28	32
5	42	49	57	63	45	36	43
6	34	42	35	46	31	18	27
7	58	64	43	59	72	50	48

8.30 The Overland Bus Company is trying to improve its municipal transit service in large cities. It is particularly interested in assigning one additional bus to each of four cities. The company has four buses of varying ages and conditions that have been removed from cross-country service because of the gas shortage problem. The company's Transportation Division has estimated that the operating profit per day for each bus in each city will be as follows:

	City			
Bus	Roanoke	Washington	Richmond	Norfolk
1	$150	$110	$130	$125
2	140	135	150	110
3	125	120	115	135
4	130	115	120	145

a. Which bus should be assigned to which city in order to maximize the total profits?

b. Are there alternative optimum solutions? If so, identify them.

8.31 Given the following computer solution of a maximization assignment problem:

```
PROGRAM: Assignment

***** INPUT DATA ENTERED *****

Maximization problem:

      !    1        2        3        4   !
      -------------------------------------------
   1 !  280.00   180.00   150.00   170.00 !
   2 !  320.00   480.00   230.00   380.00 !
   3 !  510.00   580.00   585.00   540.00 !
   4 !  430.00   410.00   410.00   440.00 !
      -------------------------------------------


*****   PROGRAM OUTPUT   *****

      ! 1  2  3  4 !
      ------------------
   1 ! 1  0  0  0 !
   2 ! 0  1  0  0 !
   3 ! 0  0  1  0 !
   4 ! 0  0  0  1 !
      ------------------


Optimal solution :  1785
```

a. Formulate a zero–one programming model for the problem.

b. Develop the opportunity cost table for the problem.

8.32 The city police department must determine the optimal assignment of five police officers to five precincts so that crime can be minimized. The department has estimated the number of crimes expected to occur daily with different officers assigned to the different precincts, based on their past records:

Officer	Crimes per Precinct				
	A	**B**	**C**	**D**	**E**
1	40	12	30	20	32
2	39	8	26	18	40
3	36	7	23	16	38
4	32	6	27	22	35
5	42	8	24	25	30

However, officer 1 cannot be assigned to precinct D, and officer 4 cannot be assigned to precinct C, due to a policy of the police department.

a. Set up a zero–one programming model for this problem.
b. Solve the problem by using a computer or the Hungarian method.

8.33 Given the following computer solution of a maximization assignment problem:

```
PROGRAM: Assignment

***** INPUT DATA ENTERED *****

Maximization problem:

   :     1        2        3        4        5        6    :
   -------------------------------------------------------------
 1 :   100.00   120.00   110.00    90.00    0.00     0.00  :
 2 :    50.00   100.00   130.00    70.00    0.00     0.00  :
 3 :   120.00   130.00    80.00   110.00    0.00     0.00  :
 4 :    80.00   150.00    90.00   130.00    0.00     0.00  :
 5 :    60.00    80.00    70.00   110.00    0.00     0.00  :
 6 :   140.00    90.00   110.00   100.00    0.00     0.00  :
   -------------------------------------------------------------


*****   PROGRAM OUTPUT   *****

    : 1  2  3  4  5  6 :
   -----------------------
 1 : 0  0  0  0  1  0 :
 2 : 0  0  1  0  0  0 :
 3 : 0  0  0  0  0  1 :
 4 : 0  1  0  0  0  0 :
 5 : 0  0  0  1  0  0 :
 6 : 1  0  0  0  0  0 :
   -----------------------


Optimal solution :  530
```

a. Formulate a zero–one programming model
b. Interpret the optimum solution.

8.34 The Lincoln Manufacturing Company has four jobs to assign to five machines. The company employs a flexible manufacturing process, arranging its machines according to the types of jobs received. The following table shows the setup time (in minutes) required for each machine for each job. Management wants to reduce the setup time to improve productivity. Job B cannot be assigned to machine 3, and job D cannot be assigned to machine 4, because of certain machine characteristics.

Job	Machine 1	Machine 2	Machine 3	Machine 4	Machine 5
			Setup Time (min)		
A	15	17	14	16	12
B	10	15	X	13	19
C	17	19	18	16	13
D	13	20	16	X	16

a. Solve the problem by using a computer software package or by the Hungarian method.

b. Interpret the solution.

8.35 The Omaha Bears professional football team has serious financial problems, and management must cut some players, including two of the seven quarterbacks. To solve this problem, management established each quarterback's probability of winning a game, based on data from games with five major rivals.

Quarterback	Des Moines Devils	Lincoln Stars	Topeka Sunflowers	Colorado Springs Miners	Warrensburg Mulls
			Winning Probability		
1	0.30	0.45	0.65	0.50	0.45
2	0.30	0.45	0.50	0.65	0.45
3	0.50	0.50	0.65	0.50	0.30
4	0.30	0.50	0.35	0.65	0.35
5	0.40	0.70	0.55	0.60	0.40
6	0.40	0.60	0.50	0.65	0.45
7	0.20	0.30	0.40	0.30	0.10

The team wants to keep the best quarterback for each rival to keep the probability of winning as high as possible.

a. Determine which two quarterbacks to cut.

b. Interpret the solution in terms of winning percentages against each rival team.

9 DECISION THEORY

A famous philosopher once said, "Don't sacrifice today for an uncertain tomorrow." But we must and do sacrifice some of today precisely because tomorrows are uncertain. In this chapter we will study how probabilities can be used for decision making under the conditions of risk and uncertainty. We will study the concepts of expected value, payoff matrix, decision-making criteria under uncertainty, Bayes' theorem, and decision trees. Collectively, these concepts are often referred to as statistical decision theory.

Learning Objectives *From the study of this chapter, we will learn the following:*

1. The four basic states of the decision environment
2. Basics of probabilities
3. The use of probabilities for decision making under risk
4. The value of perfect information
5. Application of the expected value and expected loss criterion
6. Simple inventory problem analysis by incremental analysis
7. Decision-making criteria under uncertainty
8. Application of subjective probabilities for decision making
9. Utility analysis as a decision-making tool
10. Decision tree analysis for decision making under risk
11. Computer applications to decision theory
12. The meaning of the following terms:

Conditional payoffs	*Loss due to overstocking*
Expected payoff	*Loss due to understocking*
Indifference probabilities	*Incremental analysis*
Expected loss	*Salvage value*
Perfect information	*Goodwill cost*
Maximax	*Maximin*
Dominance criterion	*Minimax*
Utility analysis	*Coefficient of optimism*
Bayes' theorem	*Decision tree*

DECISION MAKING WITH PROBABILITY

Decision making under the condition of risk or uncertainty involves the concept of probability. Probability is an important topic of statistics and mathematics — the theory of probabilities is a discipline in itself. Our discussion of probability will be limited to the basic concept and its applications.

Although *probability* is part of our daily vocabulary, it is difficult to define concisely. The generally accepted definition of probability is "the frequency with which an event occurs when a certain number of experiments or trials are performed." This concept of probability is often referred to as *objective probability*.

Many business decisions are based on the observation of past experience or occurrences. For example, suppose that over the past 50 weeks a microcomputer dealer sold at least 20 computers in each of 10 weeks. Thus, the probability of the dealer's selling at least 20 computers in any given week would be 10/50 or 0.20. This type of objective probability is called *relative frequency* probability.

Probabilities are not always based on experiments or past experience. For example, a stock market analyst states that there is a 20 percent chance that the Dow-Jones Industrial Average will reach 2,300 this month, a meteorologist predicts a 40 percent chance of snow tomorrow, or Jimmy the Greek states that the Chicago Bears have a 60 percent chance to win the Super Bowl. Such probabilities are based on specific information, knowledge, or personal feeling about circumstances surrounding the occurrence of possible events. This type of probability is called *subjective probability*.

For decision making under risk or uncertainty, let us remember the following relevant properties concerning the concept of probability.

1. The probability that an event will occur can neither be negative nor greater than one. If we define the probability that an event will occur as $p(e)$, then $0 \leq p(e) \leq 1$. If $p(e) = 0$, the event will certainly not occur; if $p(e) = 1$, the event will certainly occur. The greater the value of $p(e)$, the more likely it is that the event will occur.

2. In any situation, the sum of the probabilities of all possible and mutually exclusive alternatives must equal 1:

$$\sum_{i=1}^{n} p_i(e_i) = 1$$

For example, in a coin-tossing game, the sum of the probabilities of all possible events would be $p(\text{head}) + p(\text{tail}) = 0.5 + 0.5 = 1.0$.

3. Two events may occur simultaneously. For example, it is possible to draw a card which is both a spade and an ace at the same time. If the events are randomly distributed, their *joint probability* is the product of their two individual probabilities:

$$p(AB) = p(A) \times p(B)$$

For example, $p(\text{spade and ace}) = p(\text{spade}) \times p(\text{ace}) = 13/52 \times 4/52 = 1/52$. If the events are not randomly distributed, the joint probability must be known (it cannot be derived). For example, the number of women aged 35 to 40 who drive a BMW cannot be derived from known age and vehicle counts; the distribution is specific to this particular situation.

If two events cannot occur simultaneously (that is, they are mutually exclusive), their joint probability is 0.

4. The probability of any one of a group of possible events happening is the sum of their independent probabilities minus their joint probability.

$$p(A \text{ or } B) = p(A) + p(B) - p(AB)$$

For example, when tossing a die, the probability of getting either 1 or 6 in any given throw is $p(1 \text{ or } 6) = 1/6 + 1/6 - 0 = 2/6$ or 0.3333. For another example, when drawing one card from a deck of cards, the probability of it being an ace or a spade would be $p(\text{spade or ace}) = p(\text{spade}) + p(\text{ace}) - p(\text{spade ace}) = 13/52 + 4/52 - 1/52 = 16/52$ or 0.3077 [16 cards in the deck are aces or spades (or both)].

5. The probability of independent events occurring together is the product of multiplying their independent probabilities. This is the same principle as joint probability, but includes sequential occurrences.

$$p(A \text{ and } B) = p(A) \times p(B)$$

For example, if a coin is tossed twice, the probability of getting the head twice is $p(\text{head and head}) = p(\text{head}) \times p(\text{head}) = 1/2 \times 1/2 = 1/4$ or 0.25.

6. *Conditional probability* arises when the probability of a given event occurring is conditional on another event's occurrence. Conditional probabilities are expressed as:

$$p(A|B) = \text{probability of } A \text{ given that } B \text{ has occurred}$$

For example, from a deck of cards, the king of hearts is drawn and discarded. The probability of next drawing an ace is $p(\text{ace}|\text{king of hearts}) = 4/51$ or 0.0784 (there are 4 aces in the remaining 51 cards).

DECISION MAKING UNDER RISK

An amateur Confucian contends that Confucius once said, "Prediction is very difficult, especially when it is for the future." Life is interesting and challenging because we live in a very uncertain world. We can seldom predict or forecast future outcomes with certainty. For example, it is difficult to say what will be the inflation rate next year. Also, we don't know whether the all-star baseball game will be postponed next year because of a player strike.

People develop certain intuitive skills or a knack of making good decisions in probabilistic situations. For instance, a good investor seems to know just when to sell stocks and put the money in Treasury bills as the interest rate increases. When we are faced with a simple problem, we can be pretty adept at making good decisions. However, if a complex or a very important decision problem is confronting us, we simply cannot rely on our intuitive judgment. Thus, decision theory is useful for making decisions under the conditions of risk and uncertainty.

The type of scientific technique we use for decision making is not entirely based on the nature of the problem at hand. The decision environment also plays a major role.

For example, an inventory problem for a country seed and fertilizer store and an inventory problem for Con-Agra would require different types of analyses. As we discussed briefly in Chapter 1, there are four basic states of decision environment: certainty, risk, uncertainty, and conflict. Probabilities are especially useful for decision making under the conditions of risk and uncertainty. Decision theory based on probabilities assists the decision maker in analyzing complex problems with numerous alternatives and consequences. The basic objective of decision theory is to provide the decision maker with concrete information concerning the relative likelihood of certain consequences. Such information is useful for identifying the best course of action.

The risk condition refers to the situation in which the probabilities of certain outcomes are known. For decision making under risk, we must identify the following components:

1. Alternative courses of action that are available and feasible

2. Possible events that can occur and their probabilities

3. Conditional payoff for a given course of action under a given possible event

Alternative Courses of Action   Any decision problem must have alternative options. If a problem has only one course of action available, it is not a decision problem—we have no choice but to accept the dictated course of action. In most real-world problems, however, we have a number of alternatives open to us.

Because we cannot consider all possible courses of action, we must use our judgment in limiting the alternatives to those that are available and feasible, in terms of predetermined criteria. For example, in designing a new automobile engine, we may limit the possible fuel alternatives to gasoline, gasohol, liquefied gas, and diesel fuel. We exclude coal, solar energy, hydrogen, and other fuels because they are not economically feasible at present, though they may be technologically feasible. Selecting all the available and feasible alternatives is an art in itself.

Possible Events and Probabilities   The possible events are also referred to as the *states of nature*. An event may be a state of international situation, economy, weather condition, foreign competition, or a particular instructor in a given section of a course. An event is usually an uncontrollable condition that is the product of a complex interaction of external forces, or it may simply be an act of God. The number of possible events for most decision problems under risk is usually finite and identifiable.

The possibility or likelihood of each event occurring in the future represents the probability of that event. For example, one may ask, "What is the probability that we will have a double-digit inflation rate next year?" If the Chase Economic Forecasting model predicts it to be 0.25, then we may want to accept this figure as the probability.

Conditional Payoff   The **conditional payoff** refers to the outcome associated with each of the alternative/event combinations. For example, in deciding what courses to take, if you take Chemistry 306 under Professor Leopold Lipscovitch, say, your expected grade might be D because that has been the average grade in his class. Typically, the conditional payoff is associated with a specific time period (e.g., a grade of D after a semester or 6 percent return after 1 year). The time period associated with the conditional payoff is often referred to as the *planning horizon* or *decision horizon*.

Table 9.1   The Decision Table Structure

Course of Action	Events and Probabilities					
	e_1 p_1	e_2 p_2	.	.	.	e_n p_n
a_1	c_{11}	c_{12}	.	.	.	c_{1n}
a_2	c_{21}	c_{22}	.	.	.	c_{2n}
.	.	.	.	.	.	.
.	.	.	.	.	.	.
.	.	.	.	.	.	.
a_m	c_{m1}	c_{m2}	.	.	.	c_{mn}

The Typical Decision Problem Structure   The above three basic components of the decision-making problem under risk can be structured as a decision table. We can label the components as follows:

a_i = alternative course i (independent controllable variables)

e_j = event j (independent uncontrollable variables)

c_{ij} = payoff for the alternative i and event j combination (dependent variables)

It is not a simple task to determine the exact monetary payoff for each of the alternative/event combinations. Nevertheless, we believe that past records and work experience can be utilized to derive sufficiently accurate conditional payoffs for many decision problems under risk. The typical decision table is presented in Table 9.1. The events (column-wise) and course of action (row-wise) arrangements can be interchanged depending on the structure of the problem under analysis.

The dominant decision-making criterion under the condition of risk is the *expected value*. The expected value for a decision alternative is the weighted average outcome (e.g., payoff or loss). Thus, the expected value is determined by the sum of the products of the conditional outcome of an alternative multiplied by the probability of each possible event. In applying the expected value criterion, we can use either the expected payoff or the expected loss criterion.

The Expected Payoff Criterion

The **expected payoff** (EP) is a decision criterion that has the basic principle of maximizing the long-term economic payoff from the selection of a particular course of action. Let us consider the following casette.

Casette 9.1   *FRIENDLY INVESTMENT CLUB*

The Friendly Investment Club (FIC) is an informal investment club composed of 50 junior managers from various local banks and stock brokerage firms. Each club member contributes $100 a month, and the total monthly funds of $5,000 are invested in either stocks or bonds, but never in both. The actual selection of particular stocks or bonds (e.g., 100 shares of Baker International common stock) will be determined later.

Table 9.2   *Friendly Investment Club Problem*

Investment Alternative	Events	
	Economic Upswing	Economic Downswing
Stocks	$1,000	$250
Bonds	600	400

The Club is attempting to determine whether the investment for September should be in stocks or in bonds. The payoff is primarily dependent on the economic condition in a given month. If the economic condition indicates an upswing (falling or stable interest rates, increasing productivity, etc.), investment in stocks tends to result in a greater payoff. However, if the economic condition is in the downswing, investment in bonds brings in a greater payoff. The investment alternatives, possible events (economic conditions), and conditional payoffs are presented in Table 9.2.

One difficult aspect of the investment problem is obtaining the probabilities of the events to occur in September. The Investment Research Committee evaluated the trends of a number of important economic indicators. The Committee's estimated probability of an economic upswing condition for September is 30 percent. Consequently, the probability of an economic downswing condition would be 70 percent.

The club decided to use the expected payoff (or expected monetary value) as the decision criterion. The expected payoff for an alternative course of action is the weighted average payoff, which is simply the sum of the products of the payoff of each event multiplied by the associated probability. Thus, the expected payoff of the two investment alternatives can be computed as follows:

$$EP(a_1) = (0.3 \times 1,000) + (0.7 \times 250) = \$475$$
$$EP(a_2) = (0.3 \times 600) + (0.7 \times 400) = \$460$$

In this computation, a_1 refers to alternative 1—investment in stocks, and a_2 represents alternative 2—investment in bonds. From the expected payoffs derived above, it is obvious that the investment plan in stocks is the better alternative because its expected payoff is $15 more than that for bonds.

Before making the final recommendation, the Investment Research Committee wanted to generate more information about the investment situation. The members of the committee were interested in finding the probabilities of the two alternatives that would result in exactly equal expected payoffs. Such probabilities are referred to as **indifference probabilities.** If the outcomes are identical, we will be indifferent toward the two investment alternatives.

If we denote p_1 as the probability of event 1 (i.e., economic upswing) and p_2 as the probability of event 2 (i.e., economic downswing), then $p_1 + p_2 = 1$. Thus, $p_2 = 1 - p_1$. Then, we can compute the expected payoffs of the two alternatives as follows:

$$EP(a_1) = 1,000 \, p_1 + 250 \, (1-p_1) = 750p_1 + 250$$
$$EP(a_2) = 600 \, p_1 + 400 \, (1-p_1) = 200p_1 + 400$$

The indifference condition requires $EP(a_1) = EP(a_2)$. Therefore, we can write

$$EP(a_1) = EP(a_2)$$
$$750p_1 + 250 = 200p_1 + 400$$
$$550p_1 = 150$$
$$p_1 = 0.2727$$

Since $p_1 = 0.2727$, we can easily compute $p_2 = 0.7273$. In other words, if the probability of an economic upswing is 0.2727, and consequently the probability of an economic downswing is 0.7273, we will be completely indifferent to whether the investments are to be in stocks or in bonds. The basic question we must ask is whether or not the probability of an economic upswing condition would be less than or greater than 0.2727. If $p_1 > 0.2727$, our choice will be stocks. On the other hand, if $p_1 < 0.2727$, investment in bonds will be our choice.

The expected payoff is an important decision criterion for decision making under risk. It should be pointed out, however, that the expected payoff is not exactly the eventual outcome of a decision. For example, $EP(a_1) = \$475$ does not mean that the payoff of investment in stocks would actually be $475. If we invest in stocks (a_1) and an economic upswing condition (e_1) occurs, the payoff will be $1,000. But if an economic downswing condition (e_2) occurs, a_1 will result in a payoff of $250. If the FIC makes the same monthly investment decisions over a long period of time, the average payoff for a_1 with the given probabilities (i.e., $p_1 = 0.3$ and $p_2 = 0.7$) for the events will be about the same as the expected value of $475.

If a decision problem is a repetitive type, the same problem will occur a great number of times. Since we attempt to maximize the long-term payoff, the expected payoff is a valid criterion for decision making under risk. The investment problem of FIC is precisely such a problem. Thus, the club decided to invest in stocks.

If a decision problem under risk is not repetitive but rather a "once in a lifetime" type problem, the expected payoff would be a less appropriate criterion to use. Also, in certain problems under risk, we may not select a decision alternative if it has a very large conditional loss, even if its expected payoff is much greater than that of the other alternatives.

The Expected Loss Criterion

The expected payoff criterion is appropriate for maximizing the long-term expected payoff. If we are interested in minimizing the long-term opportunity loss from the selection of a particular course of action, the **expected loss** (or expected opportunity loss or expected regret) criterion would be appropriate. The fundamental requirement for the two criteria remains the same — the decision problem must be a repetitive type over time. As a matter of fact, the solution is exactly the same whether we use the expected payoff or the expected loss criterion.

The concept of opportunity loss or opportunity cost was introduced in Chapter 7 (Vogel's approximation method of transportation) and in Chapter 8 (assignment method). The opportunity loss is simply the difference between the outcome of the best alternative and the outcome of a given alternative.

Casette 9.2   *THE STATE FAIR CONCESSION*

The state fair will be once again in the fairgrounds during the last two weeks of August. The A&M University is assigned the same exhibition hall to demonstrate the new advances in research, instruction, and public service at the university. Each college can have three booths and a concession stand. This year Sigma Alpha Epsilon is assigned the concession stand. One stipulation imposed by the university is that each concession stand can choose to sell only one product from among the following four choices: Coke, lemonade, coffee, and popcorn.

The officers of Sigma Alpha Epsilon are determined to do well this time around. Three years ago when the fraternity chose Coke, hoping to make a real killing, it rained for 10 days and the total sales were only $149.30. The primary factor that affects the payoff is the weather condition. This year, the officers decided to minimize the expected loss rather than maximize the expected payoff. The past records indicate the relevant information shown in Table 9.3.

The opportunity losses must be computed for each possible event, in this case the weather condition. If good weather prevails during the fair, the best course of action is selling Coke because it has the highest conditional payoff ($1,200). Thus, the opportunity loss for selling Coke under a good weather condition will be 0 because it has the highest conditional payoff. The opportunity loss for the lemonade alternative will be $1,200 - 800 = 400$. Likewise, the opportunity loss for coffee is $1,200 - 400 = 800$ and for popcorn, $1,200 - 500 = 700$. If bad weather prevails, the best course of action will be to sell coffee. We can develop a conditional loss table, as shown in Table 9.4.

Table 9.3   *Sigma Alpha Epsilon Concession Problem*

	Events	
Alternatives	Good Weather $p_1 = 0.6$	Bad Weather $p_2 = 0.4$
Coke (a_1)	$1,200	$150
Lemonade (a_2)	800	400
Coffee (a_3)	400	800
Popcorn (a_4)	500	500

Table 9.4   *Conditional Loss for the Sigma Alpha Epsilon Problem*

	Events	
Alternatives	Good Weather $p_1 = 0.6$	Bad Weather $p_1 = 0.4$
Coke (a_1)	$ 0	650
Lemonade (a_2)	400	400
Coffee (a_3)	800	0
Popcorn (a_4)	700	300

Now we can compute the expected loss *(EL)* for each alternative as follows:

$$EL(a_1) = 0(0.6) + 650(0.4) = 260$$
$$EL(a_2) = 400(0.6) + 400(0.4) = 400$$
$$EL(a_3) = 800(0.6) + 0(0.4) = 480$$
$$EL(a_4) = 700(0.6) + 300(0.4) = 540$$

From this computation, it is obvious that Coke is the best alternative because it has the minimum expected loss. Thus, Sigma Alpha Epsilon once again decided to sell Coke at the concession stand during the state fair.

SIMPLE INVENTORY PROBLEMS UNDER RISK

The expected value criterion we discussed in the previous section can be applied to a number of other types of decision problems under risk. In this section, we will expand the concept further and apply it to a relatively simple inventory problem under risk.

Casette 9.3   *NEW ENGLAND FISH MARKET*

Mr. Dan Brown owns and operates the New England Fish Market. This is the only fish market in town that sells fresh Maine lobsters. Lobsters are flown in from Boston once a week and they are kept in a salt-water tank for a period of 1 week. If the lobsters are not sold within a week, they are sold to a local restaurant at a loss. Determining the optimum number of lobsters to stock is a difficult task, especially because of a wide fluctuation in the demand for lobsters.

Mr. Brown purchases lobsters (an average of 1.5 pounds each) from a dealer in Boston at $5 each. The profit per lobster is $5, as the price charged is $10. At the end of each week the leftover lobsters are sold to a restaurant for $3 per lobster, a loss of $2 each. Mr. Brown has the sales records for the past 100 weeks, as shown in Table 9.5. Demand ranges from 1 to 7 lobsters per week. Based on the number of weeks in

Table 9.5   Past Demand for Lobsters

Weekly Sales	Number of Weeks
1	5
2	10
3	25
4	30
5	20
6	5
7	5
	100

Table 9.6   Weekly Demand for Lobsters and Probability Distribution

Weekly Demand	Probability
1	0.05
2	0.10
3	0.25
4	0.30
5	0.20
6	0.05
7	0.05
	1.00

which the identical number of lobsters were sold, we can derive a probability distribution. For example, in 5 weeks out of the 100 weeks the demand for lobster was 1 lobster. Thus, the probability of demand for 1 lobster will be $5 \div 100 = 0.05$.

Table 9.6 presents the possible weekly demand for lobsters and the probability distribution based on the past demand. This table represents the possible demand for lobsters if the past market situation remains constant. However, the future market situation may not be the same as the past records indicate. Thus, if drastic changes occur in the market situation (e.g., airline strikes, shortage of lobsters), we should not rely on the past records.

The decision problem of Mr. Brown is to determine the optimum number of lobsters to order weekly in order to maximize his profit. Clearly, if Mr. Brown orders more than what will be demanded, his profit will be reduced or he may actually have a loss because the unsold lobsters will be sold to a restaurant at a loss. However, if he orders an insufficient quantity of lobsters to meet the demand, his profit will be smaller because of lost sales due to shortage and associated goodwill costs.

Conditional Profits

Before we can calculate the expected profit, we must construct a table of conditional profits. In the New England Fish Market problem, the conditional profit of stocking a certain number of lobsters will be based on two conditions: (1) demand (D) is equal to or greater than the quantity stocked (Q), and (2) demand (D) is less than the quantity stocked (Q).

Condition 1: $D \geq Q$ When the demand is equal to or greater than the quantity stocked, the market can sell all of the lobsters it has in stock. Since the cost of a lobster is $5 and it is sold for $10, the profit will be $5 per lobster. Therefore, the total profit is $5Q. For example, if Mr. Brown stocks 3 lobsters and the demand is for 3 or more lobsters, the total profit will be $5Q = \$5 \times 3 = \$15$. The conditional profit (CP) when $D \geq Q$ will be

$$CP = \$5Q$$

Condition 2: $D < Q$ When the demand for lobsters is less than the quantity stocked, Mr. Brown will have some unsold lobsters. The total cost will be $5Q$, as Mr. Brown's purchasing cost is $5 per lobster. The total revenue from the lobsters sold will be $10D$, since the selling price is $10 per lobster. The number of unsold lobsters is simply $Q - D$. Mr. Brown sells the leftover lobsters to a restaurant for $3 each. Thus, the revenue generated from the unsold lobsters will be $3(Q - D)$.

The conditional profit when $D < Q$ can be computed as follows:

$$\text{Conditional profit} = \text{Total revenue} - \text{Total cost}$$
$$= \$10D + \$3\,(Q - D) - \$5Q$$
$$= \$10D + \$3Q - \$3D - \$5Q$$
$$CP = \$7D - \$2Q$$

For example, if Mr. Brown stocks 3 lobsters but has a demand for only 2 lobsters, the conditional profit will be $(\$7 \times 2) - (\$2 \times 3) = \$14 - \$6 = \$8$. We can check this answer as follows:

$$\text{Revenue from sale of 2 lobsters} = \$10 \times 2 = \$20$$

Revenue from 1 leftover lobster
sold to a restaurant $\qquad\qquad\qquad = \underline{\$\ 3}$

$$\text{Total revenue} = \$23$$

$$\text{Total cost of purchasing 3 lobsters} = \$15$$
$$\text{Conditional profit} = \$\ 8$$

Now we can prepare a conditional profit table, as shown in Table 9.7, by using the two conditional profit functions developed above. It should be noted here that the conditional profits presented in Table 9.7 represent the actual (explicit) monetary outcomes for specific quantities stocked under various demand conditions. In other words, conditional profits include losses due to overstocking, but they do not include the opportunity (implicit) costs due to understocking.

Table 9.7   *Conditional Profit Table for Lobsters Stocked and Demanded* (dollars)

Quantity Stocked (Q)	Demand (D)						
	1	2	3	4	5	6	7
1	5	5	5	5	5	5	5
2	3	10	10	10	10	10	10
3	1	8	15	15	15	15	15
4	−1	6	13	20	20	20	20
5	−3	4	11	18	25	25	25
6	−5	2	9	16	23	30	30
7	−7	0	7	14	21	28	35

Expected Profits

In order to compute the expected profit for stocking a certain number of lobsters, we must use the expected value *(EV)* concept we discussed earlier. First, we must obtain information about the possible demands and their probabilities, as shown in Table 9.6. Then, after we combine these probabilities and the conditional profits, as shown in Table 9.7, we can compute the expected profits.

For example, for the alternative of stocking 1 lobster ($Q = 1$), the expected profit can be computed as follows:

Demand	Probability	Conditional Profit	Expected Profit
1	0.05	$5	$0.25
2	0.10	5	0.50
3	0.25	5	1.25
4	0.30	5	1.50
5	0.20	5	1.00
6	0.05	5	0.25
7	0.05	5	0.25
	1.00		Total = $5.00

Since the conditional profit is $5 for each possible demand, we can also compute the expected profit of stocking 1 lobster as $5 × 1 = $5. The same approach can be used to compute the expected profit of stocking 2 lobsters ($Q = 2$):

Demand	Probability	Conditional Profit	Expected Profit
1	0.05	$3	$0.15
2	0.10	10	1.00
3	0.25	10	2.50
4	0.30	10	3.00
5	0.20	10	2.00
6	0.05	10	0.50
7	0.05	10	0.50
	1.00		Total = $9.65

The conditional profit is $10 for 95 percent of the time and it is $3 for only 5 percent of the time. Thus, we can easily compute the expected profit by determining ($10 × 0.95) + ($3 × 0.05) = $9.65. Table 9.8 presents the expected profits of the various stock decisions.

The maximum expected profit is $15.90 when Mr. Brown stocks 5 lobsters. Thus, the optimum quantity to stock is 5 lobsters. If the New England Fish Market faces the lobster inventory problem every week over a long period of time, stocking 5 lobsters

Table 9.8   Expected Profit for Various Quantities Stocked (dollars)

| Quantity Stocked (Q) | Demand (D) and Associated Probabilities | | | | | | | Expected Profit |
	1 (0.05)	2 (0.10)	3 (0.25)	4 (0.30)	5 (0.20)	6 (0.05)	7 (0.05)	
1	5	5	5	5	5	5	5	5.00
2	3	10	10	10	10	10	10	9.65
3	1	8	15	15	15	15	15	13.60
4	−1	6	13	20	20	20	20	15.80
5	−3	4	11	18	25	25	25	15.90
6	−5	2	9	16	23	30	30	14.60
7	−7	0	7	14	21	28	35	12.95

per week will provide the highest average weekly profit under the given demand and its probability distribution, unit cost, and unit profit conditions.

Expected Profit under Certainty

If the New England Fish Market could obtain **perfect information** about the exact demand for lobsters for the next week, Mr. Brown could eliminate the condition of risk. In fact, the decision problem then becomes one under the condition of certainty. Demand may still fluctuate from 1 to 7 lobsters per week with the given probability distribution. However, if we can obtain perfect information concerning demand in advance, Mr. Brown can easily determine the optimum quantity to stock.

Referring to Table 9.8, it is obvious that the conditional profit will be maximum for each Q (i.e., row) if the quantity stocked is exactly equal to the quantity demanded. In other words, when perfect information concerning demand is available, the only thing Mr. Brown has to do is order exactly the same quantity as demanded, or $Q = D$. Then, the conditional profits for the various demand-stock combinations will be as shown in Table 9.9.

Table 9.9   Conditional Profit Table with Perfect Information

| Quantity Stocked | Demand | | | | | | |
	1	2	3	4	5	6	7
1	$5						
2		$10					
3			$15				
4				$20			
5					$25		
6						$30	
7							$35

Since $Q = D$ when certainty prevails, there will be no losses resulting from under- or overstocking. The expected profit under certainty can be derived in the same manner, as follows:

Demand	Probability	Conditional Profit	Expected Profit
1	0.05	$5	$0.25
2	0.10	10	1.00
3	0.25	15	3.75
4	0.30	20	6.00
5	0.20	25	5.00
6	0.05	30	1.50
7	0.05	35	1.75
	1.00		Total = $19.25

The expected profit under certainty (with perfect information) is $19.25. This value is the maximum profit possible under the condition of certainty. Without perfect information concerning demand, the best thing Mr. Brown could do was identify the inventory level that maximized the expected profit. The optimum quantity to stock was found to be 5 lobsters with the expected profit of $15.90. How much better off is he with perfect information than he was without it? We can easily determine that the *value of perfect information* is the difference between the expected profit of the optimum decision without perfect information ($15.90) and that with the perfect information ($19.25). Therefore, the value of perfect information will be $3.35, as this is the amount by which the profit can be increased with the additional information.

Conditional Loss

The inventory problem of the New England Fish Market can also be solved by analyzing the expected loss. First, we shall determine the conditional loss associated with the combination of quantity stocked and quantity demanded. The conditional losses are based on two types of losses: actual (accounting) loss and opportunity (implicit) loss. The actual loss results from overstocking, and the opportunity loss from understocking.

Loss Due to Overstocking ($Q > D$)   In our example, any lobster left over after one week must be sold to a restaurant at a loss of $2 (cost of $5 and selling price of $3). For example, if we stock 6 lobsters and sell only 5, the sixth lobster must be sold to a restaurant at a loss of $2. Consequently, the amount of loss due to overstocking would be $2 ($Q - D$).

Loss Due to Understocking ($Q < D$)   If we stock less than the quantity demanded, the loss would be the lost profit. For example, if Mr. Brown stocked 4 lobsters and the demand was for 5, the demand for the fifth lobster could not be satisfied. If he had stocked the fifth lobster, he could have made a $5 profit from it. Therefore, the opportunity loss due to understocking would be $5 ($D - Q$).

From our discussion of these two types of losses, it should be apparent that there will be no loss whatsoever if we stock exactly the quantity demanded. In other words,

Table 9.10 Conditional Loss Table (dollars)

Quantity Stocked (Q)	Demand (D)						
	1	2	3	4	5	6	7
1	0	5	10	15	20	25	30
2	2	0	5	10	15	20	25
3	4	2	0	5	10	15	20
4	6	4	2	0	5	10	15
5	8	6	4	2	0	5	10
6	10	8	6	4	2	0	5
7	12	10	8	6	4	2	0

$Q = D$ would be the optimum stock quantity. We already know this, of course, because we discussed it when we considered the value of perfect information. Now we can construct the conditional loss table, as shown in Table 9.10.

Expected Loss

Once we have developed the conditional loss table, the next step is to compute the expected loss for stocking a certain quantity. The possible weekly demand and the probability distribution were shown in Table 9.6.

The expected loss can be found for a given quantity stocked by computing the weighted average loss, that is, the conditional loss multiplied by its probability. For example, the expected loss of stocking 1 lobster will be:

Demand	Probability	Conditional Loss	Expected Loss
1	0.05	$0	$0.00
2	0.10	5	0.50
3	0.25	10	2.50
4	0.30	15	4.50
5	0.20	20	4.00
6	0.05	25	1.25
7	0.05	30	1.50
	1.00		$14.25

Table 9.11 presents the expected loss resulting from various stocking decisions. The expected loss is the minimum ($3.35) if we stock 5 lobsters. This optimum stock level corresponds to the one we derived in our discussion of the expected profit. It does not matter whether we utilize the expected profit or the expected loss criterion; the same optimum stock level can be determined by either means.

The optimum quantity is found when the expected profit is the maximum, or when the change in the expected profit becomes negative as the stock level is gradually in-

Table 9.11   Expected Loss for Various Stocking Decisions (dollars)

Quantity Stocked (Q)	Demand (D) Quantity and Associated Probabilites							Expected Loss
	1 (0.05)	2 (0.10)	3 (0.25)	4 (0.30)	5 (0.20)	6 (0.05)	7 (0.05)	
1	0	5	10	15	20	25	30	14.25
2	2	0	5	10	15	20	25	9.60
3	4	2	0	5	10	15	20	5.65
4	6	4	2	0	5	10	15	3.45
5	8	6	4	2	0	5	10	3.35
6	10	8	6	4	2	0	5	4.65
7	12	10	8	6	4	2	0	6.30

Table 9.12   Summary of Expected Profits and Expected Losses

Quantity Stocked (Q)	Expected Profit	Change in Expected Profit	Expected Loss	Change in Expected Loss
1	$5.00		$14.25	
		$+4.65		$-4.65
2	9.65		9.60	
		+3.95		-3.95
3	13.60		5.65	
		+2.20		-2.20
4	15.80		3.45	
		+0.10		-0.10
5	15.90		3.35	
		-1.30		+1.30
6	14.60		4.65	
		-1.65		+1.65
7	12.95		6.30	

creased. When we look at the expected loss criterion, the optimum quantity is found when the expected loss is the minimum, or when the change in the expected loss becomes positive. Although the signs are opposite, because profit is the opposite of loss, the absolute incremental changes for both of the expected values are identical. For example, if we increase the stock level from 1 lobster to 2 lobsters, the expected profit increases by $4.65. This increase is possible if there is a corresponding decrease of $4.65 in the expected loss. Table 9.12 presents the summary of the expected profits and the expected losses of various stock levels and their changes. The optimum stock quantity is 5 lobsters, as shown by the blue-number row in Table 9.12.

Value of Perfect Information

We discussed briefly the value of perfect information in the section on expected profit under certainty. The real value of perfect information is simply the difference between the expected profit ($15.90) of the optimum quantity to stock under risk and the expected profit ($19.25) under certainty, that is, $3.35. If we use the expected loss criterion, we find the minimum expected loss to be the same as the value of perfect information.

If the demand for the next week is known in advance, no matter how many lobsters it may be, we can reduce the expected loss to 0 by simply stocking exactly the quantity that will be demanded. For example, if perfect information indicates that the demand will be 5 lobsters, we will stock 5 and have no conditional loss. Therefore, the expected loss will be 0 when perfect information is available, and the value of perfect information will be exactly equal to the expected loss of the optimum stock level under risk. The expected loss of the optimum stock level (5 lobsters in Table 9.12) is $3.35. Hence, this is the value of perfect information.

Although it is highly desirable to obtain perfect information about demand, in reality it is extremely difficult to obtain such information. The main purpose of determining the value of perfect information is to place an upper bound on the value of additional information.

INCREMENTAL ANALYSIS

A more convenient short cut for the inventory problem under risk is **incremental analysis.** Incremental analysis, first suggested by Robert Schlaifer, evaluates the inventory decision one unit at a time. For example, we analyze the difference between the expected loss of stocking the first unit and the expected loss of not stocking the first unit. If stocking the first unit has less expected loss than not stocking it, then we proceed with the same incremental analysis for the second unit, and so on. If stocking the *i*th unit has a greater expected loss than not stocking the unit, the optimum stock quantity is found and the analysis terminated.

Stocking Decision for the First Unit

Let us go back to the familiar New England Fish Market problem. Table 9.13 presents the computation of the expected losses for the two possible courses of action concerning the first lobster: Stock the first lobster or do not stock it. Regardless of which course of action Mr. Brown takes, there will be only two possible events that can occur: There may be demand for the first lobster or there may not be demand for it.

Referring to Table 9.11 for the probability distribution of demand, we can easily determine that there always will be demand for the first lobster. Since the demand ranges from 1 to 7 lobsters per week, we can always sell the first lobster if we stock it. The probability of demand for the first lobster is, therefore, 1.0. Conversely, the probability of no demand for the first lobster is 0.0.

Table 9.13 *Incremental Analysis for the First Lobster* (dollars)

Course of Action	Demand and Associated Probabilities		
	D ≥ 1 (1.0)	*D* < 1 (0.0)	Total
Stock first lobster			
Conditional loss	0	2	
Expected loss (conditional loss × probability)	0	0	0
Don't stock first lobster			
Conditional loss	5	0	
Expected loss (conditional loss × probability)	5	0	5

If we stock the first lobster and there is demand for it, the conditional loss will be zero. However, if we stock the first lobster and there is no demand for it, the conditional loss will be $2, as we discussed earlier. The expected loss for stocking the first lobster will be

$$EL(Q=1) = (1.0 \times \$0) + (0 \times \$2) = \$0$$

However, if we do not stock the first lobster but there is demand, the conditional loss will be $5, the lost profit due to understocking. If we do not stock the first lobster and there is no demand, the conditional loss will, of course, be 0. The expected loss of not stocking the first lobster, therefore, will be

$$EL(Q=0) = (1.0 \times \$5) + (0 \times \$0) = \$5$$

Since the expected loss of not stocking the first lobster ($5) is greater than that of stocking it ($0), we should stock the first lobster in order to avoid the loss.

Stocking Decision for the Second Unit

We can analyze the inventory decision concerning the second lobster in the same manner, as shown in Table 9.14. When we compare Tables 9.13 and 9.14, it should be apparent that the conditional losses remain the same for each incremental analysis. For example, if we stock the second lobster and there is demand for it, the conditional loss will be 0. But if we stock the second lobster and there is no demand, the loss will be $2 due to overstocking. Now, if we do not stock the second lobster but there is demand for it, the conditional loss will be $5 due to understocking. However, if we do not stock the second lobster and there is no demand for it, there will be no loss.

The only differences we find between Tables 9.13 and 9.14 are the probabilities of demand and of no demand for the second lobster. As long as there is demand for two or more lobsters, the second lobster will be sold. Therefore, the probability of demand for the second lobster will be 0.95. The only case in which there will be no demand for the second lobster is when only one lobster is demanded. Consequently, the probability of no demand for the second lobster will be 0.05. The expected loss of stocking the second lobster ($0.10) is still less than that of not stocking the second lobster ($4.75). Thus, we will stock the second lobster.

Table 9.14   Incremental Analysis for the Second Lobster (dollars)

Course of Action	Demand and Associated Probabilities		Total
	$D \geq 2$ (0.95)	$D < 2$ (0.05)	
Stock second lobster			
Conditional loss	0.00	2.00	
Expected loss (conditional loss × probability)	0.00	0.10	0.10
Don't stock second lobster			
Conditional loss	5.00	0.00	
Expected loss (conditional loss × probability)	4.75	0.00	4.75

Stocking Decision for the *i*th Unit

As we progress with the incremental analysis, the expected loss of stocking a certain lobster will gradually increase as the probability of demand for a greater number of lobsters decreases. Consequently, the expected loss of not stocking a certain lobster will gradually decrease as the probability of no demand for the lobster increases. Then, the optimum stock level will be found at the point where the expected loss of stocking that lobster is still less than the expected loss of not stocking that unit but where stocking one more unit will result in a greater loss. If the expected loss of stocking a certain lobster is exactly equal to that of not stocking it, we should be indifferent. In other words, we can either stock or not stock that particular lobster.

We can analyze the problem by formulating a stock decision for the generalized case (i.e., stocking the *i*th lobster), as shown in Table 9.15. The probability (p) that there will be demand for the *i*th lobster is the same as the probability that demand will be equal to or greater than i lobsters. Accordingly, there will be no demand for the *i*th lobster if demand is less than i lobsters. Of course, the sum of the two probabilities is 1.

If we stock the *i*th lobster and there is demand for it, the conditional loss will be 0. But if we stock the *i*th lobster and there is no demand, the loss will be due to overstocking (L_o). The expected loss of stocking the *i*th lobster will be

$$EL(Q > i) = L_o \cdot p(D < i)$$

If we do not stock the *i*th lobster but there is demand for it, the conditional loss will be due to understocking (L_u). However, if we do not stock the *i*th lobster and there is no demand for it, there will be no loss. The expected loss of not stocking the *i*th lobster can be computed as

$$EL(Q < i) = L_u \cdot p(D \geq i)$$

The condition required for us to stock the *i*th lobster is that the expected loss of stocking it should be less than or equal to that of not stocking it. In other words, we can express the relationship as

$$L_o \cdot (D < i) \leq L_u \cdot (D \geq i)$$

Table 9.15 *Incremental Analysis for Stocking *i*th Lobster* (dollars)

| | Demand (D) Probability (P) | | |
Course of Action	$D \geq i$ $p(D \geq i)$	$D < i$ $p(D < i)$	Total
Stock *i*th lobster			
Conditional Loss	0	L_o	
Expected Loss	0	$L_o \cdot p(D < i)$	$L_o \cdot p(D < i)$
Don't stock *i*th lobster			
Conditional Loss	L_u	0	
Expected Loss	$L_u \cdot p(D \geq i)$	0	$L_u \cdot p(D \geq i)$

We can rearrange the above relationship. The sum of the probabilities of the two possible events equals 1: $p(D < i) + p(D \geq i) = 1$. Since $p(D \geq i) = 1 - p(D < i)$, we can write

$$L_o \cdot p(D < i) \leq L_u \cdot p(D \geq i)$$
$$L_o \cdot p(D < i) \leq L_u \cdot [1 - p(D < i)]$$
$$L_o \cdot p(D < i) \leq L_u - L_u \cdot p(D < i)$$

Adding $L_u \cdot p(D < i)$ to both sides, we have

$$L_o \cdot p(D < i) + L_u \cdot p(D < i) \leq L_u - L_u \cdot p(D < i) + L_u \cdot p(D < i)$$
$$L_o \cdot p(D < i) + L_u \cdot p(D < i) \leq L_u$$

Factoring out $p(D < i)$, we obtain

$$p(D < i) (L_o + L_u) \leq L_u$$

Dividing both sides by $(L_o + L_u)$, we derive

$$\frac{p(D < i) (L_o + L_u)}{(L_o + L_u)} \leq \frac{L_u}{(L_o + L_u)}$$
$$p(D < i) \leq \frac{L_u}{L_o + L_u}$$

The above relationship simply indicates that in order to stock the ith lobster, the cumulative probability of demand being less than i lobsters should be less than or equal to the ratio of loss due to understocking (L_u) over the sum of losses due to overstocking and understocking ($L_o + L_u$). The probability $p(D < i)$ is simply a cumulative probability function, as shown in Table 9.16. For example, the probability that demand is less than 1 lobster will be 0 because demand is always at least 1 lobster. The probability

Table 9.16   Cumulative Probability p(D < i)

Demand (i)	Probability	Cumulative Probability p(D < i)
1	0.05	0.00
2	0.10	0.05
3	0.25	0.15
4	0.30	0.40
5	0.20	0.70
6	0.05	0.90
7	0.05	0.95

that demand is less than 2 lobsters is the same as the probability that demand is for only 1 lobster, that is, 0.05. The probability that demand is less then 3 lobsters is the same as the probability that demand is 1 or 2 lobsters. There is 0.05 probability that demand will be 1 lobster and 0.10 probability that demand will be 2 lobsters. Therefore, the sum of these two probabilities gives the cumulative probability 0.15 that demand is less than 3 lobsters.

In our New England Fish Market example, the loss due to overstocking, L_o, is $2, and the loss due to understocking, L_u, is $5. Therefore, we can compute:

$$p(D < i) \leq \frac{L_u}{L_o + L_u}$$

$$p(D < i) \leq \frac{5}{2 + 5}$$

$$p(D < i) \leq 0.7143$$

In other words, Mr. Brown should continue to stock lobsters as long as the cumulative probability $p(D < i)$ is less than or equal to 0.7143. Referring to Table 9.16, we find that the optimum stock level should be 5 lobsters, as shown by the red-number row. This answer corresponds to the one we derived when we used the expected profit and expected loss as decision criteria.

Now then, to solve the simple inventory problem under risk, the only things we must know in order to determine the optimum stock level are: loss due to understocking (L_u), loss due to overstocking (L_o), and the cumulative probability function $p(D < i)$. By using the incremental analysis, we can avoid the cumbersome calculative work required by the expected profit and expected loss approaches.

Analysis of Salvage Value

In the New England Fish Market problem, we assumed that any lobsters left over at the end of a week are sold to a restaurant for $3 per lobster. The $3 we receive from a restaurant is nothing but a **salvage value.** If leftover lobsters are thrown out at a total loss of $5 (cost) per lobster, then there would be no salvage value. Thus, we can reformulate the net loss due to overstocking as follows:

$$\text{Loss due to overstocking} = \text{preliminary loss due to overstocking} - \text{salvage value}$$

$$L_o = PL_o - S$$

If the salvage value of the leftover lobster is only $1, rather than $3 as assumed previously, the optimum stock quantity will be

$$p(D < i) \leq \frac{L_u}{L_o + L_u}$$

$$p(D < i) \leq \frac{L_u}{(PL_o - S) + L_u}$$

Since $L_u = \$5$, $PL_o = \$5$, and $S = \$1$,

$$p(D < i) \leq \frac{5}{(5 - 1) + 5}$$

$$p(D < i) \leq 0.5556$$

Referring to the cumulative probability distribution as shown below, we can easily determine the optimum stock level of 4 lobsters.

*i*th Lobster	$p(D < i)$
1	0.00
2	0.05
3	0.15
4	0.40
5	0.70
6	0.90
7	0.95

Since loss due to overstocking is $2 greater than the previous figure ($4 vs. $2), the optimum stock level has been decreased by one lobster.

Now we can determine what kind of salvage value is required to justify stocking a certain number of lobsters. For example, we can determine the range of salvage value required to stock 5 lobsters. From the incremental analysis we know that in order to stock 5 lobsters, $L_u \div (L_o + L_u)$ should be between 0.7 and 0.9, as shown above in the cumulative probability $p(D < i)$.

The minimum salvage value required for stocking 5 lobsters can be determined by equating the $L_u \div (L_o + L_u)$ ratio to 0.7:

$$\frac{L_u}{L_o + L_u} = 0.7$$

$$\frac{L_u}{(PL_o - S) + L_u} = 0.7$$

$$\frac{5}{(5 - S) + 5} = 0.7$$

$$\frac{5}{10 - S} = 0.7$$

Multiplying both sides by $(10 - S)$, we obtain

$$5 = 0.7(10 - S)$$
$$5 = 7 - 0.7S$$
$$0.7S = 2$$
$$S = \$2.86$$

Similarly, the maximum salvage value required to justify stocking 5 lobsters can be computed as follows:

$$\frac{L_u}{(PL_o - S) + L_u} = 0.9$$

$$\frac{5}{(5 - S) + 5} = 0.9$$

$$\frac{5}{10 - S} = 0.9$$

$$5 = 0.9(10 - S)$$

$$0.9S = 4$$

$$S = \$4.44$$

To justify stocking 5 lobsters, then, the salvage value must be between \$2.86 and \$4.44. In order to stock a large number of lobsters in relation to the demand distribution, the salvage value must be relatively high. If the salvage value is higher than \$4.44, which is almost as much as the cost of purchasing a lobster, we can stock 6 lobsters.

Analysis of Goodwill Cost

In the analysis thus far, we have assumed that the loss due to understocking is simply the amount of lost profit. In reality, however, such an assumption is rarely justified. Often, the unsatisfied or unserved customer may cause considerable amount of **goodwill cost** to the firm by simply not returning to the store or by broadcasting his or her bad experience to other current or potential customers. For example, suppose that there is a customer who purchases an average of \$50 worth of seafood per month from the New England Fish Market. Let us assume that her demand for lobsters was not satisfied because of understocking. Hence, she decided not to come back to the market for a whole month. The lost sales amount to \$50, and the lost profit to the market may be as much as \$20.

It is extremely difficult to measure the actual goodwill cost. Nevertheless, in reality goodwill cost exists. Goodwill cost affects only the loss due to understocking because it occurs only when there is unsatisfied demand. Then, the total loss due to understocking L_u should include the preliminary loss due to understocking without the consideration of goodwill cost and goodwill cost per lobster:

Loss due to understocking = preliminary loss due to understocking
+ goodwill cost G

$$L_u = PL_u + G$$

Now, let us suppose that the demand for lobsters and the probability distribution remain the same as presented earlier. Also, the following parameters are given:

$$PL_u = \$5$$

$$G = \$2$$

$$PL_o = \$5$$

$$S = \$3$$

Then, by employing the incremental analysis, we obtain

$$p(D < i) \leq \frac{L_u}{L_o + L_u}$$

$$p(D < i) \leq \frac{(PL_u + G)}{(PL_o - S) + (PL_u + G)}$$

$$p(D < i) \leq \frac{5 + 2}{(5 - 3) + (5 + 2)}$$

$$p(D < i) \leq \frac{7}{2 + 7}$$

$$p(D < i) \leq 0.7778$$

Referring to the cumulative probability distribution $p(D < i)$ in Table 9.16, we can easily determine that the optimum stock level is 5 lobsters.

By utilizing the approach shown in the salvage value section, we can also determine the range of goodwill cost that will justify stocking a certain number of lobsters. For example, by using the above information, let us determine the goodwill cost range required for stocking 6 lobsters. In order to stock 6 lobsters, the ratio of $(PL_u + G) \div [(PL_o - S) + (PL_u + G)]$ should be between 0.9 and 0.95, as we can observe in the $p(D < i)$ table.

First, we can equate the ratio to 0.9 to determine the lower limit of the goodwill cost:

$$\frac{PL_u + G}{(PL_o - S) + (PL_u + G)} = 0.9$$

Since $PL_u = \$5$, $PL_o = \$5$, and $S = \$3$,

$$\frac{5 + G}{7 + G} = 0.9$$

$$5 + G = 0.9(7 + G)$$

$$5 + G = 6.30 + 0.9G$$

$$0.1G = 1.30$$

$$G = \$13.00$$

In order to find the upper limit of the range, we can equate the ratio to 0.95:

$$\frac{5 + G}{(5 - 3) + (5 + G)} = 0.95$$

$$\frac{5 + G}{7 + G} = 0.95$$

$$5 + G = 0.95(7 + G)$$

$$0.05G = 1.65$$

$$G = \$33.00$$

The above calculations indicate that the goodwill cost per understocked lobster should have a range between $13.00 to $33.00 in order for Mr. Brown to stock 6 lobsters. The above analysis clearly points out that in order to stock a relatively large number of lobsters, the per-unit goodwill cost should be quite high. Even when the exact amount of goodwill cost is not known, the analysis of goodwill cost provides management with a cost range that often contributes to a better inventory decision.

Computer Solution of Decision Problems under Risk

Although expected value and expected loss are effective decision-making criteria, manual computation can be quite cumbersome. Decision problems under the condition of risk can be solved easily by using the computer. For example, we use *Micro Manager* to solve the Friendly Investment Club problem presented as Casette 9.1 and the New England Fish Market problem presented as Casette 9.3.

Figure 9.1 presents the input data and the program output for the Friendly Investment Club problem. The optimum solution for the problem is investment in alternative 1 (stocks) with the expected payoff of $475.

Figure 9.2 presents the input data of the conditional profit table for the New England Fish Market problem and the program output. The optimum solution for the problem is stocking 5 lobsters with an expected profit of $15.90.

Figure 9.1   Computer Solution of the Friendly Investment Club Problem

```
PROGRAM: Decision Making Under Risk

***** INPUT DATA ENTERED *****


        ---------------------------------

                        Events
                  ---------------------

                     1        2
Alternative     p = 0.30 p = 0.70
        ---------------------------------

            1        1000.00   250.00
            2         600.00   400.00
        ---------------------------------


*****    PROGRAM OUTPUT    *****


        ---------------------------------

      Alternative    Expected Value
        ---------------------------------

            1              475.00 *
            2              460.00
        ---------------------------------


      * indicates optimal solution
```

Figure 9.2   Computer Solution of the New England Fish Market Problem

```
PROGRAM: Decision Making Under Risk

***** INPUT DATA ENTERED *****
```

			Events				
	1	2	3	4	5	6	7
Alternative	p = 0.05	p = 0.10	p = 0.25	p = 0.30	p = 0.20	p = 0.05	p = 0.05
1	5.00	5.00	5.00	5.00	5.00	5.00	5.00
2	3.00	10.00	10.00	10.00	10.00	10.00	10.00
3	1.00	8.00	15.00	15.00	15.00	15.00	15.00
4	-1.00	6.00	13.00	20.00	20.00	20.00	20.00
5	-3.00	4.00	11.00	18.00	25.00	25.00	25.00
6	-5.00	2.00	9.00	16.00	23.00	30.00	30.00
7	-7.00	0.00	7.00	14.00	21.00	28.00	35.00

```
*****   PROGRAM OUTPUT   *****
```

Alternative	Expected Value
1	5.00
2	9.65
3	13.60
4	15.80
5	15.90 *
6	14.60
7	12.95

```
* indicates optimal solution
```

DECISION MAKING UNDER UNCERTAINTY

Decision making in an environment where the probabilities of certain events occurring are not known constitutes decision making under uncertainty. Decision making under uncertainty involves the following elements:

1. Alternative courses of action

2. Possible events (states of nature)

3. Conditional payoffs for the action/event combinations

4. Unknown probabilities of the events

Decision making under uncertainty is not a desirable or even a pleasant situation. Yet, this is the most prevalent decision environment we face in reality. We can recall many dramatic real-world experiences—the 1973 oil embargo, the Mount St. Helens eruption, and the Mexico earthquake of 1985, for example. We often face uncertainties when completely new situations occur, such as a group of new employees, a new production process, a new inventory control system, a new market, or a new product line. For decision making under uncertainty, we can use one of several decision-making criteria to generate more information for making the optimum decision. Let us consider the following casette as a means of studying several decision criteria under uncertainty.

Casette 9.4   ***SAKURA MOTORS CORPORATION (SMC) USA***

Sakura Motors Corporation is a Japanese automotive manufacturing company. The company recently signed a contract to build a new production plant in the state of Kentucky. The plant will be a completely modern production facility with industrial robots, an interchangeable production setup, repetitive manufacturing systems, and a total quality-control system.

The company estimates that the new plant will cost approximately $100 million and that it will provide 800 new jobs in the community. Although the management of SMC is excited about this new venture, it could not decide on the best product line for the plant. The company plans to manufacture only one product in the Kentucky plant.

SMC can produce one of three products: the Sakura 1200X motorcycle, the Sakura jet ski, or the Sakura all-terrain three-wheeler. The company management believes that the conditional payoff of each alternative product line will be based on the American people's perception of the political relationship between the United States and Japan. There are three possible events: a favorable, normal, or strained relationship between the two countries. The conditional payoff matrix for the problem is presented in Table 9.17.

If SMC produces the motorcycle, the conditional payoff will be $25 million if the political relationship is favorable, $18 million under a normal relationship, and −$12 million under a strained relationship. If SMC produces the jet ski, the conditional payoff will be $20 million, $16 million, and $2 million under each of the three respective relationships. However, if SMC produces the all-terrain three-wheeler, the conditional payoff is estimated to be $10 million regardless of the political situation between the two countries.

Table 9.17   Conditional Payoff Matrix for the Sakura Motors Problem

	Payoffs *(millions)*		
Product Line	**Favorable Relationship**	**Normal Relationship**	**Strained Relationship**
Motorcycle	$25	$18	$−12
Jet ski	20	16	2
Three-wheeler	10	10	10

Decision Making with Partial Probabilities

If there is available a certain partial probability about the future political relationship between the United States and Japan, we may be able to exercise our educated judgment in decision making. For example, let us suppose that the Brookings Institute predicts that the probability of a normal relationship during the next year is 0.4.

With the available partial probability, we can at least compute the indifference probabilities for the three alternative products. The payoff of $10 million for the three-wheeler is a certainty. Therefore, we can compute the probabilities required of the favorable relationship and the strained relationship for SMC to be indifferent between the motorcycle and the jet ski alternatives. If we denote p as the probability of the favorable relationship, then $0.6 - p$ will be the probability of the strained relationship. The sum of all three probabilities of events will be 1:

$$0.4 + p + (0.6 - p) = 1.0$$

In order for us to be indifferent between the motorcycle and the three-wheeler alternatives, the two expected values must be exactly equal. Thus,

Motorcycle:

$$\begin{aligned} EV &= 25p + 18(0.4) - 12(0.6 - p) \\ &= 25p + 7.2 - 7.2 + 12p \\ &= 37p \end{aligned}$$

Three-wheeler:

$$EV = 10$$
$$EV \text{ (motorcycle)} = EV \text{ (three-wheeler)}$$
$$37p = 10$$
$$p = 0.2703$$

If the probability of the favorable relationship is 0.2703, and thus the probability of the strained relationship is 0.3297 (i.e., $0.6 - 0.2703 = 0.3297$), we will be completely indifferent between the motorcycle and the three-wheeler alternatives. If the probability of the favorable condition is greater than 0.2703, we will, of course, prefer the motorcycle alternative.

Now we can proceed to compute the indifference probabilities between the jet ski and the three-wheeler alternatives in a similar manner:

Jet ski:

$$\begin{aligned} EV &= 20p + 16(0.4) + 2(0.6 - p) \\ &= 20p + 6.4 + 1.2 - 2p \\ &= 18p + 7.6 \end{aligned}$$

Three-wheeler:

$$EV = 10$$
$$EV \text{ (jet ski)} = EV \text{ (three-wheeler)}$$
$$18p + 7.6 = 10$$
$$p = 0.1333$$

We should be indifferent between the jet ski and the three-wheeler alternatives if the probability of the favorable relationship is 0.1333. Consequently, the required probability of the strained relationship is 0.4667.

We can also compute the indifference probabilities between the motorcycle and the jet ski alternatives as follows:

$$EV \text{ (motorcycle)} = 25p + 18(0.4) - 12(0.6 - p)$$
$$EV \text{ (jet ski)} = 20p + 16(0.4) + 2(0.6 - p)$$
$$EV \text{ (motorcycle)} = EV \text{ (jet ski)}$$
$$25p + 7.2 - 7.2 + 12p = 20p + 6.4 + 1.2 - 2p$$
$$37p = 18p + 7.6$$
$$p = 0.4$$

The required probabilities of the favorable relationship and the strained relationship are 0.4 and 0.2 respectively, in order for SMC to be indifferent between the motorcycle and the jet ski alternatives.

There is at least one certain payoff in this problem. It is the $10 million from the three-wheeler alternative. By analyzing the indifference probabilities, we can at least pinpoint the critical probabilities for the product line decision. In order to get the expected return of $10 million from the motorcycle, the favorable relationship must have a probability of 0.2703. On the other hand, we can derive the same $10 million expected payoff from the jet ski if the probability of the favorable relationship is only 0.1333. This implies that if the probability of the favorable relationship is relatively small, the choice will be between the jet ski and the three-wheeler. The indifference probability of the favorable relationship between the motorcycle and the jet ski is 0.4. Now we can construct the expected payoffs with the various probabilities of the favorable relationship, as shown in Figure 9.3 (page 364).

This illustration presents two critical probabilities. First, if the probability of the favorable relationship is 0.1333 or less, the most attractive product line is the three-wheeler. If the probability is greater than 0.1333 but less than 0.4, the best alternative is the jet ski. If the probability of the favorable relationship is greater than 0.4, the motorcycle will be the best product line.

The Equal Probabilities (Laplace) Criterion

The case of partial probabilities for the events is a rare situation. In most decision problems under uncertainty, even partial probabilities do not exist. In such situations, we may apply one of several decision-making criteria under uncertainty.

Since the probabilities of future states of nature are not known, one approach we can take is to assign equal probabilities to all possible events. This approach is often referred to as the *Laplace* criterion. In our SMC problem, we should assign the identical 1/3 probability to the favorable, normal, and strained relationships. Then, the expected payoff becomes an appropriate criterion to use for decision making. For our SMC problem (see Table 9.17), the expected payoffs for the three product line alternatives can be computed as follows:

$$EP \text{ (motorcycle)} = \tfrac{1}{3}(25) + \tfrac{1}{3}(18) + \tfrac{1}{3}(-12) = \$10,333,333$$
$$EP \text{ (jet ski)} = \tfrac{1}{3}(20) + \tfrac{1}{3}(16) + \tfrac{1}{3}(2) = \$12,666,667 \leftarrow \text{optimum}$$
$$EP \text{ (three-wheeler)} = \tfrac{1}{3}(10) + \tfrac{1}{3}(10) + \tfrac{1}{3}(10) = \$10,000,000$$

Based on the Laplace criterion, the jet ski alternative has the highest expected payoff amount of $12,666,667.

Figure 9.3   Expected Payoffs and the Probability of the Favorable Relationship

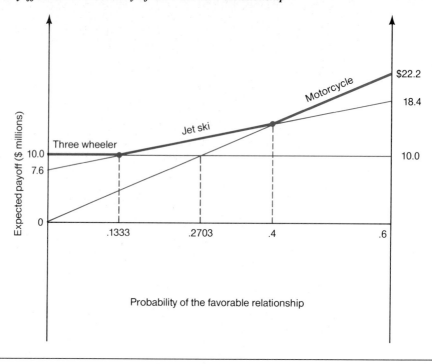

The Maximin (Wald) Criterion

The **maximin** criterion, also referred to as the *Wald* criterion (after Abraham Wald, who first suggested this criterion), is based on a completely pessimistic outlook (i.e., risk-avoiding behavior) for the future outcomes. Accordingly, we should expect the worst outcome (similar to *Murphy's law*—whatever can possibly go wrong will) for each of the alternatives. Therefore, the minimum conditional payoffs for the alternatives are compared and the alternative that yields the maximum among the minimum payoffs should be selected. In the SMC problem, the minimum payoffs are as follows:

Alternative	Minimum Payoff
Motorcycle	$ −12
Jet ski	2
Three-wheeler	10 ← optimum

Based on the above comparison, it is obvious that the optimum choice under the maximin criterion will be the three-wheeler. This alternative has the maximum-minimum payoff of $10 million. One major weakness of this criterion is that it utilizes only partial information (i.e., analysis of the minimum payoffs). Thus, this approach can be a totally unrealistic way to analyze a decision-making problem under uncertainty.

The Maximax Criterion

Since we have a very pessimistic outlook in the maximin criterion, we also ought to have a very optimistic outlook (i.e., risk-taking behavior). The **maximax** is precisely such a criterion. It is based on a very aggressive, optimistic, perhaps even a desperate outlook about the future outcomes. The maximax criterion suggests that we should select the alternative that has the maximum among the maximum payoffs. The maximum payoffs for the three alternatives are as follows:

Alternative	Maximum Payoff
Motorcycle	$25 ← optimum
Jet ski	20
Three-wheeler	10

The best alternative for SMC, according to the maximax criterion, is the motorcycle. This alternative has the highest maximum conditional payoff of $25 million. As is the case in the maximin criterion, this criterion does not utilize all the available information. This weakness makes the maximax criterion an unrealistic way to analyze a real-world problem.

The Dominance Criterion

A somewhat similar approach to the maximax criterion is the **dominance criterion.** This approach is useful for decision making under uncertainty to the extent that it can reduce the number of viable alternatives. However, it does not always yield a unique optimum alternative course of action as the other criteria do.

An alternative is said to be dominated when there is another alternative that yields a higher payoff (or a more favorable outcome) regardless of the state of nature that may occur. We then gradually eliminate all those alternatives that have been dominated by other alternatives. If there is only one alternative remaining after the elimination process, there will be an optimum course of action. But if the dominance test procedure yields a number of superior alternatives that cannot be eliminated any further, we must rely on another criterion in making the final choice.

For example, let us examine the following conditional payoff table:

Alternatives	Conditional Payoffs under Events		
	e_1	e_2	e_3
A*	$4,000	$3,000	$2,000
B	−6,000	2,000	1,500
C*	2,000	2,500	3,500
D	1,500	2,500	3,000
E*	2,000	4,000	2,500

Undominated alternatives.

When we compare alternatives A and B, A is clearly superior to B under every feasible event in terms of conditional payoffs. Thus, alternative B is dominated by A. When we compare alternatives C and D, we find that C dominates D. However, when we compare alternatives A, C, and E, none of these can be dominated. The undominated alternatives, indicated by the asterisks, must be analyzed by using another approach. In practice, the decision maker uses the dominance principle quite frequently, either consciously or unconsciously. Nevertheless, as we indicated earlier, this approach does not always yield the optimum course of action.

The Hurwicz Criterion

The *Hurwicz* criterion, suggested by Leonid Hurwicz, is somewhat of a compromise between the maximin and maximax criteria. The decision maker in reality is not completely pessimistic as the maximin criterion suggests. On the other hand, the decision maker is not completely optimistic as suggested by the maximax criterion. Rather, the decision maker usually has some degree of pessimism and some degree of optimism simultaneously.

Hurwicz suggested the **coefficient of optimism** (α) as a measure of the decision maker's degree of optimism. The coefficient of optimism ranges from 0 to 1, just like a probability distribution. If $\alpha = 0$, the decision maker's coefficient of optimism is completely 0; that is, he or she is totally pessimistic. However, if $\alpha = 1$, the decision maker is completely optimistic. Thus, the coefficient of pessimism is $1 - \alpha = 0$.

According to the Hurwicz criterion, the weighted payoff for each alternative is obtained in the following manner:

Weighted payoff $= \alpha$ (maximum payoff) $+ (1 - \alpha)$ (minimum payoff)

The best alternative is the one that has the maximum weighted payoff.

In the SMC problem, we can identify the following maximum and minimum payoffs for each alternative:

Alternative	Maximum Payoff	Minimum Payoff
Motorcycle	$25	$-12
Jet ski	20	2
Three-wheeler	10	10

Let us suppose that the decision maker's coefficient of optimism is $\alpha = 0.5$. Therefore, the coefficient of pessimism is $(1 - \alpha) = 0.5$. Now, we can compute the weighted payoffs *(WP)* as follows:

WP (motorcycle) $= 0.5(25) + 0.5(-12) = \$ 6.5$ million

WP (jet ski) $= 0.5(20) + 0.5(2)$ $= \$11.0$ million ← optimum

WP (three-wheeler) $= 0.5(10) + 0.5(10)$ $= \$10.0$ million

The jet ski alternative is the best choice as it has the highest weighted payoff of $11.0 million.

Figure 9.4   The Hurwicz Criterion Analysis

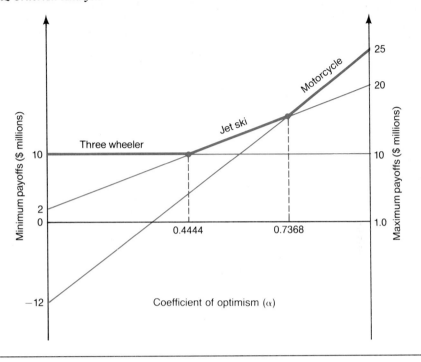

Let us suppose that the decision maker is completely optimistic ($\alpha = 1$). Then, he or she will select the motorcycle alternative because when $\alpha = 1$ the Hurwicz criterion is exactly the same as the maximax criterion:

WP (motorcycle) $= 1(25) + 0(-12) = \$25$ million $\leftarrow$ optimum

WP (jet ski) $= 1(20) + 0(2)   = \$20$ million

WP (three-wheeler) $= 1(10) + 0(10)   = \$10$ million

Conversely, if $\alpha = 0$, the approach becomes the maximin criterion. Thus, the weighted payoffs will be:

WP (motorcycle) $= 0(25) + 1(-12) = \$-12$ million

WP (jet ski) $= 0(20) + 1(2)   = \$\ \ \ 2$ million

WP (three-wheeler) $= 0(10) + 1(10)   = \$\ \ 10$ million $\leftarrow$ optimum

Thus, the optimum alternative will be the three-wheeler.

It is quite possible in reality that the decision maker cannot specify the exact α. In such a case, we can determine several critical α's and ask the decision maker whether his or her α is greater than these α's. Asking a series of questions, we can identify the best course of action.

Figure 9.4 presents the Hurwicz criterion analysis for the SMC problem. On the left side of the graph, where $\alpha = 0$, we plot the minimum payoffs, and on the right side of the graph, where $\alpha = 1$, we plot the maximum payoffs for the alternatives. Now, the minimum and maximum payoffs of each alternative are connected by a straight line.

Since there are only three straight lines, we can easily determine their intersecting points and solve for the coefficient of optimism α. For example, at the intersecting point of the three-wheeler and the jet ski lines, we will be perfectly indifferent between the two alternatives because their weighted payoffs are identical. If we express the payoff as y and the coefficient of optimism α as x, then we can derive the function of the three lines as follows:

$$\text{Motorcycle:} \quad y = -12 + 37x$$
$$\text{Jet ski:} \quad y = 2 + 18x$$
$$\text{Three-wheeler:} \quad y = 10$$

In order to find α at the intersecting point of the three-wheeler and the jet ski lines, we can equate the two expressions as follows:

$$2 + 18x = 10$$
$$18x = 8$$
$$x = 0.4444$$

We can do the same for the jet ski and the motorcycle alternatives:

$$2 + 18x = -12 + 37x$$
$$-19x = -14$$
$$x = 0.7368$$

In Figure 9.4 we can clearly see that our decision choice varies as follows:

Optimum Decision	Coefficient of Optimism
Three-wheeler	$\alpha \leq 0.4444$
Jet ski	$0.4444 \leq \alpha \leq 0.7368$
Motorcycle	$\alpha \geq 0.7368$

The Hurwicz criterion is a good compromise between the maximin and maximax criteria. This criterion also incorporates the decision maker's personal judgment about the future outcome in the form of the coefficient of optimism. However, although this criterion is conceptually attractive, it is not universally applicable to all decision problems under uncertainty. For example, if two decision alternatives have the identical miminum and maximum conditional payoffs, regardless of what kind of intermediate payoffs they have, under the Hurwicz criterion we would be indifferent between the two.

The Minimax (Regret) Criterion

The **minimax** criterion, which is also referred to as the *regret* criterion, is based on the concept of opportunity loss. The basic idea of this criterion, as proposed by L. J. Savage, is that the decision maker will experience an opportunity loss (or regret) when a

Table 9.18   *Opportunity Loss for the SMC Problem*

	Opportunity Loss *(millions)*		
Product Line	**Favorable Relationship**	**Normal Relationship**	**Strained Relationship**
Motorcycle	$0	$0	$22
Jet ski	5	2	8
Three-wheeler	15	8	0

state of nature occurs and the chosen alternative results in a payoff that is less than the maximum possible payoff for that state of nature.

The amount of opportunity loss or regret is the difference between the maximum conditional payoff and other payoffs under a given state of nature. Once the opportunity loss table is developed, we attempt to be conservative by utilizing the minimax principle — minimize the maximum opportunity loss.

In the SMC problem (see Table 9.17), we can construct the opportunity loss table as shown in Table 9.18. If we select the three-wheeler and the favorable relationship occurs, the payoff will be $10 million. However, had we selected the motorcycle alternative, the payoff would have been the maximum payoff of $25 million. Thus, the difference of $15 million represents the decision maker's opportunity loss for selecting the three-wheeler. If the jet ski alternative is chosen, the amount of opportunity loss will be $5 million. Since the motorcycle alternative has the maximum conditional payoff (i.e., $25 million), the opportunity loss for this alternative will be 0.

In Table 9.18 the maximum opportunity loss for each alternative is identified. Since we attempt to minimize the maximum opportunity loss, the jet ski alternative will be our choice, as shown below.

Alternative	**Maximum Regret**
Motorcycle	$22
Jet ski	8 ← optimum
Three-wheeler	15

Summary of Decision-Making Criteria

In this section we have discussed several of the best-known decision-making criteria under the condition of uncertainty. Since the uncertainty condition represents the most prevalent decision environment, an understanding of the various decision-making criteria is important. As we have seen, each criterion emphasizes a certain principle or assumption. Thus, the decision maker has to determine which criterion is most appropriate for the problem under consideration. We can summarize the principle or assumption for each criterion as follows:

Decision Criterion	Principal Assumption
Laplace	Equal probabilities among the states of nature—maximize the expected value
Maximin	Pessimistic view—maximize the minimum conditional payoff
Maximax	Optimistic view—maximize the maximum conditional payoff
Hurwicz	The coefficients of optimism and pessimism—maximize the weighted payoff
Minimax	Conservative view—minimize the maximum opportunity loss

For the casette problem of Sakura Motors Corporation, the optimum decision alternatives selected on the basis of different decision criteria can be summarized as follows:

Decision Criterion	Optimum Alternative
Laplace	Jet ski
Maximin	Three-wheeler
Maximax	Motorcycle
Hurwicz ($\alpha = 0.5$)	Jet ski
Minimax	Jet ski

Computer Solution of Decision Problems under Uncertainty

We have discussed five decision-making criteria under the condition of uncertainty: Laplace, maximin, maximax, Hurwicz, and minimax. If we use a computer program, we need to input the data only once to find the optimum solutions according to each of the five different criteria. We can also see how different alternatives are selected as optimum choices under various decision-making criteria.

Let's apply *Micro Manager* to the Sakura Motors problem discussed as Casette 9.4. Figure 9.5 presents the input data for the problem and the computer solution by using each of the five decision-making criteria. Note that under the Hurwicz criterion, we arbitrarily used $\alpha = 0.50$. The summary of optimum alternatives selected by different decision-making criteria is presented at the end of the computer output.

Subjective Probabilities

Another important concept about decision making under uncertainty is *subjective probability*. The traditional probability theory is based on the mathematical foundation of the *law of large numbers*. This traditional concept is often referred to as *mathematical* or *objective probability*. Subjective probability, in contrast, is based on one's degree of belief concerning the possible outcomes of a decision. Thus, it is possible that one's subjective probability may be quite different from the objective probability, if it is known. This certainly makes sense to us, as different decision makers usually do not have the same expectations concerning future outcomes. We have discussed several casettes in which we used subjective probabilities.

Many experiments and much empirical research clearly suggest that decision making under uncertainty is influenced by the decision maker's personal belief about the

Figure 9.5   *Computer Solution of the Sakura Motors Problem*

PROGRAM: Decision Making Under Uncertainty

***** INPUT DATA ENTERED *****

		Events	
Alternative	1	2	3
1	25.00	18.00	-12.00
2	20.00	16.00	2.00
3	10.00	10.00	10.00

Coefficient of optimism: .5

***** PROGRAM OUTPUT *****

Laplace

Alternatives	Expected Value
1	10.33
2	12.67*
3	10.00

Maximin

Alternatives	Maximin Payoff
1	-12.00
2	2.00
3	10.00*

Maximax

Alternatives	Maximax Payoff
1	25.00*
2	20.00
3	10.00

Hurwicz

Alternatives	Hurwicz Payoff
1	6.50
2	11.00*
3	10.00

Minimax

Alternatives	Maximum Regret
1	22.00
2	8.00*
3	15.00

* indicates the best solution.

Decision Criterion	Optimum Alternative
Laplace	2
Maximin	3
Maximax	1
Hurwicz (alpha = .5)	2
Minimax	2

likelihood of future outcomes. These studies support and reinforce the concept of subjective probability. The individual decision maker appears to be capable of assessing the value and probability of certain outcomes in the unique decision environment. Accepting this proposition, we believe the study of subjective probability will provide new insights about decision making in real-world situations.

Bayes' Decision Rule

Another important area of study related to subjective probability is Bayes' decision rule, or **Bayes' theorem.** This decision rule was pioneered by Reverend Thomas Bayes, an eighteenth-century English Presbyterian minister and mathematician. Bayes' decision rule is an orderly and consistent procedure of revising the probabilities of events (states of nature) based on additional information, experiments, or personal judgment. The basic principle of this rule is that the accuracy of event probabilities often can be improved by the utilization of additional information. The existing current probabilities are referred to as *prior probabilities,* whereas the revised or altered probabilities are referred to as *posterior probabilities.*

Let us discuss Bayes' decision rule by considering the following casette.

Casette 9.5   *CENTENNIAL PRECISION WORKS INC.*

Centennial Precision Works Inc. is a manufacturer of precision chemical instruments. The company is very concerned about defective parts produced by its new plant in Kansas City. The quality control department has determined that the defective parts produced by the Kansas City plant were due to either human or mechanical error. The breakdown of the causes of the defective parts is as follows: human error, 60 percent; mechanical error, 40 percent.

The quality control chart indicates that 80 percent of the defective parts caused by mechanical problems have been detected at the inspection station. On the other hand, only 50 percent of the defective parts caused by human errors have been detected. In order to reduce the chance that any defective part would pass the inspection station without being detected, the quality control manager decided to take one sample part and inspect it. Thus, the manager asked a machine operator to produce a sample part, and it was found to be defective upon inspection. The manager would like to know the probability that this particular defective part was caused by a machine error.

The probabilities described in this problem can be defined as follows:

$p(DH)$ = probability of a defective part produced because of human error

$p(DM)$ = probability of a defective part produced because of machine error

$p(D|DH)$ = conditional probability that a defective part is detected by an inspector, given that the part was defective because of human error

$p(D|DM)$ = conditional probability that a defective part is detected by an inspector, given that the part was defective because of mechanical error

From the information given, we can determine the following:

$$p(DH) = 0.6 \qquad p(D|DH) = 0.5$$
$$p(DM) = 0.4 \qquad p(D|DM) = 0.8$$

The posterior probability we are interested in obtaining is the conditional probability that the defective part has been caused by a mechanical error, given that the sample part is detected as defective by an inspector. This conditional probability can be described

---

Table 9.19   *Posterior Probabilities of Defective Parts*

Cause	Prior Probability	Conditional Probability	Posterior Probability
Human error	$P(DH) = 0.6$	$P(D\|DH) = 0.5$	$P(DH\|D) = 0.484$
Mechanical error	$P(DM) = 0.4$	$P(D\|DM) = 0.8$	$P(DM\|D) = 0.516$
	1.0		1.000

---

as $p(DM|D)$. According to Bayes' decision rule, we can compute the posterior probability as follows:

$$p(DM|D) = \frac{p(D|DM)p(DM)}{p(D|DM)p(DM) + p(D|DH)p(DH)}$$

$$= \frac{(0.8)(0.4)}{(0.8)(0.4) + (0.5)(0.6)}$$

$$= 0.516$$

The only information the quality control manager had previously was that 40 percent of the defective parts were due to mechanical error. After a sample part was produced and found to be defective by an inspector, the manager now knows that there is a 0.516 probability that the part is defective because of mechanical error. Thus, the sampling provides additional information that allows the manager to revise the probability estimate as to whether the defective part is due to mechanical error. The improved, more accurate estimate will certainly enhance the manager's decision-making capability concerning ways to improve the quality control effort.

A defective part detected at the inspection station is caused either by mechanical error or by human error. Therefore, the probability of selecting a defective part that was caused by mechanical error and detected by an inspector $p(DM|D)$ and the probability of selecting a defective part that was caused by human error $p(DH|D)$ are mutually exclusive. Furthermore, the sum of the two probabilities will be 1. Thus, we can write

$$p(DM|D) + p(DH|D) = 1$$

Therefore,

$$p(DH|D) = 1.0 - p(DM|D) = 1.0 - 0.516 = 0.484$$

Now we can determine the posterior probabilities concerning defective parts detected at the inspection station, as shown in Table 9.19. Such a table will be very useful to the decision maker.

Computer Solution of Bayes' Decision Rule Problem

Figure 9.6 presents the application of *Micro Manager* to the Centennial Precision Works problem discussed as Casette 9.5. The program output indicates defective parts caused by human error (state 1) and mechanical error (state 2). The column-wise states indicate the detected defective parts (state 1) and undetected defective parts.

Figure 9.6   Computer Solution of the Centennial Precision Works Problem

```
PROGRAM: Bayes' Decision Rule

##### INPUT DATA ENTERED #####

    State     Prior Probability
    ----------------------------------
      1           0.600
      2           0.400
    ----------------------------------
    Total         1.000

              Conditional Probability of Prediction
    State        1         2
    ----------------------------------------
      1         0.500     0.500
      2         0.800     0.200
    ----------------------------------------

#####   PROGRAM OUTPUT   #####

              Posterior Probability of Prediction
    State        1         2
    ----------------------------------------
      1         0.484     0.789
      2         0.516     0.211
    ----------------------------------------
```

Utility Analysis

We discussed briefly the use of utilities for multiple criteria decision making in Chapter 6. Although utility theory has been studied extensively in economics and theoretical management science/operations research, it has been severely criticized by practicing managers and pragmatic management scientists for its lack of real-world relevance and applicability. However, theoretical properties of utility theory are very neat indeed.

The word *utility* means the power to satisfy one's desires. In general, the concept of utility refers to a measure of satisfaction from the consumption of a good. Thus, it is natural that an individual's utility of a certain good differs from that of others.

Utility analysis has been suggested for decision making under uncertainty. One important problem we face in applying the minimax criterion is that the amount of opportunity loss is expressed in absolute monetary units (i.e., dollars). Since the relative value of money decreases as the amount of money increases (the diminishing marginal

Table 9.20   An Alternative Decision Problem with Uncertainty

Alternative	State of Nature		
	e_1	e_2	e_3
a_1	$1,500,000	$500,000	$-250,000
a_2	1,000,000	500,000	250,000

Table 9.21   Opportunity Costs for the Problem in Table 9.20

Alternative	State of Nature		
	e_1	e_2	e_3
a_1	$0	$0	$500,000
a_2	500,000	0	0

utility of money), utility analysis can be applied to measure and express the opportunity loss in relative values through utility. In this way the opportunity loss can represent the real loss perceived by the decision maker.

Let us examine the decision problem described in Table 9.20. The opportunity cost table for this problem is developed in Table 9.21. According to the minimax criterion, we should be completely indifferent between alternatives a_1 and a_2, since their maximum opportunity losses are identical. Are we really indifferent between the two alternatives? We should say not! Is the difference of $500,000 between the conditional payoffs of a_1 and a_2 under e_1 worth exactly the same as the difference of $500,000 we see under e_3 between a_1 and a_2? Under e_1, alternative a_2 returns $1,000,000 and a_1 returns $1,500,000. Receiving $500,000 more on $1,000,000 would be very nice, of course. Under e_3, a_2 returns $250,000 and a_1 has a conditional payoff of $-250,000. The difference is still $500,000. However, this difference may mean a survival or a bankruptcy of the firm. Certainly, under e_3 we will prefer a_2 over a_1.

Let us suppose that a decision maker has the utility function of money shown in Figure 9.7. The utility of $500,000 between $-250,000 and $250,000 is expressed by U_1. The utility of $500,000 between $1,000,000 and $1,500,000 is expressed by U_2. It is obvious that U_1 is about six times greater than U_2. Based on the analysis of marginal opportunity cost, it is clear that a_2 is a superior alternative to a_1.

Although the marginal opportunity cost approach based on utility appears to be an ideal theoretical procedure for decision making under uncertainty, there is no satisfactory general methodology to develop the utility function for individuals in various situations. Furthermore, either people do not believe in a universal measure such as utility or they tend to be inconsistent in expressing their perceived value of certain criteria. Currently, utility-based analysis is not widely applied to decision making under uncertainty. However, when all other approaches or criteria are inappropriate for a certain problem, utility analysis can be another way to analyze the problem.

Figure 9.7 *Utility Function for Monetary Payoffs*

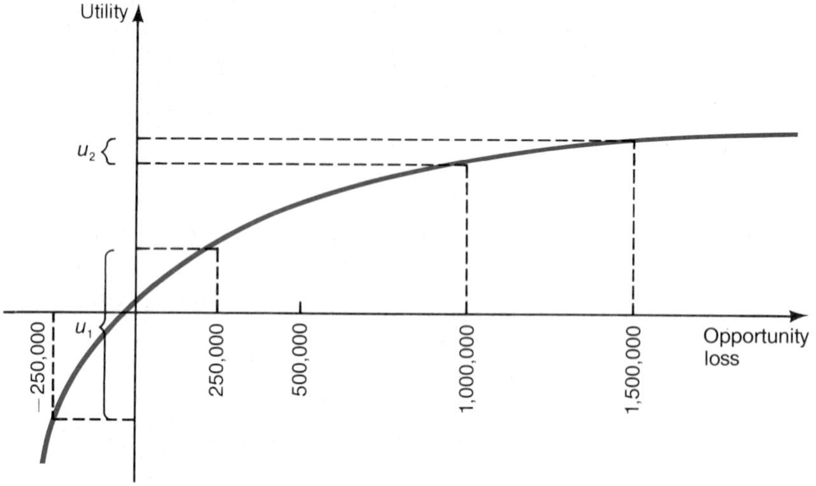

u_1 = Utility of $500,000 between −$250,000 and $250,000

u_2 = Utility of $500,000 between $1,000,000 and $1,500,000

Multiple Objectives

Decision problems under risk or uncertainty rarely involve only a single objective, such as maximizing profits or utilities, or minimizing total costs. As we discussed in Chapter 6, most decision problems involve multiple objectives. A firm may want to increase its market share, achieve a desired level of profit, develop its human resources, increase its service to the community, and develop new products or innovative management systems. Decision alternatives may yield varying measures of outcome for multiple objectives under different states of nature.

If we can somehow conveniently sum up the outcomes of a decision alternative for various multiple objectives in a cardinal measure (1, 2, 3, · · ·) such as utilities, then the problem involves single-objective decision making. However, as we have discussed previously, it is not always possible to convert heterogeneous objective measures into a common denominator.

For example, we are aware that providing job security to members of the organization is a superordinate goal in most Japanese firms. The Japanese never equate this supreme purpose of the organization with other functional objectives such as profit, market share, or operational efficiency. Furthermore, the process of converting everything into a convenient denominator like utilities often results in a fabrication or in a distortion of actualities in order to simplify the problem. In such problems, we believe that it would be a better idea to use probabilistic goal-programming methods. If you are interested in pursuing this advanced topic of goal programming, please check the References for Chapter 6.

Decision Trees

The decision making under risk and uncertainty that we have discussed thus far has been limited to cases involving a single time period as the planning horizon. Consequently, our approach has been to make a good decision at the begining of the planning horizon based on the estimated consequences at the end of a specific period of time. All the information required for decision making has been neatly presented in payoff tables for various alternative event combinations. However, many decision problems in the real world require a series of decisions ranging over several future time periods or several decision stages.

Since a decision made at a given time period may have an impact on future decisions, an analysis of the entire series of decisions is required to determine the optimum decision. A **decision tree** is a schematic presentation of a sequential or multiperiod decision-making process under risk and as such is a useful tool for evaluating sequential decision problems.

Decision trees provide a quick schematic presentation of the following sequential decision processes:

Decision points: Specific points of time when a decision must be made are shown as decision points. Alternative decisions become decision branches from a square ($\square$) decision point.

Event points: A number of states of nature that may occur are shown as event points. The possible events become event branches from a circle ($\bigcirc$) event point.

Probabilities: The known probabilities of events are presented above each of the event branches.

Conditional payoffs: The conditional payoff of each eventual branch is known and recorded at the end of each branch.

A typical decision tree is presented in Figure 9.8. A decision tree starts from the left side with one or more decision points. From the first decision point, all possible and feasible decision alternatives are branched out toward the right. At the end of each alternative branch, either an event point or another decision point is added as the problem requires. For each event branch stemming from an event point, the corresponding probability is recorded. The tree branching continues until all the sequential processes are completed and the conditional payoffs are recorded. Then, each decision branch is evaluated by computing its expected payoff (or expected value) criterion.

Figure 9.8   The Structure of a Decision Tree

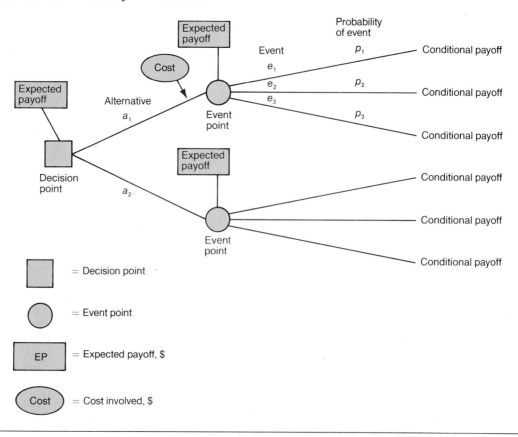

Casette 9.6   *MOSTLY NUTS OF GEORGIA, INC.*

William Joseph (Billy Joe) Bodenhammer operates the family-owned peanut farm and the nut factory Mostly Nuts of Georgia, Inc. Mostly Nuts, as the company is known nationwide, is a major producer of cocktail nuts, beer nuts for airlines, and peanut butter. The company is seriously considering a new product, a chocolate-covered candy bar with the label of Mostly Chocolate Nuts.

The developmental cost involved in introducing this new product is estimated to be $1 million. This cost includes marketing research, new equipment, new personnel, and training programs for the employees. The profit from Mostly Chocolate Nuts depends primarily on three things: (1) whether Galaxie Candy Company, the chief competitor of Mostly Nuts, would introduce a similar product; (2) the type of advertising campaign that Mostly Nuts launches; and (3) the type of advertising campaign that Galaxie uses to counter the promotional effort of Mostly Nuts.

If the company introduces Mostly Chocolate Nuts and Galaxie does not introduce a similar product, Mostly Nuts can launch a major advertising campaign and maximize profit. However, if Galaxie introduces a similar candy bar, the profit will depend on the advertising efforts of the firm and that of Galaxie. Mostly Nuts is considering three types of advertising campaigns based on the costs involved: a major campaign (with a cost of $0.5 million), a regular campaign (cost = $0.2 million), or a minor campaign (cost = $0.1 million).

Billy Joe has asked Barry Lorenzo, vice-president of marketing, to determine whether the new product should be introduced and if so which advertising campaign the company should adopt. Barry Lorenzo, after spending a considerable amount of time reviewing his old management science texts, constructed the decision tree shown in Figure 9.9 (page 380). The figure presents the sequence of decision points, event points, probabilities of events, and conditional profits involved in the problem.

At the first decision point, Mostly Nuts has two alternatives: the firm may introduce the product or it may not introduce the product. If Mostly Chocolate Nuts is not introduced, the conditional profit will of course be 0. If the company introduces Mostly Chocolate Nuts, Galaxie Candy Company has two alternatives as its reactions: (1) it may introduce a similar candy bar, or (2) it may not introduce a similar product. The probability of Galaxie introducing a similar candy bar is estimated to be 0.6 and thus the probability is 0.4 for not introducing the product.

At the second decision point, Mostly Nuts has three advertising strategies: a major campaign, a regular campaign, or a minor campaign. If Galaxie does not introduce a similar candy bar, the advertising effort of Mostly Nuts will not bring any reaction from Galaxie. However, if Galaxie introduces a similar candy bar, the advertising campaign selected by Mostly Nuts is expected to be challenged by one of the identical three types of advertising campaign of Galaxie's own.

For example, if Mostly Nuts launches a major advertising campaign, the probabilities of Galaxie's responses are: 0.5 for a major advertising campaign, 0.3 for a regular campaign, and 0.2 for a minor campaign. If Mostly Nuts' major campaign is answered by a major campaign from Galaxie, the conditional profit is estimated to be $1 million. The major-regular campaign combination results in $1.4 million, and the major-minor combination has a conditional profit of $2.5 million. These profit figures do not include the total development cost of $1 million. Other combinations of advertising campaigns, probabilities, and conditional profits are shown in Figure 9.9.

The best way to analyze the sequential decision problem of Mostly Nuts is to work from the end of each branch. Let us compare profit for each sequence of decisions. For example, the expected profit for the combination of Mostly Nuts to introduce the new product, Galaxie's introduction of a similar product, and the company's decision to launch a major ad campaign will be:

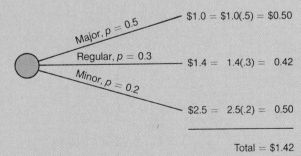

Major, $p = 0.5$ $1.0 = $1.0(.5) = 0.50

Regular, $p = 0.3$ $1.4 = 1.4(.3) = 0.42$

Minor, $p = 0.2$ $2.5 = 2.5(.2) = 0.50$

Total = $1.42

Figure 9.9 Initial Decision Tree of the Mostly Nuts Problem

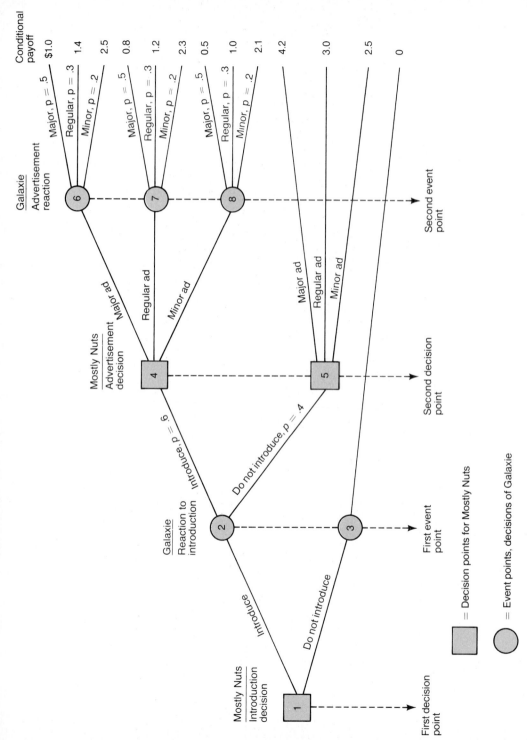

We can also compute the expected profits of events 7 and 8 as follows:

$$EP(7) = 0.8(0.5) + 1.2(0.3) + 2.3(0.2) = \$1.22 \text{ million}$$
$$EP(8) = 0.5(0.5) + 1.0(0.3) + 2.1(0.2) = \$0.97 \text{ million}$$

When Mostly Nuts initiates an advertising campaign, it incurs costs for preparing the ad and running the ad in the various media selected. Launching a major ad is estimated to cost \$0.5 million, a regular ad \$0.2 million, and a minor ad \$0.1 million. After subtracting these costs from the above computed expected profits, we obtain the following net expected profits:

$$\text{Major ad:} \quad 1.42 - 0.50 = \$0.92 \text{ million}$$
$$\text{Regular ad:} \quad 1.22 - 0.20 = \$1.02 \text{ million*}$$
$$\text{Minor ad:} \quad 0.97 - 0.10 = \$0.87 \text{ million}$$

Based on the above computation, it is obvious that if Galaxie introduces a similar product the best decision at the second decision point for Mostly Nuts is to launch a regular advertising campaign. This alternative yields a net expected payoff of \$1.02 million. This expected profit is recorded for decision point 4 in Figure 9.10 (page 382). The other two inferior strategies are eliminated, as indicated by the // signs.

If Galaxie does not introduce a similar product, the maximum conditional profit is \$4.2 million when Mostly Nuts adopts a major advertising strategy. Since a major ad campaign costs \$0.5 million, the net conditional profit for this strategy is \$3.7 million. We can compute the net conditional profits of the three advertising alternatives as follows:

$$\text{Major ad:} \quad 4.2 - 0.5 = \$3.70 \text{ million} \quad \leftarrow \text{optimum}$$
$$\text{Regular ad:} \quad 3.0 - 0.2 = \$2.80 \text{ million}$$
$$\text{Minor ad:} \quad 2.5 - 0.1 = \$2.40 \text{ million}$$

The optimum strategy is, of course, the major advertising campaign. Therefore, we can eliminate the other two strategies as shown by the double-slash signs.

Now the expected profit of the Mostly Nuts new product can be computed. It is the sum of the expected profit in the event that Galaxie introduces a similar product (\$1.02 million) multiplied by its probability (0.6) and the expected profit in the event that Galaxie does not introduce a similar product (\$3.70 million) multiplied by its probability (0.4). Thus, the expected profit for event 2 will be

$$\$1.02(0.6) + \$3.70(0.4) = \$2.092 \text{ million}$$

Developmental costs for the new product are estimated to be \$1 million. Thus, the net expected profit of the new product is \$1.092 million. Thus, Mostly Nuts of Georgia decided to introduce the new candy bar—Mostly Chocolate Nuts.

Figure 9.10 The Decision Tree and the Expected Profits

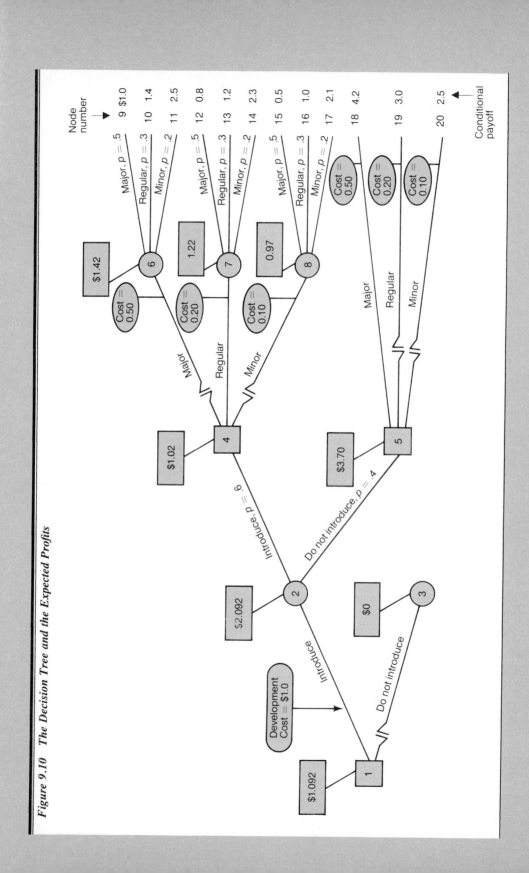

Computer Solution of Decision Tree Problems

Although decision tree analysis is effective for sequential decision making under risk, the actual solution process is quite tedious and time-consuming. This is especially true when the problem involves a large number of decision–event point sequences and many branches at each node. Obviously, these problems are best solved using easy-to-use computer programs.

Numerous computer programs are available for decision trees. Here we use *Micro Manager* to solve the Mostly Nuts of Georgia problem discussed as Casette 9.6. Figure 9.11 presents the input data and the program output. The decision tree has no set labeling procedure, but we recommend that you number the nodes commencing from the starting point and move to the next sequential point along the branch (usually from left to right and top to bottom). As long as your node-numbering system is consistent, the computer solution will be correct. (The numbering sequence used here matches Figure 9.10.) The optimum solution indicates that the expected payoff is $1.09 million along the branches 1-2, 4-7, and 5-18. Branch 1-2 indicates that at node 1 (the initial deci-

Figure 9.11   Computer Solution of the Mostly Nuts of Georgia Problem

PROGRAM: Decision Tree

INPUT DATA ENTERED

Branch	Nodes	Probability	Conditional Payoff
1	1 ---> 2	0.00	-1.00
2	1 ---> 3	0.00	0.00
3	2 ---> 4	0.60	0.00
4	2 ---> 5	0.40	0.00
5	4 ---> 6	0.00	-0.50
6	4 ---> 7	0.00	-0.20
7	4 ---> 8	0.00	-0.10
8	5 --->18	0.00	3.70
9	5 --->19	0.00	2.80
10	5 --->20	0.00	2.40
11	6 ---> 9	0.50	1.00
12	6 --->10	0.30	1.40
13	6 --->11	0.20	2.50
14	7 --->12	0.50	0.80
15	7 --->13	0.30	1.20
16	7 --->14	0.20	2.30
17	8 --->15	0.50	0.50
18	8 --->16	0.30	1.00
19	8 --->17	0.20	2.10

PROGRAM OUTPUT

Evaluated Decision Tree

Branch	Nodes	Probability	Conditional Payoff
1	1 ---> 2	Decision	1.09 *
2	1 ---> 3	Decision	0.00
3	2 ---> 4	0.60	0.61
4	2 ---> 5	0.40	1.48
5	4 ---> 6	Decision	0.92
6	4 ---> 7	Decision	1.02 *
7	4 ---> 8	Decision	0.87
8	5 --->18	Decision	3.70 *
9	5 --->19	Decision	2.80
10	5 --->20	Decision	2.40
11	6 ---> 9	0.50	0.50
12	6 --->10	0.30	0.42
13	6 --->11	0.20	0.50
14	7 --->12	0.50	0.40
15	7 --->13	0.30	0.36
16	7 --->14	0.20	0.46
17	8 --->15	0.50	0.25
18	8 --->16	0.30	0.30
19	8 --->17	0.20	0.42

* indicates preferred decision branches and payoffs

Expected payoff of the solution =   1.09

sion) we should introduce the new candy bar. If Galaxie introduces a competing product (placing us at node 4), we should mount a regular ad campaign; if Galaxie does not introduce a competing product (decision node 5), we should mount a major ad campaign.

REAL-WORLD APPLICATIONS

Decision analysis based on statistical methods, and especially on probability theories, is perhaps most popular in real-world situations. Many questionnaire surveys concerning the actual use of management science techniques, as we reviewed in Chapter 1, clearly indicate that statistical techniques are often the most widely applied tools for decision making. When we consider the use of simulation in conjunction with statistical analysis, decision theory approaches are indeed very important decision tools.

There are numerous real-world applications of decision theory techniques, from a simple newspaper delivery problem (deciding how many copies to order) to a complex investment portfolio problem. In this section we will examine two interesting real-world applications of decision theory.

Decision Analysis for Prescribing Fires in National Forests

Unpredicted and uncontrolled fires cause tremendous damage to our forests. An important tool in reducing fire hazards is the intentionally set or "prescribed" fire. The many uncertainties inherent in the use of fire pose considerable challenges in planning and executing successful burns. For example, fire behavior, weather conditions, vegetation characteristics, and pollution effects are variable as well as complex. Decision analysis techniques provide a suitable foundation for planning prescribed fires, because the key uncertainties must be clearly and individually described, with decisions made relative to each factor, in a logical fashion.[1]

After consideration of management objectives and potential alternatives, burn objectives must be set. These will help determine the fire behavior, in conjunction with the existing conditions. Logistics decisions would include crews, firing equipment, and water tankers. The actual decision sequence would involve the following decisions ($\square$) and events ($\bigcirc$) shown in the figure on page 385.

Three applications of the model were prepared, in California, Arizona, and Washington. The Tahoe National Forest (in California) burns hundreds of acres annually, both to prepare sites for fresh plantings and to reduce the hazard of wildfire. The management at Tahoe was interested primarily in making a selection of burning alone or burning with a previous cleanup using bulldozers. The model indicated that burning alone was the superior choice. In the Prescott National Forest (in Arizona), the situation included wildfire danger to 2,000 structures worth an average of $50,000 each. The decision analysis in this case attempted to minimize potential losses and recommended that a major burn program be instituted. The third case involved the Gifford Pinchot National Forest (in Washington), with potential burn areas surrounded by valuable standing timber. Here, the model indicated that once the burn decision had been made,

[1]David Cohan, Stephen Haas, David Radloff, and Richard Yancik, "Using Fire in Forest Management: Decision Making under Uncertainty," *Interfaces* 14:5 (1984), 8–19.

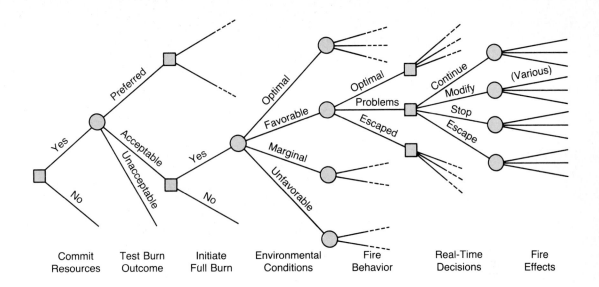

| Commit Resources | Test Burn Outcome | Initiate Full Burn | Environmental Conditions | Fire Behavior | Real-Time Decisions | Fire Effects |

marginal weather conditions should not cancel the fire. One of the key values for the model users in general is deemed to be the documentation and clear rationale underlying the decision.

Analysis of Airborne Radionuclide Health Risks from Coal-Fired Power Plants

Burning coal releases radionuclide particles which may cause cancer in humans. The particles travel with the wind, return to earth via precipitation, and enter a body through breathing or food. Regulations are constantly being proposed, and several decision models have been developed to analyze their effect. The Airborne Radionuclide Decision Analysis Tool (ARDT) is such a model, providing information in response to proposed regulations.[2] Results of operating the model include data concerning the quantity of radionuclides emitted by a specific power plant, the resulting radiation exposure, health effects, various uncertainties, and the effects of different assumptions.

ARDT is organized as a series of models, each dependent on results from the previous model. The source model determines radioactive emissions; it is followed by a dispersion model, population and exposure models, a health response model, and finally a value judgment model. The value model examines the proposed regulation's overall effect on health and costs, with risk attitudes and value trade-offs as input.

Probabilistic analyses can be performed for any input variable, with up to ten probability levels. Output can be obtained using the given distribution or by use of a decision tree. Many of the input variables have a large amount of uncertainty—such as wind speed and directionality. The program allows for a best- or worst-case result. The primary benefit of ARDT and similar programs is the potential for comparison of the results obtained using different regulation assumptions. In 1983, Environmental Protection Agency hearings on a 500-megawatt plant used radionuclide data and implications prepared (in part) with ARDT to determine that stricter standards were not warranted.

SUMMARY

Most real-world decision problems occur in an environment of risk or uncertainty. In this chapter we have studied many different approaches to decision making under risk and uncertainty. Utilizing these approaches improves the decision-making capability of the manager when faced with difficult problems under risk or uncertainty. The expected payoff or expected opportunity cost criterion based on probabilities is the dominant approach for decision making under risk. The same basic approach can be applied to simple inventory problems where the costs of overstocking and understocking are to be balanced.

When the probabilities of the states of nature are not known, decision making under the condition of uncertainty exists. Several interesting approaches and criteria have been suggested for decision making under uncertainty. Although utility theory has been developed and published extensively in the literature of management science, it is rarely used in real-world situations. In reality, decision making under uncertainty is often converted to decision making under risk by using expert opinions or subjective probabilities.

Decision trees are useful tools for analyzing sequential decision problems under the condition of risk. A decision tree contains decision points, event points, probabilities associated with the events, and conditional payoffs of alternatives. By employing the expected payoff criterion, we can gradually eliminate inferior branches and identify the optimum sequence of decisions.

Glossary

Bayes' Theorem   Existing (prior) probabilities are updated with additional information, experiments, or personal judgment through Bayes' decision rule to provide revised (posterior) probabilities, which can then be used to aid decision making.

Coefficient of Optimism   For implementation of the Hurwicz criterion, the decision maker must determine how optimistic he or she is, on a scale from 1 (totally optimistic) to 0 (totally pessimistic).

Conditional Payoff   When the decision situation reflects a change in profits or costs due to a change in conditions (such as demand or supply), conditional profits and losses may be calculated for each possible combination of factors.

Decision Table   When risk is involved in decision making, a table matching all possible decision choices with all possible events may be constructed.

Decision Tree   For multiperiod decision analysis, a decision tree presents sequential arrangements of events, showing alternatives and probabilities along each possible path.

Dominance   In decision situations under uncertainty, dominance tests may be used to eliminate any alternatives which are clearly inferior to (or dominated by) any other alternative under all possible events.

Expected Loss   In situations where a decision will be implemented repeatedly, expected loss is a valid criterion. It will yield the same result as expected payoff, by selecting the option which minimizes long-term opportunity loss.

Expected Payoff   The expected value of an alternative under risk. It directs the decision maker to select that option which maximizes long-term economic payoff, using expected value calculations.

Goodwill Cost   Understocking and thereby failing to meet demand may have undesired consequences, such as lost customers or related sales, known as goodwill cost.

Hurwicz Criterion   For decisions under uncertainty, the Hurwicz criterion utilizes the coefficient of optimism to weight each alternative's maximum and minimum payoffs to arrive at a single, comparable value.

Incremental Analysis   An alternative to decision tables, this form of decision evaluation compares the expected loss of each alternative sequentially. The optimum solution is found at the last point where the expected loss of one choice remains below the expected loss of the other choice.

Indifference Probabilities   The probabilities at which two alternatives result in equal expected values are the indifference probabilities; either choice will result in the same expected value.

Laplace Criterion   In decision situations under uncertainty, the Laplace criterion suggests that each event is assigned an equal probability, and selection is made by comparing expected values.

Loss from Overstocking or Understocking   Whenever demand does not equal supply, a loss occurs due to wasted excess supply or lost profit opportunities from insufficient supply.

Maximax   In decision making with unknown event probabilities, the maximax criterion suggests that the optimistic choice of the highest potential payoff alternative be made. This may involve considerable risk.

Maximin   In decision making with unknown event probabilities, the maximin or Wald criterion suggests that the safest choice is the one with the highest minimum payoff. The intention is to avoid risk.

Minimax   In decision making with unknown event probabilities, the minimax, or regret, criterion suggests that the alternative chosen should have the lowest maximum opportunity loss. This is perceived as a more conservative approach than maximin or maximax.

Perfect Information   The value of perfect information is the difference between the expected profits of the optimum decision made with and without the information.

Salvage Value   In an inventory problem, salvage represents value recoverable from an unsold unit.

Utility Analysis   A theoretical approach to decision making rather than a commonly used criterion, utility analysis employs marginal opportunity costs (like minimax) evaluated in light of perceived satisfaction based on a utility function to select between alternatives.

References

Holloway, C. A. *Decision Making under Uncertainty*. Englewood Cliffs, N.J.: Prentice-Hall, 1979.

Howard, R. A. "An Assessment of Decision Analysis." *Operations Research* 28:1 (1980), 4–27.

Lee, S. M., Moore, L. J., and Taylor, B. W. *Management Science*. 2d ed. Dubuque, Iowa: W. C. Brown, 1985.

Luce, R. D., and Raiffa, H. *Games and Decisions*. New York: Wiley, 1957.

Raiffa, H. *Decision Analysis*. Reading, Mass.: Addison-Wesley, 1968.

Schlaiffer, R. *Probability and Statistics for Business Decisions*. New York: McGraw-Hill, 1959.

Schlaiffer, R. *Analysis of Decisions under Uncertainty*. New York: McGraw-Hill, 1969.

White, D. J. *Decision Methodology*. London: Wiley, 1975.

Assignments

9.1 What are the four states of decision environment? Discuss which management science techniques could be useful for decision problems under each of these states.

9.2 What are the important decision components that are needed for decision making under the condition of risk?

9.3 The expected payoff and the expected loss criterion result in the same optimum solution. What is the reason for this?

9.4 In reality, no one really has perfect information. Then why should we even bother computing the value of perfect information?

9.5 Contrast the loss due to overstocking and the loss due to understocking. In addition to simple inventory problems, to what type of decision problems can we apply these cost concepts?

9.6 The salvage value and goodwill cost can be important components of an inventory problem. How do they fit into the process of determining the optimum stock quantity?

9.7 What are some of the sources where we can obtain partial probabilities of events for a certain investment problem under the condition of uncertainty?

9.8 What is the major difference between the dominance criterion and other decision-making criteria under uncertainty?

9.9 What is the major weakness of the Hurwicz criterion?

9.10 Utility analysis is a sophisticated theoretical approach to decision making. List a few of your personal decision problems that could be solved by utility analysis.

9.11 What is the difference between subjective probability and objective probability?

9.12 What are the important components of a decision tree? Explain each briefly.

9.13 Discuss a decision problem familiar to you that can be analyzed by using a decision tree.

9.14 When a decision problem under risk or uncertainty involves multiple objectives, what may be the solution approaches?

9.15 What is the major shortcoming of both the maximin and maximax criteria?

9.16 Given the following decision table, answer the questions below.

Alternative	State of Nature		
	e_1 $(p = 0.2)$	e_2 $(p = 0.3)$	e_3 $(p = 0.5)$
a_1	$3,000	$3,000	$3,000
a_2	2,800	3,600	3,600
a_3	2,600	3,400	4,200

a. Determine the expected payoff for each of the alternatives and select the optimum alternative.
b. Now construct the conditional loss table and determine the optimum alternative by the expected loss criterion.
c. What is the value of perfect information?

9.17 Given the following information, choose the best alternative by the expected value criterion.

Alternative	State of Nature	
	e_1 $(p = 0.5)$	e_2 $(p = 0.5)$
a_1	$200,000	− $40,000
a_2	0	0
a_3	400,000	− 360,000

9.18 Sugar Mountain Winter Sports Inc. has just opened up a new ski slope. There is great potential for a successful ski business in the area, since it can draw customers from all over the South. However, the key factor for success is snow. If the winter brings an average of 60 or more inches of snow, the season could be a financial success. If the snowfall is between 40 and 60 inches, the firm can operate artificial snowmakers and still manage a moderate financial gain. However, if the snowfall is less than 40 inches, as was the case during the past 3 years, the firm will be operating in the red. Recently, a large firm in Vermont has offered $500,000 to lease the ski slope from Sugar Mountain Sports. The president of Sugar Mountain is contemplating whether the firm should operate the ski slope or lease it for the coming winter. The conditional payoffs for operating the ski slope under the three snow conditions are as follows:

	Snow: 60″ or More	Snow: 40″–60″	Snow: Less than 40″
Operate ski slope	$1,500,000	$600,000	− $400,000

a. If the National Weather Bureau forecasts that there is an equal probability of 0.4 for snowfall of more than 60 inches and for snowfall of less than 40 inches, should the firm operate or lease the ski slope?

b. If the National Weather Bureau can predict only the probability of snowfall of less than 40 inches as 0.4, what kind of probability for snowfall of more than 60 inches should there be before the firm should decide to operate the ski slope?

9.19 Ernie's Fish Market sells fresh trout. Trout are bought in Denver at $1.00 per fish (including transportation costs) and sold for $1.50. Any trout left over at the end of the week is sold to a cat food plant for $0.20 per fish. According to past experience, the weekly demand for trout has been as follows:

Demand	Probability of Demand
15	0.10
16	0.20
17	0.40
18	0.20
19	0.10

a. Assuming that there is no goodwill cost involved for unmet demand, construct a payoff table for the various demand and stocking quantities.

b. Using the expected payoff criterion, determine the optimum quantity to stock per week.

c. Using the expected loss criterion, construct the conditional loss table and determine the optimum stock quantity.

d. Determine the value of perfect information.

9.20 The Cornhusker Market buys T-bone steak from the university's Animal Science Department. The purchase price is $2.50 per pound, and the market sells the steak for $4.00 per pound. Any steak left over at the end of the week is sold to a local cannery for $0.50 per pound. According to the sales records for the past 100 weeks, demand has been as follows:

Weekly Demand (lb.)	Number of Weeks
10	10
11	20
12	20
13	30
14	10
15	10
	100

a. Construct a payoff table for the various demand and stocking quantities.

b. If the market can obtain perfect information concerning the following week's demand for T-bone steak, what will be the expected profit?

c. Determine the optimum stock quantity.

9.21 The Airport Newsstand buys *House Decoration* magazine for $2.00 a copy and sells it for $3.00. Any copies remaining unsold are put on sale for $0.40 a copy in the following month. According to the requests for *House Decoration* over the past 100 months, the demand distribution has been as follows:

Number Requested	Relative Frequency
10	0.05
11	0.15
12	0.20
13	0.30
14	0.15
15	0.10
16	0.05

a. What is the loss due to overstocking?
b. What is the loss due to understocking?
c. Construct a conditional loss table and identify the optimum quantity to stock.
d. What is the value of perfect information about demand for the magazine?

9.22 Given the following payoff table, determine the best alternative based on the criteria listed below.

Alternative	State of Nature		
	e_1	e_2	e_3
a_1	$3,250	$5,000	$-2,000
a_2	3,000	4,000	500
a_3	2,500	2,500	2,500

a. Laplace
b. Maximin
c. Maximax
d. Hurwicz ($\alpha = 0.4$)
e. Minimax

9.23 The Trust Department of the First Wild West Bank is contemplating three investment alternatives for a $10 million trust fund recently acquired. The investment alternatives are stocks, bonds, and real estate. The estimated returns of each of the alternatives under three possible economic conditions are as follows:

Investment Alternative	State of Nature		
	e_1	e_2	e_3
Stocks	$1,200,000	$600,000	$-400,000
Bonds	900,000	500,000	200,000
Real estate	1,800,000	800,000	800,000

a. If the Federal Reserve Bank predicts the probability of e_1 as 0.3, in which alternative should the bank invest the money? Explain your reasoning.

b. Construct a payoff graph based on the Hurwicz criterion. Determine all critical α's and identify the optimum alternative for the various α's.

c. Determine the best alternative under each of the following criteria:

  (1) Laplace
  (2) Maximin
  (3) Maximax
  (4) Minimax

9.24 A newsstand operator buys the Sunday edition of the *Washington Post* for $1.00 per copy and sells it for $1.50. The distribution of demand for the Sunday edition over the last 100 weeks has been as follows:

Number Demanded	Relative Frequency
less than 40	0.00
40	0.02
41	0.04
42	0.07
43	0.10
44	0.12
45	0.13
46	0.14
47	0.12
48	0.10
49	0.08
50	0.05
51	0.02
52	0.01
over 52	0.00

a. Assuming that any newspaper left over has no value and that running short has no effect on any customer's tendency to return, determine the losses due to under-stocking and overstocking.

b. Based on the information from item a, determine how many copies should be stocked. Use incremental analysis.

c. If any newspaper left over can be sold to a fish market for $0.10 per copy, how many copies should be stocked?

d. What is the smallest salvage value of each of the leftover newspapers that will justify the operator's actual stocking of 50 copies?

e. Given the salvage value of $0.10 per copy, what is the range of goodwill cost that will justify stocking 50 copies?

9.25 The General Hospital is widely recognized for its pioneering surgical procedures for heart patients. The chief surgeon, Dr. Marc Crosby, is extremely concerned about the availability of rare type blood, AB negative, for open-heart surgery. In order to analyze the problem, Dr. Crosby compiled the use of the AB negative blood during the past 100 days, as shown below:

Use of AB Negative Blood (pints)	Number of Days
30	5
31	10
32	10
33	15
34	20
35	15
36	10
37	5
38	5
39	5
40+	0

The hospital purchases AB negative blood from the regional Red Cross for $100 per pint and charges the patient $300. Since only very fresh blood is used for open-heart surgery, the hospital purchases only the freshest blood (1-day old from the donation). The hospital keeps it for a maximum of 1 week, and any leftover blood is sold to other hospitals for $25 per pint.

In view of General Hospital's usage of the AB negative blood, Dr. Crosby is attempting to determine the weekly stocking policy of the blood.

a. If General Hospital is attempting to maximize the expected profit, how many pints should it stock?

b. If General Hospital runs out of blood, it can call the nearby metropolitan area Red Cross and have it delivered by helicopter in 25 minutes. However, the average cost of blood by this emergency means is $400 per pint. How many pints of blood should General Hospital stock per week?

9.26 A merchant at the farmers' market sells avocados. He purchases avocados from a dealer in California at $4 per case of 20 and sells them at $8 per case in the first week they are stocked (he sells only by the case). If there are any cases left over after the first week, he reduces the selling price to $2 per case in the following week. Any avocados that have not been sold by the end of the second week are scrapped at a total loss. The merchant, according to his previous experience, assigns the following probability distributions for the demand for fresh avocados and for week-old avocados:

Fresh Avocados		Week-old Avocados	
Demand	Probability	Demand	Probability
0	0.0	0	0.15
1	0.3	1	0.25
2	0.4	2	0.30
3	0.3	3	0.20
4+	0.0	4	0.10
	1.0		1.00

According to the merchant's experience, the demand for fresh avocados is not related to the demand for week-old avocados.

a. Construct a conditional payoff table for various stock levels.

b. How many cases of avocados should the merchant stock per week? (*Hint:* The events in the payoff table for this problem are of the type "demand for one case of avocados in the first week and demand for two cases in the second week.")

9.27 Mario's Pizza Company has four restaurants in the city. Currently, the company has a total of 200 employees. The Personnel Department files indicate the following breakdown of employees by sex and work status (full-time or part-time):

	Work Status	
Sex	**Full-Time**	**Part-Time**
Female	30	50
Male	80	40

a. If we select an employee at random, what is the probability that the employee will be a part-time employee?

b. What is the conditional probability that an employee is a female, given that she works full-time?

c. Suppose that an employee selected at random turns out to be a male. What is the chance that he is a part-time employee?

Use Bayes' decision rule in answering this question.

9.28 The United States is seriously considering a substantial amount of military aid to country A. Country A held a commanding military hardware superiority over the surrounding hostile countries before the recent outbreak. Today, however, the country maintains a relatively small superiority (55 percent on a 100 percent rating, where 50-50 is an exact balance). The U.S. government asserts that country A must maintain a considerable amount of superiority in military arms in order to sustain a long-term peace in the area. However, any arms aid to country A may result in immediate Soviet aid to the hostile countries in the area. State Department experts estimate that the probability of Soviet aid to the hostile countries subsequent to U.S. aid to country A is 0.8. The Central Intelligence Agency has informed the State Department that the Soviet Union would most likely wait and see whether the amount of U.S. aid to country A would be large, moderate, or small before it makes its move to neutralize the U.S. aid. If the U.S. aid to country A is large, the most likely Soviet reactions and their consequences in terms of country A's relative military superiority are estimated as follows:

Event: Amount of Aid to Hostile States	Probability	Country A's Position
Large	0.7	50%
Moderate	0.2	60
Small	0.1	70

However, if the United States provides country A with a moderate amount of arms aid, the expected Soviet reactions and their consequences are estimated as follows:

Event: Amount of Aid to Hostile States	Probability	Country A's Position
Large	0.1	45%
Moderate	0.6	55
Small	0.3	60

If the amount of U.S. arms aid to country A is small, the Soviet reactions are expected to be as follows:

Event: Amount of Aid to Hostile States	Probability	Country A's Position
Large	0.1	45%
Moderate	0.3	50%
Small	0.6	55%

There exists, as mentioned above, a 20 percent probability that the Soviet Union may not make any equalizing arms aid to the hostile states even when the United States provides aid to country A. In such a case, the expected outcomes are as follows:

Event: Amount of U.S. Aid to Country A	Country A's Position
Large	90%
Moderate	75
Small	60

If the U.S. government is determined to improve the military superiority of country A in order to maintain the fragile peace in the area, what kind of decisions should it make? Analyze the problem by using decision trees.

9.29 Gulf Exploration International Inc. is considering making a bid for the oil drilling rights off the Mexican shore. Through careful and thorough analysis, management of the firm has decided to set the bidding price at $520 million. The experts estimate that the firm has about a 60 percent chance of winning the contract for $520 million. Once the firm wins the contract, it has three alternatives for the extraction of oil: (1) the company can drill for oil on its own, (2) it can arrange a joint venture with Texas Oil Exploration, or (3) it can sell the drilling rights to foreign oil companies.

If the company wishes to drill on its own, the actual oil drilling operation is esti-mated to cost $80 million. The joint venture with Texas Oil Exploration is expected to cost $45 million. However, sales of the rights to foreign interests are expected to cost $2 million because of the long negotiating process.

The firm's scientists and consultants conclude that if Gulf Exploration drills on its own, the following possible outcomes and their probabilities are expected:

Event	Probability	Financial Outcome (Millions)
Big find	0.6	$900
Medium find	0.2	600
Failure	0.2	250

If the firm makes a joint drilling arrangement with Texas Oil Exploration, the expected outcomes and associated probabilities are as follows:

Event	Probability	Financial Outcome (Millions)
Big find	0.6	$750
Medium find	0.3	500
Failure	0.1	200

The sale of the rights to foreign companies is expected to return a flat $600 million. Construct a decision tree for the problem and determine the optimum decision strategy.

9.30 Smith Laboratories Inc. has just developed a new drug called "Stress Ez." This drug has been tested thoroughly in laboratories as well as through voluntary drug testing programs with human beings. The company is attempting to decide the best way to market the product.

Currently the company has the following marketing options: (1) get approval from the Food and Drug Administration (FDA) and market the drug domestically; (2) if the FDA does not approve the drug, then market it overseas only; (3) market it overseas only.

The marketing manager has constructed the decision tree, shown on page 397, with the associated conditional payoffs and probabilities. The conditional payoffs include various marketing and other related costs.

Determine the optimum marketing strategy for Smith Laboratories.

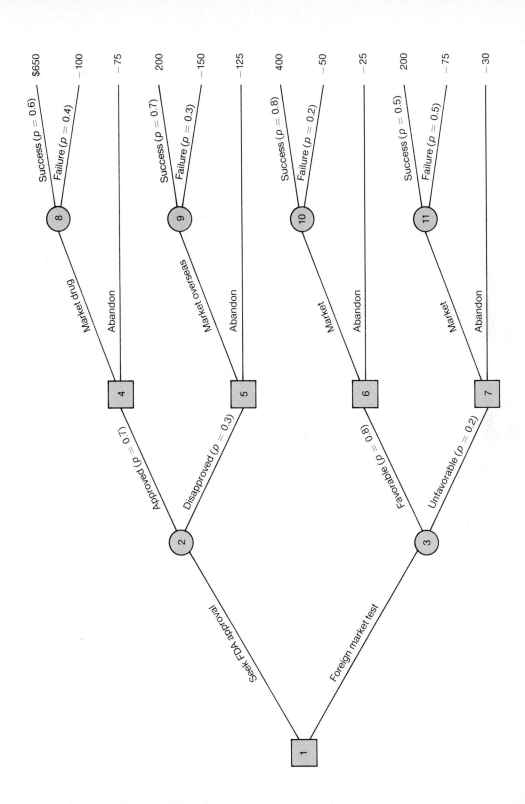

10 NETWORK MODELS

In many organizations, network analysis plays an important role in the area of operations or project management. By analyzing a network, which is a graphical representation of a series of activities and events, we can formulate, plan, and control project operations efficiently. In this chapter, we will study three network models widely applied to managerial decision making: shortest-route, minimum spanning tree, and maximum flow networks.

Learning Objectives *From the study of this chapter, we will learn the following:*

1. Characteristics of a network
2. Graphical representation of different types of networks
3. Development of networks with activities and events
4. Optimizing activity schedules for a project
5. Computer solutions of various network problems
6. Real-world applications of network models
7. The meaning of the following terms:

Activity	*Maximum flow*
Event	*Path*
Network	*Directed branches*
Shortest route	*Source node*
Minimum spanning tree	*Sink node*

CHARACTERISTICS OF A NETWORK

You may not be an expert in project planning yet, but you can certainly qualify as a frequent project planner. You may have developed detailed driving routes for your vacation, schedules to complete term projects, or a rough outline of interview schedules for a job search.

Basically, a project is an undertaking that has a clear beginning and a definite ending. In real-world situations, projects usually cost great sums of money, take a long time, require a great deal of labor, and cause frequent job stress. Examples of such large projects might be the construction of a new shopping center, the development of a new medicine to combat cancer, the strategic defense initiative ("Star Wars") project, and the Alaska pipeline project.

Projects usually involve many interrelated activities to be completed within specified limits of time and resources. Thus, we need to coordinate and schedule activities to complete a project efficiently.

Many real-world projects involve a host of activities and events that can be formulated as a **network.** Consequently, network analysis has become an important topic of management science. A network, whether involving physical operations or intellectual endeavors, complex or simple, large or small, has the following common characteristics:

A series of events and activities

Interrelationships among the activities

Issues of managing resources

A network is a graphical presentation of the flow of activities and events. An **activity** represents an operation that requires efforts, resources, or time. An **event** typically represents a junction point in time or a location, such as the beginning or ending of an operation. In a graphical model of a network, *nodes* or circles represent events and *arcs* or branches represent activities.

The originating point of a network is usually referred to as the **source node,** and the terminating point is the **sink node.** An arc indicates a relationship between two events by connecting them with a branch; if an arc is shown as an arrow, it indicates the direction of flow. Such an arc is called a *directed arc*. If an arc is a simple line without an arrow, it is an *undirected arc*. A series of nodes connected by branches is often referred to as a *chain*. A directed chain is called a *path*. If a chain connects a node to itself, it is referred to as a *cycle*.

Figure 10.1 presents a network model. In the network, six nodes are identified by numbers within circles. Nodes typically represent spatial points, such as work stations,

Figure 10.1   A Network Model

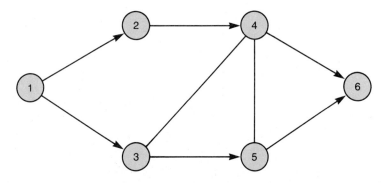

pumping stations, cities, and airports. Branches establish relationships between connected nodes. Branches represent roads that connect cities, pipelines connecting pumping stations, cables connecting switching stations, etc.

In Figure 10.1, the source node is 1 and the sink node is 6. Directed branches are: (1,2), (1,3), (2,4), (3,5), (4,6), and (5,6). Undirected branches are (3,4), (4,3), (4,5), and (5,4). One possible chain in the network is (1,3), (3,4), and (4,6). One possible path in the network would be (1→2→4→6). One possible cycle in the network is (3,5), (5,4), and (4,3).

In this chapter, we will study the three most widely used network models, namely the **shortest-route, minimum spanning tree,** and **maximum flow** models. The shortest-route problem determines the shortest route from the originating point to the termination point through alternative routes in a network. A good example of this network model would be determining the shortest travel route from Los Angeles to New York through various intermediate cities.

The minimum spanning tree problem involves identifying the optimum connections of all nodes in a network to minimize the total length of connections. For example, this model can be used to determine the best way to connect all houses with the central telephone switching point while minimizing the total telephone wire used.

The maximum flow problem determines the optimum route of flow through a capacitated network to maximize the total flow. One use of this model determines the maximum flow of water from a reservoir to a farm through an irrigation network with various flow capacities for the connecting irrigation channels.

SHORTEST-ROUTE PROBLEM

The shortest-route problem determines the shortest route from an originating point to a destination through a network, given the distance of each branch in the network. A typical shortest-route problem is the traveling plan from an originating city to a destination city over various highways and through connecting cities, given the associated distances from one city to another. The objective is to find the route which will minimize the total travel distance or time.

A number of different solution approaches have been suggested for the shortest-route problem, including the minimization model of linear programming. The most widely accepted and the simplest solution approach for the shortest-route problem is to fan out from the originating node and successively identify the next node that is the shortest route from the origin. The procedure can be summarized as follows:

Step 1 Designate the source node as the permanent set and identify the set of nodes adjacent to the permanent set.

Step 2 Identify the node in the adjacent set with the shortest distance from the source.

Step 3 Store this branch and its direction. Delete all other branches that connect the permanent set to the adjacent set node from further evaluation.

Step 4 Add the selected adjacent node to the permanent set.

Step 5 Now identify the new adjacent set of nodes and continue the evaluation process by going back to Step 2. If there is no further adjacent set of nodes to evaluate, terminate the procedure.

Casette 10.1   *PEAK SEASON TRAVEL INC.*

Peak Season Travel Inc. specializes in premium ski package tours. For 6 years, Peak Season has flown Chicagoans to various ski resorts. Due to increasing requests for western ski vacations, Peak Season has contracted with Marmot Lodge in Sun Valley, Idaho, for 50 suites. Peak Season is responsible for flying the skiers from Chicago to the Sun Valley airport and back, with two trips per week.

The company currently owns a plane that has sufficient capacity but a relatively short range — 550 miles, forcing it to land several times en route. The pilot has indicated all acceptable airports between Chicago and Sun Valley on the map, with relative distances (in miles). All other factors (such as weather) being equal, she would like to take the shortest route. The network is shown in Figure 10.2.

The shortest-route solution involves the following steps:

1. The originating node 1 (Chicago) is the initial permanent set; adjacent nodes are 2 (Lincoln) and 3 (Sioux Falls).

2. Identify node 2 (Lincoln) as the adjacent node with the shortest total distance from node 1.

3. Store branch (1→2), with a value of 475 (miles).

4. Add node 2 to the permanent set.

Figure 10.2   The Peak Season Travel Network

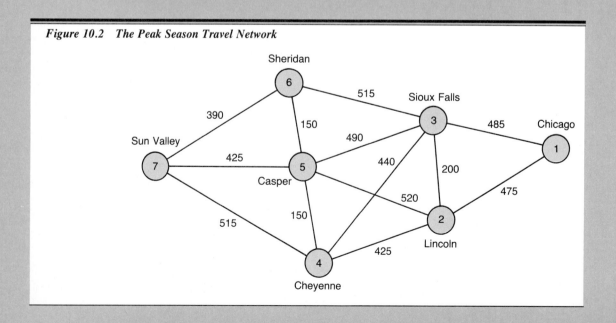

Figure 10.3(a) on page 404 presents a graphical presentation of the permanent set after one iteration. The following describes the second iteration:

1. The permanent set now contains nodes 1 and 2; the new adjacent set consists of nodes 3, 4, and 5.

2. From the table below, identify node 3 as the adjacent set node with the shortest total distance from node 1.

Branch	Permanent Set Node Value	+	Branch Value	=	Total Distance
1→3	0	+	485	=	485 ←
2→3 (X)	475	+	200	=	675
2→4	475	+	425	=	900
2→5	475	+	520	=	995

3. Store branch (1→3), with its value of 485.

4. Add node 3 to the permanent set. Delete branch (2→3), because we have reached node 3 via a shorter route.

Figure 10.3(b) shows the permanent set after two iterations. The following describes the next iteration:

Branch	Permanent Set Node Value	+	Branch Value	=	Total Distance
2→4	475	+	425	=	900 ←
2→5	475	+	520	=	995
3→4 (X)	485	+	440	=	925
3→5	485	+	490	=	975
3→6	485	+	515	=	1000

Store (2→4); delete (3→4). Figure 10.4(a) presents the permanent set after three iterations. The table below describes the fourth iteration:

Branch	Permanent Set Node Value	+	Branch Value	=	Total Distance
2→5 (X)	475	+	520	=	995
3→5	485	+	490	=	975 ←
3→6	485	+	515	=	1000
4→5 (X)	900	+	150	=	1050
4→7	900	+	515	=	1415

Figure 10.3(a)   The Permanent Set After One Iteration

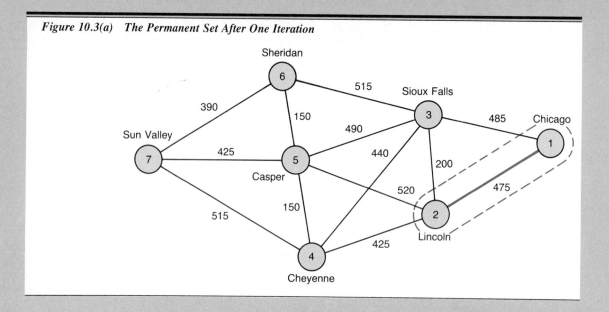

Figure 10.3(b)   The Permanent Set After Two Iterations

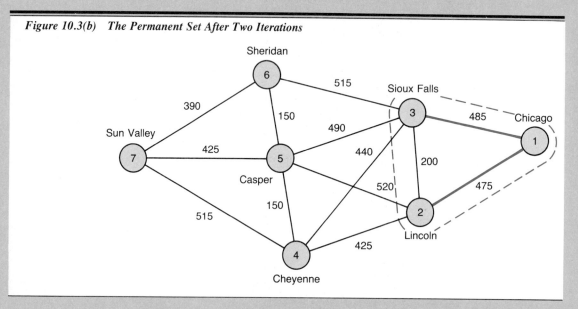

Store (3→5); delete (2→5), (4→5). Figure 10.4(b) shows the permanent set after four iterations. See the following table for the fifth iteration:

Branch	Permanent Set Node Value	+	Branch Value	=	Total Distance
3→6	485	+	515	=	1000 ←
4→7	900	+	515	=	1415
5→6 (X)	975	+	150	=	1125
5→7	975	+	425	=	1400

Figure 10.4(a)   The Permanent Set After Three Iterations

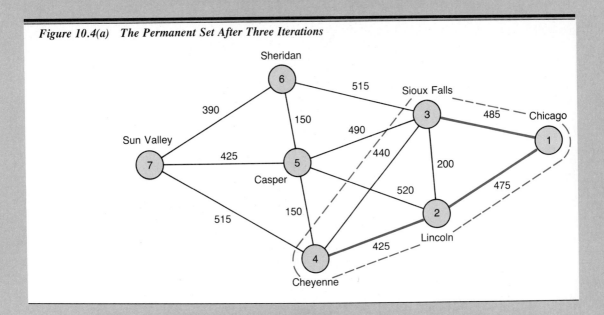

Figure 10.4(b)   The Permanent Set After Four Iterations

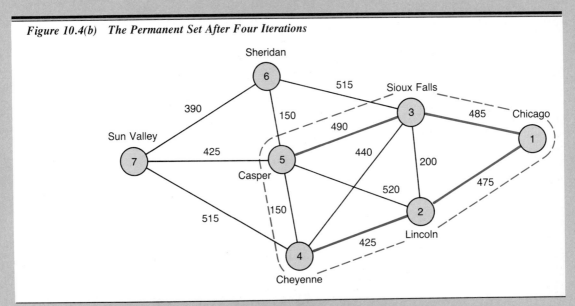

Store (3→6); delete (5→6). Figure 10.5(a) presents the permanent set after five iterations. The sixth iteration is as follows:

Branch	Permanent Set Node Value	+	Branch Value	=	Total Distance
4→7 (X)	900	+	515	=	1415
5→7 (X)	975	+	425	=	1400
6→7	1000	+	390	=	1390 ←

Figure 10.5(a)   *The Permanent Set After Five Iterations*

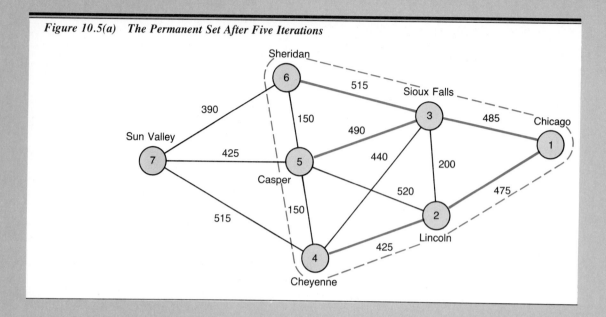

Figure 10.5(b)   *The Final Solution After Six Iterations*

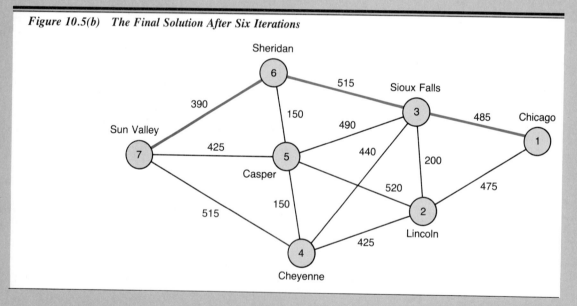

Store (6→7); delete (4→7), (5→7). Figure 10.5(b) presents the final solution after six iterations.

Storing a branch retains that branch as a possibility, but does not indicate that it is part of the final solution. Once a given node is reached and added to the permanent set, any inferior paths to that node may be deleted. In this problem, branches (1→2), (1→3), (2→4), (3→5), (3→6), and (6→7) were stored. Branches (1→2), (2→4), and (3→5) may be deleted; their final links (4→7) and (5→7) were deleted in the sixth iteration, so these two routes do not reach the sink node.

Peak Season's pilot should fly from Chicago (node 1) to Sun Valley (node 7) with refueling stops in Sioux Falls (node 3) and Sheridan (node 6), for a minimized total distance of 1,390 miles.

MINIMUM SPANNING TREE PROBLEM

The minimum spanning tree problem is a variation of the shortest-route problem. The primary objective of the minimum spanning tree problem is to connect all the network nodes while minimizing the total branch lengths. The model solution results in a tree which connects all points in the network.

Many real-world problems can be solved by the minimum spanning tree model. For example, determination of the minimum length of transmission lines required to connect all service areas of an electric utility, cable to connect all subscribing homes to a television cable system, canals to link an irrigation system, and pipelines to connect various terminals are all good application candidates for this approach. Many transportation, location-allocation, communication, and distribution problems can be analyzed by the minimum spanning tree model.

The basic solution process starts by selecting a node arbitrarily and connecting it to the closest node, in terms of time or cost. Then, select an unconnected node which is closest to either of the two connected nodes. This process is repeated until all nodes are connected.

The solution procedure for the minimum spanning tree problem is summarized as follows:

Step 1 Select a node in the network arbitrarily and connect it to the node with the shortest distance (time or cost) relative to the selected node.

Step 2 Identify the unconnected node that has the shortest distance to a connected node. Connect these two nodes. If there is a tie in selecting the shortest distance node, select one arbitrarily.

Step 3 If all nodes of the network are connected, stop. Otherwise, go to Step 2.

To demonstrate the solution procedure of the minimum spanning tree problem, let us consider the following casette.

Casette 10.2   **NATIONAL ELECTRIC COMPANY**

National Electric Company of Karelia, as a part of the national economic development plans, is attempting to install an electric transmission system in an area consisting of seven towns. Each town must be connected to the electric generating plant.

National Electric would like to lay out the transmission network that connects the towns while minimizing the total length of the transmission lines. The potential transmission paths proposed are shown in Figure 10.6. The figure also presents the required transmission line (in kilometers) for each path.

Figure 10.6   National Electric Company Network

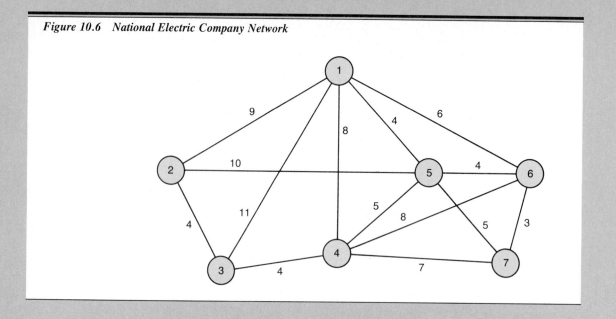

In the minimum spanning tree problem, we can initiate the solution process at any node in the network. In this sense, the minimum spanning tree problem is easier to solve than the shortest-route problem. The solution procedure can be summarized as follows:

Iteration 1: Let us select node 1 as the starting point. We search for the closest unconnected node to node 1. Node 5 is the closest to node 1, with a distance of 4 kilometers. We connect node 5 to node 1.

Iteration 2: We search for the unconnected node which is the shortest distance from the connected network, which consists of node 1 and node 5. Node 6 has the shortest distance to node 5, with 4 kilometers. Figure 10.7 presents the connections after two iterations. The spanning tree connects nodes 1, 5, and 6.

Iteration 3: Repeating the process, we identify node 7 as closest to the connected network. We connect node 7 to node 6.

Iteration 4: The next closest node is node 4, which is 5 kilometers from node 5. The spanning tree after four iterations is presented in Figure 10.8.

Iteration 5: Repeating, we select node 3 as the closest, and connect it to node 4.

Iteration 6: Node 2 is the only remaining unconnected node. The shortest distance from node 2 to any connected node is 4 kilometers, to node 3, and we therefore connect these two nodes.

Figure 10.7   Spanning Tree After Two Iterations

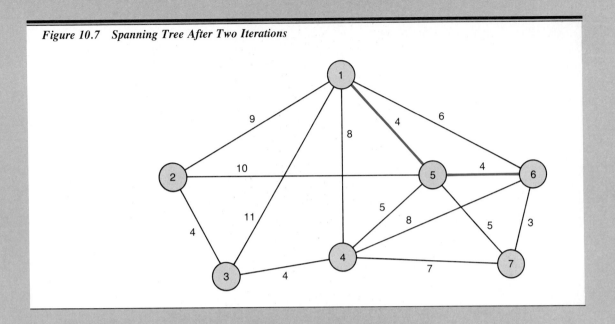

Figure 10.8   Spanning Tree After Four Iterations

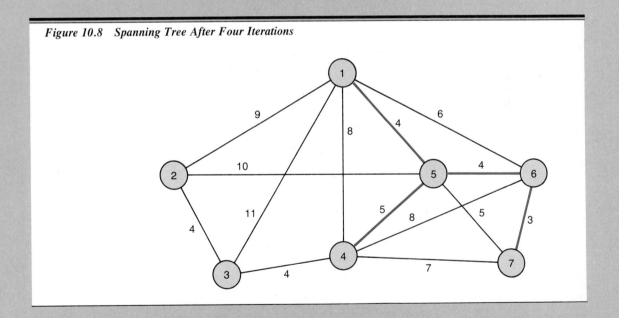

The complete spanning tree connecting all the nodes is shown in Figure 10.9. All seven towns are connected by the transmission network. The minimum length of transmission line required to connect the seven towns is 24 kilometers. This same optimum spanning tree could have been determined by starting with any node as the origin.

Figure 10.9   Optimum Spanning Tree

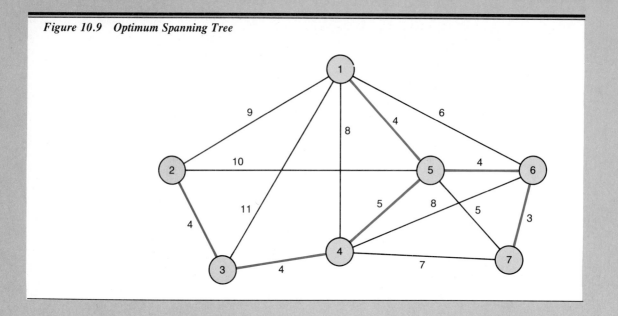

MAXIMUM FLOW PROBLEM

In many network problems, branches have limited flow capacities. In such networks, the objective is to determine a particular route that would maximize the total flow from a source point to a specified destination. Such network problems are referred to as "maximum flow problems."

Many real-world problems can be analyzed by the maximum flow approach, such as traffic flows through busy highway systems, flow of water through various irrigation systems, flow of oil through a pipeline, flow of electricity through a network of transmission systems, and flow of telephone calls through a telecommunications system. In these network systems, the branches may have different flow capacities, and the decision maker is vitally interested in determining the maximum flow through a particular **path.**

The maximum flow problem may involve branches that are **directed branches** or undirected ones. For instance, a downward-sloping irrigation canal is directed, but traffic on a two-way street is undirected. A convenient way to handle a two-way flow branch is to treat it as two separate directed branches.

The solution procedure for the maximum flow problem can be summarized as follows:

Step 1   Determine a path from the origin (source node) to the destination (sink node) with *positive* flow capacity on each branch of the path. If no such path exists, terminate the process.

Step 2   In the selected path, determine the branch with the minimum current flow capacity and denote it as *C*.

Step 3   In the same selected path, decrease the current flow capacity of each branch by C.

Step 4   Increase the flow capacity of each branch in the selected path by C in the *reverse* direction. This procedure is necessary to compute the potential redirected flow for each branch of the selected path, if branches are undirected. Go back to Step 1.

The following casette demonstrates the solution procedure of the maximum flow problem.

Casette 10.3   *PICTURESQUE CAVES TOUR*

The U.S. Forest Service operates guided tours through Picturesque Caves in Shade National Forest. These unique caves consist of a network of interconnecting tunnels and galleries that lead completely through a large hill. Once inhabited by prehistoric artists, the caves contain the only known examples of several painting techniques and styles. The Forest Service has been able to install limited air recycling equipment but still must carefully restrict the flow of tourists through the caves. The daily capacity of certain stretches is very limited, and tourist demand already exceeds the present limit.

Given the flow patterns and capacitated branches shown in Figure 10.10, the U.S. Forest Service wants to know the maximum number of tourists to view the caves without causing irreparable damage. Ranger Kim Lee has analyzed the capacity of each passage, as well as the acceptable flow patterns.

In Figure 10.10, Kim Lee indicated the flow capacity of each branch on the *immediate right* of every node. For example, the flow capacity from node 1 to node 2 is 50

Figure 10.10   The Picturesque Caves in Shade National Forest

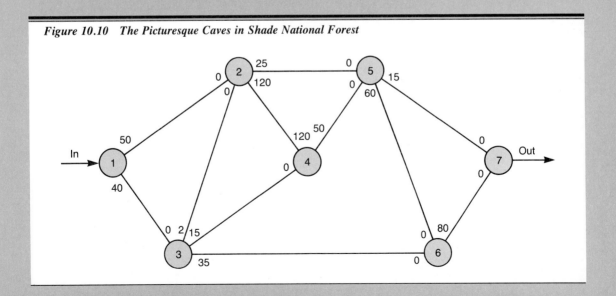

tourists. The number on the *immediate left* of each node indicates the flow capacity in the opposite direction. For example, flow capacity from node 2 to node 1 is 0. All branches with flow capacity of 0 at either end are directed branches. However, if flow is possible in both directions, such as along branch (2,4) or (4,2) in Figure 10.10, the branch is undirected.

The Picturesque Caves maximum flow problem can be solved as follows:

Iteration 1: As an initial path, we may select 1→2→5→7. The maximum flow possible on this path is 15, the flow capacity of branch (5,7). This path is shown in Figure 10.11. Adjusting the flow capacities along the route, we subtract 15 from the original capacities and obtain the remaining capacities: branch (1,2) is 35; branch (2,5) is 10. The flow capacities in the opposite direction should also be adjusted by adding the same 15. The maximum flow along the path is shown by the number in a box on each branch.

Iteration 2: Continuing along branch (1,2), we select the next path as 1→2→5→6→7, with a capacity of 10 on branch (2,5). Adjusted capacities are shown in Figure 10.12.

Iteration 3: Again starting with branch (1,2), we select the next path as 1→2→4→5→6→7. This path has a capacity of 25, the adjusted flow limit of branch (1,2). Readjusting capacities, we develop Figure 10.13.

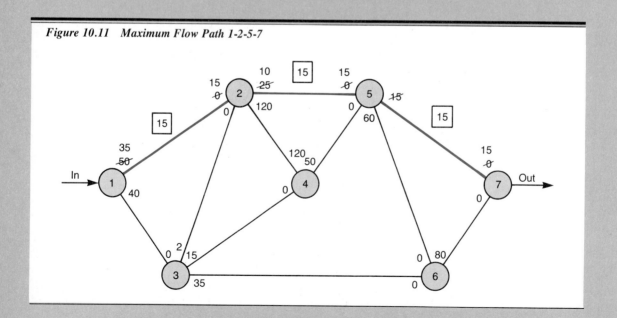

Figure 10.11   Maximum Flow Path 1-2-5-7

Figure 10.12   Maximum Flow Path 1-2-5-6-7

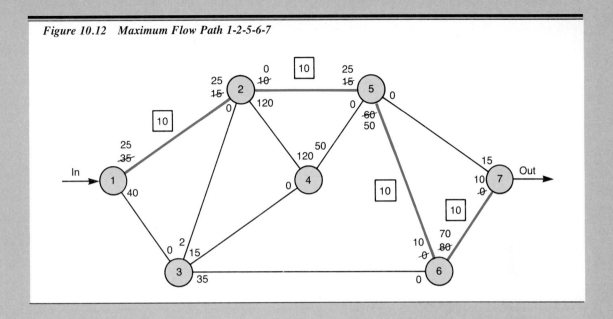

Figure 10.13   Maximum Flow Path 1-2-4-5-6-7

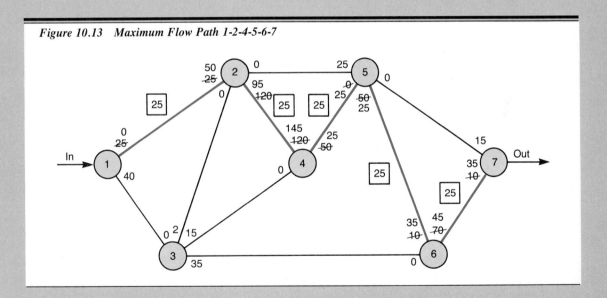

Iteration 4: Using branch (1,3) for the first time, we select the first available path as 1→3→2→4→5→6→7. This path will accommodate a maximum of two tourists, the flow restriction imposed by branch (3,2). Figure 10.14 illustrates the capacities remaining after this iteration.

Figure 10.14   Maximum Flow Path 1-3-2-4-5-6-7

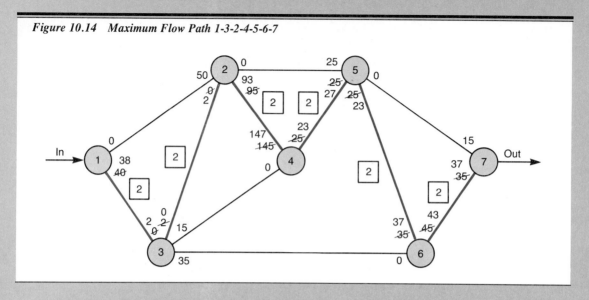

Figure 10.15   Maximum Flow Path 1-3-6-7

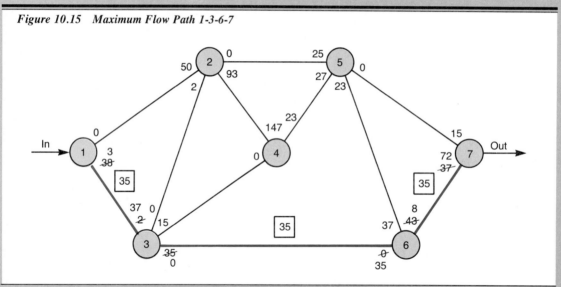

Iteration 5: Using branch (1,3) for the second time, we choose path 1→3→6→7. The maximum flow capacity along this path is 35, the restriction imposed by branch (3,6). Figure 10.15 presents the revised capacities along the path.

Iteration 6: Branch (1,3) will allow only 3 more tourists to pass through. From the listing of adjusted capacities, we can see that the only path that can handle 3 more tourists is 1→3→4→5→6→7, as shown in Figure 10.16.

Figure 10.16   Maximum Flow Path 1-3-4-5-6-7

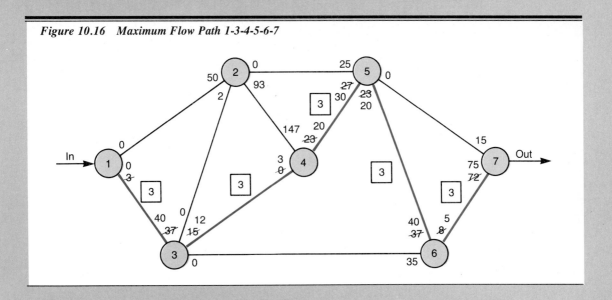

Figure 10.17   Maximum Flow for the Picturesque Caves

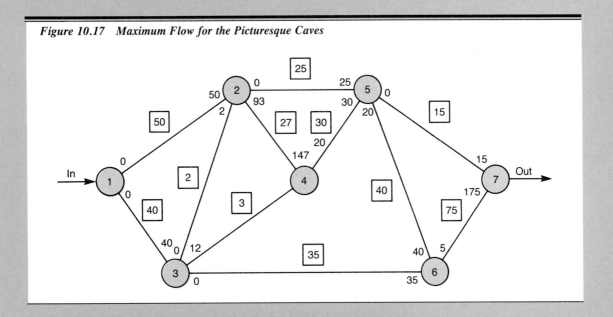

There are no more paths with available flow capacity. We completed the solution process in six iterations. The recommended flows along each branch which will maximize the total flow are shown in Figure 10.17. The maximum number of tourists that can be allowed to pass through the Picturesque Caves is 90. The solution process can also be summarized as shown in the table on the following page.

	1→2	1→3	2→4	2→5	3→2	3→4	3→6	4→5	5→6	5→7	6→7
Iteration											
1	15			15						15	
2	10			10					10		10
3	25		25					25	25		25
4		2	2		2			2	2		2
5		35					35				35
6		3				3		3	3		3
Total Flow	50	40	27	25	2	3	35	30	40	15	75
Capacity	50	40	120	25	2	15	35	50	60	15	80
Unused Capacity	0	0	93	0	0	12	0	20	20	0	5

COMPUTER SOLUTIONS OF NETWORK PROBLEMS

This section examines computer applications to network problems. As we have seen, network models can become extremely complex as the number of activities and events increases. Thus, real-world problems are never solved by hand, and a number of computer programs are available for network problems. In this section, we will discuss application examples of *Micro Manager*.

Figure 10.18 presents the computer solution of the Peak Season Travel problem presented as Casette 10.1. This problem attempts to find the shortest route from Chicago to Sun Valley. The computer output includes the input data entered and the program output. The shortest route identified is 1→3→6→7 (Chicago → Sioux Falls → Sheridan → Sun Valley), covering a distance of 1,390 miles. This result corresponds with the manual solution.

Figure 10.19 provides the computer solution of the National Electric Company of Karelia problem, which we discussed as Casette 10.2. This minimum spanning tree problem involves the electric company's attempts to lay out the transmission network that connects seven towns while minimizing the total length of the transmission lines. The minimum spanning tree network is 1-5, 5-6, 6-7, 5-4, 4-3, 3-2, with the minimum transmission line length of 24 kilometers. This solution is exactly the same as our manual solution.

Figure 10.20 presents the *Micro Manager* solution of the Picturesque Caves Tour problem which we discussed as Casette 10.3. This maximum flow problem involves a chain of caves. The solution derived by the computer is presented in the program output section. The maximum number of tourists that can be channeled through the network is 90. This solution is exactly the same as our manual solution.

REAL-WORLD APPLICATIONS

Many real-world problems involve a host of activities and events that can be analyzed as networks, and network analysis has been widely applied to real-world situations. This section discusses three real-world applications of network models.

Figure 10.18   Computer Solution of the Peak Season Travel Problem

```
PROGRAM: Shortest Route

##### INPUT DATA ENTERED #####

      --------------------------------------------
      Branch        Nodes           Value
      --------------------------------------------

        1         1 <---> 2         475.0
        2         1 <---> 3         485.0
        3         2 <---> 3         200.0
        4         2 <---> 4         425.0
        5         2 <---> 5         520.0
        6         3 <---> 4         440.0
        7         3 <---> 5         490.0
        8         3 <---> 6         515.0
        9         4 <---> 5         150.0
       10         4 <---> 7         515.0
       11         5 <---> 6         150.0
       12         5 <---> 7         425.0
       13         6 <---> 7         390.0

      --------------------------------------------

##### PROGRAM OUTPUT #####

      --------------------------------------------
      Branch        Nodes           Value
      --------------------------------------------

        2         1 <---> 3         485.0
        8         3 <---> 6         515.0
       13         6 <---> 7         390.0

      --------------------------------------------

      Total branch lengths : 1390
```

Determining Effective Highway Networks

Highway traffic assignment problems attempt either to minimize total travel time for all vehicles or to find the shortest path for a given individual vehicle. Various conditions or other cost functions, such as fuel consumption or accident hazard level, may be included. This type of problem typically eats up large volumes of computer core memory, and is often too slow to be interactive. The authors of the study discussed here applied a technique called "geographic decomposition" to divide the total area under consideration into separate subproblems, which could then be handled more efficiently.[1]

---

[1]Zachary Lansdowne and David Robinson, "Geographic Decomposition of the Shortest Path Problem with an Application to the Traffic Assignment Problem," *Management Science* 28:12 (Dec. 1982), 1380–1390.

Figure 10.19   Computer Solution of the National Electric Company of Karelia Problem

PROGRAM: Minimum Spanning Tree

***** INPUT DATA ENTERED *****

Branch	Nodes	Value
1	1 <---> 2	9.0
2	1 <---> 3	11.0
3	1 <---> 4	8.0
4	1 <---> 5	4.0
5	1 <---> 6	6.0
6	2 <---> 3	4.0
7	2 <---> 5	10.0
8	3 <---> 4	4.0
9	4 <---> 5	5.0
10	4 <---> 6	8.0
11	4 <---> 7	7.0
12	5 <---> 6	4.0
13	5 <---> 7	5.0
14	6 <---> 7	3.0

***** PROGRAM OUTPUT *****

Branch	Nodes	Value
4	1 <---> 5	4.0
12	5 <---> 6	4.0
14	6 <---> 7	3.0
14	5 <---> 4	5.0
14	4 <---> 3	4.0
14	3 <---> 2	4.0

Total branch lengths : 24

Boundary nodes are selected, forming the edge of one area, with each boundary node connecting directly to a node in another network. A new network consisting only of boundary nodes is prepared. The origin node and destination node are then linked to their respective area's boundary nodes, and the shortest overall distance can be determined.

Figure 10.20   Computer Solution of the Picturesque Caves Tour Problem

```
PROGRAM: Maximum Flow

***** INPUT DATA ENTERED *****

---------------------------------------------------------------

  Branch      Nodes        Value      Nodes        Value
---------------------------------------------------------------

    1       1 ----> 2       50.0     2 ----> 1       0.0
    2       1 ----> 3       40.0     3 ----> 1       0.0
    3       2 ----> 3        0.0     3 ----> 2       2.0
    4       2 ----> 4      120.0     4 ----> 2     120.0
    5       2 ----> 5       25.0     5 ----> 2       0.0
    6       3 ----> 4       15.0     4 ----> 3       0.0
    7       3 ----> 6       35.0     6 ----> 3       0.0
    8       4 ----> 5       50.0     5 ----> 4       0.0
    9       5 ----> 6       60.0     6 ----> 5       0.0
   10       5 ----> 7       15.0     7 ----> 5       0.0
   11       6 ----> 7       80.0     7 ----> 6       0.0
---------------------------------------------------------------

*****    PROGRAM OUTPUT    *****

-----------------------------------------------------

  Branch      Nodes        Value      Flow
-----------------------------------------------------

    1       1 ----> 2       50.0      50.0
    2       1 ----> 3       40.0      40.0
    4       2 ----> 4      120.0      27.0
    5       2 ----> 5       25.0      25.0
    3       3 ----> 2        2.0       2.0
    6       3 ----> 4       15.0       3.0
    7       3 ----> 6       35.0      35.0
    8       4 ----> 5       50.0      30.0
    9       5 ----> 6       60.0      40.0
   10       5 ----> 7       15.0      15.0
   11       6 ----> 7       80.0      75.0
-----------------------------------------------------

Total maximum flow :  90
```

The highway network of Washington, D.C., was employed to illustrate the effectiveness of the procedure. Two rivers and two major highways formed the boundaries, with bridges and access points representing boundary nodes. This model was subsequently run on a unified program as well as on a geographically decomposed version. Computer storage space required was cut in half with decomposition, processing costs were lowered by 40 percent, and running time was reduced by 40 percent.

Collecting Milk from New Zealand Farms

New Zealand's dairy industry is wholly owned by the dairy farmers themselves. The largest cooperative produces one-third of New Zealand's processed dairy products and faced a major expansion due in part to increasing milk production.[2] The co-op received milk from 4,500 farms scattered over roughly 3,600 square miles. A fleet of 300 tankers collect the milk daily, with two trips during peak season. Production is extremely seasonal, with nearly no milk processing in May, June, and July. The company wished to enhance its management's experience with a planning model that could handle location of new factories, factory expansions or shutdowns, transport policies, product mix strategies, and reliability risks.

An interactive network, named *Netplan,* was developed to portray the problem. A network formulation was chosen for its clarity in representing the situation (in particular the transport aspect), fast solution time, and ease of updating. To simplify the model, the 4,500 farms were grouped into 176 clusters containing from 5 to 50 farms. All milk produced required processing on the same day. Farm cluster nodes were connected to factory nodes by arcs labeled with factory capacity and return per unit of milk processed. Factories were connected to other factories as needed, to circumvent the need for connection between every farm cluster and every factory.

Further development of the model allowed for an arc for each process at each factory, with both input maxima and minima as well as net returns specified. Overtime possibilities were added to the system; because overtime costs exceed regular operating costs, the network program automatically fills regular hours before allocating to overtime. Demand limits for each type of product for the entire system were also included. The network model's final formulation comprised 176 farm cluster sources, 14 factories (with up to five processes each), and eight products.

Results of running *Netplan* appear in report form as well as in several useful graphic presentations. Capacity utilization and transportation maps indicated a number of problems, including optimum solutions which did not process any milk at certain factories and factory locations which were clearly suboptimal. The ease of use of the system allowed the users to test many planning possibilities, combining their experience with the model's quantitative capabilities.

Frontier Airlines Maximizes Passenger/Price Flow Via Network

Prior to deregulation, competition among airlines was strictly limited by the Civil Aeronautics Board, particularly as to pricing and routing. The only areas of real competition were frills and scheduling. Deregulation introduced low-cost, nonunion carriers and allowed regional carriers to compete with the traditional major long-distance airlines. True price competition expanded dramatically, creating the need for a more precise solution to the pricing and passenger-mix problem.[3] Complications include multiple prices on a given flight, restrictions on seats by fare for each flight, competing flights, alternative routings (on the same or another airline), seasonality, changes in daily demand, and passengers' time-of-day preferences.

[2]P. J. Mellalieu and K. R. Hall, "An Interactive Planning Model for the New Zealand Dairy Industry," *Journal of the Operational Research Society* 34:6 (1983), 521–532.

[3]Fred Glover, Randy Glover, Joe Lorenzo, and Claude McMillan, "The Passenger-Mix Problem in the Scheduled Airlines," *Interfaces* 12:3 (June 1982), 73–80.

To optimize the passenger/price mix, a user-friendly computerized model with an efficient solution method was needed. The system would affect both reservations and price/route decisions. Frontier Airlines, based in Denver, instituted a maximum flow network model, satisfying the problem's restrictions while maximizing revenue for its flight network. The network was set up as a minimum-cost flow problem with special side constraints. Forward arcs represented a flight's capacity, multiple back arcs allocated seats to various fare classes and overall passenger itineraries. Back arcs also carried revenue designators, differentiating the fare classes.

Frontier's network accommodated 600 flights, 30,000 passenger itineraries, and up to five fare classes per itinerary. Numerous side constraints guaranteed accuracy and adherence to prescribed limits. The model was set up to run on a 16-bit minicomputer. By comparison, the authors calculated that a linear-program formulation of the same problem would involve 200,000 variables and 3,000 constraints. The efficiency of the network method allows for easy manipulation of data and assumptions and permits interactive analysis. Frontier has documented an improved pricing and discount inventory capability with valuable input to scheduling functions.

SUMMARY

In this chapter, we have studied the most important network models, namely shortest-route, minimum spanning tree, and maximum flow problems. Network models have become popular topics of management science because they have a wide range of applications. Furthermore, the graphic analysis of networks has greatly enhanced the understanding and communication aspects of networks. This feature is especially important in view of one attribute common to all networks — complexity. However, the availability of many efficient computer programs has greatly enhanced the popularity of network models.

Glossary

Activity   An operation or process which requires time, effort, resources, or a combination thereof. Represented by an arc or branch (arrow or line).

Directed Branch or Arc   An activity represented by an arrow, indicating unidirectional flow. Undirected branches or arcs, represented by a plain line, allow flow in either direction.

Event   A time or location representing the beginning or end of an activity or a juncture of two or more activities. Represented by a node (circle).

Maximum Flow   A network concerned with determining flows along various branches to maximize the total flow from source node to sink node.

Minimum Spanning Tree   A network connecting all nodes in a pattern that minimizes total length of connecting branches.

Network   A graphical presentation of activities and events that shows interrelationships; useful in project planning.

Path   A series of nodes, connected by branches, with directed flow; a directed chain of nodes.

Shortest Route   A network determining the shortest directed route or path from the source node to the sink node.

Sink Node   Terminating point of a network.

Source Node   Originating point of a network.

References

Battersby, A. *Network Analysis for Planning and Scheduling*. New York: Wiley, 1970.

Cleland, D. I., and King, W. R. *Systems Analysis and Project Management*. 2d ed. New York: McGraw-Hill, 1975.

Ford, L. R., Jr., and Fulkerson, D. R. *Flows in Networks*. Princeton, N.J.: Princeton University, 1962.

Hillier, F. S., and Lieberman, G. J. *Operations Research*. 4th ed. San Francisco: Holden-Day, 1986.

Lee, S. M., Moore, L. J., and Taylor, B. W. *Management Science*. 2d ed. Dubuque, Iowa: W. C. Brown, 1985.

Assignments

10.1 What is a network? How is it useful?

10.2 Describe three kinds of networks and point out the key differences between them.

10.3 Draw a typical small network diagram and label the following components: activity, event, chain, arc, node, directed branch, sink, source, and path.

10.4 Prepare a shortest-route network illustrating potential routes you could use on your way to class from your residence.

10.5 Develop a maximum flow network connecting the parking lot with the seating area of a local auditorium, concert hall, or gymnasium. Assume one parking lot and one seating area, with several sidewalks, halls, and doorways.

10.6 Assume that you have been hired by a local supermarket to install an announcement system in its ceiling. Use a minimum spanning tree network to illustrate the project.

10.7 You have planned a long-distance vacation for next summer and now wish to ascertain the shortest route to arrive at your destination. Prepare a network using either distance or travel time as the decision factor.

10.8 Describe a project which is currently underway in your college, town, or family, and determine whether a network model might be appropriate for analyzing it.

10.9 Does it matter which node is selected as the starting node on a minimum spanning tree network?

10.10 In a shortest-route problem, when may a given branch or path be removed from further consideration?

10.11 Define *adjacent set* for each of the three types of network problems discussed in this chapter.

10.12 Does the maximum capacity of the source node or sink node necessarily determine the maximum flow for the entire network? Why or why not?

10.13 Describe at least three parameters which could be used as a decision criterion for each of the model types in this chapter.

10.14 Speed-E Trucking Corporation has just added nonstop express service to Byron to its daily schedule. The company must now select the quickest route to connect its existing network with Byron, starting at its base of Monroe. The network below shows connecting highways with estimated driving times, in units of 10 minutes. Determine the shortest route.

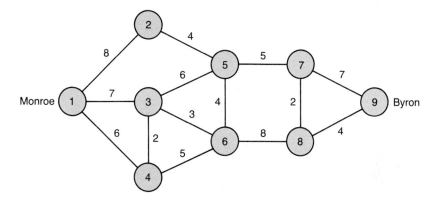

10.15 The tax office is auditing an executive's rather high deduction for commuting expenses. Mr. Brown has claimed a daily round trip of 54 miles, on average. The tax office believes it can prove this to be excessive by selecting the shortest route available to Mr. Brown, chosen from those he commonly uses. Your job is to pinpoint the shortest route; double that mileage to obtain Mr. Brown's minimum daily round-trip distance. Nodes in the following network represent intersections of major roads.

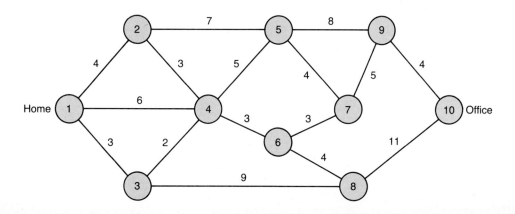

10.16 Twinkletoes Delivery Service promises rapid home delivery of meals from your favorite restaurant. A local retirement home has contracted for its Sunday lunches to be brought from the top-notch Paradise Inn, and Twinkletoes clearly desires to maintain prompt service on this order. Your task is to assist Twinkletoes in selecting the ideal (shortest distance in city blocks) route. Refer to the network below.

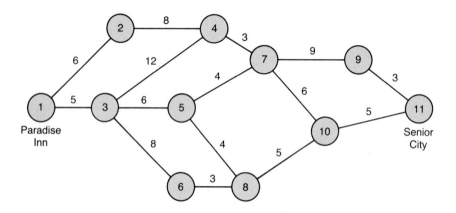

10.17 Data Base Inc. has established a new data outlet in New York. The home office in Los Angeles must relay data to New York at least 4 hours daily, so Data Base has decided to install its own long-distance microwave system. Several relay points are needed, and bits of data tend to become lost between transceivers at different rates on various routes. Data Base needs to know which route will be the most reliable; your job is to find the "shortest route" in terms of lost bits per million sent, according to the following network.

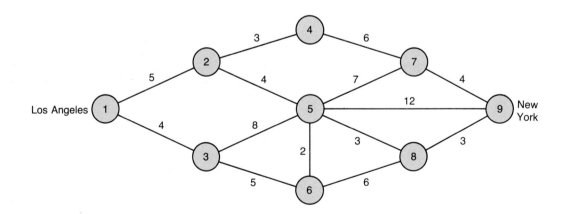

10.18 Spring Break, with the accompanying beach fever, has finally arrived at Mid-Northern University (MNU). The campus recreation department is sponsoring a bus convoy to Fort Lauderdale, and wishes to determine the shortest route there. The office has compiled the following potential routes. Please assist the department staff in determining the shortest route.

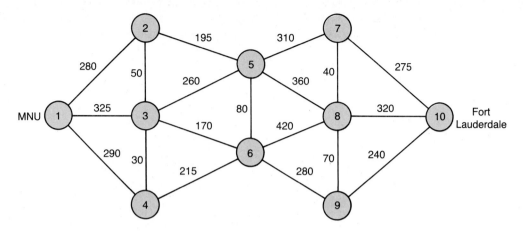

10.19 The Rural Development Agency of Upper Camumba has just received a grant that will allow it to electrify the valley of the Chinga Creek. The eight villages must be connected to the main power net at the minimum total cost; costs for each potential link, in thousands of dollars, are indicated on the network below. Determine the minimum spanning tree.

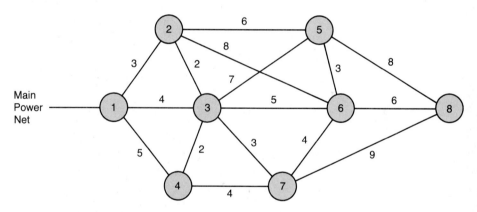

10.20 Hillstreet Developers are planning to construct eight deluxe residences and wish to construct the shortest possible paved road to connect all the homes. This road will then be connected to the main road. Distances are in 100-yard units along the potential routes shown below. Determine the minimum spanning tree.

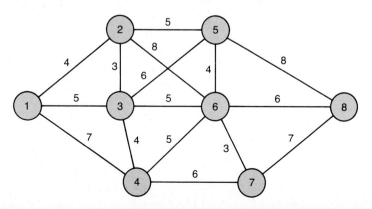

10.21 The Main Line Manufacturing Co. has decided to establish a computer network linking its floor supervisors' desks. It wishes to minimize the total distance communications wires must be strung, based on the following grid (in meters). Determine the minimum spanning tree.

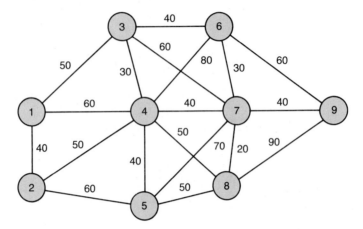

10.22 The recently developed Kansahoma Oil Field has eight producing well concentrations which must be linked by a pipeline to allow more rapid collection of the oil. The wells and their relative distances are mapped below. Determine the minimum spanning tree.

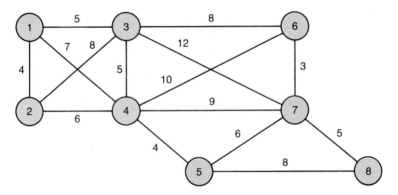

10.23 EasyGro Greenhouses has decided to install an automatic watering and fertilizing system. The greenhouses to be linked are shown below, with distances in hundreds of yards. Connect the greenhouses with the shortest possible pipe system.

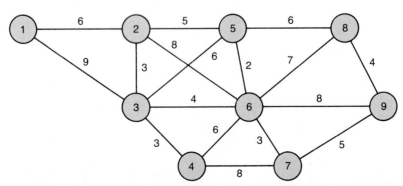

10.24 Commuters in Abingdon have complained of increasing delays and clogged arteries. The city's traffic bureau has studied capacities along the major roads and has concluded that the bottleneck is in the Charing Valley, which has a narrow entrance and exit. Using the network below, assist the traffic bureau in determining the system's maximum vehicle flow (in thousands per hour).

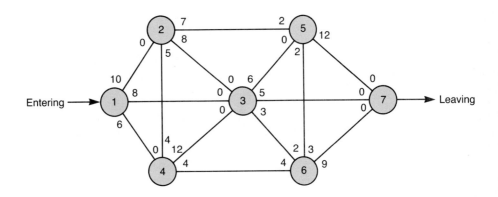

10.25 Help Cass County's electrical utility by determining the maximum energy flow through its network of transmission lines, as illustrated below. Flow may occur in either direction in equal quantities.

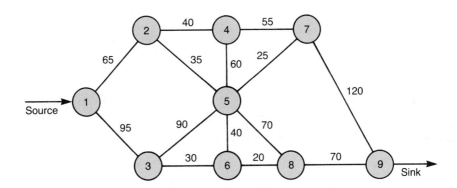

10.26 Jones's Vegetable Farm is irrigated by a system of level canals, each with a limited capacity. In anticipation of a dry spell, Farmer Jones wishes to water as much as possible now, storing excess water in a cistern at the far end of his fields. Using the illustration on the top of page 428, determine the maximum flow in thousands of gallons per hour, thereby determining how long the system will have to be wide open to fill the currently empty 800,000-gallon cistern.

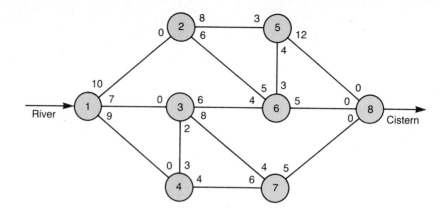

10.27 Sweetums Candy Co. wishes to perform its annual spring cleaning a week earlier than scheduled this year, due to the imminent visit of the owner's respected mother. However, the master confectioners have just filled the main bank of syrup vats with 2,168,000 pounds of special glucose syrup. These vats must be emptied before the cleaning and polishing can begin. The only way to remove the syrup is to process it into candies, through a series of work stations resembling a network. Some shuffling of partially completed candies is permitted, as shown in the diagram below. How many hours must the factory operate to clear the system? Flows given are in thousands of pounds per hour.

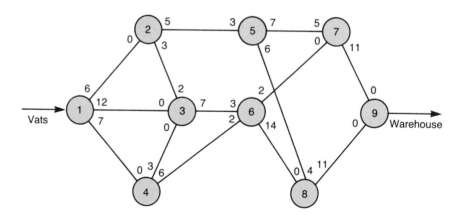

10.28 The Wheyside Dairy has constructed a detailed routing map (see page 429) for its milk-processing system in an effort to spot current inefficiencies. Wheyside asks you to find its system's current maximum flow potential, in thousands of liters per hour.

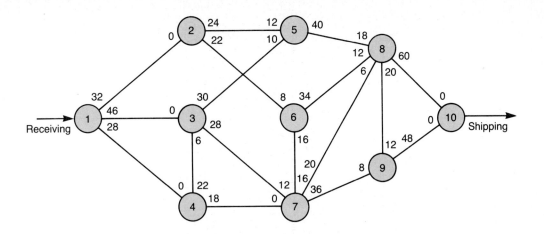

11 PROJECT PLANNING WITH PERT AND CPM

One of the most popular real-world network applications is project planning. Many important projects, such as the plan for the space shuttle program, development of a new shopping center, or construction of new road systems, are often planned as networks. By analyzing these projects as networks, which are graphical representations of a series of activities and events, we can manage required resources more efficiently. Among the several network analysis techniques available, PERT (program evaluation and review technique) and CPM (critical path method) are the best known and most widely used project-planning techniques. In this chapter, we will study the concepts and solution procedures of PERT/CPM networks for managerial decision problems.

Learning Objectives *From the study of this chapter, we will learn the following:*

1. *Several important characteristics of the project-planning problem*
2. *Development and use of the Gantt chart*
3. *Development of networks with activities and events*
4. *Development of a network from a Gantt chart*
5. *Identification of the critical path through calculation of the earliest expected time and the latest allowable time*
6. *Scheduling of activities of a project based on a network analysis*
7. *Project crashing based on a time-cost trade-off analysis*
8. *Estimation of the project completion time and associated probabilities for a PERT network*
9. *Computer solutions of PERT and CPM problems*
10. *The meaning of the following terms:*

Gantt chart	*Latest allowable time*
Activities	*Noncritical events*
Events	*Total slack*
Critical path	*Shared (floating) slack*
Dummy activities	*Free slack*
Project crashing	*Optimistic time*
Most likely time	*Pessimistic time*
Earliest expected time	

CHARACTERISTICS OF THE PROJECT-PLANNING PROBLEM

The project-planning techniques we will study in this chapter are widely applied to a variety of real-world projects. The federal government usually requests contractors to utilize project-planning techniques for most of its projects. Construction and engineering firms frequently use project-planning techniques for work planning and cost control. The project-planning techniques are extremely valuable in determining the project duration, critical tasks, and the probability of completing the project within the given resources and time.

As discussed in Chapter 10, projects usually involve a host of interrelated activities that are to be completed within specific limits of time and resources. Thus, we need to coordinate and schedule activities to complete a project efficiently. All project-planning problems have the following in common: a series of events and activities; interrelationships among the activities (beginning, process, and ending); and issues of resource management.

Project planning based on PERT/CPM may include a number of steps and procedures. However, it generally involves three basic phases: formulation, planning, and control, as shown in Figure 11.1.

The Gantt Chart

The simplest project-scheduling tool available is the **Gantt chart,** developed by Henry L. Gantt in 1918. The value of the Gantt chart rests on its flexibility, which provides ease in describing a project in terms of activities, time schedule of each activity, and the precedence relationships among some of the activities. Because of its simplicity and flexibility, the Gantt chart is a powerful project-scheduling tool. Many sophisticated network-based projects are often initiated on the basis of a good Gantt chart. The Gantt chart is undoubtedly the tool most widely used by practicing managers today.

Suppose you decided to undertake your monthly car cleaning and polishing project with a friend. The project involves the following activities: washing the car, drying the car, applying the wax, cleaning the interior while the wax is drying, and then polishing the car. Table 11.1 presents the activity label, activity description, predecessor, and duration estimates (in minutes).

Figure 11.2 presents a Gantt chart for the car cleaning and polishing project. Activities are listed vertically on the left of the bar chart. The horizontal axis represents time. The estimated duration of each project is represented by the length of the bar, from the beginning to the ending point. Since the length of the activity bar represents the total completion time, we can easily ascertain the progress of each activity. For example, in Figure 11.2 the shaded area represents the completed portions of the activities. Thus, it is clear that we are on or ahead of schedule on all activities except the polishing activity.

A Gantt chart can accommodate simple precedence relationships among the activities. For example, activity B (drying the car) cannot take place until activity A (washing the car) is completed. However, if we have a complex network under consideration, it is extremely difficult to express interrelationships among activities on the chart. This is the major weakness of the Gantt chart.

History of PERT and CPM

PERT and CPM were developed in the late 1950s as aids in the planning, scheduling, and controlling of complex, large-scale projects. PERT was developed by the U.S. Navy for planning and scheduling the Polaris missile project. CPM, however, was de-

Figure 11.1   Three Phases of PERT/CPM Application

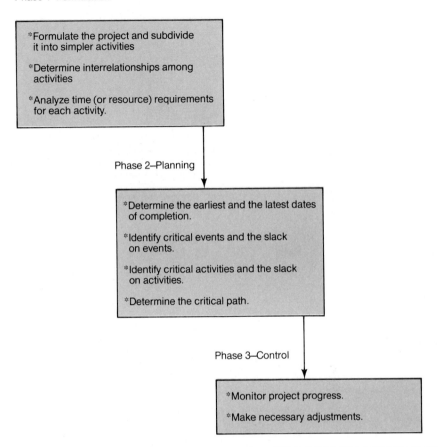

Phase 1–Formulation

*Formulate the project and subdivide it into simpler activities

*Determine interrelationships among activities

*Analyze time (or resource) requirements for each activity.

Phase 2–Planning

*Determine the earliest and the latest dates of completion.

*Identify critical events and the slack on events.

*Identify critical activities and the slack on activities.

*Determine the critical path.

Phase 3–Control

*Monitor project progress.

*Make necessary adjustments.

Table 11.1   Car Cleaning and Polishing Project

Activity	Description	Predecessor	Estimated Duration (minutes)
A	Wash the car	None	10
B	Dry the car	A	10
C	Wax the car	B	15
D	Clean the interior	B	30
E	Polish the car	C	25

veloped by the DuPont Company and the Univac Division of Remington Rand Corporation as a device to control the maintenance of chemical plants.

In many respects, PERT and CPM are similar in their basic concepts and methodology, but there is a basic difference between the two techniques. CPM is most appropriate for a project in which the activity durations are known with certainty. Thus, it

Figure 11.2   A Gantt Chart for Cleaning and Polishing a Car

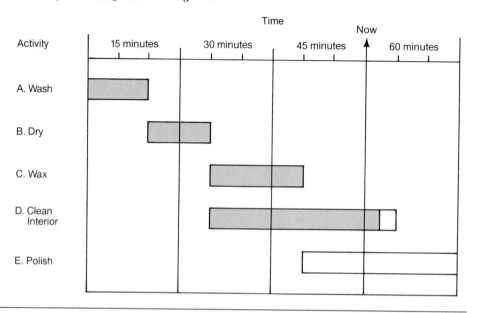

focuses on the trade-off between the project time and cost. However, PERT is useful for analyzing a project-scheduling problem in which the completion time is uncertain (probabilistic). It emphasizes the uncertainties of activity completion times and attempts to reach a particular event (milestone) in a project.

While we keep the basic difference between PERT and CPM in mind, several factors must always be considered whenever we deal with a project-scheduling problem:

The project completion time

The most critical activities that must be completed on time

The critical path (i.e., the longest path to completion) of the network

Permissible delays of noncritical activities that would not cause a delay for the entire project

The above factors are essential in understanding the critical relationships among activities and also in identifying missing elements in the network.

DEVELOPING PROJECT NETWORKS

PERT/CPM networks consist of two basic elements: **activities** and **events.** An activity represents an operation of the project that requires resources and consumes time. An event represents a certain point in time, such as the beginning or ending of an activity.

Table 11.2   A House Finishing Network

Activity	Activity Description	Start and End Nodes	Duration Estimates (Weeks)
A	Exterior finishing	(1,2)	3
B	Interior finishing	(2,3)	5

Figure 11.3   A House Finishing Network

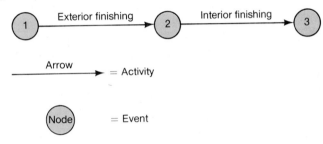

In the network model, activities are represented by arrows ($\rightarrow$) and events are shown as circles (O). The activity arrows are called *arcs,* and the event circles are referred to as *nodes*. Thus, every activity is bounded by nodes. Let us consider a simple example, the finishing process of a house construction project. There are two activities involved: the exterior finishing and the interior finishing. Table 11.2 presents a network for the finishing work process. Figure 11.3 provides the graphical representation of the two activities and the three associated events.

Each activity is identified by its starting and ending events. Event 1 represents the start of activity A (exterior finishing), and event 2 indicates the end of activity A. In other words, activity A starts from node 1 and ends at node 2. Event 2 also represents the start of activity B (interior finishing). Event 3 is the terminating point of activity B.

Transforming a Gantt Chart into a Network

In order to start a project, we can begin by developing a simple Gantt chart. We can then easily transform this chart into a network to handle complex interrelationships among activities. The Gantt chart for our car washing and polishing project is presented in Figure 11.4. As a means of transforming the chart into a network, we added circles (nodes) at the beginning and ending points of each bar.

In order to develop a network diagram, the five nodes are placed in a row, and activities are drawn as arrows connecting them. The length of an arrow has no bearing on the duration of an activity that connects two nodes. The only determining factor for the network diagram is precedence.

We have already emphasized the importance of the precedence relationship. An event or a node is not realized until all contributing or incoming activities are completed. For example, in Figure 11.4, event 5 will not be realized until both activities D and E are completed. Also, an activity cannot commence until all incoming activities to

Figure 11.4   A Gantt Chart and a Corresponding Network

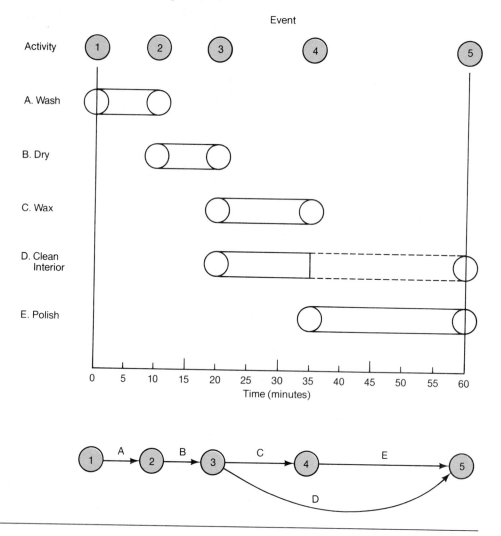

the starting event are completed. Therefore, activities C and D cannot begin until activity B is completed.

Dummy Activities

In a network, the easiest way we can identify an activity is by referring to the event numbers at the beginning and ending points. In other words, we would like to provide unique event coordinates for each activity in the network diagram. In the network diagram shown in Figure 11.5(a), we have two activities, C and D, that start at the same event (3) and also end at the same event (4). We would like to modify the diagram so that there will be only one activity between two events.

Some PERT/CPM networks must include **dummy activities** to designate proper precedence relationships. Where a doublet exists, we simply create a new event node to

Figure 11.5   Using a Dummy Activity

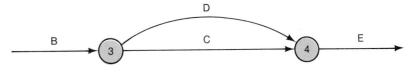

(a) A network without a dummy activity

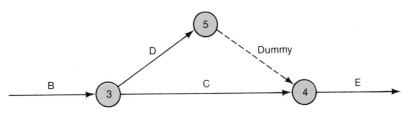

(b) A network with a dummy activity

remove one of the activities. Then, in order to preserve the precedence relationship, we also create a dummy activity that connects the new event node and the old ending event node. Since dummy activities are only artificial (e.g., a dummy destination or a dummy source in a transportation problem), they require absolutely no time or resources to complete. As shown in Figure 11.5(b), dummy activities are indicated by a dotted arrow line rather than a solid arrow line.

IDENTIFYING THE CRITICAL PATH

The **critical path** is the path that has the longest time through a network from start to finish. Identifying the critical path is of great importance as it represents the duration of the entire project. Thus, if any activity on the critical path is delayed for any reason, the entire project will be delayed accordingly. Every project network has a critical path. It is possible to have multiple critical paths if there are exact duplications among the longest paths.

Example 11.1 A SIMPLE NETWORK

Let us consider the simple network shown in Figure 11.6. There are three possible paths for the network. They are (listed by event nodes):

Path	Length of Time
① - ② - ④ - ⑥:	4 + 2 + 4 = 10 days
① - ② - ⑤ - ⑥:	4 + 7 + 2 = 13 days ← critical path
① - ③ - ⑤ - ⑥:	3 + 6 + 2 = 11 days

Figure 11.6   A Simple Network

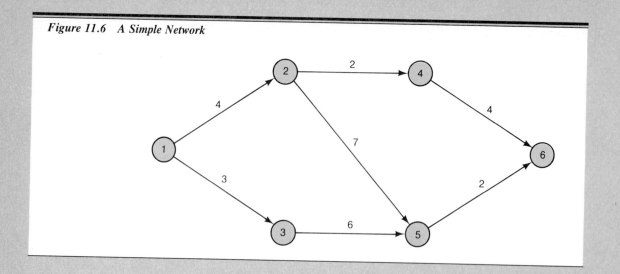

For this simple network, the critical path is found by enumerating all the possible paths to the completion point. The second path is the critical path because it requires the longest period of time to completion. Thus, if any activity on this path (① - ② - ⑤ - ⑥) is not completed within the planned time, the whole project will be delayed. For most real-world problems, enumeration of all possible paths can be cumbersome and time-consuming. There are two analytical approaches we can use to identify the critical path: the earliest expected time and the latest allowable time.

The Earliest Expected Time *(ET)*

The **earliest expected time (ET)** is based on the activity time estimate. The earliest time that an event can occur is on the latest completion of an activity terminating at that event node. This is also referred to as the *time of event realization*. ET values for each event are computed in a *forward*, or a *left-to-right*, tracing of the network.

In the CPM network, the activity time is given as a single estimate of the time required to complete each activity. In the PERT network, however, the activity time is expressed by the *mean* of each activity completion time. We will discuss how to determine the mean time of each activity in a later section of this chapter. Here, let us focus our attention on the CPM network.

In the network shown in Figure 11.6, we can see that two paths go through event 5. Event 5 cannot be realized until activities 2-5 and 3-5 are both completed. Activity 2-5 starts at event 2 and ends at event 5. Now we can compute the event realization time by tracing the activity time estimates.

The first event (the project-starting event) is assigned an *ET* value of 0 (*ET* = 0). To compute the *ET* for event 2, we add the completion time of activity 1-2 to the preceding *ET*, in this case the *ET* of event 1:

$$ET = ET \text{ (preceding event)} + \text{activity time}$$
$$ET_2 = 0 + 4 = 4$$

In general, the computation procedure for determining the earliest expected time for each network event is as follows:

$$ET_j = \text{Max } (ET_i + t_{ij})$$

where

ET_j = the earliest expected time of event j

ET_i = the earliest expected time that an activity leading to event j can

be started

t_{ij} = the estimated duration of an activity from event i to event j

Event 5 cannot be realized until activities 2-5 and 3-5 are completed. Thus, we must determine ET_5 as follows:

$$
\begin{aligned}
ET_5 &= \text{Max } (ET_2 + t_{25}; ET_3 + t_{35}) \\
&= \text{Max } (4 + 7; 3 + 6) \\
&= \text{Max } (11; 9) \\
&= 11
\end{aligned}
$$

The ET value for event 4 is computed by simply adding the completion time of activity 2-4 to ET_2. Thus, $ET_4 = ET_2 + t_{24} = 4 + 2 = 6$. The ET value for event 6, the final event, is determined by selecting the latest completion time of activities 4-6 or 5-6. Thus, the ET for event 6 would be

$$
\begin{aligned}
ET_6 &= \text{Max } (ET_4 + t_{46}; ET_5 + t_{56}) \\
&= \text{Max } (6 + 4; 11 + 2) \\
&= \text{Max } (10; 13) \\
&= 13
\end{aligned}
$$

Table 11.3 presents the computation of ET values for event 5 and event 6. Figure 11.7 presents the network with ET values for all events. The ET values are listed on the left of the T-bar above each event.

Table 11.3   Computation of ETs for Event 5 and Event 6

		EVENT 5		
Starting Event	ET_i	**Activity**	t_{ij}	ET_j
②	4	2–5	7	11*
③	3	3–5	6	9

		EVENT 6		
Starting Event	ET_i	**Activity**	t_{ij}	ET_j
④	6	4–6	4	10
⑤	11	5–6	2	13*

Figure 11.7   The Network with ET Values

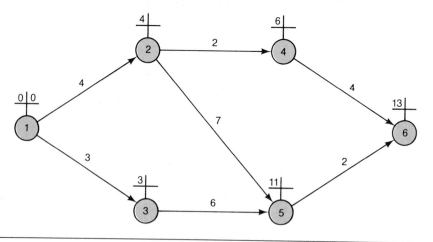

The Latest Allowable Time (*LT*)

Once the earliest expected time of the entire network is determined, the **latest allowable time (*LT*)** for an event can be computed. The *LT* for an event is the latest time that the event can be delayed without delaying the completion of the entire project.

The procedure we use in computing the *LT* value is to start from the final event of the network and work *backward* to the starting event in a *right-to-left* fashion. Let us examine our example network presented in Figure 11.6. First, the *LT* for the final event (node 6) should be set equal to the *ET* value for event 6, ET_6. In this case, $LT_6 = ET_6 = 13$. This *LT* value of 13 days is the latest time allowed to complete the entire project.

The *LT* value for an event can be computed by subtracting duration times of the activities that terminate at the last event from the preceding *LT* value. For example, the *LT* for event 4 is $13(LT_6) - 4(t_{46}) = 9$. Similarly, the *LT* for event 5 is $13(LT_6) - 2(t_{56}) = 11$. If two or more activities start from one event, such as from event 1 or event 2 in our example, we must select the *LT* value that is the smaller. Let us examine the case for event 2. Since both activities 2-4 and 2-5 start from event 2, there are two candidates for the *LT* value for event 2. One is 7 [$9(LT_4) - 2(t_{24}) = 7$], and the other is 4 [$11(LT_5) - 7(t_{25}) = 4$]. We select the smaller of the two. Thus, LT_2 is 4.

In general, the computation for the *LT* value for an event in a network is

$$LT_i = \text{Min } (LT_j - t_{ij})$$

where

LT_i = the latest allowable time of event i

LT_j = the latest allowable time of event j toward which activity i-j is headed

t_{ij} = the estimated duration for an activity from event i to event j

Table 11.4   Summary of LT Values for the Network Events

Starting Event (i)	Ending Event (j)	LT_j	Activity	t_{ij}	LT_i
6	—	13	—	—	13
5	6	13	5-6	2	11*
4	6	13	4-6	4	9
3	5	11	3-5	6	5
2	4	9	2-4	2	7
2	5	11	2-5	7	4*
1	2	4	1-2	4	0*
1	3	5	1-3	3	2

*Denotes activities along the critical path.

The *LT* value for event 3 is simply $LT_3 = 11(LT_5) - 6(t_{35}) = 5$. Activities 1-2 and 1-3 both start from event 1. Thus, we can compute the *LT* value for event 1 as follows:

$$LT_1 = \text{Min } (LT_2 - t_{12}; LT_3 - t_{13})$$
$$= \text{Min } (4 - 4; 5 - 3)$$
$$= \text{Min } (0; 2)$$
$$= 0$$

Computations of the latest allowable times for all of the events of the network are summarized in Table 11.4. It should be noted here that, by definition, at the beginning point of the network (event 1) $ET_1 = LT_1 = 0$, and at the ending point (event n) $ET_n = LT_n$.

The Critical Path

Once the values of *ET* and *LT* for all the events are determined, we can easily identify the critical path of the network. If the values of *ET* and *LT* for an event are equal, then the event is referred to as a **critical event.** All other events for which the *LT* values are not equal to the respective *ET* values are **noncritical events.** Each noncritical event has a positive *slack*.

The slack at a noncritical event is the difference between its *LT* and *ET* values ($S = LT - ET$). The slack (S) represents an excess amount of time available for the activity. In other words, we can delay this *particular* event up to the amount of slack time without risking the delay of the entire project. Figure 11.8 presents the network of our example problem with respective *ET*, *LT*, and slack values at each event. The *ET* values are listed on the left side of the T-bar, the *LT* values on the right side of the T-bar, and the slacks beneath each event node.

Now we can determine the critical path by tracing the critical events which have no slack values (i.e., $S = 0$). Thus, the critical path of our network is ①→ ②→ ⑤→ ⑥.

Figure 11.8   The Network with ET, LT, and Event Slack Values

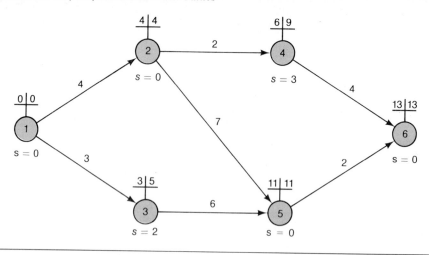

as shown in Figure 11.9. It should be noted that the events on the critical path have 0 slacks, and consequently there is no time to spare or to delay without delaying the entire project. However, at noncritical events, activities can be delayed up to their respective slack times without delaying the entire project. For example, event 3 has a slack of 2 days. Thus, we can delay activity 1-3 for up to 2 days. Since t_{13} is 3, activity 1-3 can

Figure 11.9   Critical Path of the Example Network

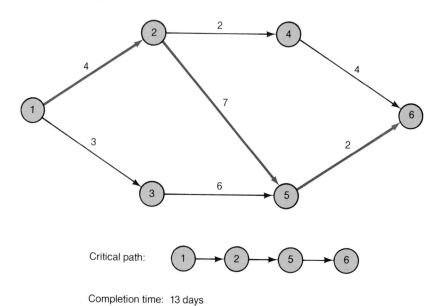

Critical path: 1 → 2 → 5 → 6

Completion time: 13 days

take up to 5 days without delaying the entire project. Alternatively, we could delay activity 3-5 for up to 2 days; we could also delay both activity 1-3 and activity 3-5 for up to a combined total delay of 2 days.

Activity Scheduling and Slack

When we computed slack times at noncritical events, we might have given the impression that we could delay activities up to the computed slack times. This is not usually the case because cumulative delays at noncritical events may actually delay the entire project. For example, we cannot delay both activity 1-3 and activity 3-5 by 2 days each without delaying the project. In this section, we will consider activity scheduling in relation to the associated slack times at various events.

The time at which an activity must be scheduled can be computed from the *ET* and *LT* values we determined earlier. For instance, in our example network presented in Figure 11.8, activity 2-4 must be scheduled to start no earlier than after 4 days ($ET_2 = 4$) and to end no later than after 9 days ($LT_4 = 9$). In other words, activity 2-4 can be scheduled as shown in Figure 11.10. We can start activity 2-4 at the beginning of the fifth day and complete it in 2 days (at the end of the sixth day). We can also start it at the beginning of the eighth day and complete it by the end of the ninth day. Or we can make any other arrangement from the fifth day to the end of the ninth day.

There are two types of slack for each activity in a network. **Total slack** represents the maximum amount of time available to schedule an activity, as discussed earlier. The

Figure 11.10   Scheduling Activity 2-4

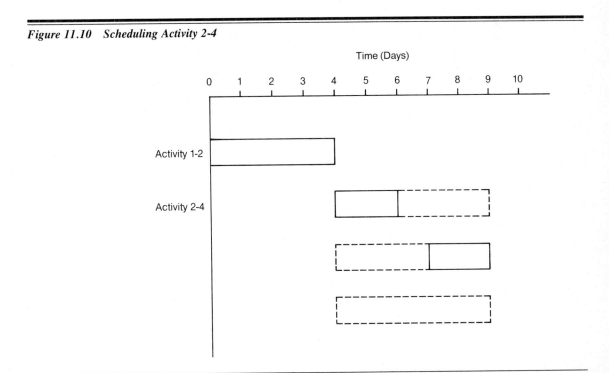

total slack for a given activity assumes that other activities on the same path will be completed during a certain time period. Total slack values can be determined as follows:

$$TS_{ij} = LT_j - ET_i - t_{ij}$$

where

TS_{ij} = total slack for activity i-j

LT_j = the latest allowable time for event j

ET_i = the earliest expected time for event i

t_{ij} = the time duration for activity i-j

For example, we can compute total slack for activities 1-3 and 2-5 as follows:

$$TS_{13} = LT_3 - ET_1 - t_{13}$$
$$= 5 - 0 - 3$$
$$= 2$$
$$TS_{25} = LT_5 - ET_2 - t_{25}$$
$$= 11 - 4 - 7$$
$$= 0$$

Free slack is the length of time a noncritical activity can be delayed without causing any delay in the completion of the entire network. Note that free slack can occur only at merge events (where two or more activities end at one event node). We can compute free slack for a given activity by the following formula:

$$FS_{ij} = ET_j - ET_i - t_{ij}$$

where

FS_{ij} = free slack for activity i-j

ET_j = the earliest expected time for event j

ET_i = the earliest expected time for event i

t_{ij} = the time duration for activity i-j

For example, we can compute free slack for activities 3-5 and 4-6 in Figure 11.11 as follows:

$$FS_{35} = ET_5 - ET_3 - t_{35}$$
$$= 11 - 3 - 6$$
$$= 2$$
$$FS_{46} = ET_6 - ET_4 - t_{46}$$
$$= 13 - 6 - 4$$
$$= 3$$

Now we can summarize the results of all our computations as shown in Table 11.5. This table is valuable in the sense that we can use the information to schedule our

Figure 11.11   The Network with Total Slack and Free Slack Values

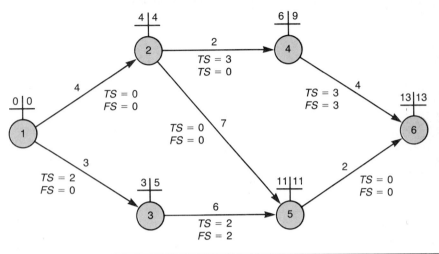

Table 11.5   Summary Information for the Network

Activity	Activity Duration	Earliest Expected Time (ET_i)	Latest Allowable Time (LT_j)	Total Slack (TS_{ij})	Free Slack (FS_{ij})	Shared Slack with
1-2	4 days	0	4	0	0	
1-3	3	0	5	2	0	2 (3-5)
2-4	2	4	9	3	0	3 (4-6)
2-5	7	4	11	0	0	
3-5	6	3	11	2	2	2 (1-3)
4-6	4	6	13	3	3	3 (2-4)
5-6	2	11	13	0	0	

☐	Critical path activities

activities, determine the critical path, determine the length of the project, and calculate the total free slack.

Whenever we have two or more noncritical activities in the same path, there may be **shared** (or **floating**) **slack.** This floating slack can be used any way we want among the activities involved. In Figure 11.8, we see that activities 1-3 and 3-5 share a slack of 2 time units. Technically, slack is only considered shared or floating once demands for free slack have been satisfied. Thus, shared slack = total slack − free slack, for any given activity. Shared slack will show up only on one activity arrow, yet applies equally to all activities in the sequence involved. It will appear as free slack at a merge event. Thus, in Figure 11.11, the shared slack for activity 1-3 and 3-5 is 2, which appears under activity 1-3 (TS − FS = 2 − 0 = 2); it appears as free slack under activity 3-5.

The values for both total slack and free slack are always 0 along the critical path. Where TS > FS, the difference represents slack which may be shared with a successor activity. When TS = FS, no sharing with successors will occur; however, a predecessor may share in the available slack. FS cannot be greater than TS.

Casette 11.1   SCHMIDT CONSTRUCTION, INC.

Hans Schmidt has been an independent contractor for over 20 years. He is a meticulous designer and worker who rejects any fast and sloppy job. This is the primary reason for his outstanding reputation as a quality builder in the city. Just recently he signed a contract to build a townhouse for a retiring banker. The contract indicates that Hans has to complete the house much faster than his normal pace will allow. He has never used any systematic approaches to conduct his building business.

His daughter Megan is home helping Hans do the bookkeeping work during the summer vacation. Megan is a management major at the university, and she has been lecturing Hans about how he should use modern management techniques in his operation. Hans decided that this is a perfect chance to test Megan and convince her that theory and practice do not always mix.

Network Construction

Megan accepted her father's challenge, although her confidence seemed to wane somewhat as she sat down and pondered where to begin. She quickly rejected linear programming, goal programming, and dynamic programming when she realized that the problem did not fit their model requirements. Finally she decided to use a network approach based on PERT/CPM.

On the basis of conversations with Hans and past contract records, Megan identified several major activities and their estimated durations. She also asked Hans about special relationships among the activities. As a result of these inquiries, she was able to compile the relevant information shown in Table 11.6. Hans reviewed the table and was pleasantly surprised to find that Megan's expensive education was not a complete waste.

Table 11.6   The Townhouse Project

Activity	Nodes	Description	Predecessor	Duration (Days)
A	1-2	Foundation and basement work	none	5
B	2-3	Erecting walls and roofing	A	10
C	2-4	Flooring work	A	6
D	3-5	Landscaping work	B	10
E	3-6	Electrical work	B	3
F	4-6	Plumbing work	B, C	4
G	6-7	Finishing work	D, E, F	15

Figure 11.12   The Townhouse Project Network Diagram

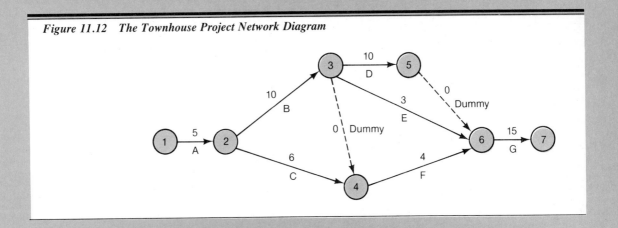

Examining the information in Table 11.6, Megan realized that she must connect events 3 and 4, because the plumbing work (activity F) can be started only when both activities B and C have been completed. Fortunately, she recalled how to add a dummy activity to accommodate such a situation. Megan constructed a network for the townhouse project as shown in Figure 11.12.

Network Analysis

In Figure 11.12, it is obvious that activities B and C can be started at the end of 5 days from the beginning of the project. On completion of activity B at the end of 15 days ($5 + 10 = 15$), activity D can be started. Similarly, on completion of activity C at the end of 11 days ($5 + 6 = 11$) and the dummy activity at the end of 15 days ($5 + 10 + 0 = 15$), we can begin activity F. Thus, activity F can be started at the end of 15 days.

In order to proceed with the network analysis, Megan decided to use the concepts of the earliest expected time and the latest allowable time by means of the following formulas:

$$ET_j = \text{Max } (ET_i + t_{ij})$$
$$LT_i = \text{Min } (LT_j - t_{ij})$$

Also, based on the *ET* and *LT* values at each event in the network derived above, Megan was able to compute total slack and free slack with the following formulas:

$$TS_{ij} = LT_j - ET_i - t_{ij}$$
$$FS_{ij} = ET_j - ET_i - t_{ij}$$

Figure 11.13 presents the townhouse project network with associated *ET*, *LT*, *TS*, and *FS* values. Megan identified four possible paths to complete the project. They are (expressed in event nodes):

Path	Length of Time	
①-②-③-⑤-⑥-⑦	5 + 10 + 10 + 0 + 15 = 40 days	← critical path
①-②-③-⑥-⑦	5 + 10 + 3 + 15 = 33	
①-②-③-④-⑥-⑦	5 + 10 + 0 + 4 + 15 = 34	
①-②-④-⑥-⑦	5 + 6 + 4 + 15 = 30	

The critical path is determined as ① - ② - ③ - ⑤ - ⑥ - ⑦ with a total duration of 40 days. On the basis of this analysis, Megan prepared for her father the summary report shown in Table 11.7. She also prepared a construction schedule for the various activities, as shown in Figure 11.14. Hans was greatly impressed by the thoroughness of the study and very proud of his favorite network person.

Figure 11.13   *The Townhouse Network with ET, LT, TS, and FS Values*

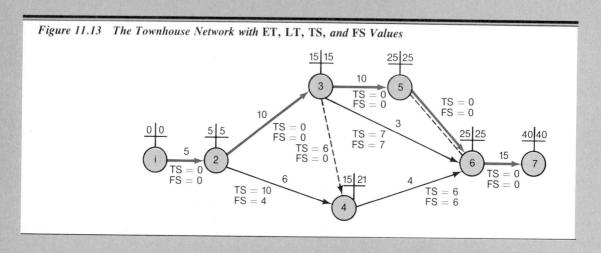

Table 11.7   *Summary Report of the Townhouse Project*

1. Critical Activities and Time Duration

Foundation and basement work	5 days
Erecting walls and roofing	10
Landscaping work	10
Finishing work	15
	Total = 40 days

2. Noncritical Activities, Duration, and Slack Time

	Duration	Total Slack	Free Slack
Flooring work	6	10	4
Electrical work	3	7	7
Plumbing work	4	6	6

3. Total Project Duration = 40 days

Figure 11.14   The Townhouse Construction Schedule

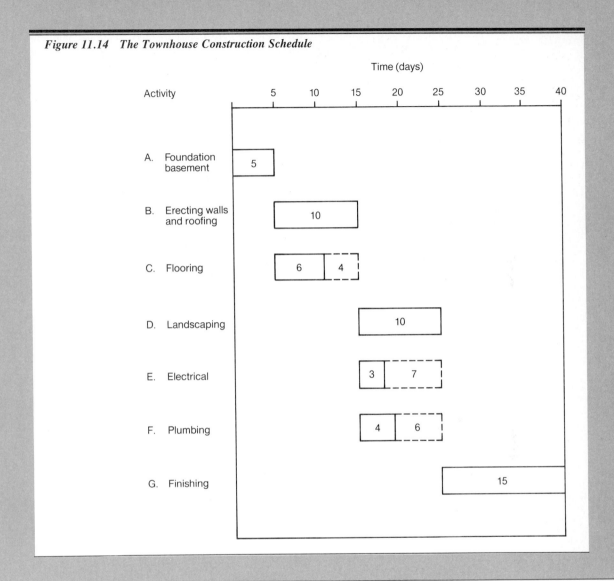

CPM TIME AND COST TRADE-OFFS

The critical path method is an effective tool in deriving valuable information about critical activities, noncritical activities, free slack times for noncritical activities, and total completion time for a project. One of the most important aspects of CPM network analysis is its capacity for evaluating alternative ways to expedite some or all the network activities and then analyze their cost implications. In many real-world problems, it is often desirable to expedite a project even at a considerable additional cost. Sometimes it is desirable not to expedite at all, depending on the nature of the project and the environment.

There was an interesting case in a Colorado ski resort town where three builders were each undertaking a large condominium project. One builder expedited his project at 50 percent cost overrun in order to open the condominium before the ski season. The second builder maintained his regular construction schedule, and the third contractor deliberately slowed down his schedule by 30 percent at a cost underrun of 15 percent. This particular ski season turned out to be a total disaster—the ski slopes were open for only 25 days out of the 140-day season because of a lack of snow. The first builder went bankrupt, the second builder sustained a substantial loss, and the third builder was not very happy either, but at least he was not complaining.

An important extension of project time analysis is project *time-cost trade-off* analysis. Expediting or rushing activities in order to shorten the project duration from the normal completion time is often referred to as **project crashing.** Cost analysis associated with project crashing is an important part of CPM analysis. However, time-cost trade-off can be applied to any project-scheduling network, whether it is a CPM or PERT type network. The basic purpose of time-cost analysis is to determine certain activities of the network that can be expedited (by how much time and at what cost).

In time-cost analysis, two time estimates and two cost estimates are used to develop the time-cost relationship. The two estimates used are: normal time (NT) versus crash time (CT), and normal cost (NC) versus crash cost (CC). The relationship between normal time and normal cost and crash time and crash cost for an activity is assumed to be linear. Let us suppose that an activity can be performed at a normal work pace requiring $200 and 4 days. Under an emergency situation, the same activity can be performed on a "crash" basis requiring $500 and only 2 days. The time-cost relationship can be developed as illustrated in Figure 11.15.

The slope of the straight line in Figure 11.15 represents the change in cost associated with one unit change in time. In other words, it represents the *crash cost per unit of time* (e.g., day, week, year). We can develop the slope as follows:

$$\text{Crash cost per unit of time} = \frac{\text{crash cost} - \text{normal cost}}{\text{normal time} - \text{crash time}}$$

$$\text{Slope} = \frac{CC - NC}{NT - CT}$$

For the problem illustrated in Figure 11.15, we can determine the crash cost per day as follows:

$$\text{Crash cost per day} = \frac{\$500 - \$200}{4 - 2}$$

$$= \frac{\$300}{2}$$

$$= \$150$$

Thus, if we are interested in reducing the total project completion time by expediting this particular activity, we can do so up to 2 days at a cost of $150 per day. One thing we must realize when crashing a project is that the critical path may change while crashing. Therefore, we should take care not to crash an activity without also affecting the project completion time.

Figure 11.15   Activity Time/Cost Relationship

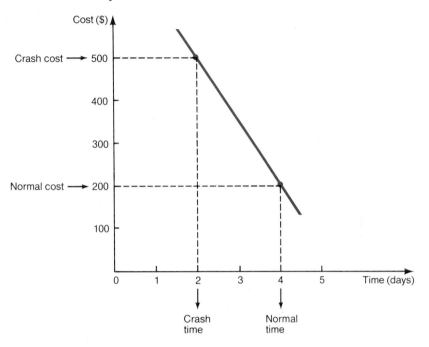

Example 11.2 *PROJECT CRASHING*

Let us consider the project network presented in Figure 11.16. The normal and crash times (in parentheses) as well as the crash cost per day are also shown in the network. The time-cost information, including the computed crash cost per day, is provided in Table 11.8.

We can easily determine the critical path of the example network by computing *ET* and *LT* values for each activity. The critical path is (1) - (2) - (4) - (5), and the normal project completion time is 58 days.

In analyzing this project crashing, the type of questions that we need to answer are: Can we complete the project faster than the critical path indicates? If so, at what additional cost? What is the minimum cost required to complete the project in 10 weeks? What would be the best way to schedule the project, given that we have a $2 million budget?

Now we are ready to examine the project crashing. As we go through the analysis procedure, we must pay close attention to any change in the critical path throughout the crashing process. The time-cost trade-off analysis involves the following steps:

Step 1   Identify and crash the critical activity that has the minimum crash cost per unit of time. In a case in which there are multiple critical paths, select the joint critical activity that has the minimum crash cost per unit of time. If no such joint critical activity

Figure 11.16   A Network for Cost Analysis

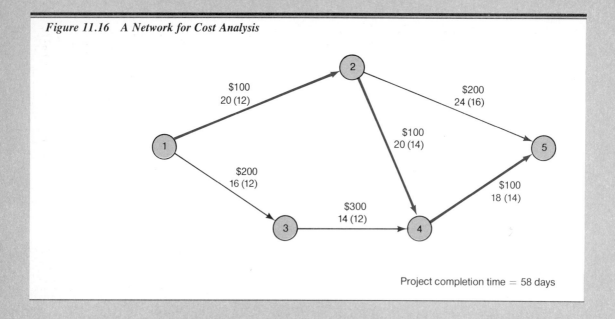

Project completion time = 58 days

Table 11.8   The Network Crashing Information

Activity	Time (days)		Cost (dollars)		Crash Cost/Day
	Normal	Crash	Normal	Crash	
1-2*	20	12	1,800	2,600	$100
1-3	16	12	800	1,600	200
2-5	24	16	3,200	4,800	200
2-4*	20	14	1,600	2,200	100
3-4	14	12	2,400	3,000	300
4-5*	18	14	800	1,200	100
			10,600	15,400	

Critical path.
The normal project completion time = 58 days.
The completely crashed completion time = 40 days.

exists, select the activity from each critical path that has the minimum crash cost per unit of time.

Step 2   Completely revise the network by adjusting the time and cost of the crashed activity. Identify the critical path. If the normal project completion time equals the crashed completion time, terminate the procedure. Otherwise, repeat the procedure by going back to Step 1.

The First Crashing

In our example, the crash costs of three critical activities, 1-2, 2-4, and 4-5, are identical, $100. Thus, we may choose any one of them. Let us arbitrarily choose activity 1-2 to crash. Activity 1-2 can be crashed by 8 days: 20 (normal time) − 12 (crash time) = 8. Thus, the associated crashing cost is $800: $100 (crash cost per day) × 8 (days) = $800.

The revised network, adjusted for the time and cost assigned to activity 1-2, is shown in Figure 11.17. The critical path is not changed but remains ①-②-④-⑤. The project completion time has been reduced by 8 days to 50 days, which is still greater than the crashed completion time of 40 days. Thus, we must continue the procedure.

The Second Crashing

Since activity 1-2 has been crashed, either activity 2-4 or activity 4-5 should be chosen for crashing based on its crash cost per day. Since both activities have the same crash costs of $100, we may choose activity 2-4 arbitrarily. Notice, however, that we cannot reduce activity 2-4 for more than 2 days, since doing so will generate a new critical path (i.e., ①-③-④-⑤). Therefore, we can crash only up to 2 days. This crash will reduce activity 2-4 to 18 days, resulting in a project completion time of 48 days. The additional cost for this crash is $200. The revised network is shown in Figure 11.18.

The Third Crashing

The project completion time of 48 days is still greater than the completely crashed completion time of 40 days. Thus, we continue our crashing procedure. As shown in Figure 11.18, now there are two critical paths: ①-②-④-⑤ and ①-③-④-⑤. By crashing activity 4-5, the only joint activity (i.e., the common activity for both critical paths), we can reduce the project completion time without crashing more than one activity. We may, in fact, crash more than one activity if we can reduce the project completion time and reduce the cost by doing so; for example, we may crash an activity

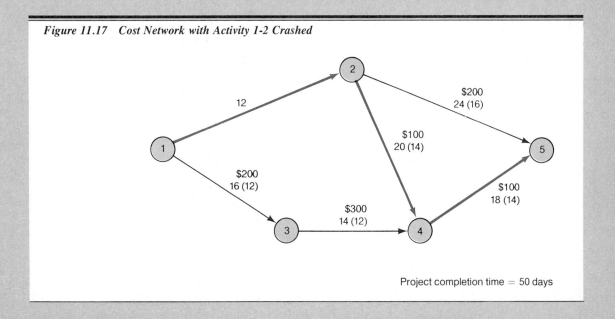

Figure 11.17   Cost Network with Activity 1-2 Crashed

Project completion time = 50 days

Figure 11.18   Cost Network with Activities 1-2 and 2-4 Crashed

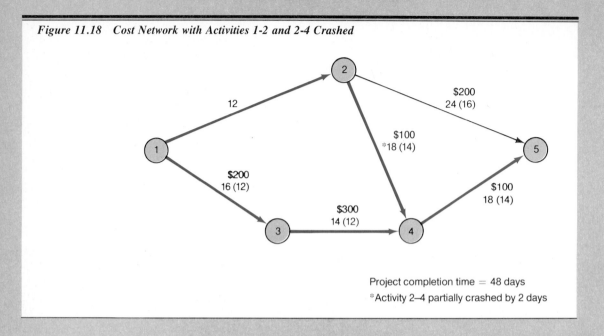

Project completion time = 48 days
*Activity 2–4 partially crashed by 2 days

Figure 11.19   Cost Network with Activities 1-2, 2-4, and 4-5 Crashed

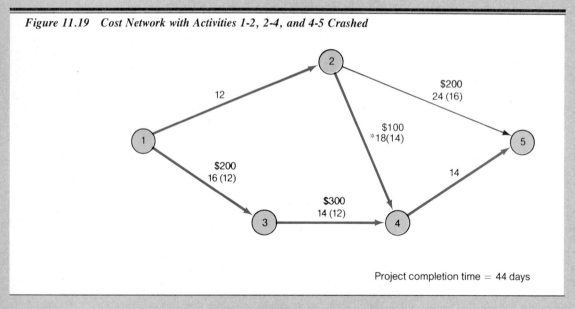

Project completion time = 44 days

on each of the two critical paths. Here, we can reduce by 4 days the duration for activity 4-5. Thus, as shown in Figure 11.19, the project completion time has been reduced to 44 days, and the resultant additional crashing cost is $400.

The Fourth Crashing

We still have two critical paths, as shown in Figure 11.19. This time, however, we cannot reduce only one activity, since there is no single uncrashed activity through

Figure 11.20   *Cost Network with Activities 1-2, 4-5, 2-4, and 1-3 Crashed*

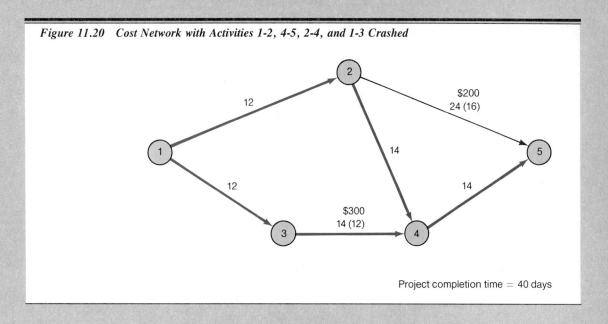

Project completion time = 40 days

which both critical paths pass. If we crash only one activity, one of the two critical paths will be still critical (unreduced), and the project completion time will remain unchanged at 44 days. Thus, in this case, both activities 1-3 and 2-4 should be crashed simultaneously. This selection is based on the fact that activity 2-4 is the only activity left to be crashed and activity 1-3 has less crash cost than activity 3-4. In general, if there are several uncrashed activities to choose from several critical paths, we should select the activity from each critical path that has the minimum crashing cost.

One more thing to note is that we can crash each activity down to the lower limit established by one of them (whichever has the minimum crash time). In this example, both activities 1-3 and 2-4 can be reduced by 4 days. Thus, activity 1-3 has been reduced to 12 days (16 − 4 = 12), whereas activity 2-4 has been reduced further to 14 days (18 − 4 = 14), as illustrated in Figure 11.20. Consequently, the total project completion time is 40 days, and the additional crashing cost is $1,200 ($200 × 4 + $100 × 4 = $1,200).

Figure 11.20 shows that the activity times of activities 1-2, 2-4, and 4-5 have been reduced to their limits. In other words, there cannot be any more crashing because the project completion time of 40 days will remain unchanged even if we crash activity 2-5, 3-4, or both. Thus, the minimum completion time for this project is 40 days, and the total additional cost for crashing the 4 activities is $2,600 ($800 + $200 + $400 + $1,200 = $2,600). The total cost of this project is then $13,200: $10,600 (normal cost) + $2,600 (additional crashing cost) = $13,200. Table 11.9 summarizes the result of this cost analysis. Figure 11.21 presents the time-cost trade-off relationship through the crashing process.

The Final Analysis

Based on our analysis, it is obvious that if the incentive of crashing the project is worth more than the crashing cost of $2,600, it is desirable to crash it. Otherwise, it is, of course, not worth crashing the project. In addition to this standard time-cost trade-off

Table 11.9   Summary of the Crashing Procedure

Crashing Step Number	Activities Crashed	Time Reduced	Revised Project Completion Time	Additional Cost	Revised Project Cost
0	—	—	58 days	—	$10,600
1	1-2	8 days	50	$ 800	11,400
2	2-4	2	48	200	11,600
3	4-5	4	44	400	12,000
4	1-3 & 2-4	4	40	1,200	13,200
		18 days		$2,600	

Figure 11.21   Time-Cost Trade-Off Relationship

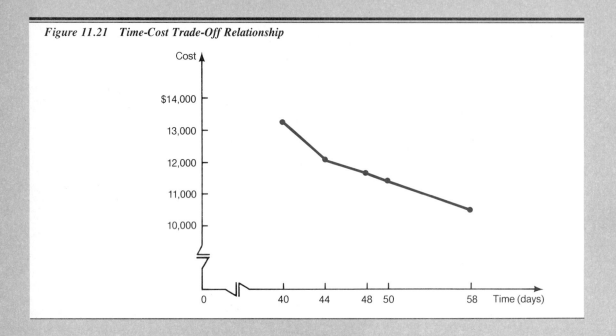

analysis, we can perform several sensitivity-type analyses. For example, we may want to find answers to questions such as: What is the minimum cost required to complete the project in 45 days? Given that we can afford only $12,000, what would be the best way to schedule the project? This type of question can be answered by using the same time-cost trade-off analysis procedure.

ESTIMATING ACTIVITY TIMES IN PERT

Thus far, our discussion has been focused on the CPM technique in which we assume that a single estimate of each activity duration can be obtained with certainty. Such an assumption is not warranted in many situations. PERT is more effective in handling cases in which activity duration times are not known with certainty.

The PERT technique makes the following basic assumptions: (1) activity times are statistically independent and could be associated with a known distribution (usually a beta distribution); (2) there are a sufficient number of activities involved in the network and thus the summed totals of activity times based on their means and variances will be normally distributed; and (3) three estimates of the activity duration can be obtained for each activity—optimistic, most likely, and pessimistic times.

We can define the three time estimates for each project activity as follows:

Optimistic (shortest) **time** represents the duration required to complete an activity under the most ideal conditions. It is denoted by a.

Most likely (model) **time** is the expected duration of an activity under normal conditions. It is denoted by m.

Pessimistic (longest) **time** represents the duration of an activity under unusual conditions, such as machine breakdowns, material shortages, bad weather. It is denoted by b.

As noted previously, it is assumed that the distribution of the three time estimates is best approximated by a *beta* distribution. In a beta distribution, it is easy to determine such parameters as mean and standard deviation by using the following formulas:

$$\textbf{Mean:} \quad t_e = \frac{a + 4m + b}{6}$$

$$\textbf{Standard deviation:} \quad \sigma_e = \frac{b - a}{6}$$

where t_e = mean duration for an activity in the PERT network.

By using t_e values, it is possible to make probability statements about the expected completion time for the project. Suppose that we have obtained the following three time estimates: $a = 8$, $m = 17$, and $b = 20$. Then, we can compute

$$t_e = \frac{8 + 4(17) + 20}{6} = \frac{96}{6} = 16$$

$$\sigma_e = \frac{20 - 8}{6} = 2$$

The expected duration of the activity is 16 days with the standard deviation of 2 days. In this example, the most likely time ($m = 17$) is closer to the pessimistic time ($b = 20$) than to the optimistic time ($a = 8$). Thus, the activity time distribution is skewed to the right, as shown in Figure 11.22. Based on the information we obtain from the three time estimates, we can further analyze the network problem. For example, we can determine the expected project completion time, the variance of the critical path, and the probability associated with completing the project before a specified period of time.

Figure 11.22   Beta Distribution of a PERT Activity Time

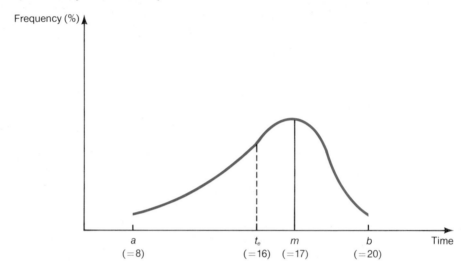

Casette 11.2   DINO'S, INC. OF CALIFORNIA

Dino's, Inc. of California is a California-based firm that operates a chain of fast food restaurants, Dino's, throughout the United States. The company has been extremely successful owing to its innovative menu and promotional activities. One of Dino's recent successful menu innovations was Beefalo Burger de Dino.

Dino's product development process is centered in two groups: the Product Development Committee, which reviews and makes final decisions on new products, and the Research and Development Department, which provides technical support. The product development process involves eight distinct activities: (1) idea generation, (2) business analysis, (3) screening, (4) development, (5) quality assurance, (6) testing, (7) approval of the committee, and (8) commercialization.

The management of Dino's has been very concerned about the duration of the product development process, and it is keenly interested in obtaining information concerning the possibility of reducing the completion time of the whole process. The Product Development Committee decided to ask Cindy Hall, a senior systems analyst, to analyze the problem and make recommendations.

Cindy is an experienced systems analyst with extensive working knowledge of PERT and CPM. Because of Dino's excellent information systems, Cindy was able to obtain time estimates (in days) for each activity without much difficulty. Cindy compiled the relevant data, as shown in Table 11.10.

In order to obtain the expected project completion time, the critical path of the network must be determined. In a PERT network, we can compute t_e (mean completion time) and σ_e (standard deviation) for each activity. The variance of the activity time distribution, $\sigma_e^2 = [(b - a)/6]^2$, is also useful for further analysis. Cindy computed t_e, σ_e, and σ_e^2 for each activity, as presented in Table 11.11. Based on the activity precedence relationship information compiled in Table 11.10 and the activity time data pre-

Table 11.10   Activity Time Estimates for Dino's, Inc.

Activity	Description	Predecessor	a (Optimistic)	m (Most Likely)	b (Pessimistic)
A	Idea generation	none	8	12	16
B	Business analysis	A	12	15	24
C	Screening	A	5	7	15
D	Development	B	4	6	14
E	Quality assurance	B	2	4	6
F	Testing	C	6	10	14
G	Approval of committee	E,F	2	4	12
H	Commercialization	D,G	13	15	23

Table 11.11   The t_e, σ_e, and σ_e^2 for Each Activity

Activity	Expected (Mean) Time $\left(\dfrac{a + 4m + b}{6}\right)$	Standard Deviation $\left(\dfrac{b - a}{6}\right)$	Variance $\left(\dfrac{b - a}{6}\right)^2$
A*	12	4/3	16/9
B*	16	2	4
C	8	5/3	25/9
D	7	5/3	25/9
E*	4	2/3	4/9
F	10	4/3	16/9
G*	5	5/3	25/9
H*	16	5/3	25/9

Critical activity.

sented in Table 11.11, Cindy developed a PERT network and its critical path, as shown in Figure 11.23.

Cindy examined the past project records and found that the distribution of each activity completion time is about *normal*. Thus, the expected activity times for critical activities (i.e., activities on the critical path) are also normally distributed. Accordingly, Cindy makes the assumption that the summation of all of the time estimates of critical activities, which is the expected project completion time, would be normally distributed according to the central limit theorem of probability theory. The expected project completion time of Dino's new product development is 53 days, as shown in Figure 11.23.

Given the normal distribution assumption, the probability of completing the project in 53 days or less is 0.5. We can develop a more precise normal curve of the project completion time if we determine the standard deviation of the time estimates for critical activities. The standard deviation is computed as follows:

$$\sigma_{cp} = \sqrt{\sum \sigma_e^2}$$

Figure 11.23   Critical Path

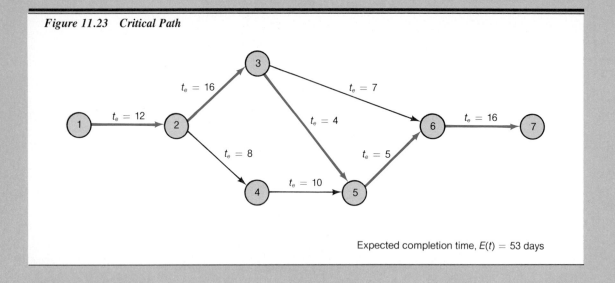

Expected completion time, $E(t)$ = 53 days

Table 11.12   *Computation of Project Standard Deviation*

Activities on Critical Path	σ_e	σ_e^2
A	4/3	16/9
B	2	4
E	2/3	4/9
G	5/3	25/9
H	5/3	25/9
		$\Sigma\sigma_e^2$ = 106/9

$$\sigma_{cp} = \sqrt{\Sigma\sigma_e^2} = \sqrt{106/9} = 3.43$$

where

$$\sigma_{cp} = \text{standard deviation of the expected project completion time}$$

$$\Sigma\sigma_e^2 = \text{sum of variance of all activities on the critical path}$$

Since Cindy has already computed the variance of each critical activity, σ_{cp} is easily computed as shown in Table 11.12. The standard deviation of the expected project completion time is 3.43 days. Now Cindy can easily find the probability of completing the project on or before a specified time (or on or after a specified time).

For some time Dino's management has been trying to complete the product development within 50 days, but without success. In order to find the probability of this completion time, Cindy decided to use the formula that computes the *standardized random variate* (Z). The formula is as follows:

$$Z = \frac{X - E(t)}{\sigma_{cp}}$$

where

$$X = \text{desired project completion time}$$
$$E(t) = \text{expected project completion time}$$
$$\sigma_{cp} = \text{standard deviation of activities on the critical path}$$
$$Z = \text{number of standard deviation of a normal distribution}$$
$$\text{(standardized random variate)}$$

Using the above formula, Cindy determined the standardized random variate, Z, as follows:

$$Z = \frac{50 - 53}{3.43} = -0.87$$

We can find the probability corresponding to any Z value in the standard normal distribution table in Appendix 4. The probability for the Z value of 0.87 is 0.80785. Since $Z = -0.87$, in this case we must subtract 0.80785 from the standard deviate of 1.0. Thus, we obtain $1.0 - 0.80785 = 0.19215$. In other words, the probability of completing Dino's new product development within 50 days is 0.19215, or 19.22 percent. This reasoning is illustrated in Figure 11.24.

Suppose that Dino's is also interested in finding the probability of completing the project in 60 days. The computation for this probability (p) is

$$p \text{ (60 or fewer days)} = p\left(Z \leq \frac{60 - 53}{3.43}\right)$$

$$= p\left(Z \leq \frac{7}{3.43}\right)$$

$$= p\left(Z \leq 2.04\right)$$

$$= 0.97932$$

Thus, the probability of completing the project in 60 days or less is 0.9793, or 97.93 percent.

In addition to determining the probability $(p = 0.1922)$ of completing the new product development project within 50 days, Cindy made several other suggestions.

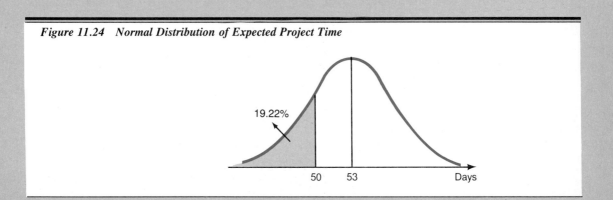

Figure 11.24   Normal Distribution of Expected Project Time

19.22%

50   53   Days

These suggestions were based on probability analysis of the earliest completion times at each node, determined by summing the activity times and variances along the critical path. Also, she analyzed the possible impact of the variances of noncritical activities on the probability of the project completion. Soon after this study, Cindy was promoted to the position of Manager of Systems Analysis.

COMPUTER SOLUTIONS OF PROJECT-PLANNING PROBLEMS

As we have seen in previous sections of this chapter, it is a time-consuming job to analyze PERT/CPM networks by hand. It might be impossible to perform certain network analyses without the help of computers, especially when the networks are large and complex. There are available today a number of computer packages that are capable of analyzing sophisticated network problems such as scheduling multiple projects simultaneously, providing cost and resource information, choosing the best procedure, and analyzing probabilistic network problems. In summary, the real-world scheduling network analysis can be performed effectively by using computers for the specific objectives of each analysis.

Once again we use *Micro Manager* to solve the casette problems. Figure 11.25 presents the input data and the program output for Casette 11.1, the Schmidt Construction, Inc. problem. The critical path, in terms of nodes, is $1\rightarrow2\rightarrow3\rightarrow5\rightarrow6\rightarrow7$, and the construction completion time is 40 days. These results correspond with the manual solutions we derived in Casette 11.1.

Figure 11.26 presents the computer solution of Casette 11.2, the Dino's Inc. of California problem. The program output shows both analysis of CPM and analysis of PERT/CPM. The critical path for the project is $1\rightarrow2\rightarrow3\rightarrow5\rightarrow6\rightarrow7$ with the completion time of 53 days. These results correspond exactly with our manual solutions. In addition, analysis of PERT/CPM presents the mean and variance of each activity time.

REAL-WORLD APPLICATIONS

Surveys of managers and practicing management scientists, similar to those cited in Chapter 1, indicate that network techniques are applied to a variety of managerial problems. Of course, it is not clear whether these surveys were referring to the actual use of PERT/CPM or to many different types of networking techniques. We believe that PERT/CPM, or stochastic network techniques such as graphical evaluation and review technique (GERT) and venture evaluation and review technique (VERT), are often used by large technology-oriented organizations and federal agencies. However, these techniques are not widely applied by medium-size or small organizations, primarily because of a lack of technical staff.

Nevertheless, we believe the Gantt chart and PERT/CPM have many sound concepts to offer, such as the precedence relationship, events, activities, the critical path, slack analysis, probabilistic analysis of the network, time-cost trade-off analysis, and the like. Thus, we believe project planning will remain an important part of management science. It is especially so with the advent of today's inexpensive but powerful micro- or personal computers.

Figure 11.25   Casette 11.1 — Schmidt Construction, Inc.

```
PROGRAM: PERT/CPM

***** INPUT DATA ENTERED *****

 CPM

-------------------------------------------------------------------------
                     Predecessor
Activity    Nodes    Activities        Duration
-------------------------------------------------------------------------
    1       1 -> 2                         5.0
    2       2 -> 3       1                 10.0
    3       2 -> 4       1                 6.0
    4       3 -> 5       2                 10.0
    5       3 -> 6       2                 3.0
    6       4 -> 6       2  3              4.0
    7       6 -> 7       4  5  6           15.0
-------------------------------------------------------------------------

*****   PROGRAM OUTPUT   *****

** Analysis of CPM **

-------------------------------------------------------------------------
                   Activity   Early    Late    Total    Free
Activity   Nodes   Duration   Start   Finish   Slack    Slack
-------------------------------------------------------------------------
    1      1 -> 2    5.0        0.0     5.0      0.0      0.0
    2      2 -> 3    10.0       5.0    15.0      0.0      0.0
    3      2 -> 4    6.0        5.0    21.0     10.0      4.0
    4      3 -> 5    10.0      15.0    25.0      0.0      0.0
    5      3 -> 6    3.0       15.0    25.0      7.0      7.0
    6      4 -> 6    4.0       15.0    25.0      6.0      6.0
    7      6 -> 7    15.0      25.0    40.0      0.0      0.0
  * 8      3 -> 4    0.0       15.0    21.0      6.0      0.0
  * 9      5 -> 6    0.0       25.0    25.0      0.0      0.0
-------------------------------------------------------------------------

The Critical Path (nodes)      1 -> 2 -> 3 -> 5 -> 6 -> 7
The Critical Path (activities)  1 - 2 - 4 - 9 - 7

The Completion Time = 40
```

Figure 11.26   Casette 11.2 — Dino's, Inc. of California

```
PROGRAM: PERT/CPM

***** INPUT DATA ENTERED *****

PERT
```

Activity	Nodes	Predecessor Activities		Optimistic	Most Likely	Pessimistic
1	1 -> 2			8.0	12.0	16.0
2	2 -> 3	1		12.0	15.0	24.0
3	2 -> 4	1		5.0	7.0	15.0
4	3 -> 6	2		4.0	6.0	14.0
5	3 -> 5	2		2.0	4.0	6.0
6	4 -> 5	3		6.0	10.0	14.0
7	5 -> 6	5	6	2.0	4.0	12.0
8	6 -> 7	4	7	13.0	15.0	23.0

```
*****   PROGRAM OUTPUT   *****

** Analysis of CPM **
```

Activity	Nodes	Activity Duration	Early Start	Late Finish	Total Slack	Free Slack
1	1 -> 2	12.0	0.0	12.0	0.0	0.0
2	2 -> 3	16.0	12.0	28.0	0.0	0.0
3	2 -> 4	8.0	12.0	22.0	2.0	0.0
4	3 -> 6	7.0	28.0	37.0	2.0	2.0
5	3 -> 5	4.0	28.0	32.0	0.0	0.0
6	4 -> 5	10.0	20.0	32.0	2.0	2.0
7	5 -> 6	5.0	32.0	37.0	0.0	0.0
8	6 -> 7	16.0	37.0	53.0	0.0	0.0

```
The Critical Path (nodes)      1 -> 2 -> 3 -> 5 -> 6 -> 7
The Critical Path (activities) 1 - 2 - 5 - 7 - 8

The Completion Time = 53

** Analysis of PERT/CPM **
```

Activity	Nodes	Optimistic	Most Likely	Pessimistic	Mean	Variance
1	1 -> 2	8.0	12.0	16.0	12.0	1.7778
2	2 -> 3	12.0	15.0	24.0	16.0	4.0000
3	2 -> 4	5.0	7.0	15.0	8.0	2.7778
4	3 -> 6	4.0	6.0	14.0	7.0	2.7778
5	3 -> 5	2.0	4.0	6.0	4.0	0.4444
6	4 -> 5	6.0	10.0	14.0	10.0	1.7778
7	5 -> 6	2.0	4.0	12.0	5.0	2.7778
8	6 -> 7	13.0	15.0	23.0	16.0	2.7778

```
The Critical Path (nodes)      1 -> 2 -> 3 -> 5 -> 6 -> 7
The Critical Path (activities) 1 - 2 - 5 - 7 - 8

The Completion Time = 53
```

CPM Aids Firefighter Manning Decisions

For nonvolunteer fire departments, personnel costs consume 90 percent or more of the total budget. Although affected by salary structure and work schedule, the major factor in determining personnel costs is the number of firefighters employed—the *manning level*.[1] The National Fire Protection Association Handbook based an effectiveness standard on a five-person crew on a pumper, and determined that a four-person crew was only 66 percent as effective, whereas a three-person crew dropped to under 25 percent as effective as a five-person crew. A test by the Dallas Fire Department found that six workers were 20 percent faster than five. A method of analyzing firefighting tactics with manning policies as a goal appeared desirable.

This study is built on the premise that firefighting activities can be decomposed into distinct activities, which may be described as activities with various precedence relationships. Once this assumption was established, the critical path method could be employed. The objective was to find the relationship between the number of firefighters present and the time needed to extinguish the fire. Effectiveness was defined as a function of time required—the faster the needed activity sequence was accomplished, the greater the effectiveness. The study concentrated on one- and two-family homes, where the majority of fire deaths and much of the property loss occur.

Structured interviews with members of the Calgary Fire Department were used to develop the network structure, define the activities, and estimate their parameters. Actual observation and data gathering was naturally difficult, so the interviews focused on standardized scenarios. Because precedence relationships were often cloudy or changeable depending on the situation, threshold probabilities were employed in several runs of otherwise identical data. Six networks were generated, with roughly 30 nodes and nearly twice as many arcs.

For all scenarios/threshold values, effectiveness leveled off at nine crew members, with no further improvement (under the given circumstances). The largest improvement comes with the addition of the seventh firefighter; the eighth and ninth are typically marginal. With fewer firefighters, effectiveness depends more on the size of the work force and less on decisions of the supervising officer. Useful information regarding critical activities was generated, and the model may serve as a valuable addition to firefighter training.

Timing of Income-Property Mortgage Loan Process

Mortgage bankers have indicated a desire for a systematic technique that would allow them to evaluate and review income-property mortgage loan processing.[2] Time is, of course, a factor in applications for such loans, and various events must occur before others are possible. Variations occur due to the preparedness of the loan applicant, as well as the quality of the request.

PERT proved well suited to the task of evaluating the time sequence involved in processing the loan application. The formulated network stretched from the initial node

---

[1] Jonathon Halpern, Efstratios Sarisamlis, and Yair Wand, "An Activity Network Approach for the Analysis of Manning Policies in Firefighting Operations," *Management Science* 28:10 (Oct. 1982), 1121–1136.

[2] V. Edward Gold, "Income Property Loans: From Start to Finish," *Mortgage Banking* 42:13 (Sept. 1982), 27–30.

(first meeting with borrower) to the seventeenth and final node (loan closing), with four merge nodes followed by a simple chain, illustrated below. Selected nodes are identified. The network proved useful in setting initial earliest closing dates and could also be used for revised estimates as various stages are completed.

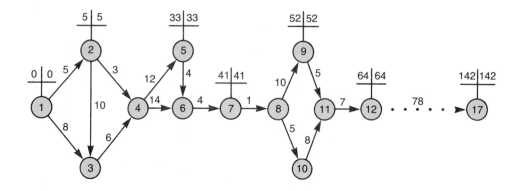

Events: 1. Initial meeting

        2. Inspection of property

        5. Receipt of all requested data

        7. Review of potential investors

      11. Loan synopsis

      12. Lending committee meeting

      17. Loan closing

SUMMARY

In this chapter we have discussed several valuable tools for project planning. They are the Gantt chart, the general project network, CPM, and PERT. Although the Gantt chart is the simplest and perhaps the most widely used tool among practicing managers, it can show only the duration of various project activities on a time scale. If we want to analyze interrelationships among project activities, we need to develop a network. A network can provide such useful information as activities, events, precedence relationships, earliest expected time, latest allowable time, total slack, free slack, and, perhaps most importantly, the critical path.

PERT and CPM techniques are built on the general concept of project networks. CPM utilizes time-cost trade-off analysis based on two time and cost estimates: normal time and crash time, and normal cost and crash cost. On the basis of this data, CPM can manipulate the critical path while establishing desired trade-offs between the project time and cost.

PERT introduces probabilistic aspects to the project network. It uses three project activity time estimates: optimistic, most likely, and pessimistic. On the basis of these time estimates, we can develop a probability distribution for project completion time. Thus, we can easily determine the probability of project completion within a certain specified time period. This information is invaluable to management in project planning.

Glossary

Activity   A portion of a project, separable as a unit from other operations within the project, which consumes resources and time.

Critical Path   The longest (in time) sequence of activities through a project, representing the duration of the entire project.

Dummy Activity   An artificial activity, consuming neither time nor resources, which is inserted into a network for the sole purpose of enabling unique event-to-event identification of activities.

Earliest Expected Time   The earliest moment at which an event can occur, based on the completion of all predecessor activities.

Event   A moment in time, typically representing the beginning or end of an activity.

Free Slack   Slack time which cannot be shared with succeeding activities; occurs only at merge events; never more than total slack.

Gantt Chart   A very widely used scheduling diagram, showing simple temporal relationships between a project's activities in a highly visible format.

Latest Allowable Time   The latest moment at which an event may be allowed to occur without delaying the entire project. On the critical path, LT = ET for each event.

Most Likely Time   In PERT analyses, the normal expected duration of an activity.

Network   A diagram or representation of a project decomposed into activities and events.

Noncritical Events   Events which are not on the critical path and therefore have slack time available.

Optimistic Time   In PERT analyses, the shortest possible duration of an activity, given ideal conditions.

Pessimistic Time   In PERT analyses, the longest expected duration of an activity, considering possible bad weather, breakdowns, shortages, etc.

Project Crashing   Shortening the total length of a project by expediting various activities, usually at increased cost.

Shared (Floating) Time   Slack time which may be shared among several noncritical activities on the same path.

Total Slack Time   Amount of time potentially available for a given activity beyond the time required, without delaying the project.

References

Cleland, D. I., and King, W. R. *Systems Analysis and Project Management*. 2d ed. New York: McGraw-Hill, 1975.

Dane, C. W., Gray, C. F., and Woodworth, B. M. "Factors Affecting the Successful Application of PERT/CPM Systems in a Government Organization." *Interfaces* 9:5 (Nov. 1979), 94–98.

Davis, E. W. *Project Management: Techniques, Applications, and Managerial Issues*. Norcross, Ga.: American Institute of Industrial Engineers, #AIIE-PP & C-76-1, 1976.

Elmaghraby, S. B. *Activity Networks: Project Planning and Control by Network Models*. New York: Wiley, 1977.

Ford, L. R., and Fulkerson, D. R. *Flows in Networks*. Princeton, N.J.: Princeton University Press, 1962.

Gallagher, C. A., and Watson, H. J. *Quantitative Methods for Business Decisions*. New York: McGraw-Hill, 1980.

Lee, S. M., Moeller, G. L., and Digman, L. A. *Network Analysis for Management Decisions: A Stochastic Approach*. Boston: Kluwer-Nijhoff, 1982.

Lee, S. M., Moore, L. J., and Taylor, B. W. *Management Science*. 2d ed. Dubuque, Iowa: W. C. Brown, 1985.

Wiest, J., and Levy, F. *Management Guide to PERT-CPM*. 2d ed. Englewood Cliffs, N.J.: Prentice-Hall, 1977.

Assignments

11.1 What is a project?

11.2 Describe a project familiar to you by listing the various activities and events of that project.

11.3 Construct a Gantt chart for the project described in Problem 11.2.

11.4 Your term project in the management science class is to analyze the inventory control system of a local manufacturing firm. Describe the necessary activities and their precedence relationships.

11.5 Your term project must be organized in the following sequences: introduction, review of the related literature, research methods, results, discussion of the results, conclusions, and bibliography. You have 10 weeks to complete the term project. Construct a Gantt chart for this project.

11.6 Develop a network for the term project based on your Gantt chart.

11.7 What is a dummy activity? Why do we need it?

11.8 Define the following terms: *critical path, noncritical activities, earliest expected time, latest allowable time, total slack, floating slack, free slack, project crashing.*

11.9 What are the two basic steps we must follow in crashing a project?

11.10 What are the important characteristics of a beta distribution?

11.11 Define the three time estimates we use in a PERT network.

11.12 Given that PERT network activities have the following time estimates, determine their mean activity times and standard deviations:

Activities	Activity Time		
	Optimistic	Most Likely	Pessimistic
A	5	10	15
B	3	9	18
C	10	14	22
D	6	10	13
E	12	20	32

11.13 A network activity has the following duration time and cost estimates. Determine the activity time-cost relationship graphically.

Activity	Time	Activity	Cost
Normal	12 days	Normal	$1,200
Crash	8 days	Crash	2,000

11.14 Construct a Gantt chart in order to schedule the following activities:

Activity	Predecessor	Duration (days)
A	—	10
B	A	7
C	A	4
D	B	9
E	C,D	6

11.15 Construct a project network for the following activities:

Activity (nodes)	Duration (days)
1-2	8
2-3	12
2-4	10
3-4	13
3-5	9
4-6	20
5-6	15

11.16 The open-heart surgery team at Methodist General Hospital has developed the following general sequence of activities for a typical patient:

Activity	Predecessor	Duration (days)
A. Patient check-in	—	1
B. Patient information file	—	1
C. General physical exam	A	2
D. Specialized lab tests	A,B	4
E. Patient rest and preparation	C,D	3
F. Surgery	E	1
G. Intensive care	F	2
H. Recovery care and discharge	G	5

   a. Construct a network for the above activities.
   b. Determine the earliest expected time for each event.
   c. Determine the latest allowable time for each event.
   d. Identify the critical path.
   e. Determine the expected project completion time.

11.17 A project being planned involves the following activities:

Activity (nodes)	Duration (weeks)
1-2	4
1-3	2
2-4	4
2-6	5
3-4	5
3-5	6
4-6	3
5-6	4

   a. Construct a network and determine the following: *ET, LT, TS,* and *FS.*
   b. Determine the critical path and the expected project completion time.

11.18 Consider the following project network:

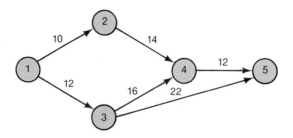

   a. Compute *ET* and *LT* at each of the events.
   b. Determine *TS* and *FS* for each activity.
   c. Identify the critical path and determine the expected project completion time.

11.19 Identify the critical path and determine the expected project completion time for the following network:

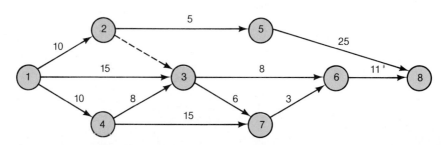

11.20 Jackie Costello has just finished her undergraduate degree in linguistics. After exploring the job market for over a year, she finally decided to go back to school and study for an MBA degree. She has not applied to any school as yet. However, she would like to find out how long it would take to get admitted to a land-grant university. Jackie has identified the following necessary activities for getting an admission:

Activity	Predecessor	Duration (days)
A. Select universities	—	14
B. Obtain application forms	A	21
C. Take GMAT and send the score	A	50
D. Complete and send applications	B	14
E. Wait for answers	C,D	30
F. Make the final decision	E	10

a. Construct a network for Jackie.

b. Identify the critical path.

c. Determine the expected time (the number of days) in which Jackie may be able to decide which university to attend.

11.21 Thomas Jones, who owns and operates a chain of grocery stores called "Groceries 4 Less," is considering a new computer system for accounting and inventory control. A local computer sales office sent the following information about the computer system installation:

Activity	Precedence	Duration (weeks)
A. Select the computer model	—	6
B. Design input/output system	A	8
C. Design monitoring system	A	8
D. Assemble computer hardware	B	20
E. Develop the main programs	B	18
F. Develop input/output routines	C	10
G. Create data base	E	8
H. Install the system	D,F	2
I. Test and implement	G,H	7

a. Construct a network for this problem.

b. Identify the critical path by computing the *ET, LT, TS,* and *FS* values.

c. Determine the project completion time.

11.22 A construction company has a shopping center development project. The project involves the following activities and relevant information:

Activity	Activity Time (weeks)		Activity Cost	
	Normal	Crash	Normal	Crash
1-2	14	10	$700	$1,100
1-3	12	6	600	900
2-4	16	12	1,600	2,400
3-4	13	10	650	950
2-6	13	10	2,600	3,500
4-6	16	12	1,600	2,600
4-5	15	11	750	950
6-7	12	8	2,400	3,600
5-7	12	6	1,800	2,400

a. Construct a network for the project.

b. Determine the project completion time and total cost based on normal activity times and costs.

c. Determine the project completion time and total cost based on crash activity times and costs.

d. Compute the minimum cost required to crash the project.

e. Compute the cost savings as compared to the total cost involved when all activities of the network are crashed.

f. If the company has only a total of $2,000 available for project crashing, which activities should be crashed?

11.23 Consider a PERT network having activity time estimates as follows:

Activity	Time (days)		
	a	m	b
1-2	12	24	46
2-3	12	15	30
3-4	9	21	45
4-5	7	9	14

a. Compute the mean time (t_e) of each activity.

b. Determine the expected project completion time.

c. Compute the standard deviation of the project completion time.

11.24 Consider a PERT network having the following activity time estimates:

Activity	Time (weeks)		
	a	m	b
1-2	2	6	10
2-3	6	14	22
3-4	4	6	20
4-5	10	10	10
5-6	2	20	26
6-7	6	12	18

a. Determine the expected project completion, *E(t)*.
b. Compute the standard deviation for the project.

11.25 Consider a project having the following activities and their time estimates:

Activity	Most Optimistic	Most Likely	Most Pessimistic
1-2	10	22	22
1-3	20	20	20
1-4	4	10	16
2-6	2	14	26
3-6	8	8	20
3-7	8	14	20
3-5	4	4	4
4-5	0	12	12
5-7	4	16	28
6-7	2	8	14

a. Construct a PERT network for the project.
b. Compute the t_e value for each activity.
c. Compute the σ_e value for each activity.
d. Identify the critical path and determine the expected project completion time.

11.26 Consider a PERT network that has the expected project completion time of 120 days and a standard deviation of 20 days.
a. Determine the probability of completing the project within 90 days.
b. Determine the probability of completing the project between 85 days and 135 days.

11.27 Consider the following network having three activity time estimates:

Activity	Predecessor	Time (days) Most Optimistic	Most Likely	Most Pessimistic
A	—	2	4	6
B	A	8	12	16
C	A	14	16	30
D	B	4	10	16
E	C,B	6	12	18
F	E	6	8	22
G	D	18	18	30
H	F,G	8	14	32

a. Construct a PERT network for the project.
b. Determine the critical path and compute the expected project completion time.

c. Determine the probability of completing the project within 80 days.

d. What is the probability the project will require at least 75 days?

11.28 Consider the following project network:

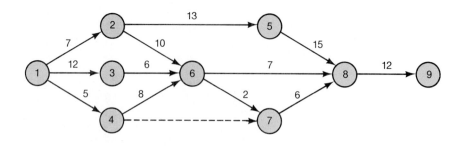

a. Compute the *ET, LT, TS,* and *FS* values.

b. Determine the critical path.

c. Determine the expected project time.

12 INVENTORY MODELS

Every company, regardless of type or size, maintains inventories of some kind. Thus, it is not surprising that maintaining and financing inventories represent a major cost of doing business. The level of inventory to carry is an important decision variable at all stages of manufacturing, marketing, financing, and distributing. Proper inventory control plays an important role in successful operations management. There are two questions that are critical to successful inventory management: (1) When should we replenish the inventory (place an order for a given item)? (2) How many units should we order at a time?

To obtain answers to these questions, quantitative models can be applied. As a matter of fact, inventory control models represent perhaps the oldest management science techniques. As such, there are almost unlimited variations of inventory models developed for unique management situations. In this chapter we will focus on the most fundamental inventory models.

Learning Objectives   From the study of this chapter, we will learn the following:

1. The importance of inventory control systems for organizational success
2. Different types of inventories
3. The purposes of holding inventories
4. Basic inventory decision problems
5. Components of total annual inventory costs
6. Understanding the EOQ model and its variations or extensions
7. Inventory models under probabilistic conditions
8. Computer solutions of inventory problems
9. The meaning of the following terms:

Holding costs
Ordering costs
Shortage costs
The economic order quantity (EOQ)
*   model*
Order quantity
Reorder point
Inventory cycles
Economic lot-size model

Setup cost
Safety stocks
Lead time
Demand during lead time
Material requirements planning (MRP)
Just-in-time (JIT) system
Kanban
Inventory system under uncertainty

CHARACTERISTICS OF INVENTORY SYSTEMS

All types and sizes of organizations, be they manufacturers, agricultural firms, wholesalers, retailers, hospitals, or government agencies, maintain inventories. The total dollar investment in inventories for any particular sector of the economy is substantial; factory inventories are worth well over $300 billion.

Inventory is any resource that is set aside for future use. We need inventories because the demand and supply of goods are usually not matched perfectly at any given time or place. As customers, we would like to see stores always carry all the items we may want on the spur of the moment. For example, we expect a grocery store to carry enough inventories of Coke, light bulbs, or detergent. However, we would not expect a car dealer to have the exact car we may want — a powder-blue sports car with white interior, compact disk player and AM-FM radio, 40-miles-per-gallon diesel engine, and genuine leather upholstery.

In many organizations, inventories represent costly unearning or idle resources. As a matter of fact, inventories have been referred to as the graveyard of U.S. business, because excess inventories cause many business failures. There are many different types of inventories. Some examples are:

Raw materials — coal, iron ore, cotton, crude oil, etc.

Semifinished products — copper wire, plastic sheets, threads, lumber, etc.

Finished products — television sets, shoes, designer jeans, frozen pizzas, etc.

Human resources — standby utility personnel such as the utility crew on an assembly line, standby cabin attendants of an airline, reserve personnel of the army, etc.

Financial or other fixed resources — cash on hand, accounts receivable, warehouse space, etc.

We tend to think that the best decision about inventories is to limit them just enough to meet future demand. However, the real-world situation is far more complex than that. Inventories are maintained for many different reasons. Some of the important reasons are:

1. *Satisfaction of fluctuating demand.* Sufficiently high levels of inventories are maintained to meet future peak demand. For example, many public utilities store excess gas or electric-generating capacity to meet peak demand during a cold winter (gas) or during a hot summer (electricity for air conditioning).

2. *Protection against a short supply of materials.* Inventories may be kept at relatively high levels to avoid a period of short supply. Some possible causes of such situations are strikes at the supplying company or in the transportation industry, international tension such as the oil embargo of 1974 or the Iranian situation in 1980, or declining natural resources.

3. *Hedge against price inflation.* Inventories may be kept at high levels as a hedge against expected price inflation. For certain goods (coal, silver, gold, copper, etc.) storage costs are negligible when compared to price increases due to inflation and materials shortage.

4. *Benefits of quantity discounts.* Another possible reason to carry high inventories may be the availability of quantity discounts for large purchases.

5. *Savings on negotiation costs.* In international trade, purchasing often requires costly and painstaking negotiations. Also, there is a general trend toward enormous increases in efforts and negotiation costs whenever a change takes place in the management of a foreign corporation. Thus, ordering large quantities of goods at one time is widely practiced.

Many other reasons prompt firms to carry high levels of inventories. A manufacturing firm, to become a dominant customer, may order large quantities for a period of time in order to establish bargaining power or control over supply sources. Or a company may carry certain levels of inventories to maintain an even production level and thus avoid the layoff of employees.

Since organizations do not have crystal balls to precisely forecast future demands, they need to carry inventory as a buffer between supply and demand. However, this approach can create chaos for management when there are many stock items (or SKUs — stock-keeping units). For example, if a company has 30,000 stock items, inventory decisions can be a real mess. Since prices change frequently and in an unorderly fashion, the items and supply sources may also change frequently. Therefore, individual items may require unique management considerations.

Another factor that further complicates the inventory situation is the literally unlimited number of ways to solve inventory problems. For example, a firm can order 10 units of an item once a week or it can order 2,600 units every 5 years. Or, to approximate the fluctuating demand, the company can order fluctuating quantities on an irregular basis.

Because of all of these characteristics of inventory systems, a seat-of-the-pants or a purely judgmental approach to the inventory problem is not a reasonable way to manage operations in today's complex environment. Mathematical models can be effectively utilized to search for good solutions to inventory problems. This is why inventory analysis was one of the first areas of application of management science principles.

One of the earliest models of inventory management was the Harris Economic Lot Size equation, developed around 1915. The Harris model was expanded by F. W. Raymond in the early 1930s. There was very little additional work published on inventory management until Moses Abramovitz published the result of his research on inventories and business cycles for the National Bureau of Economic Research in 1950. Since that time, an avalanche of research work has been reported concerning scientific inventory control.

BASIC INVENTORY DECISIONS

The two basic inventory decisions are *how much* and *when* items are to be replenished so as to minimize the total inventory costs. Although it is possible to consider these two decisions separately, they are so closely related that a simultaneous solution is usually necessary. Typically, quantity and timing decisions must be made together.

In developing inventory models, the objective is to minimize the total inventory costs. The total inventory costs have three components: holding costs, ordering costs, and shortage costs.

Holding Costs

Holding costs, or *carrying costs,* represent costs that are associated with storing a certain level of inventory. These costs include the following components:

Interest incurred or opportunity cost in having capital tied up in inventories.

Storage costs such as insurance, taxes, rental fees, utilities, and other maintenance costs of the storage space.

Warehousing or storage operation costs, including handling, record keeping, information processing, and the actual taking of a physical inventory.

Costs associated with deterioration, shrinkage, obsolescence, and damage.

The total holding costs are dependent on how many items are stored and for how long. Therefore, holding costs are expressed in terms of *dollar cost for carrying one unit of inventory per unit of time*. Holding costs can also be expressed in terms of *a percentage of the average inventory value*. Common ranges for holding costs are 15 to 20 percent of average inventory value for consumer goods, and 20 to 30 percent for industrial goods.

Ordering Costs

Ordering costs represent costs that are associated with replenishing inventories. These costs are not dependent on how many items are ordered at a time. Instead, they are based on the number of times orders are prepared. In other words, it is assumed that the cost of preparing an order is constant. Ordering costs include overhead, clerical work, data processing, and other expenses that are incurred in searching the supply sources: purchasing, expediting, transporting, receiving, inspecting. Ordering costs can be determined by dividing the total annual costs incurred in preparing orders by the number of orders processed during the year. Thus, ordering costs are usually expressed in terms of *dollar cost per order*.

Shortage Costs

Shortage costs, or *stock-out costs,* are those costs that occur when demand exceeds the available inventory in stock. These costs are dependent on how much shortage has occurred and for how long. Thus, shortage costs are expressed in terms of *dollar cost per unit of short item per unit of time.* In some cases, when only the magnitude of the shortage is considered, these costs can be expressed in terms of *dollar cost per short unit.*

Shortages and stock-outs may occur when there is unexpected high demand before inventories are replenished. Or shortages may be due to the established inventory policy of the company. If shortages can be filled by back ordering, without permanently losing the customers, the shortage costs would be only temporary and minor. Usually, however, shortages result in long-term lost customers (lost profit) or a permanent goodwill cost owing to unsatisfied customers.

ECONOMIC ORDER QUANTITY (EOQ) MODEL

The **economic order quantity (EOQ) model,** which is often referred to as the classic or basic inventory model, is the simplest and most elementary of the inventory models. Since it is so basic and simple, it may not be appropriate for many real-world inventory situations. Nevertheless, it is a good starting point for developing more realistic inventory models.

EOQ Model Assumptions

The objective of the EOQ model is to determine the optimum **order quantity** that will minimize the total inventory cost. The EOQ model is simple because it is based upon some rigid assumptions. As we develop more realistic models, we will need to modify or eliminate some of these assumptions. The EOQ model assumes the following:

The demand for inventory is known with certainty, such as one unit per day.

Inventory replenishment is instantaneous (the order is placed and received simultaneously).

No excess inventories or shortages are necessary or needed (inventory is replenished only when inventory is exactly 0).

The holding cost per unit and ordering cost are constant regardless of the order quantity.

The assumptions of the EOQ model are reflected in Figure 12.1, which represents the inventory level over a period of time. Based on the known demand rate, the inventory level decreases until it reaches 0. Then, an order is placed on the assumption of an instantaneous replenishment. When the order quantity is received, the inventory level jumps up to the previous high level. The decreasing process of the inventory level then repeats itself.

Figure 12.1   The Classic Inventory Model

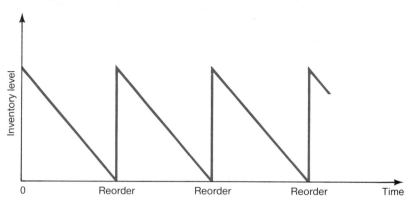

EOQ Model Symbols

To formulate the EOQ model, we must define the following symbols as model variables and parameters:

$$TC = \text{total annual inventory cost}$$
$$HC = \text{holding cost per unit per year}$$
$$THC = \text{total annual holding cost}$$
$$OC = \text{ordering cost per order}$$
$$TOC = \text{total annual ordering cost}$$
$$Q = \text{quantity per order}$$
$$D = \text{annual demand for items in inventory}$$

Before formulating the model, we should reiterate here that the objective of the EOQ model is to determine the optimum order quantity so that the sum of all of the costs related to managing the inventory system can be minimized. Shortage costs are not considered in the EOQ model because, given the model's assumptions, it is impossible for shortages to occur. Thus, inventory costs consist entirely of holding and ordering costs, and the objective is to minimize the sum of these two components.

Figure 12.2 graphically illustrates the relationships of *TC*, *THC*, and *TOC*. We will discuss the mathematical functions for each of the costs in the next section. In Figure 12.2, it is evident that the total holding cost *(THC)* is a linear function. When the quantity per order is increased, *THC* increases at a constant rate. However, total ordering cost *(TOC)* is a nonlinear function. When the quantity per order is increased, *TOC* decreases at a gradual rate.

Total inventory cost *(TC)*, which is the sum of *THC* and *TOC*, first decreases as the order quantity size increases but begins to rise from the point where the *THC* and *TOC* functions intersect. The optimum order quantity *(Q*)*, which corresponds to the minimum total inventory cost *(TC*)*, can be determined graphically at the point where *THC* equals *TOC*.

Figure 12.2   *The Classic EOQ Inventory Decision Model*

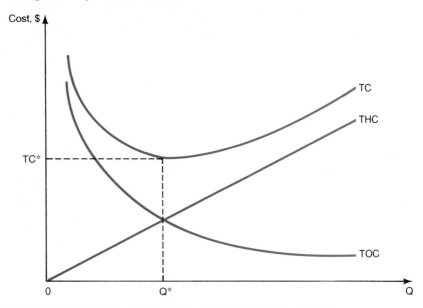

EOQ Model Formulation

Total Inventory Cost   The total annual inventory cost is the sum of two components: (1) total annual holding cost and (2) total annual ordering cost.

$$\begin{array}{ccccc} \text{Total annual} & = & \text{total annual} & + & \text{total annual} \\ \text{inventory cost} & & \text{holding cost} & & \text{ordering cost} \\ TC & = & THC & + & TOC \end{array}$$

Total Annual Holding Cost   The total annual holding cost is determined by multiplying the holding cost per unit per year *(HC)* by the inventory level measured in units. Although we can easily determine *HC*, it is not so simple to measure the inventory level, unless we do so for each day, because the inventory level fluctuates from day to day based on the demand rate.

Since the demand rate is assumed to be constant over time and to be known with certainty, we can compute the average inventory on hand and use it as the inventory level. When the demand is known and constant, the average inventory level is simply the midpoint of the highest and lowest inventory levels on hand. The highest inventory level equals Q, the order quantity, and the lowest inventory level is 0. Thus, we can compute the average inventory level as $(Q + 0)/2 = Q/2$:

$$\text{Average inventory level} = \frac{Q}{2}$$

Now we can compute the total holding cost as

$$THC = HC \cdot \frac{Q}{2}$$

Total Annual Ordering Cost   The total annual ordering cost *(TOC)* is the product of the ordering cost per order *(OC)* times the number of orders processed per year. The number of orders we need to process per year is easily computed by dividing the known annual demand *(D)* by the quantity ordered per order *(Q)*. Thus, the number of orders per year will be

$$\text{Number of orders per year } = \frac{D}{Q}$$

Now we are ready to compute the total annual ordering cost as follows:

$$TOC = OC \cdot \frac{D}{Q}$$

Optimum Order Quantity   As we already know, the total inventory cost is the sum of the total holding cost and the total ordering cost. Thus, we can write

$$TC = THC + TOC$$
$$= HC \cdot \frac{Q}{2} + OC \cdot \frac{D}{Q}$$

In the above equation, we have left out the total merchandise purchase cost because it is not usually considered to be a part of the total inventory cost. However, if we are interested in computing the total merchandising cost, we can add $(P \cdot D)$, where P is the per-unit purchase price.

Now it is possible for us to determine the optimum order quantity (Q^*). As we demonstrated in Figure 12.2, the optimum order quantity is found at the point where the total holding cost line intersects the total ordering cost curve. Thus, if we equate the total holding cost with the total ordering cost and solve for Q, we can obtain the value of Q^*:

$$THC = TOC$$
$$HC \cdot \frac{Q}{2} = OC \cdot \frac{D}{Q}$$
$$\frac{HC \cdot Q}{2} = \frac{OC \cdot D}{Q}$$
$$HC \cdot Q^2 = 2 \cdot OC \cdot D$$
$$Q^2 = \frac{2 \cdot OC \cdot D}{HC}$$
$$Q^* = \sqrt{\frac{2OC \cdot D}{HC}}$$

The optimum value of Q can also be determined at the lowest point on the total cost curve in Figure 12.2. To use this approach, the derivation of the total cost equation with respect to Q must be computed by using calculus:

$$TC = \frac{HC \cdot Q}{2} + \frac{OC \cdot D}{Q}$$
$$\frac{dTC}{dQ} = \frac{-OC \cdot D}{Q^2} + \frac{HC}{2}$$

Since this derivative represents the slope of the total cost curve, the optimum quantity of Q is the point where the slope is 0. Thus,

$$\frac{-OC \cdot D}{Q^2} + \frac{HC}{2} = 0$$

Consequently, we can obtain

$$Q^* = \sqrt{\frac{2OC \cdot D}{HC}}$$

To determine the optimum order quantity for any specific inventory model, we simply plug the values of HC, OC, and D into the EOQ model. We will now examine the application of the EOQ model and its component cost functions through a casette problem.

Casette 12.1   **TELEVISION TECHNOLOGY INC.**

Television Technology Inc. is a local retail store that specializes in the sale and service of televisions, videocassette players, and television parts. The company is an exclusive dealer for Star-Colorvision television sets. Arjay Swing, the owner of the company, wants to determine the optimum number of television sets to order each time so that the total inventory cost is minimized.

Working with the sales and accounting records, Arjay has been able to uncover the following information:

$$\text{Annual demand } (D) = 360 \text{ sets}$$
$$\text{Holding cost } (HC) = \$50 \text{ per set}$$
$$\text{Ordering cost } (OC) = \$20 \text{ per order}$$

Arjay contacted the small business center at the local university and requested some help in analyzing this inventory problem. Professor Robert Judd assigned Susan Wiseman to the project as part of her class work.

Based on available data, Susan decided that the demand for television sets is constant at one set per day. Furthermore, since the distribution center is only 20 miles away, inventory replenishment can be assumed to be instantaneous (orders can be delivered in the same day). As a matter of fact, Susan accepted all the assumptions of the EOQ model.

Total Holding Cost

The total holding cost *(THC)* can be determined by

$$THC = HC \cdot \frac{Q}{2}$$

Since $HC = \$50$, Susan could easily determine that

$$THC = \$50 \cdot \frac{Q}{2} = \$25Q$$

The above *THC* function is obviously a linear function. Thus, the total holding cost will increase at a constant rate of $25 for each unit increase in the order quantity. Susan decided to examine three possible ordering policies: (1) a yearly order, (2) quarterly orders, and (3) monthly orders.

The total annual holding cost for the three ordering policies can be determined easily as follows:

Yearly Order. A yearly order policy requires that the order quantity be equal to the total annual demand ($D = 360$):

$$Q = 360: \quad THC = \$25Q$$
$$= \$25 \times 360$$
$$= \$9,000$$

Quarterly Order. Based on a quarterly ordering policy, $Q = D/4 = 360/4 = 90$. Thus,

$$Q = 90: \quad THC = \$25Q$$
$$= \$25 \times 90$$
$$= \$2,250$$

Monthly Order. When orders are processed each month, $Q = D/12 = 360/12 = 30$. Thus,

$$Q = 30: \quad THC = \$25Q$$
$$= \$25 \times 30$$
$$= \$750$$

Susan plotted on a graph the total annual holding costs for the three ordering policies, as shown in Figure 12.3.

Total Ordering Cost

The annual total ordering cost can be computed by

$$TOC = OC \cdot \frac{D}{Q}$$

Since $D = 360$ and $OC = \$20$, Susan proceeded as follows:

$$TOC = \frac{\$20 \times 360}{Q} = \frac{\$7,200}{Q}$$

The above *TOC* function is a nonlinear function. The total ordering cost will decrease as the order quantity, Q, is increased gradually. Susan examined the behavior of the *TOC* function for the three ordering policies we examined earlier.

Yearly Order. Since only one order is processed annually, *TOC* would be

$$Q = 360: \quad TOC = \frac{\$7,200}{360} = \$20$$

Quarterly Order.

$$Q = \frac{D}{4} = \frac{360}{4} = 90: \quad TOC = \frac{\$7,200}{90} = \$80$$

Monthly Order.

$$Q = \frac{D}{12} = \frac{360}{12} = 30: \quad TOC = \frac{\$7,200}{30} = \$240$$

Figure 12.3   *Total Annual Holding Cost* (THC) *Function*

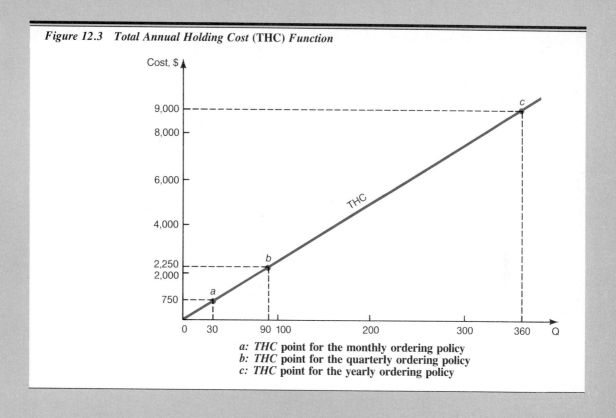

a: **THC point for the monthly ordering policy**
b: **THC point for the quarterly ordering policy**
c: **THC point for the yearly ordering policy**

Susan plotted the above *TOC* values for the three ordering policies on a graph, as shown in Figure 12.4. The *TOC* function shows that the total ordering cost decreases as the ordering quantity increases. This should make good sense, because as the order quantity is increased, the number of orders per year will decrease, and thus TOC will also decrease.

Total Inventory Cost

The total inventory cost is the sum of *THC* and *TOC*. Thus, Susan computes *THC* for the three ordering policies as follows:

Ordering Policy	THC	TOC	TC
Yearly	$9,000	$20	$9,020
Quarterly	2,250	80	2,330
Monthly	750	240	990

On the basis of the above analysis, it is clear that the monthly ordering policy is the best among the three ordering policies we have evaluated. However, the monthly ordering policy ($Q = 30$) may not be the optimum order quantity.

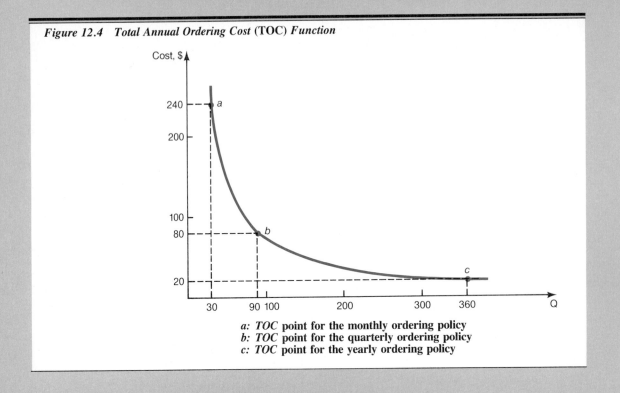

Figure 12.4   Total Annual Ordering Cost (TOC) Function

a: TOC **point for the monthly ordering policy**
b: TOC **point for the quarterly ordering policy**
c: TOC **point for the yearly ordering policy**

Determination of EOQ

To determine the optimum order quantity, Susan must determine the economic order quantity (Q^*). Since Q^* can be found when the *THC* and *TOC* functions intersect, the relationship can be written as

$$THC = TOC$$
$$\frac{HC \cdot Q}{2} = \frac{OC \cdot D}{Q}$$

Solving for Q^*, we can find

$$Q^* = \sqrt{\frac{2OC \cdot D}{HC}}$$

where
Q^* = optimum order quantity

D = annual demand

HC = holding cost per unit per year

OC = ordering cost per order

For the Television Technology problem, the optimum order quantity Q^* can be determined as follows:

$$Q^* = \sqrt{\frac{2 \times 20 \times 360}{50}} = \sqrt{\frac{1440}{5}} = \sqrt{288} = 16.97 \cong 17$$

This optimum solution indicates that the economic order quantity is 17 television sets at a time. Since the annual demand is 360 sets, we can determine the number of orders as follows:

$$\text{Number of orders } = \frac{D}{Q^*} = \frac{360}{17} = 21.18 \cong 21$$

Figure 12.5 presents the graphical solution of the Television Technology inventory problem. The minimum total inventory cost (*TC*) is found at the intersection point of the total holding cost (*THC*) and the total ordering cost (*TOC*) functions. It is obvious that Q^* is approximately 17.

Managerial Information

The EOQ model is used not only to determine the economic order quantity Q^*. We can also generate much managerial information about the inventory system under consideration. Examples of the type of valuable information we can obtain from the EOQ model are as follows:

Inventory Cycle   The inventory cycle represents the number of days the inventory would last from the day of order (receipt) to the day when it reaches 0. The length of each inventory cycle can be determined by dividing the number of business days per year by the number of orders processed per year. Thus, for the Television Technology problem we can determine the inventory cycle as follows:

$$\text{Business days per year } = 360$$

$$\text{Demand rate } = 1 \text{ set per day}$$

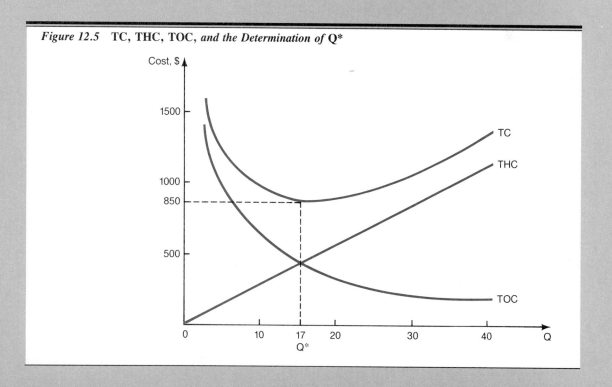

Figure 12.5*   TC, THC, TOC, *and the Determination of Q

Figure 12.6   Inventory Cycle and the Maximum and Average Inventory Levels

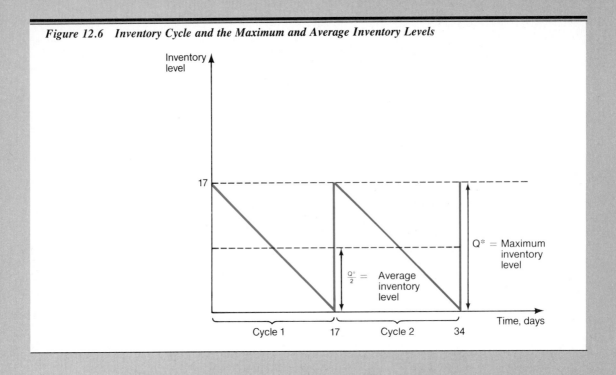

$$\text{Number of orders per year} = \frac{D}{Q^*} = \frac{360}{17} \cong 21$$

$$\text{Inventory cycle} = \text{business days} \div \text{number of orders}$$

$$= 360 \div 21 \cong 17 \text{ days}$$

The inventory cycle is presented in Figure 12.6. From this figure we can also determine the maximum inventory level and the average inventory level. The maximum inventory level is exactly the value of Q^*, and the average inventory level is, of course, $\dfrac{Q^*}{2}$:

$$\text{Maximum inventory level} = Q^* = 17$$

$$\text{Average inventory level} = \frac{Q^*}{2} = 8.5$$

It should be pointed out here that the inventory cycle equals the maximum inventory level in this particular problem. This is a coincidence caused by the values given for total demand ($D = 360$), demand rate ($DR = 1$), and business days per year (360). In most real-world problems, the inventory cycle does not equal the maximum inventory level.

Cost Information.   Once the EOQ model determines Q^*, we can determine *THC*, *TOC*, and subsequently *TC*. Furthermore, we can also determine the dollar value of each order quantity. Since we have already determined that $Q^* = 17$, we can compute *THC*, *TOC*, and *TC* as follows:

$$THC = \frac{HC \cdot Q^*}{2} = \frac{\$50 \times 17}{2} = \$425$$

$$TOC = \frac{OC \cdot D}{Q^*} = \frac{\$20 \times 360}{17} = \$424$$

$$TC = \$425 + \$424 = \$849$$

It should be noted in the above computations that *THC* and *TOC* should be equal. The difference of 1 dollar between them results because of the rounding of Q^* to 17. If we use the precise value of $Q^* = 16.97$, we would derive more accurate values for *THC* and *TOC*.

The optimum total inventory cost, TC^*, can also be derived through a general formula. For example, we can write TC^* as follows:

$$TC^* = THC + TOC$$

$$= \frac{HC \cdot Q^*}{2} + \frac{OC \cdot D}{Q^*} \qquad \left(\text{since } Q^* = \sqrt{\frac{2 \cdot OC \cdot D}{HC}} \right)$$

$$= \frac{HC \cdot \sqrt{\dfrac{2 \cdot OC \cdot D}{HC}}}{2} + \frac{OC \cdot D}{\sqrt{\dfrac{2 \cdot OC \cdot D}{HC}}} \qquad \text{(deriving a common denominator)}$$

$$= \frac{2 \cdot OC \cdot D + HC \left(\dfrac{2 \cdot OC \cdot D}{HC} \right)}{2 \cdot \sqrt{\dfrac{2 \cdot OC \cdot D}{HC}}}$$

$$= \frac{4 \cdot OC \cdot D}{2 \cdot \sqrt{\dfrac{2 \cdot OC \cdot D}{HC}}} = \frac{2 \cdot OC \cdot D}{\sqrt{\dfrac{2 \cdot OC \cdot D}{HC}}} \qquad \text{(combining all terms in the radical)}$$

$$= \sqrt{\frac{(2 \cdot OC \cdot D)^2 \cdot HC}{2 \cdot OC \cdot D}} = \sqrt{2 \cdot OC \cdot HC \cdot D}$$

Now we can find TC^* by substituting parameter values in the above formula as follows:

$$TC^* = \sqrt{2 \cdot OC \cdot HC \cdot D} = \sqrt{2 \cdot 20 \cdot 50 \cdot 360} = 848.53$$

The dollar value of each order quantity, based on Q^*, can be easily determined if the cost of each television set is known. For example, if the cost of each television set is \$500, we can determine the dollar value of an optimum order quantity as follows:

$$Q^* = 17: \qquad \text{cost of a television set} = \$500$$

$$\text{Dollar value of } Q^* = 17 \times \$500 = \$8,500$$

MODIFICATIONS IN THE EOQ MODEL

In applying the EOQ model, a number of modifications are possible. Some of these may result from the relaxation or removal of certain model assumptions, or from changed definitions of model parameters. In this section we will examine three modifications in the EOQ model. These modifications enable us to expand the model for a more realistic application or to analyze an inventory model in a different way, depending on the requirements of the situation.

Holding Cost as a Proportion of Value

As we discussed earlier in this chapter, holding cost (HC) can be expressed as a proportion or percentage of average dollar value of inventory. In other words, total annual holding cost (THC) is determined by multiplying the average dollar value of inventory by the percentage holding cost per year. This approach may be appropriate when the unit holding costs of individual items are difficult to measure.

Let us define the following new parameters:

HCP = holding cost as a percentage of the annual inventory dollar value

P = price or value per unit of inventory item

Now we can reformulate the total annual holding cost as follows:

$$THC = HCP \cdot P \cdot \frac{Q}{2}$$

In the above formula, $HCP \cdot P$ replaced the previous unit holding cost, HC. Thus, the optimum order quantity can be determined by

$$Q^* = \sqrt{\frac{2 \cdot OC \cdot D}{HCP \cdot P}}$$

In the Television Technology inventory problem presented as Casette 12.1, let us assume that the percentage holding cost *(HCP)* is 20 percent of the average annual inventory and that the price of the television set is $500. Then, the optimum order quantity becomes

$$Q^* = \sqrt{\frac{2 \cdot OC \cdot D}{HCP \cdot P}} = \sqrt{\frac{2 \times 20 \times 360}{.2 \times 500}} = \sqrt{\frac{14,400}{100}}$$

$$= \sqrt{144} = 12$$

In the above computation, the unit holding cost is in fact doubled (*HC* = *HCP* · *P* = 0.2 × $500 = $100), as compared to the previous holding cost of $50. Therefore, it makes sense to decrease the order quantity from 17 to 12. In this way we can reduce the average inventory level (from 8.5 to 6 units) to reduce *THC*. However, the number of orders, and consequently *TOC*, will increase.

Time Horizon as a Model Variable

If we specify the time horizon over which the inventory analysis is to apply, the demand for items in inventory must be specified during that time horizon. The holding cost is also specified as the cost of holding one unit in inventory per unit of time (e.g., per day). This approach is especially appropriate when holding costs change frequently over time. The following model variables need to be redefined:

$$T = \text{time horizon for the inventory analysis}$$

$$D = \text{total demand during time horizon } T$$

$$HC = \text{holding cost per unit } \textit{per unit of time} \text{ (e.g., per day)}$$

A major change in the above definition of HC is that it is measured for a unit of time (e.g., per day) rather than for the entire time horizon (e.g., per year). Now we can determine *THC*, *TOC*, and Q^* as follows:

$$THC = HC \cdot \frac{Q}{2} \cdot T$$

$$TOC = OC \cdot \frac{D}{Q}$$

$$Q^* = \sqrt{\frac{2 \cdot OC \cdot D}{HC \cdot T}}$$

Returning to our Television Technology example, suppose that the time horizon is 6 months (180 business days). Thus, the demand during the time horizon would be 180 television sets. If we assume that the holding cost per unit *per day* is 14 cents, we can determine the optimum order quantity as

$$Q^* = \sqrt{\frac{2 \times 20 \times 180}{.14 \times 180}} = 16.9 \cong 17$$

Reorder Point

Thus far in our discussion of the EOQ model, we have assumed that an order is received at the same instant it is placed. In reality, however, such a case would be a rarity. It is more realistic to assume that there exists some time lag between the time an order is placed and the time that order is received. This time lag is often referred to as **lead time.** Figure 12.7 illustrates the lead time for each of the orders (inventory cycles). Since there is a lead time, items are ordered before the inventory level reaches 0. Thus, the **reorder point** is the point at which an order is placed.

The assumptions for obtaining the reorder point are: (1) constant and known demand rate per time period (e.g., per day) and (2) constant and known lead time. We can now find the reorder point by simply finding the demand during the lead time. The demand rate per unit of time is simply the quotient of the total demand for the time horizon *(D)* divided by the number of days. Let us define the following parameters before we derive the reorder point:

$$R = \text{reorder point, expressed in terms of inventory level in units}$$

$$DR = \text{demand rate per unit of time (e.g., per day)}$$

$$LT = \text{lead time, expressed in unit of time (e.g., days)}$$

Now we can express the demand rate and reorder point as follows:

$$DR = \frac{D}{360}, \text{ assuming 360 business days per year}$$

$$R = LT \cdot \frac{D}{360}$$

Figure 12.7 Reorder Point in the Inventory Cycle

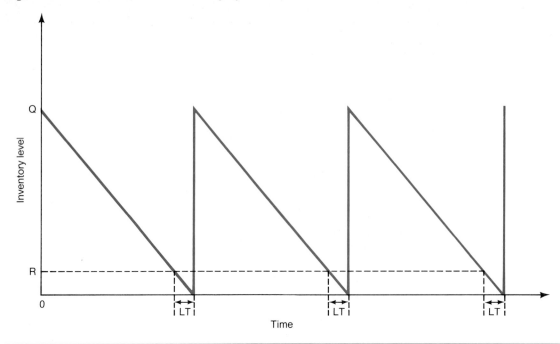

Going back to the Television Technology inventory problem of Casette 12.1, let us suppose that the company has a constant lead time of 5 days. Then, the reorder point would be

$$R = LT \cdot \frac{D}{360} = 5 \times \frac{360}{360} = 5$$

Thus, the company should reorder when the inventory level of television sets falls to 5 sets.

It should be noted here that the optimum order quantity Q^* is not affected by the existence of a lead time. However, it is important to determine the reorder point and to process orders accordingly. Otherwise, determination of Q^* and TC^* becomes impossible because all of the necessary assumptions will not be satisfied.

EXTENSIONS OF THE EOQ MODEL

There are many different extensions of the basic EOQ model that are developed either for special purposes or under specific conditions. In this section we will examine several such models.

Noninstantaneous Receipt Model

In previous models, we have assumed that once an order is placed, the entire order is received instantaneously. In other words, it has been assumed that there is no delivery lead time for replenishments. However, this assumption is not always realistic. In reality, the delivery process for most products may be gradual rather than instantaneous. In this section, we will eliminate the assumption of instantaneous receipt, but the other assumptions of the initial model will remain unchanged. In the noninstantaneous receipt model, it is necessary to assume that goods are received at a constant rate over time. Let us define the following parameters:

V = inventory receipt rate (rate at which items are received over time), assumed to start at the time the order is placed and assumed to be a constant rate

DR = demand rate per unit of time (e.g., per day), assumed to be a constant rate

All other parameters or variables are unchanged from the initial model.

Average Inventory   In the initial EOQ model, the average inventory is half the maximum inventory level (Q). In the noninstantaneous receipt model, however, the maximum inventory level must be adjusted, since the items are received over time. The average inventory can be obtained as follows:

$$\frac{Q}{V} = \text{number of days required to receive one entire order (order receipt period)}$$

$$\frac{Q}{V} \cdot DR = \text{number of units demanded (usage rate) during the order receipt period}$$

$$Q - \left(\frac{Q}{V} \cdot DR\right) = \text{maximum inventory level for a given order cycle}$$

With constant rates of receipt and use, the average inventory level is half of the maximum level. Thus,

$$\text{Average inventory level} = \frac{1}{2}\left[Q - \left(\frac{Q}{V} \cdot DR\right)\right]$$

The average inventory level can be modified to obtain

$$\text{Average inventory level} = \frac{Q}{2}\left(1 - \frac{DR}{V}\right)$$

In the above expression, $\dfrac{DR}{V}$ represents the proportion of an order receipt that will be required to meet demand. Therefore, $\left(1 - \dfrac{DR}{V}\right)$ will be the proportion of an order receipt that will become an increment to the inventory level during the delivery cycle.

The Inventory Model   The inventory level for a noninstantaneous receipt case is shown in Figure 12.8. As we can observe in the graph, the total inventory level rises gradually as the order receipt rate is assumed to be greater than the usage rate (i.e., $V > DR$). Thus, the inventory level rises at a constant rate of $V - DR$. The inventory level will reach the maximum level $Q - [(Q/V) \cdot DR]$. When the order receipt is completed for a given order, the inventory level begins to fall at the constant demand rate, DR.

Figure 12.8   *Inventory Model with Noninstantaneous Receipt*

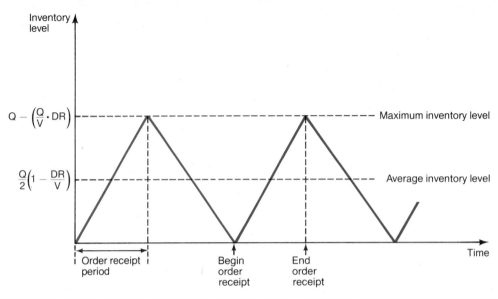

Now we can develop the inventory model:

$$THC = HC \cdot \frac{Q}{2} \left(1 - \frac{DR}{V} \right)$$

$$TOC = OC \cdot \frac{D}{Q}$$

$$TC = HC \cdot \frac{Q}{2} \left(1 - \frac{DR}{V} \right) + OC \cdot \frac{D}{Q}$$

The total inventory cost is still minimum at the point where the total holding cost equals the total ordering cost. Thus, we can write

$$THC = TOC$$

$$HC \cdot \frac{Q}{2} \left(1 - \frac{DR}{V} \right) = OC \cdot \frac{D}{Q}$$

$$Q^2 = \frac{2 \cdot OC \cdot D}{HC \, [1 - (DR/V)]}$$

Therefore, the optimum order quantity is

$$Q^* = \sqrt{\frac{2 \cdot OC \cdot D}{HC \, [1 - (DR/V)]}}$$

The basic formula for Q^* is the same as in the initial EOQ model except that the holding cost (HC) is multiplied by the proportion of the order receipt that is allocated to inventory, $1 - (DR/V)$. This multiplier takes care of the fact that items ordered are received over time rather than instantaneously.

As an example of the application of this model, let us go back to the original Television Technology problem of Casette 12.1. Let us assume the following values for the model parameters:

$$HC \text{ (holding cost per unit per year)} = \$50$$
$$OC \text{ (ordering cost per order)} = \$20$$
$$D \text{ (total annual demand)} = 360 \text{ sets}$$
$$DR \text{ (demand rate per day)} = 1 \text{ set}$$
$$V \text{ (receipt rate per day)} = 2 \text{ sets}$$

Then, the optimum order quantity would be

$$Q^* = \sqrt{\frac{2 \cdot 20 \cdot 360}{50 \, (1 - 1/2)}} = \sqrt{\frac{14{,}400}{25}} = \sqrt{576} = 24$$

In the above computation, the unit holding cost is discounted by 50 percent. This is because that 50 percent, or the proportion DR/V of the goods received, will be sold immediately; thus, no holding cost will be charged. Since the total holding cost will be reduced by 50 percent, the total inventory cost can be reduced by ordering in large quantities. The optimum order quantity is thus increased from the previous Q^* of 17 to 24.

Economic Lot-Size (ELS) Model

The **economic lot-size (ELS) model** is an interesting extension of the noninstantaneous receipt model we considered in the previous section. The ELS model is an application of the EOQ concept to the production management area. In most production problems, an important cost consideration is the *setup cost*. Setup cost represents the expenses incurred in preparing the production facilities for an upcoming run. For example, let us suppose that a furniture manufacturer is preparing to produce a specific number of colonial-style dining tables. The company must dismantle the previous production setup for Mediterranean-style sofas, prepare the machines and assemblies for the new run, and take care of any training or clerical work. Thus, the setup cost includes all expenses, both materials and personnel, that are related to dismantling the old setup and preparing for the new production run.

If the setup cost is a major component of the production cost, as it usually is in many manufacturing situations, it may be more economical to produce items in large lots rather than in small but frequent lots to meet the demand. When large lots of goods that exceed the demand rate are produced, the inventory level will gradually increase. When the inventory level reaches a certain high point, production will be stopped. Then, the inventory level decreases gradually as demand is satisfied from the existing inventory. When the inventory level is decreased to a sufficiently low level, another production lot is processed to begin the second cycle.

The ELS process is illustrated graphically in Figure 12.9. Each cycle consists of two basic phases: Phase 1 represents the production period and thus an increase of the inventory level, and Phase 2 represents the inventory depletion period.

Figure 12.9   *Inventory Level for Economic Lot-Size Model*

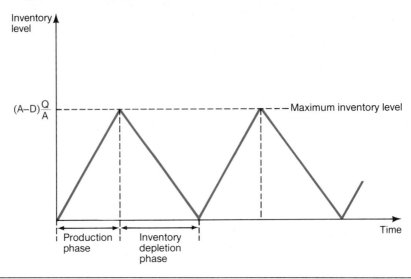

To analyze the ELS model, let us define the following parameters:

HC = holding cost per unit per year

SU = setup cost per production lot

THC = total annual holding cost

TSU = total annual setup cost

D = demand rate over time on an annual basis

A = production rate over time on an annual basis

Q = production lot size

TC = total annual production cost

Now we are ready to develop the relationships that are necessary to determine the optimum lot size Q^*.

Length of the Production Phase   During the production phase, the total production quantity would be lot Q. Since the production rate is A and the demand rate is D, the inventory level will increase at the rate of $A - D$, assuming that $A > D$. The length of the production phase in terms of days will be the lot size divided by the production rate:

$$\text{Length of production phase} = \frac{Q}{A}$$

The Maximum Inventory Level   During the production phase, the inventory level increases at the rate of $A - D$ until it reaches the maximum level at the end of this phase. Since the increase in the production level is gradual throughout the production phase, we can state:

$$\text{Maximum inventory level} = (A - D)\frac{Q}{A}$$

The Average Inventory Level Since we have determined the maximum inventory level above, the average inventory level is simply half of the maximum inventory level:

$$\text{Average inventory level} = \frac{(A - D)\,Q}{2A}$$

Total Annual Holding Cost The total annual holding cost is determined by multiplying the average inventory level by the unit holding cost per unit per year. Thus, we can write

$$THC = \frac{HC \cdot (A - D) \cdot Q}{2A}$$

Length of Inventory Depletion Phase At the end of the production phase, production stops completely. Since the demand rate continues, the inventory will be depleted gradually. The length of the inventory depletion period, then, would be simply the maximum inventory level divided by the demand rate:

$$\text{Length of inventory depletion phase} = \frac{(A - D)Q}{D \cdot A}$$

Number of Annual Inventory Cycles The number of **inventory cycles** represents the number of times the inventory level goes through the production (inventory increase) and inventory depletion phases. The number of inventory cycles will be simply the same as the number of times the production lot is processed. Thus, the number of inventory cycles is determined by the total annual demand divided by the production lot size:

$$\text{Number of inventory cycles} = \frac{D}{Q}$$

Total Annual Setup Cost The total annual **setup cost** corresponds to the total annual ordering cost in the EOQ model. Since a setup cost occurs every time we have a production phase, the total annual setup cost is the product of the setup cost per production lot multiplied by the number of annual inventory cycles:

$$TSU = \frac{SU \cdot D}{Q}$$

The optimum lot size, Q^*, is found in the usual manner, equating the total annual holding costs to the total annual setup cost:

$$\frac{HC \cdot (A - D) \cdot Q}{2A} = \frac{SU \cdot D}{Q}$$

$$HC \cdot (A - D) \cdot Q^2 = 2A \cdot SU \cdot D$$

$$Q^* = \sqrt{\frac{2A \cdot SU \cdot D}{HC\,(A - D)}}$$

Casette 12.2   *SUNERGY PRODUCTS INC.*

Sunergy Products Inc. is a relatively new firm that specializes in producing various solar energy products. The company is best known for its solar panels. It produces panels of different types, sizes, and purposes. However, it also produces various other solar energy products such as plastic pipes and valves, heat storage units, and water circulation devices.

The company is primarily concerned about determining the production lot size of its primary product, solar panels for residential use. The demand for the panels is 5,000 per year, or 25 panels per day for 200 plant operation days. The setup cost for each production run is estimated to be $1,000. The inventory holding cost per panel per year is $50. The production rate during the production phase is 30 panels per day.

Bob Reznicek, a new inventory analyst, has been assigned the task of determining the optimum production lot size and other relevant information such as total inventory cost, number of cycles, maximum inventory level, and lengths of the production and inventory depletion phases.

Bob first defined and determined the values of certain model parameters:

$$D \text{ (total annual demand)} = 5,000 \text{ panels}$$
$$A \text{ (total annual production capacity)} = 6,000 \text{ panels}$$
$$HC \text{ (holding cost per unit per year)} = \$50$$
$$SU \text{ (setup cost per production run)} = \$1,000$$

Optimum Production Lot Size

$$Q^* = \sqrt{\frac{2A \cdot SU \cdot D}{HC\,(A - D)}} = \sqrt{\frac{2(6{,}000)\,(1{,}000)\,(5{,}000)}{50\,(6{,}000 - 5{,}000)}}$$
$$= \sqrt{1{,}200{,}000} = 1{,}095.45 \cong 1{,}095 \text{ units per lot}$$

Length of Production Phase

$$\text{Length of production phase} = \frac{Q^*}{A} = \frac{1{,}095}{6{,}000} = 0.1825 \text{ years}$$

Since the company has 200 working days, the length of the production phase will be 37 operation days.

Maximum Inventory Level

$$\text{Maximum inventory level} = (A - D)\frac{Q^*}{A} = (6{,}000 - 5{,}000)\frac{1{,}095}{6{,}000}$$
$$= 182.5 \cong 182 \text{ or } 183 \text{ units}$$

Average Inventory Level

$$\text{Average inventory level} = \frac{\text{maximum inventory level}}{2}$$

or

$$\text{Average inventory level} = \frac{(A - D)\, Q^*}{2A} = \frac{(6{,}000 - 5{,}000)(1{,}095)}{2\,(6{,}000)}$$

$$= 91.25 \cong 91 \text{ units}$$

Length of Inventory Depletion Phase

$$\text{Length of inventory depletion phase} = \frac{\text{maximum inventory level}}{\text{demand rate}}$$

or

$$\text{Inventory depletion phase} = \frac{(A - D)\, Q^*}{D \cdot A} - \frac{(6{,}000 - 5{,}000)\,(1{,}095)}{(5{,}000)\,(6{,}000)}$$

$$= 0.0365 \text{ years, or 7 operation days}$$

Length of Inventory Cycles and Number of Inventory Cycles

$$\text{Length of inventory cycles} = \text{production phase} + \text{inventory depletion phase}$$

$$= 37 + 7 = 44 \text{ days}$$

$$\text{Number of inventory cycles} = \frac{D}{Q^*} = \frac{5{,}000}{1{,}095}$$

$$= 4.57 \text{ cycles per year}$$

Total Annual Holding Cost

$$THC = \frac{HC \cdot (A - D) \cdot Q^*}{2A} = \frac{\$50 \times (6{,}000 - 5{,}000)\,(1{,}095)}{(2)\,(6{,}000)}$$

$$= \$4{,}562.50$$

Total Annual Setup Cost

$$TSU = \frac{SU \cdot D}{Q^*} = \frac{(\$1{,}000)\,(5{,}000)}{(1{,}095)} = \$4{,}566.21$$

Total Annual Inventory Cost

$$TC = THC + TSU = \$4{,}562.50 + \$4{,}566.21 = \$9{,}128.71$$

In the above computation of the total annual inventory cost, the total annual holding cost does not exactly equal the total annual setup cost. These two cost components must be equal, given the optimum lot size Q^*. If we use the exact value of $Q^* = 1{,}095.4451$, the two costs will be exactly equal.

On the basis of this solution procedure, Bob was able to develop the production process of solar panels at Sunergy Products Inc. as shown in Figure 12.10.

Figure 12.10   Solar Panel Production Process of Sunergy Products Inc.

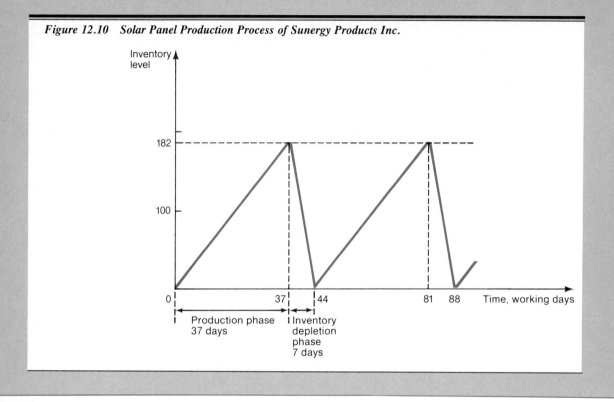

Quantity Discount Model

Quite frequently, manufacturers and vendors offer price discounts on orders of large quantities. To take advantage of such discounts, a firm will need to evaluate whether the size of a particular order should be greater than the present EOQ. If a large quantity is ordered each time in order to receive a quantity discount, the average inventory will increase. Consequently, the total annual holding cost will increase. However, when the order quantity is increased, the number of orders per year will decrease. Thus, the total ordering cost will decrease. Therefore, we can conclude that it is desirable to order a larger quantity than the EOQ if the increase in the total holding cost is less than the sum of the savings in the total ordering cost and the purchase cost of the item.

The total inventory cost for a quantity discount model would be

$$TC = \text{total holding cost} + \text{total ordering cost} + \text{total purchasing cost}$$

$$TC = HCP \cdot P\frac{Q}{2} + OC\frac{D}{Q} + P \cdot D$$

where

$$HCP = \text{holding cost as a percentage of the annual inventory dollar value}$$
$$P = \text{purchase price}$$

In the above model, it should be noted that the total holding cost is expressed as a percentage of the average dollar value of the inventory held instead of a dollar holding

Figure 12.11   *Inventory Analysis Model for Quantity Discount*

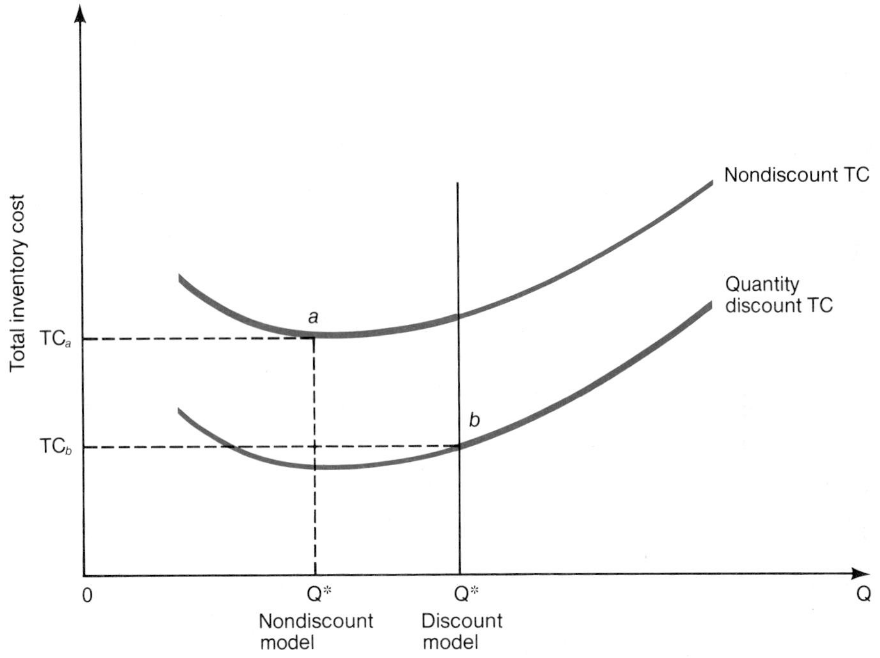

cost per unit held. We discussed this model previously as a variation of the EOQ model. Also, we added the total annual purchasing cost component to the model.

The solution procedure for this model is as follows: (1) Compute *TC with* a quantity discount; (2) compute *TC without* a quantity discount; and (3) compare the two *TC*s and determine the optimum order quantity Q^*, which results in the minimum total cost.

The quantity discount modeling approach is graphically illustrated in Figure 12.11. The nondiscount *TC* curve is higher than the discount *TC* curve, since a higher total purchasing cost is included. Point *b* indicates the minimum order quantity that is required for receiving a price break. We are interested only in the *TC* curves that are indicated by bold lines in the two *TC* curves. If our order quantity is less than the quantity required for discount, the higher price is charged and the nondiscount *TC* curve takes effect. However, if our order quantity is greater than or equal to the quantity required for a price break, the lower price is charged and the discount *TC* curve becomes relevant. In Figure 12.11, we will take the quantity discount because the total inventory cost is lower at point *b* than at point *a*.

Casette 12.3   *SMITH AUTOPARTS COMPANY*

James Robert Smith has been operating Smith Autoparts Company for the past 20 years. Jim Bob's main problem has always been inventory control. He has only 2,000 square feet of storage space. Also, he does not wish to tie up too much money in inventory.

A new vendor of a certain type of muffler that fits most foreign-made compact cars has approached Jim Bob with a quantity discount scheme. World Muffler Products Inc. is offering a 10 percent price break for orders of 50 or more mufflers. Jim Bob struggled with this proposal by putting some figures down on paper. When the figures became too complicated, he just gave up. He approached Mark Simpson, an industrial engineer at a large local manufacturing firm that produces outboard motors for boats.

Mark asked Jim Bob several questions about the operations and cost data of Smith Autoparts, and he quickly recognized the problem as a quantity discount inventory analysis case. He obtained the following information:

D (total annual demand) = 300 mufflers

HCP (holding cost as a percentage of the annual inventory dollar value) = 0.2

OC (ordering cost per order) = $20

P_1 (purchase price of muffler without discount) = $50

P_2 (unit purchase price for 50 or more mufflers) = $45

Total Inventory Cost without the Discount

To find the nondiscount TC, Mark computes the optimum order quantity as follows:

$$Q^* = \sqrt{\frac{2 \cdot OC \cdot D}{HCP \cdot P_1}} = \sqrt{\frac{2(20)(300)}{(.2)(50)}} = 35$$

Now, Mark computes TC as follows:

$$TC = HCP \cdot P_1 \frac{Q}{2} + OC \cdot \frac{D}{Q} + P_1 \cdot D$$

$$= (.2)(50)\frac{35}{2} + (20)\frac{300}{35} + (50)(300) = \$15,346.43$$

Total Inventory Cost with the Discount

$$Q^* = \sqrt{\frac{2 \cdot OC \cdot D}{HCP \cdot P_2}} = \sqrt{\frac{2(20)(300)}{(.2)(45)}} \cong 37$$

Since Q^* is less than 50, the minimum quantity required to receive the discount price, Q must be set to the required order size. Thus, Q is set to 50:

$$TC = HCP \cdot P_2 \frac{Q}{2} + OC \cdot \frac{D}{Q} + P_2 \cdot D$$

$$= (.2)(45)\frac{50}{2} + (20)\frac{300}{50} + (45)(300) = \$13,845.00$$

Comparison of the Two Total Inventory Costs

In comparing the two total inventory costs, it is clear that Smith Autoparts should order 50 mufflers at a time rather than 35, because the company can save $1,501.43 annually. Mark summarized the analysis and presented it to Jim Bob as follows:

	Q and Cost Information	
	Without Discount **(Q = 35)**	**With Discount** **(Q = 50)**
Total holding cost (*THC*)	$175.00	$225.00
Total ordering cost (*TOC*)	171.43	120.00
Total purchase cost	15,000.00	13,500.00
Total inventory cost	$15,346.43	$13,845.00

On the basis of this information, Jim Bob started a long business relationship with World Muffler Products. Mark received much satisfaction from solving an interesting problem, and, in addition, he received a $300 certificate toward automobile maintenance work at any of the shops that purchase parts from Smith Autoparts.

Inventory Model with Planned Shortages

In previous models, it has been assumed that there is no inventory shortage. In other words, an order is received at the moment the inventory level reaches 0. We will now consider an instantaneous order receipt model in which inventory shortages are allowed to occur because requested sales can be back ordered, i.e., delivery takes place after the sales request is made. Therefore, all demands will be met eventually, since all back orders will be satisfied before meeting new demands at the moment of replenishment. This approach is appropriate when the products we are dealing with are expensive or custom-made or when the specifications are very complicated. This approach is also useful when there is very little penalty cost involved with shortages. Mail order companies frequently use this inventory system.

An analysis of the inventory model with planned shortages is presented graphically in Figure 12.12. The maximum level of on-hand inventory (I) does not equal the order quantity level (Q), because back orders are filled first when an order is received. Thus, the number of items that are back ordered is represented by the difference between Q and I (or $Q - I$). Because of the lowered inventory level, we can anticipate that the total inventory holding cost will be reduced. However, we must consider shortage costs. Shortage costs are dependent on the number of back-ordered items and the duration of shortages. Shortage costs include the labor and handling costs of back-ordered items as well as the cost due to a loss of goodwill.

The definitions and descriptions of the model variables used here will be the same as in the previous models, along with several new ones:

Q = order quantity per order

HC = holding cost per unit per year

OC = ordering cost per order

SC = shortage cost per unit per year

S = shortage quantity back ordered per order

I = maximum inventory level ($Q - S$)

D = annual demand quantity

Figure 12.12   Inventory Model with Planned Shortages

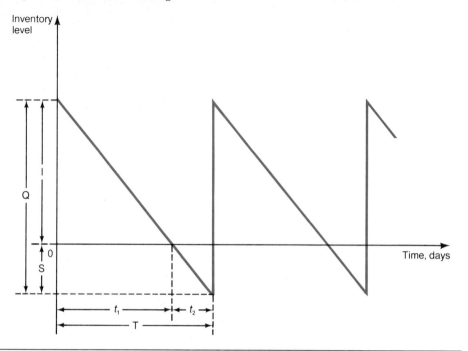

$$THC = \text{total annual holding cost}$$
$$TOC = \text{total annual ordering cost}$$
$$TSC = \text{total annual shortage cost}$$
$$TC = \text{total annual inventory cost}$$
$$T = \text{inventory cycle time period, on an annual basis}$$
$$t_1 = \text{time period when inventory is available in a cycle, on an annual basis}$$
$$t_2 = \text{time period when there are shortages in a cycle, on an annual basis}$$

The total annual inventory cost function for the model is expressed as:

Total holding cost + total ordering cost + total shortage cost

$$TC = THC + TOC + TSC$$

Now we are ready to determine each of the cost components and model variables for the inventory model with planned shortages.

Total Holding Cost   Since the inventory level ranges from 0 to I, where $I = Q - S$, the average inventory level over the time period t_1 is

$$\frac{I + 0}{2} = \frac{I}{2}$$

Thus, the total holding cost during one inventory cycle T is

$$HC \text{ per cycle } T = HC \cdot t_1 \cdot \frac{I}{2}$$

To convert this holding cost per inventory cycle into an annual cost, we must understand the geometrical relationship of t_1 to I shown by the triangular area in Figure 12.12 during period t_1. If we extend the triangular area, we obtain a similar relationship of T to Q. Thus, we can write

$$\frac{t_1}{I} = \frac{T}{Q}$$

From the above relationship we can solve for t_1 as follows:

$$t_1 = \frac{T \cdot I}{Q}$$

By substituting the above value of t_1 into the total holding cost per inventory cycle model, we obtain

$$\text{Holding cost per cycle } T = HC \cdot t_1 \cdot \frac{I}{2}$$

$$= HC \cdot \left(\frac{T \cdot I}{Q}\right) \cdot \frac{I}{2}$$

$$= \frac{HC \cdot T \cdot I^2}{2Q}$$

If there are N number of inventory cycles per year, we can write $T \cdot N = 1$ year. Thus, the number of inventory cycles per year is $N = 1/T$. The total annual holding cost is the product of the total holding cost per inventory cycle multiplied by the number of cycles per year. Thus, we can obtain

$$THC = \frac{HC \cdot T \cdot I^2}{2Q} \cdot N = \frac{HC \cdot T \cdot I^2}{2Q} \cdot \left(\frac{1}{T}\right)$$

$$THC = \frac{HC \cdot I^2}{2Q}$$

Total Ordering Cost   The total annual ordering cost is the product of the unit ordering cost multiplied by the number of orders processed per year. Thus, TOC is not affected by the allowance of shortages:

$$TOC = OC \cdot \frac{D}{Q}$$

Total Shortage Cost   In Figure 12.12, we can clearly see that the shortage level ranges from 0 to S, where $S = Q - I$. Thus, the average shortage level during the shortage time period t_2 is $S/2$. We can develop the shortage cost per inventory cycle as follows:

$$\text{Shortage cost per cycle } T = SC \cdot t_2 \cdot \left(\frac{S}{2}\right)$$

Since the geometric relationship of t_2 to S is precisely the same as the relationship of T to Q, we can write $t_2/S = T/Q$. Again, we can solve for t_2 and obtain

$$t_2 = \frac{T \cdot S}{Q}$$

By substituting the value of t_2 into the shortage cost function, we obtain the following shortage cost per inventory cycle:

$$\text{Shortage cost per cycle } T = SC \cdot t_2 \cdot \frac{S}{2} = SC \cdot \left(\frac{T \cdot S}{Q}\right) \cdot \frac{S}{2}$$

$$= \frac{SC \cdot T \cdot S^2}{2Q}$$

Since there are N number of inventory cycles per year ($N = 1/T$) and the shortage is simply the order quantity minus the maximum inventory level ($S = Q - I$), we can derive the total annual shortage cost as

$$TSC = \frac{SC \cdot T \cdot S^2}{2Q} \cdot N = \frac{SC \cdot T \cdot (Q - I)^2}{2Q} \cdot \left(\frac{1}{T}\right)$$

$$TSC = \frac{SC \cdot (Q - I)^2}{2Q}$$

Total Annual Inventory Cost   The total annual inventory cost model with planned shortages is determined by summing the three cost components:

$$TC = \frac{HC \cdot I^2}{2Q} + \frac{OC \cdot D}{Q} + \frac{SC \cdot (Q - I)^2}{2Q}$$

Determination of Optimum Values of Q, I, S, T, and TC   Next, we should find the optimum values of Q, I, and S as well as T and TC. The method for obtaining these solutions involves partial differentiation of the total cost function with respect to Q and I, setting each partial derivative to 0 and solving the resulting equations simultaneously. This method is beyond the scope of this book, but it may be found in other books such as *Management Science*, by Lee, Moore, and Taylor, and *Introduction to Operations Research* by Hillier and Lieberman.

The optimum solutions for the model variables, however, are given below:

$$Q^* = \sqrt{\frac{2 \cdot OC \cdot D}{HC}} \cdot \sqrt{\frac{HC + SC}{SC}}$$

$$I^* = \sqrt{\frac{2 \cdot OC \cdot D}{HC}} \cdot \sqrt{\frac{SC}{HC + SC}}$$

$$S^* = Q^* - I^*$$

$$T^* = \sqrt{\frac{2 \cdot OC}{HC \cdot D}} \cdot \sqrt{\frac{HC + SC}{SC}}$$

$$TC^* = \sqrt{2 \cdot HC - OC \cdot D} \cdot \sqrt{\frac{SC}{HC + SC}}$$

Casette 12.4   AMERICAN RUBBER PRODUCTS INC.

American Rubber Products Inc. is a family-owned wholesaler of rubber products for households. One of its typical stock items is a rubber belt for vacuum cleaners, which it sells to retailers in boxes. The company has had a long-standing corporate policy of no inventory shortage. However, this policy has resulted in a high level of annual holding cost of inventories. The manager of the Materials Management Division, James Hines, has been assigned the task of evaluating the implications of an inventory policy for planned shortages.

On the basis of company records, Jim has estimated the following demand and cost information:

$$D \text{ (total annual demand)} = 100 \text{ boxes}$$
$$HC \text{ (holding cost per box per year)} = \$4$$
$$OC \text{ (ordering cost per order)} = \$2$$
$$SC \text{ (shortage cost per box per year)} = \$8$$

Jim proceeded to determine the optimum values for the following decision variables:

Optimum Order Quantity

$$Q^* = \sqrt{\frac{2 \cdot OC \cdot D}{HC}} \cdot \sqrt{\frac{HC + SC}{SC}}$$

$$= \sqrt{\frac{2(2)(100)}{4}} \cdot \sqrt{\frac{4 + 8}{8}}$$

$$= 10 \cdot \sqrt{\frac{3}{2}} \cong 12 \text{ boxes}$$

Maximum Inventory Level

$$I^* = \sqrt{\frac{2 \cdot OC \cdot D}{HC}} \cdot \sqrt{\frac{SC}{HC + SC}}$$

$$= \sqrt{\frac{2(2)(100)}{4}} \cdot \sqrt{\frac{8}{4 + 8}}$$

$$= 10 \cdot \sqrt{\frac{2}{3}} \cong 8 \text{ boxes}$$

Inventory Cycle

$$T^* = \sqrt{\frac{2 \cdot OC}{HC \cdot D}} \cdot \sqrt{\frac{HC + SC}{SC}}$$

$$= \sqrt{\frac{2(2)}{4(100)}} \cdot \sqrt{\frac{4+8}{8}}$$

$$= \frac{1}{10} \cdot \sqrt{\frac{3}{2}} \cong 0.122 \text{ year}$$

Assuming 365 working days per year, $0.122 \times 365 \cong 45$ days.

Total Annual Inventory Cost

$$TC^* = \sqrt{2 \cdot OC \cdot HC \cdot D} \cdot \sqrt{\frac{SC}{HC + SC}}$$

$$= \sqrt{2(2)(4)(100)} \cdot \sqrt{\frac{8}{4+8}}$$

$$= 40 \cdot \sqrt{\frac{2}{3}} \cong \$32.65$$

On the basis of the above computations, Jim made the following conclusions:

1. The company should order 12 boxes of belts at a time.

2. The company may allow a shortage of 4 boxes before placing another order for 12 boxes.

3. The inventory reaches the maximum level of 8 boxes.

4. The optimum time between orders is approximately 45 days.

Jim Hines proceeded to compare the above results with the current no-shortage policy of the company, as shown below:

Important Variables	EOQ Model, No-Shortage Policy	Planned Shortage Model
Order quantity (Q)	10 boxes	12 boxes
Maximum inventory level (I)	10 boxes	8 boxes
Back order (S)	0 box	4 boxes
Inventory cycle (T)	37 days	45 days
Total inventory cost (TC)	$40.00	$32.65

Based on this result, American Rubber Products adopted a planned shortage inventory policy. This new policy is appropriate in view of the number of the company's diverse products (50 different rubber belts for various brands and types of vacuum cleaners as well as many other household rubber products).

THE INVENTORY MODEL UNDER UNCERTAINTY

The inventory models we have discussed thus far in this chapter require two basic assumptions: (1) demand is constant and known with certainty, and (2) lead time is constant and known with certainty. These two assumptions make the model somewhat unrealistic. In this section, we will discuss inventory models in which one or both of the above assumptions are untenable. In other words, we will discuss inventory models with an uncertain demand but with a certain lead time, as well as models with probabilistic demand and lead time.

Inventory Model with Safety Stocks

In many real-world situations, organizations maintain certain **safety stocks.** These safety stocks serve as a buffer or security for emergencies or unexpected excess demands. For example, public utility firms maintain high levels of safety stocks in anticipation of severe weather conditions (tornadoes, floods, snowstorms, etc.).

In the inventory model with safety stocks, demand is considered to be probabilistic while the lead time is assumed to be constant and known with certainty. Since the lead time is constant, the order quantity from the classic EOQ model can be utilized as an approximated order quantity. However, demand is uncertain. Thus, we should compute the expected (average) demand during lead time so that the reorder point can be determined. In other words, we are assuming that demand is constant and known over lead time. Actual demand varies continuously, of course, and consequently shortages or stock-outs may occur during any lead time period. Thus, it is desirable to hold safety stocks or buffer stocks of inventory to avoid such possible shortages.

The inventory level with safety stocks is illustrated graphically in Figure 12.13. In the second inventory cycle we would have faced inventory shortages if we did not hold

Figure 12.13   Inventory Model with Safety Stock

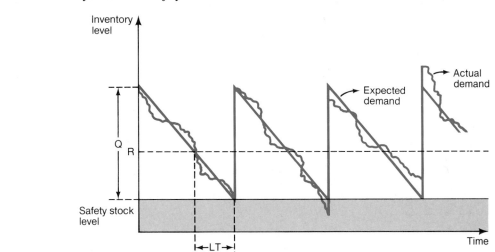

safety stock. However, in the third cycle we would have had a surplus of inventory even without the safety stock. The implication of this model is that surpluses and shortages will be balanced out over time (a year), and they will approximate the expected demand pattern. The average excess inventory held over time is shown by the shaded area in the figure.

In this model, we are primarily interested in finding the optimum quantity of safety stock to hold. As the actual demand over any period of time is uncertain, it must be considered as a probability distribution. Many firms have records of **demand during lead time (DDLT).** This information can be used to generate a probability distribution of *DDLT*. For example, let us suppose that a firm has experienced the demand during the lead time as shown in Table 12.1. On the basis of the data provided, we can easily compute the probability distribution for *DDLT*.

Annual Safety Stock Cost   In the inventory model with safety stocks, we must develop a probabilistic model that involves safety stocks, expected demand, and expected shortages. As previously mentioned, the approximated optimum order quantity is determined by using the classic EOQ model. However, the reorder point, which may include safety stock, will be determined separately as a probabilistic model.

If the level of safety stock is high, the total holding cost will be high, but the shortage (stock-out) cost will be low. However, if we lower the safety stock level sufficiently, the holding cost will be low but the shortage cost will increase. Thus, we need to achieve a balance by analyzing the trade-off between the two costs.

Let us define the following new variables:

$$SI = \text{safety stock inventory level}$$
$$SHC = \text{annual safety stock holding cost}$$

The unused safety stocks will incur holding costs that are the product of the unit holding cost (*HC*) and the safety stock level. Then, we can compute the annual safety stock holding cost as follows:

$$SHC = HC \cdot SI$$

Annual Expected Shortage Cost   Let us examine the *DDLT* distribution presented in Table 12.1. If we set the reorder point at 50 units, we would not face a shortage, since 50 units represent the maximum demand during a lead time. If the reorder point is set at 40 units, we would experience an inventory shortage for an average of 10 percent of

---

Table 12.1   Development of a Probability Distribution for **DDLT**

Demand during Lead Time (*DDLT*)	Frequency	Probability of *DDLT* (Relative Frequency)
10 units	10 times	0.10
20	20	0.20
30	40	0.40
40	20	0.20
50	10	0.10
		1.00

Table 12.2   The Expected Shortage for Selected Reorder Points

Reorder Point	Safety Stock	DDLT	Shortage	P(DDLT)	Expected Shortage E(S)
30	0	30	0	0.4	0 ⎫
		40	10	0.2	2 ⎬ 4
		50	20	0.1	2 ⎭
40	10	40	0	0.2	0 ⎫ 1
		50	10	0.1	1 ⎭
50	20	50	0	0.1	0

the time because a demand of 50 units will occur for 10 percent of the lead time. Similarly, if we set the reorder point at 20 units, we would expect shortages of 10 units for 40 percent, 20 units for 20 percent, and 30 units for 10 percent of the time.

The expected (average) demand during lead time for the above example is found as follows:

$$E(DDLT) = 0.1(10) + 0.2(20) + 0.4(30) + 0.2(40) + 0.1(50) = 30 \text{ units}$$

On the basis of the expected demand during lead time of 30 units, we can select a reorder point (R). If we select 40 units as a reorder point, the average excess of 10 units $[R - E(DDLT)]$ is regarded as the safety stock. If a reorder point of 20 units is selected, the expected shortage would be 10 units. The expected shortages for reorder points of 30, 40, and 50 can be computed as shown in Table 12.2.

Table 12.2 clearly shows that if we do not allow any safety stock, the expected shortage will be 4 units. If we allow a safety stock of 10 units (i.e., a reorder point of 40 units), the expected shortage is only one unit. If we keep a large safety stock (e.g., 20 units), then there will be no stock-outs.

The expected shortage we computed is for only one inventory order (inventory cycle). Thus, the total expected shortage per year would be found by multiplying the expected shortage cost per inventory order by the number of orders per year.

Total shortage cost = shortage cost · number of orders · expected shortage per inventory order cycle

$$TSC = SC \cdot N \cdot E(S)$$

where
SC = shortage cost per unit
N = number of annual orders, D/Q
$E(S)$ = expected shortage units per order cycle

Casette 12.5   BOLD BODYBUILDERS INC.

Bold Bodybuilders Inc. is a specialty sporting goods store that carries equipment and accessories for body builders. Since the store caters to a special group of clients, it is essential for the company to keep up with new trends in the body-building area.

Joe Staub (Super Staub), the owner and manager of the store, attends all national, regional, and local body-building contests. A popular new product made a debut at a recent Chicago contest—Geni, a piece of body-building equipment for women. Bold Bodybuilders has become the exclusive distributor of the Geni line in the three-state region.

After carrying the line for a year, Joe decided to analyze the company's inventory policy for Genies. On the basis of the past year's record, Joe has accumulated the following data:

$$HC \text{ (annual holding cost per Geni)} = \$20$$
$$SC \text{ (shortage cost per Geni per year)} = \$10$$
$$D \text{ (annual demand)} = 1,200 \text{ Genies}$$
$$N \text{ (number of orders per year)} = 10$$

Probabilistic Demand Data	
DDLT	*P(DDLT)*
100 units	0.1
110	0.2
120	0.4
130	0.2
140	0.1
	1.0

Safety Stock Holding Cost

Joe Staub easily computed the safety stock holding cost with the following equation:

$$SHC = HC \cdot SI$$

where
$$SHC = \text{safety stock holding cost}$$
$$SI = \text{safety stock inventory level}$$

Safety Stock Level (SI)	×	Holding Cost (HC)	=	Annual Safety Stock Holding Cost (SHC)
0		$20		$ 0
10		20		200
20		20		400

In the above computation, it should be noted that $Q^* = 120$. This is simple to compute as follows:

$$N = \frac{D}{Q^*}$$
$$10 = \frac{1200}{Q^*}$$
$$Q^* = 120$$

Since the company orders 120 Genies at a time, the safety stock level will be 0 if *DDLT* is 120 or greater. If *DDLT* = 100, the safety stock level will be 20 units. However, if *DDLT* = 110, then *SI* = 10.

Expected Shortage Cost

Joe realized that the expected shortage cost could be determined by computing the combined product of the shortage cost per unit, the number of orders per unit, and the expected number of shortages per order cycle (lead time or inventory cycle):

$$TSC = SC \cdot N \cdot E(S)$$

where
TSC = total annual shortage cost

$E(S)$ = expected number of shortages per order cycle

The expected number of shortages per order cycle can be computed as follows:

Reorder Point	DDLT	Shortage	P(DDLT)	E(S)	
120	120	0	0.4	0	
	130	10	0.2	2	4
	140	20	0.1	2	
130	130	0	0.2	0	
	140	10	0.1	1	1
140	140	0	0.1	0	

Now, based on the above information and computed data, the total annual shortage cost can be determined as follows:

Safety Stock Level (SI)	Shortage Cost (SC)	× Number of Orders (N) ×	Expected Shortage per Order Cycle E(S)	= Total Annual Shortage Cost (TSC)
0	$10	10	4	$400
10	10	10	1	100
20	10	10	0	0

Total Expected Cost

The total annual cost involved in the safety stock decision is the sum of the safety stock holding cost and the expected shortage cost. Joe summarized his analysis as follows:

Safety Stock Level (SI)	Safety Stock Holding Cost (SHC)	Expected Shortage Cost (TSC)	Total Expected Cost
0	$ 0	$400	$400
10	200	100	300
20	400	0	400

It is clear from the previous calculation that the total expected cost can be minimized when the company keeps a safety stock level of 10 Genies (i.e., a reorder point of 130 Genies). This solution is based on an *expected* cost value derived from the probability distribution of *DDLT* during 1 year. For the company to implement this safety stock level policy, it needs an accurate data base for a lengthy period of time. Such a data base is imperative in order to balance out variations in actual costs and to examine trade-offs between a policy of no safety stocks and one of holding an adequate level of safety stocks.

Inventory Model with Uncertain Demand and Lead Time

In this section we will consider an inventory model in which both the demand rate and the lead time are assumed to be probabilistic. Since both demand and lead time are uncertain, we cannot determine the optimum order quantity Q^* independently without considering the lead time. By the same token, the optimum reorder point R^* cannot be determined without examining the demand rate. In other words, we must determine an optimum combination of Q^* and R^*.

In this model, the total annual inventory cost will be the sum of the total holding cost, total ordering cost, and total shortage cost:

$$TC = THC + TOC + TSC$$

We shall examine each cost component in detail.

Total Holding Cost   Since both demand and lead time are uncertain, the average inventory level is dependent on the reorder point (R) as well as on the order quantity (Q). If we assume that no shortage will occur during an order cycle, the average inventory pattern will be as shown in Figure 12.14.

We can easily determine the average inventory level as

$$\text{Average inventory level} = \frac{Q}{2} + \Delta Q$$

In Figure 12.14, ΔQ is considered a safety stock level, and $\Delta \hat{Q}$ is the expected demand during a lead time. Since $R = \Delta \hat{Q} + \Delta Q$, we can determine ΔQ as follows:

$$\Delta Q = R - \Delta \hat{Q}$$

or

$$\Delta Q = R - E(DDLT)$$

Now we can determine the total annual holding cost as follows:

$$THC = HC \cdot \left[\frac{Q}{2} + R - E(DDLT) \right]$$

where

$$HC = \text{annual holding cost per unit}$$
$$Q = \text{order quantity}$$
$$E(DDLT) = \text{expected demand during a lead time}$$

Figure 12.14   *Average Inventory Pattern with Uncertain Demand Rate and Lead Time (No Shortage Assumption)*

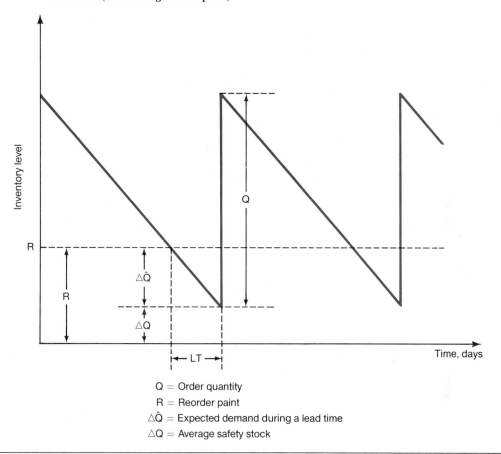

Q = Order quantity
R = Reorder paint
$\triangle\hat{Q}$ = Expected demand during a lead time
$\triangle Q$ = Average safety stock

Total Ordering Cost   The total annual ordering cost is simply the product of the ordering cost per order multiplied by the number of orders processed per year. Thus, there will be no change in the computation of *TOC:*

$$TOC = OC \cdot \frac{D}{Q}$$

where OC = ordering cost per order
                                        D = total annual demand

Total Shortage Cost   Shortages occur only when demand during a lead time is greater than the sum of the expected demand and the safety stock level. For example, suppose that the expected demand during a lead time is 2 units and the firm has a safety stock of 3 units. Then, a shortage will occur only if demand during a lead time is greater than 5 units.

Since the reorder point (R) should be equal to the expected demand during a lead time ($\Delta\hat{Q}$) plus the safety stock (ΔQ), as seen in Figure 12.14, we can write

$$R = \Delta\hat{Q} + \Delta Q$$

Then, a shortage occurs only when $DDLT > R$. The expected shortage per lead time $E(S)$ can be computed as follows:

$$\text{Expected shortage per lead time} = E(DDLT > R)$$

The total annual shortage cost is simply the product of the expected shortage per lead time multiplied by the annual per-unit shortage cost multiplied by the number of lead times. Since a lead time occurs whenever we process an order, the number of annual lead times would be D/Q. Now we can determine the total annual shortage cost as follows:

$$TSC = E(DDLT > R) \cdot SC \cdot \frac{D}{Q}$$

where

$$E(DDLT > R) = \text{expected shortage per lead time}$$
$$SC = \text{annual per-unit shortage cost}$$

Now we can obtain the total annual inventory cost:

$$TC = THC + TOC + TSC$$
$$= HC \cdot \left[\frac{Q}{2} + R - E(DDLT) \right] + OC \cdot \frac{D}{Q} + E(DDLT > R) \cdot SC \cdot \frac{D}{Q}$$

In the EOQ model section, we discussed the relationship of the order quantity (Q) to the total annual holding cost (THC) and to the total annual ordering cost (TOC). If we set Q very high, THC will be high because the average inventory level is high. However, a high-level Q will result in a low TOC because the number of orders (D/Q) will decrease. In the above TC function, we can also see that a high-level Q tends to decrease the total shortage cost (TSC) because the number of lead times (D/Q) would decrease. If we decrease the level of Q, the reverse will be true.

If we set the reorder point (R) very high, THC will increase as the average inventory level becomes high. However, a high-level Q will decrease TSC as the safety stock level increases. However, R has no direct influence on TOC. The relationships of Q and R values to THC, TOC, and TSC are summarized in Table 12.3. Because of the inter-

---

*Table 12.3 Relationships of **Q** and **R** to Inventory Cost Components*

	THC	TOC	TSC
Order Quantity (Q)			
High	↑	↓	↓
Low	↓	↑	↑
Reorder Point (R)			
High	↑	—	↓
Low	↓	—	↑

twined relationships of Q and R to the various components of the total inventory cost, the optimum order quantity Q^* and optimum reorder point R^* cannot be determined independently of each other.

Casette 12.6   **MODERN OFFICE EQUIPMENT INC.**

Modern Office Equipment Inc. specializes in designing and providing modern equipment for efficient executive offices. The company's newest line is Exec-Desk, a genuine wood desk with a built-in computer terminal, dictating machine, a small duplicating machine, and a telephone drawer. It also offers a priority filing system for confidential materials.

Exec-Desk has become an important product for the sales of other equipment and services of Modern Office Equipment. Thus, the company has decided to undergo a complete analysis of the inventory patterns of the Exec-Desk. Laura Compton, a rising systems analyst, was assigned to evaluate the system and make appropriate recommendations to the vice-president for materials management.

After an intensive review and analysis of the existing data, Laura was able to determine the following:

> Current cost of Exec-Desk: $3,000
>
> Annual holding cost per desk (HC): 5% of cost or $150
>
> Ordering cost per order (OC): $30
>
> Annual demand (D): 220 desks (for 220 working days)
>
> Annual per-unit shortage cost (SC): $80
>
> Shortage units are back ordered

The daily demand rate (DR) is uncertain with the following probability distribution:

Demand Rate	Probability
0	0.3
1	0.4
2	0.3
	1.0

The lead time (LT) is uncertain with the following probability distribution:

Lead Time	Probability
1	0.25
2	0.50
3	0.25
	1.00

To systematize the analysis process, Laura decided to evaluate the inventory system step by step. The basic inventory problem is to determine the optimum order quantity (Q^*) and optimum reorder point (R^*) that will minimize the total inventory cost (TC^*).

Expected Demand during Lead Time

Laura realizes that Q^* and R^* cannot be determined independently of each other. She has jotted down the following key points:

1. Shortage occurs only during a lead time if the demand during a lead time is greater than the reorder point ($DDLT > R$).

2. The magnitude of inventory shortage is a function of the reorder point, daily demand rate, and lead time.

3. To determine Q^* and R^*, the expected shortage during lead time $E(DDLT > R)$ must be determined.

4. The expected shortage during a lead time can be determined only if the expected demand during lead time $E(DDLT)$ is known.

5. To determine the expected demand during lead time, $E(DDLT)$, all of the possible demand quantities during a lead time must be known.

Demand during Lead Time (DDLT) and Probabilities

To analyze the demand during a lead time, Laura checked the inventory pattern during the last three lead time periods. Figure 12.15 presents the inventory pattern of the Exec-Desk. The actual inventory level and possible shortages are determined by R, DR, and LT.

Laura proceeded to determine the possible demand quantities during a lead time. We shall see only her calculation for $DDLTs$ of 6, 5, and 4 units, shown below:

Demand during Lead Time (DDLT)	Required Lead Time (LT)	Probability of Lead Time P(LT)	Demand Rate (DR)			Probability of Demand Rate P(DR)		
			Day 1	Day 2	Day 3	Day 1	Day 2	Day 3
6	3 days	0.25	2	2	2	0.3	0.3	0.3
5	3	0.25	2	2	1	0.3	0.3	0.4
			2	1	2	0.3	0.4	0.3
			1	2	2	0.4	0.3	0.3
4	3	0.25	2	2	0	0.3	0.3	0.3
			2	0	2	0.3	0.3	0.3
			0	2	2	0.3	0.3	0.3
			2	1	1	0.3	0.4	0.4
			1	2	1	0.4	0.3	0.4
			1	1	2	0.4	0.4	0.3
4	2	0.50	2	2	—	0.3	0.3	—

Since the maximum LT is 3 days and the maximum DR is 2 units, the maximum $DDLT$ would be 6. The probability of $DDLT = 6$ can be computed by $P(LT) \times P(DR)$. Thus, we can obtain

Figure 12.15 *Inventory Pattern of Exec-Desk*

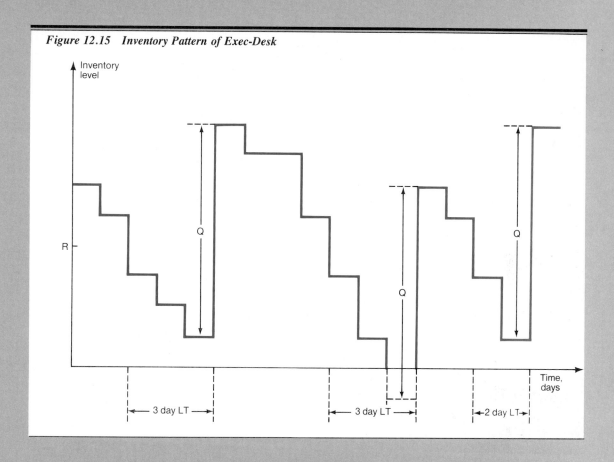

$$P(DDLT = 6) = (0.25) \times (0.3) \times (0.3) \times (0.3) = 0.00675$$

Proceeding in this fashion, Laura was able to determine $P(DDLT = 5)$ as follows:

$$P(DDLT = 5) = P(LT = 3) \cdot P(DR = 2, 2, 1 \text{ combination})$$

$$= (0.25)(0.3)(0.3)(0.4) = 0.009$$

or

$$= (0.25)(0.3)(0.4)(0.3) = 0.009$$

or

$$= (0.25)(0.4)(0.3)(0.3) = \underline{0.009}$$

Thus, $P(DDLT = 5) = 0.027$

On the basis of this computation procedure, Laura computed the *DDLT*, the $P(DDLT)$, and the cumulative probability that demand during a lead time will be greater than the given quantity $P(DDLT > Z)$, as shown in Table 12.4. The last column $P(DDLT > Z)$ is simply a cumulative probability that demand during a lead time will be greater than Z, which is the *DDLT* quantity we see in the first column. For example, the maximum *DDLT* is 6. The probability of *DDLT* = 6 is 0.00675. Then, the probability that demand during a lead time will be greater than 6 is 0. This is shown by $P(DDLT > 6)$.

Table 12.4 *Demand during Lead Time Probability Distribution*

Possible Demand during Lead Time (DDLT)	P(DDLT)	Cumulative Probability P(DDLT > Z)
0	0.12675	0.87325
1	0.24700	0.62625
2	0.30125	0.32500
3	0.19000	0.13500
4	0.10125	0.03375
5	0.02700	0.00675
6	0.00675	0.00000

Expected Shortage per Lead Time

Laura proceeded to determine the expected shortage per lead time for various reorder points (R). If R is set at 6 units (i.e., when the stock level reaches 6 units, an order is placed immediately), there will never be a shortage because $P(DDLT > 6)$ is 0. If R is set at 5, there will be a shortage of 1 unit if $DDLT$ is 6. The probability of $DDLT > 5$ is 0.00675. Then, the expected shortage per lead time for $R = 5$ units will be $(6 - 5) \times 0.00675 = 0.00675$ units.

If R is set at 4 units, Modern Office Equipment can expect shortages 3.375 percent of the lead times. Now the expected shortage per lead time can be determined as follows:

1. If $DDLT = 6$, the shortage will be 2 units $(6 - 4)$. Since $P(DDLT = 6) = 0.00675$, the expected shortage is $2 \times 0.00675 = 0.0135$.

2. If $DDLT = 5$, the shortage will be 1 unit $(5 - 4)$. Since $P(DDLT = 5) = 0.027$, the expected shortage is $1 \times 0.027 = 0.027$.

Therefore, the company would experience an expected shortage per lead time of 0.0405 units. In other words, if we examine 10,000 lead times, we would expect a total shortage of 405 units. In a similar manner, Laura determined the expected shortage per lead time for various reorder points. The expected shortage per lead time is simply a cumulative of the cumulative probabilities $P(DDLT > Z)$. The expected shortage is computed in Table 12.5.

Computation of Total Inventory Costs for Various **Q** and **R**

Laura has no formal training in simulation. Thus, she decided to solve for the optimum Q^* and R^* by means of a step-by-step search method. If she sets R at a certain low quantity and determines the optimum Q for that R, she could determine the total inventory cost (TC) with the given combination of R and Q. She can increase R by 1 unit and once again determine the optimum Q and TC. If TC increases gradually and then decreases, she would be able to find the optimum R^* and Q^* that produce the minimum TC^*.

Table 12.5   Computation of Expected Shortage per Lead Time

Reorder Point (R)	P(DDLT > R)	E(DDLT > R)
0	0.87325	2.00000
1	0.62625	1.12675
2	0.32500	0.50050
3	0.13500	0.17550
4	0.03375	0.04050
5	0.00675	0.00675
6	0.00000	0.00000

Laura's search procedure started with the following computations:

Expected Demand during Lead Time. The expected demand during lead time, $E(DDLT)$, is a component required for computing the total holding cost. $E(DDLT)$ can be easily determined if the expected lead time $E(LT)$ and the expected demand rate per day $E(DR)$ can be computed.

The probability distribution for lead time is as follows:

LT	P(LT)
1	0.25
2	0.50
3	0.25
	1.00

Then, the expected lead time is

$$E(LT) = (1 \times 0.25) + (2 \times 0.50) + (3 \times 0.25)$$
$$= 0.25 + 1.00 + 0.75 = 2 \text{ days}$$

The probability distribution for the demand rate per day is as follows:

DR	P(DR)
0	0.3
1	0.4
2	0.3
	1.0

Thus, the expected demand rate is computed as

$$E(DR) = (0 \times 0.3) + (1 \times 0.4) + (2 \times 0.3) = 0.4 + 0.6 = 1 \text{ unit per day}$$

Now Laura is able to determine the expected demand during lead time as follows:

$$E(DDLT) = E(LT) \times E(DR) = 2 \times 1 = 2 \text{ units}$$

Optimum Order Quantity.   The optimum order quantity Q^* can be determined from the total inventory cost function:

$$TC = THC + TOC + TSC$$

$$= HC \cdot \left[\frac{Q}{2} + R - E(DDLT) \right] + OC \cdot \frac{D}{Q} + SC \cdot \left(\frac{D}{Q} \right) \cdot E(DDLT > R)$$

By using the partial derivation procedure, Laura proceeded as follows:

$$\frac{d(TC)}{dQ} = \frac{HC}{2} - \frac{OC \cdot D}{Q^2} - \frac{SC \cdot D \cdot E(DDLT > R)}{Q^2}$$

At the minimum total inventory cost point, the partial derivative (slope) must be 0. Thus, we can proceed as follows:

$$0 = \frac{HC}{2} - \frac{OC \cdot D}{Q^2} - \frac{SC \cdot D \cdot E(DDLT > R)}{Q^2}$$

$$\frac{D[OC + SC \cdot E(DDLT > R)]}{Q^2} = \frac{HC}{2}$$

$$Q^2 \cdot HC = 2 \cdot D[OC + SC \cdot E(DDLT > R)]$$

$$Q^* = \sqrt{\frac{2 \cdot D[OC + SC \cdot E(DDLT > R)]}{HC}}$$

If we select a given reorder point (e.g., $R = 3$), then we can easily determine the optimum order quantity Q^* by the above formula.

Total Inventory Cost for Selected Reorder Points.   To determine the optimum Q^* and R^* that would yield the minimum TC^*, Laura decided to compute TC for selected reorder points.

   R = 2:   From Table 12.5 we can find $E(DDLT > R)$. If $R = 2$, $E(DDLT > 2)$ will be 0.5005. Now, Q^* can be determined for $R = 2$ as follows:

$$Q^* = \sqrt{\frac{2 \cdot D[OC + SC \cdot E(DDLT > 2)]}{HC}}$$

$$= \sqrt{\frac{2 \cdot 220(30 + 80 \times 0.5005)}{150}}$$

$$= \sqrt{205.45} = 14.33$$

$$\cong 14$$

Given that $Q = 14$ and $R = 2$, TC becomes

$$TC = HC \cdot \left[\frac{Q}{2} + R - E(DDLT) \right] + OC \cdot \frac{D}{Q} + SC \cdot \left(\frac{D}{Q} \right) \cdot E(DDLT > R)$$

$$= \$150 \left(\frac{14}{2} + 2 - 2 \right) + \$30 \cdot \frac{220}{14} + \$80 \times \left(\frac{220}{14} \right) \times 0.5005$$

$$= \$1,050.00 + \$471.43 + \$629.20 = \$2,150.63$$

   R = 3:   Following the same computation procedure, we can compute Q^* for $R = 3$:

$$Q^* = \sqrt{\frac{2 \cdot 220(30 + 0.1755 \cdot 80)}{150}} = \sqrt{129.184} = 11.3659$$

$$\cong 11$$

$$TC = \$975.00 + \$600.00 + \$280.80 = \$1,855.80$$

R = 4:

$$Q^* = \sqrt{\frac{2 \cdot 220(30 + 0.0404 \cdot 80)}{150}} = \sqrt{97.504} = 9.87$$

$$\cong 10$$

$$TC = \$1,050.00 + \$660.00 + \$71.28 = \$1,781.28$$

R = 5:

$$Q^* = \sqrt{\frac{2 \cdot 220(30 + 0.00675 \cdot 80)}{150}} = \sqrt{89.584} = 9.465$$

$$\cong 9$$

$$TC = \$1,125.00 + \$733.33 + \$13.20 = \$1,871.53$$

Determination of Optimum **Q*** *and* **R***

The procedure that Laura utilized in searching for the optimum order quantity (Q^*) and reorder point (R^*) was as follows:

Step 1: Set R at a low quantity.

Step 2: Determine Q^* for the given R.

Step 3: Compute TC with the given R and Q^*.

Step 4: Record TC. If this TC is greater than the previous TC, go to Step 6. Otherwise, go to Step 5.

Step 5: Increase R by 1 and return to Step 2.

Step 6: Stop and record Q^*, R^*, and TC^*.

This procedure is presented as a flowchart in Figure 12.16. Laura's computational search procedure is summarized in Table 12.6. The optimum order quantity and the reorder point are 10 and 4 respectively. With $Q^* = 10$ and $R^* = 4$, the total inventory cost is $1,781.28. It is interesting to note that as R increases, the total shortage cost decreases. When R increases, the total holding cost also increases but Q gradually decreases. Thus, the combined effect of these simultaneous changes of R and Q would first decrease THC and then increase it. As Q decreases, TOC gradually increases, of course, as the number of orders per year increases.

Laura presented the result of her analysis to the vice-president for materials management. On the basis of this analysis, Modern Office Equipment was able to develop an efficient inventory policy for Exec-Desks.

Figure 12.16   Flowchart of the Search Procedure for **Q*** *and* **R***

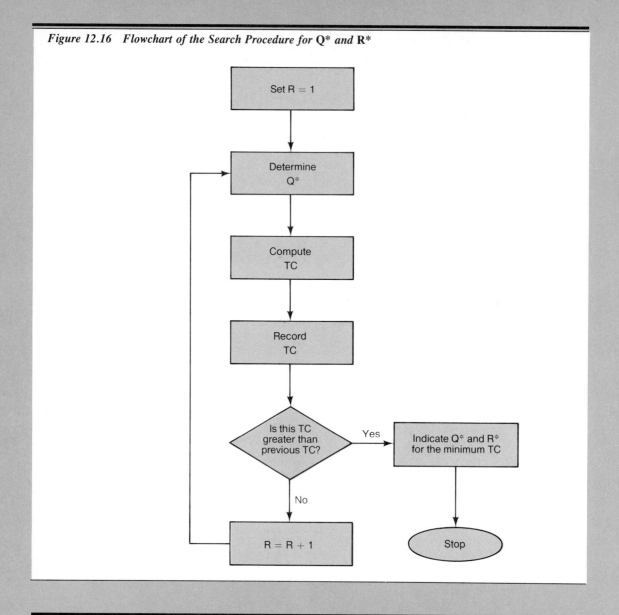

Table 12.6   Summary of the Search Procedure for **Q*** *and* **R***

R	Q	TC	THC	TOC	TSC
2	14	$2,150.63	$1,050.00	$471.43	$629.20
3	11	1,855.80	975.00	600.00	280.80
4*	10*	1,781.28	1,050.00	660.00	71.28
5	9	1,871.53	1,125.00	733.33	13.20

Q^* = optimum order quantity.
R^* = optimum reorder point.

ANALYTICAL VERSUS SIMULATION APPROACH

In developing and solving inventory models, we would like to employ analytical approaches whenever possible. Analytical approaches use a direct, or "pure," form of computation in determining the optimum order quantity by calculus. For example, the EOQ model is a good representation of the analytical approach.

In the previous section, we discussed probabilistic inventory models in which the lead time and demand rates are stochastic. In analyzing these models, we employed a search procedure that is a combination of an analytical and a simulation approach. In real-world inventory problems, many model parameters and variables are interrelated and stochastic. Frequently, therefore, the last resort in analyzing the **inventory system under uncertainty** is simulation. We will discuss simulation in Chapter 15. If you are interested in pursuing more advanced inventory models, you should consult the References at the end of this chapter.

MATERIAL REQUIREMENTS PLANNING AND JUST-IN-TIME (JIT) SYSTEMS

The inventory models we have discussed thus far are based on the general assumption that the demand pattern is essentially constant over time. Such an assumption is often valid for many finished goods. The same assumption, however, is quite unrealistic for subassembly items. The primary reason for this is that the demand for subassembly items is usually "lumpy" rather than "steady" because it is dependent on the demand for finished goods. For example, in producing a three-wheel all-terrain motorcycle, the demand for subassemblies of the three-wheelers occurs at a very high level for a short duration of the production time.

For such lumpy demand, it is very costly to hold required items in inventory for an entire production time. The usual EOQ model has very little value for such a case. If we can devise an inventory system that will deliver the required items *just in time* for them to be used, the total inventory cost will be reduced greatly. **Material requirements planning (MRP)** is such a system.

The MRP system consists of three elements: (1) a master production schedule, (2) a bill of materials file, and (3) an inventory master file. Based on the production schedule, the MRP system determines what subcomponents will be required when and in what quantities by searching through the bill of materials file and the inventory master file. The MRP system can be used advantageously in the lot-sizing problem we discussed previously. This system plans the timing of the lot so that the required subcomponents would be available in the week of production. However, MRP has no effect on economic lot-size determination of the optimum lot size.

MRP has been heralded as the best inventory control system for the job-lot production that requires various subcomponents. It is an efficient system in that it minimizes the inventory level because inventory is dependent on the production schedule.

The **just-in-time (JIT)** system, a Japanese approach to repetitive manufacturing, attempts to carry the MRP philosophy of correct order timing much further. The JIT system at Toyota, for example, is designed to allow major components to arrive just in time to go into final end products, for subcomponents to arrive just in time to go into major components, for parts to arrive just in time to go into subcomponents, and so forth. The system is supported by **kanban,** a set of delivery and reorder cards attached to subcomponents, parts, and so on that act as a sort of reorder point indicator.

The major difference between MRP and JIT is in the time frame. In MRP, "just in time" usually implies the right week of production or assembly work. In JIT, however, "just in time" means the right day or even hour of production. Although MRP can also utilize a finer time frame, it is often more economical, because of the setup costs involved, to develop lots that are sufficient in size to allow production for a period of several weeks. In JIT, an important key input, the setup cost, is altered in the EOQ model. If the setup cost is reduced, economic lot sizes can be adjusted downward. This process allows the Japanese factory to deliver parts "just in time."

Several organizations, including Hewlett-Packard, Buick, Omark Industries, and Kawasaki Motors Corporation, have reported successful implementation of the JIT system in the United States. It appears that several Japanese manufacturing systems have great potential in terms of their impact in developing more efficient inventory control systems. If you are interested in JIT, you should consult the References at the end of this chapter.

COMPUTER SOLUTIONS OF INVENTORY PROBLEMS

Most real-world inventory problems are complex. Thus, using manual solution approaches to solve real-world problems is unrealistic. The availability of various computer software and consulting services has made inventory management more systematic. A number of computer-based materials management systems are offered by such organizations as IBM, Arthur Andersen and Co., and TRES. These systems keep perpetual inventory records, analyze trends, compute EOQs, print purchase orders, and control warehousing operations and inventories. In this section, we use *Micro Manager* to solve the casette problems discussed in this chapter.

Figure 12.17 presents the input data and program output for Casette 12.1, the Television Technology Inc. problem. The optimum order quantity Q^* is 17, and the optimum total inventory cost is $848.53. These results correspond with our manual solution.

Figure 12.18 shows the computer solution of an economic lot-size problem, the Sunergy Product Inc. problem presented as Casette 12.2. Again, the solution exactly corresponds with our manual solution.

Figure 12.19 presents the solution to an inventory problem with planned shortages. We discussed this problem as Casette 12.4 — the American Rubber Product Inc. problem. The program output indicates that the optimum order quantity is 12.2 units, the shortage quantity is 4 units per order, and the optimum total annual inventory cost is $32.66. These results correspond to our manual solutions.

REAL-WORLD APPLICATIONS

Inventories represent a major business investment. Proper management and control of inventory systems are important not only for individual organizations but also for the national economy. Inventory management does not mean a physical count of every item in stock. Nor does it mean a mathematical analysis of every stock keeping unit (SKU). There is the principle of *critical few* in the inventory situation. That is, a small proportion of SKUs contributes a very large proportion of the total sales. Also, 2 percent of

Figure 12.17   Casette 12.1 Television Technology Inc.

```
PROGRAM: Inventory Models

***** INPUT DATA ENTERED *****

Basic economic order quantity (EOQ) model

Demand (annual)     :   360 units/year
Annual working days :   360 days/year
Ordering cost       : $ 20 /order
Holding cost        : $ 50 /unit/year

*****   PROGRAM OUTPUT   *****

Optimum order quantity (EOQ) :      17.0   units per order
Optimum total inventory cost :   $848.53  per year
Maximum inventory level      :      17.0   units
Average inventory level      :       8.5   units
Demand rate (DR)             :       1.0   units per day
Optimum number of orders     :      21     per year
Inventory cycle              :      17     days per cycle
```

Figure 12.18   Casette 12.2 Sunergy Products Inc.

```
PROGRAM: Inventory Models

***** INPUT DATA ENTERED *****

Economic lot-size (ELS) model

Demand (annual)     :   5000 units/year
Annual working days :   200 days/year
Setup cost          : $ 1000 /production lot
Production rate     :   6000 units/year
Holding cost        : $ 50 /unit/year

*****   PROGRAM OUTPUT   *****

Optimum production lot size        :   1095.4 units per lot
Maximum inventory level            :    182.6 units
Average inventory level            :     91.3 units
Length of inventory depletion phase :     7   days
Demand rate (DR)                   :    25.0 units per day
Number of inventory cycles         :     4.6 per year
Total annual inventory cost        :  $9128.71 per year
```

Figure 12.19   Casette 12.4 American Rubber Products Inc.

```
PROGRAM: Inventory Models

***** INPUT DATA ENTERED *****

Inventory model with planned shortages

Demand (annual)     :   100 units/year
Annual working days :   365 days/year
Ordering cost       : $ 2 /order
Holding cost        : $ 4 /unit/year
Shortage cost       : $ 8 /unit/year


*****   PROGRAM OUTPUT   *****

Optimum order quantity(EOQ):    12.2 units
Maximum inventory level    :     8.2 units
Shortage quantity          :     4   per order
Inventory cycle            :    45   days per cycle
Total annual inventory cost:   $32.66
```

inventory items cause 50 percent of inventory control problems. Thus, management must exercise good judgment in selecting certain critical items for analysis.

There are numerous published studies that deal with inventory models. Many practitioners argue that the EOQ model is abused and overused. They contend that the EOQ model is used even in situations in which the required assumptions are not satisfied. To design a proper inventory management system, the manager must understand the properties as well as the limitations of certain modeling approaches. The EOQ model remains the basic starting point for developing other advanced or modified inventory models.

Classical EOQ Model Applied to Pharmaceuticals

Rhone-Poulenc Pharma, Inc. manufactures drugs in Montreal.[1] The firm produces over 30 drugs, and a variety of forms and processes are involved (tablets, creams, liquids, etc.). In addition, a given drug may be prepared in varying doses. Thus, a total of 86 different products, in a total of 140 package sizes, are produced. The marketing department provides forecasts of monthly demand, prepared every 6 to 12 months (depending on the product class).

Each product type is produced in batches for inventory. Also, each product is made in a single process on efficient, specialized equipment, which involves substantial setup

[1]Roch Ouellet, Jacques Roy, Claude Cardinal, and Yves Rosconi, "EOQ Application in a Pharmaceutical Environment: A Case Study," *Journal of Operations Management* 3:1 (Nov. 1982), 49–55.

costs. For example, for a given capsule, 39 hours of fixed setup time must be added to the partially variable production times of 8.75 hours for 100,000 capsules, 32.25 hours for 500,000 capsules, 56 hours for 1 million units, or 81.5 hours for 2 million units. The materials control department has established reorder points for each product; when the inventory level declines to that point, an order is placed, with the order quantity derived by the EOQ model.

Ordering costs were set at $70 per order, regardless of the type of product, quantity, etc. Sensitivity analysis showed that an order cost of $0 would have a negligible impact on the solution using $70, so ordering cost had little influence on the EOQ model. Inventory holding costs were set at 30 percent of the inventory value, with sensitivity tests performed for higher and lower holding costs. Lead time was established by analyzing production data. Shortage costs were not known, but the marketing department deemed customer service important and factored it into the reorder point calculation.

Implementation of the revised order (and production) quantities led to a reduction of 164 work-hours per week and a cost savings over $85,000. Buffer stock evaluation led to annual savings of $25,000. Incidentally, all computations were so "easy and cheap" that they were performed on a hand-held calculator.

Ordering Aircraft One Piece at a Time

Companies in developing countries face all the typical inventory control problems, with additional worries thrown in: acute shortages of materials, frequent delays in supply of available items, and sometimes uncertain supplies of those. Many items must be imported. Thus, to ensure the continued viability of a company, management frequently stocks up on whatever it can obtain, often resulting in excesses of some items and shortages of others.

The Aircraft Division of Hindustan Aeronautics Limited, of India, makes and overhauls aircraft, primarily for the Indian Air Force.[2] Its inventory situation reflected management's philosophy that inventory control meant maintaining less than 1 year's supply of foreign items and 6 months' supply of domestic purchase. No systematic inventory analysis had been carried out, and data on individual items was not readily available. Most items needed by the firm were made to order and required long lead times; stock-outs occurred due to vendor delays. For example, lead time for proprietary items was 24 to 30 months; for raw materials, 36 months; and for standard parts, 18 months. Typically, issuing a purchase order took more than 90 days.

At the time of the study, the Aircraft Division had three projects underway. For one of these, inventoriable items totaled 1,950 different parts or materials, worth about $200,000 per aircraft. To reduce the size of the system, all items were grouped into categories based on their value and importance. Value, in monetary terms, was assigned a letter from *A* to *C* (decreasing value); importance was subjectively judged as "vital" (*V*), "essential" (*E*), or "desirable" (*D*), resulting in an *ABC-VED* matrix. Confidence levels of 99 percent, 95 percent, and 90 percent were established for the three importance categories, giving a safety stock level for each value-importance class, stated in terms of needed months of supply on hand. This varied from 2.6 months for *C-D* (least expensive, least important) to 5.2 for *A-V* (most expensive, most important) items.

[2]B. P. Lingaraj and R. Balasubramanian, "An Inventory Management and Materials Information System for Aircraft Production," *Interfaces* 13:5 (1983), 65–70.

Average ordering costs were set at $36 and $53 for domestic and foreign suppliers; carrying costs were fixed at 21 percent of value. An EOQ model then provided an ordering table, showing when orders should be placed based on the value of the item in terms of annual usage. A vendor-rating system was added to further refine the model, based on quality, price, delivery, and lead time; this portion of the model was intended to lower required safety stock, particularly on vital proprietary items, which constituted 67 percent of the total inventory value.

Implementation of the EOQ and materials information systems allowed for tighter control, better planning, vendor evaluation, and better use of foreign exchange. With emphasis on user involvement, Hindustan Aeronautics successfully phased in the plan without major problems. After 1 year, delivery time had been reduced by 3 months and inventory decreased by 10 percent, for an estimated annual savings of $400,000, and the firm anticipated further savings and inventory reductions. Stock-outs were greatly reduced, and materials availability (service level) increased by 25 percent.

Simulation Allows Weyerhaeuser to Reduce Wood Chip Inventories

Pulp mills carry large inventories of wood chips for two primary reasons: as a buffer against unstable supply and as a hedge against fluctuating wood prices. However, stored chips deteriorate with time and incur carrying costs. For a modern pulp mill, an inventory of 100,000 dry tons of chips at $50 per ton would represent a $5 million investment. Both supply and demand are uncertain, since weather, markets, competitors, labor, and transportation all influence inventory needs and levels. Stock-out costs are believed to be very high, even "traumatic," and thus management makes highly subjective decisions in the attempt to prevent their mill from ever running out of chips.

To assist mill procurement managers, Weyerhaeuser installed *Sprint* (Springfield Inventory Target) at six of its pulp mills.[3] *Sprint* projects chip inflows, outflows, and inventory levels for any period the user desires. Each source and use are represented by a probability distribution, based on upper, lower, and most likely estimates. Monte Carlo simulation provides results obtained by random selection from the given distributions, and the final supply, demand, and ending inventory levels are probability distributions rather than simple estimates. Bayesian statistics are then employed to translate the stock-out risk into dollar terms. Finally, inventory carrying costs are calculated.

Weyerhaeuser reports that installing the model has enabled managers to make standardized decisions not based on fear of running out of chips and has increased cooperation between mill managers and procurement managers. At the six pulp mills where *Sprint* has been used for 3 years, chip inventories were nearly cut in half, saving over $2 million annually.

SUMMARY

Inventories represent a considerable investment for many organizations. This is especially true for manufacturing, wholesaling, and retailing companies, and for public utilities, hospitals, and government agencies such as the Department of Defense. Thus, it is extremely important to minimize total inventory costs as much as possible while

[3]Gary Finke, "Determining Target Inventories of Wood Chips Using Risk Analysis," *Interfaces* 14:5 (1984), 53–58.

achieving the organization's production and/or service objectives. In this chapter, we have studied the basic EOQ model, a number of variations of the EOQ model, and inventory problems under uncertainty.

In the deterministic EOQ-type models, the optimum order quantity is determined by balancing the total holding cost and the total ordering cost. In probabilistic inventory models, the optimum order quantity and optimum reorder point must be determined in order to minimize the total inventory cost, which includes shortage costs in addition to the holding and ordering costs.

The inventory situation is usually unique for any given organization. Thus, it is difficult to develop a general inventory model that can be applied widely. In this chapter, we have studied many special models for various inventory situations. These models can be adapted to different situations. We can also use simulation to analyze inventory systems under stochastic conditions of demand and lead time. Regardless of which approach or model we develop, the basic purpose of the inventory model remains the same: to determine when and how much to order at one time so that the organization's production and/or service objectives can be achieved while minimizing the total inventory cost.

Glossary

Demand during Lead Time (DDLT)   When demand or lead time fluctuates, relative frequencies of various demands during lead time may be ascertained from a study of past records. This demand may eat into a safety stock.

Economic Lot Size   When setup costs are involved in a production and inventory situation, the production of batches in the economic lot size (quantity) will minimize total costs.

Economic Order Quantity (EOQ)   The classic basic inventory management model that relates the various costs to demand to determine what optimum order quantity will minimize total inventory costs.

Holding Cost   Costs related to carrying inventory, such as interest, insurance, warehouse rent, and recordkeeping.

Inventory Cycle   Time needed to completely use or sell one order quantity; the time between orders.

Just-in-Time System (JIT)   A production management system designed to ensure timely delivery of components for assembly and quality control while minimizing inventories at the assembly site.

Kanban   A set of cards attached to component inventories that signal reorder time and quantity when the given group of components is delivered. Typically used in a JIT system.

Lead Time   Time elapsed between the placing of an order and receipt of the items to be added to inventory.

Material Requirements Planning (MRP)   Based on a master production schedule, bill of materials (list of components), and an inventory file, an MRP system determines which components will be needed for production at what time and in what quantity.

Ordering Cost   Costs associated with replenishing inventory, including supplier decision costs, purchasing expenses, transport fees, inspection costs, etc.

Order Quantity   Amount requested from suppliers in one order.

Reorder Point   Specified inventory level which signals that an order should be placed to replenish stock.

Safety Stock   The extra quantity of inventory beyond the average expected demand that may be kept to lessen the likelihood of shortages or stock-outs when demand and lead time are uncertain.

Setup Cost   Expenses incurred in preparing facilities, machinery, and so on to produce a given item in an upcoming production run.

Shortage Cost   Costs incurred when demand exceeds available inventory, including rush-ordering costs, lost profit, lost customers, and lost goodwill; also called *stock-out cost*.

References

Buffa, E. S., and Taubert, W. J. *Production-Inventory Systems: Planning and Control* Rev. ed. Homewood, Ill.: Irwin, 1972.

Hillier, F. S., and Lieberman, G. J. *Introduction to Operation Research*. 4th ed. San Francisco: Holden-Day, 1986.

Lee, S. M., Moore, L. J., and Taylor, B. W. *Management Science*. 2d ed. Dubuque, Iowa: W. C. Brown, 1985.

McMillan, C., and Gonzales, R. *Systems Analysis*. 3d ed. Homewood, Ill.: Irwin, 1973.

Schonberger, R. J. *Japanese Manufacturing Techniques*. New York: Free Press, 1982.

Schonberger, R. J. *Operations Management*. 2d ed. Dallas: Business Publications, 1985.

Schonberger, R. J. *World Class Manufacturing*. New York: Free Press, 1986.

Starr, M. K., and Miller, D. W. *Inventory Control: Theory and Practice*. Englewood Cliffs, N.J.: Prentice-Hall, 1962.

Sugimori, Y., et al. "Toyota Production System and Kanban System: Materialization of Just-in-Time and Respect-for-Humans System." *International Journal of Production Research* 15:6 (1977), 553–564.

Turban, E., and Meredith, J. R. *Fundamentals of Management Science*. 2d ed. Dallas: Business Publications, 1981.

Assignments

12.1 Why is inventory management important for the national economy, a firm, and the customer?

12.2 What are some examples of inventories that are familiar to you?

12.3 What are some of the reasons that we keep inventories?

12.4 What are the two basic inventory decisions? Why are they important?

12.5 Holding costs represent an important component of the total annual inventory cost. Discuss some examples of costs that may be included in holding costs.

12.6 What are the three major components of the total annual inventory cost? Explain each component briefly.

12.7 The EOQ model is said to be so basic and elementary that it does not really represent complex real-world situations. Why, then, should we study the EOQ model?

12.8 Discuss several assumptions that are required in the EOQ model.

12.9 In the EOQ formulation, the optimum order quantity is found when $THC = TOC$. Why is this true?

12.10 In the economic lot-size model (*ELS*), which cost replaces the total ordering cost component?

12.11 In the inventory model under uncertainty, what conditions are assumed to be uncertain?

12.12 In an inventory model under uncertainty, which costs are affected by Q and R?

12.13 What are the major differences between MRP and JIT?

12.14 Why is it sometimes necessary to employ simulation to analyze inventory systems?

12.15 Do you think it is possible for U.S. corporations to adapt Japanese manufacturing systems? Why or why not?

12.16 You are given the following parameters:

$$D = 100 \text{ units per year}$$
$$HC = \$18 \text{ per unit per year}$$
$$OC = \$20 \text{ per order}$$

  a. Plot the *THC* on a graph for $Q = 5$, $Q = 10$, and $Q = 20$.
  b. Plot the *TOC* on the graph for $Q = 5$, $Q = 10$, and $Q = 20$.
  c. Plot the *TIC* for $Q = 5$, $Q = 10$, and $Q = 20$.
  d. Determine the optimum order quantity.
  e. What is the optimum number of orders per year?

12.17 The First Gateway Bank just introduced the "Money Now" checking system. The bank requires a minimum balance of $500 in order for the customer to be able to write as many checks as desired without paying any service charge. As a promotional scheme, Gateway will give away to new checking account customers the popular brass belt buckles that have been used as free gifts to savings accounts depositors.

The additional brass buckles required have created a new inventory problem. Mary Kaye Snyder, assistant manager of customer services, has revised the inventory data as follows:

$$D = 800 \text{ buckles per year}$$
$$HC = \$3 \text{ per buckle}$$
$$OC = \$20 \text{ per order}$$

  a. How many buckles should Mary Kaye order at a time?
  b. Determine the total annual inventory cost with the optimum order quantity.

12.18 Christenson's Television Service is a local dealer of SONY television sets. Mike Olson, the manager of the store, has been trying hard to find ways to lower the inventory level because of the increasing holding cost and the limited storage space. Mike has estimated the store sells about 800 SONY sets annually. The estimated holding cost is $30 per set and the ordering cost is $20 per order.

a. Determine the optimum order quantity.
b. Determine the number of orders.
c. Describe the inventory pattern graphically.
d. What is the total inventory cost per year?

12.19 Weber Babyfood Company can produce sugarless applesauce for infants. The company's production capacity is 200,000 jars of applesauce every year. The demand for the applesauce is estimated to be 180,000 jars per year. To produce applesauce, a setup cost of $1,000 is required for the production line. The annual inventory holding cost is estimated to be $0.25 per jar of applesauce per year.

a. Determine the economic lot size.
b. Determine the optimum number of production runs.
c. Determine the length of time between the start of each production run, assuming 300 working days in a year.

12.20 Ace Chemicals, Inc. has just introduced a new detergent, Snow-White. Ace's monthly production capacity is 20,000 boxes of Snow-White. The annual demand for the detergent has been predicted to be 200,000 boxes at a constant rate. The setup cost for the production of Snow-White is $500 per production run, and the *monthly* holding cost is estimated to be $0.25 per box.

a. Determine the optimum lot size.
b. Determine the optimum number of production runs.
c. Determine the length of time between the start of each production run, assuming 20 working days per month.

12.21 Ryan's Liquor Shoppe orders Scotch whiskey 4 times a year. The lead time for reordering is estimated to be 25 days. The average demand for Scotch whiskey is 2 cases per day (300 business days). Ryan's has estimated the stock-out cost to be $50 per case and the inventory holding cost to be approximately $30 per case per year. Based on the past reorder periods, the actual demand distribution is shown below:

Demand during Lead Time (*DDLT*)	Frequency
40 cases	32 times
45	64
50	128
55	64
60	32

Ryan's is considering carrying 0, 5, or 10 boxes of safety stock.

a. Determine the total annual shortage cost (*TSC*) and the safety stock holding cost (*SHC*).
b. Determine the optimum level of safety stock.

12.22 Mr. Dan Brown, owner of the New England Seafood Store, has the only seafood store in town that carries Maine lobsters. The demand for lobsters has been sufficiently high to warrant the continued air transportation of lobsters from Boston. However, Mr. Brown cannot order too many lobsters because of the ever-increasing holding costs and the limited salt water tank space.

Mr. Brown asked his son-in-law, Jimmy Stuart, a recent graduate of a business college, to give him some help in determining the best inventory policy for lobsters. After looking over the company's past records, Jimmy came up with the following data:

$$D = 4,000 \text{ lobsters per year}$$
$$HC = \$0.50 \text{ per lobster per year}$$
$$OC = \$40 \text{ per order (including air freight)}$$
$$LT = 3 \text{ days}$$
$$\text{Store business days} = 300 \text{ per year}$$

a. Determine the optimum order quantity (Q^*) for lobsters.
b. Determine the demand rate (DR) per day.
c. Determine the optimum order point (R^*).
d. Compute the total inventory cost with the optimum Q^* and R^*.

12.23 The purchasing manager of St. Mary's Municipal Hospital was contacted by a new vendor who offered a quantity discount for disposable syringes. The ordering cost for the item is $80 per order and the holding cost is 25 percent of the average inventory value on an annual basis. The annual demand for the syringes is 40,000 boxes at a constant rate. The hospital currently pays $80 per box for the syringes. However, the new vendor offered a $4-per-box discount if the hospital would order a minimum of 2,000 boxes at a time.

Should the hospital take advantage of this offer? Show a comparative analysis of all of the costs involved for the two alternatives.

12.24 Goldstar Electronics Company manufactures a transistor circuit that is used to produce solid-state television sets. Goldstar has agreed to supply the circuit to Panavision TV, Inc. for the next 3 years. Panavision has ordered 4,000 circuits per year during the contract period. Goldstar's annual production capacity is 8,000 circuits. The holding cost is $10 per unit per year, and the setup cost per production run is estimated to be $2,000. Given this information, determine:

a. The optimum production lot size
b. The length of the production phase
c. The average inventory level
d. The optimum total annual inventory cost

Illustrate the inventory level graphically.

12.25 Rocky Snowmobile Rental Company operates a snowmobile rental business near Vail, Colorado. The company uses an average of 2,000 gallons of gasoline each month. The ordering cost of gasoline is $50, and the holding cost is 10 percent of the unit cost. The cost of the gasoline is currently $1.40 per gallon if the company orders less than 2,000 gallons. However, the cost would be $1.30 per gallon if it orders more than 2,000 gallons.

a. How much gasoline should the company order at a time? Show a comparative analysis of the two alternatives.

b. Suppose the cost of gasoline would be $1.20 per gallon if the company orders more than 5,000 gallons. Then, how much gasoline should the company order at a time?

12.26 Mr. Howard Davis, the owner of a hardware store, is faced with an inventory problem for a particular item. Because of a high inventory holding cost, Mr. Davis is considering allowing shortages but he does not want to create any damaging goodwill problems with his customers. His estimated annual demand for the item is 4,000 units. The ordering cost is estimated to be $100 per order, and the holding cost is $5 per unit per year. The shortage cost per unit is approximately $10.

  a. Determine the optimum order quantity.
  b. Determine the maximum inventory level.
  c. Illustrate the inventory level for the first three inventory cycles.
  d. Compute the optimum total inventory cost.

12.27 Western Regional Center is a state-supported mental health institution. It has 300 patients in the minimum security ward. The patients have been engaged in various arts and crafts that are money-making activities. The center's most popular products have been hand-painted egg decorations for such special occasions as Christmas, Easter, and Mother's Day.

  Arts and crafts activities are not only money-making activities for patients and the institution, but they also have tremendous therapeutic value. Thus, the patient's activities are relatively stable over time, although the actual demand for decorated eggs is definitely seasonal. Dixie Johnson, the coordinator of arts and crafts, has been purchasing goose and duck eggs from several sources. In order to systematize the purchasing procedure, Dixie has been analyzing the egg decoration activities. She came up with the following information:

$$HC = \$2 \text{ per egg per year}$$
$$SC = \$20 \text{ per egg per year}$$
$$D = 7{,}200 \text{ eggs per year}$$
$$N \text{ (number of orders)} = 12 \text{ per year}$$

Demand during Lead Time (*DDLT*)	Probability (*DDLT*)
100	0.10
110	0.20
120	0.20
130	0.30
140	0.10
150	0.05
160	0.05

  a. Determine the total annual shortage cost (*TSC*).
  b. Compute the optimum level of safety stock.

12.28 Sprint Print Company has been an exclusive printer of all state court proceedings and legislative sessions. The company has been purchasing its paper from Continental Paper and Pulp, Inc. Inventory information currently available at Sprint Print is as follows:

$$Demand = 120,000 \text{ pounds of paper type A1}$$
$$HC = \$10 \text{ per pound per year}$$
$$OC = \$30 \text{ per order}$$
$$SC = \$5 \text{ per pound}$$

LT	P(LT)	DR	P(DR)
5	0.30	400	0.50
6	0.40	410	0.50
7	0.30	—	—
	1.00		1.00

a. Compute the expected lead time and expected demand rate.
b. Compute the expected demand during a lead time.
c. What is the expected shortage if R is set at 800 pounds?
d. If we assume that the optimum R is 1,200 pounds, what would be the optimum order quantity?

12.29 The Boshgarian Oriental Rug Company sells fine imported rugs. The company has a long-term contract with a large department store. The contract calls for a total of 5,000 oriental rugs in the 6-feet × 9-feet size. The company has been negotiating with an Indian rug dealer, and the dealer has offered the following quantity discount schedule:

Quantity	Price per Rug
0–999	$500
1,000–2,999	450
3,000–4,999	400
5,000 or more	350

The company estimates the following:

$$HC = 20 \text{ percent of price of rug per year}$$
$$OC = \$150 \text{ per order}$$

a. Determine the EOQ for each price level and ascertain its feasibility.
b. Compare the total inventory costs at various quantity levels and recommend the best inventory policy for the company.

12.30 You are given the following information:

$$HC = 10 \text{ percent of cost per unit per year}$$
$$\text{Purchase cost} = \$200 \text{ per unit}$$
$$OC = \$40 \text{ per order}$$
$$D = 500 \text{ units per year}$$
$$SC = 20 \text{ percent of cost per unit per year}$$

LT	P(LT)	DR	P(DR)
1	0.25	1	0.25
2	0.50	2	0.50
3	0.25	3	0.25
	1.00		1.00

DDLT	P(DDLT)	P(DDLT > Z)
0	0.0000	1.0000
1	0.0613	0.9387
2	0.1520	0.7867
3	0.2011	0.5856
4	0.2188	0.3668
5	0.1718	0.1950
6	0.1101	0.0849
7	0.0578	0.0271
8	0.0232	0.0039
9	0.0039	0.0000

a. Assuming that there is complete certainty concerning the lead time and the demand rate, compute the EOQ.

b. Under the condition of certainty, if the ordering cost is not known (while other cost information is known) but the EOQ is known to be 35, what will be the ordering cost?

c. Under the condition of uncertainty, if the optimum R is assumed to be 5, what should be the optimum Q?

13 WAITING LINE (QUEUING) MODELS

Waiting lines are a fact of life. From traffic lights to hamburger stands, our society forces us to wait. Although a catsup commercial glamorizes waiting with the catchword "anticipation," we usually consider any waiting experience very unpleasant. As a matter of fact, whenever we face a waiting situation, we attempt to avoid it or to shorten the waiting time.

Waiting lines occur when the time of arrival of someone needing a service and/or the time required to provide that service vary from a fixed schedule. Waiting lines not only affect our personal lives, but they can critically influence business operations. Operating systems from computer networks to production operations, from shipping docks to airports, can become inefficient because of waiting lines.

Since there is virtually an unlimited number of variations of waiting line systems, it is impossible to discuss all of them in this chapter. As a matter of fact, there are perhaps more unique and exotic models in waiting line theory than in any other management science approaches. In this chapter we will examine the foundation of queuing models in general. Three of the most common models will be discussed in detail; five others are covered in Appendix 6.

Learning Objectives *From the study of this chapter, we will learn the following:*

1. *The basic components of a waiting line system*
2. *The basic structure of a waiting line system*
3. *Waiting line decision problems*
4. *Arrival and service time distributions*
5. *Queue discipline*
6. *Kendall's notation*
7. *Different types of queuing models*
8. *The relationship between queuing problems and simulation*
9. *The implication of applying queuing models to real-world problems*
10. *Computer applications for waiting line models*
11. *The meaning of the following terms:*

Waiting line system	*Phases*
Calling population	*Poisson arrival distribution*
Service facility	*Negative exponential distribution*
Queue length	*First-come, first-served queue discipline*
Channels	*Balking*

12. *The primary parameters of a queuing system:*

$$L = \textit{Mean length of the system, including waiting and service,}$$
$$\textit{in terms of numbers of arrivals}$$

$$L_q = \textit{Mean length of the waiting line only, in number of arrivals}$$

$$W = \textit{Mean time spent by an arrival in the system, including}$$
$$\textit{waiting and service}$$

$$W_q = \textit{Mean time spent waiting by an arrival}$$

$$P_0 = \textit{Probability of no unit in the system}$$

$$P_n = \textit{Probability of n units in the system}$$

$$\rho = \textit{Utilization rate of service facility}$$

$$\lambda = \textit{Arrival rate in number of arrivals per unit of time}$$

$$\mu = \textit{Mean service rate in number of departures per unit of time}$$

THE WAITING LINE PROCESS

Having to wait is a real pain. As a student you should be an expert in waiting. Wherever you go, there seems to be a line waiting for you. You face a string of waiting lines when you seek to register for required courses, obtain a parking permit, make necessary class changes, purchase football tickets, buy books, get a haircut, and get an interview with a company recruiter. Almost everyone has experienced some waiting time at a bank, a grocery store, a highway tollbooth, a hamburger shop, or a busy discount store. At a grocery store we carefully check which line is the shortest and has customers with only a few items in their carts. But we often discover that the cashier at the short line happens to be a slow trainee and that the customer in front of us has several items without price tags. Someone has even developed a law of waiting lines to describe such a situation — "The other line moves faster."

Waiting lines are often referred to as *queues*. Queues can consist of automobiles, assembly parts, people, animals, or other objects waiting for service. People's attitudes toward waiting are quite diverse. The British are well-known for their patience and jolliness in "queuing up" at a waiting line. However, we have seen pictures of grim-faced Poles and Russians waiting in long lines leading to state-run food distribution centers.

Waiting lines are important for any organized society. Thus, the study of waiting lines, which is often referred to as *queuing theory*, is one of the oldest and most fruitful topics of management science. The pioneering work of queuing theory was done by the Danish mathematician A. K. Erlang. His study, published in 1913, involved an analysis of telephone service delays due to varying demands. Since then, queuing theory has been applied to many real-world problems.

Waiting lines may be clearly observable in many situations such as lines at theaters, grocery stores, or hotel telephone switchboards. However, the more subtle or abstract forms of waiting lines may have profound managerial implications. For example, a breakdown of equipment results in a queue for repair. Customers at a gift-wrapping service counter take a number and browse around the store while waiting. Customers at a restaurant are often seated in the bar while they wait for a table. Table 13.1 presents a variety of familiar waiting line situations we see in our daily lives.

Table 13.1   *Examples of Waiting Line Systems*

Situation	Arrivals	Queue	Service Facility
Airport	Airplanes	Stacked planes or planes on holding patterns	Runway
Air terminal	Passengers	Gate waiting room	Airplane
Assembly line	Components	Assembly line	Workers or machines
Bakery	Customers	Customers with numbers	Sales counter
Bank	Customers	Customers in line	Teller
Car wash	Automobiles	Dirty cars in line	Washing facility
Computer center	Programs or jobs	Stacked programs	Computer
Course registration	Students	Students in line	Registration desk
Doctor's office	Patients	Waiting room	Medical staff
Fire station	Fire alarms or calls	Fires	Firemen and trucks
Grocery store	Customers	Customers in line	Checkout counter
Machine repair shop	Machine breakdowns	Repair requests	Repair shop
Police department	Service calls	Crimes in progress or service needs	Policemen
Shipping dock	Ships	Waiting ships	Loading and unloading facility
Stadium	Ticket holders	Waiting line	Entrance
Street intersection	Automobiles	Cars in line	Traffic light
Telephone company	Calls	Callers on line	Operator
Tollbooth	Automobiles	Cars in line	Toll payment

Although no one likes waiting in a line, it may be extremely costly to completely eliminate waiting by increasing the service capacity. For example, a branch bank that serves about 150 people per day could completely eliminate waiting if it had 20 tellers at work at all times. Common sense tells us that we need a balance between the costs involved in waiting and the desired service level.

The manager's decision problem is to decide on the most appropriate service capacity or service rate. There will be absolutely no queuing problem if customers arrive according to a set schedule for fixed service times. The only thing the manager has to decide in such a case is the service capacity that will exactly correspond with customer arrivals. Many production assemblies are set up according to such an exact scheduling scheme.

In most real-world situations, however, customer arrivals and the service times are unpredictable. The manager at the student union can tell us when the cafeteria is busiest during the day but probably would not even be able to guess when each customer will arrive. Also, the time required to serve each customer (some people cannot quickly make up their minds about what to eat) will vary considerably. In other words, most waiting line situations may involve many unpredictable elements.

A manager with extensive experience and good judgment may intuitively come up with a pretty good balance between waiting and service cost. For example, a small family-owned grocery store owner may stop stocking shelves and run the second cash register when the customer line becomes too long. A toy store manager hires part-time help during the holiday season on the basis of the previous year's experience. In many complex waiting line situations, however, intuition is not sufficient to determine the proper balance between waiting and service capacity. Or the problem may involve such substantial cost or risk, as in capital investment problems or airport control tower operations, that queuing analysis may be very beneficial.

As we mentioned earlier, there are almost an infinite number of variations of queuing models describing particular characteristics of waiting line systems. Queuing theory encompasses all such mathematical models. The general purpose of these models is to determine the characteristics of the steady state of the system, such as the average length of the waiting line, the average waiting time, and the average service time. The steady-state behavior can provide us with a sound basis for determining optimum service capacity.

Components of a Waiting Line System

A **waiting line system** is described by the following components: *arrivals, waiting lines* or *queues, queue discipline, service facility,* and *departures,* as shown in Figure 13.1. Let us examine these components in greater detail.

Arrivals   The arrival of an entity (customer, automobile, airplane, etc.) in need of some service is the first component. Arrivals can occur in a number of different ways. Arrivals can be constant, as in an assembly line. Often, however, arrivals occur in random fashion. We may be able to describe the rate of arrivals according to some probability distribution. Then, we could infer some rational cost analysis despite the fact that arrivals do not conform to fixed schedules. The source of arrivals is often referred to as the **calling population.** We need to develop a clear description of the calling population in order to understand and analyze a waiting line problem.

Waiting Lines   When arrivals occur in such a way that they have to wait for service, waiting lines, or queues, develop. Waiting lines may be desirable if we want efficient utilization of service facilities. A waiting line ensures that the service facility will be kept busy. But if you happen to be in a waiting line, you may take a dim view of a long waiting period and may well decide to take your business to another place where the waiting time is shorter. The fast-food industry (McDonald's, Burger King, Wendy's, etc.) has prospered by catering to the desire of customers to cut down on waiting time.

Queue Discipline   From the waiting line, arrivals move to the service facility according to a decision rule that prescribes how they are to be served. This rule is referred to as "queue discipline." It is most frequently assumed that customers are served on a **first-come, first-served queue discipline.** Other decision rules are possible, of course. Last-come, first-served; random service; or some sort of priority decision rule is often found in real-world applications. In this chapter, we will consider only the first-come, first-served discipline.

Figure 13.1   A General Waiting Line System

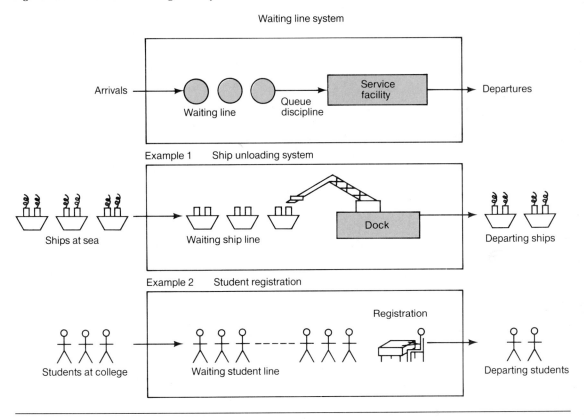

Service Facility   The **service facility** or server is the next component of the waiting line system. There are many possible configurations of service facility, such as a single server (e.g., a ticket counter), multiple servers (e.g., several bank tellers), or sequential servers (e.g., a package deal of gasoline pumping, car wash, and vacuum job). In addition, the rate of service at the facility may be constant, as in a washing machine's cycle or a blast furnace process. But service rates can vary just as arrival rates can. A visit to a dentist may be less than 10 minutes for a quick checkup, or it may drag on for hours. A letter written by a manager may take only a few minutes, or may take weeks, months, or forever. The rate of service, just as the rate of arrivals, can be described according to a number of distributions.

Departures   Once arrivals are served, they become departures. Departing customers are not usually allowed to reenter the system immediately. Of course, this happens in real-world situations—forgetting something at the grocery store and going back to the checkout counter is one example. However, frequent reentries by departing entities may affect the arrival rates. Thus, it is generally assumed that departing customers do not reenter the system immediately.

Figure 13.2   Four Basic Waiting Line Structures

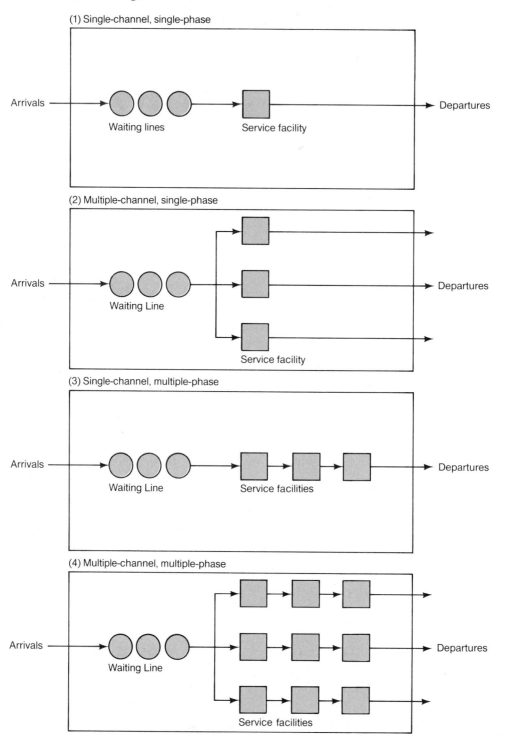

(1) Single-channel, single-phase

Arrivals ⟶ Waiting lines ⟶ Service facility ⟶ Departures

(2) Multiple-channel, single-phase

Arrivals ⟶ Waiting Line ⟶ Service facility ⟶ Departures

(3) Single-channel, multiple-phase

Arrivals ⟶ Waiting Line ⟶ Service facilities ⟶ Departures

(4) Multiple-channel, multiple-phase

Arrivals ⟶ Waiting Line ⟶ Service facilities ⟶ Departures

There are a number of specific factors in the above described components that have an impact on the analysis of the general waiting line system. The population of arrivals may consist of any positive finite number or an infinite calling population. The queue may be limited to some maximum number. There may be multiple servers. The order of service may be first-come, first-served; last-come, first-served; or some other priority system. Service itself may consist of more than one station, such as the system found in driver's license facilities. Waiting may be required to register for the license, to take a written test, to take an eye test, to take a road test, to have a photograph taken, and finally, to pay for the license.

Basic Structures of Waiting Line Systems

Waiting line systems can be classified into four basic structures, based on the nature of the service facilities involved. The four classifications are illustrated in Figure 13.2. If a service facility involves parallel service stations, they are known as **channels.** However, if numbers of sequential steps are involved in the service, they are referred to as **phases.**

The simplest waiting line structure is a single-channel, single-phase system, such as a single barber in a barbershop. Many hairstyling shops have more than one hairstylist, an example of a multiple-channel, single-phase system. If a customer wants a hairstyling and a manicure, it may require waiting for the stylist and then waiting for the manicurist, an example of a two-phase system. The same type of waiting systems is seen at places like Disney World and Universal Studios, where visitors queue to buy tickets and then wait for a tram or monorail ride.

This classification is by no means exhaustive. Multiple queues often have different characteristics at service counters, such as in department stores. In some multiple-channel waiting lines, switching between servers may be possible. Although reality is often very complex, the fundamentals of queuing theory for the basic structures we have discussed can be effectively used for the analysis of waiting line problems.

| *Casette 13.1* | *STUDENT UNION HAIRSTYLING SALON* |

Norman Dwork has been operating the Hairstyling Salon at the university student union for the past 30 years. He often talks to his customers about the good old days when the crew cut was the "in" thing. He had four barbers working for him then, and all five chairs were busy most of the time. He still has three barber chairs in his shop. But he is now the only stylist working in the shop.

The salon's service hours are 8:00 a.m. to 1:30 p.m. and 2:30 p.m. to 5:00 p.m. Monday through Friday. Although there is a definite pattern of volume during the day, customers come to the salon at random intervals during any given hour. The time required to provide a good style cut for a customer is also a random variable. Since Norman does not have an appointment system, his customers are served strictly on a first-come, first-served basis.

The busiest time during a given day is from 11:30 a.m. to 1:00 p.m., the lunch period for most of the faculty, staff, and students. Norman asked his wife, the cashier and occasional shampooer, to keep a log to check the waiting pattern of his customers

Table 13.2   *Student Union Hairstyling Salon Customer Service Data*

Customer Arrival Time	Time Styling Begins	Styling Time Required (min.)	Time Service Ends	Customer Waiting Time	Number of Customers Waiting	Norman's Idle Time (min.)
11:32 a.m.	11:32 a.m.	8	11:40 a.m.	0	0	2
11:35 a.m.	11:40 a.m.	7	11:47 a.m.	5	1	0
11:38 a.m.	11:47 a.m.	5	11:52 a.m.	9	2	0
11:45 a.m.	11:52 a.m.	12	12:04 p.m.	7	1	0
11:46 a.m.	12:04 p.m.	9	12:13 p.m.	18	2	0
12:00 p.m.	12:13 p.m.	6	12:19 p.m.	13	2	0
12:02 p.m.	12:19 p.m.	5	12:24 p.m.	17	1	0
12:07 p.m.	12:24 p.m.	9	12:33 p.m.	17	0	0
12:25 p.m.	12:33 p.m.	8	12:41 p.m.	8	0	4
12:45 p.m.	12:45 p.m.	9	12:54 p.m.	0	0	0
12:48 p.m.	12:54 p.m.	7	1:01 p.m.	6	0	0

during the busiest period. Table 13.2 presents a summary of the customer service data during the 11:30 a.m. to 1:00 p.m. period on Monday.

The table is a good summary of customer flows, customer waiting times, lengths of waiting times, styling time variances, and Norman's working time. The table clearly indicates that Norman's hairstyling work begins when a customer arrives at the salon and Norman is not already engaged in the styling work for a previously arrived customer. A waiting line is created on the basis of two elements: the customer arrival time and the styling time required for customers.

The table also provides important information about the salon operation. Since the salon has eight chairs available for customer waiting, the number of customers indicated in the table provides no special problems to Norman. However, the length of customer waiting time worries Norman. Will a customer wait 18 minutes for a haircut? Customers may perceive the waiting time as too long and not come back in the future. Such customer perceptions may cause a permanent business loss.

Norman is also concerned about a large number of customers waiting more than 7 or 8 minutes. Should he consider hiring a part-time stylist during the busy hours? Or should he subscribe to additional popular reading materials such as *National Geographic, Reader's Digest, Sports Illustrated, Time,* and *Ladies' Home Journal?* Determining accurate answers to these questions simply cannot be based on intuitive judgment. Waiting line models are helpful in answering such questions.

WAITING LINE DECISION PROBLEMS

As we indicated previously, there have been numerous queuing models developed to describe the operating characteristics of various waiting line systems. Operating characteristics are described in terms of how well a system functions in the *steady state.* The *transient states,* the starting up and shutting down of the system, are not usually analyzed. The steady state system characteristics, such as expected length of a waiting line, customer waiting time, and percentage of time that servers are idle, are described by the expected value concept. These operating characteristics are only the necessary inputs to a broader framework of analysis required for waiting line decision making.

Waiting line problem analysis must answer various service-related questions. Eventually, however, it should answer the basic question, "How can we minimize the total expected cost involved in the system's operation?" within certain managerial policies concerning service. To answer this primary question, we must determine the optimum level of service. For example, let us consider the problem of a hamburger shop owner. He or she certainly would like to see the employees working steadily throughout their working hours, generating revenue. This would require a constant waiting line in front of each and every cash register. The customers, however, may base their decision of where to take their business on the minimum waiting time required. The owner can minimize the customer waiting time by hiring more servers. Since customers do not arrive according to a desired schedule, the owner will face conflicting trade-offs between the number of servers hired, which results in increased payroll cost, and the quality or level of service provided, which results in increased waiting costs.

Most business problems that can benefit from waiting line models involve cost analysis. Businesses typically provide service facilities, and customers are usually found in waiting lines. Employees can also be found in waiting lines, eating up payroll time while waiting to use a copy machine, a telephone line, or a tool crib. Service facilities, such as drive-in teller stations, often require substantial investment. The level of service must eventually be related to the other parameters and variables of the waiting line system.

Total expected system cost is the sum of two separate cost components: *service costs* and *waiting costs*. Our objective is to minimize the total expected cost of the waiting line system. Figure 13.3 presents the relationship of our decision variable, level of service, to expected service cost, waiting cost, and total cost.

As the level of service increases (e.g., as the number of checkout counters increases in a grocery store), the cost of serving increases. However, as the level of service increases, the customer waiting time will decrease, and consequently the expected waiting cost (e.g., lost customers due to long waiting lines) will decrease. We cannot eliminate customer waiting completely. But we can minimize the expected total system cost by analyzing the relationship between the service and waiting costs. As shown in Figure 13.3, if the service cost increases monotonically and the waiting cost decreases steadily, the total system cost is minimized when the increase of service cost equals the decrease of waiting cost.

Service Costs

The service costs include payroll, equipment, facilities, and other related costs in providing the service. As the level of service increases, the service costs will naturally increase. In our hamburger shop example, if the owner hires a second checkout worker, service costs increase by the wage of the second worker, the cost of the second cash register, and the uniform and other related costs for the second worker. The exact cost of employing the second server may be straightforward. However, it may also require a careful analysis of the complexities that are unique in the given situation.

Figure 13.3   *Relationship of Level of Service to Typical Waiting and Service Costs*

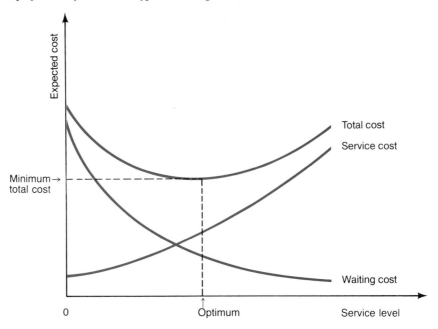

We can also analyze service costs by evaluating the costs associated with server or service facility idle time. When we increase the level of service, the idle time for servers will obviously increase. For example, when the hamburger shop installs a second check-out counter, the server idle time will naturally increase from the level experienced with only one checkout. Whether we analyze service costs through calculating the additional cost of servers or measuring the idle service time cost, we would usually derive the same result.

Waiting Costs

When the level of service is increased, we expect waiting time, and consequently wait-ing costs, to decrease. But since waiting costs usually depend on the arrival of custom-ers and customers' reactions to the waiting line, it is often difficult to measure waiting costs directly. In the hamburger shop example, it is difficult to determine how much revenue is lost because the lines are too long. Managerial judgment, perhaps tempered by experience, may provide an estimate of waiting costs. If waiting occurs in a work situation, such as workers waiting in line at a copy machine, the cost of waiting should reflect the cost of productive resources lost during the waiting time.

The Total System Cost

Now we can clearly see that the decision problem is one of balancing waiting time costs and service costs. Thus, a general decision model for a waiting line problem can be described as follows:

$$\text{Minimize } TC(S) = IC_1 + WC_2$$

where

$$TC(S) = \text{total expected cost to provide service level } S$$

$$I = \text{total expected server idle time for a specified period} \\ \text{(each hour, each day, etc.)}$$

$$C_1 = \text{cost per unit of server idle time}$$

$$W = \text{total expected waiting time for all arrivals for a specified period}$$

$$C_2 = \text{cost per unit of waiting time}$$

In our model, the level of service, S, is the decision variable. Each level of service being considered should be evaluated separately. It is important to recall that queuing theory is probabilistic; we are dealing with *expected* costs, idle times, and waiting times. Our objective is to determine which possible level of service has the minimum combination of service and waiting costs. The following example illustrates how the model can be applied.

Example 13.1 A PORT UNLOADING PROBLEM

A company has two unloading facilities at a port. The management is attempting to determine whether to use both facilities for a particular day. Since the arrival rates of customers (ships) fluctuate randomly, estimates of the expected arrivals for a given day are required for the analysis.

The company has obtained the following information:

Model Parameter	One Dock	Two Docks
Total expected dock idle time for the day (I)	1 hr.	12 hr.
Total expected ship waiting time for the day (W)	4 hr.	1 hr.
Estimated cost per unit of dock time (C_1)	\$2,000/hr.	
Estimated cost per unit of ship waiting time (C_2)	\$10,000/hr.	

On the basis of the above data, we can calculate the total expected system cost for operating one or two docks as follows:

$$TC(S = 1) = (1)(\$2,000) + (4)(\$10,000)$$

$$= \$2,000 + \$40,000$$

$$= \$42,000$$

$$TC(S = 2) = (12)(\$2,000) + (1)(\$10,000)$$

$$= \$24,000 + \$10,000$$

$$= \$34,000$$

It is apparent from the above analysis that the cost of ship waiting time outweighs the cost of dock idle time. Thus, even though manning the second dock facility results in a large amount of idle time for the dock workers and the port facility (if the company owns the port as well as the ships) the company should provide the additional dock workers to operate the second dock.

From the previously discussed example, it should be obvious that solving waiting line problems requires the assumption that model parameters are known. Management must be able to determine sufficiently accurate estimates of C_1 (cost associated with a unit of server idle time) and C_2 (cost associated with customer waiting per unit of time).

As we noted earlier, unlike linear programming or the other optimization techniques we have studied, there exists no general optimization theory for waiting line problems. The total system cost approach we discussed above is a means of analyzing waiting line problems as a decision-making model. Thus far we have identified the general components of the decision-making model for waiting line problems. The mathematical formulation required to solve queuing problems can vary widely according to the characteristics of the problem under study. Some of these formulations will be presented in this chapter. Many queuing problems, however, do not fit developed waiting line formulations. For this reason, waiting line theory has been developed primarily to provide a wide variety of descriptive measures of the system's operating performance.

ASSUMPTIONS FOR WAITING LINE MODELS

To analyze the waiting line situation, we need estimates of such operating characteristics as expected server idle time and expected customer waiting time. Waiting line theory provides formulas that allow calculation of operating characteristics based on specific assumptions.

The operating characteristics most frequently obtained in the analysis of waiting lines are:

Probability of any specified number of customers being in the system

Mean (expected) waiting time for each customer

Mean (expected) length of the waiting line

Mean time in the system (waiting plus being served) for each customer

Mean number of customers in the system

Probability that the service facility will be idle

To determine these operating characteristics, we must make certain assumptions about the waiting line situation. A waiting line system can be classified by defining six key conditions, or parameters, that affect the system's operation. The key parameters are:

1. Arrival distribution

2. Service time distribution

3. Number of servers

4. Queue discipline

5. Maximum number of customers allowed in the system

6. Number of potential customers in the calling population

In 1953, D. G. Kendall introduced a compact notational scheme to describe the characteristics of waiting line systems. The *Kendall notation* has since been widely accepted as a systematic means of describing queuing models. Kendall's notation can be used as a shorthand means of portraying a waiting line system. For example, abbreviations for the six parameters listed above can be placed in the appropriate positions of the following format:

(Arrival distribution/service distribution/number of servers):

(Queue discipline/maximum customers/calling population)

Queuing models can become rather involved, with seemingly limitless twists. A few general models have proven applicable to many management situations, and we will examine their characteristics briefly here. For a more detailed discussion of queuing theory, models, and parameters, please refer to Appendix 6.

The three models given here are identical in four of the six assumptions. All assume a **Poisson arrival distribution,** indicating that arrivals are independent of each other. The Poisson distribution is usually appropriate when arrivals are random and unscheduled (see Appendix 6). All three models assume a first-come, first-served queue discipline, or order of service. The three models also share the assumptions that both the capacity of the system and the number of potential callers are infinite. A very large calling population may be common; however, people tend to shy away from waiting lines that seem to stretch to infinity—a behavior called **balking.** In our models, infinity is used to ease computations.

WAITING LINE MODELS

Now we are ready to study the most widely used waiting line models and their required assumptions. First, however, note that waiting line systems are in a transient state when they begin operations, during which state they approach equilibrium, or steady-state conditions. Thus service facilities may begin their operations without a queue of waiting customers—at the beginning of the day, unless customers arrive before opening time, no customers are forced to wait for service. A period of system operating time may have to pass before the steady-state conditions described by queuing formulas could accurately predict system parameters.

Complex queuing models have been developed that allow an estimation of service time as a function of the time elapsed since operations began. Waiting lines begin operations empty, representing a higher probability of shorter lines. This chapter, however, will present only steady-state models. The three models presented are designated by their Kendall notations.

The operating characteristics of waiting line models are typically denoted by the following symbols:

$$\lambda = \text{mean arrival rate } (1/\lambda = \text{mean time between arrivals})$$
$$\mu = \text{mean service rate } (1/\mu = \text{mean service time})$$
$$n = \text{number of customers (units) in the system (includes those waiting and in service)}$$
$$L = \text{mean number in the system}$$
$$L_q = \text{mean number in the waiting line (queue length)}$$
$$W = \text{mean time in the system}$$
$$W_q = \text{mean waiting time (in the queue)}$$
$$\rho = \text{service facility utilization factor}$$
$$P_0 = \text{probability of no units in the system}$$
$$P_n = \text{probability of } n \text{ units in the system}$$

Note that the arrival rate, λ, must be less than the service rate, μ, or the queue will grow forever. Consider what would happen if our hamburger shop's cook took 5 minutes to prepare a burger but a new order for a burger arrived every three minutes. . . .

The Single Server, Constant Service Time Model ($M/D/1$):(FCFS/∞/∞)

A common waiting line situation consists of one line to one server who takes a specified, constant amount of time to perform the service. Queues of this nature can be found at an automatic car wash, valet parking dropoff point, pizza oven, and numerous other situations. The assumptions on which this model depends are:

1. Arrival distribution: Poisson (M)

2. Service distribution: constant, or deterministic (D)

3. Number of servers: one

4. Queue discipline: first-come, first-served (FCFS)

5. System capacity: infinity (∞)

6. Population size: infinity (∞)

Example 13.2 FAST-FOOD DINER

To illustrate the single server, constant service time model described by the assumptions listed above, let's consider a fast-food diner where all the food comes in plastic containers, with each order taking 3 minutes in the microwave. The diner has only one microwave, a constant service time, and a random customer arrival rate which works out to be about 15 per hour.

Mean arrival rate	λ = given	= 15 (per hour)
Mean time between arrivals	$1/\lambda$	= 0.0666 hours or 4 minutes
Mean service rate	μ = given	= 20 (per hour)
Mean service time	$1/\mu$	= 0.05 hours or 3 minutes

Server utilization factor

$$\rho = \frac{\lambda}{\mu} = \frac{15}{20} = 0.75$$

Empty-system probability

$$P_0 = 1 - \rho = 1 - 0.75 = 0.25$$

Probability of n units in the system

$$P_n = \rho^n(1 - \rho)$$

$P_1 = 0.75^1(0.25) = 0.1875$
$P_2 = 0.72^2(0.25) = 0.1406$
$P_3 = 0.75^3(0.25) = 0.1055$
$P_4 = 0.75^4(0.25) = 0.0791$

Probability of k or more units in the system

$$P_{n \ge k} = \rho^k \qquad P_{\ge 8} = 0.75^8 = 0.1001$$

Mean queue length

$$L_q = \frac{\rho^2}{2(1 - \rho)} = \frac{(0.75)^2}{2(0.25)} = 1.125 \text{ customers}$$

Mean system length

$$L = L_q + \rho = 1.125 + 0.75 = 1.875 \text{ customers}$$

Mean waiting time

$$W_q = \frac{L_q}{\lambda} = \frac{1.125}{15} = 0.075 \text{ hours, or 4.5 minutes}$$

Mean time in system

$$W = W_q + \frac{1}{\mu} = 0.075 + 0.05 = 0.125 \text{ hours or 7.5 minutes}$$

The model shows that on average two customers will be waiting to receive their order and that each customer will wait on average 4.5 minutes. The microwave will be in use three-fourths of the time, or idle one-fourth of the time. The line of customers waiting to be served will have an average of 1.125 people in it; there will be a large crowd (eight or more customers without food) only 10 percent of the time.

The Single Server, Random Service Time Model ($M/M/1$):(FCFS/∞/∞)

Many waiting lines involve random customer arrival coupled with fluctuating service times. For example, a queue may build at a pop machine, with different customers taking varying amounts of time to make their selection, purchase it, and move on. The most commonly used distribution assumption for service times is the **negative exponential distribution,** which is somewhat less than ideal because it assumes randomness where real waiting lines may actually affect the service times. Where the server may adjust the service time, people waiting may encourage the server to speed up—as in a bill-paying queue, where the clerk may decide not to converse as much when faced with impatient customers in a lengthening line. For this reason, the assumpion of a negative exponential service time distribution must be checked very carefully.

The assumptions on which this model depends are:

1. Arrival distribution: Poisson (M)

2. Service distribution: negative exponential (M)

3. Number of servers: one

4. Queue discipline: first-come, first-served

5. System capacity: infinity (∞)

6. Population size: infinity (∞)

Example 13.3 CORNER BOOKSHOP

To illustrate the single server, random service time model, under the assumptions listed above, we will consider the Corner Bookshop, which deals in used and out-of-print nonfiction books. Customers arrive at random and require a variety of service times from Ralph Corner, the owner. Some customers just browse, taking only a minute or two of Ralph's time when paying, and others wish to order special volumes through an interstore network and can occupy Ralph for half an hour. On what Ralph believes to be a typical day, he helped 60 customers and spent 6 of the 8 hours helping someone. To estimate his customers' average waiting time, Ralph has assumed that the negative exponential distribution represents the service time he spends.

Mean arrival time	λ = given	$= \dfrac{60}{8} = 7.5$ customers per hour
Mean time between arrivals	$1/\lambda$	$= \dfrac{1}{7.5} = 0.1333$ hours (8 minutes)
Mean service rate	μ = given	$= \dfrac{60}{6} = 10$ customers per hour
Mean service time	$1/\mu$	$= \dfrac{1}{10} = 0.10$ hours (6 minutes)
Server utilization factor	$\rho = \dfrac{\lambda}{\mu}$	$= \dfrac{7.5}{10} = 0.75$
Empty-system probability	$P_0 = 1 - \rho$	$= 1 - 0.75 = 0.25$
Probability of n units in the system	$P_n = \rho^n(1 - \rho)$	$P_1 = 0.75^1(0.25) = 0.1875$
		$P_2 = 0.75^2(0.25) = 0.1406$
		$P_3 = 0.75^3(0.25) = 0.1055$
		$P_4 = 0.75^4(0.25) = 0.0791$

Probability of k or more units in the system	$P_{n \geq k} = \rho^k$	$P_{\geq 7} = 0.75^7 = 0.1335$

Mean system length

$$L = \frac{\lambda}{\mu - \lambda} = \frac{7.5}{10 - 7.5} = 3 \text{ customers}$$

Mean queue length

$$L_q = \frac{\lambda \rho}{\mu - \lambda} = L\rho = \frac{(7.5)0.75}{10 - 7.5} = 2.25 \text{ customers}$$

Mean time in system

$$W = \frac{1}{\mu - \lambda} = \frac{1}{10 - 7.5} = 0.4 \text{ hours (24 minutes)}$$

Mean waiting time

$$W_q = \frac{\rho}{\mu - \lambda} = W\rho = \frac{0.75}{10 - 7.5} = 0.3 \text{ hours (18 minutes)}$$

Ralph can expect to have three customers in the queuing system at any given time —which means three are either waiting to be served or being served. There may be additional customers in the shop who are not requesting his attention. The average customer must wait 18 minutes to receive 6 minutes of service. Ralph can also expect to be free for one-fourth of his 8-hour shift each day.

The Multiple Servers, Random Service Time Model $(M/M/s):(\text{FCFS}/\infty/\infty)$

A single waiting line frequently funnels customers to several servers, with the first customer in the line heading to whichever server becomes available first. You may have encountered this type of queuing system at your local post office, a popular restaurant, the bank, a barber shop, or when calling a government office ("please hold for the next available operator").

The multiple-server queuing model is extremely useful when comparing service alternatives where servers may be added or removed. Using s to denote the number of servers, the single-server service rate μ becomes $s\mu$ for the multiple server system. As with any other queuing model, the mean service rate must exceed the customer arrival rate, or $s\mu > \lambda$.

The assumptions on which this model depends are:

1. Arrival distribution: Poisson (M)

2. Service distribution: negative exponential (M)

3. Number of servers: one or more (s)

4. Queue discipline: first-come, first-served

5. System capacity: infinity (∞)

6. Population size: infinity (∞)

Example 13.4 *COUNTY DEPARTMENT OF REVENUE*

To illustrate the multiple server, random service time model, we place ourselves in the tax information office of the county department of revenue just before tax season. The office manager wishes to ascertain the minimum number of phone counselors to hire to cover the crunch, while keeping complaints about slow service to a minimum. Based on a tally from the previous year, an average of 45 calls will come in per hour, with an average call requiring 10 minutes of counseling. Complaints become troublesome when the *average* waiting period exceeds 3 minutes. To simplify analysis, the service distribution is assumed to be negative exponential, and calls are received on a Poisson distribution.

Mean arrival time	λ = given	= 45 calls per hour	
Mean time between arrivals	$1/\lambda$	= 0.0222 hours, or 1.333 minutes	
Mean service rate	μ = given	= 6 customers per server per hour	
Mean service time	$1/\mu$	= 0.1667 hours, or 10 minutes	
Number of servers	s = given, or to be determined		
Mean system service rate	$s\mu$		

Server utilization factor

$$\rho = \frac{\lambda}{s\mu}$$

Empty-system probability

$$P_0 = \frac{1}{\left[\sum_{n=0}^{s-1} \frac{(\lambda/\mu)^n}{n!}\right] + \left[\frac{(\lambda/\mu)^s}{s!(1 - \lambda/s\mu)}\right]}$$

Probability of n units in the system

$$P_n = \frac{(\lambda/\mu)^n}{n!} P_0 \quad (\text{if } n \leq s)$$

$$P_n = \frac{(\lambda/\mu)^n}{s!s^{(n-s)}} P_0 \quad (\text{if } n > s)$$

Probability of k or more units in the system

$$P_{n \geq k} = 1 - \sum_{n=0}^{k-1} P_n$$

Mean queue length

$$L_q = \frac{P_0(\lambda/\mu)^s \rho}{s!(1 - \rho)^2}$$

Mean system length

$$L = L_q + \frac{\lambda}{\mu}$$

Mean waiting time

$$W_q = \frac{L_q}{\lambda}$$

Mean time in system

$$W = W_q + \frac{1}{\mu}$$

Instead of reformulating the general model parameters to determine the optimum number of servers directly, analysis is frequently performed by calculating the desired values for each s (number of servers) under consideration. For our tax information example, results for several different quantities of servers follow:

	Number of Servers (s)					
	7*	8	9	10	11	12
ρ	1.0714	0.9375	0.8333	0.7500	0.6818	0.6250
P_0	−0.0003305	0.0002032	0.0004102	0.0004941	0.0005289	0.0005343
P_5	−0.0654	0.0402	0.0811	0.0977	0.1046	0.1057
P_6	−0.0817	0.0502	0.1014	0.1221	0.1307	0.1321
P_7	−0.0875	0.0538	0.1086	0.1309	0.1401	0.1415
P_8	−0.0938	0.0505	0.1019	0.1227	0.1313	0.1327
P_9	−0.1005	0.0473	0.0849	0.1022	0.1094	0.1106
P_{10}	−0.1077	0.0443	0.0707	0.0767	0.0560	0.0353
P_{15}	−0.1520	0.0321	0.0284	0.0182	0.0121	0.0086
L_q	−18.3819	12.1089	2.5460	0.9201	0.3769	0.1570
L	−10.8819	19.6089	10.0460	8.4201	7.8769	7.6570
W_q (hours)	−0.4085	0.2691	0.0566	0.0204	0.0084	0.0035
(minutes)	−24.509	16.145	3.395	1.227	0.503	0.209
W (hours)	−0.2418	0.4358	0.2232	0.1871	0.1750	0.1702

*The 7-server evaluation is included to demonstrate the effects of an impossible situation, where $\lambda > s\mu$, or arrivals (45) exceed possible service (42) for each time period.

Examining the analysis for seven to twelve operators, we find that ten operators should prove satisfactory. Were the manager to hire ten operators, the average waiting time that a caller would be on hold should be approximately 1:14 minutes; if nine operators were hired, the waiting time would increase to 3:24 minutes, above the desired limit. With ten operators, there should be an average of just under one caller (0.92) on hold at any given time. (To confirm this, multiply 45 callers per hour by 1:14 average holding time to obtain 55 minutes per hour that someone is on hold, or 0.92 percent of the time.) With nine operators, 2.5 people would be on hold at any given time. If only eight operators were employed, 12 people would be on hold, and a typical caller would wait 16 minutes before being helped.

OTHER MODELS

The three basic models discussed above are relevant in many waiting line situations, but they are too limited or restrictive for many others. Each queuing situation must be analyzed separately, to determine which assumptions can reasonably be made. A change in any of the parameters can invalidate results obtained with a selected queuing model. Variations typically encountered in realistic situations include:

1. Arrival distribution

$$D = \text{deterministic}$$
$$M = \text{Poisson}$$
$$E_k = \text{Erlang}$$
$$\text{GI} = \text{General independent (other)}$$

2. Service time distribution

$$D = \text{Constant}$$
$$M = \text{Negative exponential}$$
$$E_k = \text{Erlang}$$
$$GS = \text{General (other)}$$

3. Number of servers: one or more

4. Queue discipline

$$FCFS = \text{First-come, first-served}$$
$$LCFS = \text{Last-come, first-served}$$
$$SIRO = \text{Service in random order}$$
$$GD = \text{General distribution (other)}$$

5. System capacity

$$\infty = \text{Infinite}$$
$$\text{Finite (particular quantity)}$$

6. Population size

$$\infty = \text{Infinite}$$
$$\text{Finite (particular quantity)}$$

In addition to changes in model parameters, changes in customer behavior may need to be entered into the model. For example, if customers perceive that the line is too long, they may balk or refuse to enter the waiting line; if the line is moving too slowly, they may *renege* or leave the line after having entered it earlier. Everyone has experienced *jockeying,* where people switch lines when they perceive another line as moving faster—such as at a grocery store or bank.

Appendix 6 presents eight queuing models, including the three presented above, illustrated with a single, varying casette. Some variations of model parameters, in particular alternative distributions, are discussed in detail. This chapter has served as an introduction to queuing models; if you are interested in applying queuing theory to any actual waiting line system, check the assumptions very carefully to ensure selection of an appropriate model.

SIMULATION OF WAITING LINE SYSTEMS

In this chapter we have looked at several analytic models of queuing systems, presenting equations that allow prediction of system parameters. However, the discussion of these models, restricted by so many assumptions and by no means exhaustive, leads one to appreciate the many real applications that defy the categorization required by the available models.

You have been given a taste of the analysis of waiting line systems in this chapter, and have obtained at least rough approximations of system operating characteristics. The techniques of simulation, which will be discussed in Chapter 15, can be employed in the analysis of queuing systems. The interested reader should therefore explore simulation with queuing applications in mind.

COMPUTER APPLICATIONS OF QUEUING MODELS

A growing number of software solution packages are available for waiting line models. Some are for use on a mainframe, and others are for use on a microcomputer; some are based on complex simulation approaches. Figures 13.4 through 13.6 present the application of *Micro Manager* to the three queuing models we discussed.

Figure 13.4   Computer Solution for Example 13.2 Fast-Food Diner

```
PROGRAM: Queuing Models

***** INPUT DATA ENTERED *****

M/D/1 type

Average service rate:  20
Average customer arrival rate:  15

*****   PROGRAM OUTPUT   *****

Number of customers    Probability
------------------------------------
        0                 0.250
        1                 0.188
        2                 0.141
        3                 0.105
        4                 0.079
        5                 0.059
------------------------------------
Mean number of customers in the system :     1.88
Mean number of customers in the queue   :     1.13
Mean time in the system                 :     0.13
Mean waiting time                       :     0.08
Traffic intensity ratio                 :     0.75
```

Figure 13.5   Computer Solution for Example 13.3 Corner Bookshop

```
PROGRAM: Queuing Models

***** INPUT DATA ENTERED *****

M/M/1 type

Average service rate:  10
Average customer arrival rate:  7.5

*****   PROGRAM OUTPUT   *****

Number of customers    Probability
--------------------------------------
         0                0.250
         1                0.188
         2                0.141
         3                0.105
         4                0.079
         5                0.059
--------------------------------------
Mean number of customers in the system :    3.00
Mean number of customers in the queue  :    2.25
Mean time in the system                :    0.40
Mean waiting time                      :    0.30
Traffic intensity ratio                :    0.75
```

REAL-WORLD APPLICATIONS

A large number of studies dealing with real-world applications of waiting line models have been reported in the management science literature. Most of these studies deal with unique characteristics of waiting line systems and related managerial decision problems. In this section we will examine two of the recently published real-world applications of waiting line models.

Change of Queuing Model Increases ATM Usage

Queues are a common occurrence at many banks, and the waiting line for teller service has been analyzed frequently. With the increasing availability of automatic teller machines (ATMs), some banks have developed queuing models specifically to study use of the ATM. A major metropolitan bank, with nearly 500 ATMs at numerous locations, faced a major expansion with some trepidation and hired representatives of the Columbia University Graduate School of Business to conduct the necessary analysis.[1] The project grew from a series of student assignments concerning queues at various banks.

[1]Peter Kolesar, "Stalking the Endangered CAT: A Queuing Analysis of Congestion at Automatic Teller Machines," *Interfaces* 14:6 (1984), 16–26.

The queuing model developed by the bank revealed various shortcomings, notably that it permitted a queue of infinite length and that it based service times and transaction counts on machine activity. Because of space limitations, actual queues of more than 10 to 12 customers were rarely observed, leading the research team to limit potential queue length. Service time was redefined to allow for ''setup'' time, where the customer occupies the ATM but the machine is not engaged. Under typical circumstances, recorded service time for a given customer began when the previous customer departed and ended when the customer in question departed. In Kendall notation, the bank had employed an $(M/M/s){:}(FCFS/\infty/\infty)$ model, while research indicted that an $(M/M/s){:}(FCFS/m/\infty)$ model would be more appropriate.

The bank had focused on customer waiting time as the decision criterion. Using various situational models, the researchers demonstrated that even with a ''supersaturated'' arrival rate, average waiting time remained under 6 minutes. Observation of customer behavior, as well as interviews, determined that balking of various types became problematic with a relatively moderate arrival rate; the new model showed that with a saturation arrival rate over half the arriving customers balked. Some just glanced in and kept on walking, others started to join the queue but turned away, and some customers learned by experience to avoid peak traffic periods altogether. Balking customers represented potential loss of business to the bank, so the decision criterion was altered to

---

Figure 13.6   Computer Solution for Example 13.4 County Department of Revenue

PROGRAM: Queuing Models

INPUT DATA ENTERED

M/M/C type

Average service rate: 6
Average customer arrival rate: 45
Number of servers: 7

PROGRAM OUTPUT

Number of customers	Probability
0	-0.000
1	-0.002
2	-0.009
3	-0.023
4	-0.044
5	-0.065

Mean number of customers in the system	: -10.89
Mean number of customers in the queue	: -18.39
Mean time in the system	: -0.24
Mean waiting time	: -0.41
Traffic intensity ratio	: 1.07

PROGRAM: Queuing Models

INPUT DATA ENTERED

M/M/C type

Average service rate: 6
Average customer arrival rate: 45
Number of servers: 8

PROGRAM OUTPUT

Number of customers	Probability
0	0.000
1	0.002
2	0.006
3	0.014
4	0.027
5	0.040

Mean number of customers in the system	: 19.61
Mean number of customers in the queue	: 12.11
Mean time in the system	: 0.44
Mean waiting time	: 0.27
Traffic intensity ratio	: 0.94

(continued)

Figure 13.6 (continued)

PROGRAM: Queuing Models

INPUT DATA ENTERED

M/M/C type

Average service rate: 6
Average customer arrival rate: 45
Number of servers: 9

PROGRAM OUTPUT

Number of customers	Probability
0	0.000
1	0.003
2	0.012
3	0.029
4	0.054
5	0.081

Mean number of customers in the system :	10.05
Mean number of customers in the queue :	2.55
Mean time in the system :	0.22
Mean waiting time :	0.06
Traffic intensity ratio :	0.83

PROGRAM: Queuing Models

INPUT DATA ENTERED

M/M/C type

Average service rate: 6
Average customer arrival rate: 45
Number of servers: 11

PROGRAM OUTPUT

Number of customers	Probability
0	0.001
1	0.004
2	0.015
3	0.037
4	0.070
5	0.105

Mean number of customers in the system :	7.88
Mean number of customers in the queue :	0.38
Mean time in the system :	0.18
Mean waiting time :	0.01
Traffic intensity ratio :	0.68

PROGRAM: Queuing Models

INPUT DATA ENTERED

M/M/C type

Average service rate: 6
Average customer arrival rate: 45
Number of servers: 10

PROGRAM OUTPUT

Number of customers	Probability
0	0.000
1	0.004
2	0.014
3	0.035
4	0.065
5	0.098

Mean number of customers in the system :	8.42
Mean number of customers in the queue :	0.92
Mean time in the system :	0.19
Mean waiting time :	0.02
Traffic intensity ratio :	0.75

PROGRAM: Queuing Models

INPUT DATA ENTERED

M/M/C type

Average service rate: 6
Average customer arrival rate: 45
Number of servers: 12

PROGRAM OUTPUT

Number of customers	Probability
0	0.001
1	0.004
2	0.015
3	0.038
4	0.072
5	0.107

Mean number of customers in the system :	7.66
Mean number of customers in the queue :	0.16
Mean time in the system :	0.17
Mean waiting time :	0.00
Traffic intensity ratio :	0.63

focus on the percentage of customers lost rather than on the average waiting time. Using a 5 percent lost-customer rate, the bank targeted certain facilities for additional ATMs or other upgrading. Actual results indicated that the "lost" customers did indeed comprise a substantial share of the total potential customers, with a considerable rise in transactions counted at the upgraded facilities.

Staffing Telephone Operator Service Systems

Telephone operators provide a variety of services to callers, including directory assistance, person-to-person, collect, and calling card services. The Bell System, employing some 85,000 operators, provided each service center with staffing tables which indicated maximum load levels allowable by set service criteria.[2] The basic service criterion dictates an average customer delay of 1.25 to 7 seconds (depending on the system's function). The operators are staffed in half-hour slots; forecast load levels are provided by a computer program.

Certain service centers couldn't quite reach the standards, so Bell anticipated an across-the-board staffing increase—with an annual cost of over $10 million. The staff of Bell Communications Research, Inc. analyzed the situation in detail and determined that the standard tables were inadequate for certain service centers for several reasons. Typical queuing models did not allow for some of this particular situation's parameters. The author's team developed a new queuing model, taking into account the large number of servers (100 to 300 operators) at each site, the desired system peak occupancy rate of 90 to 95 percent, the sharply split service time distribution (due to different types of calls, in differing quantities at different sites), caller balking (abandonment) and repeat attempts, and the need to prioritize certain calls (i.e., a discriminatory first-come, first-served service priority).

Results of three verification tests indicated a significantly greater accuracy with the new model. The tests compared predictions with actual data for sites at both extremes and in the middle of the typical service mix. New tables were prepared specifically for the centers with atypical call mixes, and the total increase in cost to the Bell System was less than 10 percent of the originally anticipated increase.

SUMMARY

In this chapter we have examined waiting line models and their applications to management decision-making problems. In a waiting line system, arrivals enter the system when they enter a line to wait their turn to be served, then they progress to the service facility where they are served, and they immediately depart the system once they are served. The basic purpose of waiting line theory is to minimize the total expected operating cost for the system. This can be achieved through a proper management of the system so that the cost of waiting and the cost of service can be balanced.

Waiting line models are not the end in decision making; they are just the beginning of the structuring of a decision-making framework. Thus, waiting line models are often developed for the purpose of understanding the operating characteristics of the system rather than of finding exact solutions to a queuing problem. Waiting line systems are

---

[2]David Sze, "A Queuing Model for Telephone Operator Staffing," *Operations Research* 32:2 (1984), 229–249.

evaluated in two phases. The first phase involves the analysis of the steady-state operating characteristics of the system by using waiting line theory or simulation. The second phase attempts to minimize the total expected operating cost of the system by using the estimated waiting and service costs.

You have been introduced to a number of different waiting line models that are useful in determining steady-state operating characteristics under different assumptions. When an appropriate model does not exist for a particular problem, a simulation approach may be used. Management scientists frequently debate the capability of waiting line models to reflect complex real-world situations. However, an increasing number of real-world applications of waiting line models appear in management science literature. This is a clear indication that queuing models are important tools for management decision making.

Glossary

Balking   Departure from or refusal to enter a queue due to momentary characteristics such as overcrowding or excessive waiting periods.

Calling Population   Entire group of persons or objects which have the potential to join the queue.

Channel   Group of parallel identical servers.

Constant Distribution   Distribution with no deviation from a specified constant value for arrival time or service time; deterministic.

Erlang Distribution   A variation of the negative exponential distribution, including the effect of multiple phases.

Exponential Distribution   A random, continuous probability distribution related to the pattern of service times and time between arrivals for some queues.

First-Come, First-Served (FCFS)   The standard queue discipline, termed "first-come, first-served" because of the strictly sequential nature of the queue.

Kendall Notation   Abbreviation format used to describe queuing models with six distinguishing parameters.

Phase   Stage of service in a chain of sequential servers.

Poisson Distribution   A probability distribution used to describe the random arrival patterns for a queue. The result in a given period is not influenced by the results obtained in prior periods.

Priority Queue Discipline   The selection rule in a waiting line system where some factor other than simple order of arrival assists in determining the order of service.

Queue   Group of persons or objects waiting to receive attention from a person or system. Those waiting usually form a line or lines; hence, queues are frequently called waiting line systems.

Service Facility (Server)   Person or system which provides the service or attention that those waiting in the queue expect.

References

Buffa, E. S. *Operations Management: Problems and Models*. 3d ed. New York: Wiley, 1972.

Feller, W. *An Introduction to Probability Theory and Its Applications*. Vol. I, 3d ed. New York: Wiley, 1968.

Hillier, F., and Lieberman, G. J. *Operations Research*. 4th ed. San Francisco: Holden-Day, 1986.

Kendall, D. G. "Stochastic Processes Occurring in the Theory of Queues and Their Analysis by Means of the Imbedded Markov Chain." *The Annals of Mathematical Statistics* 24 (1953), 338–354.

Kleinrock, L. *Queueing Systems* (2 vols.). New York: Wiley, 1975.

Kolesar, P. "Stalking the Endangered CAT: A Queuing Analysis of Congestion at Automatic Teller Machines." *Interfaces* 32:2 (1984), 229–249.

Lee, S. M., Moore, L. J., and Taylor, B. W. *Management Science.* 2d ed. Dubuque, Iowa: W. C. Brown, 1985.

Morse, P. M. *Queues, Inventories, and Maintenance.* New York: Wiley, 1958.

Panico, J. A. *Queuing Theory: A Study of Waiting Lines for Business, Economics and Science.* Englewood Cliffs, N.J.: Prentice-Hall, 1969.

Saaty, T. L. *Elements of Queueing Theory.* New York: McGraw-Hill, 1961.

Sze, D. "A Queuing Model for Telephone Operator Staffing." *Operations Research* 32:2 (1984), 229–249.

Assignments

13.1 In an operation involving waiting lines, what happens when the arrival rate exceeds the service rate?

13.2 What can be done to reestablish a stable operation if the arrival rate exceeds the service rate?

13.3 Does the existence of a very long waiting line for professional service (such as in a doctor's office) provide any indication of the economic appropriateness of the fees being charged?

13.4 How does customer impatience affect waiting lines?

13.5 Under what conditions might faster service be detrimental?

13.6 What sources exist for gathering data for queuing analysis?

13.7 Give an example of a last-in, first-out queue discipline.

13.8 Give an example of a random order queue discipline.

13.9 Give an example of a preemptive priority queue discipline.

13.10 Many business operations face uneven waiting lines. How do grocery stores, as an example, deal with fluctuating waiting lines?

13.11 In waiting line situations involving multiple servers, why is it more efficient to have a single-pooled waiting line than individual waiting lines in front of each server?

13.12 Why will limited queue lines reach a steady state even when the arrival rate exceeds the service rate?

13.13 Why will models with limited calling populations reach a steady state even though the arrival rate may exceed the service rate?

13.14 What is the effect of scheduling arrivals (such as barber appointments) on a waiting line?

13.15 The transient state of a queuing system is expected to have smaller than average waiting lines. Under what conditions might initial waiting lines be longer than average?

13.16 The Ace Wrecking Company operates a large fleet of trucks. These trucks have averaged one call for mechanical service every 4 hours. Trucks generate revenue for Ace of $20 per hour. Ace's ace mechanic, Thumbs Swenson, costs the company $12 per hour in wages, fringes, and equipment. Thumbs was found to average 20 minutes on a truck without help from the truck driver (2 hours per truck with the truck driver's help). (Assume an $M/M/1$:FCFS/∞/∞ model.)
   a. What is the probability of 0, 1, or 2 trucks in need of repair at any one time?
   b. What is the average number of trucks requiring repair at any one time?
   c. What is the average time a truck is out of service after breaking down?
   d. What is the average amount of time a truck waits for Thumbs?
   e. On the average, how many trucks are idle while waiting for Thumbs?

13.17 As the trucks got older, Ace Wrecking Company (presented in Problem 13.16) found the rate of mechanical failures increased. In the second year of operation, Ace suffered a truck breakdown once every hour. The increased severity of the mechanical failures also required additional mechanic time. The average repair time per truck increased to 30 minutes.
   a. What is the probability of 0, 1, or 2 trucks in need of repair?
   b. What is the average number of trucks that are inoperative?
   c. What is the average time a truck is inoperative?
   d. What is the average number of trucks waiting for the mechanic?
   e. What is the average idle time for a truck that is waiting for a mechanic?
   f. What is the cost to Ace in lost revenue by not having enough mechanics?
   g. Would it pay to add a mechanic?

13.18 Sal Maglie has operated a small tonsorial parlor in Poughkeepsie for a number of years. Sal has experienced a wide variety of business conditions over that time. With the development of his business, conditions have changed a great deal. Sal has kept meticulous records of operations over the years. There have been distinct changes in the distribution of customer arrivals as well as Sal's haircut time. When Sal was learning to cut hair, the rate of service varied a lot. He averaged 30 minutes per haircut, distributed exponentially. About one customer per hour, arriving randomly, risked his head in Sal's shop.

Calculate the basic parameters of this system (P_0, P_1, P_2, L, L_q, W, W_q, ρ).

13.19 Frank's Slow Cook Diner features special-order hamburgers ($M/M/1$):(FCFS/∞/∞). Customers wander in at the rate of 5 per hour. Determine the number of people who will be waiting in line, the average time they will have to wait, and the probabilities of 0, 1, 2, and more than 2 waiting customers, given the following different service rates:

    a. A service rate of five ($\lambda = 5$).
    b. A service rate of seven ($\lambda = 5$).
    c. A service rate of nine ($\lambda = 5$).

13.20 Larsen E. Whipsnade is a rising young attorney. He wants to determine the optimum time to spend consulting with each client $(M/M/1):(FCFS/\infty/\infty)$. Larsen E. feels the more time spent with clients, the more satisfied the clients will be and the more willing they will be to pay a not-so-nominal consulting fee. However, longer consulting time results in other clients having to wait longer. If clients wait too long, they are likely to consult other solicitors. Given the arrival rate of 4 clients per hour, randomly distributed, determine total clients in the office, average client time in the office, and the probabilities of 0, 1, 2, and more than 2 clients in Larsen E.'s office. Use the service rates given below.

    a. Average consulting time of 15 minutes ($\lambda = 4$).
    b. Average consulting time of 10 minutes ($\lambda = 4$).
    c. Average consulting time of 7.5 minutes ($\lambda = 4$).

13.21 Dirty Dan's Car Wash uses a fixed-time assembly line requiring 3 minutes to wash a car, including drying time $(M/D/1):(FCFS/\infty/\infty)$. If customers arrive in a random manner at the average rate of 8 per hour, calculate the expected number of cars in the system and the average time each customer can expect to spend at Dirty Dan's.

13.22 The Fourth National Bank (FNB) of Wilber is expanding. To justify a second teller, the vice-president of finance has requested a series of waiting line analyses. The initial phase involves determining current system properties. At present, customers arrive in a random fashion, about 10 per hour. The teller spends exactly 5 minutes with each customer. Define the appropriate model, stating any assumptions you have made, and determine the current operating parameters.

13.23 According to marketing staff of the FNB from 13.22, customer service times could be more accurately described by a random (negative exponential) distribution. What effect does this change in assumptions have on the current system parameters?

13.24 The board of directors of the bank has concluded that a second teller is needed. The decision was based on a complaint by the husband of one of the board members: "There were five people ahead of me!"

    a. Determine the probability of an arriving customer finding five people already in the queue (thus constituting seven customers in the system: one being served, five in line, plus the new arrival).
    b. Determine the same probability for a two-teller system.
    c. Compare the empty-system probabilities for the one- and two-teller situations.
    d. What are the server utilization factors?
    e. What is the mean queue length for each system?

13.25 The bank experienced a surge in customer arrivals immediately after the second teller window opened. The mean arrivals are now 16 per hour. Determine the current parameters, including the probability of n units in the system for $n = 0$ to 6. Analyze the change in customer behavior relative to introduction of the second teller.

13.26 Solaspa Inc. has opened a series of minioutlets in a variety of locations around town, including university dorms and major office complexes. Each minioutlet features one tanning booth, with customers served on a first-come, first-served basis. For health reasons, each customer is limited to exactly 12 minutes under the lights. The average arrival rate is 4 customers per hour; the highest arrival rate at any of the outlets was 4.8 per hour. Examine the system's operating parameters under the two stated arrival rate assumptions.

13.27 Rainer's WunderBar serves only quality imported beers and wines. Rainer prides himself on providing top-notch service to his customers. However, with increasing demand, the WunderBar is becoming crowded. A planned expansion must provide enough additional seats to restore the mean waiting time to no more than 2 minutes. Rainer estimates a peak arrival rate of 50 customers per hour, with each customer staying 20 minutes (mean). The 15 seats currently available at the bar don't meet the peak demand. How many additional seats are needed?

13.28 The Madison Avenue Pizzeria receives orders on a random basis, averaging 14 per hour. It takes the master chef only 3.5 minutes (mean) to prepare a pizza to customer specifications; plain pizzas take less time, "specials" take more. Plenty of oven space is available and boxers and drivers are numerous, so the primary constraining factor is the chef.
  a. Determine the system's operating parameters.
  b. Whenever there are more than 5 pizzas in the preparation system (1 in process, 4 in the queue), additional pizzas are not delivered within the promised "30 minutes or half price" time limit. What percentage of pizzas are late?

13.29 To improve the half-price percentage, the Madison Avenue Pizzeria has considered hiring a second chef. The number of orders and amount of preparation time will not change. Determine the improvement in the late pizza percentage and the server utilization factor.

13.30 Sudsville Auto Laundry has an option to build a new washer complex in a prime suburban location. The lot will accommodate four wash-and-wax lines, but Sudsville isn't sure that many are needed to maintain both customer satisfaction and profitability. Customers appear to be satisfied when mean waiting time is under 3 minutes, and profit will be made when the lines are operating during at least half of the available hours. A wash-and-wax job takes 8 minutes, and a car arrives every 3 minutes. How many lines should Sudsville install?

13.31 The Southwood Sports Complex features a racquetball court with climate control and sound absorption characteristics that make it "worth the wait." However, no group will enter the queue if they must wait more than 30 minutes. Court time is strictly limited to 15 minutes per group of players. Thus, balking will occur whenever there are three groups of players in the system as a newcomer approaches. If potential players arrive every 10 minutes, how many will refuse to wait in any given hour?

13.32 A canned-soft drink vending machine near the student union is generating lines long enough to interfere with sidewalk traffic. The vending company must decide whether installation of a second machine nearby is economically feasible. Potential customers have been observed to walk away rather than enter the line. Expected arrivals (and purchases) would increase 40 percent from the current arrival rate of one every 30 seconds. The machine is capable of releasing cans at a rate of 15 per minute, but with customer decision time and coin insertion delays, mean service time is 24 seconds. Both arrivals and purchases are random in their variation.

  a. What is the current (one machine) server utilization rate?
  b. What is the probability of 7 or more customers in the system?
  c. What is the mean queue length?
  d. How long does a typical customer have to wait?
  e. What would be the server utilization rate after installation of a second vendor?
  f. Calculate the change in mean queue length and the $P_n \geq 7$.
  g. What is the new mean waiting time?
  h. The second machine will cost $1,000 per month, including installation, service, utilities, and depreciation. Each machine will operate 12 hours per day, 30 days per month. Gross profit is 10 cents per can. To be economically viable, the monthly gross profit increase must exceed the monthly cost increase resulting from installation of the second machine. Will the second vendor be installed?

13.33 Oil Can Pete's promises to have your car in and out in less than 15 minutes, having performed a lube, filter check, and oil change ("your choice of five major brands!"). Peter Townsan, owner and manager, has asked his ad agency to drum up more customers — but not more than his system can handle. The actual servicing takes 10 minutes, and Pete figures that if the mean waiting is under 4 minutes, nearly all his customers will be satisfied.

  a. Using an $(M/D/1)$:(FCFS/∞/∞) model, determine how many customers (arrivals) per hour Pete's garage can handle. (Hint: Watch your time units.)
  b. Assume a negative exponential service distribution, rather than a deterministic service time, and recalculate Pete's hourly capacity. Would it be to Pete's advantage to attempt to regularize the service time?
  c. Upon hearing the results of your calculations, Pete retorts that he already averages 3.5 cars per hour. Show that this arrival rate would indicate a mean waiting time greater than the desired 4 minutes. Would the average customer be "in and out in less than 15 minutes," as advertised? Use the $(M/D/1)$ model.
  d. If Pete can schedule his customer's arrivals through an appointment service, and maintain a constant service time, how many cars per hour could be handled? The appointment service costs $2 per appointment made; gross profit per car is $5.75.

Should Pete sign up with the appointment service? (Assume that he would otherwise maintain his current arrival rate of 3.5 cars per hour and that the appointment service guarantees full bookings.)

13.34 The local Army recruiter's office has been furnished a single telephone line. When the line is busy, a secondary device plays a prerecorded message in response to any incoming call and places the call in a queue. Although the recruiter takes calls as rapidly as he can, some callers hang up (presumably to call the Navy, Air Force, or Marines instead). The regional office has requested that a queuing analysis be performed. Calls arrive according to a Poisson distribution with a mean of 4 per hour, and the length of calls is exponentially distributed with a mean of 10 minutes. Determine λ, μ, ρ, P_0, P_1, P_2, P_3, $P_{n \geq 4}$, L_q, L, W_q, and W. If callers hang up after waiting 20 minutes (mean), what percentage of callers is lost? (Note: P_0 = empty, P_1 = 1 call being served, P_2 = 1 call waiting and 1 being served, etc.)

14 DYNAMIC PROGRAMMING

Dynamic programming is a mathematical modeling technique that is useful in solving a select set of problems involving a sequence of interrelated decisions. Dynamic programming provides a systematic means of solving multistage problems over a planning horizon or a sequence of events. As an example, a stock investment problem can be analyzed by dynamic programming to determine the allocation of funds that will maximize the total profit over a number of years. Decision making in this case, as in many similar cases, requires a set of decisions separated by time. Each year can be a stage in which a decision must be made.

Dynamic programming is a powerful tool that allows segmentation or decomposition of complex multistage problems into a number of simpler subproblems. These subproblems are often much easier for us to handle. In this chapter, we will discuss the basic nature, problem formulation, and solution procedures of dynamic programming.

Learning Objectives   From the study of this chapter, we will learn the following:

1. The basic nature of dynamic programming
2. Segmentation of a problem into subproblems
3. The backward solution approach for a dynamic programming problem
4. The basic features of a dynamic programming problem
5. The complete enumeration approach for a dynamic programming problem
6. The solution approach of dynamic programming
7. The basics of probabilistic dynamic programming
8. Computer solutions of dynamic programming
9. The meaning of the following terms:

Decomposition or segmentation	*Sequential decision making*
Backward approach	*Stage*
State	*Policy decision*
Return	*Recursive relation*
Probabilistic dynamic programming	*Deterministic dynamic programming*

THE BASIC NATURE OF DYNAMIC PROGRAMMING

Most management science techniques are designed to analyze a decision problem by finding the optimum solution under a given set of conditions. The usual approach is to solve the model and derive a solution in one operation. Of course, we have seen some exceptions. In decision tree analysis, which we studied in Chapter 9, an example of sequential decision making was analyzed through various states of nature and their associated probabilities. In many ways, dynamic programming is similar to decision tree analysis in that both techniques are useful for analyzing complex problems by breaking them down into interrelated subproblems in which decisions can be made sequentially. Therefore, dynamic programming is a convenient way to analyze a complex problem by breaking it down into smaller subproblems.

This **decomposition,** or **segmentation,** approach is a unique characteristic of dynamic programming. For this reason, dynamic programming is also referred to as a *multistage* or *sequential* decision process. Since the problem is segmented into smaller interrelated subproblems, the decision outcome of a subproblem at one stage (or time period) will be affected by the decision outcome of the previous-stage subproblem.

The pioneering work in dynamic programming was done by Richard Bellman. His important work *Dynamic Programming* was published in 1957. Further development and applications have flourished since then. In dynamic programming, we do not have a universal solution method such as the simplex method for linear programming problems. Instead, dynamic programming utilizes a variety of methods to solve the multistage problem. Because of its flexibility, this technique has been applied to a variety of decision problems, including those in the areas of resource allocation, inventory control, production planning, equipment maintenance and replacement, investment planning, product assortment, process design and control, and work force planning.

Segmentation and Sequential Decisions

The first important concept of dynamic programming is the segmentation of the problem into a set of smaller subproblems. Each of the subproblems is called a **stage.** The entire problem now becomes a sequence of stages. Thus, dynamic programming becomes a sequential decision process.

For example, let us suppose that we are interested in making an investment decision during a period of 4 years. We can segment the problem into four yearly subproblems. Our investment problem is to determine where to invest and how much to invest in each year in order to maximize the total return at the end of the 4-year period. Therefore, we can segment the problem, shown in Figure 14.1, as a sequence of decisions.

The Backward Approach

In Figure 14.1, the arrows, representing the linkage between stages and the stage numbers, are arranged in a left to right order. The linkage direction is also from left to right, and it indicates the direction of the information flow required for sequential decision making. For example, the investment decision in the second quarter must be based on funds available at the end of the first quarter. In other words, we must first make the decision about what should be invested in the fourth year based on the capital available at the end of the third year. Such an approach is often referred to as the **backward,** or **rollback, approach** and is our first attempt to make the decision that is closest to the final target.

Figure 14.1 Segmentation of the Investment Problem into Four Yearly Stage Problems

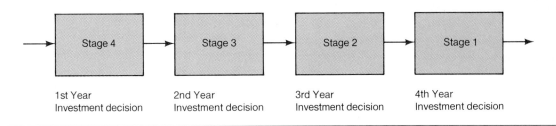

In dynamic programming, most problems are solved with this backward approach. However, this is by no means the universal solution approach of dynamic programming. In certain problems, dynamic programming may utilize the *forward* approach, which starts the solution process from the point that is farthest from the target. The appropriateness of the approach we take will depend on the unique characteristics of the problem under consideration.

Although many dynamic programming problems are segmented on the basis of time, that is not a requirement. If a problem can be segmented into a sequence of interrelated subproblems, or if it is initially composed of a set of smaller problems, dynamic programming can be applied as a solution technique. To understand the general characteristics and terminology of dynamic programming, let us examine a shortest-route problem.

Casette 14.1 THE WASHINGTON, D.C. CONFERENCE

Roger Miller is a systems analyst at Pacific Instruments, Inc., a Los Angeles-based producer of medical instruments. Roger coauthored an article with Susan Allen, a senior production engineer, entitled ''A Multistage Production Planning Model via Dynamic Programming.'' The paper has been accepted for presentation at a national conference scheduled for May in Washington, D.C.

When Roger and Susan submitted the required travel authorizations to their respective supervisors, they were told that the trip to Washington, D.C., must be by the company's plane. The company has a small Cessna plane that is available to executives for business trips. The plane requires frequent stops to refuel, and it must avoid severe weather conditions.

The pilot, after studying the typical weather conditions for May, determined a network of possible routes to Washington, D.C. The network, along with the required flying time for each leg, is presented in Figure 14.2. Roger and Susan quickly recognized that this traveling problem can be analyzed as a shortest-route problem, a typical dynamic programming application.

Figure 14.2   A Shortest-Route Travel Network

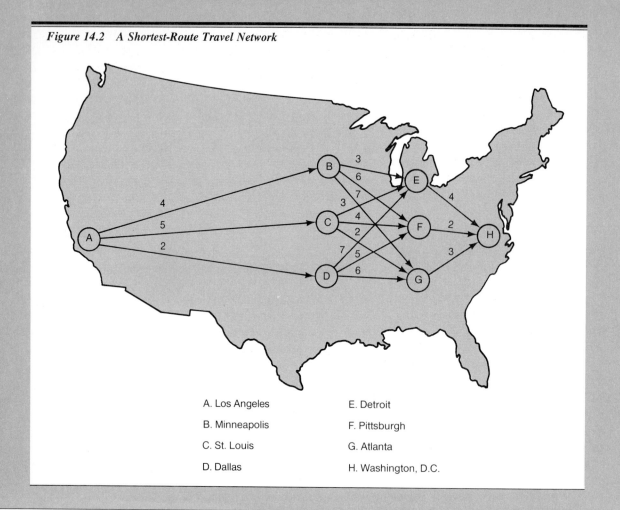

A. Los Angeles

B. Minneapolis

C. St. Louis

D. Dallas

E. Detroit

F. Pittsburgh

G. Atlanta

H. Washington, D.C.

The Basic Features of Dynamic Programming

The shortest-route problem is made up of nodes (stations) and arcs (routes). In Figure 14.2, the nodes indicate cities on the possible travel routes. The arcs indicate the flight routes from city to city. The numbers over each arc indicate the flying time required between two adjacent cities. Roger and Susan are attempting to determine the fastest route from Los Angeles to Washington, D.C. Thus, they revised the travel network as a dynamic programming problem, as shown in Figure 14.3.

Let us examine the basic features of dynamic programming in the shortest-route problem.

State   A state is the condition that a problem under analysis has in a particular stage. It is represented as a node of a system configuration and is identified by a label, such as A, B, etc. One or a number of states may be associated with a stage. In our shortest-route problem, a city corresponds to a state. For example, in stage 2 we have three states: B (Minneapolis), C (St. Louis), and D (Dallas).

Stage   A dynamic programming problem can be segmented into a number of stages. A stage is a decision point represented by an arc. In our example, Roger and Susan must decide which flying route to take for a particular leg of the journey. The stages are determined as follows: In Los Angeles they must decide which route to take—to B (Minneapolis), C (St. Louis), or D (Dallas). Once they arrive at B, C, or D, their next decision would be to travel to E (Detroit), F (Pittsburgh), or G (Atlanta). Regardless of the location in the third leg (cities E, F, or G), they must travel to Washington, D.C. Thus, this shortest-route problem can be segmented into three stages.

In each stage, Roger and Susan can be at one and only one state. Thus, a stage is a single step in a sequential decision-making process. A decision made at each step results in the transition from one state to an adjacent state. In Figure 14.2, one stage corresponds to the transition from one column of cities to the next column of cities.

Policy Decision   A policy decision refers to a plan to make a decision based on a predetermined policy under each possible condition. A policy decision must be made from the set of available alternatives at each stage. For example, in Figure 14.3, if Roger and Susan are at St. Louis, three different travel alternatives exist: to Detroit, Pittsburgh, or Atlanta. Obviously, the best decision is to travel from St. Louis to Atlanta, because this travel plan has the least flying time (2 hours versus 3 or 4).

Figure 14.3   A Network of Cities in a Shortest-Route Problem

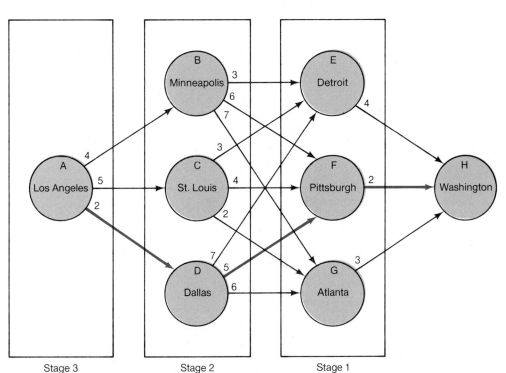

Return   A return or reward is the value of the state that is generated over one stage. It is also referred to as *immediate return*. In the shortest-route problem, the immediate return is the time (or distance, cost, etc.) required in moving from one state to the next state.

Total Return   Total return is a function of returns generated from the initial state to the current state. The function can be simply a sum, a multiplication, or a more complex operation. In the shortest-route problem, total return corresponds to the accumulated travel time from the initial state to the current state. The shortest total return will be the optimum value in our example.

Principle of Optimality   The most important concept of dynamic programming is the *principle of optimality*. Given the current state, an optimum policy decision for the remaining stages is independent of the policy decisions adopted in the previous stages. In other words, each subproblem is determined only by the solution (or the parameters from the solution) of its immediate predecessor. For example, in Figure 14.3, determining which route we should take from Dallas is based on the travel time of the immediate predecessor (Los Angeles to Dallas) and the travel time from the current state (Dallas to Atlanta, Dallas to Pittsburgh, and Dallas to Detroit). This principle must be satisfied before we try to solve a problem by dynamic programming. The principle may seem somewhat ambiguous at first glance, but it means only that *at any stage of the problem, future decisions are independent of prior decisions.*

The Complete Enumeration Approach

For a simple problem, we can easily analyze all possible alternatives. The shortest-route problem has only nine possible routes from Los Angeles to Washington, D.C., as shown in Table 14.1. It is obvious that route A–D–F–H is the best route because it provides the shortest travel time. This best route is also indicated in Figure 14.3 by the color arc lines. The minimum travel time required by the company plane is 9 hours by taking route A–D–F–H.

The complete enumeration approach is an easy way to identify the optimum solution if the problem under consideration is a very simple one. For a large and complex

Table 14.1   Complete Enumeration of the Shortest-Route Problem

Possible Routes	Travel Time
A–B–E–H	4 + 3 + 4 = 11
A–B–F–H	4 + 6 + 2 = 12
A–B–G–H	4 + 7 + 3 = 14
A–C–E–H	5 + 3 + 4 = 12
A–C–F–H	5 + 4 + 2 = 11
A–C–G–H	5 + 2 + 3 = 10
A–D–E–H	2 + 7 + 4 = 13
A–D–F–H	2 + 5 + 2 = 9 ← Minimum
A–D–G–H	2 + 6 + 3 = 11

travel network problem, however, it is unrealistic to use the complete enumeration approach. The time and effort required to evaluate every possible route may indeed be prohibitive. Thus, dynamic programming is needed for such problems.

Solution by Dynamic Programming

Step 1: Segmentation   As we discussed previously, the first step of dynamic programming is the segmentation or decomposition of the problem into smaller subproblems or stages. The shortest-route problem has been broken down into three stages, as shown in Figure 14.3. Stages are numbered from right to left so that the backward approach may be used.

Step 2: The Backward Approach   In dynamic programming, we often use the backward approach, in which the last part of the problem is analyzed first. For example, let us assume that Roger and Susan are in Washington, D.C. Now we need to examine from which state (city) they should travel in order to minimize the flying time to Washington, D.C.

Stage 1   When Roger and Susan reach Washington, D.C., they will be at the final destination. Before reaching Washington, D.C., they must be at state E (Detroit), F (Pittsburgh), or G (Atlanta) regardless of how they got there. These three states are in stage 1. Since this is the last leg of the trip, the travel route from each state to Washington, D.C., is given, and there is no other choice. For example, if Roger and Susan are in Detroit, the only route to Washington, D.C., open to them is Detroit → Washington, D.C. A similar reasoning applies to each state in stage 1. Table 14.2 presents the analysis for stage 1.

Stage 2   For Roger and Susan to reach any state in stage 1, they must have been at state B (Minneapolis), C (St. Louis), or D (Dallas) in stage 2. It is important to examine the best route from each of these states to the final destination, Washington, D.C. Since we have already examined the states of stage 1 in Table 14.2, we need only to evaluate the routes in stage 2. For example, from state B there are three alternative routes to states E, F, or G in stage 1. The first route (B–E) requires 3 hours and the time required for the last leg, E–H, was computed as 4 hours in stage 1. Of the three alternatives open for state B, the best route is B–E with the total required time of seven hours to Washington, D.C., as shown in Table 14.3. The best route is selected for each state in the table. It should be noted that the "best time from stage 1 to Washington" is obtained from the previous table, Table 14.2.

Table 14.2   The First-Stage Analysis

State	Alternative Routes	Time Required to Washington	Best Route
E	E–H	4 hours	4 hours
F	F–H	2	2
G	G–H	3	3

Table 14.3   The Second-Stage Analysis

State	Alternative Routes	Time Required to Stage 1	Best Time from Stage 1 to Washington	Total Travel Time	Best Route
	B–E	3 hours	4 hours	7 hours	←
B	B–F	6	2	8	
	B–G	7	3	10	
	C–E	3	4	7	
C	C–F	4	2	6	
	C–G	2	3	5	←
	D–E	7	4	11	
D	D–F	5	2	7	←
	D–G	6	3	9	

Table 14.4   The Third-Stage Analysis

State	Alternative Routes	Time Required to Stage 2	Best Time from Stage 2 to Washington	Total Travel Time	Best Route
	A–B	4 hours	7 hours	11 hours	
A	A–C	5	5	10	
	A–D	2	7	9	←

Stage 3   For Roger and Susan to reach stages B, C, or D in stage 2, they must start from the initial point, state A (Los Angeles). They have three alternative routes to states B, C, or D. Table 14.4 presents the computation summary.

The best route is now identified. It is A–D–F–H for a total of 9 hours of flying time. This solution corresponds to the one we obtained by the complete enumeration method. The sequence of decisions we have made at each stage is based on the backward approach, as shown in Figure 14.4.

THE STRUCTURE OF DYNAMIC PROGRAMMING

We have discussed the basic structure of the dynamic programming problem through the shortest-route problem presented as Casette 14.1. The fundamental idea of dynamic programming involves *segmentation,* **sequential decision making,** and the **recursive relation.** Segmentation is accomplished through decomposing the problem into subproblems, each of which is often referred to as a stage. Sequential decision making is required to move from a decision point in a given stage to the next decision point. The recursive relation function ties together the sequential decisions at each stage. This function represents the relationships among the immediate return, the total return, and the optimum total return.

Figure 14.4 *Sequential Optimization of the Shortest-Route Problem*

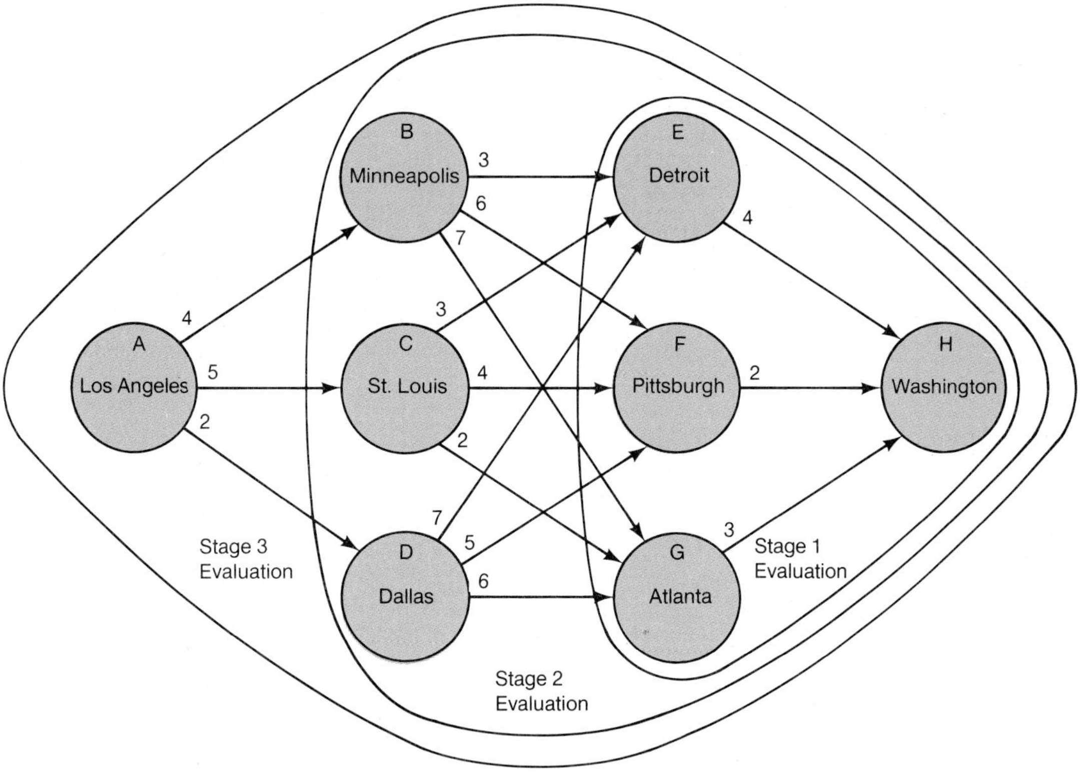

Before we present the general structure of dynamic programming, let us first define the following terminology and symbols:

Terminology	Symbol	Definition
Stage	n	A transition from a node (e.g., a city) to an adjacent node (city) for the current stage
State	s_n	A node (e.g., a city) in the current stage
Policy decision	x_n	A decision made among alternatives at stage n in a state (e.g., distance from a city to an adjacent city)
Return	c_{x_n}	Cost or payoff (e.g., travel time) incurred by x_n
Total return	$f_n(s_n)$	Total cost or payoff (e.g., travel time) from the current state (city) to the terminal stage (final destination city)
	$x_n^{\star}$	The optimum value (e.g., the distance of the best route) for each x_n
	$f_n^{\star}(s_n)$	The optimum value (e.g., the minimum total distance) for each $f_n(s_n)$

The recursive relation in a typical shortest-route problem can be developed as follows:

$$f_n^* (s_n) = \min [c_{x_n} + f_{n-1}^* (s_{n-1})]$$

For example, with two stages remaining, the recursive function $f_2^*(s_2)$ is to minimize $c_{x2} + f_1^*(s_1)$, and the optimum decision at this stage is to find the value of x_2 associated with $f_2^*(s_2)$. The subscript $n - 1$ represents the previous stage, regardless of whether we use a backward or a forward approach. Thus, the best route to take at stage 2 in the shortest-route problem, as shown in Table 14.3, is determined by finding the minimum total travel time to stage 2 $[f_2^*(s_2)]$. This minimum total travel time to stage 2 can be determined by finding the sum of the travel time from stage 2 to stage 1 (c_{x2}) and the minimum travel time from stage 1 to the final destination $[f_1^*(s_1)]$.

The exact form of the recursive function (or relationship) may differ from problem to problem. For the shortest-route problem, the functional operation required to link the immediate return with the total return was the addition $(+)$ operation. However, this may be a multiplication operation or another type of operation. Also, the objective of the problem may be to maximize the total payoff rather than to minimize the total cost. Thus, the general form of the recursive relationship can be described as

$$f_n^*(s_n) = \max \text{ or } \min [f_n^*(s_n, x_n)]$$

Since dynamic programming may utilize diverse forms of recursive relationships, subject only to the basic characteristics of the problem and the principle of optimality, the best way to examine the benefits of dynamic programming is to see how it is applied. For this purpose, we will look at several additional examples.

Before proceeding, however, we need to introduce the term **deterministic dynamic programming.** In deterministic dynamic programming, the state at the next stage is determined completely by the state and the policy decision at the current stage. In other words, we are certain of the costs of the alternatives. When the determination of the

Figure 14.5   One-Stage Shortest-Route Problem of Casette 14.1

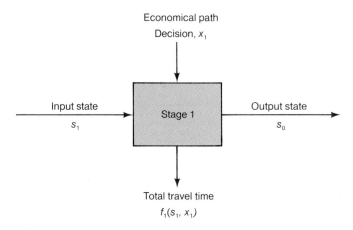

Figure 14.6   Three-Stage Shortest-Route Problem of Casette 14.1

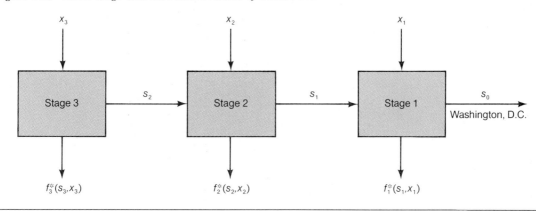

next state requires a probability distribution, such a case is referred to as **probabilistic dynamic programming.** We will discuss probabilistic problems later in this chapter.

Figure 14.5 presents a typical one-stage diagram of deterministic dynamic programming, in conjunction with the shortest-route problem. The input state, s_1, represents different routes from stage 2 to stage 1. Economical path decision, x_1, indicates the shortest travel time from stage 1 to the final destination. The total travel time, $f_1(s_1, x_1)$, represents the minimum cumulative travel time to the final destination. Finally, the output state, s_0, indicates the travel route from stage 1 to the final destination.

Figure 14.6 shows the entire three-stage diagram of the shortest-route problem presented in Casette 14.1. It is clear in Figure 14.6 that there is only one path from a state s_n to a next state s_{n+1} in deterministic dynamic programming.

The shortest-route travel problem we discussed in Casette 14.1 is clearly deterministic since every path from a city in one stage to a city in the next stage is determined by the state (i.e., city) and policy decision (i.e., minimum travel time), but not by any probability distribution. We assumed that the travel time was known with certainty.

Casette 14.2   **DOWNJOHN PHARMACEUTICAL CORPORATION**

Downjohn is the producer of the widely used cold medicine Context. The company has been successful in increasing its market share in many areas. However, the company has experienced difficult distribution problems. The product is perishable and must be refrigerated. Tardy distribution will cause the medicine to spoil. The company has recently created the product distribution department because of the importance of distribution to the company's success.

Marcia Antonelli is the newly appointed manager of the product distribution department. She has been contemplating the establishment of a systematic method of distributing the product to three primary market areas—the Northeast, Midwest, and South. The product is distributed by company airplanes because of the product's perishability. Marcia has been informed by the sales manager that the maximum quantity of

Table 14.5   Forecasted Sales and Profits in the Three Market Areas

Product Sales (thousands of pounds)	Expected Profit ($1,000)		
	Northeast	Midwest	South
0	$ 0	$ 0	$ 0
1	8	6	6
2	15	12	12
3	23	20	19
4	30	28	28
5	36	36	36
6	40	40	43

the product available for distribution in the three market areas is 6,000 pounds per month.

Marcia asked her assistant, Sam Jones, how much profit the company could expect in the three market areas. Sam, who has a master's degree in management science, analyzed the past sales data based on several forecasting models. The forecasted sales and profits in each of the market areas are presented in Table 14.5. Because of shipping costs, the company has a policy that calls for transporting the product in units of 1,000 pounds.

The basic decision problem facing Marcia is how the company should distribute its product to the three market areas to maximize profits. Initially, Marcia thought the problem was rather simple. However, as she began to analyze it, the problem soon became quite complex. Reluctantly, Marcia asked Sam for help. After a few days of study, Sam came up with a systematic method for solving this problem.

Sam's solution procedure, based on dynamic programming, begins with definitions of basic terms: ,

1. *State:* The quantity of product to be distributed to each market area.

2. *Stage:* Each market for the product.

3. *Decision:* To determine how much of the product is to be assigned to each market.

4. *Return:* Profit from each market.

5. *Total return:* Accumulated profit at each stage.

On the basis of the above definitions, Sam developed the market stage relationships shown in Figure 14.7. Unlike the shortest-route problem, there is no concern about which market is treated as the first stage and which as the last. Thus, Sam begins the solution from the Northeast market district, treating it as the first stage.

Stage 1

For the Northeast market area, the company can distribute quantities (in 1,000-pound lots) of 0, 1, 2, 3, 4, 5, or 6 units of the product. The quantity of the product available for distribution in the Northeast market area is denoted by s_1. Since our problem is

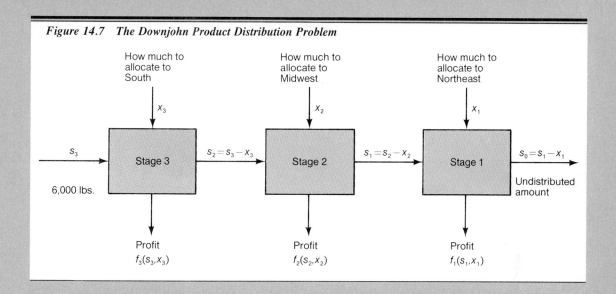

Figure 14.7   The Downnjohn Product Distribution Problem

to maximize profits, the recursive relationship for this problem can be expressed as follows:

$$f_n^*(s_n, x_n) = \max [c_{x_n} + f_{n-1}^* 1(s_{n-1})]$$

The total return, $f_1(s_1, x_1)$, in the first stage is exactly the same as the return c_{x_1}, assuming that all of the product would be sold. The computed returns from the quantities distributed and sold in the Northeast market district are presented in Table 14.6.

Stage 2

In Stage 2, we must decide how the available products need to be allocated to the Northeast and the Midwest market areas. In this stage, we can define the following:

s_2 = quantity of the product distributed to both the Northeast and the Midwest market areas

x_2 = quantity of the product allocated to the Midwest market area

$s_2 - x_2$ = quantity of the product allocated to the Northeast market area

Table 14.6   The Downnjohn First-Stage Analysis

Quantity, s_1, to Be Distributed (1,000 Pounds)	Decision x_1, Quantity to Be Allocated to Northeast (1,000 Pounds), and Associated Profit, $f_1(s_1)$ ($1,000)							Optimum Return, $f_1^*(s_1, x_1)$ ($1,000)
	0	1	2	3	4	5	6	
0	$0							$0
1	0	$8						8
2	0	8	$15					15
3	0	8	15	$23				23
4	0	8	15	23	$30			30
5	0	8	15	23	30	$36		36
6	0	8	15	23	30	36	$40	40

State variable s_2 can take a value of 0, 1, 2, 3, 4, 5, or 6, as shown earlier in Tables 14.5 and 14.6. For each possible value of s_2, we can consider several alternatives in allocating the product to the Midwest and the Northeast market areas. The recursive equation for this stage is

$$f_2^* (s_2, x_2) = \max [c_{x_2} + f_1^*(s_1)]$$

We can consider all seven possible values of s_2. For example, if $s_2 = 0$, then no allocation is possible. Thus, the expected profit (return) will be, of course, 0. If $s_2 = 1$, the value of total returns for $f_2(s_2 = 1)$ would be

$$f_2(s_2 = 1, x_2) = \max \begin{cases} c_{x_2} + f_1(s_1 = 1) = 0 + 8 = 8 & \text{(for } x_2 = 0) \\ c_{x_2} + f_1(s_1 = 0) = 6 + 0 = 6 & \text{(for } x_2 = 1) \end{cases}$$

In other words, the two alternatives open to Downjohn would be as follows:

Alternative 1	Midwest	Northeast
Allocation	0	1
Return	$0	$8

Alternative 2	Midwest	Northeast
Allocation	1	0
Return	$6	$0

From the above calculation, it is clear that when $s_2 = 1$ the first allocation scheme is a better alternative because its total return ($8 + $0 = $8) is greater than that of the second alternative ($0 + $6 = $6). In other words, if there is only one 1,000-pound lot of the product available for allocation, the entire amount should be distributed to the Northeast market.

We can use the same approach for the remaining values of s_2. For example, if $s_2 = 2$, we can evaluate three available allocation alternatives as follows:

Allocation to Midwest, x_2 (1,000 Pounds)	Allocation to Northeast, $s_2 - x_2$ (1,000 Pounds)	Immediate Return from Midwest, c_{x_2} ($1,000)	Optimum Return from Northeast, $f_1^*(s_1)$ ($1,000)	Total Return, $f_2(s_2,x_2)$ ($1,000)
0	2	$0	$15	$15
1	1	6	8	14
2	0	12	0	12

The computation becomes more tedious as the value of s_2 increases. However, the procedure is exactly the same. For example, if $s_2 = 4$, we can evaluate five possible allocation alternatives, as shown in Table 14.7. Now we are ready to develop a complete table of computations for all of the possible values of s_2, as presented in Table 14.8. In this table, the optimum decision value of x_2 (quantity to be allocated to the Midwest market) for various values of s_2 are circled.

Table 14.7   *Analysis of Allocation Alternatives for* $s_2 = 4$

Allocation to Midwest, x_2 (1,000 Pounds)	Allocation to Northeast, $s_2 - x_2$ (1,000 Pounds)	Immediate Return ($1,000)	Optimum Return in Stage 1 ($1,000)	Total Return, $f_2(s_2,x_2)$ ($1,000)	Optimum Alternative, $f_2^*(s_2,x_2)$
0	4	$0	$30	$30	←
1	3	6	23	29	
2	2	12	15	27	
3	1	20	8	28	
4	0	28	0	28	

Table 14.8   *The Downjohn Second-Stage Analysis*

Quantity, s_2, to Be Distributed (1,000 Pounds)	Decision x_2, Quantity to Be Allocated to Midwest (1,000 Pounds) and Associated Profit, $f_2(s_2,x_2)$($1,000)							Optimum Return, $f_2^*(s_2,x_2)$ ($1,000)
	0	1	2	3	4	5	6	
0	($0)							$0
1	(8)	$6						8
2	(15)	14	$12					15
3	(23)	21	20	$20				23
4	(30)	29	27	28	$28			30
5	(36)	(36)	35	35	(36)	($36)		36
6	40	42	42	43	43	(44)	$40	44

Stage 3

Now the computation for the third stage can be performed in a similar manner. The recursive relationship for the third stage is

$$f_3^*(s_3, x_3) = \max \left[c_{x_3} + f_2^*(s_2) \right]$$

For example, if $s_3 = 2$, we can evaluate the available allocation alternatives as follows:

Allocation to South, x_3 (1,000 Pounds)	Allocation to Northeast and/or Midwest $(s_3 - x_3)$ (1,000 Pounds)	Immediate Return from South, c_{x_3} ($1,000)	Optimum Return in Stage 2, $f_2^*(s_2)$ ($1,000)	Total Return, $f_3(s_3,x_3)$ ($1,000)
0	2	$0	$15	$15
1	1	6	8	14
2	0	12	0	12

Based on the return value c_{x3} and $f_2^*(s_2)$, the total return, $f_3(s_3,x_3)$, is computed in Table 14.9.

Table 14.9   The Downjohn Third-Stage Analysis

Quantity, s_3, to Be Distributed (1,000 Pounds)	Decision x_3, Quantity to Be Allocated to South (1,000 Pounds) and Associated Profit, $f_3(s_3,x_3)$($1,000)							Optimum Return $f_3^*(s_3,x_3)$ ($1,000)	Optimum Alternative
	0	1	2	3	4	5	6		
0	($0)							$0	
1	(8)	$6						8	
2	(15)	14	$12					15	
3	(23)	21	20	$19				23	
4	(30)	29	27	27	$28			30	
5	(36)	(36)	35	34	(36)	($36)		36	
6	(44)	42	42	42	43	(44)	$43	44	←

Now we are ready to identify the maximum return and the optimum decision alternative. From Table 14.9 we can easily ascertain that $f_3^*(s_3) = 44 (i.e., $44,000) and $x_3^* = 0$ or 5. If we choose $x_3^* = 0$ (no allocation to the South), we would have 6,000 pounds of the product for the Northeast and Midwest market areas. On the other hand, if we choose $x_3^* = 5$, we will have only 1,000 pounds left for sale in either the Northeast or the Midwest market. Thus, we have alternative optimum solutions. The value of state variable s_2 would be as follows:

$$\text{If } x_3 = 0, \text{ then } s_2 = 0, 1, 2, 3, 4, 5, 6$$
$$\text{If } x_3 = 5, \text{ then } s_2 = 0, 1$$

From Table 14.8 we can find the value of the two solution pairs (x_2, x_3); either (5, 0) or (0, 5). Now we can proceed to the first-stage problem to find the value of x_1. Since Downjohn would sell all of the product except 1,000 pounds in either case, the only possible value for s_1 is 1. Therefore, we can obtain $x_1 = 1$ from Table 14.6.

Summarizing the result, we can derive the following two solutions:

Market	Solution 1 Allocation (1,000 Pounds)	Solution 1 Profit ($1,000)	Solution 2 Allocation (1,000 Pounds)	Solution 2 Profit ($1,000)
Northeast	1	8	1	8
Midwest	5	36	0	0
South	0	0	5	36
Total	6	44	6	44

In the previous two casettes, we dealt with typical problems that could be solved by dynamic programming. In Casette 14.3, we will study another example of a typical application of dynamic programming — production scheduling and inventory control.

Casette 14.3   ACE MANUFACTURING COMPANY

Hagar Prudence, a systems engineer in the Ace Manufacturing Company, developed a new component to be used in mining equipment. Hagar was promoted to production manager of Ace's newly established mining tool plant. As a new production manager, Hagar felt he should develop a systematic way of minimizing production cost while satisfying customer demand. Hagar sought to make his department the most productive in the company.

The first thing Hagar analyzed was future demand. He knew future demand for the new component would be very unstable and subject to great fluctuation. He decided the only reliable forecast would be relatively short term. The estimated demands for four future planning periods are shown in Table 14.10.

The production cost of this new component is $1 per unit. Setup cost is $90. Ace produces the product in batches of 30 units owing to the very expensive setup cost and marketing problems. Because of packing and delivery operations, the product has been sold wholesale also in batches of 30 units. The maximum production capacity is 180 units per period. Other fixed costs associated with production are not included here because those costs are not affected by the decision at each period. The total production cost is expressed as follows:

$$\text{Total production cost} = \$90 + \$30x_i \quad (\text{for } 0 < x_i \le 6)$$

or
$$\$0 \quad (\text{for } x_i = 0)$$

where x_i = the multiple of 30 units of products for period i.

Hagar estimates that the inventory holding cost is $15 for a batch of 30 units per period. Since this is a new product, he can safely assume the final period to be 0 to avoid the unnecessary cost of storage. After determining the important cost factors and demand, the objective is clear: minimize total production and inventory costs while satisfying customer demand. Since the problem is one of multiperiod optimization, he decides to use dynamic programming.

Hagar defined the basic terms as follows:

1. *Stage:* The number of periods remaining n.

2. *State:* The amount of inventory at the beginning of the stage I_n.

3. *Decision:* The production level at each stage. The decision variable is expressed by x_n.

Table 14.10   Demand Forecast for Ace Manufacturing

Planning Period	Estimated Batches (units)
1	$S_4 = 2$ (60)
2	$S_3 = 3$ (90)
3	$S_2 = 2$ (60)
4	$S_1 = 4$ (120)

4. *Return:* Total production cost for the current stage f_n (I_n).

5. *Total return:* The accumulated sum of total production costs up to the current stage.

Figures 14.8 and 14.9 show one-stage and four-stage diagrams of the problem.

To find the current inventory level, Hagar made the transition equation for inventory level a function of three variables: the previous inventory level I_n, the production level of the previous period x_n, and the product sold in the previous period S_n. It is assumed that the product sold in any period is equal to the demand forecast given in Table 14.10.

The transition equation for inventory level is

$$I_{n-1} = I_n + x_n - S_n$$

The total production cost (i.e., return) for each stage is

$$c_n (x_n, I_n) = 90 + 30x_n + 15I_n \quad \text{(for } 0 < x_n \leq 6\text{)}$$

or

$$0 \quad \text{(for } x_n = 0\text{)}$$

Finally, the general recursive relationship was easily obtained using the functions described above. The recursive function for total production cost is

$$f_n(I_n) = \min [c_n(x_n, I_n) + f^*_{n-1}(I_n + x_n - S_n)]$$

subject to

$$x_n + I_n \geq S_n$$

$$0 \leq x_n \leq 6$$

Once all the necessary relationships were established, Hagar started with the last period (i.e., period 4) and proceeded backward. Since at every stage the optimum decision (the production level that yields the minimum production cost) is determined by the previous optimum value, he was confident that the principle of optimality was satisfied.

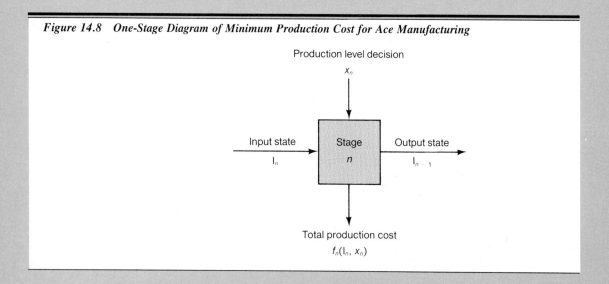

Figure 14.8   One-Stage Diagram of Minimum Production Cost for Ace Manufacturing

Production level decision

x_n

Input state   Stage   Output state

I_n n I_{n-1}

Total production cost

$f_n(I_n, x_n)$

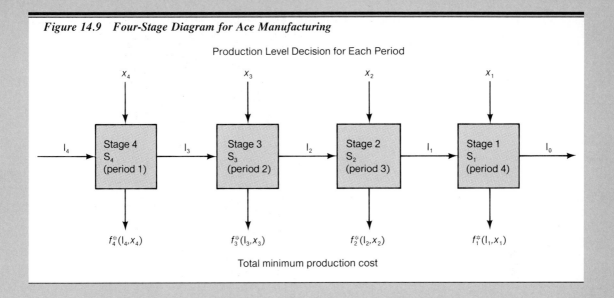

Figure 14.9 Four-Stage Diagram for Ace Manufacturing

Production Level Decision for Each Period

Total minimum production cost

Stage 1

First, we will examine the single-stage problem for stage 1. The total production cost associated with the state variable I would be

$$f_1(I_1) = \min [c_1 (x_1, I_1) + f_0^* (I_1 + x_1 - S_1)]$$

However, $f_0^* (I_1 + x_1 - S_1) = 0$, since it is assumed that there will be no inventory at the end of period 4. Therefore

$$f_1 (I_1) = \min c_1 (x_1, I_1)$$

Using the above equation, we find that the total production cost $f_1(I_1)$, the minimum production cost $f_1^*(I_1)$, and the optimum decision variable x_1^* are determined as shown in Table 14.11.

Table 14.11 Single-Stage Problem

State Variable I_1	Total Production Cost $f_1(I_1)$ x_1					Minimum Return $f_1^*(I_1)$	Optimum Decision x_1^*
	0	1	2	3	4		
0					$210	$210	4
1				$180 +15		195	3
2			$150 +30			180	2
3		$120 +45				165	1
4	$60					60	0*

Note that the possible values of inventory levels are the integer values from 0 to 4. Since there is a demand for 120 units (i.e., 4 batches of 30 units) for period 4, depending on the different values of inventory level I_1, we can make different decisions. Since $S_1 = 4$ (120 units), $I_1 + x_1 = 4$. For example, if $I_1 = 4$, then $x_1 = 0$. In this case, the only cost involved will be the inventory cost of $15 per batch, or $60. However, if $I_1 = 3$, then $x_1 = 1$. In this case, the total cost will be $90 (setup cost) + $30 ($1 × 30 units) + $45 (inventory cost, $15 × 3 batches) = $120 + $45 = $165.

Stage 2

Now let us look at the two-stage problem, which includes periods 3 and 4. The sum of production and inventory must be greater than or equal to the forecast demand of 6 batches (180 units) for periods 3 and 4. Thus, the possible values of I_2 would range from 0 to 6. We can calculate the sum of production and inventory costs in a similar manner.

The total production cost is calculated by summing the production cost in the current stage [i.e., $c_2(x_1, I_2)$] and the total production cost in the previous stage [i.e., $f_1^*(I_2 + x_2 - S_2)$]. Mathematically, the function is

$$f_2(I_2) = \min [c_2(x_2, I_2) + f_1^*(I_2 + x_2 - S_2)]$$

The results of the two-stage problem are presented in Table 14.12. Each cost entry consists of two costs — production cost (including setup cost) and inventory cost. For example, if $I_2 = 0$ and $x_2 = 2$, then the production cost for period 3 will be $90 + $60 = $150 and the inventory cost will be 0. However, since the total demand is 6

Table 14.12   Two-Stage Problem

State Variable I_2	Total Production Cost $f_2(I_2)$							Minimum Return $f_2^*(I_2)$	Optimum Decision x_2^*
	0	**1**	**2**	**3**	**4**	**5**	**6**		
0			$150 +210	$180 +195	$210 +180	$240 +165	$270 +60	$330	6*
1		$135 +210	165 +195	195 +180	225 +165	255 +60		315	5
2	$30 +210	150 +195	180 +180	210 +165	240 +60			240	0
3	45 +195	165 +180	195 +165	225 +60				240	0
4	60 +180	180 +165	210 +60					240	0
5	75 +165	195 +60						240	0
6	90 +60							150	0

batches (180 units), production for period 4 will be $x_1 = 4$. The minimum return for this decision is $210, as shown in Table 14.11. Thus, the return $f_2(I_2 = 0, x_2 = 2)$ is $360. This calculation procedure identifies the optimum value of x_2.

Stage 3

We now face the three-stage problem, which includes periods 2, 3, and 4. At the beginning of period 1, there was no inventory. Thus, we know that inventory in period 2 is determined by subtracting the sales in period 1 from the production in period 1. In other words, $I_3 = x_4 - S_4$. The forecasted sales in period 1 are determined as 2 ($S_4 = 2$). Thus, we can easily determine that I_3 can range from 0 to 4.

The total production and inventory cost $f_3(I_3)$ is determined by

$$f_3(I_3) = \min [c_3(x_3, I_3) + f_2^*(I_3 + x_3 - S_3)]$$

The computation is exactly the same as the previous stage. The minimum total production cost $f_3^*(I_3)$ is obtained with optimum decision x_3^*. The results are shown in Table 14.13. For example, if $x_3 = 3$ and $I_3 = 2$, then the total production cost would be $90 (setup cost) + $90 (production cost of 3 batches) = $180, and the inventory cost will be $30. Since the forecast demand for period 2 is 3 batches (90 units), if $I_3 = 2$, we must produce at least 1 batch. If we produce 3 batches in period 2, then $x_3 = 3$ and we will have 2 surplus batches. Since the total demand for periods 3 and 4 is 6 batches, we must still produce 4 more batches during periods 3 and 4. Thus, $I_2 = 2$. We find $f_2^*(I_2 = 2) = $240 in Table 14.12. Thus, the total cost for $x_3 = 3$ and $I_3 = 2$ will be $210 + $240 = $450, as shown in Table 14.13.

Stage 4

The last stage is easy to calculate because the only value of I_4 is 0. The total production cost $f_4(I_4)$ is

$$f_4(I_4) = \min [c_4(x_4, I_4) + f_3^*(I_4 + x_4 - S_4)]$$

Table 14.13   Three-Stage Problem

State Variable I_3	Total Production Cost $f_3(I_3)$ x_3							Minimum Return $f_3^*(I_3)$	Optimum Decision x_3^*
	0	1	2	3	4	5	6		
0				$180 +330	$210 +315	$240 +240	$270 +240	$480	5
1			$165 +330	195 +315	225 +240	255 +240	285 +240	465	4
2			$150 +330	180 +315	210 +240	240 +240	270 +240	300 +240	450	3
3		$45 +330	165 +315	195 +240	225 +240	255 +240	285 +240	315 +150	375	0*
4	60 +315	180 +240	210 +240	240 +240	270 +240	300 +150		375	0

Table 14.14 Four-Stage Problem

State Variable I_4	Total Production Cost $f_4(I_4)$ x_4						Minimum Return $f_4^*(I_4)$	Optimum Decision x_4^*
	0	1	2	3	4	5	6		
0			$150 +480	$180 +465	$210 +450	$240 +375	$270 +375	$615	5*

Using the same computation procedure, we obtain the optimum solution of the four-stage problem as shown in Table 14.14. This is the optimum solution for the entire problem. The minimum total production cost for the four periods is $615.

Optimum Solution

Now we have to determine the optimum decision variable at each stage:

Stage 4 Clearly, $x_4^* = 5$.

Stage 3 Since $I_3 = I_4 + x_4 - S_4$, while $I_4 = 0$, $x_4 = 5$, and $S_4 = 2$, we obtain $I_3 = 3$. From Table 14.13, we obtain $x_3^* = 0$.

Stage 2 Since $I_2 = I_3 + x_3 - S_3$, while $I_3 = 3$, $x_3 = 0$, and $S_3 = 3$, we obtain $I_2 = 0$. From Table 14.12, we obtain $x_2^* = 6$.

Stage 1 Since $I_1 = I_2 + x_2 - S_2$, while $I_2 = 0$, $x_2 = 6$, and $S_2 = 2$, we obtain $I_2 = 4$. From Table 14.11, we obtain $x_1^* = 0$.

The optimum solution is shown below:

Period	Production Quantity (batches)	Production Cost ($)	Demand (batches)	Inventory Quantity (batches)	Inventory Cost ($)	Production and Inventory Cost ($)
1	5	240	2	3	45	285
2	0	0	3	0	0	0
3	6	270	2	4	60	330
4	0	0	4	0	0	0
					Total cost =	615

PROBABILISTIC DYNAMIC PROGRAMMING

In the previous section, we discussed deterministic dynamic programming. We know that deterministic dynamic programming deals with problems in which a transition from one state to another is known with certainty, yielding a series of returns that result in a total return. However, in many cases we face situations in which a transition from one state to another is associated with a probability distribution. In other words, a state of the next stage is determined by the probability distribution, which in turn is determined by the previous state. This probability, referred to as *transition probability*, is an important concept in decision making under risk. This advanced topic of dynamic programming is beyond the scope of this book. If you are interested in this topic, consult the books listed in the References.

COMPUTER SOLUTIONS OF DYNAMIC PROGRAMMING

Dynamic programming is an effective tool for multistage problems. However, many real-world problems involve a large number of stages and are just too complex to solve by hand. Thus, computer-based solution is a prerequisite for any complex dynamic programming problem. In this section, we will discuss computer solutions of casette problems we have discussed in this chapter, through *Micro Manager*.

Figure 14.10 presents the Washington, D.C. Conference problem that we discussed as Casette 14.1. The computer solution presents the input data entered and the program output. The solution indicates that the shortest route is 1→4→6→8 (Los Angeles → Dallas → Pittsburgh → Washington, D.C.) with the total of 9 hours of flying time. This result corresponds exactly with our manual solution.

Figure 14.11 shows the computer solution of the Downjohn Pharmaceutical Corporation problem presented as Casette 14.2. The optimum solution indicates that allo-

Figure 14.10   Computer Solution of the Washington, D.C. Conference Problem

PROGRAM: Dynamic Programming

***** INPUT DATA ENTERED *****

Network/Minimization problem

Stage	State	Nodes	Return value
3	1	1 ---> 2	4.00
		1 ---> 3	5.00
		1 ---> 4	2.00
2	2	2 ---> 5	3.00
		2 ---> 6	6.00
		2 ---> 7	7.00
	3	3 ---> 5	3.00
		3 ---> 6	4.00
		3 ---> 7	2.00
	4	4 ---> 5	7.00
		4 ---> 6	5.00
		4 ---> 7	6.00
1	5	5 ---> 8	4.00
	6	6 ---> 8	2.00
	7	7 ---> 8	3.00

Recursion function: f(n) = R(n) + f(n-1)

(continued)

Figure 14.10   (continued)

```
*****    PROGRAM OUTPUT    *****
```

Stage 1

S(n)	D(n)	R(n)	S(n-1)	f(n-1)	f(n)
5	5 --> 8	4.000	8	0.000	4.000
6	6 --> 8	2.000	8	0.000	2.000
7	7 --> 8	3.000	8	0.000	3.000

Stage 2

S(n)	D(n)	R(n)	S(n-1)	f(n-1)	f(n)
2	2 --> 5	3.000	5	4.000	7.000
2	2 --> 6	6.000	6	2.000	8.000
2	2 --> 7	7.000	7	3.000	10.000
3	3 --> 5	3.000	5	4.000	7.000
3	3 --> 6	4.000	6	2.000	6.000
3	3 --> 7	2.000	7	3.000	5.000
4	4 --> 5	7.000	5	4.000	11.000
4	4 --> 6	5.000	6	2.000	7.000
4	4 --> 7	6.000	7	3.000	9.000

Stage 3

S(n)	D(n)	R(n)	S(n-1)	f(n-1)	f(n)
1	1 --> 2	4.000	2	7.000	11.000
1	1 --> 3	5.000	3	5.000	10.000
1	1 --> 4	2.000	4	7.000	9.000

Final Solution

Stage	Optimal Dn	Optimal Rn
3	1 --> 4	2.000
2	4 --> 6	5.000
1	6 --> 8	2.000
	Total	9.000

Figure 14.11   Computer Solution of the Downjohn Pharmaceutical Corporation Problem

PROGRAM: Dynamic Programming

***** INPUT DATA ENTERED *****

Nonnetwork/Maximization problem

Maximum value of decisions: 6
Value of state in stage 3 : 6

Transition function: S(n-1) = S(n) - D(n)

Recursion function: f(n) = R(n) + f(n-1)

Return function

		Stages	
Decisions	3	2	1
0	0.00	0.00	0.00
1	8.00	6.00	6.00
2	15.00	12.00	12.00
3	23.00	20.00	19.00
4	30.00	28.00	28.00
5	36.00	36.00	36.00
6	40.00	40.00	43.00

***** PROGRAM OUTPUT *****

Stage 1

S(n)	D(n)	R(n)	S(n-1)	f(n-1)	f(n)
0	0	0.000	0	0.000	0.000
1	0	0.000	0	0.000	0.000
1	1	6.000	0	0.000	6.000
2	0	0.000	0	0.000	0.000
2	1	6.000	0	0.000	6.000
2	2	12.000	0	0.000	12.000
3	0	0.000	0	0.000	0.000
3	1	6.000	0	0.000	6.000
3	2	12.000	0	0.000	12.000
3	3	19.000	0	0.000	19.000

(continued)

Figure 14.11 *(continued)*

4	0	0.000	0	0.000	0.000
4	1	6.000	0	0.000	6.000
4	2	12.000	0	0.000	12.000
4	3	19.000	0	0.000	19.000
4	4	28.000	0	0.000	28.000
5	0	0.000	0	0.000	0.000
5	1	6.000	0	0.000	6.000
5	2	12.000	0	0.000	12.000
5	3	19.000	0	0.000	19.000
5	4	28.000	0	0.000	28.000
5	5	36.000	0	0.000	36.000
6	0	0.000	0	0.000	0.000
6	1	6.000	0	0.000	6.000
6	2	12.000	0	0.000	12.000
6	3	19.000	0	0.000	19.000
6	4	28.000	0	0.000	28.000
6	5	36.000	0	0.000	36.000
6	6	43.000	0	0.000	43.000

Stage 2

$S(n)$	$D(n)$	$R(n)$	$S(n-1)$	$f(n-1)$	$f(n)$
0	0	0.000	0	0.000	0.000
1	0	0.000	1	6.000	6.000
1	1	6.000	0	0.000	6.000
2	0	0.000	2	12.000	12.000
2	1	6.000	1	6.000	12.000
2	2	12.000	0	0.000	12.000
3	0	0.000	3	19.000	19.000
3	1	6.000	2	12.000	18.000
3	2	12.000	1	6.000	18.000
3	3	20.000	0	0.000	20.000
4	0	0.000	4	28.000	28.000
4	1	6.000	3	19.000	25.000
4	2	12.000	2	12.000	24.000
4	3	20.000	1	6.000	26.000
4	4	28.000	0	0.000	28.000
5	0	0.000	5	36.000	36.000
5	1	6.000	4	28.000	34.000
5	2	12.000	3	19.000	31.000
5	3	20.000	2	12.000	32.000
5	4	28.000	1	6.000	34.000
5	5	36.000	0	0.000	36.000

(continued)

Figure 14.11   (continued)

6	0	0.000	6	43.000	43.000
6	1	6.000	5	36.000	42.000
6	2	12.000	4	28.000	40.000
6	3	20.000	3	19.000	39.000
6	4	28.000	2	12.000	40.000
6	5	36.000	1	6.000	42.000
6	6	40.000	0	0.000	40.000

Stage 3

$S(n)$	$D(n)$	$R(n)$	$S(n-1)$	$f(n-1)$	$f(n)$
6	0	0.000	6	43.000	43.000
6	1	8.000	5	36.000	44.000
6	2	15.000	4	28.000	43.000
6	3	23.000	3	20.000	43.000
6	4	30.000	2	12.000	42.000
6	5	36.000	1	6.000	42.000
6	6	40.000	0	0.000	40.000

Final Solution

Stage	Optimal Dn	Optimal Rn
3	1.000	8.000
2	0.000	0.000
1	5.000	36.000
Total	6.000	44.000

cations should be: stage 1 (Northeast) — 1,000 pounds; stage 2 (Midwest) — 0; and stage 3 (South) — 5,000 pounds. The total profit of the solution is $44,000. This solution corresponds with our manual solution.

REAL-WORLD APPLICATIONS

There have been a number of interesting real-world applications of dynamic programming. Some of these studies deal with such diverse problems as inventory control, investment analysis, work force scheduling, resource allocation, police force development, and network optimization. Most of these studies report design and implementation of dynamic programming models for sequential decision-making problems. In this section, we will consider three application examples of dynamic programming.

Sporting Events Planning Benefits from Dynamic Programming

Sport has proven a fertile ground for the application of management science, particularly dynamic programming. This may be attributable in part to the competitive nature of sports—participants are eager to attain the optimum "solution." Orienteering requires careful planning on the part of event organizers, as destinations, controls, and rescue teams must be strategically located. Annual orienteering competitions held in the Lake District of England attempt to present challenging courses with less-than-obvious route selection, providing a chance to apply dynamic programming.[1]

The problem facing an orienteering competitor is to reach a control or destination point as fast as possible—preferably ahead of all other participants. Elevation contours and ground conditions vary continuously by minute increments, making an exact model suitable for simple programming. A condensed version of the landscape to be traversed must be generated; in this case, a grid was placed over the map, with every intersection assigned values corresponding to its elevation and estimated travel time to each adjacent point in the eight standard compass directions. However, possible options multiply very rapidly under this type of network and quickly become unmanageable. This is where dynamic programming steps in, with a shortest-route function matching the one discussed in this chapter:

$$f_n(i) = \min_j Nt(i, j) + f_{n-1}(j)$$

where

$f_n(i)$ = optimal time from i to goal in at most n steps

$t(i, j)$ = time from i to j

$f_{n-1}(j)$ = previously determined minimum time from j to goal in at most $n - 1$ steps

The computer model suggested various routes converging at the selected goal, each route representing the optimal route from various starting points or intermediate points that competitors might select. Time data are indicated for each route at key points. Tested against the winner of the Mountain Trail, the computer-generated optimal route rather closely followed the winner's route (which incidentally did not remotely resemble a straight line). Only near the end of the stretch did the actual winner divert from the suggested route—because he factored in his desire for fresh water from a known spring on a different track and his superior running ability (whereas the computer output indicated a shorter route that required walking up a steep slope). In addition to suggesting optimal routes, the program also indicates points where convergence of several routes is likely—these are suitable for aid stations or monitors.

Blue Bell Trims Inventories to Bolster Profits

Inventory carrying costs can substantially affect the well-being of a company, particularly if it is engaged in manufacturing apparel. Blue Bell, Inc. is one of the world's largest clothing manufacturers, better known by its business names of Wrangler, Red Kap, and Jantzen.[2] Over 27,000 people work for Blue Bell in 95 plants and 49 distri-

---

[1] M. Hayes and J. M. Norman, "Dynamic Programming in Orienteering: Route Choice and the Siting of Controls," *Journal of the Operational Research Society* 35:9 (1984), 791–796.

[2] Jerry Edwards, Harvey Wagner, and William Wood, "Blue Bell Trims Its Inventory," *Interfaces* 15:1 (1985), 34–52.

bution centers worldwide. Fiscal 1983 sales totaled $1.2 billion, with $48 million net income.

Blue Bell's averge inventory before implementation of a management science program was over $371 million, more than half of the company's total asset base. High interest rates on short-term borrowing and warehousing and obsolescence costs caused inventory carrying charges that were believed to total at least 25 percent of the inventory investment. In terms of dollars spent, inventory carrying costs were double the actual net income.

Market conditions were changing, with a dramatic rise in the number of stock keeping units (detailed product types), less inventorying by Blue Bell's customers and hence a shorter order lead time for Blue Bell, and greater demands by the major customers for on-time, complete shipments. Blue Bell found itself manufacturing for stock and absorbing huge inventory carrying costs.

The decision to reduce inventory while maintaining service levels required a concentrated task force effort. The first target was the Wrangler group of products, comprised of four profit centers. Thirty-seven plants and over 10,000 individual inventory units were involved in the annual production of 35 million pairs of men's jeans—only one part of one of the profit centers. The task force approached the problem in three stages: diagnosis of the potential inventory reduction, program development, and implementation. Seasonal demand, materials contracts, and desired service levels were reconciled with management's constant work force policy. Sales forecasts and safety stocks were incorporated in the plan. In addition, a linear programming model was developed to reduce fabric waste in the cutting operation.

Once the decision to implement the inventory planning model had been made, dynamic programming systems were installed to forecast sales, plan capacity, plan lots, forecast sizes, plan sizes, and establish cutting patterns. Intense interest and involvement by top management filtered through the company and ensured successful implementation. A parallel test with the old planning system actually used for production was run on one lot. This was followed by a "live" test where production was actually scheduled by the new model. With high user involvement, the test was expanded to a group of lots, then a product line, then to all the Wrangler divisions.

Results were almost immediately apparent. With no reduction in product line or sales, inventory was reduced by 31 percent to $256 million. Short-term debt dropped by nearly 60 percent, and cash and securities increased from $8 million to $90 million in 1 year. Interest expense declined by $16 million, and fabric cost savings were increased, and the service level was maintained or improved throughout Blue Bell's divisions.

Oil Supply Disruption Motivates Preventive Stockpiling

The availability of oil in international markets depended until recently on the internal policies of the Organization of Petroleum Exporting Countries (OPEC). The potential for disruption of OPEC oil supplies was a matter of major concern to many nations, with analysis of several options following naturally.[3] Chief among possible government or private policies was the idea of stockpiling oil—in essence, buying while it was

---

[3]Hung-Po Chao and Alan Manne, "Oil Stockpiles and Import Reductions: A Dynamic Programming Approach," *Operations Research* 31:4 (1983), 632–651.

available (even though this would raise the price) and saving it for troubled times. Stockpiling oil isn't cheap—both physical storage and capital costs must be considered. Oil stockpiles serve as an insurance policy, preventing huge losses during problem years.

Both the value of the insurance and the cost of oil vary with time, international demand, and OPEC politics. A break-even probability exists, given various values, where the cost of insurance (stockpiling oil) matches the expected loss based on the probability of a disruption occurring. Sequential decision analysis allows for an objective evaluation of this situation. Dynamic programming serves as a guide to the optimum decision at each succesive point in time, based on historical information and known oil inventories.

The *Stockpile* dynamic programming model evaluates alternative policies by their expected impact on future consumption. Required inputs include labor force, capital, and rate-of-investment data. The objective is to maximize future consumption, valuing each year's consumption with a discount factor and incorporating stockpiling recommendations based on the probability of disruptions. Prices react to demand by U.S. and foreign importers, with increases in stockpiles causing increases in demand. Further inputs to the base-case model were based on assumptions of disruption probabilities, price-demand reactions, coordinated efforts by oil-importing countries, OPEC production capacities, general demand increases, physical storage costs, net discount rate, GNP loss function, and time intervals.

Stockpile showed that maintaining oil stockpiles of varying sizes would reduce adverse effects of disruptions but not eliminate them. A 1.4 billion barrel stockpile was indicated as optimal (for 1985). A stockpile of 0 would indicate replenishment of 1 million barrels per day; as the inventoty approaches the optimum level, the fill rate would decrease. A stockpile over 1.4 billion barrels would provide oil for current use, declining more rapidly as the size of the excess inventory increased. In years when disruptions in the oil market occur, the stockpile should be drawn down by a minimum critical amount, plus a marginal amount of the remaining stockpile.

Economic effects of a policy such as that recommended by *Stockpile* would show loss reductions in troubled years, paid for in part by higher oil prices and inventory costs during calm years. The model showed that for a major disruption, based on an original oil price of $30 per barrel, the absence of a U.S. stockpile would cause prices to rise to just over $100 per barrel, whereas a 1 billion barrel inventory would hold the imported oil cost (on the world market) to just under $68 per barrel. Other oil importers would naturally benefit from the lower price but would have paid higher prices while the United States built its stockpile. The authors indicate that following an optimum stockpile policy from 1980 to 1995 would produce expected net benefits of $13 billion, or a 9 percent reduction in losses from oil production disruptions.

SUMMARY

Dynamic programming is a powerful technique for solving multistage problems. Dynamic programming deals with state variables, stages, decisions (variables), returns, and a recursive relationship for subproblems (e.g., single-stage, two-stage). Dynamic programming uses decomposition of complex programs into smaller and simpler subproblems. The computation procedure is almost identical for each subproblem, and for each subproblem a suboptimum solution is obtained. Dynamic programming eliminates much of the computational effort required in complete enumeration. Depending on the characteristics of the operators in recursive relationships, the computational procedure may be rather cumbersome. Nevertheless, it is much better than enumeration of all of the possible solution vectors.

In this chapter we have dealt only with finite-stage deterministic dynamic programming. If you are interested in more advanced techniques and applications of dynamic programming, consult the following References.

Glossary

Backward Approach Process of solving dynamic programming problems by beginning with the last decision to be made then moving sequentially back to the earliest decision.

Decomposition The breaking up of a problem into smaller, interrelated subproblems (or stages) to simplify solution—a primary characteristic of dynamic programming.

Deterministic Dynamic Programming Programming that involves no probabilities in the decision to select the next state; all values involved are known and fixed.

Policy Decision The intention to make a decision based on a previously established guideline or policy, allowing for all possible conditions.

Probabilistic Dynamic Programming When the decision value associated with a transition from one state to another involves a probability distribution, the advanced techniques of probabilistic dynamic programming must be used.

Recursive Relation The mathematical expression of the decision policy, indicating the relationship between stages and decision variables, which is to be optimized (maximized or minimized) for each stage of the problem.

Return The value derived by attaining a given state during a particular stage (decision). Return may be in terms of costs or rewards.

Segmentation See **Decomposition.**

Sequential Decision Making Based on a series of stages, dynamic programming provides information about the decisions that should be made in an orderly sequence.

Stage A decision point in a dynamic programming problem, involving selection of one of several available states. A stage is one step in the sequential decision process.

State The current condition of a problem in a given stage. Several alternative states may exist in a particular stage.

References

Bellman, Richard. *Dynamic Programming*. Princeton, N.J.: Princeton University Press, 1957.

Bellman, Richard, and Dreyfus, Stuart. *Applied Dynamic Programming*. Princeton, N.J.: Princeton University Press, 1962.

Howard, Ronald A. "Dynamic Programming." *Management Science* 12:5 (Jan. 1966), 317–345.

Kaufman, Arnold, and Cruon, R. *Dynamic Programming: Sequential Scientific Management*. New York: Academic Press, 1967.

Nemhauser, George L. *Introduction to Dynamic Programming*. New York: Wiley, 1966.

Wagner, Harvey M. *Principles of Operations Research*. Englewood Cliffs, N.J.: Prentice-Hall, 1969.

White, D. J. *Dynamic Programming*. San Francisco: Holden-Day, 1969.

Assignments

14.1 What is the difference between dynamic programming and linear programming?

14.2 Explain the following terms: *decomposition* (or *segmentation*), *multistage* (or *sequential*) decisions.

14.3 Discuss the principle of optimality.

14.4 Discuss the differences and similarities between the *backward* approach and the *forward* approach.

14.5 Why is dynamic programming a better method than complete enumeration?

14.6 Define the following terms: *stage, state, policy decision, return, total return*.

14.7 List the typical application areas of dynamic programming.

14.8 Describe the additive recursive relationship and explain it by using the terms in Problem 14.6.

14.9 How does probabilistic dynamic programming differ from deterministic dynamic programming?

14.10 John Lynch inherited $3,000 from his grandmother and decided to invest it in stocks. A local brokerage firm suggested three stocks: X, Y, and Z. The following table indicates the probable return for each stock:

Investment ($1,000)	Return on Investment		
	Stock X	Stock Y	Stock Z
0	0%	0%	0%
1	5	5	4
2	15	15	26
3	40	40	40

Obviously, John wants to maximize the total return, which is the sum of the individual returns. It is assumed that the return from each stock is independent of investments in other stocks.
   a. Illustrate the problem graphically with states, stages, decisions, and returns.
   b. Determine the transition function.
   c. Determine the optimum mix of stocks by using dynamic programming.

14.11 The Harwell Software Company plans to develop an efficient procurement plan over the next 2 years. The estimated demand for the critical items the company intends to purchase is given as follows:

Year:	1	2
Demand:	100	200

The procurement cost is estimated to be 20¢ per unit with the condition that the quantities be purchased in multiples of 100 at the beginning of each period; a maximum of 400 units can be purchased. Holding cost is $0.10 per unit per year. The current maximum storage capacity is 200 units. Total cost is expressed as the sum of procurement cost and holding cost for 2 years. Assume that there is no stock on hand at the beginning of the first year and at the end of the second year.

    a. Develop the dynamic programming formulation with the illustration of states, stages, decisions, returns, and transition function.

    b. Determine the optimum quantity of procurement.

14.12 The Harwell Software Company has developed a new mathematical programming software for mini- and microcomputers and has contracted to develop the package over the next four production periods. The lack of skilled programmers and other engineering capabilities limits the production of the package to 10 units per period. The storage cost per unit of software is $20. The table below shows the production costs and sales contracted:

Period	Production Cost	Sales Contracted
1	$350	6
2	360	7
3	400	12
4	380	6

Jim Harwell, president and chief system analyst, wants to satisfy the contracts within the current capacity of the firm; he also wants to minimize cost. Note that the ending state is expressed as the beginning inventory plus the production quantity minus sales.

    a. Formulate a dynamic model for the problem.

    b. Show the solution procedure stage by stage. (*Hint:* Four stages are needed.)

    c. Determine the optimum quantity of product and total cost.

14.13 The Water Resource Management Council of the county is responsible for providing water to the towns in the county. This council decided to provide water to the newly developing town of Plainview. A systems analyst group has estimated the costs to be incurred for adding new capacity such as pipes and other necessary equipment.

The estimated costs are given in the illustration below:

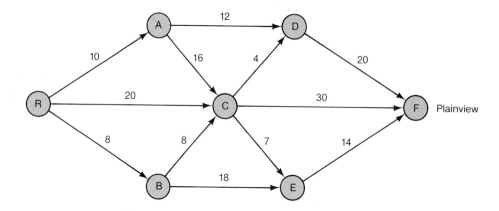

a. Formulate a dynamic programming model for the problem.
b. Solve the problem by the complete enumeration method.
c. Show the solution procedure step by step.
d. Determine the most economic path to use for providing water to Plainview.

14.14 The Jensen Laboratories has three popular products for general health care: Comtol I, Comtol II, and Comtol X. The company currently has three machines that can produce any of the three products. The production scheduling is prepared in such a manner that once a machine is set up for one product that machine must run for a week without being changed. The production scheduler is responsible for determining how many machines are to be used to produce each product. The following table presents the estimated profit for the three products in terms of machines scheduled:

Number of Machines	Forecast Profit per Week ($100)		
	Comtol I	Comtol II	Comtol X
1	50	45	15
2	57	75	48
3	82	96	84

a. Formulate the problem by using dynamic programming.
b. Determine the optimum number of machines to be assigned to each product for the coming week.

14.15 Refer to Problem 14.14. To maximize the profit, the production manager decides that two more machines will be installed to produce any one of the three products. The new machines are assumed to have the same capability as the machines currently in use. The estimated profits for the fourth and fifth machines to be added are as follows:

Number	Forecast Profit per Week ($100)		
of Machines	Comtol I	Comtol II	Comtol X
4	95	105	92
5	108	112	110

a. Formulate the problem by using dynamic programming.

b. Determine the optimum number of machines to be assigned to each product for the coming week.

14.16 Richard Armando, a Maine fisherman, owns his own fishing boat. His boat is usually inspected every 2 years. At a time of inspection, he decides whether the boat is to be overhauled or replaced. If the boat does not pass the inspection, he sells it for scrap material. The cost figures for overhaul and the scrap values of boats with different ages are given in the table below:

Boat's Age (years)	Overhaul Cost	Scrap Value
2	$ 3,000	$20,000
4	7,000	10,000
6	10,000	4,000

The current market price for a new fishing boat is about $50,000. The boat that Mr. Armando owns is about 4 years old. When the boat is 6 years old, Mr. Armando plans to sell it for scrap material.

    a. Formulate the problem by using dynamic programming. (*Hint:* There are only two decision variables—replace and overhaul.)

    b. Determine the optimum replacement plan.

14.17 Refer to Problem 14.16. Mr. Armando decided to continue using the fishing boat because of a lack of cash on hand. He figured out that he could use the fishing boat up to 8 years and that the overhaul cost and the scrap value of the boat at the eighth year would be $15,000 and $2,000 respectively.

    a. Formulate the problem by using dynamic programming.

    b. Determine the optimum replacement plan.

    c. Is his new replacement plan the same as the one in Problem 14.16?

14.18 General Aviation International has developed a medium-range plan for developing a new type of computerized aviation system called Project OWL. Since the top management insists upon efficiency and effectiveness in planning any project, the manager of the planning department is very concerned about the risk of failure. The operations research group estimated the probability of success for three different projects as follows:

Amount Invested ($ Million)	Probability of Success		
	Project OWL I	Project OWL II	Project OWL III
1	0.7	0.6	0.8
2	0.8	0.7	0.9
3	0.95	0.95	0.9

Note that the manager decided to allocate the budget in block amounts of $1 million. The maximum amount for each project is $3 million, and the total available budget is $5 million.

a. Determine the optimum allocation of the budget for each project that will maximize the probability of success.

b. Show the dynamic programming formulation by using a state, stage, return, and transition function.

14.19 Refer to Problem 14.18. The operations research group also estimated the probability of failure for the three projects as follows:

Amount Invested ($Million)	Probability of Failure		
	Project OWL I	OWL II	OWL III
$1	0.3	0.4	0.2
2	0.2	0.3	0.1
3	0.05	0.05	0.1

What would be the optimum budget allocation in order to minimize the probability of failure? Is the answer to this problem the same as the answer to Problem 14.18?

14.20 Karen Oliver, the marketing manager of Ragoo Toy Company, faces a pricing decision for a new toy, Walking Bear. She is considering three different prices: $10, $12, and $14. Since the toy market is very competitive and demand fluctuates, she has to decide on a price for each of the next 3 years. After studying the market, she calculated the potential profit over 3 years as shown below:

Price	Potential Profit ($ Million)		
	1st year	2d year	3d year
$10	7	3	5
12	5	4	7
14	3	7	8

Ms. Oliver wants to maximize the potential profit during the next 3 years.
   a. Formulate the problem by using dynamic programming.
   b. Determine the optimum pricing plan over 3 years.
   c. What is the maximum profit?

14.21 Refer to Problem 14.20. After conferring with her boss, the vice-president of marketing, Ms. Oliver is told that the price of Walking Bear should not fluctuate very much, up or down. After considering the possible solutions to this restriction, she decides that any price change, up or down, should be made within a range of $2.
   a. Formulate the problem by using dynamic programming.
   b. Determine the maximum profit and the optimum prices.

14.22 The Alaskan Tourist Company owns four small but luxurious sailboats for traveling the Alaskan coastal sea via three different routes. The management of the company wants to optimize the allocation of these four boats on the three routes in terms of profit. The expected profits per month are as follows:

Number of Boats Allocated	Expected Profit ($1,000)		
	Route 1	Route 2	Route 3
1	2.8	0.8	1.8
2	3.6	2.0	2.4
3	4.0	3.6	3.8
4	4.2	5.2	4.8

   a. Formulate the problem by using dynamic programming.
   b. Determine the optimum allocation of the sailboats.

14.23 Refer to Problem 14.22. Assume that the Alaskan Tourist Company wants to purchase two more sailboats because of expanding tourism. The expected profits for the additional two boats are as follows:

Number of Boats Allocated	Expected Profit ($1,000)		
	Route 1	Route 2	Route 3
5	4.7	5.6	5.5
6	5.0	6.0	6.2

What would be the new optimum allocation plan?

14.24 The Miller and Associates Construction Company obtained a new contract for constructing a football stadium for Lakeview High. The construction schedule is determined as follows:

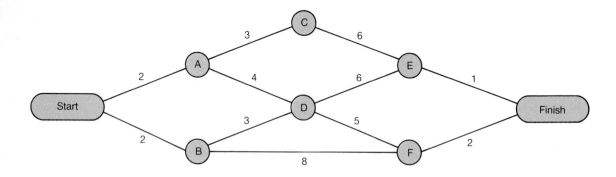

a. Use dynamic programming to isolate the longest-time path.
b. Use dynamic programming to isolate the shortest-time path.

14.25 Refer to Problem 14.24. The company is reconsidering the problem in terms of costs. The cost data are shown in the following table:

Node	A	B	C	D	E	F
Cost ($1000)	20	40	60	100	36	200

a. Determine the minimum cost path by using dynamic programming.
b. Determine the maximum cost path by using dynamic programming.

14.26 The Red Valley Mine Company wants to purchase a new custom truck for delivering coal and other materials. The current price of this truck is $15,000. Recently the operating cost for this truck became a concern because of skyrocketing gasoline prices. The local chamber of commerce provided the following data for the operating costs and resale prices of the truck:

Year	Operating Cost ($1,000)	Resale Price ($1,000)
1	5	12
2	7	10
3	10	7

Since this type of truck is heavily used in the mine, no single truck can be used for more than 3 years. Every year the company decides whether it should buy a new truck. Assume that all the values are adjusted as present values.

a. Show the solution procedure of dynamic programming by using a state, stage, return, and transition function.
b. Determine the optimum replacement plan of the company.

14.27 Refer to Problem 14.26. The Rock Valley Mine Company wants to extend the current replacement plan through a fifth year period. The operating costs and resale prices for the additional two years are given below:

Year	Operating Cost ($1,000)	Resale Price ($1,000)
4	12	6
5	15	5

Determine the new optimum replacement plan of the company.

14.28 The Portland Shipbuilding Company produces three types of racing sailboat: Snipe, Hampton, and Lightning. Each type of boat needs a certain amount of fiberglass for its hull construction. Currently, the company has 20 tons of fiberglass in stock and cannot receive more fiberglass in the near future because of a labor strike. Thus, the allocation of fiberglass to each type of sailboat is critical at present. The probable returns for these three different types of sailboats, shown below, depend on the quantity of fiberglass allocated. Note that the allocation of fiberglass is made in units of 5 tons.

Fiberglass (5-ton unit)	Expected Profit		
	Snipe	Hampton	Lightning
5	$200,000	$120,000	$160,000
10	350,000	350,000	220,000
15	N/A	N/A	380,000

a. Develop the dynamic programming formulation by using a state, stage, return, and transition equation.

b. Determine the optimum allocation plan of the company to maximize the return.

14.29 Refer to Problem 14.28. The Portland Shipbuilding Company wants to diversify its products to meet the demand. After conferring with the chief engineer, the management of the company decided to add another type of sailboat, to be called the "Rebel." The probable returns for this type of boat are $170,000, $320,000, and $390,000 for each successive level of allocation, respectively.

a. Determine the optimum allocation plan and probable total return.

b. Did the company make the right decision in terms of probable return?

15 SIMULATION

For all the prowess of management science, many real-world problems cannot be easily analyzed by the modeling techniques we have discussed thus far in this text. Many standard analytical techniques based on algorithms, such as linear programming and transportation methods, are often too restrictive for dynamic decision problems. Some decision problems are characterized by complex interrelationships among the decision variables, random events, and simultaneous changes of the model parameters. When all available analytical models fail, one possible avenue open to us is to conduct an experiment. Simulation is one such experimentation technique. It is based on mathematical models or logical trial-and-error approaches. Simulation is widely applied to evaluate the behavior of many real-world systems, such as inventory, production, sales, and labor. In this chapter, we will study the basic nature, characteristics, and important approaches of simulation.

Learning Objectives   *From the study of this chapter, we will learn the following:*

1. Many different types of simulation in real-world situations
2. The advantages and disadvantages of simulation
3. The various characteristics of simulation models
4. The general process of simulation
5. Application of the Monte Carlo process
6. Generation of random numbers and their transformation for determining random variables
7. Incorporation of optimization in simulation
8. The application areas of simulation
9. The meaning of the following terms:

Simulation	*Transformation*
Random number	*GPSS*
Descriptors	*SIMSCRIPT*
Flowchart	*SIMULA*
Monte Carlo	*GASP IV*
Uniform probability distribution	*DYNAMO*
Artificial intelligence	*Heuristics*
Business games	*Industrial dynamics*

THE NATURE OF SIMULATION

We are most familiar with physical simulations. "It's great . . . things are just spectacular. Voyager 2 is racing by Saturn at 54,000 mph, skimming just 63,000 miles over the ringlets within the C-ring, surrounded by B-ring," an excited scientist at the Jet Propulsion Laboratory comments on the television set. He continues, "After examining Enceladus, one of Saturn's collection of at least 17 moons, Voyager 2 will continue its long journey to distant Uranus. Please watch the simulator." Now we see an artist's simulated journey of Voyager 2 far into the dark universe.

We are exposed to many such physical simulations. The ground flight simulator duplicates flying conditions for training pilots. Most experiments conducted by the manned space flight programs of NASA are based on simulated space conditions. Many of the board games children play are also simulations—Monopoly, Acquire, Life, and the like. Other simulations we often see are:

Management games used for training and development

Simulation models of the world, urban systems, and corporations

Corporate-planning simulation models

Water resource simulation models

Inventory-production simulators

Probabilistic network models

Queuing models for airport traffic control

Air-quality simulation models

Econometric models to predict economic conditions

World energy models

As we mentioned in Chapter 1, simulation is one of the most widely used techniques of management science. The primary reason for this popularity is its applicability to a wide range of management problems. Simulation is effective in generating a large amount of information concerning the performance or behavior of a system under various conditions and/or assumptions.

What Is Simulation?

Simulation is much like a model. A model is a representation of reality. Instead of representing reality, however, simulation simply imitates it. The process of simulation involves "operating" or "running" the model to obtain operational information of the system. Operational information should be so designed to help the manager in making the decision. Today, simulation generally refers to computer-based simulation. Thus, we can define simulation in the management science context as: *A numerical technique of experimentation to determine the dynamic behavior of a management system on the digital computer*. Although powerful computers allow us to simulate complex systems, simulation can also be carried out manually for simple problems.

In simulation, instead of seeking an optimum solution through algorithms as in analytical modeling approaches, we attempt to obtain descriptive information through experimentation. The descriptive results of simulation are often referred to as **descriptors.** The system descriptors can be valuable for predicting behavior or performance of a system under various conditions. For example, change in the inventory level under various combinations of daily demand and lead time, as we studied in Chapter 12, gives us a pretty good idea of what to expect when the demand rate changes.

Although simulation output is always in the form of descriptive results, it is certainly possible to include a search rule in the simulator so that the results can be evaluated in such a way that the optimum solution to the decision problem can be identified. Thus, we can visualize the model solution phase of the management science process as shown in Figure 15.1. The dashed arrow in the figure, leading from the block containing descriptive results to the block containing optimization results, represents the optimum solution possibility of simulation.

A simplified version of the simulation process is illustrated in Figure 15.2, where the model is shown as a box. The simulation process requires the generation of input data to be fed into the model, and the model should be designed in such a way as to provide the output that can be used to measure or evaluate the performance (objective criteria) variables. In order to design an effective simulation model, we must identify the system under study by carefully considering its important variables and performance criteria.

Figure 15.1   *Management Science Modeling Solution Process*

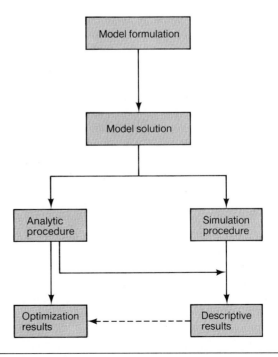

Figure 15.2   The Simulation Process

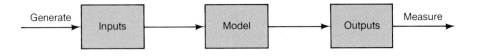

On the basis of our discussion thus far, we can summarize the characteristics of simulation as follows:

Simulation is a technique of experimentation to determine the behavior of a system under various conditions.

A computer-based model is used to generate descriptive results.

An optimum solution routine can be included in the simulation process.

Simulation requires data, and its results must be evaluated based on objective criteria.

Simulation does not necessarily represent reality but merely imitates it.

Simulation is usually applied when a decision problem under analysis is too complex to be solved by analytical models (e.g., linear programming and EOQ models).

Why Simulate?

In recent years, computers have become more powerful in terms of speed and computational power. Speed of computation is getting faster, even for large-scale models, while the cost is decreasing dramatically. A small personal computer costing less than $2,000 can be as powerful as a gigantic computer that used to fill up a room in the 1960s. Another significant development is in the area of dedicated (specially designed) simulation languages for various managerial problems.

Although the attempts to simulate a situation under investigation have not always been successful, simulation has grown rapidly as a decision-making tool in many organizations. The increasing application of simulation is a good indication that simulation has many advantages. Table 15.1 presents the major advantages and disadvantages of simulation. Let us discuss the advantages and disadvantages of simulation in greater detail.

Advantages   Computer-based simulation has the following advantages:

1. The first, and perhaps the most important, advantage of simulation is that it provides a means to study the real-world system or situation without actually changing it. In many social systems, it is often impossible to experiment, or an experiment may involve a high level of risk. For example, a change of price for a product can be a risky business. Even when such a change is made on the basis of a rigorous analysis, it can still lead to disaster. There are many such cases in real-world situations: change of tax systems, tactical changes in warfare, psychological experiments, policy changes in dé-

Table 15.1   *Advantages and Disadvantages of Simulation*

Advantages	Disadvantages
Allows controlled experimentation.	Model development can be costly and/or time-consuming.
Reveals new facts about the problem.	
Allows a patchwork approach to model formulation.	Requires powerful computers.
	Is very sensitive to model formulation.
Is an effective training tool.	Gives no guaranteed optimum solution.
Has a broad range of applications.	Encourages tendency to overlook other techniques.
Allows "what if" questions.	

tente with the Soviet Union, change of government regulations, a gasoline coupon system, and the like.

If such real-world systems can be simulated on a computer, the decision maker can observe the potential outcome of various changes without altering the real system. Thus, many alternatives can be explored and their results can be studied in a formal way. Simulation is especially valuable for analyzing complex systems that defy other analytical techniques.

2. Simulation requires a thorough analysis of the problem in order to generate the required data. This process can reveal some hidden interrelationships or previously unrecognized defects in the system.

3. The simulation model, regardless of the complexity of the problem, does not need to be an overwhelming large-scale model at the beginning. Usually, a simulation model is the aggregate of many simple models representing interrelationships among system variables and components. Thus, the simulation model can be built slowly, step by step.

4. The simulation model is usually designed on the basis of the manager's perspective of the system rather than on that of the management scientist. This is an important factor in the eventual implementation of the model results. We will discuss implementation thoroughly in Chapter 18.

5. Simulation can be an effective training tool for managers and employees alike. Management games based on simulation are widely used by business schools and the in-house training programs of many organizations.

6. Simulation has a broad range of applications, from such operations problems as inventory control to such strategic planning problems as mergers and capital budgeting. Computer-based simulation is particularly effective for analyzing complex organizational problems.

7. Simulation provides descriptive results rather than prescriptive (optimum) results. Thus, the manager has ample opportunity to ask "what if" sensitivity analysis questions. Such information provides much confidence concerning the range of possible outcomes to a certain decision alternative.

Disadvantages   Although computer simulation is a very effective technique for many decision problems, it has some disadvantages:

1. Development of a simulation model, especially a complex computer-based model, can be a very costly and slow proposition. Since an effective simulation model requires accurate data and precise interrelationships among the variables, it may become a formidable task in terms of cost, labor, time, and expertise.

2. Most simulation models require powerful digital computers for computation. Therefore, simulation is not a quick and inexpensive approach to complex decision problems.

3. Simulation model results are usually very sensitive to model formulation. Thus, if the model contains some inaccurate relationships or interdependencies, the results may be quite misleading.

4. Simulation provides descriptive model results. Thus, either an optimum solution (or a very good solution) cannot be guaranteed or identification of an optimum (or a good) solution becomes an additional task after the simulation work is completed.

5. Simulation may become the jack-of-all-trades to some managers. Thus, some analytical techniques, which are simpler and more effective for finding even better solutions, may be overlooked.

Besides the advantages and disadvantages of simulation, we had better remember the adage, ''When all else fails, simulate.'' This implies that simulation should be the last resort only if other available techniques cannot solve the problem. As we pointed out earlier, the purpose of simulation is to conduct systematic experiments for a real system. Therefore, the results obtained from simulation must be complementary to analytical solutions, regardless of whether analytical solutions exist.

Characteristics of Simulation Models

There are many different types of simulation models, depending on the nature of the problem under investigation. Let us discuss the following characteristics:

Static versus Dynamic   We can use simulation to analyze both static and dynamic situations. In most cases, the simulation models we construct are dynamic in nature. For example, economic forecasting models and national energy models are dynamic simulation models that analyze real-world systems. Examples of static simulation models might be plant layout design, space allocation, warehouse location, and the like.

Deterministic versus Stochastic   Virtually all of the real-world situations we face are stochastic (probabilistic) rather than deterministic. Whenever a system involves randomness in its variables or parameters, the model we construct should be stochastic. For example, if a hamburger shop has a waiting line, the customer waiting time in the line is a random variable. If we design a simulation model to observe the customer waiting patterns, it will be a stochastic model. However, if the expected value of the waiting time is available, we can use this information to construct a deterministic simulation model.

Continuous versus Discrete   A variable is said to be continuous if its value changes continuously over time. However, a variable is said to be discrete if its value changes discretely (in stages or irregularly) over time. We must choose appropriate variables for the problem under study because the variable selection greatly affects the nature of a simulation model. Continuous simulation models are often used for large-scale problems such as econometric (economic forecasting) models and energy planning models. Discrete simulation is used for detailed operational problems such as production scheduling, inventory control, and labor force planning.

Aggregated versus Detailed   The level of detail and the degree of aggregation are perhaps the most important characteristics of simulation. These two characteristics are determined according to the purpose of the particular simulation modeling. For example, if the top decision maker is interested in gross quantities such as total sales, total inventories, total production, or work force capacity, a simulation model should be an aggregated model. However, if a middle manager of a manufacturing firm is concerned with detailed operational information, the simulation model should be a detailed one.

Time Slice   In most problem situations, the variables involved in a simulation model change over time. Therefore, the simulation process should be capable of revealing the current status of the important variables at each time period. Thus, determining the appropriate size of the time slice between time periods is a critical concern. In a simulation model designed for weekly analysis, such as material requirements planning (MRP) models, the time slice can be a day or even an hour. However, in an econometric simulation model designed for forecasting economic conditions, the time slice can be a month, a quarter, or a year.

THE PROCESS OF SIMULATION

Simulation is usually carried out in a sequence of several steps. These steps are important elements of the successful system experimentation process. The simulation process is presented in Figure 15.3.

Step 1: Problem Formulation   A simulation model may be designed to generate information about the behavior of an existing system or to help develop a new system. Because a hospital may be experiencing rising operation costs, it may design a simulation model to uncover the contributing causes of the increasing costs. Similarly, an investment firm may experiment with alternative financing schemes for a new shopping center development project.

The initial step of the simulation process is to identify and formulate the problem or the purpose of the study. Objective or performance criteria, variables, decision rules, and parameters must be clearly defined. If the experimental objectives are not clearly specified by management, the simulation process has no definite guidelines. Thus, it is necessary to modify abstract objectives to more definite operational goals whenever possible.

Figure 15.3   The Process of Simulation

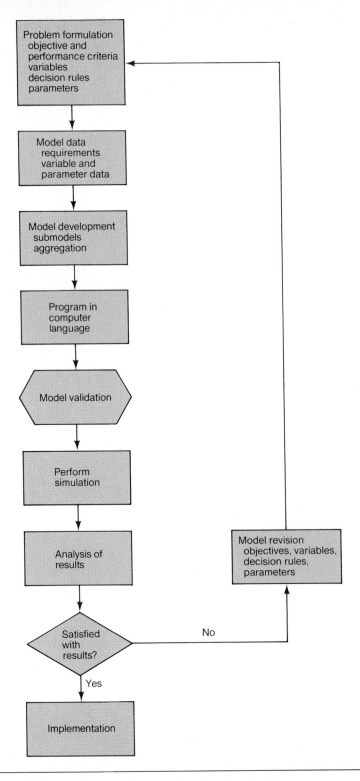

Step 2: Analysis of Model Requirements   In this step, all of the required data concerning variables and parameters must be identified. It is important to determine which variables and parameters are needed to measure the system performance. It is important in this step to classify the variables into two basic types: controllable and uncontrollable (see Chapter 2). Controllable variables are those within the influence of the decision maker. Uncontrollable variables are those influenced by exogenous factors. The simulation model should include controllable variables while holding other variables constant. The division of variables into two classifications is not always clear, and some experience is needed for proper definition.

Generally, data for parameters can be obtained from historical data. If such historical data are not available, they can be estimated from other information sources or judgments. It is also possible at this step to identify which variables are deterministic or stochastic.

Step 3: Model Development   In most situations, it is effective to formulate a number of submodels according to their functions before aggregating them into a whole model. Obviously it is much easier to analyze smaller subsystems separately than to analyze a large and complex system in one operation. Once a number of submodels are formulated, the whole model can be developed by linking the submodels according to their logical relationship. The linkage must have a flexibility that allows easy revisions for possible changes.

In developing a simulation model, flowcharts are often very useful. A **flowchart** is simply a graphic aid that simplifies the logical process being used in simulation — it provides a visual aid to the mental process of simulation. We have already used flowcharts throughout this text. The most widely used flowchart outlines are shown in Figure 15.4.

Step 4: Programming the Model by Computer Language   In this step, a model written by a natural language is transformed into a model written by a computer language. This transformation, often the most time-consuming and painful step, is necessary in order to run the model on the computer. However, a proper formulation of submodels makes this step much simpler. Also, a proper selection of a simulation language can be an important factor in the success of the model.

Step 5: Validation of the Simulation Model   In order to validate the simulation model, a number of test runs are often required. The results of these runs should be compared with the real data under similar conditions. If the test outputs deviate significantly from the real data, the whole process of modeling should be reexamined carefully.

Step 6: Perform Simulation   Once the simulation model is designed and validated, it is run according to the scheme or purpose of the experiment. The simulation results under various experimental schemes are observed, and, if necessary, revisions are made in the model. In this step, user participation is extremely important in order to obtain practical results.

Step 7: Analysis of Results   Simulation usually yields operating statistics in the form of averages and probability distributions. Thus, analysis of results can be either simple or complex depending on the characteristics of the simulation objectives. In addition to the many technical aspects of analysis, successful interpretation is an important factor in this step.

Figure 15.4   Basic Flowchart Outlines

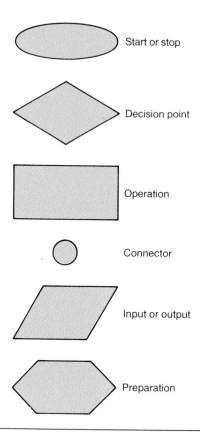

In practice, the seven steps described above are not necessarily distinct steps nor are they in a rigid sequence. Some of these steps overlap, some can be simplified, and others may need to be expanded. The basic determining factors are: the objective of the study, the type of model, the capability of the simulation, the language used, and the availability of data. What is important is the completeness of the required analysis rather than strict adherence to the sequence of steps.

SIMULATION OF STOCHASTIC MODELS

Many decision problems that involve probabilistic (stochastic) events are difficult to solve by applying analytical techniques. This is especially true if a problem involves several random variables. We remember studying inventory problems with random lead times and random demand rates. Also, many waiting line problems involve random arrival rates and random service times. Such problems are good candidates for a simulation study. The majority of real-world applications of simulation are based on stochastic models.

Figure 15.5   The Monte Carlo Process

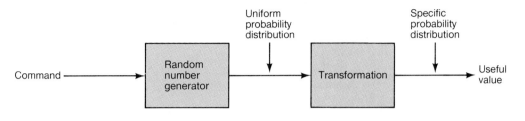

The Monte Carlo Process

The **Monte Carlo** process is a procedure that generates values of a random variable based on one or more specific probability distributions. Thus, the Monte Carlo process is not a simulation method or a simulation model per se, although it has become almost synonymous with stochastic simulation. In actuality, the Monte Carlo process is simply an important technique that is extensively used for stochastic simulation.

The Monte Carlo process was originated from the statistical sampling process. The basic idea of Monte Carlo is that the probabilities of certain events can be approximated by a sampling process based on a certain probability distribution. In general, the use of the Monte Carlo technique is attributed to John von Neumann and associates, who used the technique in various research efforts, including the development of the atomic bomb during World War II.

The Monte Carlo process is basically a two-stage procedure, as presented in Figure 15.5. In the first stage, when a command is given, a **random number** generator produces a number. By definition, the random numbers generated have a uniform probability distribution. In other words, each number should have an equal probability of being selected. The random number generator can be a simple device such as a deck of cards, a die, or colored balls in a hat, or it can be a complex computer-based device.

The second stage of the Monte Carlo process is the **transformation** procedure. This manipulates the random number into the value that is useful, according to a specified distribution. For example, in an inventory problem the Monte Carlo process involves the following:

1. Generate a random number in order to determine a lead time.

2. Fit the random number generated into the probability distribution of the lead time.

3. Transform the random number into an appropriate lead time.

The basis of the Monte Carlo process is the generation of the values of random variables included in the simulation model. The following examples of random variables can provide us with useful insights:

Waiting line model
    Time between customer arrivals at a service location
    Time between machine breakdowns
    Service time (to serve a customer or repair a machine)

Project management model
Time to complete an activity in a project

Inventory model
Lead time for a specific order
Demand per day
Time to process an order after it is received
Order quantity, when it is received

Since random variables are included in almost all simulation models, we need to know how to obtain the random values for random variables. First we will look at the simple manual method of generating random values. Then, we will proceed to computer-based methods of generating uniform random numbers and their transformation into appropriate probability distributions.

Simple Random Number Generation and Transformation   For simple problems, we can easily generate uniformly distributed random numbers without using a computer-based system. For example, we can use such methods as reading down the table of random numbers (see Appendix 5), rolling dice, flipping coins, spinning a number wheel, or the numbers-in-a-hat method.

Let us assume that the probability distribution given in Table 15.2 represents the demand per day for a particular product. Here, the random variable is the quantity demanded on a particular day. We are going to use an unbiased spinning wheel, as shown in Figure 15.6. Each segmented sector represents a demand according to its corresponding probability. For example, 10 percent of the spinning wheel area is occupied by $D = 0$. By *unbiased* we mean that the result of a spin will be the same regardless of the starting position of the roulette wheel or the spinning power.

Spinning a roulette wheel can generate a random number for a random variable, in this case the demand on a particular day. If we continue using this method, over many spins of the wheel the relative frequency of demand generated will approximate the probability distribution given in Table 15.2. This procedure is, in fact, a Monte Carlo process.

Although the spinning wheel method provides us with the randomly selected daily demand in one operation, most Monte Carlo processes require the transformation stage.

Table 15.2   Probability Distribution of Demand per Day

Demand (D)	P(D)
0	0.1
1	0.2
2	0.3
3	0.3
4	0.1

Figure 15.6   Simulated Sampling by Spinning a Roulette Wheel

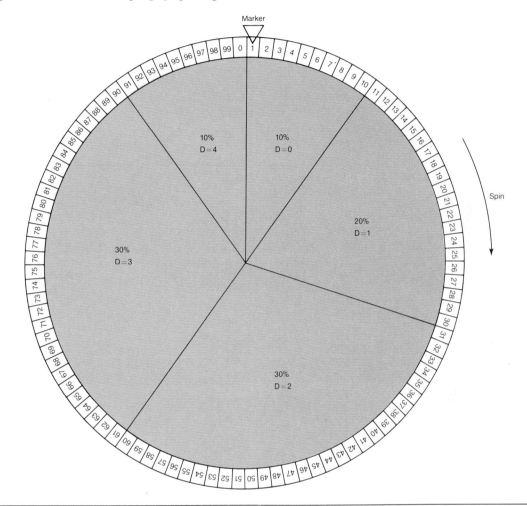

The transformation stage may be based on a tabular form, a graphical method, or a mathematical transformation technique. Here we will examine the tabular and graphical methods. The mathematical transformation will be discussed later in this chapter.

Tabular Method   The tabular method is perhaps the simplest and easiest way to transform a random number. This method is based on the cumulative probability function. Table 15.3 presents the same basic data presented in Table 15.2 but with two additional columns. The third column presents the cumulative probability distribution of daily demand, *F(D)*. The fourth column is for the intervals of random numbers that match the cumulative probability distribution. For example, the probability of 2 units demanded is 0.3. In the cumulative probability column, we can see that the range of this demand

Table 15.3　Cumulative Probability Distribution of Daily Demand

Demand (D)	$P(D)$	Cumulative Probability $F(D) = P(\text{Demand} \leq D)$	Random Number Interval	
0	0.1	0.1	0.01–0.10	
1	0.2	0.3	0.11–0.30	
2 ←	0.3 ←	0.6 ←	0.31–0.60 ←	$r = 0.50$
3	0.3	0.9	0.61–0.90	
4	0.1	1.0	0.91–1.00	

Figure 15.7　Cumulative Probability Distribution of Daily Demand

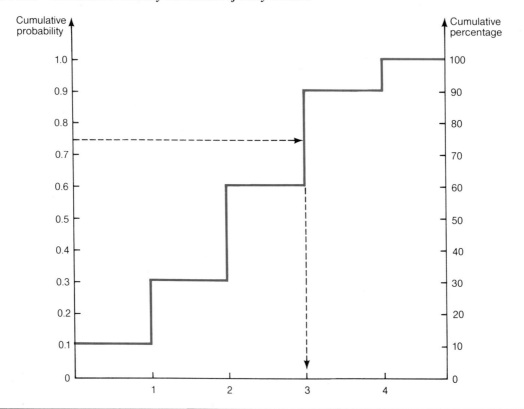

($D = 2$) is between 0.3 and 0.6. Thus, if we generate a 2-digit random number between 0 and 1, then the random number interval should be exactly as shown in the fourth column.

Now we are ready to make any transformation. For example, suppose we generated a random number r. The number we found is 0.50. Since 0.50 falls in the 0.31–0.60 range of intervals, the daily demand represented by this random number can be easily determined by simply following the arrows in Table 15.3. In this case, the daily demand will be 2 units.

Graphical Method   The graphical method is also a simple way to transform a uniformly distributed random number into a meaningful number in a specific distribution. In order to use the graphical method, we must prepare a graph of the cumulative probability distribution. For our daily demand determination example, the cumulative probability distribution of daily demand is expressed by $F(D)$, as shown in Table 15.3. Figure 15.7 provides the graphical presentation of $F(D)$.

Suppose that a random number is generated and it is found to be 0.75. By tracing the graph we can easily determine that the corresponding daily demand for this particular random number is 3 units, as shown in Figure 15.7. Notice that the length of the vertical lines at each demand D corresponds exactly to the probability of each demand $P(D)$. For example, let us consider $D = 1$. The probability of a daily demand for 1 unit $P(1)$ is shown by the vertical line from 0.1 to 0.3, yielding a probability of 0.2, or 20 percent.

Casette 15.1   THE MILWAUKEE CONSTRUCTION COMPANY

The Milwaukee Construction Company is a medium-sized construction firm specializing in erecting professional office buildings. Currently, .the company has three identical cranes. These cranes represent the most valuable equipment the company has in terms of cost and use. The company has only one repairperson for the cranes. Thus, in case of a crane breakdown, construction work may be delayed. Mr. William Cane, president of the company, is naturally very interested in finding ways to reduce the breakdown rate of the three cranes.

Another of Mr. Cane's concerns is reducing repair time. No accurate statistics are currently available for both the frequency of crane breakdown and repair time. After conferring with his staff, Mr. Cane decided to ask a local consulting firm, Infotech, for help. Bert Erlanger, a management scientist at Infotech, paid a visit to Milwaukee Construction and examined the problem.

Bert concluded that there was little chance of utilizing any analytical technique to study the crane breakdown problem. Thus, he decided to use a simulation approach to collect the data about crane utilization. Bert is a firm believer in user participation. Hence, he explained to Mr. Cane how the simulation process works and showed that the study results come from a valid representation of the real system.

Modeling the Machine Shop Operation

Bert decided that the best way to demonstrate the simulation process is to first work the problem out manually. Thus, he developed a simple model to represent the machine shop operation, as shown in Figure 15.8.

Every block in Figure 15.8 indicates the location where a miniature crane (or a simpler indicator, such as a card) is to be put. We can easily note that the condition of the machine shop can be broken down into three stages: normal operation, breakdown, and repair. When all three crane blocks are filled up, it is obvious that all cranes are in normal operation. When a crane is moved into the queue or repair block, it is waiting

Figure 15.8   *Functional Block Diagram for the Machine Shop Operation*

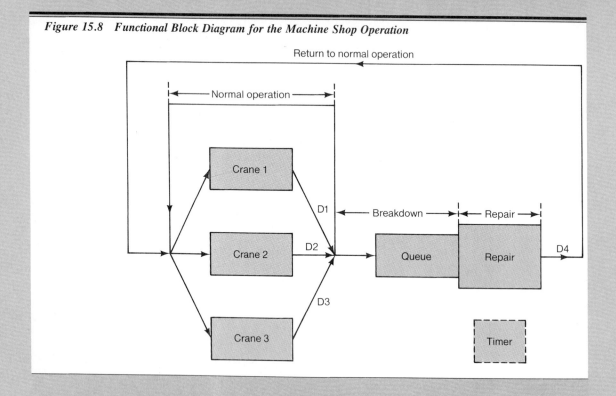

for repair or is being repaired. Since there are three cranes, three of the five blocks must be filled at all times.

The next thing Bert introduced in the model is a timer. This is not necessarily a real timer. Nevertheless, it indicates the amount of time elapsed during operation. For example, let us get a deck of 24 cards, with a numerical label, ranging from 1 to 24, printed on each card. In order to represent a 12-hour operation period, each card will represent 1 half-hour time block. Thus, by putting these 24 cards in sequence on the timer block and checking the number of the card on the top, we can ascertain the duration of crane operation time. In simulation, it is important to store the timed operational statistics.

Table 15.4 presents the crane-status tabulation. The first column indicates the passage of time (i.e., time period). The time period number must be identical to the card number on the timer block. For each crane, there are three condition columns: operating, queuing, and repairing. One of these columns must be checked at a given time period for each crane, depending in which block in Figure 15.8 each crane is located. Then, at the end of simulation, crane downtime can be easily computed by counting the number of checkmarks in the queue and repair columns and multiplying them by one half-hour.

Stochastic Variables

As we discussed earlier, it is important to classify variables as either deterministic or stochastic. For a deterministic variable, there is no need to generate random numbers.

Table 15.4   *Crane-Status Table*

Time Period (half-hours)	Crane 1			Crane 2			Crane 3		
	Oper.	Queue	Repair	Oper.	Queue	Repair	Oper.	Queue	Repair
1	√					√	√		
2	√					√	√		
3	√					√	√		
4		√				√	√		
5			√	√			√		
.									
.									
.									
23			√	√				√	
24	√			√				√	

However, for a stochastic variable, we need some sort of mechanism that generates random numbers according to an appropriate statistical distribution.

In the machine breakdown problem of the Milwaukee Construction Company, there are basically two stochastic variables: (1) a variable that indicates whether a crane is in normal operation or in need of repair, and (2) a variable that indicates whether a crane under repair can be returned to normal operating condition.

Stochastic Variable — Crane Breakdowns. Since there exist no reliable data on crane breakdowns, Bert Erlanger decided to assume that a crane breakdown occurs in a random fashion. On the basis of his observations and interviews with the crane operators, however, he roughly estimated that a crane breakdown occurs once in every 12 half-hours (i.e., every 6 hours). In other words, the probability that a crane breakdown occurs in a given time period (half hour) is approximately 0.083.

Now we are ready to generate random numbers. Let us prepare three decks of cards, each deck containing cards from 0 to 9. The reason for preparing three card decks is that we need to generate a number that has three digits below the decimal point (e.g., 0.125 is derived when we draw a one from deck 1, two from deck 2, and five from deck 3). Since we draw each of three cards from a different card deck, the randomness of the value generated is guaranteed.

The random number (r) that we generate by this mechanism is always between 0 and 1 (i.e., $0 \leq r < 1.000$). It should be obvious by now that we are generating a number that represents a probability. Since the probability of machine breakdown is estimated to be 0.083, we can establish the following decision rule:

If $r > 0.083$, crane is in normal operation.

If $r \leq 0.083$, crane is in need of repair.

For example, let us suppose that the cards we drew from the three decks at time period 10 are 1, 3, and 5. Then, we have a probability value of 0.135. This number is clearly greater than the probability of crane breakdown of 0.083. Thus, the crane under analysis is considered to be in normal operating condition. Conversely, if we draw a

Table 15.5   *Repair Time and Probability of Occurrence*

Repair Time Period (half-hours)	Probability of Occurrence
1	0.3
2	0.2
3	0.3
4	0.2

Figure 15.9   *Crane Repair Time under Uniform Distribution*

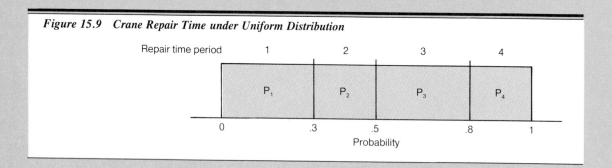

random number that is less than or equal to 0.083, the crane will be considered broken down and in need of repair.

Stochastic Variable—Repair Time.   A similar mechanism can be developed to generate random numbers for repair time. On the basis of historical data, Bert could estimate the repair time. The repair time duration ranges from one time period (a half-hour) to four time periods (2 hours). Table 15.5 presents the repair time duration and corresponding probabilities.

Since the probability is represented by one number below the decimal point, we can use a single deck of cards containing cards from 0 to 9. We shuffle the deck and draw a card. If the number drawn is 5, then the probability is 0.5. Now we must check the area in which this probability falls. Figure 15.9 presents four probability areas for the four possible repair time periods. Since probability 0.5 falls in area P_2, we can interpret that the required repair is 2 half-hour periods, or 1 hour.

We developed two random-number-generating mechanisms in order to determine values of the two stochastic variables: breakdown and repair time. These values determined by random numbers must be checked at points D1, D2, D3, and D4 in Figure 15.8. These points represent *decision points*.

The Simulation Procedure

In the previous section, Bert Erlanger introduced two important concepts: simulation modeling and random number generation. Now we are ready to perform simulation for the machine repair problem. The simulation procedure can be either very simple or very complex, depending on the level of detail needed. The simulation procedure of the machine repair problem, presented on pages 630 and 631 in Figure 15.10 as a flowchart diagram, attempts to obtain information about crane utilization.

The entire procedure consists of five subprocedures: (1) initialization, (2) time-advance, (3) check-crane-breakdown, (4) check-repair, and (5) compute-output. Notice that each subprocedure is named according to its basic task. Now, let us examine each subprocedure in detail.

Initialization.   This subprocedure prepares for the simulation run. Block 0 sets all three cranes in operating positions (i.e., the three blocks of cranes in Figure 15.8) and also sets the timer at 0 by putting time card 0 on the timer block in Figure 15.8. Preparation of a set of card decks for random number generation and the crane status table are not included in the flowchart. However, they are assumed to be included in this subprocedure. Admittedly, this step is simple, but without a proper initialization step no valid simulation is possible.

Time-Advance.   Blocks 1 and 2 accomplish the task of advancing time. These blocks check the available time cards on the timer, and if a card is available, then time is advanced by putting a new time card on top of the previous time cards on the timer. The time-advance is an important function of the simulation procedure.

Check-Crane-Breakdown.   Blocks 3 and 10 perform the task of determining whether each crane is broken down. First, crane 1 is examined for its operational condition. If it is operational, a random number is generated by drawing three numbers from three different card decks, as we explained earlier. By comparing this random number with the probability of machine breakdown ($P = 0.083$), we can determine whether or not the crane is broken down. If the crane is broken down ($r \leq 0.083$), we record this change of status for crane 1 in the crane-status table and move the crane to the queue block (see blocks 7 and 8). If the crane is not broken down, we proceed to the next crane until the operational conditions of all of the cranes are checked (blocks 3, 9, and 10).

Check-Repair.   In this subprocedure, we determine whether the repair of a crane is completed. We determine the repair time through the second random number generator, as explained earlier. Thus, if a crane is already in the repair shop, we can simply compare the timer time and return time. If these two times are identical, the crane has been repaired, and it returns to normal operating condition (blocks 11 to 14).

After a crane completes its repair service, we must examine the queue block to see whether there is any other crane waiting for repair work (block 15). If there is no crane waiting for repair, then, because no additional checking is necessary, we go back to block 1 and advance to the next time period. If there are one or more cranes in queue, we move the rightmost crane to the repair block and indicate this change in the appropriate column of the crane-status table.

There is one more task remaining. That is to determine the repair time of the crane that just moved into repair by using the second random number generator. By simply adding the repair time to the current time, we can obtain the return time of the crane. Blocks 16 to 18 accomplish this task.

Compute-Output.   This subprocedure concludes the simulation procedure. We attempt to obtain information about crane utilization. Thus, we first compute the downtime and then compute the crane utilization time by the simple formula presented in block 21.

Figure 15.10   Simulation Procedure for the Machine Repair Problem

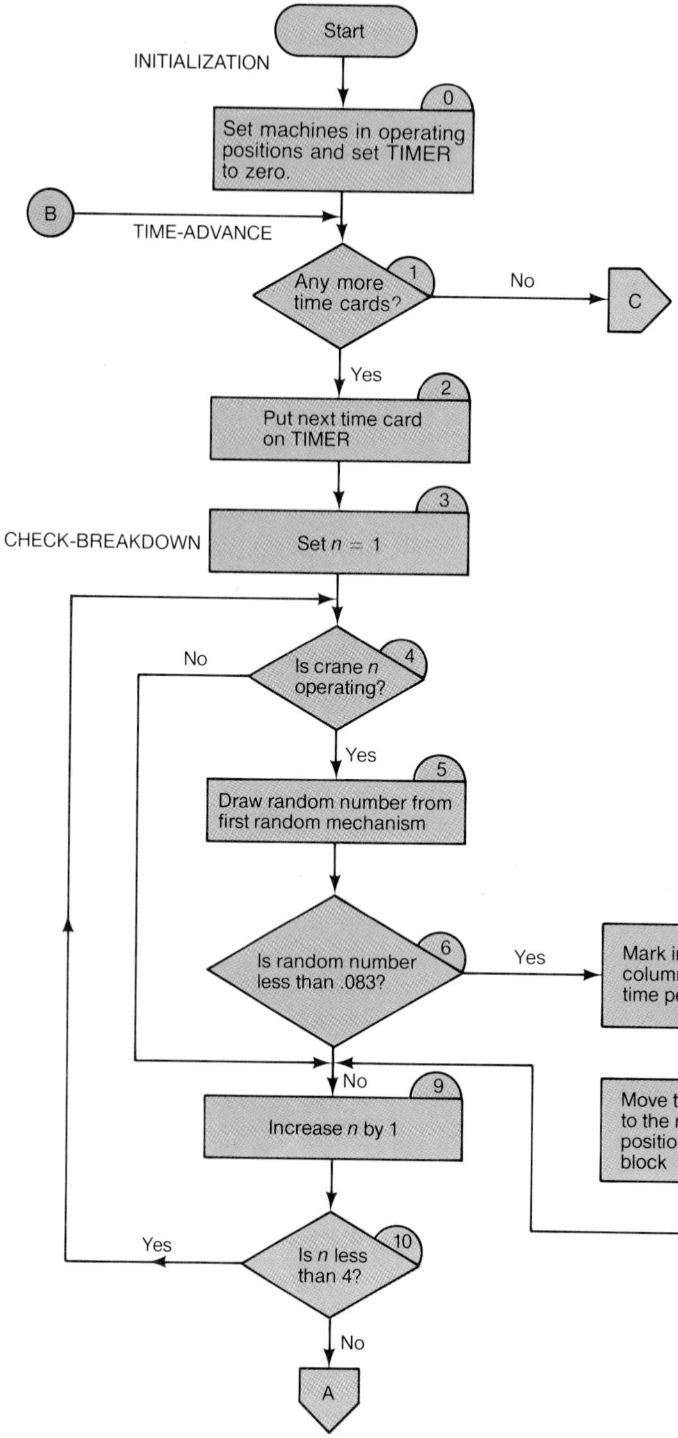

Figure 15.10 *(continued)*

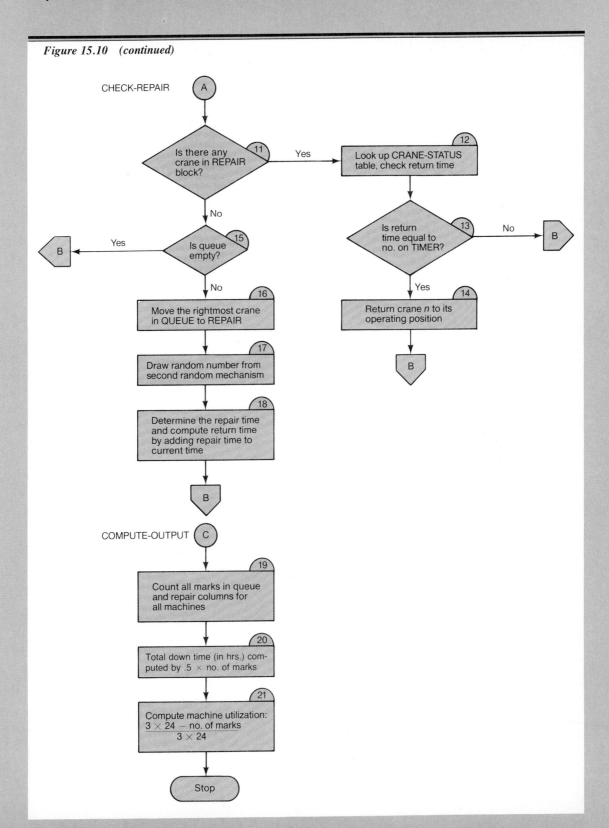

Result of a Single Simulation Run

Let us examine the *event list* of one actual simulation run for the span of 24 time periods (12 hours), as shown in Table 15.6. This event list is actually based on the information in the crane-status table shown in Table 15.7. Table 15.8 summarizes the downtime and waiting time for each crane during the 24 time periods; the table also presents the total crane downtime and crane utilization in terms of percentage (68.1 percent).

After completing the simulation work for the Milwaukee Construction Company, Bert Erlanger made the following observation: "In order to obtain reliable output, Milwaukee Construction should run a lot more simulations than 24 time periods, perhaps about 10,000 time periods." This statement clearly makes sense. Since there are two stochastic variables, a great number of runs would make the results more reliable. Nevertheless, it must be added here that it is not a simple matter to determine exactly how many simulation runs would guarantee valid results. In order to answer this question, we need much experience in applying various simulation approaches to real-world problems and perhaps a great deal of rigorous analytical work.

Table 15.6   *Event List of a Single Simulation Run*

Time	Events (or Transactions)
1	Crane 2 is in repair, repair time = 4 units.
2	—
3	—
4	Crane 1 is broken down and in queue.
5	Crane 2 returns to operation. Crane 1 is in repair; repair time = 3 units.
6	—
7	—
8	Crane 1 returns to operation.
9	—
10	—
11	Crane 3 is broken down and in repair; repair time = 3 units.
12	—
13	Crane 2 is broken down and in queue.
14	Crane 3 returns to operation. Crane 2 is in repair; repair time = 2 units.
15	—
16	Crane 2 returns to operation.
17	—
18	Crane 3 is broken down and in repair; repair time = 4 units.
19	Crane 1 is broken down and in queue.
20	—
21	—
22	Crane 3 returns to operation. Crane 1 is in repair; repair time = 2 units.
23	—
24	Crane 1 returns to operation.

Table 15.7   Crane-Status Table for a Single Run

Time Period (half-hours)	Crane 1			Crane 2			Crane 3		
	Oper.	Queue	Repair	Oper.	Queue	Repair	Oper.	Queue	Repair
1	✓					✓	✓		
2	✓					✓	✓		
3	✓					✓	✓		
4		✓				✓	✓		
5			✓	✓			✓		
6			✓	✓			✓		
7			✓	✓			✓		
8	✓			✓			✓		
9	✓			✓			✓		
10	✓			✓			✓		
11	✓			✓					✓
12	✓			✓					✓
13	✓				✓				✓
14	✓					✓	✓		
15	✓					✓	✓		
16	✓			✓			✓		
17	✓			✓			✓		
18	✓			✓					✓
19		✓		✓					✓
20		✓		✓					✓
21		✓		✓					✓
22			✓	✓			✓		
23			✓	✓			✓		
24	✓			✓			✓		

Table 15.8   Machine Utilization for a Single Run

Machine	Downtime (hours)	Waiting Time (hours)
Crane 1	4.5	2.0
Crane 2	3.5	0.5
Crane 3	3.5	0

Machine utilization = 0.681.
Total waiting time = 2.5 hours
Waiting time in worst case = 2 hours

GENERATING RANDOM NUMBERS

An essential element of stochastic simulation is the generation of random numbers. In a simple simulation model, we can use a manual procedure to generate random numbers (dice, a roulette wheel, a deck of cards, numbers in a hat, etc.). However, in most simulation models we need a more systematic way to generate random numbers as they play such a significant role in the validity of the simulation results.

Table of Random Numbers

Appendix 5 presents an excerpt from a random number table. The random numbers in the table were generated by a numerical technique. A long sequence of numbers generated by a numerical technique usually repeats itself after a certain number of iterations. Thus, these numbers are not true random numbers. Consequently, they are often referred to as *pseudorandom numbers*. True random numbers are usually generated by some physical process such as electrical noise, which is naturally random.

In using the random number table, we can use one of two approaches: (1) select a number in a random fashion (e.g., close your eyes and place your pencil on the random number table); or (2) select a number according to a fixed pattern (e.g., pick every third number from the top). You can use your creativity in using the table.

Mid-Square Method

The mid-square method was first studied by John von Neumann. This method employs a starting number, referred to as a *seed* value, and generates a series of random numbers. For example, if we use 4,745 as the initial value, then it is squared and selected middle-digit numbers are used as a random number. Then, this random number is squared to find the next random number, and so on, as in the following example:

$$\text{Seed value} = 4{,}745$$
$$(4{,}745)^2 = 22\boxed{5150}25;\ r_1 = 5{,}150$$
$$(5{,}150)^2 = 26\boxed{5225}00;\ r_2 = 5{,}225$$
$$(5{,}225)^2 = 27\boxed{3006}25;\ r_3 = 3{,}006$$
$$(3{,}006)^2 = \cdots,\ \text{etc.}$$

Of course, these random numbers must be divided by 10,000 in order to generate a decimal number between 0 and 1. This method yields a set of pseudorandom numbers that can be used in a simulation model. However, this is not an efficient way to generate random numbers because of its computational complexities and time requirement.

Mid-Product Method

The mid-product method is similar to the mid-square method in that both use a seed value and select middle-digit numbers. The only difference is that in the mid-product method, instead of squaring the value, we multiply a constant. For example, let us use the same seed value as before (4,745) and a constant of 123. Then the random number generation process will be:

$$\text{Seed value} = 4{,}745;\ \text{constant} = 123$$
$$123(4{,}745) = 5\boxed{8363}5;\ r_1 = 8{,}363$$
$$123(8{,}363) = 10\boxed{2864}9;\ r_2 = 2{,}864$$
$$123(2{,}864) = 3\boxed{5227}2;\ r_3 = 5{,}227$$
$$123(5{,}227) = \cdots,\ \text{etc.}$$

This method generates a set of pseudorandom numbers as does the mid-square method. However, it also shares the same basic inefficiency as the mid-square method.

Random Number Transformation

There are a number of different methods to generate random numbers by the computer. Some of these methods use complex procedures, such as the multiplicative congruential method. Discussions of these procedures are beyond the scope of this text. Instead, we will discuss how uniform random numbers are transformed into random numbers for a given distribution. There are a number of methods of transformation, such as the inverse transformation, the tabular method, the method of convolution, and so on. We will study the *inverse transformation* method because it is the simplest and the most fundamental technique of generating random numbers from a probability distribution.

The basic approach of inverse transformation is to get random numbers from the cumulative probability distribution that may be based on historical data. Suppose that we wish to generate random numbers from a probability distribution $F(x)$. If we have a uniform random number, r, and if we know how to determine x from $F(x)$, then we can generate numbers with distribution $F(x)$ by first generating r and then taking $x = F^{-1}(x)$. This inverse transformation method is illustrated in Figure 15.11.

The inverse transformation method is the same basic approach we used in the tabular method (Table 15.3) and the graphical method (Figure 15.7), where we used a discrete distribution. If we had a continuous distribution, the cumulative distribution would be represented by a continuous function, as shown in Figure 15.11.

In a computer-based simulation model, we can use one of a number of different random number generators as a subroutine in the system. Even though random number generators have a wide variety of computational schemes and their purposes differ

Figure 15.11   Inverse Transformation Procedure

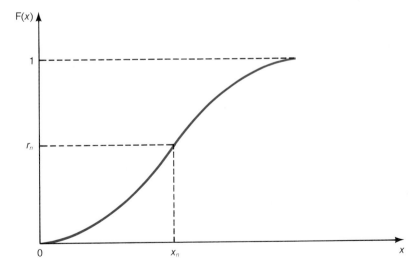

(1) Generate uniform random number r_n

(2) Find x_n by using $F^{-1}(x)$.

Figure 15.12   Flowchart of Random Generation of Daily Demand

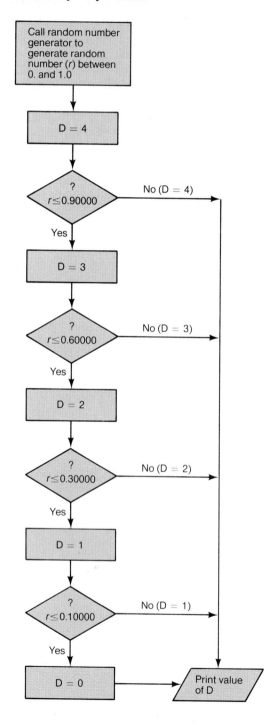

sometimes (e.g., a normal random number generator or an exponential random number generator), the basic approach used is almost the same. Figure 15.12 presents a flow-chart for the random generation of daily demand that we discussed in Table 15.3.

Casette 15.2   **PEACH COMPUTERS INC.**

Peach Computers Inc. specializes in selling various personal computers. Recently, the company has been experiencing widely fluctuating inventories for its Saturn X comput-ers. William Sharpe, the office manager, is interested in experimenting with various inventory policy options before selecting an acceptable one. The primary policy deci-sions are concerned with the order quantity and the reorder point.

The office has good historical data concerning past lead time, weekly demand, and associated inventory costs. Although Bill has not been able to pinpoint the unit shortage cost, there are some lost sales when computers are not available for sale. Thus, Bill would like to obtain information about the total inventory cost and the probability of computer shortage associated with a given order quantity and reorder point.

After a thorough search of the historical data, Bill was able to determine the following:

Annual holding cost per computer (HC): $104 ($2/week)

Ordering cost per order (OC): $30

Weekly Demand Distribution	
Computers	Probability
0	0.3
1	0.4
2	0.3
	1.0

Lead Time Distribution	
Weeks	Probability
1	0.25
2	0.50
3	0.25
	1.00

Simulation Procedure

Bill would like to experiment with order quantities ranging from 5 to 10 and reorder points from 2 to 5. In order to establish a valid pattern for inventory levels throughout a year (52 weeks) for each of the 24 combinations of order quantities and reorder points (6 order quantities × 4 reorder points = 24), Bill would like to run a sufficient number

Table 15.9   Monte Carlo Process for the Inventory Problem

Weekly Demand

Units	Probability	Cumulative Probability	Random Number Intervals
0	0.3	0.3	1–30
1	0.4	0.7	31–70
2	0.3	1.0	71–100

Lead Time

Weeks	Probability	Cumulative Probability	Random Number Intervals
1	0.25	0.25	1–25
2	0.50	0.75	26–75
3	0.25	1.00	76–100

of simulation runs to draw valid conclusions. Table 15.9 presents the cumulative probabilities and random number intervals for the weekly demand and lead time.

In order to determine the total annual inventory cost for various combinations of order quantity (Q) and reorder point (R), the simulation model is designed as shown in Figure 15.13. This process adjusts the inventory level, initiates the necessary orders, and computes the total inventory cost for various combinations of Q and R.

Simulation Results

The beginning inventory level of Saturn X computers in the first week is assumed to be 7 units. Table 15.10 presents the results of the first five runs based on an order quantity of five units and a reorder point of two.

Bill first conducted a complete simulation of the problem for 24,000 runs, 1,000 runs for each combination of the order quantity (Q) and reorder point (R). The result of the computer run is presented in Figure 15.14. Although the difference in the average total annual inventory cost is relatively small among the 24 combinations, there are significant differences in the average annual stock-out.

Table 15.10   Five Inventory Simulation Runs ($Q = 5$, $R = 2$)

Week	Lead Time Random Number	Lead Time Weeks	Weekly Demand Random Number	Weekly Demand Units	Ending Inventory	Holding Cost/ Week	Ordering Cost	Total Cost/Week
0					7			
1	—	—	56	1	6	$12	—	$12
2	—	—	91	2	4	8	—	8
3	62	2	88	2	2	4	$30	34
4	—	—	16	0	2	4	—	4
5	—	—	59	1	6	12	—	12

Figure 15.13   *Peach Computer Inventory Simulation Model*

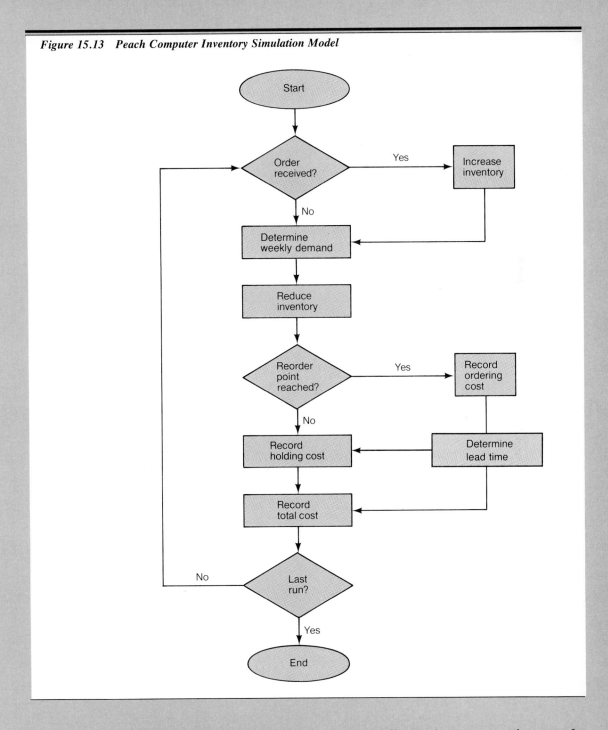

Bill believes that Peach Computers cannot afford to lose customers because of a continuous shortage of Saturn X computers. Thus, the absolute ceiling of average stockouts is set at 5 computers per year. On the basis of this policy decision, Peach Computers decided to adopt an inventory policy of EOQ = 9, $R = 3$. With this policy, the company can expect the minimum total inventory cost of \$1,586.15 per year.

Figure 15.14   *Inventory Simulation Results, 24,000 runs*

.invensim output

Q = 5	R	AVERAGE ANNUAL ORDER & HOLDING COST	AVERAGE ANNUAL STOCK-OUT
	2	1596.02	13.93
	3	1598.43	4.88
	4	1597.22	1.17
	5	1594.08	0.19

Q = 6	R	AVERAGE ANNUAL ORDER & HOLDING COST	AVERAGE ANNUAL STOCK-OUT
	2	1601.60	14.02
	3	1601.47	4.96
	4	1596.31	1.14
	5	1596.89	0.19

Q = 7	R	AVERAGE ANNUAL ORDER & HOLDING COST	AVERAGE ANNUAL STOCK-OUT
	2	1598.00	14.16
	3	1594.87	4.85
	4	1594.09	1.12
	5	1598.15	0.19

Q = 8	R	AVERAGE ANNUAL ORDER & HOLDING COST	AVERAGE ANNUAL STOCK-OUT
	2	1592.07	13.79
	3	1592.80	4.91
	4	1591.65	1.15
	5	1603.15	0.17

Q = 9	R	AVERAGE ANNUAL ORDER & HOLDING COST	AVERAGE ANNUAL STOCK-OUT
	2	1595.23	13.94
	3	1586.15	4.79
	4	1594.31	1.05
	5	1599.98	0.16

Q = 10	R	AVERAGE ANNUAL ORDER & HOLDING COST	AVERAGE ANNUAL STOCK-OUT
	2	1595.62	14.01
	3	1594.00	4.90
	4	1593.09	1.16
	5	1595.02	0.18

OPTIMIZATION IN SIMULATION

As we discussed earlier, the simulation model usually provides descriptive results about the behavior of a system under study. However, for certain problems, we may be able to use a subroutine in the model in such a way that simulation, through its search process, will provide us with the best solution. The best solution selected by this procedure is *optimum* in the sense that it is the best among the solutions generated by simulation. However, it is not the same as the optimum solution that we obtain from a linear program.

Table 15.11   Total Inventory Cost for Various Q and R Combinations

Quantity Ordered (Q)	Reorder Point (R)			
	3	**4**	**5**	**6**
10	$1,215	$1,110	$980	$1,025
11	1,079	1,002	874	926
12	945	836	746	795
13	926	812	728	774
14	981	864	769	821

The optimum solution derived by an analytical technique such as linear programming is truly optimum. The best solution derived by a simulation model is only approximate or quasi-optimum. Nevertheless, if the simulation process is carefully designed and includes a large enough number of runs to derive valid conclusions, simulation can produce a "good" approximate optimum solution.

As we demonstrated in Casette 15.2, we can easily determine the best combination of order quantity (Q) and reorder point (R) that yields the minimum total inventory cost. For example, suppose that the total inventory cost (TC) function is given as follows:

$$TC = THC + TOC + TSC$$

where

$$THC = \text{total annual holding cost}$$
$$TOC = \text{total annual ordering cost}$$
$$TSC = \text{total annual stock-out cost}$$

Now, we can set Q to a certain number and vary the value of R and determine the total inventory cost for that combination by selecting the lead time and demand rate through a Monte Carlo process. If we simulate 100 runs for each combination, the average TC of the combination can be taken as a good approximation. On the basis of this process, the simulation model can compare the average TC for each Q and R combination and select the best inventory policy. In order to assist the decision maker, we can construct a summary table as shown in Table 15.11. In this summary, the minimum total inventory cost ($728) is obtained when $Q = 13$ and $R = 5$.

SIMULATION LANGUAGES

Construction of a simulation model usually requires the development of a computer program. This phase of simulation modeling is often a very time-consuming step. Fortunately, there are several widely used general simulation languages available. A selection of the most appropriate simulation language for the given problem can save us much time and cost.

Most simulation programs have many similar functions, such as generating random numbers, advancing time, recording intermediate results for analysis, and the like. In recognition of such similarities, a generalized simulation language was developed in the 1950s. Since then, several other simulation languages have been developed.

The best-known and most widely available simulation languages are GPSS (General Purpose Simulation System), Simscript, Simula, Slam, and Dynamo. We will discuss each of these simulation languages briefly.

GPSS

This is one of the most widely used simulation languages available today. It was developed by IBM in the early 1960s. Its latest version is GPSS/H from Wolverine Software. Although GPSS is often classified as a flowchart-oriented language, it is also effective for systems with complex processes. Thus, it is quite compatible with problems that involve queues or networks. Knowledge of computer programming is not a prerequisite for using GPSS.

SIMSCRIPT

SIMSCRIPT, developed by the RAND corporation in the early 1960s, is a dedicated high level simulation language for discrete event simulation. Its latest version called SIMSCRIPT II.5 was updated by CACI in 1983. This language is particularly effective for process-oriented simulation modeling. This version of SIMSCRIPT, with a much-improved interface, is one of the most popular languages in the industry today.

SIMULA

SIMULA was developed by O. J. Dahl and K. Nygaard and released by the Norwegian Computing Center in 1965. The latest version is SIMULA 67. This language is quite similar to SIMSCRIPT.

SLAM II

SLAM II is a FORTRAN based simulation language. It was originally developed by Alan P. Pritsker in 1979. SLAM II is an effective tool for process-oriented simulation modeling with other capabilities including continuous modeling. The basic feature of SLAM is similar to the block structures of GPSS. The advanced features of this language are somewhat difficult to use due to the requirement of understanding FORTRAN subroutines.

DYNAMO

DYNAMO was developed by P. Fox and A. Pugh at M.I.T. in 1959. This language was an outgrowth of J. Forrester's *Industrial Dynamics* modeling approach. It is particularly efficient in analyzing the dynamic behaviors of large-scale industrial systems. DYNAMO requires very little computer programming knowledge for its use.

The aforementioned simulation languages have been developed for the mainframe. Recently, most of these languages are available in a microcomputer version. GPSS/PC, SIMSCRIPT PC, and Micro-DYNAMO are languages for microcomputers. In addition, there are many special-purpose simulation languages for microcomputers on the market. They include ASSE, DYNSIM, GASS, HYSIM, MAXSIM, Micro-NET, SLAM II, SIMAN, and TUTSIM.

APPLICATIONS OF SIMULATION

Simulation has been applied to many decision problems that are too complex to be analyzed by analytical techniques. What is impressive about simulation is that a great number of the studies dealing with this topic are about applications to real-world problems. Let us briefly discuss some of the best-known application areas of simulation.

Queuing Problems

Perhaps the most prevalent application area of simulation is queuing problems. As we discussed in Chapter 13, in many real-world queuing problems, the only avenue open to systematic analysis is simulation.

Inventory Problems

Many inventory problems involve several random variables such as lead time, demand rate, time required to process an order, and quantity received. As we saw in Casette 15.2, simulation is an effective tool for analyzing complex inventory problems.

Network Problems

In many network problems, all parameters are not provided as neatly as we need for using PERT or CPM. There are many random events we must deal with in network systems, such as probabilistic activity times, branching, and performance. Many stochastic network simulation programs have been developed recently. Five of these are GEMS-II, Q-GERT, VERT III, NETWORK II.5, and Micro-NET. NETWORK II.5 is specially designed for finding bottlenecks in a proposed computer system. Micro-NET is a discrete event language for microcomputers.

Operations Planning

Many operations management problems, including production, inventory control, warehousing, plant layout, assembly line balancing, location-allocation, and maintenance, involve complex stochastic processes. Simulation has been applied extensively to these problems. SIMAN is a continuous/discrete general purpose language specially designed for the modeling of manufacturing systems.

Financial Planning

Many financial problems are influenced by external factors (e.g., state of the economy, interest rates, monetary policy, and foreign trade). Thus, it is difficult to use analytical techniques for such problems. Simulation has been applied to such financial problems as overall corporate financial planning, capital budgeting, working capital management, and cash flow analysis. SIMPLAN is a special purpose simulation language for the modeling of financial and economic systems.

Policy Analysis

Recently there have been reported many interesting applications of simulation that deal with public policies. Among these are operational policy decisions for schools, police departments, fire departments, sewage treatment plants, judiciary systems, land development, water resources, environmental protection, and tax systems.

Artificial Intelligence, Expert Systems, and Heuristic Programming

Artificial intelligence deals with simulating human thought through computers. Although the attempt to make the computer think intelligently is still far from complete, much progress has been made in using the computer to search, recognize patterns, prove mathematical relationships, and learn from experience.

Expert systems, also referred to as "knowledge systems" or "knowledge engineering," have received increasing attention as a subfield of artificial intelligence. An expert system is a computer program that behaves very much as a human expert would when solving problems; it differs only in that it represents and applies knowledge electronically. Many expert systems, such as medical diagnosis, tax preparation, and accounting analysis, are constructed for specific objectives; they are rule-based systems used for analysis.

An area related to artificial intelligence is heuristic programming. **Heuristics** are basically step-by-step procedures that are used to obtain satisfying solutions to complex problems. Heuristic programming is the general approach that uses heuristics to derive "good enough" solutions to poorly structured problems. Simulation has a great potential in these new areas of human decision making.

Business Games

Many **business games** (management games, decision games, simulation games, marketing games, investment games, operational games, and the like) are useful educational or training tools that simulate realistic settings for decision making. The basic purpose of simulation games is to provide the participants with an intuitive feel for the effect of interrelated variables on a decision outcome.

System Simulation

System simulation usually involves an analysis of the dynamic behavior of a very large-scale system, such as the national economic system, the world population problem, or an urban system. System simulation is based on the **industrial dynamics** modeling approach developed by J. Forrester. The simulation model includes many mathematical equations for the flow of resources or their interactions in a computer program. Then, through time lags and feedback systems built into the model, the simulation model provides information concerning the effects of various policies or inputs.

REAL-WORLD APPLICATIONS

In view of the general applicability of simulation and today's easy access to inexpensive computing facilities, it is natural to expect wide applications of simulation. The literature of management science certainly supports this trend. Furthermore, we expect that this trend will continue at an accelerating rate. We believe that simulation will play an even greater role in the application of management science to real-world decision problems in the years to come. In this section we will briefly review two interesting real-world applications of simulation.

Railway Simulation Guides Canadian National Expansion

Canada's economy depends to a large extent on exports carried by its railways, in particular the western route of Canadian National (CN).[1] Much of CN's western line is single track, although current transportation demands exceed what many railways consider possible for single track. Traffic forecasts indicate steadily growing shipments on this line through 1990, with over 50 percent growth for the entire line. Expansion to double track was clearly called for, yet any such expansion would be financially strenuous, costing CN $3 to 5 million (Canadian dollars) per mile, plus bridges and tunnels. For the years 1985 to 1989, forecast capital expenditures totaled $3.5 billion (Canadian dollars). Any scientific assistance in reducing or delaying any part of this sum was highly desirable.

Several models were prepared to analyze and optimize train assignment to individual segments of track. The established centralized traffic control (CTC) signal system was used as a control mechanism, with two simulation models providing train speed information and route-capacity–induced delays. Maintenance efforts were represented by selected track outages and slow orders. Distance between trains, or headway, was minimized to emulate the signal system's effect. The decision simulator used a global feasibility check to prevent unresolvable conflicts and a local heuristic involving priority and delays to arrange train meets and overtakes.

Written in SIMSCRIPT II.5, the major route capacity model simulates 2 weeks of operations in less than 1 minute, giving a 95 percent confidence interval of 10 percent. Program development took 15 months and cost $250,000 (Canadian dollars). Among the early results was the decision to install a system of intermediate signals, a low-cost move that allowed for shorter headways. Detailed analysis was performed for four maintenance scenarios and zero to five intermediate signals. The addition of five intermediates between each pair of control signals gave the same capacity results as double-tracking 40 percent of the line, at a comparative cost of $8 million (Canadian dollars) per subdivision for signals and $150 million for double track. Partial double track, close to subdivision terminal portals, was also recommended.

Maintenance procedures were also analyzed, with deferral of double track installation possible where work shifts were broken up into 4-hour rather than 8-hour blocks and where temporary tracks were installed to store equipment rather than blocking a siding. Smaller equipment with higher working costs provided a net benefit in decreasing delay time. Running this simulation reduced double track plans by 27 percent and allowed deferral of $350 million of capital expenditures. In addition, Seaboard System Railway bought the models designed by CN and has used them extensively.

Improving the Efficiency of a Health-Care System

The health institutions of Nigeria were plagued by ineffectiveness and inefficiency, usually blamed on inadequate personnel levels. Studies conducted in the health services industry in Western nations were not applicable to the situation in Nigeria, because the systems, personnel, and other factors differed so. To determine where the problem could

[1]Norma Welch and James Gussow, "Expansion of Canadian National Railway's Line Capacity," *Interfaces* 16:1 (1986), 51–64.

best be attacked, management science techniques were employed.[2] The analysis focused on the Rural Health Center in Ikire, a major component of the Nigerian health-care system.

Two sets of models were designed. Linear programming provided optimal solutions with respect to patient delegation patterns and determined the adequacy of the current staffing pattern and the marginal productivity of each category of worker. Simulation allowed for variation of operational and management policies, as recommended by experienced personnel. Simulation was used to determine conflict between various clinics of the health center should a patient require attention at more than one clinic. The impact of increases in case load at the center was also evaluated by the simulation model.

Optimal results indicated that the clinic could increase its patient load by 75 to 100 percent, depending on the day of the week. Various policies were endorsed, such as task delegation procedures and the timing of records preparation. Both model types showed that bottlenecks arose from misallocation of personnel rather than insufficient staffing. With the support of the Ministry of Health and the workers, changes in operating policies were implemented. Average patient time in the center has declined by up to 45 minutes, and a new policy of free medical services increased the average number of patients by almost 60 percent. No staffing change was needed, and all concerned appreciate the center's improved efficiency.

SUMMARY

Most of the management science techniques we have studied prior to this chapter are designed for specific types of problems. For example, linear programming is an optimization technique for constrained decision problems. These techniques are based on restrictive and sometimes unrealistic assumptions. Many of the real-world problems we face are often too complex to impose such restrictive assumptions.

Simulation is a method for conducting experiments based on logical procedures or mathematical models. As such, simulation does not require any inherent assumptions. Simulation is a highly flexible and powerful management science tool for many real-world problems. This flexibility results in some undesirable side-effects, such as the diverse model structures, the problem of model validity, and the complexity of output analysis. However, individual creativity and a strict set of technical procedures can help us to alleviate most of these problems.

Perhaps the most significant element of simulation is the Monte Carlo process. It is an extremely useful process to generate values of random variables. The Monte Carlo process involves basically two phases: (1) generation of a uniformly distributed random number, and (2) transformation of the selected random number into a corresponding value for the random variable.

Simulation has been widely applied to a variety of real-world problems. In addition to typical operational problems, such as queuing, inventory control, financial planning,

---

[2]Eyitayo Lambo, ''An Optimization-Simulation Model of a Rural Health Center in Nigeria,'' *Interfaces* 13:3 (1983), 29–35.

and production operations, it is becoming increasingly important in the area of artificial intelligence and heuristic programming. The computer-based simulation approach is a valuable management science tool today and will be more so in the future.

Glossary

Artificial Intelligence   The simulation of human thought through computers, especially in the areas of pattern recognition and learning from experience.

Business Games   Techniques of using simulation to provide training in business methods. Usually interactive, these games may focus on management decisions, marketing, investments, production, etc.

Descriptor   Information describing characteristics of a system, obtained through simulation.

Expert System   A computer program that behaves very much as a human expert would when solving problems based on preset rules.

Flowchart   Diagram analyzing the steps involved in a process in terms of actions, processes, and decisions.

Heuristic Programming   Method of obtaining acceptable (rather than optimal) solutions to complex problems by use of a series of decision-rule-type procedures.

Industrial Dynamics   Large-scale simulation technique involving numerous mathematical equations representing the flow of resources, time lags, feedback, and interaction between various model components.

Monte Carlo   Process of sampling based on selection of a random number which corresponds to a given outcome, based on a known probability distribution.

Pseudorandom Number   Value generated by a numerical technique, which typically is part of a pattern that eventually repeats itself. Not truly random, but frequently useful as such.

Random Number   Member of a group of numbers which all have a uniform (equal) probability of being selected.

Simulation   An experimentation technique allowing use of a model (representing a system) to determine the operating characteristics of the system in descriptive terms.

Transformation   Conversion of a selected random number into a value appropriate for describing a model parameter, such as lead time or daily demand.

Uniform Probability Distribution   Distribution in which every item in the group under consideration has an equal probability of occurring.

References

Forrester, J. *Industrial Dynamics*. Cambridge, Mass.: M.I.T. Press, 1961.

Kiviat, P. J., Villaneuva, R., and Markowitz, H. M. *The Simscript II Programming Language*. Englewood Cliffs, N.J.: Prentice-Hall, 1969.

Kluyver, C., and McNally, G. "Corporate Planning Using Simulation." *Interfaces* 10:3 (June 1980), 1–7.

Lee, S. M., Moore, L. J., and Taylor, B. W. *Management Science*. 2d ed. Dubuque, Iowa: W. C. Brown, 1985.

Meier, R. C., Newell, W. T., and Pazer, H. L. *Simulation in Business and Economics*. Englewood Cliffs, N.J.: Prentice-Hall, 1969.

Pritsker, A. A. B. *The GASP IV Simulation Language*. New York: Wiley, 1974.

Pritsker, A. A. B. *Modeling and Analysis Using Q-GERT Networks*. 2d ed. New York: Wiley, 1977.

Pugh, A. L. *DYNAMO II User's Manual*. Cambridge, Mass.: M.I.T. Press, 1970.

Schriber, T. S. *Simulation Using GPSS*. New York: Wiley, 1974.

Wheelwright, S. C., and Makridakis, S. G. *Computer-Aided Modeling for Managers*. Reading, Mass.: Addison-Wesley, 1972.

Wyman, F. P. *Simulation Modeling: A Guide to Using SIMSCRIPT*. New York: Wiley, 1970.

Assignments

15.1 What is simulation? Define it by using your own words.

15.2 What are the major differences between an analytical solution procedure and simulation?

15.3 Describe any decision problem familiar to you that could be analyzed by simulation more appropriately than by analytical techniques.

15.4 What are the types of results we can obtain from simulation of a model?

15.5 Describe a decision problem that is not suited for simulation. (*Hint:* Consider several of the disadvantages of simulation discussed in this chapter.)

15.6 Define the following terms briefly: *random variable, pseudorandom number, cumulative distribution, random number generation, transformation, Monte Carlo method*.

15.7 Among all of the advantages of simulation we discussed in this chapter, what is the most important advantage in your opinion? Why?

15.8 Briefly describe the basic steps of the simulation process and indicate how various types of information are processed through each step.

15.9 Explain briefly how the tabular method and the graphical method work in the random-number generation process.

15.10 Categorize simulation languages in terms of their orientation toward flowchart or process.

15.11 Briefly define the following terms: *artificial intelligence, business games, heuristics, industrial dynamics*.

15.12 It is possible to incorporate an optimization process in simulation. Does that mean that the optimum solution we derive through simulation would be exactly the same as the true optimum solution?

15.13 What are the major characteristics of simulation models?

15.14 Why is the transformation procedure necessary in the Monte Carlo process?

15.15 What is the primary reason that many random-number generators produce pseudorandom numbers rather than true random numbers?

15.16 By using a random selection procedure, generate 10 random numbers from the table of random numbers (Appendix 5).

15.17 Generate 10 random numbers by the mid-square method. Use 1,779 as the initial seed value and select 4 middle-digit numbers.

15.18 Generate 10 random numbers by the mid-product method. Use 1,779 as the seed value and 253 as the constant. Select the middle 4 digits as numbers.

15.19 The time between arrivals of customers at the information desk of a local IRS office is given by the following probability distribution:

Time between Arrivals (minutes)	Probability
1	0.10
2	0.25
3	0.35
4	0.20
5	0.10

a. Construct a cumulative probability distribution.
b. Simulate the arrival of 10 customers by the tabular method.
c. Compute the expected time between arrivals and compare it with the mean time between arrivals derived by simulation.

15.20 Customer service time of the teller machine at the Midland Commercial Bank is considered as a random variable and is defined by the following probability distribution:

Service Time (minutes)	Probability
3	0.10
4	0.20
5	0.30
6	0.25
7	0.10
8	0.05

a. Construct a cumulative probability distribution.

b. Suppose there are 10 customers to be served. Simulate their service time by using the graphical method.

15.21 Aqua-Science Laboratories produces a number of different types of marine science equipment. This company has two different assembly lines to produce its most popular sonar equipment, Aqua-Sonics. The process time for each assembly line is regarded as a random variable and is described by the following probability distribution:

Process Time (minutes)	Assembly 1	Assembly 2
3	0.10	0.15
4	0.40	0.35
5	0.30	0.25
6	0.20	0.25

a. Construct a cumulative probability distribution of the process time for each assembly line.

b. Develop a random number mechanism to generate the process time for 20 units of the product and compute the average process time for the product.

15.22 The time between two consecutive customers arriving at an auto repair shop is considered a random variable and has the following probability distribution:

Time between Arrivals (10-minutes)	Probability
1	0.10
2	0.20
3	0.30
4	0.15
5	0.13
6	0.12

a. Construct a cumulative probability distribution of the interarrival time.

b. Simulate the customer arrival for 10 customers and compute the mean time between arrivals.

15.23 Abdul Mohammed has been the port manager in the state of Oman. After several hectic years of his tenure, he has learned to manage the port efficiently. Realizing the importance of the port as the major window of export for his country, Mohammed would like to establish an effective port management policy. Since simulation appears to be the best method for analyzing this type of problem, he organized a management science group to conduct a feasibility study of this project.

Assume that you are a member of the management science group. Given the probability distribution for interarrival time between ships as shown below, construct a cumulative probability distribution and illustrate it graphically. Indicate on the graph how the time between ship arrivals can be obtained as a random variable based on the generation of random numbers between 0 and 1.

Time between Ship Arrivals (days)	Probability
1	0.05
2	0.10
3	0.20
4	0.30
5	0.20
6	0.10
7	0.05

15.24 By using the probability data in Problem 15.23 and the random number table in Appendix 5, generate uniform random numbers first and then determine the corresponding interarrival times for the first 20 ships. In selecting random numbers from Appendix 5, select any two-digit number (e.g., 35, 74) at a time. Complete the following table of 20 observations:

	Random Number	Interarrival Times
No ship—1st ship		
1st ship—2d ship		
2d ship—3d ship		
.		
.		
.		
19th ship—20th ship		

15.25 Assume that most ships entering this port, described in Problem 15.23, need about 5 days to unload, clean, and prepare for departure. Determine by simulation the values for the random variables specified in the following table. (Use the Monte Carlo process and let the days start with day 0.)

Ship Number	Arrival Day	Time to Arrival of Next Ship	Day Unloading Begins	Departure Day	Waiting Time	No. of Ships Waiting
1						
2						
3						
.						
.						
.						
10						

15.26 Compute the following summary statistics for the ship docking simulation of Problem 15.25:
  a. Mean time between ship arrivals
  b. Mean time that ships wait to unload
  c. Mean number of ships waiting to unload
  d. Mean time that ships spend waiting to unload and being unloaded
  e. Proportion of arrivals that enter an empty port
  f. Frequency distribution of ship waiting time
  g. Frequency distribution of number of ships waiting

15.27 Refer to Problem 15.25. Assume that the time required to unload, clean, and prepare for departure is a random variable that ranges from 3 days to 6 days with the following probability distribution:

Time to Unload, Clean, and Prepare for Departure (days)	Probability
3	0.1
4	0.2
5	0.4
6	0.3

  a. For the first 20 ships, construct a cumulative probability distribution and determine the time to unload, clean, and prepare for departure by using the random number table in Appendix 5.
  b. Assuming a random unloading time for this case, construct a new table similar to the table shown in Problem 15.25. (Note that the simulation results now include the joint interaction of two random variables, interarrival time and unloading time.)

15.28 On the basis of the processes used to obtain simulation results from Problems 15.23 through 15.27 (regarding unloading time as a random variable), develop a flowchart of ship docking simulation and identify five basic components of the Monte Carlo process.

15.29 John Demsky is the inventory manager for the Weight Watchers' Clinic. Recently, the demand for Diet 15 has shown wide fluctuations. John wants to determine the expected demand for Diet 15 in stock during a reorder period, i.e., the time lapse from the stock reorder until the ordered goods are received. The most important information John is seeking is how far in advance he should reorder before the stock level is reduced to 0. On the basis of the historical data concerning lead time and demand, John realizes that these two variables are random variables, described by the following probability distributions.

Lead Time (days)	Probability	Demand per Day	Probability
1	0.5	1	0.1
2	0.3	2	0.3
3	0.2	3	0.4
		4	0.2

a. Simulate this problem by using the Monte Carlo process. Show the demand during lead time (*DDLT*) for 30 reorders and determine the expected demand during lead time. (*Hint:* The lead time must first be randomly generated, followed by separate random generations of daily demand rates for each day of lead time.)

b. From the simulation results, construct a frequency distribution of the demand during lead time.

15.30 Refer to Problem 15.29. After determining the frequency distribution of the demand during lead time, John wishes to set his reorder point so that the probability of stock-out during a lead time is no greater than 0.1 (the percentage of reorder periods during which shortages occur should be no more than 10 percent). This policy represents a 90 percent service level for customers.

a. At what level should John set his reorder point in order to provide a 90 percent service level to his customers?

b. Where should the reorder point be set to maintain a service level of 80 percent? Of 60 percent?

16 FORECASTING

One of management's most important functions is planning. A successful organization must have an effective planning system that accurately forecasts future events and develops appropriate strategies. Experience and judgment can give a decision maker a good "feel" for what the future holds. However, many difficult management decisions require more concrete data because of the magnitude or the importance of such decisions. For example, a production manager needs accurate predictions of expected demand, a financial officer of a bank needs a good forecast of the interest rate, and the treasurer of a state government needs an accurate estimate of the future tax revenues. In this chapter, we will study several important forecasting methods that are essential for effective management decision making.

Learning Objectives *From the study of this chapter, we will learn the following:*

1. The basic nature of forecasting
2. The use of time series methods: moving averages, weighted moving averages, exponential smoothing, and trend projection
3. The use of regression forecasting methods: simple and multiple regression models
4. The use of qualitative methods to forecast: Delphi and nominal group techniques
5. Computer solutions of forecasting methods
6. Real-world applications of forecasting methods
7. The meaning of the following terms:

Time series	*Regression analysis*
Forecast	*Multiple regression model*
Trend	*Correlation coefficient*
Moving averages	*Coefficient of determination*
Weighted moving averages	*Delphi method*
Exponential smoothing	*Nominal group techniques*
Mean absolute deviation (MAD)	

FORECASTING METHODS

Forecasting involves prediction of future events. Wall Street analysts forecast the stock market movements, meteorologists predict the weather conditions, sports odds makers predict the point spreads of basketball games, and sales managers attempt to estimate the future demand for their products. An accurate forecast is extremely important for effective decision making.

A sales manager attempts to predict future sales volumes as accurately as possible because so many important functions of the organization depend on these estimates. For example, production schedules, inventory policies, purchasing, sales quotas, work force planning, training and development, and cash flow management all depend on the sales volume forecast.

To make an accurate sales forecast for a product, we may first review the general industry sales trend during the past several years. Then, we need to analyze the company's past sales data to establish a general trend, such as an 8 percent average annual increase. Also, we may identify seasonal patterns in sales, such as peak sales occurring in the Christmas season and sales volume bottoming out in the summer season. With such data, we are in a good position to predict relatively accurately a product's future sales.

The historical sales data described above can be referred to as a time series. A **time series** is a set of historical data measured or observed over a sequence of points in time. We are quite familiar with time series, such as interest rates, unemployment rates, trade deficits, sales, housing starts, the Dow-Jones Industrial Average, etc.

Forecasting methods can be classified into quantitative and qualitative approaches. Quantitative forecasting methods include time series methods and causal methods. Time series methods attempt to predict a time series based on its historical data. In these methods, we are assuming that what has happened in the past will continue to occur in the future. Moving average, exponential smoothing, and trend projection are the time series methods discussed in this chapter.

Causal methods are used to predict a time series by analyzing historical data of the factors or variables that are related to the time series we are attempting to forecast. For example, the number of tourists coming to Florida in December can be forecasted based on the temperature, snowfall (in inches), and air fare specials in the northern part of the country. In addition, we may also want to include historical data on tourists coming to Florida in December. We will discuss regression analysis as a causal method.

Qualitative methods incorporate subjective or judgmental factors into forecasting. In general, qualititative methods use the opinions, judgment, or experiences of experts to make appropriate forecasts. These methods are especially useful when no historical data are available or the decision is extremely important but rarely occurs. In this chapter, we will discuss the Delphi method and the nominal group technique. Figure 16.1 presents the forecasting methods to be discussed in this chapter.

There are a number of ways to **forecast** the future. As individuals, we predict traffic patterns at different times, lengths of time required to do our daily chores, the weather conditions in the afternoon, and the like. These estimates are often subjective. Many managers, especially in small businesses, often use qualitative or seat-of-the-pants methods of forecasting based on their judgment or experience.

Many quantitative methods are useful to forecast time series, such as moving averages, exponential smoothing, trend analysis, and regression analysis. A forecasting method's applicability depends on the objective of the procedure, the time horizon, the existence of patterns (e.g., trend, seasonality, peak and valley), and the number of variables associated with the item in question. Regardless of the forecasting method we select, the forecasting process requires the following basic steps:

Figure 16.1   Classification of Forecasting Methods

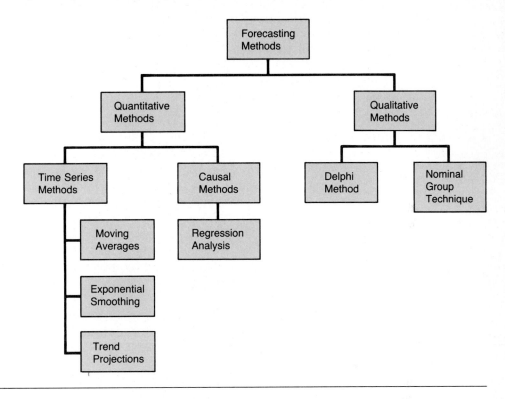

Step 1   Determine the objective of the forecast—what are we trying to find out?

Step 2   Determine the items or variables to be forecasted—sales, labor requirements, tax revenue, etc.

Step 3   Determine the time horizon for the forecast—short term (weekly), intermediate term (quarterly), or long term (yearly).

Step 4   Determine the forecasting method—moving average, regression model, etc.

Step 5   Collect the required data—past sales records, past student enrollments, number of housing permits issued, etc.

Step 6   Validate the forecasting model.

Step 7   Make the forecast.

Step 8   Implement the results and update the forecasting process through a feedback system.

The above steps are quite similar to the management decision-making process. An effective forecasting process solidly establishes the above steps so that they function on a continuous basis.

TIME SERIES METHODS

In general, time series forecasting can be analyzed according to different time frames. *Short-term* forecasts usually involve a relatively short time, such as daily sales during the next several weeks to 3 months. *Medium-term,* or *intermediate-term,* forecasts typically involve time frames from 1 quarter (3 months) to 1 year. A medium-term forecast may reveal peaks and valleys of inventory levels for seasonally demanded products. *Long-term* forecasting usually encompasses several years to discern the long-term trend of time series data.

Elements of Time Series

In analyzing time series data, we should look for several components in the data. A time series typically consists of four components—trend, cycles, seasonal patterns, and random movements. A **trend** is a long-term movement of a time series. For example, the treasurer of a state government closely monitors monthly tax revenues. In a careful scrutiny of the data over the past 5 years, the treasurer can establish a gradual increasing trend in the long term, although there are short-term variations. The long-term trend may be in a linear, nonlinear, or no-trend form. Figure 16.2 presents three possible trends: (a) a linear increasing trend; (b) a nonlinear trend; and (c) no trend.

Whereas a trend indicates the long-term pattern of movement for a time series, we may observe regular movements below or above the trend line. For example, the long-term rate of increase in U.S. productivity, although a linear increasing trend, has definite *cycles,* such as the one shown in Figure 16.3.

The trend and cycles are long-term movements typically encompassing a number of years. A *seasonal pattern* is a regular variability that occurs repetitively within 1-year periods. For example, a producer of Christmas ornaments experiences peak sales in the fall and very low sales in the spring. This seasonal pattern repeats itself year after year.

A time series may also include *random movements* that do not follow any predictable patterns. Random movements, also called ''noise'' or ''residual,'' would be left after we forecast the time series through analyzing the trend, cycles, and seasonal patterns. Random movements represent unanticipated and unpredictable variability in the time series. Thus, a time series with a great deal of random movement would be quite difficult to forecast accurately.

Figure 16.2   Long-Term Trends

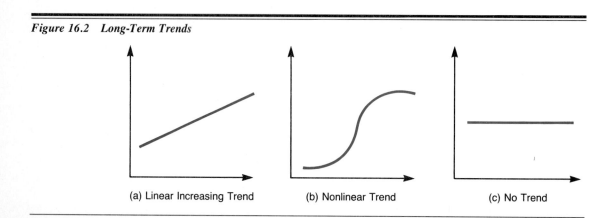

(a) Linear Increasing Trend   (b) Nonlinear Trend   (c) No Trend

Figure 16.3 A Time Series with a Trend and Cycles

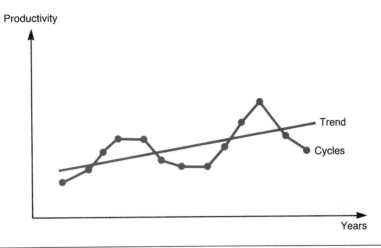

The Moving Average

Time series methods are statistical smoothing techniques that use historical data exclusively. Consequently, these methods forecast a variable against only one factor—time. *Moving averages* compute an average of the most recent data of a time series and then use this average to forecast a measure for the next period. The moving average is computed as follows:

$$\text{Moving average} = \frac{\Sigma \text{ (most recent } n \text{ measures)}}{n}$$

where
$$n = \text{number of data measures}$$

The following casette explains the use of moving averages.

Casette 16.1   *CENTENNIAL CORPORATION*

Centennial Corporation specializes in the sales and service of Comet video cameras. The cameras are imported from Japan on monthly orders made through telex. A 1-month lead time makes accurate forecast of the expected demand in the next month extremely important.

The company had monthly sales during the past 12 months as shown in Table 16.1. These sales data are presented graphically in Figure 16.4.

To compute the moving average, we must first decide how many measures to include in the average. Moving averages are frequently based on three or five time periods. As an example, we will first compute forecasts based on a 3-month moving average.

The moving average for the first 3 months of Comet camera sales is:

$$\text{Moving average (months 1 to 3)} = \frac{1{,}850 + 1{,}920 + 1{,}800}{3} = 1{,}856.67$$

Table 16.1   Monthly Sales of Comet Cameras during the Past Year

Month	Camera Sales
1	1,850
2	1,920
3	1,800
4	1,875
5	1,960
6	2,040
7	1,980
8	2,100
9	2,070
10	2,150
11	2,210
12	2,180

Figure 16.4   Monthly Sales of Comet Cameras during the Past Year

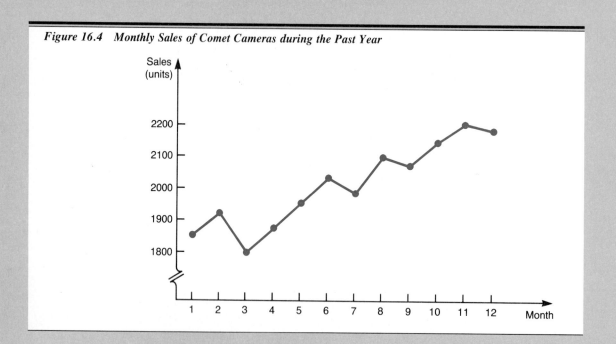

This value can be used as a prediction of the sales in month 4. The sales forecast for month 5 is:

$$\text{Moving average (months 2 to 4)} = \frac{1,920 + 1,800 + 1,875}{3} = 1,865$$

Table 16.2 presents the moving averages for the remaining months, in rounded figures. We can also compute moving averages based on 5-month periods. For example, the moving average for month 6 based on the sales of the first 5 months would be:

$$\begin{array}{c}\text{Moving average}\\ \text{(months 1 to 5)}\end{array} = \frac{1,850 + 1,920 + 1,800 + 1,875 + 1,960}{5} = 1,881$$

Table 16.2   Summary of 3- and 5-Month Moving Averages

Month	Actual Camera Sales	Forecast Sales	
		3-Month Moving Average	5-Month Moving Average
1	1,850		
2	1,920		
3	1,800		
4	1,875	1,857	
5	1,960	1,865	
6	2,040	1,878	1,881
7	1,980	1,958	1,919
8	2,100	1,993	1,931
9	2,070	2,040	1,991
10	2,150	2,050	2,030
11	2,210	2,107	2,068
12	2,180	2,143	2,102
13		2,180	2,142

Table 16.2 also presents the moving averages for the remaining months based on the 5-month averages.

The manager of Centennial is interested in forecasting the demand in the thirteenth month. The forecast based on the 3-month moving average is 2,180 cameras. The forecasted demand for the thirteenth month using the 5-month moving average is 2,142 cameras. The manager can base the monthly order on the moving averages derived in Table 16.2.

Although the moving average can be used to forecast a time series in the next period, we can also extend the forecast farther by identifying the general pattern of moving averages. Moving average forecasts represent the smoothed measures of an actual time series because they are averages of several time periods. Thus, moving averages plotted on a graph can reveal the general pattern of the time series under study.

Figure 16.5 presents the 3-month and 5-month moving averages of monthly camera sales: Clearly the jagged actual monthly sales observed are smoothed out by the 3-month moving averages, and they are even further smoothed by the 5-month moving averages. Thus, the response to a drastic change in monthly sales would be much slower in the 5-month moving averages than in the 3-month moving averages.

One crucial disadvantage of the moving average method is its inability to reflect chart variations that have significant meanings such as seasonality or cyclical movements. Nevertheless, this method is a relatively inexpensive and simple means to obtain a good forecast for the immediate future.

Weighted Moving Averages

The moving average method provides equal weights to actual data observed in each period. That is one of the reasons for its slow reaction to more recent variations in the time series. A modified version, using the **weighted moving averages,** assigns a greater weight to the more current data.

Figure 16.5   Monthly Sales, 3-Month and 5-Month Moving Averages

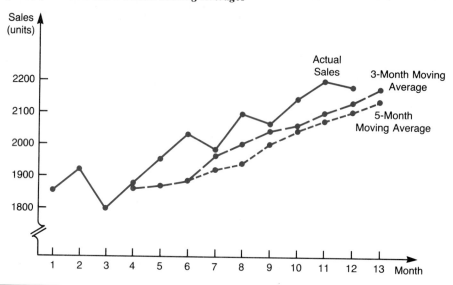

In our Centennial Corporation example, we may wish to assign a weight of 3 to the most current sales data, a weight of 2 to the previous month's data, and a weight of 1 to the data of 2 months ago. For example, computation of the four-month forecast of sales by the 3-month moving average method is:

Weighted 3-month average (months 1 to 3)

$$= \frac{3(1,800) + 2(1,920) + 1(1,850)}{6} = 1,848$$

Since the actual sales in month 3 are lower than in previous months, and a greater weight was assigned to these most-current sales data, the weighted moving average (1,848) is slightly lower than the previously computed nonweighted moving average (1,857). Be careful in determining the most appropriate weight distribution. If too great a weight is assigned to the current data, the weighted average may overreact to an irregular movement. However, if the weight assigned to current data is not much greater than that assigned to other data, the meaning of the weighted average would be lost.

Exponential Smoothing

The **exponential smoothing** forecast method attempts to predict the time series in the next period based on the moving average of the current period. This method also weights the most current data more heavily than older data. Consequently, the most recent changes are strongly reflected in the forecast.

The exponential smoothing model is as follows:

$$F_t = \alpha A_{t-1} + (1 - \alpha) F_{t-1}$$

where $\quad F_t$ = forecast of the time series for period t

$\quad A_{t-1}$ = actual or observed time series value in period $t-1$

$\quad F_{t-1}$ = forecast of the time series for period $t-1$

$\quad \alpha$ = smoothing factor ($0 \le \alpha \le 1$)

The smoothing factor α has a value between 0 and 1. This value represents the weight assigned to the previous period's actual data. For example, if we assign a weight of 0.3 to α, the exponential smoothing model becomes:

$$F_t = 0.3A_{t-1} + 0.7F_{t-1}$$

The above model indicates that the forecast for the upcoming period is based on 30 percent of the actual time series value in the previous period and 70 percent of past time series data. F_{t-1} is nothing but the forecast value based on past data. Consequently, if α is 1, the forecast for this period is based entirely on the actual data in the previous period. However, if α is 0, then the forecast is based entirely on previous data and ignores the actual data in the immediately preceding period.

Let us consider the Centennial Corporation problem presented as Casette 16.1. In computing the forecast value for each period, F_2 for month 2 must be based on only the actual data in month 1 (no forecast for period 1, or F_1, can be calculated from the data given). In other words, $F_2 = A_1$. Suppose we assign $\alpha = 0.2$. Then,

$$F_3 = 0.2A_2 + 0.8F_2$$
$$= 0.2(1{,}920) + 0.8(1{,}850)$$
$$= 1{,}864$$

$$F_4 = 0.2A_3 + 0.8F_3$$
$$= 0.2(1{,}800) + 0.8(1{,}864)$$
$$= 1{,}851$$

Table 16.3 presents the exponential smoothing forecast based on $\alpha = 0.2$ and $\alpha = 0.4$. Figure 16.6 presents monthly sales and exponential smoothing forecasts based

Table 16.3 Exponential Smoothing Forecast

Month	Actual Camera Sales	Exponential Smoothing Forecast $\alpha = 0.2$	Exponential Smoothing Forecast $\alpha = 0.4$
1	1,850		
2	1,920	1,850	1,850
3	1,800	1,864	1,878
4	1,875	1,851	1,847
5	1,960	1,856	1,858
6	2,040	1,877	1,899
7	1,980	1,910	1,955
8	2,100	1,924	1,965
9	2,070	1,959	2,019
10	2,150	1,981	2,039
11	2,210	2,015	2,083
12	2,180	2,054	2,134
13	—	2,079	2,152

Figure 16.6   *Monthly Sales and Exponential Smoothing Forecasts*

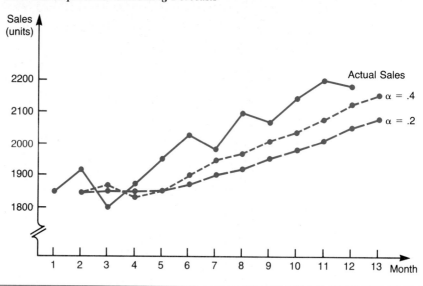

on $\alpha = 0.2$ and $\alpha = 0.4$. The figure shows that a forecast with a higher smoothing factor ($\alpha = 0.4$) reacts more sensitively to changes in sales than that with a lower smoothing factor ($\alpha = 0.2$). The exponential smoothing forecasts usually lag behind the trend. Thus, the forecast lines in Figure 16.6 are below the actual demand figures, since the general trend is a steady increase.

Trend Projections

The last forecasting method for a time series we will discuss is trend projection. This method is especially useful for medium- or long-term forecasts based on a trend line that fits historical time series data. Although several trend projection methods are available, we will discuss the linear projection method only.

Let us go back to the Centennial Corporation case. The actual monthly sales data, as shown in Table 16.3, are plotted in Figure 16.7. This scatter diagram gives us a general visual relationship between the two variables of time and sales.

A convenient way to develop a statistical trend line is the *least squares method*. This method determines a trend line that minimizes the sum of the squares of vertical differences between the projection line and each of the actual sales observations. The least squares line is:

$$\hat{Y} = a + bX$$

where $\hat{Y}$ = predicted value of the dependent variable (sales)
X = value of the independent variable (time)
a = Y intercept
b = slope of the least squares line

Figure 16.7   Scatter Diagram of Monthly Camera Sales

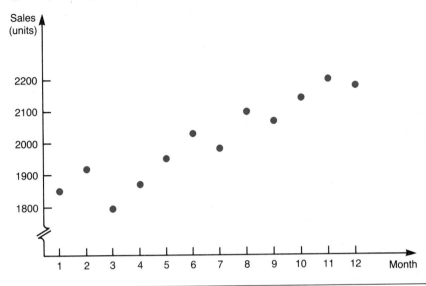

The equations we use to determine values of a and b are

$$b = \frac{\Sigma XY - n\overline{XY}}{\Sigma X^2 - n\overline{X}^2}$$

$$a = \overline{Y} - b\overline{X}$$

where
Y = value of the dependent variable (sales)
$\overline{Y}$ = average of the values of the Ys, or $(\Sigma Y)/n$
$\overline{X}$ = average of the values of the Xs, or $(\Sigma X)/n$
n = number of observations (12 monthly sales)

Table 16.4 presents the computations of the various components of the formulas. Now we can compute the trend line as follows:

$$b = \frac{\Sigma XY - n\overline{XY}}{\Sigma X^2 - n\overline{X}^2} = \frac{161{,}890 - 12(6.5)(2{,}011)}{650 - 12(42.25)} = 35.19$$

$$a = \overline{Y} - b\overline{X} = 2{,}011 - (35.19)(6.5) = 1{,}782.26$$

Thus, the least square equation is

$$\hat{Y} = 1{,}782.26 + 35.19X$$

To project sales for the 13th month, we can compute as follows:

$$\hat{Y} = 1{,}782.26 + 35.19(13) = 2{,}239.73 \cong 2{,}240$$

We can project sales of additional future months using the same least squares equation. Figure 16.8 presents the least squares line projected along with the scatter diagram. This line has the $\hat{Y}$ intercept of 1,782.26 and a slope of 35.19.

Table 16.4 Least Squares Line Computations

X (Month)	Y (Sales)	X²	XY
1	1,850	1	1,850
2	1,920	4	3,840
3	1,800	9	5,400
4	1,875	16	7,500
5	1,960	25	9,800
6	2,040	36	12,240
7	1,980	49	13,860
8	2,100	64	16,800
9	2,070	81	18,630
10	2,150	100	21,500
11	2,210	121	24,310
12	2,180	144	26,160
$\Sigma X = 78$	$\Sigma Y = 24{,}135$	$\Sigma X^2 = 650$	$\Sigma XY = 161{,}890$

Figure 16.8 The Least Squares Line for Comet Cameras

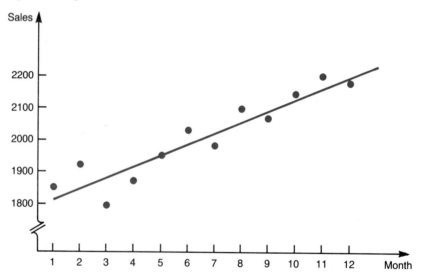

Forecast Reliability

An important aspect of forecasting is the reliability or accuracy of the forecast. No forecast method provides a perfect projection for the future event. Thus, it is important to test the accuracy of the forecast. We can use several reliability tests; here we present one widely used reliability measure, the **mean absolute deviation (MAD).**

MAD is simply the average of the sum of the absolute deviations, or the mean forecast error. MAD is computed as follows:

$$\text{MAD} = \frac{\Sigma \,|\, \text{actual} - \text{forecast}\,|}{\text{number of periods}}$$

Table 16.5   Three-Month Moving Averages and Absolute Deviations

Month	Camera Sales	3-Month Moving Averages	Absolute Deviation
1	1,850		
2	1,920		
3	1,800		
4	1,875	1,857	18
5	1,960	1,865	95
6	2,040	1,878	162
7	1,980	1,958	22
8	2,100	1,993	107
9	2,070	2,040	30
10	2,150	2,050	100
11	2,210	2,107	103
12	2,180	2,143	37
			$\Sigma AD = 674$

For example, our 3-month moving average forecasts for Centennial Corporation as presented in Table 16.2 are presented in Table 16.5 with the appropriate absolute deviations. MAD can be computed as follows:

$$\text{MAD} = \frac{\Sigma AD}{n} = \frac{674}{9} = 74.89$$

Although interpretation of MAD is not always easy, the smaller the value of MAD, the more accurate the forecast. In our example problem, the mean absolute deviation of the forecast is approximately 75 cameras.

REGRESSION FORECASTING METHODS

Exponential smoothing and moving averages are time series methods that are based on historical data of the forecasted variable. **Regression analysis,** however, is a statistical technique that measures the relationship between two or more variables. Because regression analysis forecasts are based on factors that affect or cause trends, cycles, and seasonal fluctuations, this technique is also referred to as a *causal forecasting method*. Regression analysis is usually more powerful and accurate than time series methods.

Regression analysis forecasts many types of variables, such as sales volume of a product, productivity of an organization, employment in a community, and employee job satisfaction. For example, the sales volume of a product can be estimated based on the firm's sales force, advertising budget, quality improvement, price of the product, and competitors' strategies for pricing, advertising, and personal selling. In this case, the sales volume is the *dependent* variable, and other variables are the *independent* variables.

Simple linear regression relates only two variables. Least square regression analysis takes the same linear equation for trend projections. The only difference is that in the regression model, the independent variable can be any variable, whereas in the time series in the trend projection model, only time could be the independent variable.

$$\hat{Y} = a + bX$$
$$\hat{Y} = \text{predicted value of the dependent variable}$$
$$a = Y \text{ intercept}$$
$$b = \text{slope of the regression line}$$
$$X = \text{independent variable}$$

Casette 16.2 THE EXECUTIVE MBA PROGRAM

The Great Plains University has a very successful evening executive master of business administration (MBA) program. This program is designed for middle- and upper-level managers who desire graduate management education. The program has grown from a class of 25 students 10 years ago to the current enrollment of 148 students.

The university administration believes that the program's growth has resulted primarily from its well-organized promotional programs. To analyze the relationship between enrollment in the program and promotional expenditures, data covering the past 10 years are collected as shown in Table 16.6. The scatter diagram for the data is presented in Figure 16.9. Although the dots on the diagram do not show a perfectly linear relationship, a positive relationship definitely exists between the enrollment and promotional expenditures. Thus, we can develop a regression model from the data.

To predict the dependent variable (enrollment) by an independent variable (promotional expenditures), we must compute two components of the regression model: a, the intercept, and b, the slope. The slope represents the change in Y associated with a unit change in X. For example, if we increase the promotional expenditures by $1,000, the resulting change in student enrollment would be expressed by b. The intercept is a

Table 16.6 *Student Enrollment and Promotional Expenditures*

Year	Student Enrollment (Y)	Promotional Expenditures (X) ($ thousands)	XY	X²
1	25	3	75	9
2	38	4	152	16
3	75	6	450	36
4	86	10	860	100
5	102	11	1,122	121
6	98	12	1,176	144
7	115	14	1,610	196
8	128	14	1,792	196
9	130	15	1,950	225
10	148	18	2,664	324
	$\Sigma Y = 945$	$\Sigma X = 107$	$\Sigma XY = 11,851$	$\Sigma X^2 = 1,367$

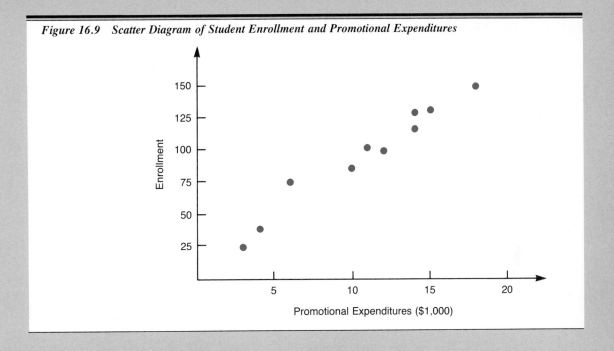

Figure 16.9   Scatter Diagram of Student Enrollment and Promotional Expenditures

constant value of Y when X is 0. In other words, the intercept represents the point where the linear equation intersects the Y axis.

$$a = \overline{Y} - b\overline{X}$$

$$b = \frac{\Sigma XY - n\overline{X}\overline{Y}}{\Sigma X^2 - n\overline{X}^2}$$

where

$x =$ promotional expenditures (in \$1,000)

$y =$ student enrollment

$n =$ number of observations (10 years)

$$\overline{X} = \frac{\Sigma X}{n}$$

$$\overline{Y} = \frac{\Sigma Y}{n}$$

Thus, using the computations derived in Table 16.6, we obtain

$$b = \frac{11{,}851 - 10(94.5)(10.7)}{1{,}367 - 10(114.5)} = \frac{1{,}739.5}{222.1} = 7.83$$

$$a = 94.5 - (7.83)10.7 = 10.70$$

$$\hat{Y} = 10.70 + 7.83X$$

If the Great Plains University has allocated \$20,000 for promotional expenditures of the executive MBA program, we can estimate the student enrollment as follows:

$$\hat{Y} = 10.70 + 7.83(20) = 167.3$$

In other words, the student enrollment in the program is expected to reach 167 students.

Figure 16.10   A Regression-Line Approximation

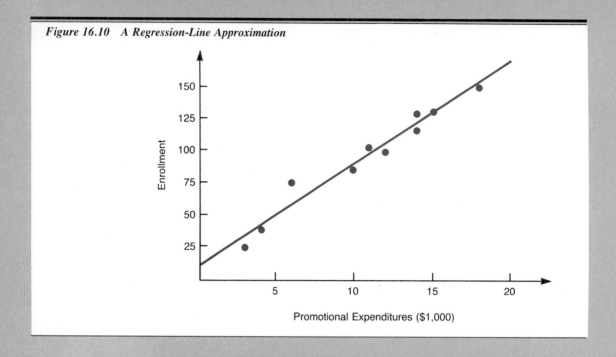

Figure 16.10 presents the regression line drawn on the scatter diagram. The straight line provides a good approximation of the relationship between the student enrollment and promotional expenditures. Since the slope is positive, the relationship between the two variables is positive. The slope of 7.83 indicates that an increase of promotional expenditures by $1,000 is associated with an increase of approximately eight new students in the executive MBA program.

COEFFICIENT OF DETERMINATION

A regression model can be an effective forecasting tool if the relationship between the two variables is strong. An indicator of the regression model's reliability and, consequently, the strength of the relationship between the variables is the **coefficient of determination** (r^2). The coefficient of determination is simply the square of the **correlation coefficient** (r). The correlation coefficient represents the degree of association between the two variables:

$$r^2 = \left[\frac{n\Sigma XY - \Sigma X \Sigma Y}{\sqrt{[n\Sigma X^2 - (\Sigma X)^2][n\Sigma Y^2 - (\Sigma Y)^2]}} \right]^2$$

Although the equation looks very complicated, we already have computed most of the components. The only component remaining for us to compute is ΣY^2, which is 103,511. Thus, the coefficient of determination is:

$$r^2 = \left[\frac{10(11{,}851) - (107)(945)}{\sqrt{[10(1{,}367) - (11{,}449)][10(103{,}511) - 893{,}025]}} \right]^2$$

$$= (0.9792)^2 = 0.9588$$

The coefficient of determination 0.9588 means that 95.88 percent of the variance in student enrollment during the 10-year period can be explained by promotional expenditures. The remaining 4.12 percent is the unexplained portion of the total variance in student enrollment. Although some forecast error exists using this regression model, the coefficient of determination indicates a very reliable forecast.

MULTIPLE REGRESSION

Regression analysis with more than one independent variable is *multiple regression*. For example, the Great Plains University executive MBA problem presented as Casette 16.2 may have two independent variables—promotional expenditures and the number of business firms in the community. These two independent variables can be used to forecast the student enrollment. The **multiple regression model** can be developed in the following form:

$$\hat{Y} = a + b_1 X_1 + b_2 X_2$$

where

$\hat{Y}$ = the estimated value of the dependent variable (e.g., enrollment)

a = Y intercept

b_1 = regression coefficient for the first independent variable

b_2 = regression coefficient for the second independent variable

X_1 = value of the first independent variable (e.g., promotion)

X_2 = value of the second independent variable (e.g., firms)

The mathematical formulas required to develop the multiple regression model are quite involved. Because of the computational burden, multiple regression analysis is performed using computer programs. A number of programs are available on the mainframe or on the microcomputer (for example, SPSS, SAS, and BMD).

QUALITATIVE FORECASTING METHODS

We have discussed several quantitative forecasting methods—techniques that are quite effective as long as the required historical data exist for the variables under consideration. However, even when such historical data are available for time series, if drastic changes occur in the environment, such past data may no longer be valid for predicting future values of the time series in question. For example, government deregulation of natural gas would make it impossible to forecast natural gas sales based on historical data.

In addition to their quantitative orientation, most forecasting techniques are intended for individual decision making. To date, only scattered attempts have been made for qualitative techniques that also accommodate group decision making. Recently, the

Delphi method and **nominal group techniques** have emerged to offer some help in making broad long-range forecasts.

The Delphi technique was developed by N. C. Dalkey and his associates in 1950 at the Rand Corporation. Only recently has this technique become popular as a long-term forecasting method using group consensus. Today, many organizations in business, government, education, health, and the military are using Delphi to forecast long-term economic, technological, military, and health-care trends. Although no forecasting technique, especially a qualitative one, can precisely predict the future, the Delphi technique is one of the best currently available.

The technique has many variations but, in general, involves the following steps:

Step 1   A panel of experts on the particular problem or topic under consideration is formed from both inside and outside the organization. These experts usually do not interact on a face-to-face basis.

Step 2   Each expert is asked to make a prediction on a particular subject on an anonymous basis.

Step 3   Each member then receives a composite feedback of the entire panel's answer to the question.

Step 4   New estimates or predictions are made on the basis of the feedback; the process is repeated as desired.

A number of organizations have reported successful application of Delphi. For example, McDonnel Douglas Aircraft has used the technique to forecast the future of commercial air transportation; Weyerhaeuser used it to predict the long-term trend of the construction industry; and Smith-Kline used the technique to study the uncertainties of medicine.

Closely related to Delphi is the nominal group technique. This technique has been used by social psychologists in their research for almost three decades. The basic steps used by the technique are as follows:

Step 1   A group generates ideas in writing.

Step 2   Round-robin feedback comes from group members; each idea is recorded on a flip chart.

Step 3   Each idea is discussed for evaluation, clarification, or modification.

Step 4   Individual members vote on the recorded ideas for priority, and the group decision is accommodated mathematically, based on rank ordering or other rating systems.

This technique and Delphi differ primarily in that the nominal group technique usually uses panelists who are acquainted and allows them face-to-face contact and direct communication. Although more research is needed, some empirical evidence suggests that the nominal group technique tends to generate more good ideas and its members tend to forecast better than do groups using the Delphi technique.

There are other qualitative forecasting methods, such as *scenario writing, brainstorming sessions,* and other group technologies. These techniques have been widely practiced to forecast the future based on different sets of assumptions. Artificial intelligence and expert systems have recently shown real promise as effective tools for long-term forecasting.

COMPUTER SOLUTIONS OF FORECASTING MODELS

Forecasting is an important part of management planning. Thus, virtually every organization uses some forecasting techniques. Most forecasting is done through the use of computers, and a large number of computer programs are available for the mainframe or the microcomputer. In this section, we will examine the computer solution of the Great Plains University problem we discussed as Casette 16.2. The program we used is the *Statistical Analysis System (SAS)*.

Figure 16.11 (page 674) presents the output summary, including various unfamiliar significance test data. However, the results we *are* looking for are indicated by the shaded boxes. The regression equation is $\hat{Y} = 10.697 + 7.832X$ and the coefficient of determination (r^2) is 0.959. These results correspond exactly with our hand calculations.

REAL-WORLD APPLICATIONS

Forecasting methods have been used quite extensively by all types of organizations. For example, government agencies, hospitals, universities, banks, insurance firms, and trade companies rely heavily on forecasting methods to reduce uncertainty involved in future operations. For many government agencies and regulated industries, systematic forecasting is often required by law. Consequently, forecasting methods have numerous real-world applications. We will examine three examples of real-world applications of forecasting methods.

Texas Legislative Budget Ceiling Imposed by Forecast

The Texas constitution requires that the Legislative Budget Bureau forecast the growth rate of Texas personal income over 2-year periods and imposes that rate as a limit on the growth rate of state appropriations for that period. The first appropriations determined under these limitations were for the biennium 1982–1983. Careful analysis of a variety of models led the authors to select a bivariate time series model.[1] To test their model, the last 8 quarters of data were reserved for validation, leaving 52 quarters of data upon which to base the equation. The time series included both a weighted average of previous Texas personal income statistics and gross national product (GNP) growth rate forecasts. The actual model, shown below, predicted a growth rate of 33 percent over the 2-year period, resulting in a constitutionally imposed legislative spending limit of $15,220,439,216 for 1982–1983.

$$tpy_t = 0.00680 + 0.105tpy_{t-1} + 0.035tpy_{t-2} + 0.237tpy_{t-3} + 0.503gnp_t + a_t$$

where
tpy = Texas personal income growth rate (biennial)

t = time period

gnp = GNP forecast

a = random error term

---

[1] Richard Ashley and John Guerard, "Applications of Time Series Analysis to Texas Financial Forecasting," *Interfaces* 13:4 (1983), 46–55.

Figure 16.11 Computer Output for Casette 16.2

MODEL: MODEL01

DEP VAR: Y1

	SSE	584.635750	F RATIO	186.43
	DFE	8	PROB>F	0.0000
	MSE	73.079469	R-SQUARE	0.9589

VARIABLE	DF	PARAMETER ESTIMATE	STANDARD ERROR	T RATIO	PROB>\T\	VARIABLE LABEL
INTERCEPT	1	10.696983	6.706681	1.5950	0.1494	
X1	1	7.832058	0.573619	13.6538	0.0001	

VARIABLE	N	MEAN	STD DEV	SUM	MINIMUM	MAXIMUM
Y1	10	94.50000000	39.73313758	945.00000000	25.00000000	148.00000000
X1	10	10.70000000	4.96767328	107.00000000	3.00000000	13.00000000

PEARSON CORRELATION COEFFICIENTS / PROB > \R\ UNDER HO:RHO=0 / N = 10

	Y1	X1
Y1	1.00000 0.0000	0.97921 0.0001
X1	0.97921 0.0001	1.00000 0.0000

To Test or Not to Test the Market

Test marketing is one of the last and most vital steps in the decision to launch or abandon a new product. A test market isn't cheap, usually costing from $1 to $2 million. Data compiled by the A. C. Nielsen Company show a major increase in test market failures, from 45.6 to 53.4 to 64.5 percent over 16 years. With success rates falling and costs climbing, many companies wished to pretest their product, allowing them to abandon doomed items before sinking money into a test-marketing program. An integrated modeling and measurement system, *Assessor,* was designed at the Massachusetts Institute of Technology (MIT) to perform such analyses, with three goals: (1) to predict long-run sales or market share quickly and inexpensively, (2) to recommend product improvements, and (3) to permit comparison of alternative marketing plans.[2]

Assessor requires input from management and from consumers. Management inputs delineate the positioning strategy and marketing plan, and consumer research involves both laboratory and home testing. Two mathematical models predict brand share, with similar results desired on both models. One model analyzes preferences, and the other represents the trial-repeat process. A mini market test shows a selected sample of consumers advertising and gives them the opportunity to purchase the new product or its established competition. Follow-up interviews determine the likelihood of repurchase.

Over a 10-year period, 450 new products were evaluated for more than 100 clients in 15 countries. Food, cleaning agents, health and beauty aids, and pharmaceuticals have been tested. Initial resistance to *Assessor* was high, because formal new product evaluation was generally believed to be inaccurate. As more firms used the model, acceptance increased. A follow-up study collected actual share data for 44 of the 215 new products tested; some had not been introduced, and no share data were obtained for others. The correlation coefficient for the known data proved to be 0.95, with *Assessor* tending to predict a bit high. Of the products receiving a favorable evaluation, 34 percent failed in the test market—almost half the failure rate of 64.5 reported in the Nielsen study. Of the few products which were test marketed after receiving a negative pretest, all were judged to be "big" failures in the test market.

The authors' personal evaluation of *Assessor* concluded that the firms that used it enjoyed a net increase of $126 million profit. Frequent users who wrote the authors of this article with favorable comments include Armour-Dial, Procter & Gamble, Richardson-Vicks, Bristol-Myers, L'Oréal, Unilever, and S. C. Johnson & Son. Richardson-Vicks indicated total savings of roughly $5 million, and Nippon Lever saved over $4 million on a single campaign by changing the focus of the launch to match *Assessor*'s recommendations. *Assessor* analyses currently number about 100 annually, and benefits of $20 million are anticipated per year.

A Delphi Forecast on Diversification Strategies for Alaska's Future

The government of Alaska, nervous about its budget base, commissioned an elaborate Delphi-style study to forecast "Alaska's energy, economy, and resource development future."[3] The oil industry so dominates the Alaskan economy that over 90 percent of the state government's budget comes from oil. The oil will eventually run out, and oil

---

[2]Glen Urban, Gerald Katz, Thomas Hatch, and Alvin Silk, "The ASSESSOR Pre-Test Market Evaluation System," *Interfaces* 13:6 (1983), 38–59.

[3]Ted Eschenbach and George Geistauts, "A Delphi Forecast for Alaska," *Interfaces* 15:6 (1985), 100–109.

prices are volatile. Alaska's problem is thus a classic development problem: diversification based on revenues from one currently dominant industry.

Resource development is the key to Alaska's future; its harsh climate, small population, and remoteness limit the manufacturing and service sectors. Among the major resources of international stature are oil, natural gas, coal, zinc and other metals, salmon and other fish, timber, agricultural land, scenery, and wildlife. The world market prices for these resources will in large part determine their development, making forecasts of market conditions crucial to state policy and project planning.

The volatility of the situation and the political nature of many policy decisions precluded use of statistical forecasting. Economic factors may limit certain choices, but political considerations will guide the final decisions. The necessary forecasts thus become not only a prediction but also an element of policy formulation, depending on their believability. Predicting the critical events in the development process can only be done using human judgment, with guidelines to ensure objectivity and provide credibility.

The Delphi panel was organized to include as many recognized Alaskan leaders and experts as possible, with emphasis on a balance in viewpoints, responsibilities, etc. Sixty percent of those contacted accepted the invitation, with a resulting initial panel of 91 members. After 60 pages of questions and feedback, representing over 800 responses per individual, 85 percent of the panelists remained. In addition to the established Delphi process, input was sought in several native areas through interviews with local leaders. Cross-impact analysis, examining interaction between various events, concluded the formal process.

With time horizons of 1990, 2000, 2020, and beyond, no objective evaluation of the results is yet possible. However, acceptance of the report appears encouraging—it is being reprinted a fourth time and has been frequently cited by state officials. A major bank adopted the Delphi forecast for its long-range planning, and other private sector interest has been strong.

SUMMARY

In this chapter, we studied several basic methods of time series analysis and forecasting. More specifically, we concentrated on the two most popular forecasting techniques— time series and regression. Although there are many other forecasting techniques, they are variations of the time series or regression methods.

Forecasting models do not provide answers for management planning. Instead, these models are used to generate concrete information that is useful to management decision making. Quantitative methods may not be useful when historical data are inappropriate for forecasting because of some structural changes in the environment. In such cases, we may use the Delphi or nominal group technique, the two best-known qualitative group techniques available for long-term forecasting.

Glossary

Coefficient of Determination (r^2) Square of the correlation coefficient r; indicates reliability of the regression model and strength of relationship between the dependent and independent variables.

Correlation Coefficient (*r*)   Degree of association between dependent and independent variables.

Delphi Method   An involved, systematic method for obtaining a group consensus. Typically used to consult experts when major decisions or drastic changes are involved in a forecast.

Exponential Smoothing   Time series prediction device that allows weighting of past predictions and current actual data to project a value for the next period.

Forecast   Prediction of future values or events based on quantitative or qualitative methods.

Mean Absolute Deviation (MAD)   Mean forecast error, average of the sum of the absolute deviations of forecast values from actual results.

Moving Average   Time series smoothing device which combines the preceding periods as an averaged prediction tool.

Multiple Regression Model   A regression equation involving more than one independent variable as a predictor of the dependent variable.

Nominal Group Technique   Method of obtaining a group decision through a sequence involving idea generation, comments, and a voting procedure.

Regression   Forecasting technique employing statistical analysis to seek causal relationships between dependent and independent variables.

Time Series   Observations or data collected at successive points during a time period.

Trend   Long-term, regular movement in a time series.

Weighted Moving Average   A time series smoothing tool which allows emphasis to be placed on selected periods, typically the most recent ones.

References

Benton, W. K. *Forecasting for Management*. Reading, Mass.: Addison-Wesley, 1972.

Box, G. E. P., and Jenkins, G. M. *Time Series Analysis, Forecasting and Control*. San Francisco: Holden-Day, 1970.

Buffa, E. S., and Dyer, J. S. *Essentials of Management Science/Operations Research*. New York: John Wiley and Sons, 1978.

Delbecq, A. L., Van deVen, A. H., and Gustafson, D. H. *Group Techniques for Program Planning*. Glenview, Ill.: Scott, Foresman, 1975.

Huang, D. S. *Regression and Econometric Methods*. New York: John Wiley and Sons, 1970.

Nelson, C. R. *Applied Time Series Analysis for Managerial Forecasting*. San Francisco: Holden-Day, 1973.

Tersine, R. J. *Production/Operations Management*. New York: Elsevier North Holland, 1980.

Van deVen, A. H. *Group Decision Making Effectiveness*. Kent, Ohio: Kent State University Center for Business and Economic Research Press, 1974.

Wheelwright, S. C., and Makridakis, S. *Forecasting Methods for Management*. New York: John Wiley and Sons, 1973.

Younger, M. S. *A Handbook for Linear Regression*. North Scituate, Mass.: Duxbury Press, 1979.

Assignments

16.1 Why is forecasting important?

16.2 How do quantitative and qualitative forecasts differ?

16.3 Distinguish between simple average, moving average, and weighted moving average.

16.4 Comment on the importance of the weighting scheme selected for a weighted moving average forecast.

16.5 Under which circumstances would each of the three techniques in problem 16.3 be most appropriate?

16.6 Distinguish between the weighted moving average and exponential smoothing techniques.

16.7 Is validation of a forecasting model appropriate, or is reliance on statistical techniques sufficient?

16.8 What are the basic assumptions made when using time series techniques and causal techniques?

16.9 Describe the concept of forecast horizon or time frame, and select a method appropriate for each term you mention.

16.10 What are the four components of a time series? How do they differ? Which is most important?

16.11 Explain each component's meaning in the following exponential smoothing model: $F_t = 0.4A_{t-1} + 0.6F_{t-1}$.

16.12 Why would a company select a smoothing factor of 0.8 as opposed to 0.2?

16.13 What is the function of the least squares method?

16.14 If the average value of a set of data is 1,800 and a forecasting model results in a MAD of 25, what is your opinion of the model? Would your opinion change if the average value were 10 and the MAD 6?

16.15 Does regression analysis prove causality?

16.16 What distinguishes regression analysis from the time series analysis?

16.17 Prepare a general regression model using the following four variables (use common sense to select dependent and independent variables): marriages, housing starts, personal income, interest rates.

16.18 Would all the factors in problem 16.17 have an immediate impact on the dependent variable, or are time lags possible? Explain.

16.19 Would you prefer a regression model where $r^2 = 0.98$ or $r^2 = 0.02$? Why?

16.20 Suggest three situations for which qualitative forecasting techniques would be more appropriate than quantitative methods.

16.21 Distinguish between the Delphi and nominal group techniques and explain which you prefer.

16.22 Given the following actual demand figures for January through September:

Month	Demand
January	90
February	86
March	97
April	103
May	94
June	105
July	101
August	110
September	108

a. Describe any trend in these data.
b. Can you derive any seasonality conclusions from the data given?
c. Compute the simple average. Would this be an appropriate estimate for demand in October?
d. Prepare an October forecast using a 3-month moving average. Would you expect demand to exceed, match, or be less than this value?

16.23 Using the data given in problem 16.22, prepare both 3-month and 5-month moving average forecasts for each month that this is possible.
   a. Without using statistical techniques, make an eyeball judgment as to which of these averages seems more accurate.
   b. Is it possible to make forecasts for November and December? Try doing so, taking forecast values where actual data are not available.

16.24 Prepare a scatter diagram of the data in assignment 16.22, and draw a rough line through the diagram to form a projection or trend line. Read the values you obtained for the last 3 months of the year, and compare them with your results in 16.22c, 16.22d, and 16.23b.

16.25 Warmamaker Inc. has experienced the following demand for kerosene heating units during the past 7 months:

Month	Demand
June	10
July	20
August	40
September	80
October	160
November	300
December	480

a. What is your opinion of the nature and probable continuity of the apparent trend?

b. Predict January demand using a simple average and a 3-month moving average. Is either appropriate?

c. A regression could be performed, linking time and demand. Would such a regression be useful? Would simple statistical tests indicate that it might be useful?

d. What forecasting method or methods would you recommend in this situation?

16.26 Sales of floppy disks at the downtown Abacus Computer Shop have peaked and are starting to decline, as hard-shell disks become more popular. Sales data for the past 2 years are given below, in thousands of floppies.

	Year 1	Year 2
January	48	53
February	48	51
March	50	51
April	51	48
May	49	46
June	52	47
July	54	45
August	54	44
September	56	40
October	55	42
November	54	40
December	55	38

How would you handle these data when preparing forecasts using time series analysis techniques? Prepare forecasts for January of year 3 using at least three techniques.

16.27 The Abacus Computer Shop (in the last problem) feels that year 3 sales should total 474,000 disks, projecting a trend from year 1 (total sales = 626) and year 2 (545). Would you agree or disagree? Explain.

16.28 The Abacus Computer Shop from problem 16.26 has settled on a 4-month weighted average projection, with weights as follows, from most recent to least recent: 0.4, 0.3, 0.2, 0.1. Use this method to forecast sales in January of year 3. What is your opinion of the results? Would a different weighting scheme be more suitable?

16.29 The nonprofit Medicure Clinic has experienced a fairly steady increase in outpatient visits. New staff must go through a 3-month training period, so future demand for services must be projected at least 3 months in advance. The chief administrator has heard of the exponential smoothing technique and believes it would be a useful forecasting tool.

Month	Outpatient Visits
1	632
2	691
3	764
4	837
5	960
6	1054
7	1122
8	1248

a. Prepare an exponential smoothing model in both formulas and words, so that the administrator will be able to understand and use the model.
b. Using a smoothing factor of 0.3, predict demand for months 9, 10, and 11. Explain the results.
c. Prepare a forecast for month 9, using a factor of 0.7. Which prediction for month 9 seems more accurate to you?
d. Given the needs of the Medicure Clinic, would you recommend use of this model?

16.30 The Medicure Clinic from problem 16.29 now wishes to use a weighted average forecasting technique. Given two weighting schemes, determine anticipated demand in month 9, and evaluate the results.

Scheme 1: 0.6, 0.3, 0.1 (most recent month first)

Scheme 2: 0.4, 0.3, 0.2, 0.1

16.31 Analyze the Medicure Clinic's (16.29) increase in visits by determining each monthly increase, both as a quantity and as a percentage of the total number of visits. Use the average percentage increase over the whole 8 months to project demand for the next 4 months.
   a. Do these forecast values appear reasonable? How do they compare with the forecasts prepared in 16.29 and 16.30?

b. Plot a time series diagram, including your projections prepared by the various methods you have used. Draw a straight trend line through the actual data to aid your analysis; a visual estimate is good enough.

16.32 Hot Off The Rack (HOTR) has a virtual monopoly on the pizza market in Thrushburg, a small community with no population growth and little likelihood of attracting new fast-food restaurants. HOTR wishes to predict pizza demand for next month, based on its sales records. A prediction for each of three types of pizza is desired, as well as an overall total forecast. Use exponential smoothing, with a smoothing factor of your choice. Explain your choice of factor, as well as the results.

	Demand					
	Month 1	Month 2	Month 3	Month 4	Month 5	Month 6
Pizza:						
Combo	85	83	86	84	85	85
Special	43	46	40	44	42	43
Extra	24	27	31	36	42	47
Total	152	156	157	164	169	175

16.33 Prepare a least squares trend line for Hot Off The Rack (16.32), for each of its pizzas. Plot your projections for the next month, and comment on the fit.
   a. What is the meaning of the slope constant (*b*) in each case?
   b. Project sales for each type of pizza throughout the rest of the year. What are total sales for each month? How do you account for this rise? Is it likely that the trend for Extra pizzas will continue indefinitely?

16.34 On separate scatter diagrams, plot the following sets of data, prepare a least squares line for each, and project demand for the next 3 periods.

	Period 1	Period 2	Period 3	Period 4	Period 5	Period 6	Period 7	Period 8	Period 9	Period 10
Item:										
Dog biscuits	64	72	81	88	97	106	120	123	134	
BMW 320i	15	16	18	17	19	21	22	24		
Sunday papers	862	881	893	899	912	919	929			

What is the one assumption common to the three forecasts you have just prepared?

16.35 Analyze the accuracy of your results for each item in 16.34 using the MAD criterion. Explain your confidence in each of the projections.

16.36 Prepare a regression equation for the following data, and explain the components of the formula. (Remember that regression is a *causal* approach.)

Year	Number of dogs registered	Quantity of leashes sold
1	286	392
2	324	440
3	300	414
4	270	370
5	248	346
6	320	430
7	330	441

a. Use MAD to judge the reliability of your model.

b. Find the correlation coefficient and the coefficient of determination for this model. Explain your findings.

c. The police department indicates that 295 dogs will likely be registered next year. How many leashes would you expect to sell?

d. Is there a reasonable explanation for why more leashes are sold than dogs registered?

e. In your opinion, is the independent variable a suitable predictor for the dependent variable?

16.37 Airborne Radionuclide Scrubbers Inc. has found an interesting correlation between demand for its exhaust filters and antipollution sentiment as expressed in an annual opinion poll. The data which caught ARS's attention are as follows:

				Year				
	1	2	3	4	5	6	7	8
Poll results	0.40	0.48	0.48	0.56	0.58	0.59	0.61	0.63
Filter sales (thousands)	180	200	208	225	230	240	260	265
Population (thousands)	3,200	3,250	3,310	3,360	3,390	3,450	3,510	3,540
Advertising (thousands)	8	9	10	12	14	14	14	15

Poll results represent the fraction of respondents who indicated concern with air pollution; filter sales, population, and advertising are in thousands.

a. Prepare a simple (single) regression equation linking filter sales to popular sentiment. Note that you have several options here—select whichever seems most reasonable to you.

b. If a computer program is available, run this model and interpret the results.

c. The current opinion poll indicates 62 percent of the total population of 3,570 is concerned about air pollution. How many filters should you expect to sell? How confident are you that this is accurate?

d. Prepare a multiple regression model using three independent variables to explain sales. If a computer program is available, run and interpret this model.

16.38 Use the nominal group technique to predict your class average score on the next exam.

16.39 Use the nominal group technique to project the inflation rate and prime interest rate for 6 months hence. Involve at least seven people in your analysis.

17 MARKOV ANALYSIS

Markov analysis involves probabilistic movement from one situation or state to another over time. For example, the probability that a customer buying one brand of soda this week will purchase the same brand next week, or that a good accounts receivable this month will turn into a bad debt next month, are typically evaluated using Markov analysis. Markov analysis is a probabilistic technique and thus does not provide the optimum solution per se. Instead, Markov analysis provides probabilistic information about various conditions of a decision problem that can be used for decision making. Consequently, Markov analysis is a descriptive rather than an optimization technique.

Learning Objectives   From the study of this chapter, we will learn the following:

1. Properties of Markov processes
2. Developing transition probabilities
3. Developing steady-state probabilities
4. Computer solutions of Markov models
5. Real-world application of Markov analysis
6. The meaning of the following terms:

Stochastic processes   *Markov process*
State of the system   *Transition probabilities*
State probability   *Steady-state probability*
Absorbing state   *Transition matrix*

PROPERTIES OF MARKOV PROCESSES

Markov analysis was originally introduced by A. A. Markov, a Russian probability theorist. The technique was refined through the efforts of many researchers and developed into a distinct management science tool. The basic objective of Markov analysis is to provide to the decision maker probabilistic information about a particular state of the problem.

Markov analysis consists of a particular class of probabilistic models that are useful for analyzing decision problems in organizations. The general probabilistic models of systems whose current state depends on all previous states are **stochastic processes.** In a **Markov process,** however, the current state of the system depends only on the immediately preceding state.

Many real-world problems can be analyzed by Markov analysis. For example, customer brand-switching behavior, changes in accounts receivable, machine maintenance and operating characteristics, and certain classes of inventory and queuing problems can be studied by Markov analysis. Customer brand switching involves the examination and forecasting of the behavior of customers from the standpoint of their loyalty to one particular brand in one state and their switching patterns to other brands in the next state.

A Markov process requires two basic elements: (1) the possible *states* of the system; and (2) the probabilities associated with moving between states, known as **transition probabilities.** A **state of the system** represents the status of the system at a certain point in time, such as what different brands customers are using, whether a piece of equipment is operating, or whether an account receivable has been paid. Transition probabilities represent the probability associated with the system moving from one state to another during a specified period, such as the probability that a customer using brand A this period will switch to brand B in the next period.

Casette 17.1   STATE HISTORICAL SOCIETY

The state historical society has been providing valuable services to various visitors. One of the society's most popular places is its genealogy library. Many visitors across the country come to the library to trace their family history through various census records, old newspapers, vital records, and other genealogical research materials. Most of these records are on microfilm.

The most valuable research tool for the visitors is the microfilm reader. The society currently has only five microfilm readers; four readers are old-style hand-cranked machines, and the fifth is a new electronic reader with quick advance and rewind. The new machine is fast but it breaks down quite frequently. Thus, the librarian has been concerned with this machine's operating state.

The new microfilm reader is either in the operating state or out of order and being repaired on any given day. Thus, the machine can be in one of two possible states: operation or broken. We can define the states as follows:

State 1: Microfilm reader is in operation.

State 2: Microfilm reader is broken and being repaired.

The librarian conducted a daily check during the past 100 working days. In reviewing the data, she found that when the machine was in operation (state 1) on a given day, the machine was also in operation (state 1) on the following day 90 percent of the time, although 10 percent of the time the machine was broken (state 2) on the following day. Also, when the machine was in the broken state (state 2) on a given day, the machine was in operation (state 1) on the following day 70 percent of the time, and 30 percent of the time the machine remained in the broken state (state 2) on the following day.

The probabilities that the machine moves from a state in a given period to a state in the following period are transition probabilities. These probabilities are provided in

Table 17.1   Transition Probabilities for the Machine

	To:	
From	State 1: Operation	State 2: Broken
State 1: Operation	0.9	0.1
State 2: Broken	0.7	0.3

Figure 17.1   Markov Transition Probability Diagram: Operation (O) and Broken (B)

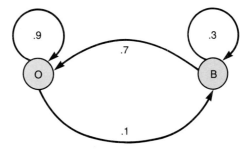

Table 17.1. The Markov process in the table can be illustrated as a transition probability diagram in Figure 17.1. Now we can summarize the properties or assumptions of a Markov process using our casette example.

Property 1

The transition probabilities depend only on the current state and are independent of the states prior to the present state. For example, in our state historical society problem, the probability of moving to either operation or broken state in the next day (time period) is conditional only on the current state of the microfilm reader and not on the state of the reader in any prior days.

Property 2

The transition probabilities are constant over time. In our example, the probability of moving from the operation state to the broken state remains 0.1 in any future time period.

Property 3

Given the present state in the current time period, the transition probabilities of moving to alternative states in the next time period must sum to 1.0. In our historical society problem, the transition probabilities of moving to either the operation or broken state in the next period, given the current state of operation, are 0.9 and 0.1, which sum to 1.0. The broken state in the current period also has transition probabilities to the next period — 0.7 for the operation state and 0.3 for the broken state — that sum to 1.0.

PREDICTING FUTURE STATES

The primary reason for obtaining the transition probabilities in a Markov process is to predict future states. For example, in our state historical society problem, what is the predicted condition of the microfilm reader in future periods? Once the initial state of the machine is specified and the transition probabilities are known, we can predict future states of the machine. The sequence of successive future states is often referred to as a *chain*. Thus, Markov processes are also known as Markov chains.

The machine can be in one of two possible states, operation or broken. Let us label the time periods as time 1 for today and time 2 for the next day (tomorrow). We are now interested in predicting the status of the machine in time 3 (the third day). *Decision trees* are convenient ways to analyze the problem for a limited number of transitions.

Figures 17.2 and 17.3 illustrate the probabilities of the machine states for two initial cases: The machine is in the operation state in the present period, and the machine is in the broken state in the present period, respectively. As we move from one time period to the next, two possible states are given: operation and broken. Thus, the ending branch probabilities of independent events are computed by multiplying the probabilities of the events on the same branch.

To determine the probability of the machine being in operation on the third day, given that the machine is in operation on the first day, we must compute the following probabilities from Figure 17.2:

	Day 1	**Day 2**	**Day 3**	
Case 1				
State 1	Operation	Operation	Operation	
Probabilities		0.9 ×	0.9	= 0.81
Case 2				
State 2	Operation	Broken	Operation	
Probabilities		0.1 ×	0.7	= 0.07
			Total probability	= 0.88

Consequently, we can easily obtain the probability of the machine being in the broken state on the third day, given that the machine is in operation on the first day, as follows:

	Day 1	**Day 2**	**Day 3**	
Case 1				
State 1	Operation	Operation	Broken	
Probabilities		0.9 ×	0.1	= 0.09
Case 2				
State 2	Operation	Broken	Broken	
Probabilities		0.1 ×	0.3	= 0.03
			Total probability	= 0.12

Figure 17.2   Probabilities of Future States, Given That the Machine Is in the Operation State Today

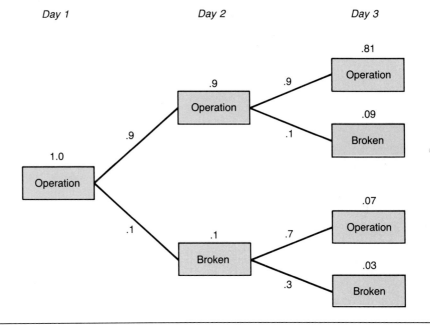

Figure 17.3   Probabilities of Future States, Given That the Machine Is in the Broken State Today

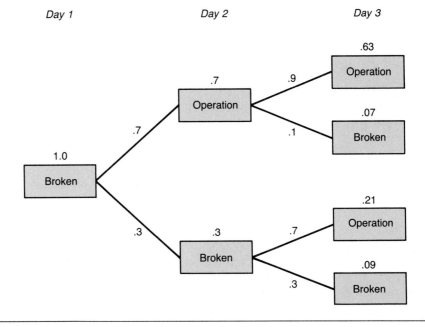

The same type of analysis can be made for the condition that the machine is broken on the first day as shown in Figure 17.3. The probabilities of the two possible states in the third day are:

$$\text{Operation:} \quad 0.63 + 0.21 = 0.84$$
$$\text{Broken:} \quad 0.07 + 0.09 = 0.16$$

For each starting state in the first day, operation or broken, the probabilities of two possible states on the third day sum to 1.0, as shown below:

State in Day 1	Probability of State in Day 3		Sum of Probabilities
	Operation	Broken	
Operation	0.88	0.12	1.0
Broken	0.84	0.16	1.0

Although the decision tree analysis is simple and easy to understand, it becomes extremely complex when the number of time periods increases in the analysis. For example, if the librarian is interested in knowing the machine breakdown state on day 50, the decision tree can be a total mess. *Matrix algebra* is a convenient tool to perform the same analysis.

Matrix Approach

Matrix algebra techniques can be used to predict the state of a Markov system at some future time period. For example, the transition probabilities of the microfilm reading machine moving from one state on one day to the other state on the next day, presented in Table 17.1, can be presented as a matrix. A *matrix* is simply a rectangular array of numbers. The **transition matrix T** is presented below:

$$
\begin{array}{cc}
\textit{Day 1} & \textit{Day 2} \\
 & \begin{array}{cc} \text{Operation} & \text{Broken} \end{array} \\
\begin{array}{c} \text{Operation} \\ \text{Broken} \end{array} \; T = & \begin{bmatrix} 0.9 & 0.1 \\ 0.7 & 0.3 \end{bmatrix}
\end{array}
$$

To compute the probability of a certain state in a future period, let us define several symbols. The probability of the machine being in operation in future period (day) i, given that the machine was initially in operation on the first day, can be defined as follows:

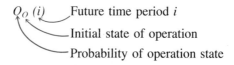

$$Q_O(i)$$ — Future time period i
— Initial state of operation
— Probability of operation state

Likewise, we can also define the probability of the machine being broken in future time period i, given that the machine was initially in operation on the first day, as follows:

$$B_O \ (i)$$

where (i) = Future time period i

O = Initial state of operation

B = Probability of broken state

The initial state represents an absolute beginning state with the probability of 1.0. Now we can write various symbols for possible probabilities of future machine states. The subscript symbol always refers to the initial state. For the first day, the probabilities of machine states are as follows:

$$O_O \ (1) \ = \ 1.0$$
$$B_O \ (1) \ = \ 0.0$$

In the above-stated probabilities, the initial state is operation. Thus, O_O (1) will always be 1.0, and B_O (1) will always be 0. Likewise, we can also define the following probabilities:

$$B_B \ (1) \ = \ 1.0$$
$$O_B \ (1) \ = \ 0.0$$

The above described probabilities can be expressed in matrix form as follows:

$$[O_O \ (1) \quad B_O \ (1)] \ = \ [1.0 \quad 0.0]$$
$$[B_B \ (1) \quad O_B \ (1)] \ = \ [1.0 \quad 0.0]$$

The above matrices represent the starting conditions of the state historical society problem.

Once we determine the initial conditions of the system, we can compute the subsequent probabilities of the machine being in operation or broken on day 2 by multiplying the initial state matrix above by the transition probability matrix. Day 2:

$$[O_O \ (2) \quad B_O \ (2)] \ = \ [O_O \ (1) \quad B_O \ (1)] \ [T]$$

$$= \ [1.0 \quad 0.0] \begin{bmatrix} 0.9 & 0.1 \\ 0.7 & 0.3 \end{bmatrix}$$

$$= \ [1.0(0.9) \ + \ 0.0(0.7) \quad 1.0(0.1) \ + \ 0.0(0.3)]$$

$$= \ [0.9 \quad 0.1]$$

The above probabilities, 0.9 and 0.1, correspond exactly with those we obtained in Figure 17.2.

If we have forgotten matrix algebra, a quick review may refresh our memory. To multiply two matrices, the number of columns in the first matrix must equal the number of rows in the second matrix. We will review two simple cases here.

$$[a_1 \quad a_2] \begin{bmatrix} b_1 & b_2 \\ c_1 & c_2 \end{bmatrix} \ = \ [(a_1b_1 \ + \ a_2c_1) \quad (a_1b_2 \ + \ a_2c_2)]$$

$$\begin{bmatrix} a_1 & a_2 & a_3 \\ b_1 & b_2 & b_3 \end{bmatrix} \begin{bmatrix} c_1 & c_2 \\ d_1 & d_2 \\ e_1 & e_2 \end{bmatrix} \ = \ \begin{bmatrix} (a_1c_1 \ + \ a_2d_1 \ + \ a_3e_1) & (a_1c_2 \ + \ a_2d_2 \ + \ a_3e_2) \\ (b_1c_1 \ + \ b_2d_1 \ + \ b_3e_1) & (b_1c_2 \ + \ b_2d_2 \ + \ b_3e_2) \end{bmatrix}$$

Now we can use the same procedure to determine the probabilities on day 3 as follows:

$$[O_O(3) \quad B_O(3)] = [O_O(2) \quad B_O(2)] \, [T]$$

$$= [0.9 \quad 0.1] \begin{bmatrix} 0.9 & 0.1 \\ 0.7 & 0.3 \end{bmatrix}$$

$$= [(0.9 \times 0.9 + 0.1 \times 0.7) \quad (0.9 \times 0.1 + 0.1 \times 0.3)]$$

$$= [0.88 \quad 0.12]$$

The above probabilities correspond exactly with those we obtained through the decision tree in Figure 17.2. Any additional state probabilities would be very cumbersome to determine through the decision tree analysis. However, it is an easy task using the matrix approach:

$$\text{Day } 4 = [O_O(4) \quad B_O(4)] = [0.88 \quad 0.12] \begin{bmatrix} 0.9 & 0.1 \\ 0.7 & 0.3 \end{bmatrix}$$

$$= [0.876 \quad 0.124]$$

$$\text{Day } 5 = [O_O(5) \quad B_O(5)] = [0.8752 \quad 0.1248]$$

$$\text{Day } 6 = [O_O(6) \quad B_O(6)] = [0.8750 \quad 0.1250]$$

$$\text{Day } 7 = [O_O(7) \quad B_O(7)] = [0.8750 \quad 0.1250]$$

As we move further into future time periods, the incremental changes in the state probabilities become extremely small, and eventually there are absolutely no changes. For example, the **state probabilities** for day 6 and day 7 are exactly identical. These probabilities are referred to as **steady-state probabilities.** The steady-state probabilities represent average probabilities that the system will be at certain states after a large enough number of time periods. Figure 17.4 presents the probability $O_O(i)$ over various time periods until it reaches the steady-state probability of 0.875.

Figure 17.4   The Movement of Probability O$_O$ (i) Toward a Steady State

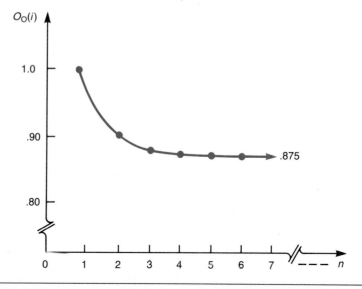

The same steady-state characteristic can be found for $B_O(i)$. After 6 days, $B_O(i)$ reaches the steady-state probability of 0.125. The steady-state probabilities provide valuable information to the decision maker. In the state historical society problem, the librarian can conclude that after 6 days the electronic microfilm reader will be in the operating state with 0.875 probability, and conversely in the broken state with 0.125 probability, provided that the machine was initially in an operation state. Another way to interpret the steady-state probabilities is that in a period of 1,000 days, the machine will be in the operating state about 875 days, and for 125 days it will be in the broken state.

The same computation procedure can be used to analyze the starting condition that the machine was in the broken state, as shown in Figure 17.3. The state probabilities for a number of time periods can be computed as follows:

$$\text{Day } 1 = [O_B(1) \quad B_B(1)] = [0.0 \quad 1.0]$$

$$\text{Day } 2 = [O_B(2) \quad B_B(2)] = [0.0 \quad 1.0] \begin{bmatrix} 0.9 & 0.1 \\ 0.7 & 0.3 \end{bmatrix}$$

$$= [0.0(0.9) + 1.0(0.7) \quad 0.0(0.1) + 1.0(0.3)]$$

$$= [0.7 \quad 0.3]$$

$$\text{Day } 3 = [O_B(3) \quad B_B(3)] = [0.7 \quad 0.3] \begin{bmatrix} 0.9 & 0.1 \\ 0.7 & 0.3 \end{bmatrix}$$

$$= [0.84 \quad 0.16]$$

$$\text{Day } 4 = [O_B(4) \quad B_B(4)] = [0.868 \quad 0.132]$$

$$\text{Day } 5 = [O_B(5) \quad B_B(5)] = [0.8736 \quad 0.1264]$$

$$\text{Day } 6 = [O_B(6) \quad B_B(6)] = [0.8747 \quad 0.1253]$$

$$\text{Day } 7 = [O_B(7) \quad B_B(7)] = [0.8749 \quad 0.1251]$$

$$\text{Day } 8 = [O_B(8) \quad B_B(8)] = [0.8750 \quad 0.1250]$$

$$\text{Day } 9 = [O_B(9) \quad B_B(9)] = [0.8750 \quad 0.1250]$$

Note that in the above computation the steady-state probabilities are exactly the same regardless of the starting state. In other words, whether we start the Markov analysis with the initial state of operation or broken, the same steady-state probabilities will be obtained. However, the number of time periods required to reach the steady state was greater when the starting state was broken—8 days were required to reach the steady state when we began with the broken state as compared with only 6 days when we began with the operation state.

STEADY-STATE PROBABILITIES

The steady-state probabilities we obtained in the above analysis are 0.875 for the operation state and 0.125 for the broken state. The probabilities are obtained as the state probabilities converge as we go through a sufficient number of time periods. In other words, when the time period i increases, the difference between the state probabilities for period i and period $i + 1$ becomes extremely small and negligible. Thus, as i becomes large, we can assume that the state probabilities at the $(i + 1)$th period are exactly equal to those at the ith period. This observation allows us to derive a simple and direct algebraic determination of steady-state probabilities.

Since state probabilities are the same for the ith and $(i + 1)$th periods, we can even eliminate the time period designation as follows:

$$[O_O(i + 1) \quad B_O(i + 1)] = [O_O(i) \quad B_O(i)] \, [T]$$

$$[O_O \quad B_O] = [O_O \quad B_O] \begin{bmatrix} 0.9 & 0.1 \\ 0.7 & 0.3 \end{bmatrix}$$

Now we can carry out the matrix operation as follows:

$$O_O = 0.9O_O + 0.7B_O$$
$$B_O = 0.1O_O + 0.3B_O$$

Since the sum of the state probabilities must equal 1.0, we obtain

$$O_O + B_O = 1.0$$

and

$$B_O = 1.0 - O_O$$

Substituting this value of B_O into our equation $O_O = 0.9O_O + 0.7B_O$, we obtain

$$O_O = 0.9O_O + 0.7 \, (1.0 - O_O)$$
$$O_O = 0.9O_O + 0.7 - 0.7O_O$$
$$O_O = 0.7 + 0.2O_O$$
$$0.8O_O = 0.7$$
$$O_O = 0.7 \div 0.8 = 0.875$$

We can then obtain the state probability B_O as follows:

$$B_O = 1.0 - O_O$$
$$B_O = 1.0 - 0.875$$
$$B_O = 0.125$$

The steady-state probabilities we obtained algebraically are exactly the same as those we obtained through the step-by-step procedure:

$$[O_O \quad B_O] = [0.875 \quad 0.125]$$

Casette 17.2   SUPER-SAVER MARKET INC.

Super-Saver Market is the largest supermarket in Star City. The store sells the four best-known brands of detergent: Action, Gentle, Clear, and Sun. The management of the store is very interested in knowing how many customers switch from one brand to another. Although the total demand has been relatively stable, demands for different brands appear to fluctuate widely.

The president of the company decided to conduct some marketing research to use in deciding the order quantity for each brand of detergent. The research team of the company interviewed 1,000 customers randomly selected at the store. Based on the sample of 1,000 customers, data were obtained about their brand switching from one month to the next. Last month, 100 customers stated that they purchased Action, 400 purchased Gentle, 300 used Clear, and 200 customers bought Sun. Of the 100 Action purchasers last month, only 60 people purchased Action this month, 20 switched to Gentle, 10 to Clear, and 10 switched to Sun. Of the 400 purchasers of Gentle last month, 120 people again purchased Gentle this month, 80 of them switched to Clear, and 200 to Sun. Of the Clear purchasers, 60 people out of 300 still purchased Clear this month, 90 switched to Action, 120 to Gentle, and 30 to Sun. The interview also indicated that of the 200 users of Sun last month, 100 still remained loyal to Sun this month, 80 switched to Action, and 20 switched to Gentle.

The total sales of detergents at the Super-Saver Market have been relatively stable during the past several months. Sales for each brand this month were: 10,000 boxes of Action, 40,000 boxes of Gentle, 30,000 boxes of Clear, and 20,000 boxes of Sun. By analyzing the sales record, the research team concluded that the interview results accurately reflected the customers' detergent brand-switching behavior.

The management of the Super-Saver Market wants to know the expected demand for each brand of detergent next month and in subsequent future months to determine the monthly order quantity for each brand.

As the first step of Markov analysis for this problem, the matrix of transition probabilities needs to be developed based on the interview results. The transition probability of Action to Action is obtained as 0.6 from 60 divided by 100. The rest of the transition probabilities are obtained in a similar manner in Table 17.2.

The expected demand for the next month for each branch of detergent can be determined as follows:

$$\begin{array}{cccc} \text{Action} & \text{Gentle} & \text{Clear} & \text{Sun} \end{array} \begin{bmatrix} 0.6 & 0.2 & 0.1 & 0.1 \\ 0 & 0.3 & 0.2 & 0.5 \\ 0.3 & 0.4 & 0.2 & 0.1 \\ 0.4 & 0.1 & 0 & 0.5 \end{bmatrix}$$

$$[10{,}000 \quad 40{,}000 \quad 30{,}000 \quad 20{,}000]$$

$$\begin{aligned} \text{Action} &= (10{,}000 \times 0.6 + 40{,}000 \times 0 + \\ & \quad 30{,}000 \times 0.3 + 20{,}000 \times 0.4) = 23{,}000 \end{aligned}$$

Likewise, we can determine the other brands as follows:

$$\begin{aligned} \text{Gentle} &= 28{,}000 \\ \text{Clear} &= 15{,}000 \\ \text{Sun} &= 34{,}000 \end{aligned}$$

Table 17.2   Transition Probabilities for the Detergents

	To			
From	**Action**	**Gentle**	**Clear**	**Sun**
Action	0.6	0.2	0.1	0.1
Gentle	0.0	0.3	0.2	0.5
Clear	0.3	0.4	0.2	0.1
Sun	0.4	0.1	0.0	0.5

The steady-state probabilities are determined using the same algebraic computation procedure, although the steps are much more involved and complex. The steady-state probabilities obtained after 13 periods are as follows:

Action   Gentle   Clear   Sun
[0.3822   0.2104   0.1004   0.3070]

In the long run, the above probabilities represent percentages of the total detergent sales by brand at the Super-Saver Market. If the store sells 100,000 boxes per month, as the trend indicates, the expected sales of each brand in the future would be:

Action   Gentle   Clear   Sun
[38,220   21,040   10,040   30,700]

SPECIAL CASES OF MARKOV ANALYSIS

A number of special cases cannot be easily analyzed by the approach we have discussed thus far in this chapter. Detailed discussion of many of these cases is beyond the scope of this book, but we will discuss some so that you can easily recognize them when you do encounter such cases.

Suppose we obtained the following matrix of transition probabilities for a problem.

$$
\begin{array}{c}
 & \begin{array}{ccc} 1 & 2 & 3 \end{array} \\
T = \begin{array}{c} 1 \\ 2 \\ 3 \end{array} & \begin{bmatrix} 0 & 0 & 1.0 \\ 0 & 0.64 & 0.36 \\ 0 & 0.75 & 0.25 \end{bmatrix}
\end{array}
$$

In the above matrix, state 1 is often referred to as a *transient* state. States 2 and 3 both have 0.0 probability of moving to state 1. But, since state 1 has a probability of 1.0 of moving to state 3, once state 3 is achieved, the system will not be able to return to state 1 again.

Another special case is a problem with a *cyclic* transition matrix. In the following matrix, the system cycles back and forth between the two states and never gets out of the cycle.

$$
\begin{array}{c}
 & \begin{array}{cc} 1 & 2 \end{array} \\
T = \begin{array}{c} 1 \\ 2 \end{array} & \begin{bmatrix} 0.0 & 1.0 \\ 1.0 & 0.0 \end{bmatrix}
\end{array}
$$

Another interesting case is demonstrated by the following transition matrix:

$$
\begin{array}{c}
 & \begin{array}{ccc} 1 & 2 & 3 \end{array} \\
T = \begin{array}{c} 1 \\ 2 \\ 3 \end{array} & \begin{bmatrix} 0.25 & 0.60 & 0.15 \\ 0.00 & 1.00 & 0.00 \\ 0.40 & 0.15 & 0.45 \end{bmatrix}
\end{array}
$$

State 2 in this matrix is called an **absorbing,** or trapping, **state.** State 2 has only one nonzero probability, 1.00 in the state 2 column. That means once state 2 is achieved, the system cannot move out of this state. Thus, in the future periods, there will be no movement from this absorbing state.

Casette 17.3   **ST. ELIZABETH COMMUNITY HOSPITAL**

St. Elizabeth Community Hospital is considered to be the best hospital in River City. The hospital is well-known for its practice of accepting patients regardless of their abilities to pay the medical bills. Thus, the hospital has horrendous accounts receivable problems. The hospital's accounting department has a long-standing procedure for handling accounts receivable. The department has established the following four categories for all medical accounts:

1. Fully paid

2. Bad debt, written off

3. Current and due within 30 days

4. Delinquent, 31 to 120 days old

The accounting department analyzed the past data and came up with the following transition probability matrix based on a weekly status report. The transition matrix is valid both for number of accounts and for the dollar value of the receivables.

$$T = \begin{array}{c} \\ 1 \\ 2 \\ 3 \\ 4 \end{array} \begin{array}{cccc} 1 & 2 & 3 & 4 \\ \begin{bmatrix} 1.0 & 0.0 & 0.0 & 0.0 \\ 0.0 & 1.0 & 0.0 & 0.0 \\ 0.6 & 0.0 & 0.2 & 0.2 \\ 0.4 & 0.2 & 0.0 & 0.4 \end{bmatrix} \end{array}$$

The transition probabilities matrix indicates several interesting characteristics of the Markov process of the accounts receivable:

1. Absorbing (trapping) states exist for categories 1 (paid) and 2 (bad debt). In other words, once an account receivable is paid in full and makes a transition to state 1, there is no probability of making a transition to any remaining states. Also, if an account turns into a bad debt and makes a transition to state 2, the probability of making a transition to other states is 0.

2. The probability of an account in the current 30-day category (state 3) making a transition to the paid category (state 1) in the next period (week) is 0.6; it is 0.0 to the bad-debt category (state 2), 0.2 to remain in the same category (state 3), and 0.2 to turn into the category of delinquent for 31 to 120 days.

3. The probability of a dollar in the category of delinquent 31 to 120 days (state 4) moving to the paid category (state 1) is 0.4; it is 0.2 to the bad-debt category (state 2), 0.0 to move up to the current category (state 3), and 0.4 to remain in the same (delinquent) category.

4. Since we have absorbing states in this process, computing the steady-state probabilities is not necessary. Eventually, the Markov process will settle in the absorbing states.

The only information we may want to determine is the probabilities of accounts receivable ending up in each of the two absorbing states.

To determine the probability that a dollar starting in state 3 or in state 4 will end up in each of the absorbing states (state 1 and state 2), let us partition the transition matrix as follows:

$$T = \begin{array}{c} \\ 1 \\ 2 \\ 3 \\ 4 \end{array} \begin{array}{cccc} 1 & 2 & 3 & 4 \\ \left[\begin{array}{cc|cc} 1.0 & 0.0 & 0.0 & 0.0 \\ 0.0 & 1.0 & 0.0 & 0.0 \\ \hline 0.6 & 0.0 & 0.2 & 0.2 \\ 0.4 & 0.2 & 0.0 & 0.4 \end{array}\right] \end{array}$$

The four parts of the transition matrix can be labeled as follows:

$$T = \left[\begin{array}{c|c} I & O \\ \hline R & Q \end{array}\right]$$

where

$$I = \begin{array}{c} \\ 1 \\ 2 \end{array} \begin{array}{cc} 1 & 2 \\ \left[\begin{array}{cc} 1 & 0 \\ 0 & 1 \end{array}\right] \end{array} \qquad \text{An } \textit{identity matrix} \text{ with diagonal values of 1}$$

$$O = \begin{array}{c} \\ 1 \\ 2 \end{array} \begin{array}{cc} 3 & 4 \\ \left[\begin{array}{cc} 0 & 0 \\ 0 & 0 \end{array}\right] \end{array} \qquad \text{A matrix of 0 values}$$

$$R = \begin{array}{c} \\ 3 \\ 4 \end{array} \begin{array}{cc} 1 & 2 \\ \left[\begin{array}{cc} 0.6 & 0.0 \\ 0.4 & 0.2 \end{array}\right] \end{array} \qquad \text{A matrix of absorbing transition probabilities in the next period (week)}$$

$$Q = \begin{array}{c} \\ 3 \\ 4 \end{array} \begin{array}{cc} 3 & 4 \\ \left[\begin{array}{cc} 0.2 & 0.2 \\ 0.0 & 0.4 \end{array}\right] \end{array} \qquad \text{A matrix of transition probabilities between all nonabsorbing states}$$

The first operation required is to determine the *fundamental matrix N* as follows:

$$N = (I - Q)^{-1}$$

Again, if we have forgotten matrix algebra, the "-1" exponent simply refers to the *inverse* of the matrix. To refresh your memory, we will examine the computation used to obtain the inverse for a 2-by-2 matrix.

$$M = \begin{bmatrix} a_1 & a_2 \\ b_1 & b_2 \end{bmatrix}$$

$$M^{-1} = \begin{bmatrix} a_1 & a_2 \\ b_1 & b_2 \end{bmatrix}^{-1}$$

$$= \begin{bmatrix} b_2/D & -a_2/D \\ -b_1/D & a_1/D \end{bmatrix}$$

where D is the determinant of the matrix M and is defined as

$$D = a_1 b_2 - b_1 a_2$$

Now we can go back to our problem and determine the fundamental matrix N:

$$N = (I - Q)^{-1}$$

$$N = \left(\begin{bmatrix} 1 & 0 \\ 0 & 1 \end{bmatrix} - \begin{bmatrix} 0.2 & 0.2 \\ 0.0 & 0.4 \end{bmatrix} \right)^{-1}$$

$$= \begin{bmatrix} (1.0 - 0.2) & (0.0 - 0.2) \\ (0.0 - 0.0) & (1.0 - 0.4) \end{bmatrix}^{-1}$$

$$= \begin{bmatrix} 0.8 & -0.2 \\ 0.0 & 0.6 \end{bmatrix}^{-1}$$

$$= \begin{matrix} 1 \\ 2 \end{matrix} \begin{matrix} 1 & 2 \\ \begin{bmatrix} 1.250 & 0.417 \\ 0.0 & 1.667 \end{bmatrix} \end{matrix}$$

Next, by multiplying N times R we obtain the new matrix of transition probabilities that the dollar in the nonabsorbing states will end up in the two absorbing states.

$$N \times R = \begin{matrix} 3 \\ 4 \end{matrix} \begin{matrix} 3 & 4 \\ \begin{bmatrix} 1.25 & 0.417 \\ 0.0 & 1.667 \end{bmatrix} \end{matrix} \times \begin{matrix} 3 \\ 4 \end{matrix} \begin{matrix} 1 & 2 \\ \begin{bmatrix} 0.6 & 0.0 \\ 0.4 & 0.2 \end{bmatrix} \end{matrix}$$

$$NR = \begin{matrix} 3 \\ 4 \end{matrix} \begin{matrix} 1 & 2 \\ \begin{bmatrix} 0.917 & 0.083 \\ 0.667 & 0.333 \end{bmatrix} \end{matrix}$$

The transition matrix NR reflects the probability that a dollar in state 3 (due in 30 days) will eventually be absorbed into state 1 (paid in full) or state 2 (bad debt). Thus, the dollar in the category of current and due in 30 days has the probability of 0.917 that it will be fully paid and 0.083 probability that it will turn into a bad debt. However, the dollar in state 4 (delinquent, 31 to 120 days) has a 0.667 probability of being paid in full in the future and 0.333 probability of turning into a bad debt.

Let us suppose that the St. Elizabeth Hospital has \$150,000 in state 3 and \$50,000 in state 4. To determine how these accounts will end up in the fully paid (state 1) and bad-debt (state 2) categories, we can compute as follows:

$$\text{Accounts receivable} = \begin{matrix} 3 & 4 \\ [150,000 & 50,000] \end{matrix} \times \begin{matrix} 3 \\ 4 \end{matrix} \begin{matrix} 1 & 2 \\ \begin{bmatrix} 0.917 & 0.083 \\ 0.667 & 0.333 \end{bmatrix} \end{matrix}$$

$$= \begin{matrix} 1 & 2 \\ [171,900 & 29,100] \end{matrix}$$

Clearly, of the $200,000 total accounts receivable, the hospital can expect payments of $171,900, and the remaining $29,100 is expected to turn into bad debts. Such information is extremely useful to the decision maker in establishing the organization's long-term strategies as well as short-term operating policies.

COMPUTER SOLUTIONS OF MARKOV PROBLEMS

Markov analysis can be very involved and complex when the problem has a large number of states and the analysis covers a long series of time periods. Thus, Markov analysis is a natural for computers applications. In this section, we will apply *Micro Manager* to solve the Super-Saver Market problem discussed as Casette 17.2.

Figure 17.5 presents the input data for the transition probabilities and the output in terms of the steady-state probabilities and steady-state values (boxes sold for each brand of detergent). The results correspond, except for minor rounding errors in our manual calculations, with the solution we derived earlier.

REAL-WORLD APPLICATIONS OF MARKOV ANALYSIS

A number of interesting real-world applications of Markov analysis have been reported in the management science literature. Some of these applications have been for decision problems in business and industry, and others have been for decision problems in non-profit organizations and government agencies. Most of these applications involve descriptive probabilistic information about various conditions of decision problems under consideration.

Ascertaining Human Resource Values for Depreciation Purposes

As the U.S. economy becomes increasingly service oriented, companies are recognizing that their people are the most important and valuable asset. This transition has led to the creation of human resource accounting (HRA). HRA attempts to measure and properly account for the economic value that people represent to their organization.[1] Tax laws in the United States allow for the depreciation of the value of intangible assets provided that the asset's useful life is limited and determinable and that the asset is clearly separable from goodwill. The intangible asset goodwill cannot be deducted for tax purposes, leading companies to search for a valid method of distinguishing human resource values from goodwill value. This situation occurs most frequently when one company buys another for a price exceeding its net book value, as in this real-world application. Due to the sensitive nature of the evaluation, the acquiring corporation and the purchased securities brokerage firm were not identified.

A Markov process was assumed to represent the annual change in earnings attributable to the account executives (AE) whose services were acquired. Several qualifying assumptions allowed for use of the Markov modeling technique: (1) Each AE could be in one of the four states in each year. These states represented high, medium, and low

[1]Eric Flamholtz, George Geis, and Richard Perle, "A Markovian Model for the Valuation of Human Assets Acquired by an Organizational Purchase," *Interfaces* 14:6 (1984), 11–15.

Figure 17.5   Computer Solution of the Super-Saver Market Problem

PROGRAM: Markov Models

***** INPUT DATA ENTERED *****

Transition probability table

```
---------------------------------------------------
States:  to      1     2     3     4
from
  1            0.600 0.200 0.100 0.100
  2            0.000 0.300 0.200 0.500
  3            0.300 0.400 0.200 0.100
  4            0.400 0.100 0.000 0.500
---------------------------------------------------
```

Number of iterations (periods): 99

```
        Initial vector
        States      Value
        ---------------------------
          1          10000
          2          40000
          3          30000
          4          20000
        ---------------------------
```

*****   PROGRAM OUTPUT   *****

```
-----------------------------------------------------------
States   Steady state probability   Steady state Value
-----------------------------------------------------------
  1             0.38                     38223.94
  2             0.21                     21042.47
  3             0.10                     10038.61
  4             0.31                     30694.98
-----------------------------------------------------------
```

After 13 iteration(s) steady state is approached.

---

earnings and the absorbing state of retirement or termination. (2) Movement between the states is permitted, except out of the termination state. (3) AEs' states in any year depend only on their state in the previous year. (4) Transition probabilities are constant over time. (5) All AEs share the same transition probabilities. The actual transition matrix follows:

From Year n	To Year n + 1			
	High	**Medium**	**Low**	**Terminated**
High	0.7430	0.1927	0.0000	0.0643
Medium	0.0786	0.6900	0.1921	0.0343
Low	0.0042	0.1081	0.7500	0.1377
Terminated	0.0000	0.0000	0.0000	1.0000

The transition coefficients were determined by analyzing the previous 6 years' transitions for all the AEs in the firm. After a setup run to compensate for the 2 months remaining in the year of acquisition, initial probabilities for each state were determined: high, 0.1149; medium, 0.2425; low, 0.6222; and terminated, 0.0176. The total depreciable value was calculated using a present value of future earnings equation, which was decomposed into 40 separate yearly amounts. For accounting and tax purposes, differing amortization schedules were prepared based on the human asset valuation derived via the Markov model. The model served to meet the Internal Revenue Service's criterion that the useful life of an asset must be determined with reasonable accuracy and that its value must be separable from the goodwill value.

A Triple Markov Chain Predicts College Enrollment

As the pool of available college students decreases, colleges become more sensitive to changes in their enrollment.[2] Retention rates are of particular interest. Recent college students have become more erratic, with far fewer attending consecutive terms and graduating in the traditional eight terms. Parks College of St. Louis University divides its academic year into trimesters—fall, winter, and spring. It is assumed that students will attend all sessions consecutively, but this is often not the case. The spring trimester, covering much of the summer, is prone to enrollment drops of 35 to 40 percent. This effect varies by department. To determine overall college enrollment, departmental projections are necessary.

The Transportation, Travel and Tourism Department's (TTT) published schedule assumes that a student will graduate after eight consecutive trimesters. The fact that many students interrupt their schooling requires the department to offer spring session classes during other terms as well—leading to low section enrollments and the associated costs and inefficiencies. To apply Markov analysis to the TTT situation, required assumptions were that a student's progress could be viewed as transition between states and that historical transition rates can be used to provide the transition matrix.

Five states were defined: F (full-time student), P (part-time student), L (leave of absence), G (graduated), and W (withdrawn permanently). G and W are absorbing states. All transitions are assumed to occur at the end of a trimester. Data on 712 transitions, representing 117 students, were used to obtain the following transition matrix.

[2]N. K. Kwak, Raymond Brown, and Marc Schniederjans, "A Markov Analysis of Estimating Student Enrollment Transition in a Trimester Institution," *Socio-Economic Planning Science,* forthcoming.

From	To				
	G	W	F	P	L
G	1.000	0.000	0.000	0.000	0.000
W	0.000	1.000	0.000	0.000	0.000
F	0.104	0.064	0.655	0.058	0.119
P	0.263	0.123	0.333	0.193	0.088
L	0.000	0.000	0.755	0.078	0.167

Analysis of the transition matrix above showed overall, annual usefulness, but it was not an accurate representation of the transition between particular trimesters. Thus, a new model was developed, employing three distinct transition matrices—one for the break between each of the trimesters—connected in a circle. These matrices correlated well with data for the trimester transitions they were to represent. This matrix chain predicted more full-time students in the fall and winter, and more on-leave students during the spring, than did the single matrix. Use of the matrix allowed TTT to determine that approximately 20 new students would be needed each fall to maintain enrollment. Statistical tests showed that the triple Markov model produced projections which were statistically significant in 19 out of 21 trimesters, whereas the single matrix was accurate for only 8 of 21. A combined annual matrix, obtained by multiplying the three individual matrices, showed that over 1 year, 26 percent of full-time students will graduate, 16 percent will drop out, and 52 percent will still be full-time students.

SUMMARY

This chapter has presented an overview of Markov analysis, a particular class of probabilistic models that are useful for analyzing decision situations over time. We discussed simple but widely applied problem areas: machine breakdown and brand switching. Although Markov analysis is quite useful and mathematically interesting, this technique has seen only limited real-world applications. A primary reason appears to be that Markov analysis requires strict assumptions that are difficult to satisfy in real-world situations. For example, many problems do not have transition probabilities that are constant over time.

Numerous effective computer software packages are available for Markov analysis, and thus some of the limitations imposed by the necessary assumptions could be alleviated. For example, we can experiment with various changing transition probabilities without too much effort. Since the basic purpose of Markov analysis is to obtain descriptive information that is useful to the decision maker, the interactive computer approach becomes an important tool to enhance the value of this technique.

Glossary

Absorbing State   A condition or state which accepts transitions from other states but does not permit transitions to any other states.

Markov Process   A special form of stochastic process where a given state of the system depends on the single preceding state exclusively rather than on several or all previous states.

State of Probability   For a given time period, the likelihood that the system will be in a particular state.

State of the System   Conditions or parameters of a situation measured at one particular moment, disregarding past or future changes in these values.

Steady-state Probability   After a sufficient sequence of time periods, a typical Markov process will result in constant probabilities for the occurrence of each possible state, valid for all subsequent periods.

Stochastic Processes   Probabilistic models in which the current state of the system depends on previous states of the system.

Transition Matrix   Presentation of transition probabilities in matrix form.

Transition Probabilities   The set of probabilities representing the likelihood of change from each state (at a given moment) to all possible states in the next time period.

References

Feller, W. *An Introduction to Probability Theory and Its Applications*. Vol. I, 3d ed. New York: Wiley, 1968.

Howard, R. A. *Dynamic Programming and Markov Processes*. Cambridge, Mass.: M.I.T. Press, 1960.

Kemeny, J. G., and Shall, J. L. *Finite Markov Chains*. Princeton, N.J.: D. Van Nostrand, 1960.

Lee, S. M., Moore, L. J., and Taylor, B. W. *Management Science*. 3d ed. Dubuque, Iowa: W. C. Brown, 1985.

Searle, S. R., and Hausman, W. H. *Matrix Algebra for Business and Economics*. New York: Wiley, 1970.

Assignments

17.1 Discuss whether Markov analysis can be classified as deterministic or probabilistic.

17.2 Describe the major elements of Markov process models.

17.3 Name several possible business situations where the Markov process can be applied to predict the future.

17.4 Describe assumptions necessary for the valid application of a Markov process.

17.5 How can we tell that we have reached the steady state?

17.6 In computing transition probabilities for the steady state, what equation must we add in addition to equations developed from the given matrix of transition probabilities?

17.7 What is an absorbing state? Give some examples.

17.8 Can Markov analysis be considered as a decision-making model for optimization like dynamic programming? Discuss.

17.9 Can we use tree diagrams in lieu of a Markov process? Discuss.

17.10 Discuss whether the sum of the probabilities in each row and each column in a transition probability matrix should be 1.

17.11 Recall the steady-state condition from the queuing theory chapter: Are there any common characteristics between the terminology in steady-state conditions from Markov analysis and queuing theory?

17.12 Given the following 1-year transition matrix, compute the transition matrix for a period of 2 years.

	To	
From	**A**	**B**
A	0.35	0.65
B	0.60	0.40

17.13 Compute the following matrix:

$$[1{,}000 \quad 2{,}000] \begin{bmatrix} 0.1 & 0.9 \\ 0.8 & 0.2 \end{bmatrix}$$

17.14 Given the following transition matrix, determine the steady-state condition.

	To		
From	**A**	**B**	**C**
A	0.10	0.20	0.70
B	0.30	0.50	0.20
C	0.45	0.20	0.35

The initial states of *A, B,* and *C* are assumed to have 1,000 units each.

17.15 Bruce County's population is 1,000, and Lee's is 1,500. A study indicated that 10 percent of Bruce's population moves to Lee each year, but only 5 percent of Lee's population moves to Bruce.
   a. Construct the transition matrix for switching population.
   b. Compute the expected population for each county 5 years later.
   c. Compute the expected populations in the long-run situation.

17.16 Qing and Orange are manufacturing and selling personal computers. Over any given year, Qing loses 5 percent of its customers to Orange, but Orange loses only 2 percent to Qing. The market share for Qing computers is 40 percent; Orange has the rest.

a. Develop the transition matrix from year to year.
b. What will be the market share for each company in the long run?

17.17 Suppose that the management of Qing (from problem 17.16) has decided to use a promotional campaign to increase its market share. If the company employs this campaign, which costs $150,000, they can decrease the percentage of customers lost to Orange to 2 percent while gaining 5 percent of the customers held by Orange every year. If each percentage increase in market share is worth $20,000, is the promotional campaign a worthwhile venture?

17.18 Central American Shopping Center wants to predict the behavior of customers in paying their credit card debts. The credit department has developed the following monthly transition matrix for payment patterns, by using historical data:

From	To	
	Paid	Not Paid
Paid	0.7	0.3
Not Paid	0.9	0.1

a. If customers do not pay their bills in month k, what will be the probability that they will pay within the next 4 months?
b. What will be the probabilities for paying and not paying the bills on any given month in the long run?

17.19 Santa Manufacturing Company wants to predict its machine operation pattern in the future. The firm has collected past records for this type of machine and has found that the probability of not breaking down on the following day given not breaking down on any given day is 75 percent, and the probability of breakdown given breakdown in the previous day is 30 percent.

a. Set up the transition matrix for the problem.
b. Determine the steady-state condition.

17.20 Recalling problem 17.19, let us suppose that the company presently has 120 new machines. The company also found that the average repair cost per machine is $15. What will be the total average repair cost per day in the steady-state condition?

17.21 The director of the marketing department of the *Morning Journal* newspaper has found that readers have been switching from one newspaper to another. She has established the following matrix table showing readers' switches between last month and this month.

| | | To | |
From	Morning Journal	Star Herald	Others
Morning Journal	10,000	1,000	300
Star Herald	3,500	25,000	100
Others	150	50	2,500

The director is very interested in forecasting the expected demand 3 months in advanced to prepare production plans. If each subscriber above 15,000 (break-even point) generates $1.00 profit, how much monthly profit or loss will the *Morning Journal* have 3 months from now?

17.22 The accounting department of Bell Manufacturing Co. has secured a breakdown on the transition among three categories of accounts receivable by its customers. Because all invoices are payable within 21 days and the firm has a liberal reinstatement policy, customers can shift between any of the categories.

| | | From | | | |
Class	June	Clear	Current	Delinquent	July
Clear	1,650	1,500	200	200	1,900
Current	2,500	50	2,000	50	2,100
Delinquent	1,050	100	300	800	1,200

What percentage of credit customers will be classified in each category in December? Assume that no new credit customers are added.

17.23 Steve is an independent taxi driver working in Murchison. To maintain his taxi's condition, he makes it a rule to have his car inspected every month. If any problem is found, it will be fixed. However, the repair does not guarantee that the car's excellent condition will be reattained. If there is no way to fix it, Steve will replace it with a new car. His car's condition can be classified into four levels. These levels and average repair cost for each level are presented below.

Condition	Average Repair Cost
Excellent	$ 0
Average	150
Acceptable	1,000
Junk (no way to repair)	8,000

Suppose that the transition matrix for his car's condition from month to month is as follows:

| | To | | | |
From	Excellent	Average	Acceptable	Junk
Excellent	0.90	0.05	0.05	0.0
Average	0.10	0.80	0.10	0.0
Acceptable	0.05	0.10	0.75	0.1
Junk	1.00	0.00	0.00	0.0

What will be the average cost per month per car in the long run? Suppose his car's condition now is excellent.

17.24 Tom is making and selling gloves for a living. His productivity varies with his mood on any particular day. The type of mood that Tom has on a given day and the average number of pairs of gloves that he can produce while in that mood are shown below.

Type of Mood	Average Number of Pairs
Inspired	250
Average	200
Depressed	120

Tom's mood on a given day depends on his mood on a previous day. Information for his mood swings from day to day is given as follows:

| | To | | |
From	Inspired	Average	Depressed
Inspired	0.50	0.25	0.25
Average	0.30	0.60	0.10
Depressed	0.10	0.20	0.70

How many pairs of gloves, on average, can he produce per day in the steady-state condition?

17.25 Three close friends are retiring to Sunny City in Florida and have decided to play poker every Saturday night. They have agreed to play only with a bag of distinctive chips they acquired many years ago. Players take home all their chips, including the ones they won that night. On the following Saturday, they bring those chips again and start with that number of chips. Following is the transition matrix based on the number of chips:

Player	Last Week	From A	B	C	This Week
A	200	190	20	40	250
B	200	10	170	30	210
C	200	0	10	130	140

Assuming that the trend continues over time, how many chips will player *A* have at the end of next week's game? How many chips is each player going to have in the steady-state condition?

17.26 The Abraham General Hospital has three departments which depend on the help of nursing volunteers. Volunteers can choose the department where they want to work. The number of volunteers moving from one department to another between January and February is shown below.

Department	January	From A	B	C	February
A	30	25	10	5	40
B	25	1	15	2	18
C	35	4	0	28	32

Assume that the total number of volunteers working in the hospital will not change and that each department needs at least 30 nurses. How many paid nurses will be needed in each department in March, if any department with fewer than 30 volunteers must hire nurses to maintain the minimum level of 30?

17.27 Theresa plans to open a retail shoe store specializing in the Tiger brand. She has hired a marketing research consultant to gather information about brand-switching behavior of the residents in the two cities where Theresa is considering locating her store —Warrensburg and Boonville. The cities have roughly the same population.

	Warrensburg To		
From	**Tiger**	**Lion**	**Moth**
Tiger	0.60	0.30	0.10
Lion	0.30	0.25	0.45
Moth	0.25	0.65	0.10
	Boonville		
Tiger	0.80	0.10	0.10
Lion	0.30	0.30	0.40
Moth	0.10	0.20	0.70

Which city is the better choice?

17.28 Swan University has four colleges: business, education, art/science, and engineering. The yearly expense for educating one student and current enrollment for each college are as follows:

College	Expense per Student	Enrollment
Business	$200	2,500
Education	180	800
Art/Science	350	500
Engineering	500	1,200

The transition matrix for enrollment from year to year is shown below.

	To			
From	Business	Education	Art/Science	Engineering
Business	0.80	0.10	0.10	0.00
Education	0.20	0.50	0.10	0.20
Art/Science	0.40	0.15	0.30	0.15
Engineering	0.15	0.10	0.10	0.65

Find the expected enrollment and budget for each college in the long run.

17.29 Andrew Company rents out its fleet of 300 cars. The company has three branches: Lincoln, Kansas City, and St. Louis. Customers can return the car at their destination or at the place they rented it. The probabilities representing the customers' behavior in renting cars are as follows:

	To		
From	Lincoln	Kansas City	St. Louis
Lincoln	0.50	0.30	0.20
Kansas City	0.20	0.65	0.15
St. Louis	0.35	0.25	0.40

a. Figure out the steady-state probabilities for each branch.
b. Suppose that each branch has 100 cars right now. How many cars (on average) will each branch expect to have in the long run?

17.30 Frez is the only ice cream shop in a small town. Because the daily demand for ice cream depends on the weather condition, Frez's owner wishes to predict the weather.

Through his experience, he has found that the weather on any day depends on the previous day's weather. Only three types of weather exist in this town: fair, cloudy, and rainy. The daily transition matrix for the weather is presented below.

From	To Fair	Cloudy	Rainy
Fair	0.70	0.20	0.10
Cloudy	0.25	0.50	0.25
Rain	0.40	0.40	0.20

a. What are the steady-state probabilities for each kind of weather?

b. If the daily demand for ice cream is 150 gallons on a fair day, 80 gallons on a cloudy day, and 20 gallons on a rainy day, what will be the average demand per day in the steady-state condition?

18 MANAGEMENT SCIENCE IMPLEMENTATION AND DECISION SUPPORT SYSTEMS

Most of the readers of this book are likely to become decision makers. Thus, it is perfectly fitting to close this book with a discussion of management science implementation and management science in the decision support context. We have seen enough evidence that the successful application of management science requires more than just a good knowledge of management science techniques. There is no question whatever that management science has a great potential for improving management decision making. Nevertheless, we are far from reaching this potential. As a matter of fact, there is increasing concern among practicing managers about the role and direction of management science. Management science is a discipline of systematic analysis intended to provide useful information for effective decision making. A decision support system (DSS) is a computer-based information system that provides support to the decision maker. Since most management science techniques are applied to real-world situations with computer support, management science can be an important part of a DSS.

In this chapter, we will first explore ways to improve organizational effectiveness and performance through successful implementation of management science. Then we will discuss the concept of DSS, DSS structure, different levels of DSS, artificial intelligence, expert systems, and application of DSS in real-world situations.

Learning Objectives *From the study of this chapter, we will learn the following:*

1. *The meaning of management science implementation*
2. *Several typical problems involved in implementation*
3. *Differences between managers and management scientists in the perceived barriers to the application of management science*
4. *The basic role of the management scientist*
5. *Factors that are important for successful management science implementation*
6. *Strategies for managing resistance to organizational change*
7. *Several ways to improve each phase of the management science process*
8. *Evolution of decision support systems from data processing and management information systems*
9. *The relationship between decision support systems and management science*
10. *Reasons behind the rapid development of decision support systems*
11. *The basic structure of decision support systems*
12. *Different levels of decision support systems*
13. *Evolution of artificial intelligence and expert systems*
14. *The meaning of the following terms:*

Implementation   *Situational normativism*
Cost-benefit analysis   *Data processing*
Management information systems   *Decision support systems*
Interactive system   *DSS generators*
DSS tools   *Artificial intelligence*
Robotics   *Natural language*
Voice recognition   *Expert systems*

MANAGEMENT SCIENCE IMPLEMENTATION

As we have discussed throughout the previous chapters, a phenomenal advance has been made in the field of management science since the end of World War II. Many new techniques have been developed through technical breakthroughs, new applications of existing techniques have been explored, and complex decision problems have been solved through the use of computers. In this book we have purposely selected the most widely used basic management science techniques for study.

We need a good working knowledge of modeling techniques in order to analyze decision problems. Nevertheless, modeling is only a part of the entire process of management science application. Today, more than ever, management scientists and practicing managers are concerned about the actual **implementation** of management science. For example, over 400 studies have been published that deal with the implementation issue of management science. This concern clearly indicates the growing maturity of the management science field as a profession.

According to a number of studies, approximately 50 percent of the manufacturing firms surveyed use management science. Over 90 percent of these firms rate the results of the management science applications as very good to excellent. However, the actual picture of management science implementation in organizations is not always that rosy. We are beginning to find reports of failures in applying management science to decision problems. One study even had this catchy title: ''How to Fail with OR in Government without Really Trying.'' We have seen many claims of successful management science implementation of one sort or another. Yet management science is increasingly concerned about its future, especially its role in the most important part of the management science process — implementation.

What Is Implementation?

Implementation of management science basically means the actual use of the output of a management science project by managers to improve organizational performance. It is not easy to define what degree of use would be required to label a management science project as implemented. There are differing views about successful implementation. The practicing manager tends to declare implementation a success when management science output helps the manager to achieve his or her intended objectives. However, the management scientist tends to think that a successful implementation has occurred if the project provided valuable new information, experience, or insights about the problem.

A broader and more realistic index of implementation is to view implementation as a continuous cycle or process of management science. In this framework, implementation does not start after the solution to a model is obtained or the recommendation is accepted by the manager. Instead, implementation encompasses the entire process of management science, involving all of the following phases:

Identification and formulation of a problem

Development of a model

Solution of the model

Testing of the solution

Recommendation and implementation

Figure 18.1 presents the process of management science. This process is not a series of isolated operating steps. Typically there are feedback and feedforward activities at each phase. For example, the model formulation effort may indicate that the needed data are not available. Then, we may need to go back to the first step to examine the problem once again. This process will be more fully discussed when we examine implementation strategies in a later section of this chapter.

The concept of a continuous life cycle of implementation has been supported by a number of researchers. Gupta reported an interesting study about implementation difficulties of management science in the U.S. Postal Service. His study clearly demonstrates that a successful implementation requires successful achievement of various criteria at each phase of the entire process of management science.

Obviously we do not have a unified definition of implementation. Nevertheless, a successful implementation is often associated with the following characteristics:

1. An improved organizational performance through the use of the model results or information generated by the process

2. An improved communication or work relationship among the interdisciplinary parties involved (the manager, management scientist, operations personnel, staff specialists, and others)

Figure 18.1   The Process of Management Science

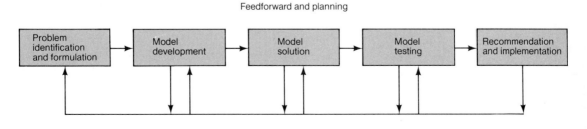

3. Carefully planned and monitored activities in each phase of the entire process

4. A continuous and dynamic process of updating, feedforward, feedback, review, control, and communication

Typical Problems Involved in Implementation

The kind of picture we have drawn in this book may look rosy for management science. In some organizations, such an optimistic picture may be justified. However, numerous organizations are experiencing many difficulties in their attempts to apply management science to decision analysis. In reality, we often see practicing managers and management scientists operate as two separate groups, each with its own language, methods, and goals. Each has much to contribute to and learn from the other. Yet, managers often accuse management scientists of dealing with "technological nonsense," whereas management scientists scorn managers as "ignorant pragmatists." The British philosopher C. P. Snow once observed that science and the humanities operate as two distinct cultures. His advice was: "What we need to do is humanize the scientist and simonize the humanist."

When organizations face certain problems in implementation, the typical causes listed are often opinionated finger pointing such as: lack of interpersonal and communication skills on the part of management scientists, cultural and educational differences between managers and management scientists, improper identification of the problem by managers, unworkable model formulation by management scientists, lack of understanding of the decision environment by management scientists, lack of understanding of management science by managers, and formulating too complex models for simple problems (the scalpel for a hamburger syndrome).

C. Jackson Grayson, a student of management science and former chair of the Price Commission in the federal government, lists the following reasons for not applying management science:

1. *Shortage of Time.*   Most important decisions require immediate solutions; no time to fool around with problem formulation, data collection, model design, testing the model solution, etc.

2. *Lack of Data.*   Often the required data for the model are inaccessible, nonexistent, or not in the form usable to the model.

3. *Resistance to Change.*   Implementation requires organizational change, which is often resisted by managers and operational personnel.

4. *Long Response Time.*   The management scientist tends to take a systematic but time-consuming way to analyze a problem, and managers would rather use a quick judgmental decision than wait for a good solution for 6 months.

5. *Simplifications and Assumptions.*   Important environmental or behavioral constraints are often swept under the rug by the management scientist in designing the model. For

Table 18.1   *Management Scientists' Perception of Barriers to Management Science Application*

Rank	Barrier
1	Selling management science techniques to management meets with resistance.
2	Neither top nor middle management has the educational background to appreciate management science techniques.
3	Lack of good clean data.
4	There is never time to analyze a real problem using a sophisticated approach.
5	Lack of understanding by those who need to use the results.
6	Hard to define problems for applications.
7	The payoff from using unsophisticated methods is sufficient.
8	Shortage of personnel.
9	Poor reputation of management scientists as problem solvers.
10	Individuals feel threatened by management scientists and their techniques.

Source: H. J. Watson and P. G. Marett, ''A Survey of Management Science Implementation Problems,'' *Interfaces* 9:4 (1979), 124–128.

example, time constraints, data inaccessibility, bureaucratic power structures, organizational values, and the manager's priority structure of objectives are often simplified out of the model.

Although the previously discussed five reasons may sound reasonable, they are more eloquent excuses than legitimate causes for not applying management science. These five reasons exist for any major project that organizations undertake. For example, a change of organizational structure, which is usually not a management science project, may encounter the same five problems.

We may be able to shed some light on more meaningful causes of implementation difficulties by citing a recent study conducted by Watson and Marett in 1979. This study presents practicing management scientists' perceptions about the barriers to management science implementation. Table 18.1 presents the survey results.

There is a general trend of agreement between managers and management scientists concerning the major barriers to application. Some of the important barriers appear to be educational or technical knowledge, perceptional differences about the value of management science, and lack of appropriate data. However, there also are some differences on several important issues. Managers generally tend to be more cost or time conscious. Thus, they often pursue ''quick and dirty'' solutions. However, management scientists tend to be more concerned with developing mathematically elegant models than with attempting to just extract information that is needed by managers.

Perhaps the most important factor for successful implementation of management science is the corporate culture. The organization should exhibit a prevailing set of values and philosophies that encourage systematic analysis for productivity improvement. Otherwise, organizational change based on management science application becomes simply a nuisance created by a handful of people who are trying to justify their jobs.

Many other recent studies have identified a number of factors that are important for successful implementation of management science. Some of these factors are:

An appropriate corporate culture

The degree of management participation and support

Technical competence and organizational influence of the management scientist

Relevance of management science to organizational problems

Effectiveness of the model—simplicity, robustness, adaptability, and ease of communication

Resources allocated to management science projects

Organizational climate for innovation and change

Organizational commitment to long-range strategic planning

Commitment of all personnel to organizational values and purpose

Communication among all levels of the organization

Unique aspects of the organization, problem, decision environment, or personnel

MANAGEMENT PERSPECTIVE OF IMPLEMENTATION

Role of the Management Scientist

Management science implementation is much like the successful introduction of a new product. In order to introduce a new product, an organization must go through a market research, feasibility study, product design, production, distribution, sales, and maintenance or service. Each phase of the process must be successfully completed in order to have a successful result. For example, a sloppy sales effort will certainly ruin a fine product.

Many empirical studies suggest that for successful implementation the management scientist must work harmoniously with the manager. We believe management scientists should take the initiative in changing their work behavior. It is extremely difficult for managers to change their work patterns. Furthermore, the end product is supposed to be management, not management science.

Traditional educational programs train a student of management science to formulate and solve models. Rarely is a student exposed to the relationship between the abstract organizational purpose and the model. Worse yet, most management science courses are technique-oriented rather than implementation-oriented. Thus, most management scientists do not have the broad management perspective required for successful implementation.

H. Z. Halbrecht, the president of a management consulting firm, told the following story in a professional meeting:

A recent Ph.D. in operations research was hired by a metropolitan city government. His job was to find a good location for a sewage disposal plant somewhere in one of the boroughs. A few weeks later he came to his supervisor. He had the model; he had spent an awful lot of money on computer time; and he announced, "I've got the optimum location for it." When his supervisor heard "optimum" he started to duck, but thought he would listen to him anyway. Then the fellow showed how he came up with the location. Now, everybody who is high-up in any city administration (who has also got a little bit of brains and who has lasted more than six months) has an address book in his pocket, because it's great to know all the theories about public administration and city management, but before you do anything drastic, it's nice to know who lives in the area that you are going to pick for the sewage disposal plant. And, by an odd coincidence, the optimum location picked was two blocks from the Chairman of the City Finance Committee's home. The supervisor suggested that that was not the "optimum" location, and this fellow got furious. He said, "I will tell you that this is the optimum location. Are you looking for a political solution or for a truthful solution?" The man who replaced the first fellow was put on that assignment and was told to find the best "workable" solution.[1]

The above story tells us that the management scientist should know more than the analytical techniques to design models and that he should help implement the results of the design model. There have been several recent attempts to narrow the gap between management and management science. First, there has been a rapid decentralization of management science activities in organizations. Instead of maintaining a separate management science group, many firms have sprinkled management scientists throughout the organization in areas where they can be really valuable. Many management scientists are assigned to significant functional management positions, or as aides to the top managers. They are given line responsibilities for results.

Another trend is the managers' demand for implementation of the model by management scientists. This approach helps alleviate the problem of unworkable, theoretical model design on the part of management scientists. A third trend has been thorough on-the-job training of management scientists in the broad organizational purpose and values, unique organizational characteristics, and behavioral aspects of management science implementation. *It is the responsibility of management to integrate management scientists into the mainstream of the organization's operations.*

The basic problem of implementation is not the weaknesses inherent in management science itself. Rather, the root of the problem lies in two factors: (1) management's failure to develop and articulate a proper organizational culture that integrates all functions of organization members into its basic purpose, and (2) management scientists' failure to broaden their views and insights about their roles in the organization. Thus, the basic problem of implementation rests on the misconception, by both managers and management scientists, of the role and purpose of management science in organizations.

IMPLEMENTATION STRATEGIES

The success of management science application is determined by the organization's efforts in implementing the model results. If implementation is properly planned with appropriate effort, time, resources, and determination, the organization will most likely enjoy maximum benefits from the management science process.

---

[1]Quoted with the permission of *Decision Sciences* from H. Z. Halbrecht, "If Your Students Aren't Marketable, What's Your Future?" *Decision Sciences* 4:3 (1973), xx.

Numerous implementation strategies of management science have been suggested by many researchers and practitioners. In order to attain successful implementation, there are several key issues that need to be addressed. Some of these issues are:

Who should be responsible for the implementation?

Who should be involved in the process?

What problems are most likely to be encountered?

What strategies should be used to resolve these problems?

What are the required resources for implementation?

How can we plan ahead for implementation?

We will briefly discuss these questions from both empirical and theoretical viewpoints and provide important guidelines and strategies for implementation.

Organizational Factors Important for Successful Implementation

The organizational factors discussed below have been pointed out by many empirical studies as important for successful implementation.

Top Management Involvement and Support   Many studies have pointed out that visible involvement and support of top management are crucial for the management science process to succeed. The very purpose of management science is to improve the organizational performance and effectiveness outlined by top management. Also, implementation usually requires large-scale changes in organizational structure, policy and work procedures, and job responsibilities. Thus, top management involvement is imperative.

Consistent Management Philosophy   Management science projects are based on the belief that greater efficiency can be achieved in the organization when systematic analysis is applied to decision making for long-term organizational objectives. If management's philosophy is contrary to the underlying principles of management science, implementation cannot be successful. The organization must have a management philosophy that encourages creativity, innovation, and change.

Effective Communication   The management science process, contrary to what many people think, is a human process. In order to bring out the best imagination, creativity, and efforts from various members of the organization, clear communication is essential. Effective communication results in *commitment* to the common purpose rather than reluctant *compliance* on the part of organization members.

Effective Management Information System   A **management information system** is concerned with collecting, storing, processing, and transmitting information that is essential for effective decision making. The management science process is an important element of the broad concept of **decision support systems** (DSS). An effective information system is required to carry out such important steps as quantification of organizational objectives, formulation of the model, model testing, and feedback analysis.

Managerial and Technical Skills   Management science implementation requires various managerial and technical skills. Managers must possess conceptual skills in formulating and communicating organizational objectives. However, management scientists must have technical competence in order to collect required data, quantify many abstract objective criteria, construct models, and analyze the implications of the model solutions. Perhaps the most crucial skills required of everybody are human skills— abilities to listen and communicate, develop human relationships, coach and counsel, and motivate others to work toward a common goal.

Proper Integration of Management Science with Other Functions   Management science cannot exist in a vacuum. It must be properly integrated with the other functions of management. Many successful organizations integrate management science within each of their line functions. Thus, management scientists work as line personnel while practicing their professional skills.

Commitment to Reduce Bureaucracy   Implementation of management science model results usually requires a great deal of interaction, coordination, communication, and cooperation among personnel and departments. Thus, management science projects frequently require additional paperwork and bureaucracy for implementation. In order to avoid the ''bogged down'' situation, it is important that top management make a commitment to reduce bureaucracy and paperwork as much as possible.

Preparing for Organizational Change

Implementation frequently results in significant changes in the organization, not only in management practice and organizational structure but also in work policies and procedures. Thus, organization members may need to work, behave, and think differently. For an effective implementation, we must minimize the negative consequences of such change. Organizational change is a complex field in itself, and our discussion here can only be brief. Let us simply discuss some of the important issues involved in preparing for organizational change.

Management Assessment   The first major step required for organizational change is managerial assessment of the problem at hand, the situation, the cost-benefit considerations, and whether the organization is ready to use management science. The assessment should involve more than an appraisal of expected benefits versus associated costs (including organizational disturbance and unrest). It is not advisable to embark on a management science project because of the ''other firms do it'' syndrome without fully recognizing the required organizational change.

Planning for Organizational Change   Planning is essential for any significant organizational change. The planning process for implementation should produce and communicate the following information:

What needs to be changed

Why change is necessary

How change will be carried out

Who will be involved in the change process

When change will take place

Expected organizational benefits from change

The planning period for implementation is perhaps the most sensitive phase for organization members. The way implementation planning is carried out has enormous impact upon the eventual effectiveness of implementation. Once a go-ahead decision has been made to implement the model results, the operational manager must take charge and outline the following important aspects:

Immediate changes that are necessary.

Appointment of a task force or planning group for implementation.

Needs assessment for change in policies, work procedures, information requirements and flows, training and development programs, job descriptions, functional relationships among various work units, and communication systems.

Perhaps the best way to initiate implementation planning is through a task force group composed of all key operational personnel (linking pin concept), management scientists, and some external experts (if appropriate). In order to provide prestige and credibility as well as appropriate responsibility to the task force group, top managers must be actively involved in the implementation planning process.

Managing Resistance to Change   According to a theory of social change proposed by Kurt Lewin, any situation in which change is proposed has dynamic forces working in opposing directions. The *driving forces* attempt to move the situation toward the direction of a desired change. The opposing forces, referred to as *restraining forces,* attempt to resist the driving force and keep the situation from moving toward the desired change. A dynamic equilibrium is achieved between the two sets of opposing forces. Lewin contends that any increase in the driving force will most likely be accompanied by an increase in the restraining forces. Thus, the achievement of a desired change in a smooth and permanent way would be through three basic steps: (1) identifying and blunting the courses of the restraining forces, (2) increasing the driving forces toward the desired change, and (3) achieving a new level of equilibrium between the opposing forces closer to the desired change by reinforcing positive behaviors.

Some of the most widely accepted strategies of managing resistance to change are:

Involve key personnel throughout the process.

Open channels of communication — no secrets.

Create and maintain top management's interest in and commitment to the desired changes.

Recognize and honor established work procedures or group norms as much as possible.

Provide reinforcement for positive behaviors toward the desired change.

Improving the Process of Management Science

We have already stressed the importance of successful completion of each phase of the management science process for a successful final implementation. Let us briefly discuss several essential factors that must be considered in each phase.

Problem Identification and Formulation   The identification and formulation of a decision problem is the responsibility of the manager. The manager must determine the existence of a gap between where the organization ''is or will be at'' and where it ''ought to be at'' at the end of a planning horizon in a given area of operation. This identification process requires a clear understanding of the organizational purpose, long-range goals, intermediate objectives, and activities that would contribute to the improvement of organizational effectiveness. Therefore, it is imperative for the management scientist to have a clear understanding of the managerial decision process. We must avoid and reject the general tendency to believe that the identification and formulation of a problem phase is conditioned by the management scientist's knowledge of management science techniques. In other words, management should not allow the management scientist to construct a model for the problem simply because he or she can solve it. Instead, the manager must work with the management scientist in identifying, formulating, and solving the actual problem that needs to be analyzed.

Several practitioners have reported that one approach that is useful for avoiding such problems is **situational normativism,** proposed by M. L. Shakun. This behavioral approach advocates the construction of a descriptive model of a real-world situation involving participants, their values and aspirations, and the decision rules of the existing system. This model can be used as a gaming device to test the applicability of various management science models. Furthermore, it encourages and necessitates an interaction between the manager and the management scientist. Consequently, this approach can lead to a successful implementation.

Model Development   There is no doubt that this phase is the most exciting and interesting part for the management scientist. Thus, some inexperienced management scientists may want to jump right into this phase and have fun rather than labor over problem identification and formulation. A model hastily developed without proper effort to identify and formulate the problem may be based on many unverified assumptions. Models with untested assumptions are not only unrealistic but they can also lead to unsuccessful implementation.

Another critical problem involved in model development is inaccessibility or nonavailability of required data. Management scientists frequently design models first and hope that the manager will somehow come up with the required data. Obviously a model can dictate its data requirement. However, a model does not and cannot generate data for itself. Therefore, the actual model development phase must be preceded by a data securing system.

Model Solution   Once the model is properly developed, usually very few problems are faced in the model solution phase. Of course, large-scale models based on sophisticated techniques (e.g., nonlinear integer programming) may not be easy to solve, even with the help of the most advanced computer. This phase is an appropriate time to test the various model assumptions. Also, the problem should be attacked by using the simplest possible tool rather than the most sophisticated technique available.

Solution Testing   Before the final recommendations are prepared for the manager, the model solution should be thoroughly tested. Some researchers have suggested the gaming approach, based on a simulation of the decision environment, as a testing device. In testing the solution, actual data should be used whenever possible. Furthermore, it is very important to test the sensitivity of the model to the various model assumptions and to changes in model parameters. Sensitivity analysis based on an analytical or simulation-based approach can provide valuable information for "what if" questions.

Recommendation and Implementation   Management scientists are trained to obtain the optimum solution. If the management scientist simply presents the optimum solution to the decision maker, the manager has only two options: accept the recommended solution or reject it. We are already familiar with the story of the sewage disposal plant fiasco for a large city. A much better and more pragmatic approach is to provide the manager with a number of different options with associated resource requirements and benefits. Such a recommendation enables the manager to select a workable decision based on rich information concerning the various decision options.

Also, the management scientist can be directly involved with the manager in exploring different options before arriving at a good solution. The shared purpose and commitment are important factors for successful implementation.

Gupta, on the basis of his real-world experience in the U.S. Postal Service, suggests the following strategies for successful implementation:

Analyze the decision situation and construct its descriptive model.

Establish the cause and effect relationship of decision factors influencing the manager's thinking.

Explore or develop appropriate information systems to secure the needed data.

Construct a mathematical model with explicit recognition of data requirements and availability.

Identify the managerial and organizational changes required by the model.

Obtain multiple and competitive solutions to the model.

Analyze each solution in terms of the consequences on decision factors.

Prepare a realistic **cost-benefit analysis** of each competitive solution.

Provide the manager with multiple solutions with consequences and cost-benefit analysis.

Aid managers and their staff in implementing the managers' decision, if they request it.

Cost-Benefit Analysis for Implementation

When people are involved in an exciting management science project, cost considerations are often completely overlooked or put aside. However, it is important to derive a good estimate of the total cost of the project. The easiest cost components to estimate are direct personnel costs, indirect personnel costs (external consultants), computer time costs, and other required resources for developing the model. However, the often neglected but significant costs are those stemming from work disruptions, decreased employee productivity and morale, and possible failure of the final implementation process.

Management scientists and managers who are directly involved often exaggerate the benefits of management science projects. The possible benefits are often expressed in terms of estimated increases in profit, sales, or employee productivity, and decreases in costs, waste, or resource requirements. However, what is often ignored or neglected are the lasting implicit costs associated with employee dissatisfaction, obsolescence of skills, decrease in employee commitment to organizational goals, and the like. Similarly, the lasting benefits such as new skills acquired by employees and increased worker involvement are often ignored.

COMPUTER-BASED DECISION SUPPORT SYSTEMS

No single change during the past 10 to 15 years has affected our lives more profoundly than the rise of the computer. Today, almost everything we do, see, touch, hear, or experience has some relationship with computers. We take our courses based on the computerized registration system, we get bills from various places based on computerized accounting systems, we make airline reservations on a computerized system, we watch television programs monitored by computer systems, and we often rely on medical diagnosis based on computer systems.

The original computer-based information systems can be traced back to **data processing** (DP) systems of the late 1950s and early 1960s. DP systems were concerned primarily with recordkeeping and the automation of routine information-handling processes for employee payrolls, customers and their orders, inventory, vendor files, and accounting data. Since the late 1960s, *management information systems* (MISs) have become popular. MISs have built upon and expanded the DP feature of providing pertinent information for management, focusing on providing up-to-date or on-line information for such management functions as planning, controlling, organizing, and decision making.

In essence, an MIS is an integrated computer-based system composed of a set of processes that provide information to management to support operations, analysis, and decision making in an organization. An MIS may use a combination of such supporting tools as computer hardware and software, quantitative models, manual procedures, and a data base.

Decision support systems (DSSs) have enhanced an important feature of MIS— decision-making support. It is difficult to draw a clear demarcation line between an MIS and a DSS. MISs are primarily concerned with decision support for those problems that are routine, highly structured, or programmable. For example, assignment of workers to different work stations based on weekly demand analysis by a computer system is a typical decision support function of an MIS. However, DSSs are concerned with those problems that are unique, semistructured, or unprogrammable. For example, design of a product for a new market is a typical problem that can be supported by a DSS.

A decision support system is typically an **interactive system** that allows the user a friendly dialogue with the system. The interactive DSS helps generate useful information for decision making through the use of analytic and information-providing capabilities of the system. Figure 18.2 presents a summary of different characteristics of management science, MIS, and DSS. This figure clearly shows that modern DSS and

Figure 18.2   *Characteristics of Management Science, MIS, and DSS*

System	Problem Types Supported	Input	Process	Output
Management Science	Well structured Clear objectives and constraints Optimization, satisficing, or solution recommendations required Can be modeled	Processed data Some managment oriented data	Solution Simulation Analysis	Solution Recommendation Descriptive result
MIS	Routine Well structured Programmable Operational or tactical	Processed data Some management oriented data Preprogrammed model results	Generate reports Data management Simple models Some query-driven	Summary List of exceptions Routine decisions Answers to queries
DSS	Unique Semi- or unstructured Strategic Unprogrammable	Some processed data Management generated data Unique models or approaches	Query-driven Management science models Intelligence generating programs	Special reports Recommendations Answers to management queries

management science are very closely related to each other. Many decision support systems include different management science techniques in their processes.

Another important feature of DSS that can be observed in Figure 18.2 is that a DSS emphasizes *support* rather than *solution* of decisions. In other words, a DSS provides valuable information that can be used for effective decision making for a semi- or unstructured problem rather than simply providing a solution to a well-structured problem. Thus, in the DSS context, management science techniques generate useful data for decision making rather than providing solutions to problems. In our view, this concept of management science is most appropriate, and this philosophy has been emphasized throughout the book.

There are many reasons for the rapid development of DSS in the past 10 years. The following are some factors that have provided important impetus for DSS development.

Decision Complexity   Decision-making environments have become extremely complex. A decision problem cannot be analyzed easily based on available internal data and quantitative tools. Many external factors, which are quite uncertain and volatile, often have direct impact on decision making. For example, the 1973–1974 oil crisis, the oil glut of 1985–1986, severe international competition in many manufacturing and service industries, terrorist threats in foreign operations, and the increased federal reporting requirements all contribute to the increasing complexity of the turbulent decision environments. Consequently, management needs more support for decision making.

Advances in Computer Technology   Advances in computer technology made it possible to design and use various decision support systems. Many different computers (super computers, mainframes, minicomputers, microcomputers, and portable computers) and different system configurations (networking, time-shared terminals, access to various data bases) have allowed the widespread use of the DSS. In addition to the advances in hardware (i.e., physical computer equipment and peripheral devices), availability of user-friendly software (i.e., a set of programs that provides instructions to use the hardware for specific purposes) has exploded. Furthermore, much easy-to-use software with intelligence-providing capabilities has become available. These programs are often based on artificial intelligence or expert systems.

Technical Expertise of Decision Makers   One of the traditional barriers to the use of management science or computer technology by decision makers has been the lack of technical expertise on the part of decision makers. In the early 1970s, a widely quoted statement of an executive was ''most managers would rather live with problems they can't solve than use a solution they don't understand.'' However, times have changed. Today, not only do many decision makers understand management science and computer technology, but they often know how to use them. The managers are often business school graduates who had sufficient training in mathematics, management science, statistics, and computer science. Furthermore, sprinkling management scientists throughout the organization rather than forming a centralized management staff department is a definite trend. Consequently, decision makers can work with management scientists in solving problems that they face together.

DSS Structure

The structure of a DSS depends on many factors, such as the purpose of the DSS, DSS levels, and the hierarchy of management activities being analyzed. However, the general structure of a DSS consists of the following elements: data base, computer hardware and software systems, analytical tools, reports or model results, interactive process, and decision making. The general structure of a DSS is shown in Figure 18.3

Figure 18.3   The General Structure of DSS

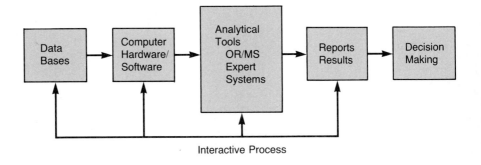

Suppose an electronics firm is interested in marketing a new videotape camera. The company must develop the following elements of a DSS:

1. *Data Base.*   The type of cameras that are in the market; competition in price, quality, service, product innovation, and corporate images; potential market; accounting data for production; the future market conditions.

2. *Computer Hardware and Software.*   The company must have necessary computer hardware and software to analyze data through interactive analytical tools.

3. *Analytical Tools.*   The company may use various management science tools, statistical techniques, or available expert systems to analyze the market potential for a new product, product design, production process design, distribution and service logistics, and the like.

4. *Reports and Results.*   The computer system will generate required reports and model results through the computer system.

5. *Interactive Process.*   The decision maker may experiment with various "what if" changes in the data, such as the changes in the market share projection, cost, price, quality control, and competition. The new results or reports generate new information which may be very valuable to the final decision.

6. *Decision Making.*   The final step of the DSS is making a plan of action. The action may be a clearly specified set of plans such as the product design, production plans, distribution plans, market penetration plans, service activity plans, product innovation activities, labor allocation, capital allocation, and expected financial consequences.

An important aspect of the DSS structure which requires our attention is the need for interdepartmental cooperation, since the problem under consideration (e.g. a new-product development) requires information and input from various departments. Thus, interdependence among the various departments must be recognized and an interdisciplinary approach should be planned accordingly. In this process, top management involvement and participation play important roles for the success of DSS implementation.

Levels of DSS

Decision support systems can be viewed in terms of different levels of roles and their relationships. Three basic levels of DSS generally recognized are: specific DSS, **DSS generators,** and **DSS tools.** We will discuss each level in greater detail.

Specific DSS   A DSS can be developed to support a specific decision-making task. For example, a computer-based DSS may be built specifically for materials management, including such components as the vendor data base, material selection criteria, purchasing procedures, warehousing, inventory control, and material accounting systems. Specific systems can be developed for various functional areas of the organization—personnel, production planning, portfolio management, capacity planning, accounting, customer services, international marketing, and the like.

DSS Generators   DSS generators are computer hardware or software packages used in developing a specific DSS. A large number of computer hardware systems are available, including super, mainframe, mini, and personal computers. Also, many specific software packages are available that possess special capabilities such as statistical analysis routines, optimization techniques, risk analysis, graphic display routines, financial analysis, and data management. Some DSS generators are: *Interactive Financial Planning Systems (IFPS),* developed by Execucom Systems Corporation; *Executive Information Services (EIS),* available from Boeing Computer Services; and *Express,* marketed by Tymshare.

DSS generators are used quite extensively for DSS development. A DSS generator is a package that combines a number of capabilities important for a specific DSS. Typically, a DSS generator has a user-friendly procedure that uses **natural language** much like ordinary English and *nonprocedural language,* which is free of restrictions of procedure-oriented programming language.

DSS Tools   DSS tools function like building blocks for a DSS. A set of selected tools can be used to develop a specific DSS. Many DSS generators include a set of DSS tools that can be used to build different types of systems. Some of the most commonly used DSS tools include programming languages, statistical analysis packages, optimization packages, and data management systems.

Many different programming languages are available for DSS development. The procedure-oriented languages often used for DSS development are FORTRAN, BASIC, COBOL, and PL/1. These languages define systematic procedures that the computer should follow to complete certain tasks. Structure-oriented languages, such as APL and PASCAL, are also useful for building a DSS through special features for structural logic or data-handling capabilities. A number of problem-oriented languages have also been used for DSS development — GPSS, DYNAMO, GASP, and the like.

Decision support systems typically require some type of statistical analysis, and many statistical packages have found wide use for DSS development, including SAS, SPSS, IMSL, and BMDP.

Optimization techniques can be effective tools if a DSS requires the best solution to a certain problem. For example, a production-scheduling DSS may require the optimum product mix solution based on linear programming. In such a case, we can include such linear programming packages as LINDO or MPSX as a DSS tool.

Every DSS requires efficient data management capabilities. The system must be capable of entering new data, updating existing data files, retrieving required data, analyzing data through other DSS tools, and reporting data in appropriate formats. Some of the popular data base management systems are *TOTAL, IDMS,* and *ADABAS.* These systems are available not only on mainframe computer systems but also on mini- and microcomputers.

Artificial Intelligence

The development of computer technology has taken two broad directions: number processing and symbol processing. Number processing has made information available on a much more accessible, retainable, and transferable basis than ever before. Thus, decision support systems have relied heavily on such number-processing systems as optimization, statistical analysis, and data management.

Symbol processing is generally referred to as **artificial intelligence** (AI). AI is a field of study where the computer attempts to mimic the capabilities that are considered signs of an intelligent person. These capabilities stem from sensor perception and locomotion, from the ability to reason and solve problems, and from the logic of natural languages. Today, AI is rapidly becoming an important DSS tool.

There are five major subfields of AI: robotics, vision systems, natural language, voice recognition, and expert systems. Many firms have been developing **robotics**—intelligent robots to perform repetitive industrial jobs. Although much progress has been made in this field, robots that can see, feel, think logically, and take appropriate actions are yet to be developed. One of the interesting works in vision systems is recognition by the computer of moving objects and the determination of their motion characteristics.

Natural language is fairly self-descriptive; the basic process calls for the development of computers that can understand English and the syntax of a natural language. In their AI work at MITRE Corportion, the researchers have designed King Kong Parser, a portable natural language interface that depends upon the theory of relational grammar to provide a bridge between its syntactic and semantic components. A number of software companies market programs that check for grammatical errors on microcomputers.

Voice recognition is presently being worked on by a number of firms. Although voice recognition software is intriguing, it has seen only limited practical use thus far. However, the potential of this technology is so enormous that a large number of firms are continuing their research work, including Bell Laboratories, IBM, ITT, Nippon Electric Company (NEC), Sperry Univac, and Texas Instruments.

Voice recognition systems can be applied in many functional areas, such as manufacturing, materials handling, equipment control, office automation through voice messages and word processing, finance and banking, retailing, hospitals and laboratories, and military operations. Although more than 60 firms are working on voice recognition systems, the number of products and manufacturers in the current commercial market is fairly small. Among them, those intensively marketing products are Interstate Electronics, Threshold Technology, Votan, Verbex, and NEC. The prices for the commercial systems range from a low of $1,000 to a high of $65,000. Currently, voice recognition systems have only limited value as DSS tools. Nevertheless, their potential is unlimited if technological progress makes them as reliable as other information-processing systems.

Expert Systems

The most promising AI application to DSS is in **expert systems;** some authorities refer to expert systems as "knowledge systems" or "knowledge engineering." An *expert system* is an intelligent computer program that uses knowledge and inference procedures to solve problems that are sufficiently different to require significant human expertise for their solution. The knowledge to perform analysis or reasoning and the inference procedures employed can be thought of as a model of the expertise of the best-known practitioners in the specific field.

The knowledge base of an expert system consists of facts and heuristics. The *facts* constitute a body of information that is publicly shared and generally agreed upon among the experts in the field. The *heuristics* are little-known rules of good judgment that characterize expert decision making.

The basic structure of an expert system consists of the following three components: (1) the knowledge base and heuristics associated with problems and if-then rules — the ''if'' part of a rule represents the situation as a condition (premise), and the ''then'' part represents the response; (2) the inference mechanism for using the knowledge base in the solution of the problem — the inference engine uses information provided by the knowledge base and the system user to arrive at a conclusion based on facts; (3) the working memory keeps track of the system status in terms of what has been done thus far on the problem under consideration.

Expert systems approach a problem quiet differently than conventional programs. In conventional programs, the approach to a problem is predetermined by the programmer, who specifies procedures, algorithms, or mathematical formulas. An expert system can perform the same functions as the conventional programs do. However, it can also manipulate data to provide a meaningful answer to a partially specified question; it can request additional information from the user; it may provide appropriate partial solutions, suggest the general area where the complete solution exists, and explain its reasoning behind recommending certain solutions. In other words, an expert system can act much like a human adviser. The only difference is that it represents and applies knowledge electronically.

Recent advances in expert systems have led to their applications in many real-world settings. Some interesting applications are in the areas of medical diagnosis and decision making, maintenance of telephone switching equipment, management of business operations, oil and mineral exploration, government operations, and accounting. Some of the best-known expert systems currently available are shown in Table 18.2.

Although expert systems have enormous potential as a DSS, they also have some significant problems. First, expert systems are often very expensive to develop, because they require human experts and much of their time for system development. Furthermore, eliciting knowledge from an expert in such a way that it would be useful in all occasions is difficult. Also, designing an expert system in a simple manner so that a nonexpert user can easily use an expert's knowledge base has not always proved possible.

Table 18.2   Some Commercially Available Expert Systems

Expert System	Application
Auditor	Analysis of accounts receivable
Caduceus	Medical consulting
Compass	Maintenance of telephone equipment
Dendral	Analysis of mass spectrograms
Dipmeter Advisor	Oil exploration
EDAAS	Protection of confidential information
Expert Strategist	Analysis of financial statements
Genesis	Genetic engineering and molecular research
Mycin	Medical consulting
Pomme	Apple orchard management
Preceptor	Medical diagnosis
Prospector	Mineral exploration
Puff	Diagnosis of lung disease
R1	Computer configuration
Taxadvisor	Tax consulting

Figure 18.4   DSS and Related Systems and Techniques

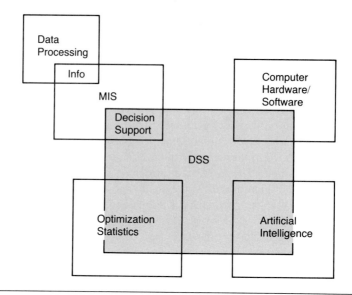

Now we have a general understanding about the roles of DSS and the relationships of DSS to such closely related areas as data processing, MIS, management science, artificial intelligence, and expert systems. Figure 18.4 presents a general overview of DSS relationships with other related systems and techniques.

REAL-WORLD APPLICATION OF DECISION SUPPORT SYSTEMS

An increasing number of organizations are using decision support systems. Some use their own customized DSS for specific purposes, and others use commercially available interactive software packages for general decision support.

Maximizing Profit at a Sawmill

The Weyerhaeuser Company decided to implement a DSS to guide management at its new small log mill at Raymond, Washington.[1] Composed of two interlocking systems, the DSS was supposed to ensure that the maximum possible value would be extracted from the wood. Decisions relating to single logs, called "merchandising," were modeled in a merchandising decision system (MDS), which was incorporated into a concurrent simulation system, named *Compass*. The MDS analyzes the structure of each stem as it is received from inventory, indicating where cuts should be made to maximize profit. *Compass* was designed to help mill management evaluate the decisions made through the MDS and to examine alternative merchandising strategies.

[1]M. T. Hehnen, S. C. Chou, H. L. Scheurman, G. J. Robinson, T. P. Luken, and D. W. Baker, "An Integrated Decision Support and Manufacturing Control System," *Interfaces* 14:5 (1984), 44–52.

Initial resistance to the new system was profound. Established mill standards related to measurable items, such as logs per hour or board feet per shift. By shifting users' perceptions from these surrogate measures of profit to an actual estimated profit, the system developers learned that user acceptance could make or break the system. To resolve the communications problems, mill managers and their teams were brought into the creation process. Demonstration of the simulation aspects proved valuable in developing staff understanding of the merchandising calculations. Presenting the results in terms meaningful to the mill staff led to their gradual acceptance of the new system. Specific situations would still cause conflicts, such as when an operator disagrees with an MDS evaluation and overrides it, although most such problems were alleviated by comparisons of such factors as margin, cost, and greater profit. In evaluating the program, the mill manager wrote that managers "were able to quantify to our satisfaction the annual profit increment attributable to using the system . . . these test results indicate an investment payback period of slightly more than one year, equivalent to a return on investment in excess of 40 percent under reasonable assumptions."

Helicopter Program Development

The U.S. Marine Corps needed to find a replacement for its aging helicopter fleet.[2] To be called the "Marine Medium Assault Transport (V/HXM)," the new vehicles would be required to meet selected criteria (speed, reliability, etc.). A cost-benefit analysis DSS with multiattribute weighting was used to consider a range of designs beyond those of the current CH-46E helicopter. The main thrust of the DSS was to assist in identifying the "efficient frontier," that is, the best design candidates for different levels of funding.

Two 2-day design conferences set up and refined a cost-benefit model, incorporating the participants' rationale for their selections. Nine design areas or variables were considered in the prototype, with eight variables in the revised model (two variables were combined during revision). The eight selected decision variables were hover design point, maximum continuous power speed, spotting and troops capacity, troop mission radius and external-cargo carrying ability, presence of a ramp, reliability and maintainability, survivability and vulnerability, and crashworthiness. Minimum and maximum feasible limits were set for each variable, and the intermediate levels most realistically reflected the desired design capabilities. Technical personnel established cost figures for each level of each variable, and operations personnel defined benefits in terms of value relative to other designs. (Actual cost and benefit estimates were classified and therefore not published.) The prototype model resulted in 2,822,400 possible design configurations, considering all possible combinations of the decision variables. An efficient frontier curve was constructed; all points on the curve represented the maximum possible benefit for a given cost.

The originally proposed design was then compared with the efficient frontier and was found to be suboptimal. Revised design features placed the proposed V/HXM very close to the efficient frontier. The resulting final design model was well supported by the participants and served as the basis for subsequent decisions about the new helicopter. The model provided rapid feedback under various estimates of benefits and costs, inflation, schedules, etc. and improved group discussion by providing structure as well

[2]Leonard Adelman, "Real-Time Computer Support for Decision Analysis in Group Setting: Another Class of Decision Support Systems," *Interfaces* 14:2 (1984), 75–83.

as an object (the model) that could be addressed, rather than other people. The results of the two conferences were acted upon within 1 week after presentation. The director of the Systems Engineering Management Division responsible for the DSS indicated that it was highly satisfactory and that the technique would continue to be used by his office for other projects.

SUMMARY

This chapter has attempted to provide an overview of what management science implementation involves. Implementation is generally regarded as a continuous process encompassing the entire cycle of the management science project. There are many possible problems that can arise during the implementation process. We have studied some innovative strategies that can be used to alleviate some of the problems of implementation. However, the most important factor for successful implementation appears to be a proper management perspective about the role of management science.

We have seen many successful applications of management science. In order to ensure continued success, the management scientist must broaden his or her vision beyond the model building stage. There are many people who are competent model builders. But there are few who have the broad management perspective, creativity, and conceptual and human skills to make a real impact on the organization. The future decision environment cries out for sophisticated analysis in the hands of creative professionals who can work with managers.

Decision support systems are integrated systems consisting of various components, including computer-based information processing, quantitative analysis, and technological innovations, to support management decision making. A DSS should support decision-making activities at all levels of management. Since a DSS has special support characteristics for semi- and unstructured decision problems, the systems emphasize middle- and top-level decision-making situations.

Decision support systems can be classified into three basic levels: specific DSS, DSS generators, and DSS tools, and new technological advances are making the DSS even more valuable in today's organizations. Artificial intelligence, especially in the form of expert systems, has enormous potential as a DSS.

Glossary

Artificial Intelligence   Computer procedure involving symbol processing (rather than simple number crunching) and incorporating selection criteria that resemble rational thought. Subfields include robotics, vision systems, natural languages, voice recognition, and expert systems.

Cost-Benefit Analysis   Overall comparison of the financial and organizational effects of a project to determine its desirability.

Data Processing   Routine information-processing needs, such as recordkeeping, handled on computers.

Decision Support System   Advanced form of a management information system, suitable for unique or semistructured problems, such as new product decisions.

DSS Generators   Computer hardware and/or software systems designed to assist in developing DSS for specific applications.

DSS Tools   Components used in establishing a DSS, such as programming languages, statistical analysis packages, optimization procedures, and data management systems.

Expert System   Computerized information-processing system with built-in data base and heuristics (decision or judgment rules); intended to provide decision assistance similar to consultation of leading experts in the given field.

Implementation   Management science techniques used to assist decision makers from conception of the problem through recommendations and constructive use of the results.

Interactive Process   Adjustment of input data from a DSS, with sensitivity analysis or target values the primary consideration.

Management Information System   Computerized information system that provides management with processed data for routine planning, controlling, organizing, and decision-making procedures.

Natural Language   Computer-intelligible language similar to everyday language (such as English) that simplifies operator-system communication.

Robotics   Developing field of information processing that incorporates some degree of artificial intelligence in robots, including sensory perception and (potentially) responsive actions.

Situational Normativism   Behavioral approach to implementation of management science that constructs a descriptive model of the situation, including the participants, their values and aspirations, and the currently practiced decision rules.

Voice Recognition   A computer system's ability to accept verbal information and instructions, in addition to input from keyboards or storage media.

References

Alter, S. L. *Decision Support Systems: Current Practice and Continuing Challenges.* Reading, Mass.: Addison-Wesley, 1980.

Bennett, J. L. (ed). *Building Decision Support Systems.* Reading, Mass.: Addison-Wesley, 1983.

Boulding, K. "The Specialist with a Universal Mind." *Management Science* 14:12 (1969), 647–653.

Churchman, C. W., Ackoff, R. L., and Arnoff, E. L. *Introduction to Operations Research.* New York: Wiley, 1958.

Davis, G. B., and Olson, M. H. *Management Information Systems.*2d ed. New York: McGraw-Hill, 1985.

Deal, T. E., and Kennedy, A. A. *Corporate Cultures.* Reading, Mass.: Addison-Wesley, 1982.

Grayson, C. J., Jr. "Management Science and Business Practice." *Harvard Business Review* 51:4 (1973), 41–48.

Griener, L. "Patterns of Organizational Change." *Harvard Business Review* 45 (1967), 119–130.

Gupta, J. N. D. "Management Science Implementation: Experiences of a Practicing O.R. Manager." *Interfaces* 7:3 (1977), 84–90.

Halbrecht, H. Z. "If Your Students Aren't Marketable, What's Your Future?" *Decision Sciences* 4:3 (1973), xiii–xix.

Harvey, A. "Factors Making for Implementation Success and Failure." *Management Science* 16 (1970), 312–321.

Hayes, R. H., and Abernathy, W. J. "Managing Our Way to Economic Decline." *Harvard Business Review* 58 (1980), 67–77.

Jones, S., and Smithen, T. "Using MS for the Practice of MS." *Interfaces* 14:3 (1984), 68–75.

Keen, P. G. W. "Decision Support Systems: Translating Analytic Techniques with Useful Tools." *Sloan Management Review* (Spring 1980) 33–44.

Keen, P. G. W., and Morton, Scott. *M.S. Decision Support Systems: An Organizational Perspective.* Reading, Mass.: Addison-Wesley, 1978.

Kroeber, D. W., and Watson, H. J. *Computer-Based Information Systems.* New York: Macmillan, 1984.

Lee, S. M., Moore, L. J., and Taylor, B. W. *Management Science.* 2d ed. Dubuque, Iowa: W. C. Brown, 1985.

Lewin, K. "Group Decision and Social Change." In *Readings in Social Psychology,* ed. T. N. Newcomb and E. L. Hartley. New York: Holt, Rinehart & Winston, 1947, 340–344.

Schultz, R. L., and Slevin, D. P. (eds.). *Implementing Operations Research/Management Science.* New York: Elsevier, 1975.

Shakun, M. L. "Management Science and Management: Implementing Management Science via Situational Normativism." *Management Science* 18 (1972), 367–377.

Sprague, R. J., and Carlson, E. D. *Building Effective Decision Support Systems.* Englewood Cliffs, N.J.: Prentice-Hall, 1982.

Watson, H. J., and Marett, P. G. "A Survey of Management Science Implementation Problems." *Interfaces* 9:4 (1979), 124–128.

Wynne, B. E. "A Domination Sequence—MS/OR; DSS; and the Fifth Generation." *Interfaces* 14:3 (1984), 51–58.

Wysocki, R. K. "OR/MS Implementation Research: A Bibliography." *Interfaces* 9:2 (1979), 37–41.

Assignments

18.1 Is management science implementation different from other projects in organizations? Why or why not?

18.2 What are the basic steps of the management science process?

18.3 Do you agree with C. Jackson Grayson's reasons for not applying management science? Provide your argument on each reason listed by Grayson.

18.4 Why do you think there are significant differences between the manager and management scientist in the perceived barriers to the management science application?

18.5 Is management science always applicable to management problems? Why or why not?

18.6 Why is there a definite gap between management practice and the management science approach?

18.7 In solving a difficult problem, should a management scientist take the initiative and lead the manager toward implementation? Why or why not?

18.8 Some organizations have separate management science departments. Such departments usually operate as service departments. Their services to other departments are usually charged based on a profit-generating scheme (each department is operated as a profit center). At the end of the fiscal year, the management science department is responsible for its profit or loss positions. What are some advantages and disadvantages to the profit center concept of management science service?

18.9 What are some workable strategies that could be used to manage the following organizational change?

Notice to Students:
Effective immediately, any student who did not get the desired courses through the general registration must go to each individual department and go through the priority system. The priority system allows into the class only a handful of students who desperately need the course. Items required on the priority slip are:

1. Undergraduate advisor's verification
2. Instructor's approval
3. Department chairperson's approval
4. Dean's signature
5. Stamp of the registrar

18.10 Management scientists are said to be very competent for certain tasks but ineffective in others. Discuss the overall process of management science and point out the steps or phases in which management scientists are usually either competent or ineffective.

18.11 Do you think the advances in computer technology will enhance or decrease the use of management science in the future?

18.12 Management science projects are usually undertaken by a team (group). The composition of team members is crucial for successful implementation. Suppose an automobile company is considering production of a new model. The company president wants to organize a management science team to analyze the feasibility of this new model. What kind of people should be involved in this team?

18.13 Explain the development of attempts to provide management with reliable information useful for decision making.

18.14 In what types of information systems would you expect to find management science techniques?

18.15 Describe several advantages that interaction provides the decision maker.

18.16 Analyze the basic philosophy behind use of decision support systems.

18.17 Consider again this quote: ''Most managers would rather live with problems they can't solve than use a solution they don't understand.'' Relate your experiences with this type of attitude.

18.18 Explain the components of a typical DSS.

18.19 What could be some of the results of improper DSS implementation and lack of interdepartmental cooperation?

18.20 Distinguish between specific DSS, DSS generators, and DSS tools.

18.21 How cost-effective are decision support systems?

18.22 What sort of statistical analyses could be useful in a DSS?

18.23 What is "artificial intelligence"?

18.24 Give examples of real applications for the five subfields of artificial intelligence.

18.25 Consider a large, modern automobile factory. What types of DSS would you expect to find there? What functions would the systems serve?

18.26 What are the advantages and disadvantages of using an expert system rather than a human expert (or group)?

18.27 Analyze the basic structure of an expert system.

Appendix 1   POISSON PROBABILITY VALUES

r	λ 0.10	0.20	0.30	0.40	0.50	0.60	0.70	0.80	0.90	1.00
0	.9048	.8187	.7408	.6703	.6066	.5488	.4966	.4493	.4066	.3679
1	.0905	.1637	.2222	.2681	.3033	.3293	.3476	.3595	.3659	.3679
2	.0045	.0164	.0333	.0536	.0758	.0988	.1217	.1438	.1647	.1839
3	.0002	.0011	.0033	.0072	.0126	.0198	.0284	.0383	.0494	.0613
4	.0000	.0001	.0003	.0007	.0016	.0030	.0050	.0077	.0111	.0153
5	.0000	.0000	.0000	.0001	.0002	.0004	.0007	.0012	.0020	.0031
6	.0000	.0000	.0000	.0000	.0000	.0000	.0001	.0002	.0003	.0005
7	.0000	.0000	.0000	.0000	.0000	.0000	.0000	.0000	.0000	.0001

r	λ 1.10	1.20	1.30	1.40	1.50	1.60	1.70	1.80	1.90	2.00
0	.3329	.3012	.2725	.2466	.2231	.2019	.1827	.1653	.1496	.1353
1	.3662	.3614	.3543	.3452	.3347	.3230	.3106	.2975	.2842	.2707
2	.2014	.2169	.2303	.2417	.2510	.2584	.2640	.2678	.2700	.2707
3	.0738	.0867	.0998	.1128	.1255	.1378	.1496	.1607	.1710	.1804
4	.0203	.0260	.0324	.0395	.0471	.0551	.0636	.0723	.0812	.0902
5	.0045	.0062	.0084	.0111	.0141	.0176	.0216	.0260	.0309	.0361
6	.0008	.0012	.0018	.0026	.0035	.0047	.0061	.0078	.0098	.0120
7	.0001	.0002	.0003	.0005	.0008	.0011	.0015	.0020	.0027	.0034
8	.0000	.0000	.0001	.0001	.0001	.0002	.0003	.0005	.0006	.0009
9	.0000	.0000	.0000	.0000	.0000	.0000	.0001	.0001	.0001	.0002

r	λ 2.10	2.20	2.30	2.40	2.50	2.60	2.70	2.80	2.90	3.00
0	.1225	.1108	.1003	.0907	.0821	.0743	.0672	.0608	.0550	.0498
1	.2572	.2438	.2306	.2177	.2052	.1931	.1815	.1703	.1596	.1494
2	.2700	.2681	.2652	.2613	.2565	.2510	.2450	.2384	.2314	.2240
3	.1890	.1966	.2033	.2090	.2138	.2176	.2205	.2225	.2237	.2240
4	.0992	.1082	.1169	.1254	.1336	.1414	.1488	.1557	.1622	.1680
5	.0417	.0476	.0538	.0602	.0668	.0735	.0804	.0872	.0940	.1008
6	.0146	.0174	.0206	.0241	.0278	.0319	.0362	.0407	.0455	.0504
7	.0044	.0055	.0068	.0083	.0099	.0118	.0139	.0163	.0188	.0216
8	.0011	.0015	.0019	.0025	.0031	.0038	.0047	.0057	.0068	.0081
9	.0003	.0004	.0005	.0007	.0009	.0011	.0014	.0018	.0022	.0027
10	.0001	.0001	.0001	.0002	.0002	.0003	.0004	.0005	.0006	.0008
11	.0000	.0000	.0000	.0000	.0000	.0001	.0001	.0001	.0002	.0002
12	.0000	.0000	.0000	.0000	.0000	.0000	.0000	.0000	.0000	.0001

					λ					
r	3.10	3.20	3.30	3.40	3.50	3.60	3.70	3.80	3.90	4.00
0	.0450	.0408	.0369	.0334	.0302	.0273	.0247	.0224	.0202	.0183
1	.1397	.1304	.1217	.1135	.1057	.0984	.0915	.0850	.0789	.0733
2	.2165	.2087	.2008	.1929	.1850	.1771	.1692	.1615	.1539	.1465
3	.2237	.2226	.2209	.2186	.2158	.2125	.2087	.2046	.2001	.1954
4	.1733	.1781	.1823	.1858	.1888	.1912	.1931	.1944	.1951	.1954
5	.1075	.1140	.1203	.1264	.1322	.1377	.1429	.1477	.1522	.1563
6	.0555	.0608	.0662	.0716	.0771	.0826	.0881	.0936	.0989	.1042
7	.0246	.0278	.0312	.0348	.0385	.0425	.0466	.0508	.0551	.0595
8	.0095	.0111	.0129	.0148	.0169	.0191	.0215	.0241	.0269	.0298
9	.0033	.0040	.0047	.0056	.0066	.0076	.0089	.0102	.0116	.0132
10	.0010	.0013	.0016	.0019	.0023	.0028	.0033	.0039	.0045	.0053
11	.0003	.0004	.0005	.0006	.0007	.0009	.0011	.0013	.0016	.0019
12	.0001	.0001	.0001	.0002	.0002	.0003	.0003	.0004	.0005	.0006
13	.0000	.0000	.0000	.0000	.0001	.0001	.0001	.0001	.0002	.0002
14	.0000	.0000	.0000	.0000	.0000	.0000	.0000	.0000	.0000	.0001

					λ					
r	4.10	4.20	4.30	4.40	4.50	4.60	4.70	4.80	4.90	5.00
0	.0166	.0150	.0136	.0123	.0111	.0101	.0091	.0082	.0074	.0067
1	.0679	.0630	.0583	.0540	.0500	.0462	.0427	.0395	.0365	.0337
2	.1393	.1323	.1254	.1188	.1125	.1063	.1005	.0948	.0894	.0842
3	.1904	.1852	.1798	.1743	.1687	.1631	.1574	.1517	.1460	.1404
4	.1951	.1944	.1933	.1917	.1898	.1875	.1849	.1820	.1789	.1755
5	.1600	.1633	.1662	.1687	.1708	.1725	.1738	.1747	.1753	.1755
6	.1093	.1143	.1191	.1237	.1281	.1323	.1362	.1398	.1432	.1462
7	.0640	.0686	.0732	.0778	.0824	.0869	.0914	.0959	.1002	.1044
8	.0328	.0360	.0393	.0428	.0463	.0500	.0537	.0575	.0614	.0653
9	.0150	.0168	.0188	.0209	.0232	.0255	.0281	.0307	.0334	.0363
10	.0061	.0071	.0081	.0092	.0104	.0118	.0132	.0147	.0164	.0181
11	.0023	.0027	.0032	.0037	.0043	.0049	.0056	.0064	.0073	.0082
12	.0008	.0009	.0011	.0013	.0016	.0019	.0022	.0026	.0030	.0034
13	.0002	.0003	.0004	.0005	.0006	.0007	.0008	.0009	.0011	.0013
14	.0001	.0001	.0001	.0001	.0002	.0002	.0003	.0003	.0004	.0005
15	.0000	.0000	.0000	.0000	.0001	.0001	.0001	.0001	.0001	.0002

					λ					
r	5.10	5.20	5.30	5.40	5.50	5.60	5.70	5.80	5.90	6.00
0	.0061	.0055	.0050	.0045	.0041	.0037	.0033	.0030	.0027	.0025
1	.0311	.0287	.0265	.0244	.0225	.0207	.0191	.0176	.0162	.0149
2	.0793	.0746	.0701	.0659	.0618	.0580	.0544	.0509	.0477	.0446
3	.1348	.1293	.1239	.1185	.1133	.1082	.1033	.0985	.0938	.0892
4	.1719	.1681	.1641	.1600	.1558	.1515	.1472	.1428	.1383	.1339
5	.1753	.1748	.1740	.1728	.1714	.1697	.1678	.1656	.1632	.1606
6	.1490	.1515	.1537	.1555	.1571	.1584	.1594	.1601	.1605	.1606
7	.1086	.1125	.1163	.1200	.1234	.1267	.1298	.1326	.1353	.1377
8	.0692	.0731	.0771	.0810	.0849	.0887	.0925	.0962	.0998	.1033
9	.0392	.0423	.0454	.0486	.0519	.0552	.0586	.0620	.0654	.0688
10	.0200	.0220	.0241	.0262	.0285	.0309	.0334	.0359	.0386	.0413
11	.0093	.0104	.0116	.0129	.1043	.0157	.0173	.0190	.0207	.0225
12	.0039	.0045	.0051	.0058	.0065	.0073	.0082	.0092	.0102	.0113

r	5.10	5.20	5.30	5.40	5.50	λ 5.60	5.70	5.80	5.90	6.00
13	.0015	.0018	.0021	.0024	.0028	.0032	.0036	.0041	.0046	.0052
14	.0006	.0007	.0008	.0009	.0011	.0013	.0015	.0017	.0019	.0022
15	.0002	.0002	.0003	.0003	.0004	.0005	.0006	.0007	.0008	.0009
16	.0001	.0001	.0001	.0001	.0001	.0002	.0002	.0002	.0003	.0003
17	.0000	.0000	.0000	.0000	.0000	.0001	.0001	.0001	.0001	.0001

r	6.10	6.20	6.30	6.40	6.50	λ 6.60	6.70	6.80	6.90	7.00
0	.0022	.0020	.0018	.0017	.0015	.0014	.0012	.0011	.0010	.0009
1	.0137	.0126	.0116	.0106	.0098	.0090	.0082	.0076	.0070	.0064
2	.0417	.0390	.0364	.0340	.0318	.0296	.0276	.0258	.0240	.0223
3	.0848	.0806	.0765	.0726	.0688	.0652	.0617	.0584	.0552	.0521
4	.1294	.1249	.1205	.1161	.1118	.1076	.1034	.0992	.0952	.0912
5	.1579	.1549	.1519	.1487	.1454	.1420	.1385	.1349	.1314	.1277
6	.1605	.1601	.1595	.1586	.1575	.1562	.1546	.1529	.1511	.1490
7	.1399	.1418	.1435	.1450	.1462	.1472	.1480	.1486	.1489	.1400
8	.1066	.1099	.1130	.1160	.1188	.1215	.1240	.1263	.1284	.1304
9	.0723	.0757	.0791	.0825	.0858	.0891	.0923	.0954	.0985	.1014
10	.0441	.0469	.0498	.0528	.0558	.0588	.0618	.0649	.0679	.0710
11	.0244	.0265	.0285	.0307	.0330	.0353	.0377	.0401	.0426	.0452
12	.0124	.0137	.0150	.0164	.0179	.0194	.0210	.0227	.0245	.0269
13	.0058	.0065	.0073	.0081	.0089	.0099	.0108	.0119	.0130	.0142
14	.0025	.0029	.0033	.0037	.0041	.0046	.0052	.0058	.0064	.0071
15	.0010	.0012	.0014	.0016	.0018	.0020	.0023	.0026	.0029	.0033
16	.0004	.0005	.0005	.0006	.0007	.0008	.0010	.0011	.0013	.0014
17	.0001	.0002	.0002	.0002	.0003	.0003	.0004	.0004	.0005	.0006
18	.0000	.0001	.0001	.0001	.0001	.0001	.0001	.0002	.0002	.0002
19	.0000	.0000	.0000	.0000	.0000	.0000	.0001	.0001	.0001	.0001

r	7.10	7.20	7.30	7.40	7.50	λ 7.60	7.70	7.80	7.90	8.00
0	.0008	.0007	.0007	.0006	.0006	.0005	.0005	.0004	.0004	.0003
1	.0059	.0054	.0049	.0045	.0041	.0038	.0035	.0032	.0029	.0027
2	.0208	.0194	.0180	.0167	.0156	.0145	.0134	.0125	.0116	.0107
3	.0492	.0464	.0438	.0413	.0389	.0366	.0345	.0324	.0305	.0286
4	.0874	.0836	.0799	.0764	.0729	.0696	.0663	.0632	.0602	.0573
5	.1241	.1204	.1167	.1130	.1094	.1057	.1021	.0986	.0951	.0916
6	.1468	.1445	.1420	.1394	.1367	.1339	.1311	.1282	.1252	.1221
7	.1489	.1486	.1481	.1474	.1465	.1454	.1442	.1428	.1413	.1396
8	.1321	.1337	.1351	.1363	.1373	.1381	.1388	.1392	.1395	.1396
9	.1042	.1070	.1096	.1121	.1144	.1167	.1187	.1207	.1224	.1241
10	.0740	.0770	.0800	.0829	.0858	.0887	.0914	.0941	.0967	.0993
11	.0478	.0504	.0531	.0558	.0585	.0613	.0640	.0667	.0695	.0722
12	.0283	.0303	.0323	.0344	.0366	.0388	.0411	.0434	.0457	.0481
13	.0154	.0168	.0181	.0196	.0211	.0227	.0243	.0260	.0278	.0296
14	.0078	.0086	.0095	.0104	.0113	.0123	.0134	.0145	.0157	.0169
15	.0037	.0041	.0046	.0051	.0057	.0062	.0069	.0075	.0083	.0090
16	.0016	.0019	.0021	.0024	.0026	.0030	.0033	.0037	.0041	.0045
17	.0007	.0008	.0009	.0010	.0012	.0013	.0015	.0017	.0019	.0021
18	.0003	.0003	.0004	.0004	.0005	.0006	.0006	.0007	.0008	.0009
19	.0001	.0001	.0001	.0002	.0002	.0002	.0003	.0003	.0003	.0004

					λ				
r	7.10	7.20	7.30	7.40	7.50	7.60	7.70	7.80	7.90	8.00
20	.0000	.0000	.0001	.0001	.0001	.0001	.0001	.0001	.0001	.0002
21	.0000	.0000	.0000	.0000	.0000	.0000	.0000	.0000	.0001	.0001

					λ				
r	8.10	8.20	8.30	8.40	8.50	8.60	8.70	8.80	8.90	9.00
0	.0003	.0003	.0002	.0002	.0002	.0002	.0002	.0002	.0001	.0001
1	.0025	.0023	.0021	.0019	.0017	.0016	.0014	.0013	.0012	.0011
2	.0100	.0092	.0086	.0079	.0074	.0068	.0063	.0058	.0054	.0050
3	.0269	.0252	.0237	.0222	.0208	.0195	.0183	.0171	.0160	.0150
4	.0544	.0517	.0491	.0466	.0443	.0420	.0398	.0377	.0357	.0337
5	.0882	.0849	.0816	.0784	.0752	.0722	.0692	.0663	.0635	.0607
6	.1191	.1160	.1128	.1097	.1066	.1034	.1003	.0972	.0941	.0911
7	.1378	.1358	.1338	.1317	.1294	.1271	.1247	.1222	.1197	.1171
8	.1395	.1392	.1388	.1382	.1375	.1366	.1356	.1344	.1332	.1318
9	.1256	.1269	.1280	.1290	.1299	.1306	.1311	.1315	.1317	.1318
10	.1017	.1040	.1063	.1084	.1104	.1123	.1140	.1157	.1172	.1186
11	.0749	.0776	.0802	.0828	.0853	.0878	.0902	.0925	.0948	.0970
12	.0505	.0530	.0555	.0579	.0604	.0629	.0654	.0679	.0703	.0728
13	.0315	.0334	.0354	.0374	.0395	.0416	.0438	.0459	.0481	.0504
14	.0182	.0196	.0210	.0225	.0240	.0256	.0272	.0289	.0306	.0324
15	.0098	.0107	.0116	.0126	.0136	.0147	.0158	.0169	.0182	.0194
16	.0050	.0055	.0060	.0066	.0072	.0079	.0086	.0093	.0101	.0109
17	.0024	.0026	.0029	.0033	.0036	.0040	.0044	.0048	.0053	.0058
18	.0011	.0012	.0014	.0015	.0017	.0019	.0021	.0024	.0026	.0029
19	.0005	.0005	.0006	.0007	.0008	.0009	.0010	.0011	.0012	.0014
20	.0002	.0002	.0002	.0003	.0003	.0004	.0004	.0005	.0005	.0006
21	.0001	.0001	.0001	.0001	.0001	.0002	.0002	.0002	.0002	.0003
22	.0000	.0000	.0000	.0000	.0001	.0001	.0001	.0001	.0001	.0001

					λ				
r	9.10	9.20	9.30	9.40	9.50	9.60	9.70	9.80	9.90	10.00
0	.0001	.0001	.0001	.0001	.0001	.0001	.0001	.0001	.0001	.0000
1	.0010	.0009	.0009	.0008	.0007	.0007	.0006	.0005	.0005	.0005
2	.0046	.0043	.0040	.0037	.0034	.0031	.0029	.0027	.0025	.0023
3	.0140	.0131	.0123	.0115	.0107	.0100	.0093	.0087	.0081	.0076
4	.0319	.0302	.0285	.0269	.0254	.0240	.0226	.0213	.0201	.0189
5	.0581	.0555	.0530	.0506	.0483	.0460	.0439	.0418	.0398	.0378
6	.0881	.0851	.0822	.0793	.0764	.0736	.0709	.0682	.0656	.0631
7	.1145	.1118	.1091	.1064	.1037	.1010	.0982	.0955	.0928	.0901
8	.1302	.1286	.1269	.1251	.1232	.1212	.1191	.1170	.1148	.1126
9	.1317	.1315	.1311	.1306	.1300	.1293	.1284	.1274	.1263	.1251
10	.1198	.1210	.1219	.1228	.1235	.1241	.1245	.1249	.1250	.1251
11	.0991	.1012	.1031	.1049	.1067	.1083	.1098	.1112	.1125	.1137
12	.0752	.0776	.0799	.0822	.0844	.0866	.0888	.0908	.0928	.0948
13	.0526	.0549	.0572	.0594	.0617	.0640	.0662	.0685	.0707	.0729
14	.0342	.0361	.0380	.0399	.0419	.0439	.0459	.0479	.0500	.0521
15	.0208	.0221	.0235	.0250	.0265	.0281	.0297	.0313	.0330	.0347
16	.0118	.0127	.0137	.0147	.0157	.0168	.0180	.0192	.0204	.0217
17	.0063	.0069	.0075	.0081	.0088	.0095	.0103	.0111	.0119	.0128
18	.0032	.0035	.0039	.0042	.0046	.0051	.0055	.0060	.0065	.0071
19	.0015	.0017	.0019	.0021	.0023	.0026	.0028	.0031	.0034	.0037

r	9.10	9.20	9.30	9.40	λ 9.50	9.60	9.70	9.80	9.90	10.00
20	.0007	.0008	.0009	.0010	.0011	.0012	.0014	.0015	.0017	.0019
21	.0003	.0003	.0004	.0004	.0005	.0006	.0006	.0007	.0008	.0009
22	.0001	.0001	.0002	.0002	.0002	.0002	.0003	.0003	.0004	.0004
23	.0000	.0001	.0001	.0001	.0001	.0001	.0001	.0001	.0002	.0002
24	.0000	.0000	.0000	.0000	.0000	.0000	.0000	.0001	.0001	.0001

r	11.	12.	13.	14.	λ 15.	16.	17.	18.	19.	20.
0	.0000	.0000	.0000	.0000	.0000	.0000	.0000	.0000	.0000	.0000
1	.0002	.0001	.0000	.0000	.0000	.0000	.0000	.0000	.0000	.0000
2	.0010	.0004	.0002	.0001	.0000	.0000	.0000	.0000	.0000	.0000
3	.0037	.0018	.0008	.0004	.0002	.0001	.0000	.0000	.0000	.0000
4	.0102	.0053	.0027	.0013	.0006	.0003	.0001	.0001	.0000	.0000
5	.0224	.0127	.0070	.0037	.0019	.0010	.0005	.0002	.0001	.0001
6	.0411	.0255	.0152	.0087	.0048	.0026	.0014	.0007	.0004	.0002
7	.0646	.0437	.0281	.0174	.0104	.0060	.0034	.0019	.0010	.0005
8	.0888	.0655	.0457	.0304	.0194	.0120	.0072	.0042	.0024	.0013
9	.1085	.0874	.0661	.0473	.0324	.0213	.0135	.0083	.0050	.0029
10	.1194	.1048	.0859	.0663	.0486	.0341	.0230	.0150	.0095	.0058
11	.1194	.1144	.1015	.0844	.0663	.0496	.0355	.0245	.0164	.0106
12	.1094	.1144	.1099	.0984	.0829	.0661	.0504	.0368	.0259	.0176
13	.0926	.1056	.1099	.1060	.0956	.0814	.0658	.0509	.0378	.0271
14	.0728	.0905	.1021	.1060	.1024	.0930	.0800	.0655	.0514	.0387
15	.0534	.0724	.0885	.0989	.1024	.0992	.0906	.0786	.0650	.0516
16	.0367	.0543	.0719	.0866	.0960	.0992	.0963	.0884	.0772	.0646
17	.0237	.0383	.0550	.0713	.0847	.0934	.0963	.0936	.0863	.0760
18	.0145	.0256	.0397	.0554	.0706	.0830	.0909	.0936	.0911	.0844
19	.0084	.0161	.0272	.0409	.0557	.0699	.0814	.0887	.0911	.0888
20	.0046	.0097	.0177	.0286	.0418	.0559	.0692	.0798	.0866	.0888
21	.0024	.0055	.0109	.0191	.0299	.0426	.0560	.0684	.0783	.0846
22	.0012	.0030	.0065	.0121	.0204	.0310	.0433	.0560	.0676	.0709
23	.0006	.0016	.0037	.0074	.0133	.0216	.0320	.0438	.0559	.0669
24	.0003	.0008	.0020	.0043	.0083	.0144	.0226	.0329	.0442	.0557
25	.0001	.0004	.0010	.0024	.0050	.0092	.0154	.0237	.0336	.0446
26	.0000	.0002	.0005	.0013	.0029	.0057	.0101	.0164	.0246	.0343
27	.0000	.0001	.0002	.0007	.0016	.0034	.0063	.0109	.0173	.0254
28	.0000	.0000	.0001	.0003	.0009	.0019	.0038	.0070	.0117	.0181
29	.0000	.0000	.0001	.0002	.0004	.0011	.0023	.0044	.0077	.0125
30	.0000	.0000	.0000	.0001	.0002	.0006	.0013	.0026	.0049	.0063
31	.0000	.0000	.0000	.0000	.0001	.0003	.0007	.0015	.0030	.0054
32	.0000	.0000	.0000	.0000	.0001	.0001	.0004	.0009	.0018	.0034
33	.0000	.0000	.0000	.0000	.0000	.0001	.0002	.0005	.0010	.0020
34	.0000	.0000	.0000	.0000	.0000	.0000	.0001	.0002	.0006	.0012
35	.0000	.0000	.0000	.0000	.0000	.0000	.0000	.0001	.0003	.0007
36	.0000	.0000	.0000	.0000	.0000	.0000	.0000	.0001	.0002	.0004
37	.0000	.0000	.0000	.0000	.0000	.0000	.0000	.0000	.0001	.0002
38	.0000	.0000	.0000	.0000	.0000	.0000	.0000	.0000	.0000	.0001
39	.0000	.0000	.0000	.0000	.0000	.0000	.0000	.0000	.0000	.0001

r	25.0	30.0	40.0	50.0	75.0	λ 100.0
0	.0000	.0000	0	0	0	0
1	.0000	.0000	0	0	0	0
2	.0000	.0000	0	0	0	0
3	.0000	.0000	0	0	0	0
4	.0000	.0000	0	0	0	0
5	.0000	.0000	0	0	0	0
6	.0000	.0000	.0000	0	0	0
7	.0000	.0000	.0000	0	0	0
8	.0001	.0000	.0000	0	0	0
9	.0001	.0000	.0000	0	0	0
10	.0004	.0000	.0000	0	0	0
11	.0008	.0000	.0000	.0000	0	0
12	.0017	.0001	.0000	.0000	0	0
13	.0033	.0002	.0000	.0000	0	0
14	.0059	.0005	.0000	.0000	0	0
15	.0099	.0010	.0000	.0000	0	0
16	.0155	.0019	.0000	.0000	0	0
17	.0227	.0034	.0000	.0000	0	0
18	.0316	.0057	.0000	.0000	0	0
19	.0415	.0089	.0001	.0000	0	0
20	.0519	.0134	.0002	.0000	0	0
21	.0618	.0192	.0004	.0000	0	0
22	.0702	.0261	.0007	.0000	0	0
23	.0763	.0341	.0012	.0000	0	0
24	.0795	.0426	.0019	.0000	0	0
25	.0795	.0511	.0031	.0000	0	0
26	.0765	.0590	.0047	.0001	.0000	0
27	.0708	.0655	.0070	.0001	.0000	0
28	.0632	.0702	.0100	.0002	.0000	0
29	.0545	.0726	.0138	.0004	.0000	0
30	.0454	.0726	.0185	.0007	.0000	0
31	.0366	.0703	.0238	.0011	.0000	0
32	.0286	.0659	.0298	.0017	.0000	0
33	.0217	.0599	.0361	.0026	.0000	0
34	.0159	.0529	.0425	.0038	.0000	0
35	.0114	.0453	.0485	.0054	.0000	0
36	.0079	.0378	.0539	.0075	.0000	0
37	.0053	.0306	.0583	.0102	.0000	0
38	.0035	.0242	.0614	.0134	.0000	0
39	.0023	.0186	.0629	.0172	.0000	0
40	.0014	.0139	.0629	.0215	.0000	0
41	.0009	.0102	.0614	.0262	.0000	0
42	.0005	.0073	.0585	.0312	.0000	.0000
43	.0003	.0051	.0544	.0363	.0000	.0000
44	.0002	.0035	.0495	.0412	.0000	.0000
45	.0001	.0023	.0440	.0458	.0001	.0000
46	.0001	.0015	.0382	.0498	.0001	.0000
47	.0000	.0010	.0325	.0530	.0001	.0000
48	.0000	.0006	.0271	.0552	.0002	.0000
49	.0000	.0004	.0221	.0563	.0003	.0000

r	25.0	30.0	40.0	50.0	75.0	100.0
50	.0000	.0002	.0177	.0563	.0005	.0000
51	.0000	.0001	.0139	.0552	.0007	.0000
52	.0000	.0001	.0107	.0531	.0011	.0000
53	.0000	.0000	.0081	.0501	.0015	.0000
54	.0000	.0000	.0060	.0464	.0021	.0000
55	.0000	.0000	.0043	.0422	.0028	.0000
56	.0000	.0000	.0031	.0376	.0038	.0000
57	.0000	.0000	.0022	.0330	.0050	.0000
58	.0000	.0000	.0015	.0285	.0065	.0000
59	.0000	.0000	.0010	.0241	.0082	.0000
60	.0000	.0000	.0007	.0201	.0103	.0000
61	.0000	.0000	.0004	.0165	.0126	.0000
62	.0000	.0000	.0003	.0133	.0153	.0000
63	.0000	.0000	.0002	.0105	.0182	.0000
64	.0000	.0000	.0001	.0082	.0213	.0000
65	0	.0000	.0001	.0063	.0246	.0000
66	0	.0000	.0000	.0048	.0279	.0001
67	0	.0000	.0000	.0036	.0313	.0001
68	0	.0000	.0000	.0026	.0345	.0002
69	0	.0000	.0000	.0019	.0375	.0002

r	25.0	30.0	40.0	50.0	75.0	100.0
70	.000	.0000	.0000	.0014	.0402	.0003
71	0	.0000	.0000	.0010	.0424	.0004
72	0	.0000	.0000	.0007	.0442	.0006
73	0	0	.0000	.0005	.0454	.0008
74	0	0	.0000	.0003	.0460	.0011
75	0	0	.0000	.0002	.0460	.0015
76	0	0	.0000	.0001	.0454	.0020
77	0	0	.0000	.0001	.0442	.0026
78	0	0	.0000	.0001	.0425	.0033
79	0	0	.0000	.0000	.0404	.0042
80	0	0	.0000	.0000	.0379	.0052
81	0	0	.0000	.0000	.0350	.0064
82	0	0	.0000	.0000	.0321	.0078
83	0	0	.0000	.0000	.0290	.0094
84	0	0	.0000	.0000	.0259	.0112
85	0	0	.0000	.0000	.0228	.0132
86	0	0	.0000	.0000	.0199	.0154
87	0	0	.0000	.0000	.0172	.0176
88	0	0	.0000	.0000	.0146	.0201
89	0	0	0	.0000	.0123	.0225
90	0	0	0	.0000	.0103	.0250
91	0	0	0	.0000	.0085	.0275
92	0	0	0	.0000	.0069	.0299
93	0	0	0	.0000	.0056	.0322
94	0	0	0	.0000	.0044	.0342
95	0	0	0	.0000	.0035	.0360
96	0	0	0	.0000	.0027	.0375

r	25.0	30.0	40.0	50.0	75.0	λ 100.0
97	0	0	0	.0000	.0021	.0387
98	0	0	0	.0000	.0016	.0395
99	0	0	0	.0000	.0012	.0399
100	0	0	0	.0000	.0009	.0399
101	0	0	0	.0000	.0007	.0395
102	0	0	0	.0000	.0005	.0387
103	0	0	0	.0000	.0004	.0376
104	0	0	0	0	.0003	.0361
105	0	0	0	0	.0002	.0344
106	0	0	0	0	.0001	.0325
107	0	0	0	0	.0001	.0303
108	0	0	0	0	.0001	.0281
109	0	0	0	0	.0000	.0258
110	0	0	0	0	.0000	.0234
111	0	0	0	0	.0000	.0211
112	0	0	0	0	.0000	.0188
113	0	0	0	0	.0000	.0167
114	0	0	0	0	.0000	.0146
115	0	0	0	0	.0000	.0127
116	0	0	0	0	.0000	.0110
117	0	0	0	0	.0000	.0094
118	0	0	0	0	.0000	.0079
119	0	0	0	0	.0000	.0067
120	0	0	0	0	.0000	.0056
121	0	0	0	0	.0000	.0046
122	0	0	0	0	.0000	.0038
123	0	0	0	0	.0000	.0031
124	0	0	0	0	.0000	.0025
125	0	0	0	0	.0000	.0020
126	0	0	0	0	.0000	.0018
127	0	0	0	0	.0000	.0012
128	0	0	0	0	.0000	.0010
129	0	0	0	0	.0000	.0007
130	0	0	0	0	.0000	.0006
131	0	0	0	0	.0000	.0004
132	0	0	0	0	.0000	.0003
133	0	0	0	0	.0000	.0003
134	0	0	0	0	.0000	.0002
135	0	0	0	0	.0000	.0001
136	0	0	0	0	.0000	.0001
137	0	0	0	0	.0000	.0001
138	0	0	0	0	.0000	.0001

Appendix 2 VALUES OF e^x AND e^{-x}

x	e^x	e^{-x}	x	e^x	e^{-x}
0.00	1.000	1.000	3.00	20.086	0.050
0.10	1.105	0.905	3.10	22.198	0.045
0.20	1.221	0.819	3.20	24.533	0.041
0.30	1.350	0.741	3.30	27.113	0.037
0.40	1.492	0.670	3.40	29.964	0.033
0.50	1.649	0.607	3.50	33.115	0.030
0.60	1.822	0.549	3.60	36.598	0.027
0.70	2.014	0.497	3.70	40.447	0.025
0.80	2.226	0.449	3.80	44.701	0.022
0.90	2.460	0.407	3.90	49.402	0.020
1.00	2.718	0.368	4.00	54.598	0.018
1.10	3.004	0.333	4.10	60.340	0.017
1.20	3.320	0.301	4.20	66.686	0.015
1.30	3.669	0.273	4.30	73.700	0.014
1.40	4.055	0.247	4.40	81.451	0.012
1.50	4.482	0.223	4.50	90.017	0.011
1.60	4.953	0.202	4.60	99.484	0.010
1.70	5.474	0.183	4.70	109.95	0.009
1.80	6.050	0.165	4.80	121.51	0.008
1.90	6.686	0.150	4.90	143.29	0.007
2.00	7.389	0.135	5.00	148.41	0.007
2.10	8.166	0.122	5.10	164.02	0.006
2.20	9.025	0.111	5.20	181.27	0.006
2.30	9.974	0.100	5.30	200.34	0.005
2.40	11.023	0.091	5.40	221.41	0.005
2.50	12.182	0.082	5.50	244.69	0.004
2.60	13.464	0.074	5.60	270.34	0.004
2.70	14.880	0.067	5.70	298.87	0.003
2.80	16.445	0.061	5.80	330.30	0.003
2.90	18.174	0.055	5.90	365.04	0.003
3.00	20.086	0.050	6.00	403.43	0.002

Appendix 3   VALUES OF P_0 FOR VARIOUS COMBINATIONS OF $\dfrac{\lambda}{s\mu}$

FOR MULTICHANNEL POISSON/EXPONENTIAL QUEUING PROCESS: PROBABILITY OF ZERO IN SYSTEM

$R = \lambda/s\mu$

NUMBER OF CHANNELS: s

R	2	3	4	5	6	7	8	9	10	15
0.02	0.96079	0.94177	0.92312	0.90484	0.88692	0.86936	0.85215	0.83527	0.81873	0.74082
0.04	0.92308	0.88692	0.85215	0.81873	0.78663	0.75578	0.72615	0.69768	0.67032	0.54881
0.06	0.88679	0.83526	0.78663	0.74082	0.69768	0.65705	0.61878	0.58275	0.54881	0.40657
0.08	0.85185	0.78659	0.72615	0.67032	0.61878	0.57121	0.52729	0.48675	0.44933	0.30119
0.10	0.81818	0.74074	0.67031	0.60653	0.54881	0.49659	0.44933	0.40657	0.36783	0.22313
0.12	0.78571	0.69753	0.61876	0.54881	0.48675	0.43171	0.38289	0.33960	0.30119	0.16530
0.14	0.75439	0.65679	0.57116	0.49657	0.43171	0.37531	0.32628	0.28365	0.24660	0.12246
0.16	0.72414	0.61838	0.52720	0.44931	0.38289	0.32628	0.27604	0.23693	0.20190	0.09072
0.18	0.69492	0.58214	0.48660	0.40653	0.33959	0.28365	0.23693	0.19790	0.165530	0.06721
0.20	0.66667	0.54795	0.44910	0.36782	0.30118	0.24659	0.20189	0.16530	0.13534	0.04979
0.22	0.63934	0.51567	0.41445	0.33277	0.26711	0.21437	0.17204	0.13807	0.11080	0.03688
0.24	0.61290	0.48519	0.38244	0.30105	0.23688	0.18636	0.14660	0.11532	0.09072	0.02732
0.26	0.58730	0.45640	0.35284	0.27233	0.21007	0.16200	0.12492	0.09632	0.07427	0.02024
0.28	0.56250	0.42918	0.32548	0.24633	0.18628	0.14082	0.10645	0.08045	0.06041	0.01500
0.30	0.53846	0.40346	0.30017	0.22277	0.16517	0.12241	0.09070	0.06720	0.04978	0.01111

0.32	0.51515	0.37913	0.27676	0.20144	0.14644	0.10639	0.07728	0.05612	0.04076	0.00823
0.34	0.49254	0.35610	0.25510	0.18211	0.12981	0.09247	0.06584	0.04687	0.03337	0.00610
0.36	0.47059	0.33431	0.23505	0.16460	0.11505	0.08035	0.05609	0.03915	0.02732	0.00452
0.38	0.44928	0.31367	0.21649	0.14872	0.10195	0.06981	0.04778	0.03269	0.02230	0.00335
0.40	0.42857	0.29412	0.19929	0.13433	0.09032	0.06065	0.04069	0.02729	0.01830	0.00248
0.42	0.40845	0.27559	0.18336	0.12128	0.07998	0.05267	0.03465	0.02279	0.01498	0.00184
0.44	0.38889	0.25802	0.16860	0.10944	0.07080	0.04573	0.02950	0.01902	0.01226	0.00136
0.46	0.36986	0.24135	0.15491	0.09870	0.06265	0.03968	0.02511	0.01587	0.01003	0.00101
0.48	0.35135	0.22554	0.14221	0.08895	0.05540	0.03442	0.02136	0.01324	0.00825	0.00075
0.50	0.33333	0.21053	0.13043	0.08010	0.04896	0.02984	0.01816	0.01104	0.00671	0.00055
0.52	0.31579	0.19627	0.11951	0.07207	0.04323	0.02586	0.01544	0.00920	0.00548	0.00041
0.54	0.29870	0.18273	0.10936	0.06477	0.03814	0.02239	0.01311	0.00767	0.00448	0.00030
0.56	0.28205	0.16986	0.09994	0.05814	0.03362	0.01936	0.01113	0.00638	0.00366	0.00022
0.58	0.26582	0.15762	0.09119	0.05212	0.02959	0.01673	0.00943	0.00531	0.00298	0.00017
0.60	0.25000	0.14599	0.08306	0.04665	0.02601	0.01443	0.00799	0.00441	0.00243	0.00012
0.62	0.23457	0.13491	0.07550	0.04167	0.02282	0.01243	0.00675	0.00366	0.00198	0.00009
0.64	0.21951	0.12438	0.06847	0.03715	0.01999	0.01069	0.00570	0.00303	0.00161	0.00007
0.66	0.20482	0.11435	0.06194	0.03304	0.01746	0.00918	0.00480	0.00251	0.00131	0.00005
0.68	0.19048	0.10479	0.05587	0.02930	0.01522	0.00786	0.00404	0.00207	0.00106	0.00004
0.70	0.17647	0.09569	0.05021	0.02590	0.01322	0.00670	0.00338	0.00170	0.00085	0.00003
0.72	0.16279	0.08702	0.04495	0.02280	0.01144	0.00570	0.00283	0.00140	0.00069	0.00002
0.74	0.14943	0.07875	0.04006	0.01999	0.00986	0.00483	0.00235	0.00114	0.00055	0.00001
0.76	0.13636	0.07087	0.03550	0.01743	0.00846	0.00407	0.00195	0.00093	0.00044	0.00001
0.78	0.12360	0.06335	0.03125	0.01510	0.00721	0.00341	0.00160	0.00075	0.00035	0.00001
0.80	0.11111	0.05618	0.02730	0.01299	0.00610	0.00284	0.00131	0.00060	0.00028	0.00001
0.82	0.09890	0.04933	0.02362	0.01106	0.00511	0.00234	0.00106	0.00048	0.00022	0.00000
0.84	0.08696	0.04280	0.02019	0.00931	0.00423	0.00190	0.00085	0.00038	0.00017	0.00000
0.86	0.07527	0.03656	0.01700	0.00772	0.00345	0.00153	0.00067	0.00029	0.00013	0.00000
0.88	0.06383	0.03060	0.01403	0.00627	0.00276	0.00120	0.00052	0.00022	0.00010	0.00000
0.90	0.05263	0.02491	0.01126	0.00496	0.00215	0.00092	0.00039	0.00017	0.00007	0.00000
0.92	0.04167	0.01947	0.00687	0.00377	0.00161	0.00068	0.00028	0.00012	0.00005	0.00000
0.94	0.03093	0.01427	0.00627	0.00268	0.00113	0.00047	0.00019	0.00008	0.00003	0.00000
0.96	0.02041	0.00930	0.00403	0.00170	0.00070	0.00029	0.00012	0.00005	0.00002	0.00000
0.98	0.01010	0.00454	0.00194	0.00081	0.00033	0.00013	0.00005	0.00002	0.00001	0.00000

Appendix 4

AREA UNDER THE STANDARD NORMAL CURVE

Z	.00	.01	.02	.03	.04	.05	.06	.07	.08	.09
0.0	.50000	.50399	.50798	.51197	.51595	.51994	.52392	.52790	.53188	.53586
0.1	.53983	.54380	.54776	.55172	.55567	.55962	.56356	.56749	.57142	.57535
0.2	.57926	.58317	.58706	.59095	.59483	.59871	.60257	.60642	.61026	.61409
0.3	.61791	.62172	.62552	.62930	.63307	.63683	.64058	.64431	.64803	.65173
0.4	.65542	.65910	.66276	.66640	.67003	.67364	.67724	.68082	.68439	.68793
0.5	.69146	.69497	.69847	.70194	.70540	.70884	.71226	.71566	.71904	.72240
0.6	.72575	.72907	.73237	.73536	.73891	.74215	.74537	.74857	.75175	.75490
0.7	.75804	.76115	.76424	.76730	.77035	.77337	.77637	.77935	.78230	.78524
0.8	.78814	.79103	.79389	.79673	.79955	.80234	.80511	.80785	.81057	.81327
0.9	.81594	.81859	.82121	.82381	.82639	.82894	.83147	.83398	.83646	.83891
1.0	.84134	.84375	.84614	.84849	.85083	.85314	.85543	.85769	.85993	.86214
1.1	.86433	.86650	.86864	.87076	.87286	.87493	.87698	.87900	.88100	.88298
1.2	.88493	.88686	.88877	.89065	.89251	.89435	.89617	.89796	.89973	.90147
1.3	.90320	.90490	.90658	.90824	.90988	.91149	.91309	.91466	.91621	.91774
1.4	.91924	.92073	.92220	.92364	.92507	.92647	.92785	.92922	.93056	.93189
1.5	.93319	.93448	.93574	.93699	.93822	.93943	.94062	.94179	.94295	.94408
1.6	.94520	.94630	.94738	.94485	.94950	.95053	.95154	.95254	.95352	.95449
1.7	.95543	.95637	.95728	.95818	.95907	.95994	.96080	.96164	.96246	.96327
1.8	.96407	.96485	.96562	.96638	.96712	.96784	.96856	.96926	.96995	.97062
1.9	.97128	.97193	.97257	.97320	.97381	.97441	.97500	.97558	.97615	.97670
2.0	.97725	.97784	.97831	.97882	.97932	.97982	.98030	.98077	.98124	.98169
2.1	.98214	.98257	.98300	.98341	.98382	.98422	.98461	.98500	.98537	.98574
2.2	.98610	.98645	.98679	.98713	.98745	.98778	.98809	.98840	.98870	.98899
2.3	.98298	.98956	.98983	.99010	.99036	.99061	.99086	.99111	.99134	.99158
2.4	.99180	.99202	.99224	.99245	.99266	.99286	.99305	.99324	.99343	.99361
2.5	.99379	.99396	.99413	.99430	.99446	.99461	.99477	.99492	.99506	.99520
2.6	.99534	.99547	.99560	.99573	.99585	.99598	.99609	.99621	.99632	.99643
2.7	.99653	.99664	.99674	.99683	.99693	.99702	.99711	.99720	.99728	.99736
2.8	.99744	.99752	.99760	.99767	.99774	.99781	.99788	.99795	.99801	.99807
2.9	.99813	.99819	.99825	.99831	.99836	.99841	.99846	.99851	.99856	.99861
3.0	.99865	.99869	.99874	.99878	.99882	.99886	.99899	.99893	.99896	.99900
3.1	.99903	.99906	.99910	.99913	.99916	.99918	.99921	.99924	.99926	.99929
3.2	.99931	.99934	.99936	.99938	.99940	.99942	.99944	.99946	.99948	.99950
3.3	.99952	.99953	.99955	.99957	.99958	.99960	.99961	.99962	.99964	.99965
3.4	.99966	.99968	.99969	.99970	.99971	.99972	.99973	.99974	.99975	.99976
3.5	.99977	.99978	.99978	.99979	.99980	.99981	.99981	.99982	.99983	.99983
3.6	.99984	.99985	.99985	.99986	.99986	.99987	.99987	.99988	.99988	.99989
3.7	.99989	.99990	.99990	.99990	.99991	.99991	.99992	.99992	.99992	.99992
3.8	.99993	.99993	.99993	.99994	.99994	.99994	.99994	.99995	.99995	.99995
3.9	.99995	.99995	.99996	.99996	.99996	.99996	.99996	.99996	.99997	.99997

TABLE OF RANDOM NUMBERS

39 65 76 45 45	10 90 69 64 61	20 26 36 31 62	58 24 97 14 97	95 06 70 99 00
73 71 23 70 90	65 97 60 12 11	31 56 34 19 19	47 83 75 51 33	30 62 38 20 46
72 20 47 33 84	51 67 47 97 19	98 40 07 17 66	23 05 09 51 80	59 78 11 52 49
75 17 25 69 17	17 95 21 78 58	24 33 45 77 48	69 81 84 09 29	93 22 70 45 80
37 48 79 88 74	63 52 06 34 30	01 31 60 10 27	35 07 79 71 53	28 99 52 01 41
02 89 08 16 94	85 53 83 29 95	56 27 09 24 43	21 78 55 09 82	72 61 88 73 61
87 18 15 70 07	37 79 49 12 38	48 13 93 55 96	41 92 45 71 51	09 18 25 58 94
98 83 71 70 15	89 09 39 59 24	00 06 41 41 20	14 36 59 25 47	54 45 17 24 89
10 08 58 07 04	76 62 16 48 68	58 76 17 14 86	59 53 11 52 21	66 04 18 72 87
47 90 56 37 31	71 82 13 50 41	27 55 10 24 92	28 04 67 53 44	95 23 00 84 47
93 05 31 03 07	34 18 04 52 35	74 13 39 35 22	68 95 23 92 35	36 63 70 35 33
21 89 11 47 99	11 20 99 45 18	76 51 94 84 86	13 79 93 37 55	98 16 04 41 67
95 18 94 06 97	27 37 83 28 71	79 57 95 13 91	09 61 87 25 21	56 20 11 32 44
97 08 31 55 73	10 65 81 92 59	77 31 61 95 46	20 44 90 32 64	26 99 76 75 63
69 26 88 86 13	59 71 74 17 32	48 38 75 93 29	73 37 32 04 05	60 82 29 20 25
41 47 10 25 03	87 63 93 95 17	81 83 83 04 49	77 45 85 50 51	79 88 01 97 30
91 94 14 63 62	08 61 74 51 69	92 79 43 89 79	29 18 94 51 23	14 85 11 47 23
80 06 54 18 47	08 52 85 08 40	48 40 35 94 22	72 65 71 08 86	50 03 42 99 36
67 72 77 63 99	89 85 84 46 06	64 71 06 21 66	89 37 20 70 01	61 65 70 22 12
59 40 24 13 75	42 29 72 23 19	06 94 76 10 08	81 30 15 39 14	81 83 17 16 33
63 62 06 34 41	79 53 36 02 95	94 61 09 43 62	20 21 14 68 86	84 95 48 46 45
78 47 23 53 90	79 93 96 38 63	34 85 52 05 09	85 43 01 72 73	14 93 87 81 40
87 68 62 15 43	97 48 72 66 48	53 16 71 13 81	59 97 50 99 52	24 62 20 42 31
47 60 92 10 77	26 97 05 73 51	88 46 38 03 58	72 68 49 29 31	75 70 16 08 24
56 88 87 59 41	06 87 37 78 48	65 88 69 58 39	88 02 84 27 83	85 81 56 39 38
22 17 68 65 84	87 02 22 57 51	68 69 80 95 44	11 29 01 95 80	49 34 35 86 47
19 36 27 59 46	39 77 32 77 09	79 57 92 36 59	89 74 39 82 15	08 58 94 34 74
16 77 23 02 77	28 06 24 25 93	22 45 44 84 11	87 80 61 65 31	09 71 91 74 25
78 43 76 71 61	97 67 63 99 61	80 45 67 93 82	59 73 19 85 23	53 33 65 97 21
03 28 28 26 08	69 30 16 09 05	53 58 47 70 93	66 56 45 65 79	45 56 20 19 47
04 31 17 21 56	33 73 99 19 87	26 72 39 27 67	53 77 57 68 93	60 61 97 22 61
61 06 98 03 91	87 14 77 43 96	43 00 65 98 50	45 60 33 01 07	98 99 46 50 47
23 68 35 26 00	99 53 93 61 28	52 70 05 48 34	56 65 05 61 86	90 92 10 70 80
15 39 25 70 99	93 86 52 77 65	15 33 59 05 28	22 87 26 07 47	86 96 98 29 06
58 71 96 30 24	18 46 23 34 27	85 13 99 24 44	49 18 09 79 49	74 16 32 23 02
92 22 53 64 39	07 10 63 76 35	87 03 04 79 88	08 13 13 85 51	55 34 57 72 69
78 76 58 54 74	92 38 70 96 92	52 06 79 79 45	82 63 18 27 44	69 66 92 19 09
61 81 31 96 82	00 57 25 60 59	46 72 60 18 77	55 66 12 62 11	08 99 55 64 57
42 88 07 10 05	24 98 65 63 21	47 21 61 88 32	27 80 30 21 60	10 92 35 36 12
77 94 30 05 39	28 10 99 00 27	12 73 73 99 12	49 99 57 94 82	96 88 57 17 91

SUPPLEMENTARY SECTION ON WAITING LINE MODELS

Appendix 6 presents eight queuing models through a refinery port's tanker docking and unloading operations. Model assumptions are discussed in greater detail, particularly the distribution characteristics.

MODEL PARAMETERS: DISTRIBUTIONS

Arrival Distribution

The pattern of arrivals is described by the arrival distribution. The number of arrivals per unit of time is not usually based on a precise schedule but occurs in a random fashion according to one of many probability distributions. The most frequently used assumption about customer arrivals is the *Poisson distribution*.

In the Poisson distribution, named after the French mathematician Siméon D. Poisson (1781–1840), the number of arrivals during a certain time interval is independent of the number of arrivals in previous time intervals. The Poisson distribution has proven useful for the simple reason that many statistical studies of queuing processes have resulted in Poisson-distributed arrivals.

The general formula for the Poisson probability distribution is

$$P(r) = \frac{e^{-\lambda}(\lambda)^r}{r!}$$

where

$$r = \text{number of arrivals per unit of time}$$
$$P(r) = \text{probability of } r \text{ arrivals}$$
$$\lambda = \text{mean arrival rate}$$
$$e = \text{the base of natural logarithms, 2.71828}$$
$$r! = r(r - 1)(r - 2) \cdots (3)(2)(1)$$

Assuming random independent arrivals, we can describe the arrivals as a Poisson distribution.[1] Each arrival is also independent of the state of the system. The Poisson

[1] Appendix 1 presents a table of Poisson probability values for various values of r and λ.

distribution has the unique feature that the mean is equal to the variance. Therefore, if we know the mean, we can describe the entire Poisson distribution. The Poisson distribution is a *discrete* probability distribution, since it provides the probability of the number of arrivals per unit of time. This means that we need to deal only with whole numbers. Figure A6.1 portrays the shape of the general Poisson distribution. As the mean (λ) becomes larger, the distribution becomes flatter and more bell-shaped.

Let us consider an example. If the mean arrival rate of ships at a port is one every 12 hours, the probabilities associated with a different number of arrivals per hour would be

$$P(r) = \frac{e^{-\lambda}(\lambda)^r}{r!}$$

For $r = 1$, $P(1) = \dfrac{2.71828^{(-1/12)}(1/12)^1}{1!} = 0.9200(1/12) = 0.0767$

r	P(r)
0	0.9200
1	0.0767
2	0.0032
3	0.0001
4	0.0000

If the number of arrivals per unit of time can be described by a Poisson distribution, with a mean rate of λ, then the time between arrivals is distributed as a *negative exponential* probability distribution, with a mean of $1/\lambda$. The negative exponential distribution is continuous, allowing any fraction. For example, if the mean arrival rate per

Figure A6.1   The General Shape of the Poisson Distribution

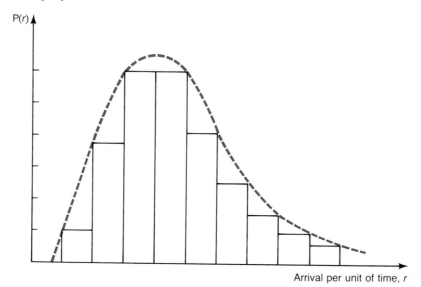

1-hour period is 6, then the mean time between arrivals is 10 minutes (1 hour ÷ 6). The relationship between the arrival rate and the time between arrivals is as follows:

Arrival Rate	Time between Arrivals
Poisson	Negative exponential
Mean $= \lambda$	Mean $= 1/\lambda$
$\lambda = 6$ arrivals per hour	$1/\lambda = (1/6)(1 \text{ hour}) = 10$ minutes

Arrival rates can be described by other distributions as well. If arrivals follow a schedule, without variance, they are deterministic. Assembly line processes may be set at this arrival distribution.

The *Erlang distribution* assumption is very important in waiting line theory. As we noted in Chapter 13, queuing theory was pioneered by A. K. Erlang to analyze waiting effects on a telephone system. Most of the empirically determined distributions can be described as Erlang distributions. This is a very important value of the Erlang distribution. The Erlang distribution density function is:

$$f(t) = \frac{(\mu k)^k}{(k-1)!} t^{k-1} e^{-k\mu t}$$

where

$$t = \text{service time}$$
$$f(t) = \text{probability density associated with } t$$
$$k = \text{number of service phases}$$
$$\mu = \text{mean service rate}$$
$$e = \text{natural number (2.71828)}$$

In the above formula, μ is the mean and k is the parameter that determines the dispersion of the distribution. This distribution is shown, with several values of k, in Figure A6.2. If $k = 1$, we obtain the negative exponential distribution; if $k = \infty$, we obtain a constant distribution. It should be noted that k must be a positive integer.

A general explanation of k can be obtained by considering a multiple-phase queuing operation, in which a server can perform several functions. For example, a druggist can take the prescription, fill it, make the proper records, and ring up the cash register. If a single server performs several functions for a customer during one service operation, and all the k service functions have identical exponential distributions with mean $1/k\mu$, then the aggregate service distribution will be $1/\mu$, and the variance σ^2 will be $1/k^2$. Even if the physical process does not fit this description, the Erlang distribution may fit the arrival distribution.

The arrival distribution symbols in Kendall's notation are given below:

Symbol	Description
M	Poisson
D	Deterministic
E_k	Erlang, with parameter k
GI	General independent

Any arrival distribution not described by the first three symbols can be noted by the symbol GI.

Figure A6.2   Erlang Distribution for Selected Values of **k**

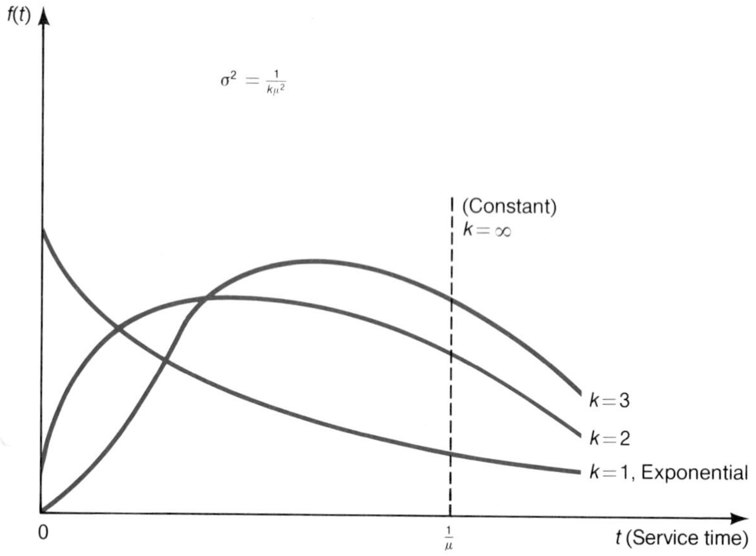

Service Time Distribution

Service times in a waiting line process may also be described by any one of a large number of different probability distributions. The most commonly assumed distribution for service times is the negative exponential distribution.

The assumption of negative exponential service times is not valid nearly as often as is the assumption of the Poisson arrival distribution. Therefore, we must check this assumption very carefully before selecting the service time distribution.

The general formula for the negative exponential probability density function is

$$f(t) = \mu e^{-\mu t}$$

where

$$t = \text{service time}$$
$$f(t) = \text{probability density associated with } t$$
$$\mu = \text{mean service rate}$$
$$1/\mu = \text{mean service time}$$
$$e = 2.71828$$

The negative exponential service time assumes random time for service. The probability of serving a customer is independent of how much time has already elapsed on the service for that customer or for any prior customers. It is also independent of the number of customers waiting for service. (This last assumption limits us a great deal, as service in reality may speed up when people are waiting.)

As pointed out before, the negative exponential distribution is continuous. Figure A6.3 illustrates the negative exponential distribution. In this figure we can easily see that short service times have the highest probability of occurrence. As service time increases, the probability function diminishes gradually toward 0.

Figure A6.3   *Negative Exponential Probability Density Distribution*

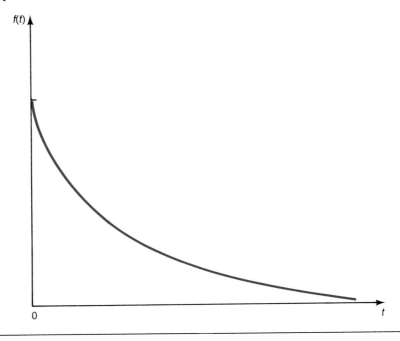

The area under the curve for the negative exponential distribution is obtained from its cumulative distribution function. The area under the curve to the left of T (T being any time selected) is described as

$$F(T) = f(t \leq T) = 1 - e^{-\mu T}$$

As an example, if the mean service time $(1/\mu)$ of a dock unloading facility is 1 ship unloaded every 8 hours, the probability that service would take T or fewer hours would be calculated from the formula given[2]:

Service Times of at Most T (hours)	$F(T)$ Probability
0	0.0000
1	0.1175
2	0.2212
3	0.3127
4	0.3935
5	0.4647
8	0.6321
12	0.7769
18	0.8946
24	0.9507
40	0.9933

[2]A table of values of e^x and e^{-x} is presented in Appendix 2.

T	F(T)
1	$1 - e^{-\mu T} = 1 - 2.71828^{-(1/0)(1)} = 1 - 0.8825 = 0.1175$
2	$1 - e^{-\mu T} = 1 - 2.71828^{-(1/0)(2)} = 1 - 0.7788 = 0.2212$
3	$1 - e^{-\mu T} = 1 - 2.71828^{-(1/0)(3)} = 1 - 0.6873 = 0.3127$

Service time distributions can take the same distribution forms as arrival distributions. Service distribution symbols in Kendall's notation are:

Symbol	Description
M	Negative exponential
D	Constant
E_k	Erlang, with parameter k
GS	General distribution

Number of Servers

The next waiting line system characteristic we will consider is the number of parallel servers. Servers can be equipment (washing machines, cranes, etc.), people (barbers, bank tellers), or systems combining both. If there is more than one server in a system, these servers can be arranged in a parallel system in which each server provides the same type of service to different customers. Alternatively, when servers are in series, services are performed in sequence. In Kendall's notation, the number of parallel servers is indicated by the appropriate integer.

It is important to remember that in a waiting line system the service rate (from all servers combined) must exceed the arrival rate; otherwise the waiting line will grow infinitely long. If the arrival rate exceeds the service rate, it will be necessary to add parallel servers to ensure that arrivals will receive service. It should be apparent that if an average of four customers an hour arrives at a barbershop with only one barber, and the barber services three customers per hour, every hour will find an additional customer in the waiting line. To restore reasonable schedules to the lives of all concerned, an additional server (barber) will be required. For the queuing system to attain equilibrium, the rate of service multiplied by the number of parallel servers must exceed the rate of arrival. This is demonstrated in Figure A6.4.

Queue Discipline

Queue discipline, as we discussed in Chapter 13, is the decision rule that determines the order in which waiting customers will be selected for service. It is normally assumed that customers are serviced on a first-come, first-served basis. Other decision rules are possible, however. Last-come, first-served, random service, or some other sort of priority decision rule is often found in real-world applications. The symbols and descriptions of queue discipline are shown below:

Symbol	Description
FCFS	First-come, first-served
LCFS	Last-come, first-served
SIRO	Service in random order (random service order)
GD	General distribution (other decision rules)

Figure A6.4   Relationship of Waiting Line Length to Arrival/Service Rate Ratio

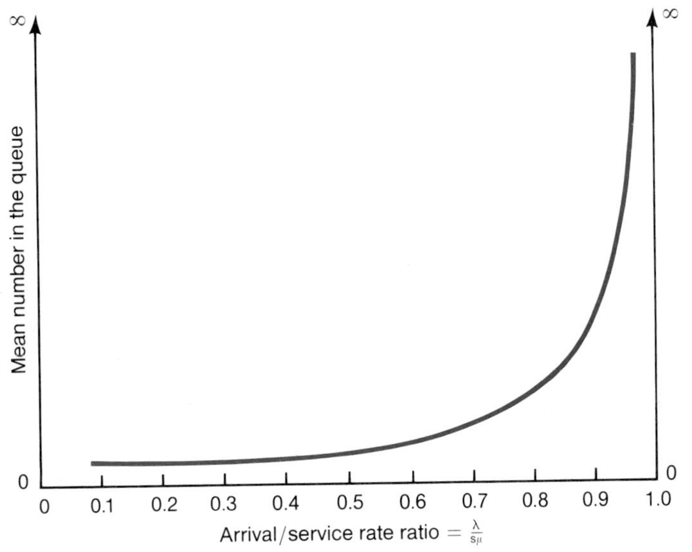

Infinite versus Finite Waiting Line Length

The maximum number of customers awaiting service can affect the waiting line model. Many models may be appropriately described by an unlimited queue length. But there may be limited space available for customers awaiting service. For example, the driveway and parking lot at a hamburger establishment may have a limited capacity. Although cars attempting to enter a car wash often back up into the street, there may be traffic ordinances against such a situation.

The behavior of customers may also be such that a limited queue length may be appropriate for a model. Customers may refuse to enter a long line even if space is available. For example, your hunger pains may cause you to seek another source of food if your favorite hamburger shop has 64 customers awaiting service. This decision to not enter a waiting line is referred to as *balking*. Balking can result in an effective limited queue despite ample space available for waiting. Although infinite queues are easier to work with from a mathematical standpoint, finite queues are often more realistic. In Kendall's notation, the maximum queue length is indicated by the appropriate integer or by the symbol ∞.

Maximum Population in the System

The calling population in waiting line theory is the source of arrivals to be served. If you are considering a waiting line problem in which there is a large number of potential customers, it would be reasonable to assume that the calling population is infinite. However, if the source of arrivals for service is such that removal of one member of that population would affect the probability of arrival, it would be appropriate to use a model having a finite calling population. In Kendall's notation, the calling population is indicated by the appropriate integer or by the symbol ∞.

EIGHT WAITING LINE MODELS

This section presents eight waiting line models, including the three we covered in Chapter 13, through casettes.

Casette A6.1   *THE TITANIC QUEUE*

Barney Harrelson reported to work in June, fresh from a business college and armed with the latest in quantitative tools. He had obtained a position with Titantic Oil Port Systems Inc. (TOPSI), a new petroleum refinery company, and had been assigned to the North Atlantic Division.

The North Atlantic Division of TOPSI came into being to meet the critical demand for petroleum products in the northeastern United States. TOPSI's president, Eric Reed, had long held an interest in a small but unproductive farm just south of Thule, Greenland. TOPSI built a refinery on the farm site, obtained agreements with various crude oil producers, and was set for operations. Mr. Reed decided to go to Boston himself to set up marketing operations, entrusting the details of the refinery operation to his executive vice-president (and favorite nephew), Lafe Erickson.

Lafe was interested in efficiency and had drawn up a plan of operations for the terminal where crude oil is to be delivered at the average rate of two 480,000 barrel tankers per day during the open shipping season (when ice conditions allowed). Lafe designed the unloading facilities to handle that delivery rate. The tankers charge demurrage of $600 per hour for idle waiting time. Lafe calculated the port facility cost $800 per hour to build and operate. Lafe's proposed schedule for the first week of operation is shown in Table A6.1.

Table A6.1   The Titantic Oil Port Systems: Constant Arrival/Constant Service Time

Ship	Arrival Hour	Service Begins	Service Time (hours)	Service Ends	Ship Waiting Time (hours)	Dock Idle Time (hours)	Ships Waiting
Ill Wind	0	0	12	12	0	0	0
Typhoon	12	12	12	24	0	0	0
Zephyr	24	24	12	36	0	0	0
Sirocco	36	36	12	48	0	0	0
Monsoon	48	48	12	60	0	0	0
Whirlwind	60	60	12	72	0	0	0
Gale	72	72	12	84	0	0	0
Tokyo Maru	84	84	12	96	0	0	0
Squall	96	96	12	108	0	0	0
Mistral	108	108	12	120	0	0	0
Simoom	120	120	12	132	0	0	0
Trade Wind	132	132	12	144	0	0	0
Samiel	144	144	12	156	0	0	0
Levanter	156	156	12	168	0	0	0
14 ships unloaded:			168		0	0	

(*D*/*D*/1):(FCFS/∞/∞)

The deterministic waiting line is actually a special case of the stochastic (probabilistic) waiting line model, with no variance in arrival and service time rates. This model depends on the following assumptions:

1. Deterministic (constant) arrival

2. Deterministic (constant) service time

3. Number of servers = 1, or a single-channel system

4. Queue discipline is first-come, first-served

5. Maximum number of customers is assumed to be infinite (∞)

6. Calling population is also assumed to be infinite (∞)

Based on the constant arrival and constant service time, the following analysis can be made.

$$\text{Mean arrival rate, } \lambda = \frac{14 \text{ ships}}{168 \text{ hours}} = \frac{1 \text{ ship}}{12 \text{ hours}}$$

$$\text{Mean service rate, } \mu = \frac{14 \text{ ships}}{168 \text{ hours}} = \frac{1 \text{ ship}}{12 \text{ hours}}$$

Mean length of the system, L = 1 ship in system

Mean time in the system, W = 12 hours in system

Mean length of the waiting line, L_q = 0 ships waiting

Mean waiting time, W_q = 0 hours waiting

Now the total cost per week can be calculated as follows:

Demurrage (W_q):	0 hours × $600/hour =	$0
Operation:	168 hours × $800/hour =	$134,000
	Total cost =	$134,000

Casette A6.2 *OPERATION THULE*

Barney Harrelson had been hired to help in planning operations at Thule. Lafe Erickson, who believed in motivation, informed Barney that his bonus would be based on the efficiency of the crude oil receiving operation. Barney examined the schedule. It did not appear promising, and his career at Thule seemed doomed. All would be well if the ships arrived on schedule and the unloading operation progressed smoothly. But Barney had always been the worrying sort. There were many sources of delay for shipping en route to Thule, including storms and icebergs. The unloading operation was also fraught with potential delays. The tankers required secure anchoring for unloading, and it took time to hook up the piping system in rough weather (which occurred at Thule 364 days a year, and 179 of the 180 annual operating days). And even though Lafe had obtained a very favorable price on some pumps from the Arctic Pump Wholesaling Company, Barney was somewhat concerned with pump reliability.

Table A6.2   Operation Thule — Poisson Arrival/Exponential Service

Ship	Arrival Hour	Service Begins	Service Time (hours)	Service Ends	Ship Waiting Time (hours)	Dock Idle Time (hours)	Ships Waiting
Ill Wind	0	0	1	1	0	0	0
Typhoon	9	9	7	16	0	8	0
Zephyr	53	53	28	81	0	37	5
Sirocco	61	81	5	86	20	0	4
Monsoon	64	86	4	90	18	0	3
Whirlwind	66	90	2	92	24	0	3
Gale	76	92	4	96	16	0	3
Tokyo Maru	79	96	17	113	17	0	3
Squall	90	113	3	116	23	0	3
Mistral	93	116	2	118	23	0	2
Simoom	99	118	12	130	19	0	2
Trade Wind	114	130	20	150	16	0	2
Samiel	119	150	1	151	31	0	1
Levanter	138	151	6	157	13	0	0
						11	
End of week	168		112		224	56	

Barney recalculated the schedule of operations based upon a Poisson distribution rate of arrival and an exponentially distributed rate of service time. Using the system set up by Lafe, Barney found little probability of unloading all of the tankers arriving during the open-sea season before the ice closed in, and calculated an infinite demurrage expense. Although Lafe felt the young man tended to worry too much, Lafe also was concerned a bit when faced with the contingencies that he had overlooked. To be on the safe side, Lafe agreed to increase the pumping system from a capacity of 40,000 barrels per hour to 60,000 barrels per hour, yielding a cost to TOPSI of $1,200 per hour for operation and depreciation. Lafe had Barney recalculate the schedule of operations, based upon a Poisson rate of tanker arrival and an exponential rate of service. The first week's operation proceeded as shown in Table A6.2.

$(M/M/1)$:$(FCFS/\infty/\infty)$

This model is based on the same assumptions as the deterministic model presented above, except that arrivals are assumed to be Poisson, and service time is negative exponential. This is the classical model of waiting line theory. The model characteristics can be determined with the following formulas, which are applied to the operations at Thule as an illustration.

Mean arrival rate $\qquad \lambda = \text{given} \qquad = \dfrac{14 \text{ ships}}{168 \text{ hours}} = \dfrac{1 \text{ ship}}{12 \text{ hours}}$

Mean service rate $\qquad \mu = \text{given} \qquad = \dfrac{14 \text{ ships}}{112 \text{ hours}} = \dfrac{1 \text{ ship}}{8 \text{ hours}}$

Server utilization factor $\qquad \rho = \dfrac{\lambda}{\mu} \qquad = \dfrac{1/12}{1/8} = \dfrac{2}{3}$

Empty-system probability	$P_0 = 1 - \rho$	$= 1 - \dfrac{2}{3} = \dfrac{1}{3}$
Probability of n units in the system	$P_n = \rho^n(1 - \rho)$	$P_3 = \left(\dfrac{2}{3}\right)^3 \left(1 - \dfrac{2}{3}\right) = 0.099$
Probability of k or more units in the system	$P_{n \geq k} = \rho^k$	$P_{n \geq 3} = \left(\dfrac{2}{3}\right)^3 = 0.296$
Mean system length	$L = \dfrac{\lambda}{\mu - \lambda}$	$= \dfrac{1/12}{1/8 - 1/12} = 2$ ships in harbor
Mean queue length	$L_q = \rho L$	$= \dfrac{2}{3} \times 2 = \dfrac{4}{3}$ ships waiting
Mean time in system	$W = \dfrac{1}{\mu - \lambda} = \dfrac{L}{\lambda}$	$= \dfrac{1}{1/8 - 1/12} = 24$ hours per ship
Mean waiting time	$W_q = \dfrac{\rho}{(\mu - \lambda)} = \rho W$	$= \dfrac{2}{3} \times 24 = 16$ hours per ship
Total waiting time	$W_q \times$ total arrivals	$= 16$ hours $\times$ 14 ships $= 224$ hours

The total cost per week is calculated as follows:

Demurrage:	224 hours × \$600/hour	= \$134,400
Operation:	112 hours × \$1,200/hour	= \$134,400
	Total cost	= \$268,800

Mr. Reed found the first week's account of unloading operations somewhat unsettling in that there was as much cost for demurrage as for operation. Also, the shipping companies had complained because their crews were getting unruly while waiting in Thule. There is a saying, "If you find out that you have only a month to live, spend it in Thule. It will seem like a lifetime."

Mr. Reed gently reminded Lafe that his future would be much more pleasant if he found a way to reduce costs in the unloading operation. Lafe took his favorite uncle's advice to heart and told Barney to come up with better alternatives by morning.

Since days in Thule are quite long in the open season, Barney had time to gather information on three alternative systems. The primary cause of unloading delay appeared to be the pumping system. It was true that the tankers arrived in a most haphazard manner, but TOPSI had no control over arrivals.

The existing dock facility allowed only one ship to berth at a time. Barney gathered information on three proposals, each involving a different pump arrangement. Pump reliability was related to cost, and since Barney was attempting to develop a cost-effective operation, he conducted the following analysis with the objective of minimizing total cost:

Pump System	Capacity (barrels/hour)	Cost of Operating per Hour	Distribution of Service Time
Brand X	1 × 60,000	$2,100	Normal: $\sigma_\mu = 3.5$
Brand Y	1 × 60,000	$2,400	Constant: $\sigma_\mu = 0$
Brand Z	2 × 30,000	$1,800	Erlang ($k = 2$): $\sigma_\mu = 5.63$
Existing	1 × 60,000	$1,200	Exponential: $\sigma_\mu = 8$

Barney brushed the snow off his quantitative methods book and analytically examined the expected outcome of the three alternatives. As a check, he developed distributions of service times conforming to the three alternatives, and examined the expected outcome of each alternative against the first week's distribution of arrival times. We will now look at three queuing models, each using a different distribution of service time.

$(M/GI/1){:}(FCFS/\infty/\infty)$

This model makes the same assumptions as the previous model but expands the service time distribution to include any kind of distribution—normal, beta, Poisson, negative exponential, or any other distribution with a known mean $(1/\mu)$ and standard deviation (σ).

Casette A6.3   Operation Thule—Pump X

Barney's analysis of the Brand X pump, with normally distributed service time, is presented in Table A6.3.

Table A6.3   Operation Thule—Pump X: Poisson Arrival/Normal Service ($\sigma_\mu = 3.5$)

Ship	Arrival Hour	Service Begins	Service Time (hours)	Service Ends	Ship Waiting Time (hours)	Dock Idle Time (hours)	Ships Waiting
Ill Wind	0	0	4	4	0	0	0
Typhoon	9	9	8	17	0	5	0
Zephyr	53	53	5	58	0	36	0
Sirocco	61	61	8	69	0	3	2
Monsoon	64	69	6	75	5	0	1
Whirlwind	66	75	8	83	9	0	2
Gale	76	83	7	90	7	0	1
Tokyo Maru	79	90	12	102	11	0	3
Squall	90	102	10	112	12	0	2
Mistral	93	112	5	117	19	0	2
Simoom	99	117	13	130	18	0	2
Trade Wind	114	130	15	145	16	0	2
Samiel	119	145	3	148	26	0	1
Levanter	138	148	8	156	10	0	0
						12	
End of week	168		112		133	56	

The operating characteristics of this type of waiting line system can be determined with the following formulas, which have been applied to the operations at Thule as an illustration.

Mean arrival rate	λ = given	$= \dfrac{14 \text{ ships}}{168 \text{ hours}} = \dfrac{1 \text{ ship}}{12 \text{ hours}}$
Mean service rate	μ = given	$= \dfrac{14 \text{ ships}}{112 \text{ hours}} = \dfrac{1 \text{ ship}}{8 \text{ hours}}$
Standard deviation	σ_μ = given	$= 3.5$
Server utilization factor	$\rho = \dfrac{\lambda}{\mu}$	$= \dfrac{1/12}{1/8} = \dfrac{2}{3}$
Empty-system probability	$P_0 = 1 - \rho$	$= 1 - \dfrac{2}{3} = \dfrac{1}{3}$
Mean queue length	$L_q = \dfrac{\lambda^2\sigma_\mu^2 + \rho^2}{2(1 - \rho)}$	$= \dfrac{(1/12)^2(3.5)^2 + (2/3)^2}{2(1 - 2/3)} = 0.7943$ ships
Mean system length	$L = \rho + L_q$	$= 2/3 + 0.7943 = 1.461$ ships
Mean waiting time	$W_q = \dfrac{L_q}{\lambda}$	$= \dfrac{0.7943}{1/12} = 9.531$ hours
Mean waiting time	$W = W_q + \dfrac{1}{\mu}$	$= 9.531 + \dfrac{1}{1/8} = 17.531$ hours
Total waiting time	$W_q \times$ total arrivals	$= 9.531 \times 14$ ships $= 133.4$ hours

The total cost per week is calculated as follows:

$$
\begin{array}{llll}
\text{Demurrage:} & 133 \text{ hours} \times \$600/\text{hour} & = & \$\ 79,800 \\
\text{Operation:} & 112 \text{ hours} \times \$2,100/\text{hour} & = & \underline{\$235,200} \\
& & \text{Total cost} = & \$315,000
\end{array}
$$

$(M/D/1):(FCFS/\infty/\infty)$

This model assumes Poisson arrival rates, with constant service time rates. This model is very useful for those applications in which there is no variance in service rate. One example among many might be an analysis of the waiting line system at an automatic car wash. Many services relying on a high degree of automation have deterministic service times.

Casette A6.4   *OPERATION THULE—PUMP Y*

The analysis of the Brand Y pump, with constant service time, is shown in Table A6.4.

The operating characteristics of this type of waiting line system can be determined with the following formulas, which Barney has applied to the Pump Y analysis for Operation Thule.

Table A6.4 *Operation Thule — Pump Y: Poisson Arrival/Constant Service*

Ship	Arrival Hour	Service Begins	Service Time (hours)	Service Ends	Ship Waiting Time (hours)	Dock Idle Time (hours)	Ships Waiting
Ill Wind	0	0	8	8	0	0	0
Typhoon	9	9	8	17	0	1	0
Zephyr	53	53	8	61	0	36	0
Sirocco	61	61	8	69	0	0	2
Monsoon	64	69	8	77	5	0	1
Whirlwind	66	77	8	85	11	0	2
Gale	76	85	8	93	9	0	2
Tokyo Maru	79	93	8	101	14	0	3
Squall	90	101	8	109	11	0	2
Mistral	93	109	8	117	16	0	2
Simoom	99	117	8	125	18	0	2
Trade Wind	114	125	8	133	11	0	1
Samiel	119	133	8	141	14	0	1
Levanter	138	141	8	149	11	0	0
End of week	168		112		112	56	

Mean arrival rate	λ = given	= 1 ship/12 hours
Mean service rate	μ = given	= 1 ship/8 hours
Standard deviation	$\sigma_\mu = 0$	= 0
Server utilization factor	$\rho = \dfrac{\lambda}{\mu}$	$= \dfrac{1/12}{1/8} = \dfrac{2}{3}$
Empty-system probability	$P_0 = 1 - \dfrac{\lambda}{\mu}$	$= 1 - \dfrac{2}{3} = \dfrac{1}{3}$
Mean queue length	$L_q = \dfrac{\rho^2}{2(1 - \rho)}$	$= \dfrac{(2/3)^2}{2(1 - 2/3)} = \dfrac{2}{3}$ ship
Mean system length	$L = L_q + \rho$	$= \dfrac{2}{3} + \dfrac{2}{3} = \dfrac{4}{3}$ ships
Mean waiting time	$W_q = \dfrac{L_q}{\lambda}$	$= \dfrac{2/3}{1/12} = 8$ hours
Mean time in system	$W = W_q + \dfrac{1}{\mu}$	$= 8 + \dfrac{1}{1/8} = 16$ hours
Total waiting time	$W_q \times$ total arrivals	= 8 hours $\times$ 14 ships = 112 hours

The total cost per week is calculated as follows:

$$\begin{aligned} \text{Demurrage:} \quad &112 \text{ hours} \times \$600/\text{hr} = \$\ 67{,}200 \\ \text{Operation:} \quad &112 \text{ hours} \times \$2{,}400/\text{hr} = \underline{\$268{,}800} \\ &\text{Total cost} = \$336{,}000 \end{aligned}$$

$(M/E_k/1):(FCFS/\infty/\infty)$

This model includes service times following the Erlang distribution, and it has proved to be highly useful in practice because of the flexibility of the service distribution. We should remember that the negative exponential and constant service distributions are special cases of the Erlang distribution, with k parameters of 1 and 0 respectively.

To analyze the operating characteristics for the Erlang service time model, we can set $\sigma^2 = 1/k\mu^2$ and use the model for arbitrary service times:

Casette A6.5 *OPERATION THULE—PUMP Z*

Barney worked up an analysis for the Brand Z pump as shown in Table A6.5.

Table A6.5 *Operation Thule—Pump Z: Poisson Arrival/Erlang Service (k = 2)*

Ship	Arrival Hour	Service Begins	Service Time (hours)	Service Ends	Ship Waiting Time (hours)	Dock Idle Time (hours)	Ships Waiting
Ill Wind	0	0	6	6	0	0	0
Typhoon	9	9	7	16	0	3	0
Zephyr	53	53	11	64	0	37	1
Sirocco	61	64	5	69	3	0	2
Monsoon	64	69	4	73	5	0	1
Whirlwind	66	73	21	94	7	0	·4
Gale	76	94	6	100	18	0	4
Tokyo Maru	79	100	3	103	21	0	3
Squall	90	103	10	113	13	0	2
Mistral	93	113	8	121	20	0	3
Simoom	99	121	19	140	22	0	3
Trade Wind	114	140	3	143	26	0	2
Samiel	119	143	4	147	24	0	1
Levanter	135	147	5	152	9	0	0
						16	
End of week	168		112		168	56	

On the basis of this analysis, he calculated the weekly operation cost as follows:

Mean arrival rate	λ = given	= 1 ship/12 hours
Mean service rate	μ = given	= 1 ship/8 hours
Variance	$\alpha^2 = \dfrac{1}{k\mu^2}$	$= \dfrac{1}{2(1/8)^2} = 32$
Server utilization factor	$\rho = \dfrac{\lambda}{\mu}$	$= \dfrac{1/12}{1/8} = \dfrac{2}{3}$
Empty-system probability	$P_0 = 1 - \rho$	$= 1 - \dfrac{2}{3} = \dfrac{1}{3}$

$$\text{Mean queue length} \qquad L_q = \frac{(k+1)\rho^2}{2k(1-\rho)} \qquad = \frac{(2+1)(2/3)^2}{2 \times 2(1-2/3)} = 1 \text{ ship}$$

$$\text{Mean system length} \qquad L = L_q + \rho \qquad = 1 + \frac{2}{3} = 1.67 \text{ ships}$$

$$\text{Mean waiting time} \qquad W_q = \frac{(k+1)\rho}{2k(\mu-\lambda)} = \frac{L_q}{\lambda} \qquad = \frac{1}{1/12} = 12 \text{ hours}$$

$$\text{Mean time in system} \qquad W = W_q + \frac{1}{\mu} \qquad = 12 + 8 = 20 \text{ hours}$$

$$\text{Total waiting time} \qquad W_q \times \text{total arrivals} \qquad = 12 \text{ hours} \times 14 \text{ ships} = 168 \text{ hours}$$

The total cost per week is calculated as follows:

$$\text{Demurrage:} \quad 168 \text{ hours} \times \$\ 600 = \$100{,}800$$
$$\text{Operation:} \quad 112 \text{ hours} \times \$1{,}800 = \underline{\$201{,}600}$$
$$\text{Total cost} = \$302{,}400$$

Barney prepared a recap of his analysis of available pump alternatives for Lafe, summarized as follows:

Pump System	Service Time Distribution (σ_μ)	Ship Waiting Time per Week	Demurrage ($600/hour)	Operating Cost/Hour	Operating Cost (112 hours)	Total Expected Cost
Brand X	Normal (3.5)	133	$ 79,800	$2,100	$235,200	$315,000
Brand Y	Constant (0)	112	67,200	2,400	268,800	336,000
Brand Z	Erlang (5.6)	168	100,800	1,800	201,600	302,400
Existing	Exponential (8)	224	134,400	1,200	134,400	268,800

This analysis indicated that the excessive cost of operating more reliable pumping systems outweighed the expected gains in reducing demurrage. Lafe relayed the analysis to Mr. Reed, who, when presented with the costs of reducing the tanker waiting time, responded by sending Thule four Ping-Pong tables to keep unruly mariners occupied.

$(M/M/1){:}(FCFS/m/\infty)$

This model is the same as the classical model we investigated earlier, with the added restriction of a limited queue. The model is very useful in practice, both for those cases where waiting is actually limited and for those cases that experience a high degree of balking activity by potential customers when there are waiting lines of some length.

We must modify our model to consider the limited length of waiting lines. For this model, the service rate does *not* have to exceed the arrival rate ($\mu > \lambda$) for us to obtain steady-state conditions.

Casette A6.6 THE ICELAND CONNECTION

With the passage of summer, tanker captains averted mutinous action from overexposure to Thule by exchanging radio messages. If two tankers were already in the harbor at Thule, other inbound tankers would divert to the more comfortable climes of Iceland.

The operating characteristics for this type of system, with the results of the tankers' reaction limiting the queue, follow:

Mean arrival rate	λ = given	= 1 ship/12 hours
Mean service rate	μ = given	= 1 ship/8 hours
Maximum in system	m = given	= 2 ships
Potential maximum server utilization factor	$\rho = \dfrac{\lambda}{\mu}$	$= \dfrac{1/12}{1/8} = \dfrac{2}{3}$
Empty-system probability	$P_0 = \dfrac{1 - \rho}{1 - (\rho)^{m+1}}$	$= \dfrac{1 - 2/3}{1 - (2/3)^3} = 0.4737$
Server utilization factor	$= 1 - P_0$	$= 1 - 0.4737 = 0.5263$
Lost customer probability	$P_m = P_0 \rho^m$	$= (0.4737)(2/3)^2 = 0.2105$
Probability of n units in the system	$P_n = P_0 \rho^n$ for $n \leq m$	$P_1 = (0.4737)(2/3) = 0.3158$ $P_2 = (0.4737)(2/3) = 0.2105$
Probability of k or more units in the system	$P_{n \geq k} = 1 - \displaystyle\sum_{n=0}^{k-1} P_n$	
Mean system length	$L = \dfrac{\lambda \mu}{1 - \lambda \mu} - \dfrac{(m + 1)(\rho)^{m+1}}{1 - (\rho)^{m+1}}$	= 0.74 ship
Mean queue length	$L_q = L - \dfrac{\lambda(1 - P_m)}{\mu}$	= 0.21 ship
Mean time in system	$W = \dfrac{L}{\lambda(1 - P_m)}$	= 11.2 hours
Mean waiting time	$W_q = W - \dfrac{1}{\mu}$	= 11.2 − 8 = 3.2 hours

Of 14 ships bound for Thule, 21.05 percent are "lost" or diverted. Thus, 78.95 percent continue, for an average of 11.05 ships per week arriving at Thule.

The total cost per week is calculated as follows:

Demurrage: 11.05 ships $\times$ 3.2 hours $\times$ $600 = \$ 21,216

Operation: (since crew costs are unchanged)   = \$134,400

Total cost = \$155,616

With the 78.95 percent productivity level, the total cost of $155,616 is the equivalent of $197,107 cost at the full operation level. This result actually provided a benefit to TOPSI, because demurrage was reduced more than productivity fell. Because the reduction in production bolstered the market, Mr. Reed sent his nephew Lafe a hearty thank-you note.

(M/M/1):(FCFS/∞/m)

This model allows consideration of limited calling populations. The probabilities of arrival in this model depend on the number of customers already in the system. This model assumes that the exponential distribution can be used to describe both the time spent outside the system between services and the service times, with means of $1/\lambda$ and $1/\mu$ respectively. An important distinction between this model and the other models presented is that λ is defined as the mean arrival rate for *each* customer, rather than for all customers. Included in the model is the consideration that a customer cannot arrive while already being served. This model is typically employed in machine breakdown analyses.

Casette A6.7   *END OF OPEN-SEA SEASON AT THULE*

Deep into the open-sea season, there was a cutback in the number of companies renewing contracts to deliver crude oil to Thule. Only the braver (or more desperate) risked the oncoming ice. Barney found that there were only six tankers in the Atlantic that would schedule delivery. This obviated the limited queue length, and any queue length up to the maximum of five was possible. Of course, there usually was no waiting line. The rate of arrivals declined, on average, to one every 48 hours. This meant that only 3.5 ships arrived per week, one-fourth the usual number. As a result, the pumping system was operating at only one-sixth of capacity. The mean arrival rate for each ship became once every 288 hours (48 hours between arrivals times six ships in the system); each ship thus spent 280 hours away from the pump during a complete cycle lasting 288 hours.

The operating characteristics for this type of system, as well as the results for Thule, considering the above changes in the situation, are:

Mean arrival rate for each customer	$\lambda^* $ = given	= 1/48
Mean service rate	μ = given	= 1 ship/8 hours

Population size	$N = $ given	$= 6$

Probability that a given customer will enter service during a given time period

$$\lambda = \frac{\mu\lambda^*}{N\mu - \lambda^*}$$

$= 0.00357$ or $1/280$

Empty-system probability

$$P_0 = \frac{1}{\displaystyle\sum_{n=0}^{N} \frac{N!}{(N - n)!} \left(\frac{\lambda}{\mu}\right)^n}$$

$= 0.83406$

Probability of n units in the system

$$P_n = \frac{N!}{(N - n)!} \left(\frac{\lambda}{\mu}\right)^n P_0 \; (n \leq N)$$

$P_1 = 0.14298$
$P_2 = 0.02043$
$P_3 = 0.002334$
$P_4 = 0.0002001$
$P_5 = 0.00001143$
$P_6 = 0.00000033$

Probability of k or more units in the system

$$P_{n \geq k} = 1 - \sum_{n=0}^{k-1} P_n$$

Mean queue length

$$L_q = N - \frac{\lambda + \mu}{\lambda} (1 - P_0)$$

$= 0.026066$ ship

Mean system length

$$L = L_q + (1 - P_0) = N - \frac{\mu}{\lambda} (1 - P_0)$$

$= 0.192009$ ships

Mean waiting time

$$W_q = \frac{L_q}{(N - L)\lambda}$$

$= 1.26$ hours

Mean time in system

$$W = W_q + \frac{1}{\mu}$$

$= 9.26$ hours

Total waiting time

$W_q \times$ total arrivals

$= 1.26 \times 3.5$
$= 4.398$ hours/week

With one ship arriving every 48 hours, $\dfrac{168}{48} = 3.5$ ships would arrive every week. The total cost per week is calculated as follows:

Demurrage:	1.26 hours $\times$ 3.5 ships $\times$ \$600 $=$	\$ 2,646
Operations:		\$134,400
	Total cost $=$	\$137,046

At the 25 percent productivity level, the total cost of $137,046 is the equivalent of $548,184 cost at the full operation level. When Mr. Reed saw the equivalent cost of operating, he became extremely concerned with tanker safety and closed down operations at Thule for the winter.

$(M/M/s):(FCFS/\infty/\infty)$

This model allows consideration of multiple-channel servers. It is extremely useful in cost analysis that compares alternative service systems, for it allows us to predict the impact of adding servers.

In this model, we will assume Poisson arrivals and exponential service times. Arrivals are assumed to come from an infinite pool of customers. There is no limit to the length of the queue. Service is first-come, first-served. Other conditions would require model modifications.

The mean effective service rate for the system is $s(\mu)$, where s is equal to the number of servers. Here, again, we have to have $s\mu$ exceed the customer arrival rate, λ. We assume that the service time distribution for each server is the same.

Casette A6.8 **PLANNING FOR THE NEW SEASON AT THULE**

Since operations were shut down for the winter, Lafe kept Barney occupied with analysis of the coming summer's operations. TOPSI had found the rewards for providing fuel to New England to be great. Mr. Reed obtained a larger share of the market, and operations for the coming year were to be doubled.

The arrival rate of tankers at Thule was to be one every 6 hours, or 28 ships per week. Clearly, the existing unloading system, with capacity of unloading a tanker every 8 hours on average, was inadequate. Lafe had developed the dock system so that up to four berths were possible. This allowed Mr. Reed to assure shippers that diversion of tankers was no longer necessary. Barney was assigned the task of determining how many pumping systems TOPSI should install at Thule. Each system would be similar to the existing one, costing $134,400 per week to operate.

Steady-state operating characteristics for this multiple-server model follow, with an analysis of the three possible pumping systems at Thule. Because calculations of P_0 can become quite involved, published tables of P_0 for various combinations of $\lambda/s\mu$ have been made available. Such a table is reproduced here as Appendix 5.

Number of servers	s = given		= 2	3	4
Mean arrival rate	λ = given		= 1/6		
Mean service rate	μ = given		= 1/8		
Server utilization factor	$\rho = \dfrac{\lambda}{s\mu}$		= 2/3	4/9	1/3

Empty-system probability	$P_0 = \dfrac{1}{\left[\displaystyle\sum_{n=0}^{s-1} \dfrac{(\lambda/\mu)^n}{n!}\right] + \left[\dfrac{(\lambda/\mu)^s}{s!(1 - \lambda/s\mu)}\right]}$		= 0.2	0.2542	0.2621

Probability of n units in the system
$$P_n = \frac{(\lambda/\mu)^n}{n!} P_0 \ (\text{if } n \le s)$$

$$P_n = \frac{(\lambda/\mu)^n}{s!s^{(n-s)}} P_0 \ (\text{if } n > s)$$

Probability of k or more units in the system
$$P_{n \ge k} = 1 - \sum_{n=0}^{k-1} P_n$$

Mean queue length	$L_q = \dfrac{P_0(\lambda/\mu)^s \rho}{s!(1 - \rho)^2}$	ships =	1.067	0.145	0.0259
Mean system length	$L = L_q + \dfrac{\lambda}{\mu}$	ships =	2.4	1.478	1.359
Mean waiting time	$W_q = \dfrac{L_q}{\lambda}$	hours =	6.4	0.87	0.155
Mean time in system	$W = W_q + \dfrac{1}{\mu}$	hours =	14.4	8.87	8.155
Total waiting time	$W_q \times$ total arrivals	hours =	179.2	24.36	4.34

The total weekly cost to operate the Thule dock with the different quantities of pumping systems follows.

	s = 2	s = 3	s = 4
Demurrage ($600 × W_q)	$107,520	$14,616	$2,604
Operations ($134,400 × s)	268,800	403,200	537,600
	$376,320	$417,816	$540,204

Therefore, TOPSI prepared for the oncoming season, looking forward to a prosperous year with two unloading systems. Table A6.6 on page 776 presents a summary of the operating characteristics and formulas for the various waiting line models we have discussed.

Table A6.6 Operating Characteristics and Formulas for Various Queuing Models

	(M/M/1):(FCFS/∞/∞)	(M/G/1):(FCFS/∞/∞)	(M/D/1):(FCFS/∞/∞)	(M/E_k/1):(FCFS/∞/∞)	(M/M/1):(FCFS/m/∞)	(M/M/1):(FCFS/∞/m)	(M/M/s):(FCFS/∞/∞)
Arrival distribution	Poisson	Poisson	Poisson	Poisson	Poisson	Poisson	Poisson
Service distribution	Exponential	Arbitrary	Constant	Erlang	Exponential	Exponential	Exponential
σ_μ^2	$1/\mu^2$	σ^2	0	$1/k\mu^2$	$1/\mu^2$	$1/\mu^2$	$1/\mu^2$
Servers	1	1	1	1	1	1	s
Queue limit	∞	∞	∞	∞	m	∞	∞
Population	∞	∞	∞	∞	∞	m	∞
Service stages	1	1	1	k	1	1	1
ρ	λ/μ	λ/μ	λ/μ	λ/μ	λ/μ	λ/μ	$\lambda/s\mu$
P_0	$1-\rho$	$1-\rho$	$1-\rho$	$1-\rho$	$\dfrac{1-\rho}{1-\rho^{m+1}}$	$\dfrac{1}{\displaystyle\sum_{n=0}^{N}\frac{N!}{(N-n)!}\,\rho^n}$	$\dfrac{1}{\displaystyle\sum_{n=0}^{s-1}\frac{(\lambda/\mu)^n}{n!} + \frac{(\lambda/\mu)^s}{s!(1-\lambda/s\mu)}}$
P_n	$(1-\rho)\rho^n$	$(1-\rho)\rho^n$	$(1-\rho)\rho^n$	$(1-\rho)\rho^n$	$P_0(\rho)^n$	$\dfrac{N!}{(N-n)!}\,\rho^n P_0$	If $n \le s$, $\dfrac{(\lambda/\mu)^n}{n!}P_0$; If $n > s$, $\dfrac{(\lambda/\mu)^n}{s!\,s^{(n-s)}}P_0$
$P_{n \ge k}$	ρ^k	$1-\displaystyle\sum_{n=0}^{k-1}P_n$	$1-\displaystyle\sum_{n=0}^{k-1}P_n$	$1-\displaystyle\sum_{n=0}^{k-1}P_n$	$1-\displaystyle\sum_{n=0}^{k-1}P_n$	$1-\displaystyle\sum_{n=0}^{k-1}P_n$	$1-\displaystyle\sum_{n=0}^{k-1}P_n$
L	$\dfrac{\lambda}{\mu-\lambda}$	$L_q + \rho$	$L_q + \rho$	$L_q + \rho$	$\dfrac{\rho}{1-\rho} - \dfrac{(m+1)\rho^{(m+1)}}{1-\rho^{(m+1)}}$	$L_q + (1-P_0)$	$L_q + \dfrac{\lambda}{\mu}$
L_q	$\dfrac{\lambda^2}{\mu(\mu-\lambda)}$	$\dfrac{\lambda^2\sigma_\mu^2 + \rho^2}{2(1-\rho)}$	$\dfrac{\rho^2}{2(1-\rho)}$	$\dfrac{(k+1)\rho^2}{2k(1-\rho)}$	$L - \dfrac{\lambda(1-P_m)}{\mu}$	$N - \dfrac{\lambda+\mu}{\lambda}(1-P_0)$	$\dfrac{P_0(\lambda/\mu)^s\rho}{s!(1-\rho)^2}$
W	$\dfrac{1}{\mu-\lambda}$	$W_q + \dfrac{1}{\mu}$	$W_q + \dfrac{1}{\mu}$	$W_q + \dfrac{1}{\mu}$	$\dfrac{L}{\lambda(1-P_m)}$	$W_q + \dfrac{1}{\mu}$	$W_q + \dfrac{1}{\mu}$
W_q	$\dfrac{\rho}{\mu-\lambda}$	$\dfrac{L_q}{\lambda}$	$\dfrac{L_q}{\lambda}$	$\dfrac{(k+1)\rho}{2k(\mu-\lambda)}$	$W - \dfrac{1}{\mu}$	$\dfrac{L_q}{(N-L)\lambda}$	$\dfrac{L_q}{\lambda}$

Appendix 7   GAME THEORY

Decision making is not restricted to only one individual. In many real-world situations, a decision maker is engaged in a competitive decision game such as bidding for a contract. Such an environment is decision making under the condition of conflict. Game theory is primarily concerned with decision-making strategies that may be applied in such situations. The primary objective in a game situation is to develop plans of action to win in the competition with an opponent. In this appendix, we will study several game situations and different strategies in such situations.

THE NATURE AND TYPES OF GAMES

Most management science techniques that we have studied in this book are oriented toward aiding an individual decision maker in an organization. We have assumed that there is no competitive or conflict situation. However, in many real-world situations parties are competing for different outcomes or consequences. We are all familiar with many athletic games where one person (or team) wins at the expense of others through competitive action plans. In game theory, a number of mathematical techniques can be used in selecting the best course of action.

One primary difference between game theory and decision theory is that in game theory the decision maker competes with other intelligent opponents. In decision theory, there is no such competitor except the passive states of nature. Game theory dates back to 1944 when John von Neumann and Oscar Morgenstern published their classic book, *Theory of Games and Economic Behavior*. The book has received much praise as a landmark in decision theory. However, practical application of game theory to real-world decision problems under the condition of conflict has been very limited.

The most important contribution of game theory is its conceptual framework for analyzing competitive situations where competing players use logical thought processes to determine optimum strategies for winning. Game situations can be classified by two criteria: (1) the number of *players*, or competing decision makers; and (2) the outcome of the game in terms of each player's gains and losses.

A game situation which involves only two players is a *two-person game*. Two-person games may involve war games, card games, management-labor negotiations, and the like. When the game situation consists of more than two players, it is referred to as an *n-person game*.

Games can be classified according to the outcome or stake of the game. If the sum of the players' gains and losses equals 0, the game is a *zero-sum game*. In other words, one person's gains should exactly equal the other person's loss. Suppose that two players are playing a poker game. If one player won $25 from the game, the other player's loss should be exactly equal to $25. Thus, the sum of gains and losses will be $25 − 25 = 0. If the sum of one player's gains does not equal the sum of the other player's losses, the game is referred to as a *nonzero-sum game*. For example, in an expanding market of microcomputers, the sum of market gains and losses of various computer firms may not equal 0.

Game theory can be complex, depending on the number of players and varying outcome situations. The simplest form of game theory is the *two-person, zero-sum game*—this appendix considers this particular game situation. This will serve as an introduction to the nature of game theory. More involved game situations are described in numerous advanced texts of management science, including those listed as references at the end of this appendix.

THE TWO-PERSON, ZERO-SUM GAME

Two-person, zero-sum games are relevant in many real-world situations, including (1) management-labor negotiations for new union contracts; (2) two political parties competing for a vacant legislative seat; (3) two competing stores trying to gain customers; (4) an athlete negotiating with a ball club. To demonstrate the game situation, let us consider the following casette.

Casette A7.1   *FLEET THE FOOT*

Anthony Fleet is an All-American football player at Pacific Central University. Tony, as he is known to his friends, is a special-team player. He is a place-kicker who has recently broken the NCAA records for the longest field goal (72 yards) and the most field goals in one season (48). Thus, Tony is known to the fans as Fleet the Foot.

Fleet is a graduating senior, and he was drafted in the second round by the Kansas City Jays. Fleet hired a New York agent to represent him in the contract negotiations. The agent has been meeting with the Jays' vice-president for personnel during the past several months. The negotiating process is complex. The ball club has proposed several package deals including a mixture of a signing bonus, special performance incentives, long-term loans at a very low interest rate, special pensions, insurance coverage for career-threatening injuries, employment opportunities in the ball club after retirement, off-season contracts, and the like. The payoff table for the problem is summarized in Table A7.1.

Table A7.1 is organized so that the player who attempts to maximize the outcome of the game is on the left (row-wise) and the player who attempts to minimize the outcome is on the top (column-wise). Fleet attempts to maximize the outcome, and thus he can be regarded as the offensive player. The ball club attempts to minimize the outcome, becoming the defensive player. In game theory, we must accept the assumption, although unrealistic, that the payoff table is known to both players.

Table A7.1   Payoff Table for Fleet the Foot

Athlete's Strategies	Ball Club's Strategies		
	A	B	C
1	$500,000	$400,000	$550,000
2	600,000	350,000	450,000

Each player in a game situation has two or more strategies from which only one is selected. A *strategy* is a course of action open to a player. In Table A7.1, Fleet has two strategies available to him (1 and 2) and the ball club has three strategies open to it (A, B, and C). The payoff table is quite similar to ones we had in decision theory (Chapter 9).

Fleet has two strategies that represent different types of contracts. The ball club's strategies also represent different contract proposals. The outcomes are in terms of present value equivalents in dollars. For example, if Fleet selects strategy 2 and the ball club selects strategy B, the outcome is a $350,000 gain for Fleet and a $350,000 loss for the ball club. The sum of the two outcomes is 0: $350,000 − $350,000 = 0. The amount of the outcome, $350,000, is the *value of the game*.

For each player, the purpose of the game is to select the strategy which will result in the best outcome regardless of the opponent's strategy. Such a best strategy is often known as the *optimum strategy*.

Pure Strategy Games

In certain game situations, the optimum strategy each player selects will always be the same regardless of the opponent's actions. This is called a *pure strategy* game. In a pure strategy game situation, the value of the game is exactly the same for both players. If the game is played a number of times and the players adopt a mixture of strategies, a *mixed strategy* game situation exists.

A pure strategy game can be solved based on the *minimax* criterion, which we discussed in decision theory (Chapter 9). In minimax, the decision maker attempts to minimize the maximum possible loss. The offensive player selects the strategy which will result in the largest of the minimum payoffs, or adopts the *maximin* strategy. The defensive player, however, selects the strategy which will result in the smallest of the maximum payoffs, adopting the *minimax* strategy.

In our casette problem, Fleet selects the maximin strategy to choose between the two strategies open to him. The minimum payoff for strategy 1 is $400,000, as opposed to $350,000 for strategy 2, as circled in Table A7.2. The maximum of these two minimum payoffs is $400,000. Thus, Fleet will select strategy 1. However, the ball club uses the minimax criterion. The maximum payoffs for each of the three strategies are: A, $600,000; B, $400,000; and C, $550,000, as indicated by the boxes in Table A7.2. The minimum among these three maximum payoffs is $400,000 for strategy B. The value of the game is thus $400,000, which is the payoff for Fleet and also the loss to the ball club. This value is indicated by both a circle (Fleet) and a box (the ball club).

Table A7.2   *Payoff Table with Maximin and Minimax Strategies*

Athlete's Strategies	Ball Club's Strategies		
	A	B	C
1	$500,000	$400,000	$550,000
2	600,000	350,000	450,000

☐ *Athlete's maximin choice*

◯ *Ball Club's minimax choice*

Table A7.3   *Payoff Table and Dominated Strategies*

Athlete's Strategies	Ball Club's Strategies		
	A	B	C
1		$400,000	
2		350,000	

Dominant Strategy Games

The *dominance* criterion was discussed in decision theory (Chapter 9). A choice is said to be dominated by another choice when the outcomes of the second choice are better than that of the first choice under every state of nature. In the context of game theory, a strategy dominates another when the payoffs of the first strategy are better than the corresponding payoffs of the second strategy.

In our example, for the Kansas City Jays, strategy B dominates strategies A and C. In Table A7.3, we eliminated strategies A and C. Thus, the only strategy left for the ball club is strategy B. Consequently, Fleet will select strategy 1. The optimum strategy selected by each player results in the same payoff value of $400,000. This value of the game resulting from a pure strategy is known as an *equilibrium point* or *saddle point*. An equilibrium point is a payoff that is simultaneously the minimum for a row and the maximum for a column; $400,000 in row 1 and column B in Table A7.3 is the saddle point.

Mixed Strategy Games

When the players use the maximin and minimax criteria for a game and still find no equilibrium point, they are playing a mixed strategy game. Let us consider the following casette problem.

Casette A7.2   *K'S RESTAURANT*

K's Restaurant is a family style restaurant featuring home-cooked meals established by Mrs. Kaye Dwark. The restaurant has built a fine reputation and a group of regular customers. However, 6 months ago another family eatery, South Street Diner, opened for business only one block from K's. Since then, fierce competition has resulted between the two restaurants.

K's Restaurant introduced a new menu, a special Sunday brunch, discounts for senior citizens and children, and new home-baked pies. South Street Diner countered K's offensive by advertising in the local newspaper, with discount coupons, the Saturday "All-You-Can-Eat" special and "Kids Eat Free" when accompanied by an adult.

The two restaurants' payoff table is provided in Table A7.4. The values in the table represent the percentage changes in their market share. The first thing we should check is whether we can simplify the table by using the dominance test. For K's Restaurant, strategy 1 dominates strategy 3. Thus, we can eliminate row 3 from the table. For South Street Diner, strategy B dominates strategy C. Now, the payoff table is much simplified as shown in Table A7.5.

The next step is to apply the maximin criterion for K's Restaurant. The minimum payoff for strategy 1 is 3 percent, and for strategy 2, it is 2 percent. Thus, the optimum strategy for K's is strategy 1 as shown in Table A7.6.

Next, for South Street Diner's strategies, we apply the minimax criterion. The maximum payoff for strategy A is 4 percent, and it is 8 percent for strategy B. The minimum value between the two maximum payoffs is 0.04. Thus, the optimum strategy for South Street Diner is strategy A as shown in Table A7.7.

Table A7.4   *Payoff Table for the Restaurants*

	South Street Diner's Strategies		
K's Strategies	**A**	**B**	**C**
1	4	3	5
2	2	8	9
3	4	2	2

Table A7.5   *Payoff Table after the Dominance Test*

	South Street Diner's Strategies	
K's Strategies	**A**	**B**
1	4	3
2	2	8

Table A7.6   *Payoff Table for K's Maximin Criterion*

	South Street Diner's Strategies	
K's Strategies	**A**	**B**
1	4	③
2	②	8

Table A7.7   Loss Table for South Street Diner's Minimax Criterion

	South Street Diner's Strategies	
K's Strategies	A	B
1	[4]	3
2	2	[8]

Table A7.8   Optimum Strategies for the Restaurants

	South Street Diner's Strategies	
K's Strategies	A	B
1	[4] ⟶ ③
2	2 ⟵ 8

The optimum strategies for K's Restaurant and South Street Diner are indicated in Table A7.8. It is clear in Table A7.8 that there is no equilibrium point for this problem. Thus, this is not a pure strategy game but a mixed strategy game.

Normally, K's Restaurant selects strategy 1 to maximize its market share increase. South Street Diner selects strategy A to minimize K's market share increase. However, when K's selects strategy 1, South Street Diner will select strategy B instead so as to minimize the market share gain of K's to only 3 percent. When South Street Diner selects strategy B, K's will not stay with strategy 1. It will swiftly select strategy 2 to increase its market share to 8 percent. Then, South Street Diner would select strategy A to reduce K's market increase to only 2 percent. Thus, we make a complete circle as shown in Table A7.8.

Several techniques have been suggested for solving mixed strategy games. We will study two: the expected outcome approach and linear programming.

Expected Outcome Approach

The basic philosophy of this approach is that in a mixed strategy game, each player can develop a plan of strategies in such a way that the expected outcome (gain) for the offensive player and the expected outcome (loss) of the defensive player will be the same, regardless of the opponent's strategies. This approach is exactly the same as the expected value approach which we discussed in decision theory (Chapter 9). As a vehicle to discuss the expected outcome approach, let us go back to the K's Restaurant problem presented as Casette A7.2. K's Restaurant attempts to develop a plan of mixed strategies that will be implemented regardless of what South Street Diner does. To determine the expected outcome for each player, we need to define the probabilities that each player will select each strategy. For K's Restaurant, we can define the following probabilities:

$$P = \text{probability that K's will select strategy 1}$$
$$1 - P = \text{probability that K's will select strategy 2}$$

First, let us assume that South Street Diner will select strategy A. In such a case, the expected outcome for K's will be, based on the information given in Table A7.8:

$$\text{Expected outcome (K's)} = 4P + 2(1 - P)$$
$$= 2 + 2P$$

Next, let us assume that South Street Diner will select strategy B. Then, the expected outcome for K's will be:

$$\text{Expected outcome (K's)} = 3P + 8(1 - P)$$
$$= 8 - 5P$$

Since our goal in developing a plan of mixed strategies is to obtain the same expected outcome regardless of the opponent's actions, the expected outcome for K's should be exactly the same whether South Street Diner selects strategy A or strategy B. Thus, we can equate the two outcomes as follows:

$$2 + 2P = 8 - 5P$$
$$7P = 6$$
$$P = 0.8571$$

The probability of selecting strategy 1 on the part of K's Restaurant should be 0.8571. Consequently, the probability of using strategy 2 is $(1 - P) = 0.1429$. The expected outcome in terms of the gain in market share for K's will be, in the case of South Street Diner taking strategy A:

$$\text{Expected gain (K's)} = 0.8571(4) + 0.1429(2)$$
$$= 3.7142 \cong 3.71 \text{ percent market share gain}$$

We should be getting the same market share gain on the part of K's Restaurant if we assume that South Street Diner will take strategy B.

$$\text{Expected gain (K's)} = 0.8571(3) + 0.1429(8)$$
$$= 3.7145 \cong 3.71 \text{ percent market share gain}$$

As anticipated, the expected market share gain is the same 3.71 percent. We can also evaluate the above computations graphically as shown in Figure A7.1. K's Restaurant's conditional gains are listed vertically for strategy 1 on the left and strategy 2 on the right. Then, if South Street Diner selects strategy A, the conditional payoffs will be 4 for strategy 1 and 2 for strategy 2. We connect these two points by a straight line. We also perform the same operation for the case of South Street Diner selecting strategy B.

On the horizontal axis, we will now list the probability values. For K's Restaurant to be perfectly indifferent, the expected payoff (gain) for K's under strategy A or B on the part of South Street Diner should be exactly equal. This point is where the two lines intersect and $P = 0.8571$; consequently, $1 - P = 0.1429$.

Figure A7.1   Expected Payoff Graph for K's Restaurant

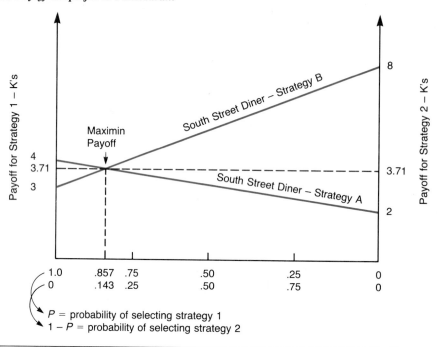

We can also go through the same procedure for the defensive player, South Street Diner. South Street Diner is trying to minimize the loss of market share to K's Restaurant. Let us define the probabilities for South Street Diner as follows:

$$q = \text{probability that South Street Diner will select strategy A}$$

$$1 - q = \text{probability that South Street Diner will select strategy B}$$

If K's Restaurant selects strategy 1, the expected outcome in terms of loss will be

$$4q + (1 - q)3 = 3 + q$$

We also need to compute the expected loss for South Street Diner provided that K's Restaurant selects strategy 2, as follows:

$$2q + (1 - q)8 = 8 - 6q$$

Now, equating the two expected loss functions, we obtain the following:

$$3 + q = 8 - 6q$$
$$7q = 5$$
$$q = 0.7143$$

The probability that South Street Diner will select strategy A is 0.7143. Consequently, the probability that South Street Diner will select strategy B is $1 - q = 1 - 0.7143 = 0.2857$. The expected loss in terms of market share for South Street Diner, given that K's Restaurant selects strategy 1, will be:

Expected loss (South Street Diner) $= 0.7143(4) + 0.2857(3)$

$$= 3.7143 \cong 3.71 \text{ percent market share loss}$$

We should get the same result if K's Restaurant selects strategy 2:

Expected loss (South Street Diner) = 0.7143(2) + 0.2857(8)

= 3.7142 ≅ 3.71 percent market share loss

When South Street Diner employs strategy A about 71 percent of the time and strategy B about 29 percent of the time, the expected market share loss will be about 3.71 percent regardless of what K's Restaurant does. We can also use a graphic approach as shown in Figure A7.2. The intersecting point of the two expected loss lines indicates the point where South Street Diner is indifferent about K's Restaurant choice of strategies. At this point, $q = 0.7143$ and $1 - q = 0.2857$. South Street Diner's expected market loss is 3.71 percent.

Clearly, the expected increase in market share for K's Restaurant and the expected loss in market share for South Street Diner are exactly the same, 3.71 percent. Consequently, the mixed strategies for each restaurant have resulted in an equilibrium point.

The expected outcome based on the mixed strategies is the average value over a long time if decisions are made repeatedly. Each restaurant will never experience a gain or loss of 3.71 percent in market share. Consequently, the expected outcome is always better than the optimum strategy based on the maximin or minimax criterion. For example, the optimum strategy for K's Restaurant based on the maximin criterion resulted in a 3 percent increase in market share, as shown in Table A7.6. Also, the optimum strategy for South Street Diner based on the minimax criterion resulted in a 4 percent loss in market share, as shown in Table A7.7. The expected outcome of 3.71 percent from the mixed strategies is a better outcome for both K's Restaurant and South Street Diner.

Figure A7.2   Expected Loss Graph for South Street Diner

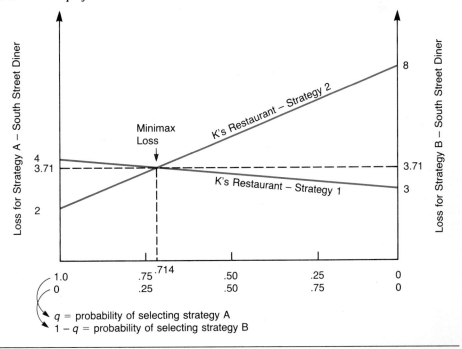

Linear Programming Approach

Although the expected outcome may appear simple to you for Casette A7.2, it may become extremely complex and cumbersome when a large number of strategies are available to the players. For large games, the linear programming approach is an attractive alternative for determining the outcome of the mixed strategies. Nevertheless, formulating a linear programming model for a game is somewhat more complex than the typical model formulation we discussed in Chapter 3.

The K's Restaurant problem we discussed as Casette A7.2 is presented again in Table A7.9. Although this is a simple game, by formulating a linear programming model for this problem we can demonstrate how linear programming can be used for complex games. We will first formulate a linear programming model for K's Restaurant and then formulate the second model for South Street Diner.

Linear Programming Model for K's Restaurant   As the first step in formulating a linear programming model, let us define the following decision variables, one for each strategy open to K's.

$$P_1 = \text{probability of K's selecting strategy 1}$$

$$P_2 = \text{probability of K's selecting strategy 2}$$

Previously, we defined P_2 as $(1 - P_1)$ because we had only two strategies. However, to make the model general enough to handle games that have more than two strategies, we changed the variable notation here. Since the game has two strategies open to South Street Diner, we can formulate two constraints for these two strategies. For each strategy that South Street Diner may select, K's Restaurant attempts to obtain the expected payoff (gain) which is equal to or greater than the value of the game V. Thus, we formulate the following constraints.

$$4P_1 + 2P_2 \geq V \qquad \text{strategy A—South Street Diner}$$

$$3P_1 + 8P_2 \geq V \qquad \text{strategy B—South Street Diner}$$

The value of the game (V) is the expected or average gain for K's when South Street Diner selects strategy A or strategy B. Since K's Restaurant is trying to maximize its gains, the inequality sign indicates "greater than or equal to."

In addition to the two constraints that are based on South Street Diner's selection of strategies, we need a constraint which assures that the sum of the probabilities assigned to selection of strategies should be 1.0. In our problem, there are only two strategies for K's. Thus, the constraint becomes:

$$P_1 + P_2 = 1.0$$

Table A7.9   Payoff Table for the K's Restaurant Game

K's Strategies	South Street Diner's Strategy	
	A	B
1	4	3
2	2	8

The three constraints we have formulated can be further simplified for linear programming solution.

$$\frac{4P_1}{V} + \frac{2P_2}{V} \geq 1$$

$$\frac{3P_1}{V} + \frac{8P_2}{V} \geq 1$$

$$\frac{P_1}{V} + \frac{P_2}{V} = \frac{1}{V}$$

We can redefine our decision variables as follows:

$$x_1 = \frac{P_1}{V}$$

$$x_2 = \frac{P_2}{V}$$

Now, the three simplified constraints are:

$$4x_1 + 2x_2 \geq 1$$

$$3x_1 + 8x_2 \geq 1$$

$$x_1 + x_2 = \frac{1}{V}$$

The objective of this game for K's Restaurant is to maximize the expected gain or the value of the game (V). Thus, the objective function can be either maximize $Z = V$, or, alternatively, minimize $Z = \frac{1}{V}$. For our problem, the minimization problem is much simpler to handle as $\frac{1}{V} = x_1 + x_2$. Consequently, the model becomes:

$$\text{Minimize } Z = x_1 + x_2$$
$$\text{subject to} \quad 4x_1 + 2x_2 \geq 1$$
$$3x_1 + 8x_2 \geq 1$$
$$x_1, x_2 \geq 0$$

Once the solution is derived for the model, we need to convert back the variables as follows:

$$x_1 = \frac{P_1}{V}, P_1 = Vx_1$$

$$x_2 = \frac{P_2}{V}, P_2 = Vx_2$$

Linear Programming Model for South Street Diner   The same basic approach can be used to formulate a linear programming model for South Street Diner. Only two differences exist:

1. Since South Street Diner is a defensive player, it attempts to minimize the expected gain on the part of K's Restaurant. This has the following two consequences. First, the strategy constraints are less-than-or-equal-to types ($\leq$). Second, the objective function is to minimize $Z = V$ or maximize $Z = \dfrac{1}{V}$.

2. The decision variables are defined as follows:

q_1 = probability of South Street Diner selecting strategy A

q_2 = probability of South Street Diner selecting strategy B

$$y_1 = \frac{q_1}{V}$$

$$y_2 = \frac{q_2}{V}$$

Thus, the final linear programming model is:

$$\text{Maximize } Z = y_1 + y_2$$
$$\text{subject to} \quad 4y_1 + 3y_2 \leq 1$$
$$2y_1 + 8y_2 \leq 1$$
$$y_1, y_2 \geq 0$$

When we compare the two linear programming models, clearly K's is the primal model, and the South Street Diner model is the dual model. Thus, once we solve the primal model, we can also obtain the solution to the dual model, as we discussed in Chapter 5.

The computer-based solution for the primal model (K's Restaurant) is provided in Figure A7.3. We can interpret the solution as follows:

$$Z = \frac{1}{V}$$

$$\frac{1}{V} = 0.27$$

$$V = \frac{1}{0.27} = 3.70$$

$$x_1 = \frac{P_1}{V}$$

$$\frac{P_1}{3.70} = 0.23$$

$$P_1 = 0.851$$

$$x_2 = \frac{P_2}{V}$$

$$\frac{P_2}{3.70} = 0.04$$

$$P_2 = 0.148$$

The above results generally correspond with our manual solution presented earlier. Small discrepancies result from the rounded solutions in linear programming. The solution process used values down to only two places below the decimal point, resulting in the rounding errors. Nevertheless, the solution is approximately correct.

Figure A7.3 Linear Programming Solution of the K's Problem

```
PROGRAM: Linear Programming I

***** INPUT DATA ENTERED *****

Min  Z =  1 x 1 + 1 x 2

Subject to:

C 1    4 x 1 + 2 x 2 >= 1
C 2    3 x 1 + 8 x 2 >= 1

*****   PROGRAM OUTPUT   *****

Simplex tableau: Iteration 2
```

\Cj			1.00	1.00	0.00	0.00	9999.00	9999.00
Cb	Basis	Bi	x 1	x 2	S 1	S 2	A 1	A 2
1.00	x 1	0.23	1.00	0.00	-0.31	0.08	0.31	-0.08
1.00	x 2	0.04	0.00	1.00	0.12	-0.15	-0.12	0.15
	Zj	0.27	1.00	1.00	-0.19	-0.08	0.19	0.08
	Zj-Cj		0.00	0.00	-0.19	-0.08	-9998.81	-9998.92

```
Final optimal solution
```

Variable	Value
x 1	0.23
x 2	0.04
Z	0.27

```
Sensitivity Analysis
```

	Right-hand side Ranging		
Constraint Number	Lower Limit	Current Value	Upper Limit
1	0.67	1.00	1.75
2	-2.00	1.00	1.25

	Contribution Rate Ranging		
Variable	Lower Limit	Current Rate	Upper Limit
x 1*	0.38	1.00	2.00
x 2*	0.50	1.00	2.67

```
* indicates basic variable
```

We can also find the solution to the dual model (South Street Diner) from the Z_j row and S_1 and S_2 columns as follows:

$$Z = \frac{1}{V}$$

$$\frac{1}{V} = 0.27$$

$$V = 3.70$$

$$y_1 = \frac{q_1}{V}$$

$$\frac{q_1}{3.70} = 0.19$$

$$q_1 = 0.703$$

$$y_2 = \frac{q_2}{V}$$

$$\frac{q_2}{3.70} = 0.08$$

$$q_2 = 0.296$$

These solution values also correspond approximately with our manual solution.

Figure A7.4   *Computer Solution of the Fleet the Foot Problem*

```
                    GAME TYPE?  2 & 3

                    INPUT DATA?

                    ROW 1 COLUMN 1 :   500
                    ROW 1 COLUMN 2 :   400
                    ROW 1 COLUMN 3 :   550
                    ROW 2 COLUMN 1 :   600
                    ROW 2 COLUMN 2 :   350
                    ROW 2 COLUMN 3 :   450

                    CHECK INPUT DATA

                     500   400   550
                     600   350   450

                    ARE DATA CORRECT ? YES

                    PURE STRATEGY: ROW:  1  COLUMN:  2

                    VALUE OF THIS GAME: 400

                    DO YOU WANT TO RUN THIS GAME AGAIN? YES
```

COMPUTER SOLUTIONS OF GAMES

Game theory can become extremely complex when a game involves a number of players and many different strategies. Consequently, a computer-based solution becomes necessary. In this section, we will apply the microcomputer to the Fleet the Foot problem presented as Casette A7.1. The program was developed by the author.

Figure A7.4 presents the computer solution to the problem. The results correspond exactly with the manual solution we derived earlier. The value of the game is $400,000, which is the payoff for Fleet and also the loss to the Kansas City Jays.

SUMMARY

Most management science techniques are oriented toward aiding an individual decision maker under the condition of certainty, risk, or uncertainty. In many real-world situations, parties compete for different outcomes or consequences from the decision situation. The decision-making situation under conflict is the subject of game theory.

In this appendix, we have presented an overview of game theory, concentrating on the two-person zero-sum game. Game theory is quite interesting and mathematically neat; nevertheless, it has found very limited real-world applications, primarily because it cannot closely reflect reality when a large number of competitors are involved and payoffs change frequently. Also, such a game situation is almost impossible to solve based on the current state of game theory.

As a means for conceptualizing the logic of decision making under the condition of conflict, game theory is a very effective technique. The concepts and techniques presented in this chapter can provide useful insight to decision makers for their strategic planning.

Glossary

Equilibrium or Saddle Point   A value of a game where the payoff is simultaneously the minimum for a given offensive strategy and the maximum for a defensive strategy.

Mixed Strategy   Repetition of a game may lead players to select different strategies rather than express a constant preference (pure strategy).

n-Person Game   Game situation involving more than two competing players.

Nonzero-sum Game   Game situation in which playing the game either increases or decreases the total value of the stakes so that the sum of all the players' gains and losses do not total 0.

Player   Decision maker in competition with other decision makers in a game situation.

Pure Strategy   Each player always selects the same strategy, regardless of others' strategy choices.

Two-person Game   Game situation involving only two competing players.

Value of a Game   Amount of the outcome of a game, typically expressed as the gain for the winner (which equals the loss of the loser in a zero-sum, two-player game).

Zero-sum Game   Game situation in which the sum of all the players' gains and losses equals 0.

References

Batlin, Carl Alan, and Hinko, Susan. "A Game Theoretic Approach to Cash Management." *Journal of Business* 55:3 (1982), 367–381.

Baumol, W. J. *Economic Theory and Operations Analysis*. Englewood Cliffs, N.J.: Prentice-Hall, 1961.

Davis, M. *Game Theory: A Nontechnical Introduction*. New York: Basic Books, 1970.

Dorfman, R., Samuelson, P. A., and Solow, R. M. *Linear Programming and Economic Analysis*. New York: McGraw-Hill, 1958.

Kwak, N. K. *Mathematical Programming with Business Applications*. New York: McGraw-Hill, 1973.

Lucas, W. "An Overview of the Mathematical Theory of Games." *Management Science* 8:5 (1972), 3–19.

Luce, R. D., and Raiffa, H. *Games and Decisions*. New York: John Wiley & Sons, 1957.

Rapaport, A. *Two Person Game Theory*. Ann Arbor, Mich.: University of Michigan Press, 1966.

Sheehan, Michael, and Kogiku, K. C. "Game Theory Analyses Applied to Water Resource Problems." *Socio-Economic Planning Sciences* 15:3 (1981), 109–118.

Shubik, M. *The Uses and Methods of Game Theory*. New York: American Elsevier, 1957.

Von Neumann, J., and Morgenstern, O. *Theory of Games and Economic Behavior*. Princeton, N.J.: Princeton University Press, 1944.

William, J. D. *The Complete Strategyst*. Rev. ed. New York: McGraw-Hill, 1966.

INDEX

SOLUTIONS TO EVEN-NUMBERED ASSIGNMENTS

Chapter 1

1.2   *See* "Management and Decision Making"
1.4   *See* "Management and Decision Making"
1.6   *See* "The Concept of Economic Person"
1.8   *See* "Management Science and the Systems Approach"
1.10   Student's own ideas (*See* "The Role of Management Science")
1.12   *See* "The Role of Management Science"
1.14   Student's own discussion

Chapter 2

2.2   *See* "Introduction to Modeling"
2.4   *See* "Management Science Modeling"
2.6 $I = .95S + .83WS$,

    where I = the dependent variable
         S = an independent variable
      WS = an independent variable
  .95 and .83 = constant parameters

2.8   *See* "Decision-Making Environment"
2.10   *See* "Decision-Making Environment"
2.12   *See* "The Process of Management Science Modeling"
2.14   Student's own discussion

Chapter 3

3.2   *See* "Basic Concepts of Linear Programming"
3.4   Student's own ideas
3.6   *See* "Graphical Solution Method"
3.8   *See* "A Simple Maximization Problem"
3.10   *See* "A Simple Maximization Problem"
3.16 $x_1 = 18$, $x_2 = 4$, $Z = 380$
3.18 $x_1 = 2.4$, $x_2 = 4$, $Z = 34.4$
3.20   (a)   Maximize $Z = \$13x_1 + \$20x_2$

    subject to $x_1 + x_2 \geq 800$
                $.2x_1 + .4x_2 \leq 400$
                $.4x_1 + .4x_2 \leq 600$
                $x_1, x_2 \geq 0$

    (b) $x_1 = 1{,}000$, $x_2 = 500$, $Z = 23{,}000$
3.22   (a)   Maximize $Z = x_1 + x_2$

    subject to $5x_1 + 2x_2 \leq 900$
              $2x_1 + 7x_2 \leq 700$
              $x_1, x_2 \geq 0$

    (b) $x_1 = 158\tfrac{23}{31}$, $x_2 = 54\tfrac{26}{31}$, $Z = 212.90$
3.24   (a)   Minimize $Z = \$150x_1 + \$100\, x_2$

    subject to $30x_1 + 40x_2 \geq 360$
              $20x_1 + 80x_2 \geq 400$
              $15x_1 + 5x_2 \geq 75$
              $x_1, x_2 \geq 0$

    (b) $x_1 = 2\tfrac{2}{3}$, $x_2 = 7$, $Z = 1{,}100$
3.26   (a)   Minimize $Z = .1875x_1 + .3125x_2$

    subject to $1{,}100x_1 + 1{,}500x_2 \geq 49{,}000$
              $2.25x_1 + 1.5x_2 \leq 75$
              $x_1 + x_2 = 42$
              $x_1, x_2 \geq 0$

    (b) $x_1 = 16$, $x_2 = 26$, $Z = 11.125$
    (c)   Minimize $Z = .1875x_1 + .3125x_2$

    subject to $1{,}100x_1 + 1{,}500x_2 \geq 49{,}000$
              $x_1 + x_2 = 42$
              $x_1, x_2 \geq 0$
optimum solution: $x_1 = 35$, $x_2 = 7$, $Z = 8.75$
3.28   (a)   Minimize $Z = .2x_1 + x_2$

    subject to $x_1 + 3x_2 = 250$
              $x_1 + 2x_2 \geq 200$
              $x_1, x_2 \geq 0$

    (b) $x_1 = 250$, $x_2 = 0$, $Z = 50$
    (c)   Minimize $Z = .2x_1 + x_2$

    subject to $x_1 + 3x_2 \leq 250$
              $x_1 + 2x_2 \geq 200$
              $x_1, x_2 \geq 0$
3.30   (a)   Minimize $Z = \$\,3{,}000x_1 + \$\,2{,}400x_2$

    subject to $9x_1 + 3x_2 \geq 18$
              $3x_1 + 3x_2 \geq 12$
              $6x_1 + 18x_2 \geq 36$
              $x_1 \leq 7$
              $x_2 \leq 7$
              $x_1, x_2 \geq 0$

    (c) $x_1 = 1$, $x_2 = 3$, $Z = \$10{,}200$
    (d) $Z = 2{,}250x_1 + 2{,}400x_2$
         $x_1 = 3$, $x_2 = 1$, $Z = 9{,}150$
3.32   Minimize $Z = x_1 + x_2$

    subject to $10.2x_1 + 4.5x_2 \geq 1{,}000$
                $5.4x_1 + 20.25x_2 \geq 2{,}000$
                $x_1, x_2 \geq 0$
optimum solution : $x_1 = 62$, $x_2 = 83$, $Z = 145$

Chapter 4

4.2   *See* "The Simplex Method"
4.4   *See* "The Simplex Solution Procedure"
4.6   *See* "The Simplex Solution Procedure"
4.8   *See* "Some Problem Situations"
4.10 $x_1 = 60$, $x_2 = 40$, $Z = 3{,}600$
4.12 $x_1 = 5$, $x_2 = 4$, $Z = 22$
4.14   (a)   Minimize $Z = .72x_1 + .18x_2$

    subject to $90x_1 + 45x_2 \geq 90$
                $6x_1 + 18x_2 \geq 18$
                $120x_1 + 120x_2 \geq 360$
                $x_1, x_2 \geq 0$

    (b) $x_1 = 0$, $x_2 = 2$, $Z = 36$
    (c) $x_2 = 2.0$, $s_2 = 18$, $s_3 = 120$
    (d) $90x_1 + 45x_2 \geq 90$
         $6x_1 + 18x_2 \leq 24$
         $120x_1 + 120x_2 \leq 360$
    (e)   Minimize $Z = .72x_1 + .54x_2$

    subject to $90x_1 + 45x_2 \geq 90$
                $6x_1 + 18x_2 \geq 18$
                $120x_1 + 120x_2 \geq 360$
                $x_1, x_2 \geq 0$
optimum solution: $x_1 = .6$, $x_2 = .8$, $Z = .864$
4.16   (a)   Maximize $Z = 60x_1 + 50x_2 + 45x_3 + 50x_4$

    subject to $x_2 \leq 20$
                     $x_4 \leq 15$
              $10x_1 + 5x_2 \leq 120$
              $8x_3 + 6x_4 \leq 135$

    (b) $x_1 = 2$, $x_2 = 20$, $x_3 = 5.63$, $x_4 = 15$, $Z = 2{,}123.13$
4.18   (a)   Minimize $Z = 40x_1 + 50x_2 + 45x_3$

    subject to $200x_1 + 300x_2 + 325x_3 \geq 5{,}000$
                       $x_1 \geq 10$
                       $x_2 \geq 5$
                       $x_3 \geq 5$
                    $x_1, x_2, x_3 \geq 0$

    (b) $x_1 = 10$, $x_2 = 5$, $x_3 = 5$, $Z = 875$
4.20   (a)   Minimize $Z = 7x_1 + 15x_2 + 9x_3 + 12x_4$

    subject to $x_1 + x_3 = 8$
                  $x_2 + x_4 = 10$
                  $x_3 + x_4 \leq 7$
                  $x_1 + x_2 \leq 14$
                $-x_1 + x_3 \leq 2$
                  $x_1 - x_3 \leq 2$
                $-x_2 + x_4 \leq 2$
                  $x_2 - x_4 \leq 2$
                $x_1, x_2, x_3, x_4 \geq 0$

    (b) $x_1 = 5$, $x_2 = 6$, $x_3 = 3$, $x_4 = 4$, $Z = 200$
4.22   (a) $x_1 = 4$, $Z = 60$
    (b)   Yes, because there is no positive $Z_j - C_j$ value
4.24   (a)   Maximize $Z = 5x_1 + 25x_2 + 75x_3$

    subject to $200{,}000x_1 + 800{,}000x_2 + 2{,}000{,}000x_3 \leq 6{,}000{,}000$
                         $x_3 \leq 1$
       $5x_1 + 25x_2 + 75x_3 \geq 187.5$
                  $x_1, x_2, x_3 \geq 0$

    (b) $x_2 = 5$, $x_3 = 1$, $z = 200$
4.26   (a)   Maximize $Z = 10x_1 + 6x_2$

    subject to $x_1 \leq 5$
                     $x_2 \leq 6$
             $4x_1 + 2x_2 \leq 20$
                 $x_1, x_2 \geq 0$

(b) $x_1 = 2$, $x_2 = 6$, $Z = 56$

4.28 (a) Maximize $Z = \$\ 12x_1 + \$\ 14x_2$

subject to
$$6x_1 + 4x_2 \leq 120$$
$$6x_1 + 7.5x_2 \leq 135$$
$$4x_1 + 10x_2 \leq 150$$
$$x_1, x_2 \geq 0$$

(b) Basic: $x_1 = 17.14$, $x_2 = 4.28$, $s_3 = 38.57$, $Z = 265.714$
Nonbasic: s_1, $s_2 = 0$

(c) SCIII, 38.57 minutes

4.30 $x_2 = 6.67$, $x_3 = 4$, $Z = 58.67$

Chapter 5

5.2 *See* "Duality in Linear Programming"
5.4 *See* "Duality in Linear Programming"
5.6 *See* "Sensitivity Analysis"
5.8 *See* "Sensitivity Analysis"
5.10 *See* "Other Topics in Advanced Linear Programming" (*chapter 6*)
5.12 Student's own discussion
5.14 Minimize $Z = 12u_1 + 24u_2$

subject to
$$3u_1 + 6u_2 \geq 240$$
$$9u_1 + 15u_2 \geq 225$$
$$u_1, u_2 \geq 0$$

5.16 Minimize $Z = 80u_1 - 80u_2 + 8u_3$

subject to
$$16u_1 - 16u_2 \geq 40$$
$$8u_1 - 8u_2 + 2u_3 \geq 36$$
$$u_1, u_2, u_3 \geq 0$$

5.18 (a) Maximize $Z = 8x_1 + 12x_2$

subject to
$$x_1 + 2x_2 \leq 9$$
$$3x_1 + 2x_2 \leq 16$$
$$x_1 + x_2 \leq 6$$
$$x_1, x_2 \geq 0$$
optimum solution: $x_1 = 3$, $x_2 = 3$, $Z = 60$

(b) Minimize $Z = 9u_1 + 16u_2 + 6u_3$

subject to
$$u_1 + 3u_2 + u_3 \geq 8$$
$$2u_1 + 2u_2 + u_3 \geq 12$$
$$u_1, u_2, u_3 \geq 0$$

(c) $x_1 = 3$, $x_2 = 3$, $Z = 60$
(d) $12 \leq c_1 \leq 18$
(e) $x_2 = 6$, $s_1 = 6$, $s_2 = 4$, $Z = 72$
(f) $x_2 = 6$, $s_1 = 3$, $s_2 = 4$, $Z = 72$

5.20 Maximize $Z = 30x_1 + 20x_2$

subject to
$$120x_1 + 120_2 \leq 6,000$$
$$30x_1 + 60x_2 \leq 2,400$$
$$30x_1 + 15x_2 \leq 1,200$$
$$x_1 \leq 35$$
$$x_1, x_2 \geq 0$$

(b) $x_1 = 30$, $x_2 = 20$, $Z = 1,300$
(c) $x_1 = 20$, $x_2 = 30$, $Z = 1,650$
(d) The shadow prices are $s_1 = .083$ and $s_3 = .667$
$5,400 \leq b_1 \leq 6,400$
$1,050 \leq b_3 \leq 1,275$

5.22 (a) $x_1 = 10$, $x_2 = 50$, $x_3 = 0$, $x_4 = 10$, $Z = 1,830$
(b) 19.20; L.L. $= 103\frac{1}{3}$ U.L. $= 136\frac{2}{3}$
(c) $x_2 = 45$, $x_3 = 10$, $x_4 = 10$.
$s_3 = 505$, $s_4 = 20$, $s_5 = 6$, $Z = 1,830$
(d) No purchase of additional resource because there are already 10 units left over ($s_4 = 10$).
(e) Yes, at least 50
(f) $x_1 = 8$, $x_2 = 50\frac{2}{3}$, $x_4 = 10\frac{2}{3}$, $s_3 = 538\frac{2}{3}$, $s_4 = 12$, $s_5 = 16$, $s_6 = \frac{2}{3}$, $z = 1781\frac{1}{3}$

5.24 $x_1 = 333\frac{1}{3}$, $x_2 = 166\frac{2}{3}$, $z = 28,333\frac{1}{3}$

5.26 $x_2 = 345.46$, $x_3 = 172.73$, $z = 1727.27$

5.28 (a) $4 \leq b_1 \leq 12$, $8 \leq b_2 \leq 48$, $b_3 \leq 8$
(b) $x_1 \leq 33.4$, $2.93 \leq x_2 \leq 12$, $5 \leq x_3 \leq 25$

(c) No effect
(d) $s_3 = 2$, $x_3 = .8$, $x_2 = 3.6$, $Z = 40.8$

5.30 (a) Yes; there are no positive $C_j - Z_j$ values
(b) Since the current $C_j - Z_j$ value in the x_1 column is -50.63, the positive change in the contribution rate of x_1 should be at least 50.63 before x_1 can become a basic variable.
(c) $x_2 = 20$, $x_3 = 6$, $s_3 = 25$, $x_4 = 1$, $Z = 2,095$
(d) $0 \leq b_1 \leq 44$, $1 \leq b_2 \leq 33$, $75 \leq b_3$, $20 \leq b_4 \leq 70$
(e) $x_2 = 20$, $x_3 = 6$, $s_3 = 25$, $s_5 = 1$, $x_4 = 1$, $Z = 2,395$
(f) No; x_5 would add $(60 - (2 \times 22.50) - (2 \times 16.25)) = -17.50$ per unit to the current optimum solution.

Chapter 6

6.2 *See* "Real-World Applicatons of Integer and Goal Programming"
6.4 *See* "The Rounding Approach"
6.6 *See* "Goal Programming"
6.8 *See* "Goal Programming"
6.10 *See* "Casette 6.2"
6.12 *See* "The Modified Simplex Method of Goal Programming"
6.14 $x_1 = 334$, $x_2 = 166$, $z = 1666$
6.16 $x_1 = 2$, $x_2 = 3$ or $x_1 = 3$, $x_2 = 2$; $z = 2.5$
6.18 $x_1 = 2$, $x_3 = 8$, $z = 66$
6.20 $x_1 = 90$, $x_2 = 50$, $d_2 = 10$, $d_3 = 18$; p_1, p_2, $p_3 =$ achieved, $p_4 =$ not achieved $(d_2^+ = 10$, $d_3^+ = 18)$
6.22 Minimize $Z = p_1d_1^- + 2p_2d_2^- + p_2d_3^- + p_3d_1^+$

subject to
$$3x_1 + 3x_2 + d_1^- - d_1^+ = 120$$
$$x_1 + d_2^- - d_2^+ = 25$$
$$x_2 + d_3^- - d_3^+ = 30$$
$$x_j, d_i^+, d_i^- \geq 0$$
$$x_1 = 25, x_2 = 30$$
$$p_1, p_2 =$$ achieved
$$p_3 =$$ not achieved

6.24 Minimize $Z = p_1d_1^- + p_2d_2^+ + 6p_3d_3^+ + 5p_3d_4^+ + 5p_4d_3^- + 6p_4d_4^-$

subject to
$$5x_1 + 6x_2 + d_1^- - d_1^+ = 550$$
$$x_2 + d_2^- - d_2^+ = 47$$
$$x_1 + d_3^- - d_3^+ = 46$$
$$x_2 + d_4^- - d_4^+ = 46$$
$$x_j, d_i^+, d_i^- \geq 0$$
$$x_1 = 53.6, x_2 = 47$$
$$p_1, p_2, p_4 =$$ acheived
$$p_3 =$$ not achieved

6.26 Minimize $Z = p_1d_1^+ + p_2d_2^- + p_3d_3^+ + p_4d_4^-$

subject to
$$50x_1 + 300x_2 + 100x_3 + d_1^- - d_1^+ = 1,000,000$$
$$50x_1 + 300x_2 + d_2^- - d_2^+ = 300,000$$
$$100x_3 + d_3^- - d_3^+ = 200,000$$
$$50x_1 + 250x_2 + 200x_3 + d_4^- - d_4^+ = M$$
$$x_j, d_i^+, d_i^- \geq 0$$
Note: M must exceed 1,700,000
$$x_1 = 6,000, x_3 = 7,000,$$
$$p_1, p_2, p_3 =$$ acheived

6.28 Minimize $Z = p_1d_1^- + p_2d_2^- + p_2d_3^- + p_2d_4^- + p_3d_5^+ + p_4d_6^- + p_4d_7^- + p_4d_8^- + p_5d_1^+$

subject to
$$5x_1 + 8x_2 + 12x_3 + d_1^- - d_1^+ = 200$$
$$x_1 + d_2^- - d_2^+ = 5$$
$$x_2 + d_3^- - d_3^+ = 5$$
$$x_3 + d_4^- - d_4^+ = 8$$
$$5x_1 + 8x_2 + 12x_3 + d_5^- - d_5^+ = 200$$
$$x_1 + d_6^- - d_6^+ = 15$$
$$x_2 + d_7^- - d_7^+ = 12$$
$$x_3 + d_8^- - d_8^+ = 12$$
$$x_i, d_i^+, d_i^- \geq 0$$
$$x_1 = 15, x_2 = 6.13, x_3 = 8$$
$$p_1, p_2, p_3 =$$ achieved
$$p_4, p_5 =$$ not achieved

6.30 (a) Maximize $Z = 20x_1 + 12x_2$

subject to
$$4x_1 + 2x_2 \leq 240$$
$$2x_1 + 6x_2 \leq 300$$
$$100x_1 + 60x_2 \leq 8,000$$
$$x_1 \leq 55$$
$$x_2 \leq 65$$
$$x_1, x_2 \geq 0$$

(b) $x_1 = 42$, $x_2 = 36$, $Z = 1,272$
(c) Minimize $Z = p_1d_1^- + p_2d_2^+ + p_3d_3^- + p_3d_4^- + p_4d_{11}^+ + p_5d_5^- + p_6d_3^+ + p_6d_4^-$

subject to
$$x_1 + d_1^- - d_1^+ = 55$$
$$100x_1 + 60x_2 + d_2^- - d_2^+ = 8,500$$
$$4x_1 + 2x_2 + d_3^- - d_3^+ = 240$$
$$2x_1 + 6x_2 + d_4^- - d_4^+ = 300$$
$$d_{11}^- + d_3^+ - d_{11}^+ = 40$$
$$x_2 + d_5^- - d_5^+ = 65$$
$$x_j, d_i^+, d_i^- \leq 0$$

6.32 Minimize $Z = p_1d_1^- + p_2d_2^- + p_3d_3^-$

subject to
$$.25x_1 + .3x_2 + .125x_3 \leq 20$$
$$x_1 + 4x_2 + 6x_3 + d_1^- - d_1^+ = 500$$
$$50,000x_1 + 100,000x_2 +$$
$$25,000x_3 + d_2^- - d_2^+ = 4,000,000$$
$$4,000x_1 + 8,000x_2 +$$
$$6,000x_3 + d_3^- - d_3^+ = 250,000$$
$$x_j, d_i^+, d_i^- \geq 0$$

6.34 (a) Minimize $Z = p_1d_1^- + p_2d_2^+ + p_3d_3^- + p_4d_4^-$

subject to $2.5x_1 + 3x_2 + d_1^- - d_1^+ = 2,000$
$$5x_1 + 8x_2 + d_2^- - d_2^+ = 5,280$$
$$x_2 + d_3^- - d_3^+ = 400$$
$$x_1 + d_4^- - d_4^+ = 500$$
$$x_j, d_i^+, d_i^- \geq 0$$

(b) $x_1 = 416$, $d_1^+ = 240$, $x_2 = 400$, $d_4^- = 84$
(c) p_1, p_2, $p_3 =$ achived, $p_4 =$ not achieved $(d_4^- = 84)$
(d) Conflict exists. Third and fourth goals $(1 : 1.6)$; second and fourth goals $(1 : 0.2)$

Chapter 7

7.4 *See* "Developing an Initial Solution"
7.6 *See* "Determining the Optimum Solution-The Modified Distribution Model"
7.8 *See* "Determining the Optimum Solution-The Modified Distribution Model"
7.10 *See* "Degeneracy"
7.12 *See* "Multiple-Optimum Solutions"
7.14 *See* "Prohibited or Impossible Transportation Routes"
7.16 (a) NW : 1-a,40, 1-b,10, 2-b,10, 2-c,30, 2-d,10, 3-d,60, *TC* = 830
MC : 1-b,20, 1-c,30, 2-d,50, 3-a,40, 3-d,20, *TC* = 890
VAM : 1-a,20, 1-c,30, 2-a,20, 2-b,20, 2-d,10, 3-d,60, *TC* = 750

(b) 1-*b*,20, 1-*c*,30, 2-*d*,50, 3-*a*,40, 3-*d*,20, $TC = 890$

7.18 (a) 1-*a*,35, 1-*b*,7, 2-*b*,30, 3-*b*,3, 3-*c*,25, $TC = 9,340$

(b) 1-*a*,2, 1-*b*,40, 2-*a*,30, 3-*a*,3, 3-*c*,25, $TC = 9,010$

(c) Minimize $Z = 80x_{11} + 90x_{12} + 100x_{13} + 90x_{21} + 110x_{22} + 110x_{23} + 100x_{31} + 120x_{32} + 90x_{33}$

subject to
$$x_{11} + x_{12} + x_{13} = 42$$
$$x_{21} + x_{22} + x_{23} = 30$$
$$x_{31} + x_{32} + x_{33} = 28$$
$$x_{11} + x_{21} + x_{31} = 35$$
$$x_{12} + x_{22} + x_{32} = 40$$
$$x_{13} + x_{23} + x_{33} = 25$$
$$x_{ij} \geq 0$$

7.20 (a) 1-*a*,260, 1-*b*,100, 2-*b*,250, 3-*b*,50, 3-*c*,250, dummy-*d*,300, $TC = 76,200$

(b) 1-*a*,260, 1-*b*,100, 2-*c*,250, 3-*b*,300, dummy-*d*,300, $TC = 61,200$

7.22 (a) 1-*d*,20, 1-*a*,30, 2-*a*,40, 2-*b*,10, 2-*e*,10, 3-*d*,40, 4-*b*,20, 4-*c*,50, 5-*e*,10, 5-dummy,40, $TC = 2,630$

(b) 1-*e*,50, 2-*a*,40, 2-*c*,20, 3-*d*,40, 4-*b*,30, 4-*c*,30, 4-*d*,10, 5-*d*,10, 5-dummy,40, $TC = 2,530$

7.24 (a) Minimize $Z = 4x_{11} + 6x_{12} + 2x_{13} + 8x_{21} + 7x_{22} + 10x_{23} + 6x_{31} + x_{32} + 4x_{33}$

subject to
$$x_{11} + x_{12} + x_{13} = 100$$
$$x_{21} + x_{22} + x_{23} = 60$$
$$x_{31} + x_{32} + x_{33} = 80$$
$$x_{11} + x_{21} + x_{31} = 40$$
$$x_{12} + x_{22} + x_{32} = 90$$
$$x_{13} + x_{23} + x_{33} = 110$$
$$x_{ij} \geq 0$$

(b) MC : 1-*m*,100, 2-*f*,40, 2-*j*,10, 2-*m*,10, 3-*j*,80, $TC = 770$
VAM : 1-*m*,100, 2-*f*,40, 2-*j*,10, 2-*m*,10, 3-*j*,80, $TC = 770$

(c) 1-*f*,40, 1-*j*,60, 2-*j*,30, 2-*m*,30, 3-*m*,80, $TC = 1,350$, cell (1,*m*),-7, maximum $= 30$

(d) 1-*m*,100, 2-*f*,40, 2-*j*,20, 3-*j*,70, 3-*m*,10, $TC = 770$

(e) 1-*m*,100, 2-*f*,40, 2-*j*,10, 2-*m*,10, 3-*j*,80, $TC = 770$

7.26 (a) Minimize $Z = 20x_{11} + 19x_{12} + 17x_{13} + 23x_{21} + 21x_{22} + 20x_{23} + 18x_{31} + 24x_{32} + 22x_{33}$

subject to
$$x_{11} + x_{12} + x_{13} \leq 175$$
$$x_{21} + x_{22} + x_{23} \leq 150$$
$$x_{31} + x_{32} + x_{33} \leq 125$$
$$x_{11} + x_{21} + x_{31} = 200$$
$$x_{12} + x_{22} + x_{32} = 100$$
$$x_{13} + x_{23} + x_{33} = 100$$
$$x_{ij} \geq 0$$

(b) *e*-*c*,75, *e*-*v*,100, *n*-*s*,100, *n*-dummy,50, *c*-*c*,125, $TC = 7,550$

(c) yes, should be assigned to the cells of *e*-*s*,*e*-dummy, *n*-*c*-, *n*-*v*, *c*-*s*, *c*-dummy

(d) *e*-*c*,100, *e*-*v*,100, *n*-*s*,100, *n*-dummy,50, *c*-*c*,125, $TC = 7,550$

7.28 (a) MC : 1-*c*,5.5, 1-*n*,17.5, 1-dummy,3, 2-*t*,33.5, 2-dummy,1.5,3-*c*,18.5, $TC = 863$
MODI : 1-*c*,5.5, 1-*n*,17.5, 1-dummy,3, 2-*t*,33.5, 2-dummy,1.5, 3-*c*,18.5, $TC = 863$

(b) 1-*c*,4, 1-*n*,17.5, 1-dummy,4.5, 2-*c*,1.5, 2-*t*,33.5, 3-*c*,18.5, $TC = 863$

7.30 (a) *a*-3,90, *b*-1,30, *b*-3,20, *c*-2,80,*d*-1,40, *d*-2,20, dummy-1,50, $TC = 1,590$

(b) *a*-3,90, *b*-1,30, *b*-3,20, *c*-2,80, *d*-1,40, *d*-2,20, dummy-1,50, $TC = 1,590$

(c) yes, CII for cell $c_1 = 0$, *a*-3,90, *b*-3, 20, *c*-1,40, *c*-2,40, *d*-2,60, dummy-1,50, $TC = 1,590$

7.32 (b) *a*-*a*,500, *a*-*b*,130, *b*-*b*,370, *b*-*g*,260, *b*-*ch*,80, *c*-*c*,500, *c*-*ch*,160, *g*-*g*,410, *g*-*cr*,90, *ch*-*ch*,500, *cr*-*cr*,500, $TC = 2,730$

7.34 Minimize $Z = 80x_{11} + 120x_{12} + 90x_{13} + 100x_{21} + 70x_{22} + 50x_{23} + 60x_{31} + 100x_{32} + 70x_{33}$

subject to
$$x_{11} + x_{12} + x_{13} = 50$$
$$x_{21} + x_{22} + x_{23} = 80$$
$$x_{31} + x_{32} + x_{33} = 70$$
$$x_{11} + x_{21} + x_{31} = 60$$
$$x_{12} + x_{22} + x_{32} = 90$$
$$x_{13} + x_{23} + x_{33} = 50$$
$$x_{ij} \geq 0$$

7.36 Maximize $Z = 8x_{11} + 3x_{12} + 9x_{13} + 6x_{21} + 7x_{22} + 10x_{23} + 4x_{31} + 11x_{32} + 8x_{33}$

subject to
$$x_{11} + x_{12} + x_{13} = 17$$
$$x_{21} + x_{22} + x_{23} = 23$$
$$x_{31} + x_{32} + x_{33} = 19$$
$$x_{11} + x_{21} + x_{31} \leq 30$$
$$x_{12} + x_{22} + x_{32} \leq 30$$
$$x_{13} + x_{23} + x_{33} \leq 30$$
$$x_{ij} \geq 0$$

7.38 Maximize $Z = 16x_{11} + 23x_{12} + 14x_{13} + 19x_{14} + 17x_{21} + 16x_{22} + 13x_{23} + 14x_{24} + 18x_{31} + 20x_{32} + 17x_{33} + 15x_{34} + 25x_{41} + 18x_{42} + 15x_{43} + 17x_{44}$

subject to
$$x_{11} + x_{12} + x_{13} + x_{14} = 96$$
$$x_{21} + x_{22} + x_{23} + x_{24} = 123$$
$$x_{31} + x_{32} + x_{33} + x_{34} = 79$$
$$x_{41} + x_{42} + x_{43} + x_{44} = 85$$
$$x_{11} + x_{21} + x_{31} + x_{41} \leq 125$$
$$x_{12} + x_{22} + x_{32} + x_{42} \leq 200$$
$$x_{13} + x_{23} + x_{33} + x_{43} \leq 75$$
$$x_{14} + x_{24} + x_{34} + x_{44} \leq 150$$
$$x_{ij} \geq 0$$

Chapter 8

8.2 See chapter preview

8.4 See "The Nature of the Assignment Problem"

8.6 See "The Hungarian Method of Assignment"

8.8 See "The Branch-and-Bound Approach"

8.10 See "Impossible (or Prohibited) Assignments"

8.12 1-*a*,40, 2-*b*,40, 3-*c*,50, $TC = 130$

8.14 1-*e*,18, 2-*c*,15, 3-*d*,19, 4-*a*,18, 5-*b*,16, $TC = 86$

8.16 Both methods : *a*-2,8, *b*-3,8, *c*-4,12, *d*-1,8, Total $= 36$

8.18 (a) and (b) 1-*b*, 2-*d*, 3-*a*, 4-*e*, 5-*c*, or, 1-*c*, 2-*d*, 3-*a*, 4-*e*, 5-*b*, Total $= 47$

8.20 1-*e*,12, 2-*a*,17, 3-*d*,16, 4-*c*,6, Total $= 51$

8.22 *f*-*kp*,1, *h*-*d*,3, *l*-*cq*,2, *o*-*gd*,1, Total $= 7$

8.24 *a*-5,27, *b*-1,20, *c*-3,4, *d*-2,12, *e*-4,26, Total $= 89$

8.26 *dc*3-*dk*,17, *dc*7-*oc*,8, *b*707-*nr*,34, *b*727-*slp*,32, *b*747-*ld*,12, Total $= 103$

8.28 (a) 1-*b*,15, 2-*a*,24, 3-*c*,21, Total $= 60$
(b) 1-*b*,15, 2-*a*,24, 3-*c*,21, Total $= 60$

8.30 (a) 1-Roanoke,150, 2-Richmond,150, 3-Washington,120, 4-Norfolk,145, Total $= 565$
(b) no

8.32 (a) Minimize $Z = 40x_{1a} + 12x_{1b} + 30x_{1c} + Mx_{1d} + 32x_{1e} + 39x_{2a} + 8x_{2b} + 26x_{2c} + 18x_{2d} + 40x_{2e} + 36x_{3a} + 7x_{3b} + 23x_{3c} + 16x_{3d} + 38x_{3e} + 32x_{4a} + 6x_{4b} + Mx_{4c} + 22x_{4d} + 35x_{4e} + 42x_{5a} + 8x_{5b} + 24x_{5c} + 25x_{5d} + 30x_{5e}$

subject to
$$x_{1a} + x_{1b} + x_{1c} + x_{1d} + x_{1e} = 1$$
$$x_{2a} + x_{2b} + x_{2c} + x_{2d} + x_{2e} = 1$$
$$x_{3a} + x_{3b} + x_{3c} + x_{3d} + x_{3e} = 1$$
$$x_{4a} + x_{4b} + x_{4c} + x_{4d} + x_{4e} = 1$$
$$x_{5a} + x_{5b} + x_{5c} + x_{5d} + x_{5e} = 1$$
$$x_{1a} + x_{2a} + x_{3a} + x_{4a} + x_{5a} = 1$$
$$x_{1b} + x_{2b} + x_{3b} + x_{4b} + x_{5b} = 1$$
$$x_{1c} + x_{2c} + x_{3c} + x_{4c} + x_{5c} = 1$$
$$x_{1d} + x_{2d} + x_{3d} + x_{4d} + x_{5d} = 1$$
$$x_{1e} + x_{2e} + x_{3e} + x_{4e} + x_{5e} = 1$$
$$x_{ij} = 0 \text{ or } 1$$

(b) assign, 1-*e*, 2-*b*, 3-*d*, 4-*a*, 5-*c*, Total $= 112$

8.34 (a) optimal, 53 minutes
(b) assign, *a*-3, *b*-4, *c*-5, *d*-1, *e*-*b*, Total Setup time $= 53$ minutes

Chapter 9

9.2 See "Decision Making under Risk"

9.4 See "Value of Perfect Information"

9.6 See "Analysis of Salvage Value" and "Analysis of Goodwill Cost"

9.8 See "Decision Making with Partial Probabilities"

9.12 See "Decision Trees"

9.14 See "Subjective Probabilities"

9.16 (a) $EP(a_1) = 3,000$, $EP(a_2) = 3,440$, $EP(a_3) = 3,640$, optimum $= a_3$
(b) $EOL(a_1) = 780$, $EOL(a_2) = 340$, $EOL(a_3) = 140$, optimum $= a_3$
(c) 140

9.18 (a) $EP(\text{operate}) = 560,000$, $EP(\text{lease}) = 500,000$; operate
(b) $p = .333$ (indifference point)

9.20. (b) $EP = 18.60$
(c) 12

9.22 (a) a_2 or a_3 (2,500)
(b) a_3 (2,500)
(c) a_1 (5,000)
(d) a_3 (2,500)
(e) a_2 (2,000)

9.24 (a) $L_u = 0.50$, $L_o = 1.0$
(b) 44
(c) 45
(d) 0.96
(e) $G = 9.85$

9.26 (b) two ($EP = 6.83$)

Chapter 10

10.2 See "Shortest-Route Problem", "Minimum Spanning Tree Problem", and "Maximum Flow Problem"

10.10 See "Shortest-Route Problem"

10.12 See "Maximum Flow Problem"

10.14 $1 \rightarrow 3 \rightarrow 6 \rightarrow 8 \rightarrow 9$ (22 minutes)

10.16 $1 \rightarrow 3 \rightarrow 5 \rightarrow 8 \rightarrow 10 \rightarrow 11$ (25)

10.18 $1 \rightarrow 4 \rightarrow 3 \rightarrow 6 \rightarrow 9 \rightarrow 10$ (1,010)

10.20 1-2, 2-3, 3-4, 4-6, 6-5, 6-7, 6-8 (29)

10.22 1-2, 1-3, 3-4, 4-5, 5-7, 6-7, 7-8 (total 32)

10.24 24

10.26 21,000 per hour, or 38 hours

10.28 106

Chapter 11

11.6 See "The Gantt Chart"

11.8 Project crashing : See "CPM Time and Cost Trade-offs" ; Others : See "Identifying the Critical Path"

11.10 See "Estimating Activity Times in PERT"

11.12 (a) $t_e = 10$, $\sigma_e = 1.67$
(b) $t_e = 9.5$, $\sigma_e = 2.5$
(c) $t_e = 14.67$, $\sigma_e = 2$

(d) $t_e = 9.83$, $\sigma_e = 1.17$
(e) $t_e = 20.67$, $\sigma_e = 3.33$

11.14 *Consult* "The Gantt Chart"

11.16 (b) $ET_1 = 0$, $ET_2 = 1$, $ET_3 = 1$,
$ET_4 = 5$, $ET_5 = 8$, $ET_6 = 9$, $ET_7 = 11$,
$ET_8 = 16$,
(c) $LT_1 = 0$, $LT_2 = 1$, $LT_3 = 1$, $LT_4 = 5$,
$LT_5 = 8$, $LT_6 = 9$, $LT_7 = 11$, $LT_8 = 16$
(d) Critical path :
$1\rightarrow2\rightarrow3\rightarrow4\rightarrow5\rightarrow6\rightarrow7\rightarrow8$ or
$1\rightarrow3\rightarrow4\rightarrow5\rightarrow6\rightarrow7\rightarrow8$
(e) 16 days

11.18 (a) $ET_1 = 0$, $ET_2 = 10$, $ET_3 = 12$,
$ET_4 = 28$, $ET_5 = 40$, ; $LT_1 = 0$,
$LT_2 = 14$, $LT_3 = 12$, $LT_4 = 28$,
$LT_5 = 40$
(b) Activity 1–2: $TS = 4$, $FS = 0$;
Activity 1–3: $TS = 0$, $FS = 0$;
Activity 2–4: $TS = 4$, $FS = 4$;
Activity 3–4: $TS = 0$, $FS = 0$;
Activity 3–5: $TS = 6$, $FS = 6$;
Activity 4–5: $TS = 0$, $FS = 0$
(c) Critical path :$1\rightarrow3\rightarrow4\rightarrow5$, $E(t) = 40$

11.20 (b) Critical path :$1\rightarrow2\rightarrow4\rightarrow5\rightarrow6$
(c) $E(t) = $ 104 days

11.22 (b) $E(t) = $ 58 weeks $(CP{:}1\rightarrow2\rightarrow4\rightarrow6\rightarrow7)$,
Cost = $12,700
(c) $E(t) = $ 42 weeks $(CP{:}1\rightarrow2\rightarrow4\rightarrow6\rightarrow7)$,
Cost = $16,750
(d) $400 + 200 + 250 + 750 + 900 + 350 + 1,200 = \$4,050$
(e) $(5,700 - 4,050) = \$1,650$
(f) Activity 1–2(4 weeks), 2–4(4 weeks),
4–6(2 weeks), 1–3(3 weeks), and
4–5(1 week); Total cost = $1,900

11.24 (a) $E(t) = $ 68 weeks
(b) $\sigma_{cp} = $ 6 weeks

11.26 (a) $P(x \le 90) = P(Z \le -1.50) = 1 - .93319 = .06681$
(b) $P(85 \le x \le 135) = P(1.75 \le Z \le 0.75) = .77337 - (1 - .95994) = .73331$

11.28 (a)

Activity	ET	LT	TS	FS
1–2	0	7	0	0
1–3	0	21	9	0
1–4	0	19	14	0
2–5	7	20	0	0
2–6	7	27	10	1
3–6	12	27	9	0
4–6	5	27	14	5
5–8	20	35	0	0
6–8	8	35	10	10
6–7	18	29	9	0
7–8	20	35	9	9
8–9	35	47	0	0

(b) $1\rightarrow2\rightarrow5\rightarrow8\rightarrow9$
(c) 47

Chapter 12

12.4 *See* "Basic Inventory Decisions"
12.6 *See* "Basic Inventory Decisions"
12.8 *See* "EOQ Model Assumptions"
12.10 Setup cost per production lot
12.12 *See* "The Inventory Model under Uncertainty"
12.14 *See* "Analytical versus Simulation Approach"
12.16 (a) $THC = HC \cdot Q/2$
(b) $TOC = OC \cdot D/2$
(c) $TIC = THC + TOC$
(d) $Q = 15$
(e) Number of orders = 7
12.18 (a) $Q = 33$ sets
(b) Number of orders = 24
(c) Inventory cycle = 15 days
(d) $TIC = \$980$
12.20 (a) $Q = 20,000$ boxes
(b) Number of production runs = 10
(c) Length of time between production = 20 days

12.22 (a) $Q = 800$
(b) $DR = 13$
(c) $R = 40$
(d) $TIC = \$335$
12.24 (a) $Q = 1,789$
(b) $Q/A = $ .22 years
(c) $(A{-}D)Q/2A = 447$
(d) $TIC = \$8,945$
12.26 (a) $Q = 490$
(b) $I = 327$
(c) $S = 163$, $T = $ .12 years, $t_1 = $ .08,
and $t_2 = $ .04
(d) $ITIC = \$1,633$
12.28 (a) $E(LT) = 6$, $E(DR) = 405$
(b) $D(DDLT) = 2,430$
(c) Expected shortage = 128.51
(d) $Q = 880$ pounds
12.30 (a) $Q = 45$
(b) $OC = \$24.50$
(c) $Q = 51$

Chapter 13

13.2 Increase service rate or number of servers
13.4 *See Appendix 6* "Infinite versus Finite Waiting Line Length"
13.6 *See* "Assumptions for Waiting Line Models"
13.12 *See* "$(M/M/1){:}(FCFS/\infty/\infty)$"
13.14 *See* "The Waiting Line Process"
13.16 (a) $P(0) = .917$, $P(1) = .076$, $P(2) = .006$
(b) $L = .09$ trucks
(c) $W = .036$ hours
(d) $W_q = .303$ hours
(e) $L_q = .0076$ trucks
13.18 $P(0) = .5$, $P(1) = .25$, $P(2) = .125$, $L = 1$ customer, $L_q = .5$ customers, $W = 1$ hour, $W_q = .5$ hours, $\mu = .5$
13.20 (a) $L = $ infinity, $W = $ infinity, $P(0) = 0$, $P(n) = 0$
(b) $L = 2$, $W = .5$, $P(0) = .33$, $P(1) = .22$, $P(2) = .15$, $P(n{>}2) = .3$
(c) $L = 1$, $W = .25$, $P(0) = .5$, $P(1) = .25$, $P(2) = .125$, $P(n{>}2) = .125$
13.22 $L = 2.92$ customers, $L_q = 2.08$, $W = .29$ hours, $W_q = .21$ hours
13.24 (a) $P(7) = .046$
(b) $P(7) = .0018$
(c) $P(0/s = 1) = .17$, $P(0/s = 2) = .58$
(d) $(s = 1) = .83$, $(s = 2) = .42$
(e) $L_q(s = 1) = 4.17$, $L_q(s = 2) = .18$
13.26 $\lambda = 4$:$P(0) = .2$, $L = 2.4$, $L_q = 1.6$, $W = .6$ hour, $W_q = .4$ hours; $\lambda = 4.8$: $P(0) = .04$, $L = 12.48$, $L_q = 11.52$, $W = 2.60$ hours, $W_q = 2.40$ hours
13.28 (a) $P(0) = .183$, $L = 4.46$ orders, $L_q = 3.64$ orders, $W = .32$ hours, $W_q = .26$ hours
(b) $P(n{>}5) = .296$
13.30 $L_q(s = 4)$ 2.4 minutes $L_q(s = 3) = 19.2$ minutes. Therefore, 4 lines
13.32 (a) $\mu = .8$
(b) $P(n \ge 7) = .2096$
(c) $L_q = 3.2$ customers
(d) $W_q = 1.6$ minutes
(e) $\mu = .4$
(f) $L_q = .15$ customers, $P(n \ge 7) = .0015$
(g) $W_q = .08$ minutes
(h) Install new one ($1,718 > $1,000)
13.34 $\lambda = 4$ hours, $u = 6$/hours, $\mu = .67$, $P(0) = .33$, $P(1) = .222$, $P(2) = .148$, $P(3) = .099$, $P(n \ge 4) = .6797$, $L_q = 1.33$ calls, $L = 2$ calls, $W_q = .33$ hours (19.8 minutes), $W = .5$ hours, $W_q = 19.8$ minutes Therefore, no calls would be lost.

Chapter 14

14.2 *See* "The Basic Nature of Dynamic Programming"

14.4 *See* "The Backward Appraoch"
14.6 *See* "The Basic Features of Dynamic Programming"
14.8 *See* "The Structure of Dynamic Programming"
14.10 (a) Stage 3(Stock Z);$S_3 = 3$, $X_3 = \{0,1,2,3\}$, $C_{x3} = \{0, 40, 520, 1,200\}$; Stage 2(Stock Y): $S_2 = S_3 - X_3$, $X_2 = \{0, 1, 2, 3\}$, $C_{x2} = \{0, 50, 300, 1,200\}$; Stage 1(Stock X): $S_1 = S_2 - X_2$, $X_1 = \{0, 1, 2, 3\}$, $C_{x1} = \{0, 50, 300, 1,200\}$; $S_0 = S_1 - X_1$
(b) $S_{n-1} = S_n - X_n$
(c) Alternative 1:Stock $Z = 0$, Stock $Y = 0$, Stock $X = \$3,000$; Alternative 2: Stock $Z = 0$, Stock $Y = \$3,000$, Stock $X = 0$; Alternative 3: Stock $Z = 0$, Stock $Y = 0$, Stock $X = 0$; Total $ROI = \$1,200$
14.12 (a) Let $C = $ unit production cost in stage i, $X_i = $ Policy decision of producing units of software in stage i, $I_i = $ units of software on hand at the beginning of stage i, and $S_i = $ units of sales contracted in stage. Then, total cost$(TC_i) = C_iX_i + 20 I_i$, $I_i = I_{i-1} + X_i - S_i$, and recursive function $[f_i (I_i)] = $ min $\{TC_i(X_i, I_i) + f^*_{i-1} (I_{i-1})\}$ where $f_0(S_0) = 0$.
(c) $X = 10$, $X = 10$, $X = 5$, $X = 6$; and total cost = $11,600
14.14 (a) Stage: products (Comtol I, Comtol II, Comtol X); State: number of machines; and recursive relationship: $f_n(S_n) = $ maximun $\{C_{xn} + f^*_{n-1} (S_{n-1})\}$ where $C_{xn} = $ forecasted profit for each X_n.
(b) Comtol I = 1, Comtol II = 2, and Comtol X = 0; and total profit = $12,500
14.16 (a) Stage: the number of even years remaining to the planning horizon; State: boat's age; Decision: Replace(R) or Overhaul (O); return: costs associated with stage and state; and recursive relation: $f_n(S_n) = $ min $\{C_{xn} + f^*_{n-1} (S_{n-1})\}$ where $X_n = $ either R or O, and trantsion rule, $S_{n-1} = 2$ if $X_n = R$ or $S_{n-1} = S_n + 2$ if $X = O$.
(b) Current year: overhaul: and the year after next year:overhaul. Total cost = $17,000
14.18 (a) Stage: each project; State: the amount of money left after an allocation; Decision: the allocation of money to each project; return: the expected probability of success; and the rescursive relation: $f_n (S_n) = $ max $\{C_{xn} + f^*_{n-1} (S_{n-1})\}$ where $C_{xn} = $ expected probability of success for X_n and the transition rule is $S_n = 3$ for $n = 3$, $S_n - X_n = S_{n-1}$ for $n = 1,2$
(b) OWL I = 1, OWL II = 3, OWL III = 1, and the sum of probability of success in each project is 2.45
14.20 (a) Stage: years in reverse year; State: the price at each year; Decision: the price decision; return: the potential profit associated with price decision and current state; and the recursive relation: $f_n(S_n) = $ max $\{C_{xn} + f^*_{n-1} (S_{n-1})\}$
(b) 1st year: $ 10; 2nd year: $ 14: and 3rd year:$ 14
(c) Total profit = $22 million
14.22 (a) Stage: each route; State: number of boats remaining for allocation; and recursive relation: $f_n(S_n) = $ max $\{C_{xn} + f^*_{n-1} (S_{n-1})\}$ where $C_{xn} = $ the expected profit by decision X_n

(b)   Route 1:1; Route 2:0; and Route 3:3
       or Route 1:1; Route 2:2; and Route
       3:1. Maximum profit: $ 6.6 million

14.24 (a)   The longest time path:
              Start→A→D→E or F→Finish
       (b)   The shortest time path:
              Start→B→Dummy→F→Finish

14.26 (a)   Stage: years remaining in the
              planning horizon; State: age of the
              truck; Decision: whether or not to buy
              a new truck; Return: costs; the

recursive function: $f_n(S_n) = $ min $\{C_{xn}$
$+ f^*_{n-1}(S_{n-1})\}$; $C_{xn} = O(S_n) +$
$\{N(S_n) - R(S_n)\}(1 - X_n)$ where $O(S_n) = $
operating cost, $N(S_n) = $ new truck
price, and $R(S_n) = $ resale price; and
$X_n = 1$ if company wants to keep, and
$X_n = 0$ if company wants to buy new
truck

(b)   1st year: buy; 2nd year: sell and buy;
       and 3rd year: sell and buy

14.28 (a)   Stage: each type of sailboat; State:

the unused amount of fiberglass;
return: the estimated return; Decision:
the allocation of fiberglass; the
recursive relation: $f_n(S_n) = $ max $\{C_{xn}$
$+ f^*_{n-1}(S_{n-1})\}$; and $S_{n-1} = S_n - X_n$
where $n = 2$, and $S_n = 20$ where $n = 1$

(b)   Snipe = 5 tons, Hampton = 10 tons,
       Lighting = 5 tons, and Total return =
       $710,000